Department of Romance Languages and Literatures Harvard University
Boylston Hall, 4th Floor
Cambridge, MA 02138

Distributed by Harvard University Press

Cultural Agents Reloaded: The Legacy of Antanas Mockus
1st Edition.

ISBN: 9780674088559

Editor
Carlo Tognato
Series Editor in Chief
José Luis Falconi
Editorial Management
Art Life Lab, LLC. (Miami and Boston) www.artlifelaboratory.com

For Art Life Lab:
Artistic Directors
Santiago Montoya and José Luis Falconi
Editorial Manager and Visual Dossier Research
Laura Oliveros Sánchez
Design
Arturo Higa Taira (Lima, Perú) (www.sputnik.pe)
and Natalia Gómez (Ciudad de México, México) (www.miheladodevanilla.com)
Color Separation
Alejandra Bonilla
Translation
Lisa Crossman, Amanda Gokee, Cydney Gottlieb
Copyeditors
Lisa Crossman, Baird Campbell, Bronte Velez, Amanda Gokee, Cydney Gottlieb, Madelyn Stroik, Lina Cepero
Printer
Panamericana Formas e Impresos S.A. (Bogotá, Colombia)

The printing and distribution of this volume was made possible by the generous contribution of *AVIANCA S. A.* and Mr. Gastón Abello, his wife Pilar Arteaga and their daughters María and Ilana.

This publication has been made possible due to the support of the Universidad Nacional de Colombia (Centro de Estudios Sociales - CES), Arte GT 2021 (Guatemala City, Guatemala) and Centro Nicanor Restrepo Santamaría para la Reconstrucción Civil - CeNiRS (Bogotá and Mexico City).

Publisher's Cataloging-In- Publication Data
(Prepared by The Donohue Group, Inc.)
Names: Tognato, Carlo, editor. | Crossman, Lisa A., translator.
Title: Cultural agents reloaded : the legacy of Antanas Mockus / edited by Carlo Tognato ; translation, Lisa Crossman.
Description: 1st edition. | Cambridge, MA : Department of Romance Languages and Literatures, Harvard University, [2017]
| [Cambridge, Massachusetts] : Harvard University Press, [2017] |
Essays in English; some essays translated into English. | Includes bibliographical references.
Identifiers: ISBN 978-0- 674-08855- 9
Subjects: LCSH: Mockus, Antanas-- Political and social views. | Art and state-- Colombia. |
Arts and society-- Colombia. | Social change--Colombia. | Colombia-- Cultural policy.
Classification: LCC F2260 .C85 2017 | DDC 303.409861-- dc23

Cultural Agents RELOADED: The Legacy of Antanas Mockus

Cultural Agents RELOADED: The Legacy of Antanas Mockus

Edited by Carlo Tognato

Distributed by
Harvard University Press

To my dear father, Mario
To my beloved daughter, Martina

Contents

Acknowledgements

I n October 2008, Doris Sommer came to Bogotá to participate in a symposium entitled "Cultural Agency, Aesthetics, and Politics," organized by the Center for Social Studies at the Universidad Nacional de Colombia (National University of Colombia), the Banco de la República (Central Bank of Colombia), and Corpovisionarios. (Corpovisionarios is the think-tank Antanas Mockus founded after the end of his second term as mayor of Bogotá to generate ideas in support of his later attempts to run as a presidential candidate and to channel his expertise into consulting). The Cultural Affairs Department of the Central Bank of Colombia is the most important cultural institution in the country. Its director, Ángela Pérez, former Associate Professor of Latin American Literature and Women's, Gender, and Sexuality Studies at Brandeis University, has been supportive of the work of Doris Sommer and the Cultural Agents Initiative at Harvard University. Francisco Ortega, then Associate Professor of History and member of the Center for Social Studies at the National University of Colombia, helped establish the link between Doris Sommer and a group of the Center's faculty members who participated in the event and some of whom later contributed to this book. Ortega had worked with Sommer at Harvard as a postdoctoral fellow before taking his position as Assistant Professor at the University of Wisconsin at Madison.

During the symposium, Doris floated the idea of publishing a book about Antanas Mockus in the *Cultural Agents Series*, published by Harvard University Press. One month later, I visited the Center for Cultural Sociology at Yale, of which I am a Faculty Fellow, and made it to Cambridge to discuss the idea with her and José Luis Falconi, the editor of the series. We then realized our mutual interest in finding ways to collaborate more closely.

In the winter and spring of 2009, I brought together an initial group of contributors to the book project with the idea of meeting again one year later with the preliminary versions of our chapters. I would like to express my special thanks to Enrique Chaux and Andrea Bustamante for submitting their piece in 2010 and even greater thanks to them for holding on throughout the long incubation period of this project.

In 2010 the Faculty of Human Sciences at the National University of Colombia launched its Doctoral Program in Human and Social Sciences. At that point, I thought that building a concentration on "Cultural Agents" within the program would allow us to institutionalize our collaboration with the Cultural Agents Initiative. Paolo Vignolo, one of the contributors to this book, enthusiastically welcomed the idea and since then has been a driving force within that concentration. Over the years, various doctoral students from the National University of Colombia and from Harvard have visited one another's institutions, and in 2012-2013, Paolo Vignolo spent a year at the David Rockefeller Center for Latin American Studies as the Santo Domingo Visiting Scholar. Meanwhile, in 2011 I left Colombia for Australia—I thought back then for good—and Paolo took up the entire coordination of the concentration on Cultural Agents within the Doctoral Program.

In April 2013 I returned to Bogotá. At the beginning of 2014, one last chapter came in, but we were still five chapters short regarding my initial design of the book. We contacted another group of contributors, which added another year to this venture. Meanwhile, the Faculty of Human Sciences at the National University of Colombia offered its institutional support for this project, as well as some financial support and a pledge of further backing for the Spanish edition of this book.

Throughout this incredibly long process, the project—and more generally Cultural Agents–Bogotá—has faced numerous challenges. Some critics of Antanas Mockus interpreted this book venture as a sophisticated operation in favor of a Colombian politician. Skeptics about North-South collaborations, for their part, politely reminded us that structural asymmetries would prevent local contributors from making their voices heard and questioned the possibility for Cultural Agents-Bogotá to be anything but a colonial outpost of Cultural Agents-Cambridge.

Pessimists about Colombian political culture, in turn, insisted that complex critical mediations have become impossible within such an extraordinarily polarized public sphere as that in Colombia; there would be hardly any way out of the opposition between friends and enemies. Scouting for valuable insights on both sides simultaneously or between them, as a result, might ultimately look suspicious and might turn out to be socially harmful.

At this point, I am confident that we managed to keep the promises we made at the beginning of this venture to ourselves, to the people who supported us, and also to our critics who observed us from afar. We took their concerns very much to heart from the beginning to the end. At the same time, we also recognized that in spite of their criticism, their skepticism, and their pessimism, all of us shared an irreducible hope that independent scholarship is possible in and from Colombia, that structural determinations are not perfectly tight, and that actors in the South *and* in the North may still stumble into some wiggle room, if they give up their reciprocal comfort zones and take the risk of looking for it. Finally, we acknowledged that all of us might have come to the realization that, in order to move the Colombian public sphere out of its current pragmatics of civil war and polarization into a new pragmatics of peace, one cannot avoid exposing oneself to the reactions and retaliations of those who may find criticism or unobvious mediations simply unbearable. In this sense, an expression drawn from Mockus's imaginative vocabulary, *dar papaya* (exposing one's own flank to possible attacks), is definitely pertinent. To authentically show one's own intentions and build trust, one needs to expose oneself to potential attacks, and risk whatever outcomes may arise.

This project capitalized on a broad range of resources that its participants, both those appearing in this book and those who have supported it from the outside, brought to it: a good deal of intellectual integrity, some audacity, a lot of patience, and a flinch of stubbornness. The broader institutional framework that ties Cultural Agents-Cambridge with Cultural Agents-Bogotá at the National University, the existence of a plurality of visions and styles within and between both, and the impossibility of composing all of them into a coherent whole (either because we did not mean to or because we lacked the time and resources to do so or both), may also have played a role in the successful completion of this project.

It is inevitable for a venture that has lasted more than six years to accumulate a debt of gratitude to a long list of people. Apart from the authors that appear in this book, I would like to thank a number of colleagues who took part in it at different stages: Terry Clark, Guillermo Hoyos, Amparo Vega, and Fernando Viviescas.

Although their contributions do not appear in this book, they added richly to our exchanges, and I am grateful to them for generously contributing to this project.

The quiet diplomacy of Yuri Jack Gómez, former Director of the Center for Social Studies at the National University of Colombia, was extremely important in obtaining institutional (and some financial) support from the National University for this project.

The contributions of the Editorial Office of the Center for Social Studies and that of the Faculty of Human Sciences at the National University and, in particular, of Catalina Hernández, Estéban Giraldo, and Claudia Roncancio were also fundamental at different stages of this publication process.

Without the support of two Deans of the Faculty of Human Sciences at the National University, Sergio Bolaños and Ricardo Sánchez, this project would have not seen the light of day.

Sebastián Cuellar assisted in the editorial process, transcribed three of the four interviews, and contributed together with Harvard's Julia Morse Leitner and with Cathy Girvin to the translation of different parts of this book. Sebastián, Cathy, and Javier Sáenz Obregón helped in translating Jesús Martín-Barbero's essay while Julia helped with those of Carlos Augusto Hernández and with Lucas Ospina. Sebastían also helped with the translation of the first three interviews. María Alejandra Ochoa transcribed Elster's interview, and Dennis Garzón provided her editorial assistance at a later stage for the interviews with Bromberg, Londoño, and Sánchez. I would like to express my thanks to all of them for volunteering to support this project. Finally, Patricia Simonson did a great job with the translation, in record time, of Antanas Mockus's "Conclusion."

Arturo Higa did a remarkable job with the graphic conception and the design of the book. Laura Oliveros, in turn, provided competent research assistance in the preparation of *Part Two*.

Doris Sommer was the first to imagine this book and provided the institutional platform that made it happen. My debt of gratitude to her is enormous. Additionally, interacting with her over the years has been inspiring in another way; her work has been a continuous reminder that beauty can, and must, be an important part of both scholarship and life.

Elaborating on the framework that ultimately brought together the contributions that appear in this book and finding a viable narrative for the argument that I make in the "Introduction" have been anything but a linear process. I am particularly grateful to José Luis Falconi, whose encouragement at a critical juncture was crucial to make this happen. Working with him has been indeed refreshing. His generosity throughout the editorial process has been simply unique.

I elaborated my introduction, which marked a flex-point in my conception of this entire project, as I was accompanying my father, Mario, in Turin, through a particularly painful stage of his cancer. I dedicate this book to him and to all the unforgettable moments we shared throughout our lives as well as to my sweet daughter, Martina, hoping that one day she will be able to say the same about me.

Translator's Note

Throughout this book, *Cultura Ciudadana* has been translated as "Civic Culture" in order to stress the civic nature of the concept.

Likewise, we have preferred to translate Mockus's campaign *Caballeros de la cebra* not as "Knights of the Zebra," as it is usually found, but as "Knights of the Crosswalk," as it is clearer in English. Additionally, his campaign *Bogotá coqueta* is translated here as "Bogotá Flirts"—as its direct translation would include the borrowed French term "coquette," which is seldom used in English.

PART ONE: INTRODUCTION

Carlo Tognato

1

Cultural Agents Reloaded through Antanas Mockus

Carlo Tognato

> To judge something, you have to care about it. If we don't care, the faculty of judgment will fail us.
> —*Doris Sommer, The Work of Art in the World*

> I felt I have not the right to want to change another if I am not open to be changed by him as far as it is legitimate.
> —*Martin Buber, The Knowledge of Man*

> Unlike the amphibian, the mere chameleon does not foster an interrelation between the cultural worlds to which it adapts.
> —*Antanas Mockus, Anfibios culturales y divorcio entre ley, moral y cultura* (Cultural Amphibians and Divorce Between Legality, Morality, and Culture)

L atin America has traditionally been the site for daring innovations in all avenues of social life that at times have resulted in incredible successes, other times in resounding failures, and on some occasions in an enervating mix of excitement and frustration for the hopes they raised and for the omissions they made. Some innovations have had the ambition to radically transform society. Others have concentrated all of their clout on individual communities; and yet others have started out small with the prospect of sending shock waves of change throughout broader and broader segments of society. This book is about one of these Latin American stories, that of Antanas Mockus, former mayor of Bogotá. It is a story that over the past two decades has been the focus of enthusiasm, passion, and admiration, but also of disappointment and disbelief.

We were intrigued from the start by the case of Antanas Mockus because he sets an example as a cultural agent who markedly departs from previous historical instances in his use of the arts on the part of government. Nazi Germany and the Soviet Union employed the arts to consolidate their totalitarian rule. In Latin America, on the other hand, the arts have been used in a more emancipatory fashion. In Mexico, José Vasconcelos employed the arts to celebrate cultural hybridity, allowing for national coherence, and supporting national reconstruction after the revolutions that took place between 1910 and 1920. In Brazil, Augusto Boal introduced his Legislative Theatre to give free reign to the political imagination of his underprivileged audiences, and to channel their innovative solutions to social problems that emerged on stage into the legislative process of Rio de Janeiro. Antanas Mockus also used the arts in government in an emancipatory fashion, but he did so in a radically different manner, embedding his cultural interventions within a technocratic framework that set a clear break with respect to earlier Latin American experiences in cultural agency. This feature paradoxically identifies the site of one of his strengths, as well as one of his major weaknesses.

When in the fall of 2008, we laid out our vision for this project, we believed that Mockus's story would give us the opportunity to bring together scholars from Latin America and the United States to systematically reflect on one prototypical case of "cultural agent." In the end, Mockus did much more than that. His case made it possible to look more carefully into our initial idea of cultural agency with an eye to decentering it and hoping to better orient its application within the field of practice. In this introduction, I will address this point of arrival and urge the reader to dive into the following essays to appreciate the many reasons that prompted us to embark on this long intellectual journey.

Antanas Mockus, Cultural Agent

The son of Lithuanian immigrants, Antanas Mockus studied at the *Lycée Français* in Bogotá in the 1960s, and graduated in mathematics from the University of Dijon in France in 1970. In 1975, he joined the academic staff of the Department of Mathematics at the National University of Colombia in Bogotá, and during the 1980s he was a member and then the director of the Federici Group—a research group working on the pedagogy of science, which ultimately played an important role in the Colombian pedagogic movement. In 1988 Mockus earned a Master's degree in philosophy at the National University. He then served as academic vice-chancellor of the same university, and in 1990, at the age of 38, he was appointed chancellor.

His term as chancellor was marked by a series of pedagogic initiatives that tapped into symbolism and performance for the purpose of promoting peaceful coexistence and free debate on campus. In 1993, during a speech before a thousand students in the majestic León de Greiff Auditorium of the National University, Mockus mooned his audience to shock a group of protestors into silence. He then pulled up his pants and went on with his speech. As a result, he was forced to resign, but public debate over the incident suddenly turned him into a popular public figure. Although he did not belong to Bogotá's elite, nor was he part of the political machinery of traditional Colombian parties, in 1994, he decided to run for mayor of Bogotá. In spite of running his campaign on what turned out to be the smallest budget in Colombian electoral history, and to the dismay of many and the satisfaction of many more, he won. Various analysts have regarded that event as a watershed in the political history of Bogotá (Gilbert and Dávila 2002; Skinner 2004; Martin 2007; Martin and Ceballos 2005; Passotti 2009; Beckett and Godoy 2010; Pérez Fernández 2010; Kalandides 2011).

When Mockus took office as mayor in 1995, Bogotá was plagued by violence and its inhabitants felt they had little in common with one another. Mockus responded to the fragmentation by seeking to build some common ground among the inhabitants of Bogotá. He addressed violence and crime by attempting to bring the legal, moral, and cultural forms of regulating conduct back into line. This orientation constituted the backbone of his cultural policy *Cultura Ciudadana* (Civic Culture), which resulted in an extensive pedagogization of the everyday life of Bogotá, and touched upon a wide variety of issues, such as recreation, transportation, public utilities, the environment, taxation, and security, to name just a few.

Mockus's use of the arts to execute his pedagogic agenda as mayor of Bogotá marked an important element of continuity with his previous engagement with performance as chancellor of the National University of Colombia. As mayor, Mockus continued to tap into creative practices to deliver his pedagogic messages and to change people's conduct. He did so by using, for example, four hundred mimes to bring order to Bogotá's chaotic traffic; by staging the so-called "Days of Inoculation Against Violence" to tackle domestic violence, which involved approximately fifty thousand people; by prompting his fellow citizens to voluntarily pay more taxes to their city than they owed; by distributing 350,000 thumbs-up and thumbs-down cards to his fellow citizens to allow people to publicly display their approval or disapproval for warranting behaviors; and by encouraging citizens to voluntarily surrender to the city administration 2,538 small arms that would be later melted into baby spoons with the inscription "*Arma Fui*" (I Was a Weapon) (Nogueira 2009; Bromberg 2003).

Over the years, Mockus's pedagogic practices have received the praise of many observers both in Colombia and internationally, and his experience has earned him a long series of mentions by various respected institutions. For example, in October 2002, the United Nations declared Bogotá to be "an exemplary city for Latin America from which other cities may learn" (Abers 1998; Souza 2001; *El Tiempo* 2002; Gilbert 2006:394).

Antanas Mockus and his *Cultura Ciudadana*, however, have also been targets for criticism. Some have insinuated a right-wing bias in his policy. Others have maintained that quantitative evidence does not support the success that he and his supporters have claimed for themselves, particularly as far as the improvement of security in Bogotá is concerned (Nogueira 2009; Hoyos Vásquez 2008; Casas Dupuy and González Cepero 2005; Valenzuela Aguilera 2008), a point on which Jaime Ramos insists in Essay 6 of this book. And yet others, while recognizing the merits of his action, have also brought into focus a series of fronts, along which improvement might be sought. For example, Javier Sáenz Obregón (2011:138-139) argues that Mockus's pedagogization of city life practiced "a one-dimensional distrustful depiction of the culture of the city's population," which took into account only the negative aspects of its knowledge, values, and practices that needed to be changed and that almost completely overlooked any positive traits that might deserve to be strengthened or capitalized on. Furthermore, *Cultura Ciudadana* focused almost exclusively on the construction of cultural agreements and tended to disregard cultural difference. Paolo Vignolo, for his part, pushes this critique even further in Essay 11. Mockus, he argues, ended up curtailing the creative potential of collective participation by only concentrating on his own role as an artist and a catalyst of social change.

Still, while considering the broad spectrum of opinions that different analysts have held in relation to Mockus's experience and legacy, there seems to be consensus over the idea that with him creative practices became so central to the exercise of government as to blur the border between art and government. Sommer (2006:1-3) uses the term "cultural agency" to signify a family resemblance that may recognize a broad "range of social contributions through creative practices." Based on that, Mockus's practice as mayor of Bogotá makes him a remarkably meaningful example of a cultural agent and therefore constitutes one important point of departure for this book.

To Mockus, or Not to Mockus

It is not uncommon for Antanas Mockus to inspire irritatingly ambivalent feelings, even among those who sincerely appreciate his contributions and cherish his legacy. This may be due to his enigmatic position along the surfaces of contact between the liberal, radical, and conservative political cultures of Colombia that contend the definition of legitimacy in social life. At first sight, what appears to be an unsettling drawback of this cultural agent surprisingly turns out to constitute a potentially useful resource, on closer inspection, that may paradoxically help bridge the dramatically deep divides that visibly partition the Colombian public sphere. Uribe Celis (2003:209) once remarked that "Mockus is many things altogether, probably contradictory ones, which gives him a political advantage: 'This is confusing!' It is very difficult for voters to box him into one single camp." This point about confusion or deception, however, ends up completely missing the latent functional accomplishment that Mockus was able to carry out within Colombian society, as he contributed to zipping together the liberal, radical, and conservative camps into which the Colombian public sphere is divided.

Liberal democracy has traditionally surfaced in Mockus's discourse and practice. Since his time as chancellor of the National University and throughout his two terms as mayor of Bogotá, his words and actions have repeatedly cued an appreciation for those attributes that have traditionally identified legitimate agency, legitimate social relationships, and legitimate political institutions in liberal democratic cultures. His unyielding pursuit of an interlocution with dissenters, for example, has indicated his confidence in individuals' autonomy, rationality, and reasonableness. His blunt acknowledgement during his first political campaign that he would raise taxes as his first decision as mayor of Bogotá, in turn, appealed to the expectation that in liberal democracies social relations should be open, trusting, truthful, and straightforward. Finally, his insistence on the sacredness of public money and the importance of abiding by the law reaffirmed the ideas of office and rule of law that are ingrained in the democratic codes of liberal political cultures.

Even so, there are elements of Mockus's discourse and practice that seem to elude standard expectations of leadership in liberal democratic cultures, both in Colombia and abroad. Although his term as visiting fellow at the Kennedy School of Government at Harvard University drew interest and appreciation on the part of the School's academic staff, by his own admission, Mockus's interlocution was much more fluid with scholars in the faculty of Humanities.[1] Possibly his highly imaginative approach to policy and his not-always-solemn enactment of public office have placed him, in the eyes of some, at the very edge of standard liberal understandings of democratic leadership. This point also resurfaces in the words of one of his long-standing collaborators, Efraín Sánchez, as he recalls in Interview 3 of this book that when Mockus visited Britain at the end of the 1990s, the British political and economic establishment was extremely suspicious of his eccentricity. Circuses, they remarked back then, are not a stage for true political leaders. And Antanas Mockus had publicly celebrated his second wedding in a circus, riding an elephant before the amused gaze of his fellow citizens. Other observers, such as Carlos Alberto Montaner (2010), have further insisted on Mockus's eccentricity by pointing out that his histrionic character, which turns him into "the political expression of surrealism," prevents him from squarely fitting into our classical understanding of a democratic leader. A segment of the Colombian public would have no problems sympathizing with these reactions.

Mockus's taste for eccentric performances and his persistent blurring of the border between art and government, however, may cue an alternative conception of politics and of political subjectivity that goes beyond standard liberal understandings—one whereby all power goes to the imagination to use a well-known slogan of the Parisian 1968 student movement. In particular, it may reflect some of the values and aspirations that might be more closely attuned with a radical political culture.

As we acknowledge the potential radicalism that might characterize some dimensions of his discourse and practice, however, we must also accept that many elements within them elude standard understandings of Latin American radicalism. Radicals across Latin America, and surely in Colombia, have pursued systemic transformations of society and sought to more directly and explicitly address such important structural issues as poverty or inequality than Mockus did. To them, Mockus has evaded the big questions and has downgraded the political vocation of practice to a problematic form of light radicalism. Also, to some Colombian radicals, Mockus's insistence on the need to abide by the rules and to use all established democratic channels to change them has often come across as unbearably authoritarian, as they believe that the Colombian state has been built on illegitimate foundations; therefore, the enforcement of its rules on the people constitutes an act of authoritarianism, while an in-good-faith acceptance or use of those rules entails a servile ratification of the status quo.

That said, it is important to recognize that other elements of Mockus's practice manage to puzzlingly elude both a liberal and a radical reading. For example, in 1991, Colombia passed a new constitution. Despite its new emphasis on the sacredness of the individual, on human dignity, personal autonomy, rationality and freedom, the new system of secular collective representations underpinning the new constitution did not provide a common political vocabulary for all Colombian society (Palacios 1999; Estrada 2004; Gutiérrez 1999; Morales 1998). Instead, the old corporatist political culture that had traditionally been built on an organic understanding of society, and that underpinned the older 1886 constitution, continued to shape the everyday understandings of legitimacy in social life among broad segments of the Colombian public.[2]

Such a culture builds on a system of binary oppositions that define what is legitimate in social life and what must be, instead, resisted. The attributes on the positive side make up the *patrón/peón* code whereas those on the negative side identify the bandit code. The notion of *patrón* collapses elements that are political, religious, familiar, moral, and economic into one figure. The *patrón* is the protector, the shelter, the moral authority, the saint, the person in charge of the workers, the lord that rules over his fief, and the owner of the house where everyone else is a guest. The *peón*, on the other hand, is the subordinate who submits to the superior wisdom of the *patrón*, the docile follower, the listener, the modest person who knows his own place in society and accepts his humble part in it. If the *patrón* is the head of the social body, then the *peón* is its hand and can claim dignity only until he fulfills his own function. On the other hand, the "bandit" is the *peón* who went rogue and decided to rebel against social, and therefore natural, harmony.

Many have identified former Colombian President Álvaro Uribe as the quintessential embodiment of the *patrón* and have therefore read his political leadership within this later corporatist political culture. It would be a mistake, however, to attribute such a cultural horizon to just those segments of the Colombian public that identify with the political right. The organic understandings of society based on patriarchy and Catholicism that underpin this political culture are quite widespread in Colombia, and even creep into the discourse of the leftist guerrillas. During the Conference the FARC summoned to celebrate its 43rd Anniversary, for example, the guerrilla group issued a communiqué that called on Colombians "to struggle for a new government capable of reconciling the Colombian *family*," [emphasis added] which, in turn, recasts the idea of society into a symbolic field that is much closer to an organic understanding of it.[3]

Quite surprisingly, there are elements in Mockus's performance of political leadership that echo this same political culture. During the 2010 presidential elections, Mockus led the so-called "Green Wave," which managed to mobilize broad segments of the Colombian urban population, particularly among the younger generations, and that at some point appeared to stand a solid chance of winning the elections and defeating the Colombian establishment. The results of the first-round election, however, froze all enthusiasm and Mockus was subsequently defeated in the second round by his opponent. The night of that first round, when polls closed and bad news started to come in at his campaign headquarters, Mockus appeared on stage in front of a mass of followers who rhythmically chanted "*Mi Profesor, mi Presidente*" (My Professor, My President), a situation that hardly squared with the image of a liberal democratic leader or a radical leader, and matched instead more closely the persona of a pastor on stage.

It is not uncommon for liberal democratic leaders to take part in charismatic rituals. When that happens, though, their followers seldom indulge in chants with psalmic overtones. They may well celebrate their victory or repeat with enthusiasm the political slogans of their campaign, such as "Yes, We Can" or "Forward." They may even hysterically shout out the name of their winning champion, but they hardly cue in their words a personal, almost intimate submission to their leader. On the other hand, Latin American radical leaders have traditionally managed to project a prophetic aura based on their own political eschatologies. Mockus, however, has not been the forbearer of any eschatology. His practices have relied on small steps that might lead far, and the horizon of his proposal has been the long term, within which his pedagogic approach might have a chance to leave a mark. His prophecy, as a result, has not beaten the tempo of urgency, that characterizes the revolutionary agenda of Latin American radical prophets.

During Mockus's first administration, Paul Bromberg was at the forefront of the *Cultura Ciudadana* as the Director of the Bogotá Institute of Tourism and Culture. Later, he took over Mockus's office as mayor of Bogotá when Mockus decided to abandon his mandate before the end of his term to run as a presidential candidate. Bromberg considers that there are two types of leadership. Some leaders are prophets, others are engineers. Prophets, Bromberg (2003) says, are the vessels of a revelation. They are visionaries. They are masters who teach, preach, and predict. Prophets, Bromberg continues, transform individuals by converting their values, their attitudes and their beliefs. Those who work with them are apostles, not officials. Prophets are the bearers of a message, and people around them tend to believe that their message—more than the organization that supports it—constitutes the true source of power of the prophet. Actually, Bromberg adds, prophets are themselves convinced that their word and their personal intervention is what really matters as the very source of efficacy of their action. Engineers, on the contrary, do not believe in the self-efficacy of the prophetic word. They are concerned, instead, with how many people hear their message, if they actually listen to it, to what extent they remember it, and whether they care at all about it. Prophets, on the other hand, are convinced that "everyone listens to them, believes in them, trusts them" (ibid.:20). Bromberg concludes that Mockus comes closer to the former style of leadership, while Bromberg identifies himself with the latter.

On some occasions Mockus's narrative style comes close to church sermons or apostolic letters, thereby adding plausibility to Bromberg's interpretation. In a piece of writing entitled "Seven Letters about Living Together," Mockus addresses, in a most intimate fashion, a number of different social groups. In the letter to "those who take illegal shortcuts in life," he reminds them that worse than facing prosecution by law enforcement agencies, and even worse than being exposed to public scorn, they will ultimately have to deal with "the torment of their conscience." Self-deception, he warns, cannot help them elude their feeling of guilt. One cannot be forever deaf, he adds, to the voice of one's own conscience. Instead, "an option for those who have explored such dramas is to share their lessons, teach, and communicate what they learnt. Pedagogic authority can be a replacement, humanly a very satisfactory one, of the authority that is granted by the arms or by money [...]. How many confessions on the part of tormented consciences await the moment when they will tell their lesson!" (Mockus 2009:6-7). In short, given Mockus's pedagogic take on politics, here he appears to come quite close to an invitation to "convert yourself and follow me" (ibid.:10).

Granting that some of Mockus's reception on the part of the Colombian public might actually fall within the horizon of meaning of the more conservative strand of Colombian political culture, it is still important to warn that one cannot take such interpretation of Mockus too far without quickly losing its plausibility. Mockus, after all, does not meet the expectations of this more corporatist political culture as far as the treatment of dissenters is concerned. The latter treats them as bandits, whereas Mockus does not. In this respect he is squarely aligned with liberal democratic codes.

Now, according to Mockus, teachers are "cultural amphibians" who are capable of recontextualizing knowledge within new contexts that lend themselves to more effective learning on the part of their pupils. Mockus developed this idea on the ground of Basil Bernstein's understanding of the educator as a translator who takes knowledge from one context and recasts it into another (Narvaez-Goldstein 2002-2003:126). When he left academia to become mayor, Mockus extended this concept to refer to people who competently move across different cultural traditions. In his view, cultural amphibians are crucial for realigning legal with moral and cultural norms whenever they are out of line. To suggest that Mockus is a cultural amphibian across liberal, radical, and conservative political cultures would presuppose an element of intentionality on his part each time we find him zipping together the edges of these three cultural spaces. Here, I am not going that far. More than his own intentionality, what matters to me at this point is his public reception and the latent accomplishment that might result from carrying out that function.

To conclude, many observers have found value in Mockus's practice in light of his impact on a broad spectrum of social issues. In that vein, I have suggested that his role is also politically significant in one further respect. In Colombia, three political cultures contend for the definition of legitimacy in social life. Very often, it is difficult to foster dialogue among them. One reason probably has to do with the fact that there are very few leaders in Colombia who can authentically bridge them, and almost no institutional spaces that systematically cultivate adequate cultural competences for new leaders to emerge and build those bridges. Thus, in line with generalized processes of segregation within Colombian society, Colombian universities have too often ended up playing into the logic of segregation have generally given up their role as potential sites for bridging and integration. By ambivalently oscillating within his practice across those three different political cultures, Mockus contributes on exactly that front. As a result, his ambivalence, however troubling it might look and feel to some, may carry out an important latent function within Colombian society.

Antanas Mockus and the Public Humanities

Since his recent passage through Harvard University in 2004, Antanas Mockus has been exposed to the US movement that advocates more public engagement on the part of scholars in the humanities than has conventionally been practiced. In a way, Mockus's professional biography—first as an academic, then as chancellor of the National University, and finally as mayor of Bogotá—provides a remarkable example of the accomplishments that may await the humanities once they dare go public. After briefly recalling what the public humanities are about in the United

States, why they started, and what they pursue, I will here discuss which elements of Mockus's practices as a cultural agent seem to converge with the intellectual project of public humanities, where they appear to take divergent paths, and how they may inform one another.

In the 1980s and early 1990s, the "culture wars" waged by neoconservative intellectuals, journalists, and academics also targeted the humanities for pursuing a revision of "Western canons, national narratives, and the relations among culture, society, and politics" (Bartha 2010:92) and pressured humanists to enter the public sphere to defend themselves and their field. In 1999, seventy-eight colleges and universities established a consortium, *Imagining America: Artists and Scholars in Public Life (IA)*, to strengthen "the public role and democratic purposes" of the humanities, arts, and design through practice and theory (Ellison 2009:2). Inspired, the public humanities followed the path that the arts had already taken in their attempt to step beyond public performance into the terrain of public engagement (Jay 2013:54). Such a move in the direction of public scholarship has reflected a general trend that has also involved the social sciences. In 2004, for example, Michael Burawoy, then President of the American Sociological Association, called for a "Public Sociology" that would acknowledge the existence of a gap between self-referential professional legitimacy and its public legitimacy (Bartha 2010:89).

Public humanists have put forward a broad spectrum of reasons why the humanities would gain from going public, and why society would gain from it as well. According to Said (2004), for example, going public does not only help the humanities become "democratic, open to all classes and backgrounds," it also disposes them to "a process of unending disclosure, discovery, self-criticism, and liberation" (Said 2004:22; Sandy 2013:315). Other leading humanists have stressed the public contribution of the humanities to society. Martha Nussbaum (2010) has insisted on the fact that they cultivate many competences that are crucial for democratic life, such as critical thinking, the respect for difference, empathy, "the ability to recognize fellow citizens as people with equal rights," "the ability to think about the good of the nation as a whole," and "the ability to see one's own nation, in turn, as part of a complicated world order" (Bell 2010:70; Sandy 2013:315). Doris Sommer (2014:6) adds that not only does aesthetic training help develop imagination and judgment, which are so important for civic life but also helps support "innovation, reorganization, and communication" by allowing multiple perspectives, by capturing contradictions through figurative language, and by creating as a result "a common understanding out of uncommon sense," which in turn may help us to make it through "our volatile times" (ibid.:88).

To go public in the United States, humanists have had to take steps on two fronts. First, they have had to cross over to other spheres of society and, to that end, they have had "to engage, displace, and transform existing paradigms of knowing and scholarship" (Bartha 2010:86). Second, they have had to develop a broad spectrum of new competencies and institutional capabilities, including "the will to understand, to inquire, to make things work, and to change," as well as fostering humility, curiosity, and commitment. "Situating knowledge, challenging habitual frames for knowing, facilitating selectively adapted repertoires, and remaking site specific practices" have demanded from humanists the "capacity to coordinate inquiry and activity, to mediate and negotiate, to engage personal and organizational differences and to sustain tensions around them" (ibid.:102).

Seen from the South, and particularly from Latin America, the intellectual project pursued by the US public humanities sounds intimately familiar. After all, when one travels south, one stumbles upon a multiplicity of instances in which the humanities, the arts and even the social sciences have managed to fruitfully establish a pretty close encounter, if not outright collaboration, with various spheres of society. Experiences such as those of Mockus are a typical example of that. Still, one should not rush to conclude that the public humanities in the North and the public humanities in the South stand for just the same, and that what is urgent for the former is for the latter, as well.

In the South, "serious work" in the humanities includes an urgent front of action and reflection that so far has not been sufficiently apparent or recognized in the agenda of the public humanities in the North.[4] And when public humanists from the North travel south, that front tends to fall all too easily and all too quickly off their radar. Over the past two decades, public humanists in the North have sought to push the humanities towards a closer embrace of society. To accomplish that goal, they have tried to carry out a plethora of projects that have attempted to realize in multiple ways the vision of that embrace. Getting such projects off the ground, adjusting their institutional capabilities to be able to run them successfully, and showcasing those cultural agents that have distinguished themselves for their extraordinary accomplishments have been urgent items at the top of the agenda. In light of those priorities, it has also made sense for public humanists in the North to look south. The South, after all, can be a source of ideas and inspiration for engaged scholarship. It can provide exemplary platforms that can help enhance the cause of public humanities in the North. More pragmatically, since neo-conservatism at first, and the economic crisis later, have dramatically reduced the funding pool at home, the

South has not only provided a market where "consumers" do not need to be convinced about the virtues of engaged scholarship, but it has also allowed public humanities in the North to tap into alternative lines of funding for their ventures in the South. This has resulted in some clear gains from trade. On the one hand, institutions in the South have been able to satisfy their constant craving for external legitimation, while public humanists from the North have had the opportunity to expand their portfolios of interventions and to diversify their sources of funding.

While the humanities in the South have benefited from such opportunities for exchange with mutual benefit, it is important not to lose sight of the fact that, together with public social science in the South, the major challenge in the South is not to get engaged scholarship off the ground. The real challenge is to sustain it and prevent it from dying out. This generally means two things. First, empirically speaking, successful engagements in the South are generally tied to the work of single charismatic figures and hardly ever manage to get institutionalized. Second, they generally struggle to maintain their legitimacy in the long term. Now, it is important to recognize why this is the case, and why the obstacle along the path to long-term legitimation is connected to the impossibility of moving beyond person-alistic forms of public engagement.

Although public engagement on the part of the humanities (and the social sciences) in the South is local, today the quest for its long-term legitimacy is both local and global. It is local because the recipients of public engagement need to manifest at least some support for it, and it is global, because such engagements need to be grounded in expert knowledge, which in turn emerges from global circuits of knowledge creation. In other words, without being properly grounded at the epistemic level, it will be increasingly difficult to defend them in the long run.

A robust epistemic grounding of a practice does not only recognize its strengths, but it also systematically addresses its weaknesses. It sheds light on its anomalies, and it is very much interested in extending its realm of application. Generally, it is along this path of discovery of the potential extension of a practice that one may unveil the conditions under which the practice may be reproduced without the intervention of the person who championed it from the start. Securing an epistemic basis that can back the practice, in turn, is no straightforward task. Since circuits of knowledge creation are global nowadays, it is an exercise that very of-ten transcends the local settings within which the practice is carried out and exercises its impacts. Sometimes the epistemic base for a specific practice comes ready-made, possibly from the outside, and it fits the practice. Other times, however, it does not, and instead fits like a suit that is too tight and constantly at risk of ripping apart.

Both the public humanities and the public social sciences in the South are therefore bound to ask whether the epistemic basis that underlies a practice is fitting and, in case it is not, they have to evaluate the costs and benefits of keeping it that way. If they decide to alter the epistemic base or to change it altogether, they will have to embed that alteration within the global circuit of knowledge production. The new epistemic ground that will back the practice, after all, will need to have a global currency for the purpose of legitimizing that practice in the long term, beyond the punctual institutional conditions under which the practice was developed in the first place. In short, doing "serious work" in the public humanities along the North-South axis means intervening in the global circuit of knowledge generation and reassembling the institutional resources put together by northern and southern partners to allow the emergence of new knowledge that can sustain a given practice in the long term.

For the public humanities and the public social sciences in the South, as a result, practice alone is not the only relevant issue. Theory is of paramount importance, too. For public humanists in the North, practice is the focus and the fact that a successful practice of public engagement may appear to be indissolubly attached to a single person is quite irrelevant. After all, their interest in recognizing successful practices has to do with the urgent imperative of showcasing the public humanities to be relevant for society.

When cultural agents in the South carry out successful practices that do not address the urgent questions about the epistemic grounds that legitimize their action; when they refrain from imagining their practices beyond themselves and after themselves, thereby precluding any systematic reflection along the route of institutionalization of those practices; when they mistake the appreciation on the part of their colleagues in the North as all there is to it, neglecting that each side is responding to different agendas, to different priorities and to different questions; then cultural agents in the South are undermining the possibility of sustaining their practices for the long-run, while their counterparts in the North may contribute to undermining the exemplary cases they use to meet their own strategic objectives.

The Cultural Agents Initiative at the National University in Bogotá and Cambridge has become aware of such stakes. They have understood what new problems appear at the horizon of the public humanities when they decide to go global, and have tried to meet the challenges—epistemic, pragmatic, and institutional—that come along with it. This book bears witness, however imperfectly, to that effort and to that aspiration. Here we try to take steps in the direction recently pointed out by Julie Ellison (2009:7), founding Director of Imagining America:

> Public scholarship is grounded in local partnerships; dedicated to diversity; and based on a concrete grasp of the "new cosmopolitanism" that reveals the connections between the local and the global. (P. 7)

At the same time, we recognize the specific challenges that the public humanities in the North may face as they open themselves to an encounter with the South and project their own ethos on it. Again, Ellison (ibid.) suggests:

> Public scholarship is carried out by people who are "called" to civic leadership. Public work in the arts and humanities needs to boldly claim and more fully realize this role, at a time of transition and flux in the nation's politics and identity. Voicing and answering this call does not come easily to artists and humanists, especially in academic settings. (P. 1)

Exercising a call in one's own context of origin is a sure sign of passion, dedication, and generosity. The history of North-South relations, however, obliges us to be cautious as we frame our North-South engagement, along with the language of the call. Too often "calls" have led to problematic distinctions between saviors and saved that have often resulted in negative outcomes. At the beginning of the path along which the public humanities go global, there stands a sign: "*Please, no calls!*"

Mockus is surely a prototypical model for the public humanities. From the public humanities he has been able to gain greater international exposure and some very useful conceptual and theoretical anchors to sustain his practice. Boosting its philosophical foundations does not, however, automatically translate into securing a solid epistemic basis on which his practice can be sustained in the long run and institutionalized beyond Mockus himself. For that to happen, it is necessary to count on a research program that systematically addresses the limits and criticalities of Mockus's practice with an eye to paving the way to its extension in ways that are robust enough to apply beyond the contexts and circumstances where it was originally carried out. This is something that the public humanities have not been able to provide Mockus, at least so far.

Bearing this in mind, the encounter between Mockus and the public humanities confronts both the aforementioned with the risks that come from each side sticking to its own comfort zone. By treating Mockus merely as a model to enhance their own agenda, the US public humanities may miss the opportunity to recognize all that is at stake in the practices carried out by public humanists in the South, and with particular reference to Mockus they may end up underplaying the peculiar way in which the humanities and the social sciences do and must weave into each other to underpin his practice. On the other hand, while being treated as a model, Mockus may be tempted to insist on the performative end of his practice all the more, laying even greater emphasis on its personalistic dimension, and overlooking the fact that the power of that practice as an example of the public humanities holds only insofar as he can show that his practice can be reproduced in other settings, without his direct intervention.

More generally, public engagement predicated upon charismatic figures cannot be a business for the public humanities. If the public humanities are to convince society that they matter, they will need to show that they can lay the ground for practices that have a chance of being replicated and spreading outside their own contexts of origin. Also, they will need to show that the success of these practices isnot contingent on the occasional charisma of some remarkable cultural agent. After all, treading too deeply into the terrain of charisma and giving in to the seductive appeal of "charismatic churches," to paraphrase Bromberg, would be an ironic point of arrival for a field that emerged in response to the neoconservative wave that threatened the very existence of the US humanities in the first place.

To step away from that dangerous edge, we need to ask whether the social theory underpinning the strands of public humanities that have acknowledged the practice of Antanas Mockus actually matches his practice and whether it is consistent with the rest of his intellectual framework. Before that, though, it is necessary to clear up one further issue.

I have suggested that the public humanities have provided an enriching field that has been nurturing Mockus's practice. On the other hand, I have argued that their seductive appeal may orient Mockus in directions that might not necessarily work in favor of sustaining his own practice. But Mockus has the option to tie himself to a mast to avoid that. For that purpose, however, he must have a clear sense of which mast he should hold onto and why. A discussion of his intellectual production and of the scholarship that has been generated in Colombia and around the world with reference to his practices may provide some useful indications in this respect.

The Hidden Trap: Cultural Agency without Epistemic Legitimacy

Over the years, different elements of *Cultura Ciudadana* have been transplanted to other cities in Colombia. Such injunctions like "Life is Sacred," or exhortations such as "Everyone contributes, everyone gains," which had been part of the vocabulary of *Cultura Ciudadana*, started to gain wider currency across the Colombian public, though Mockus (2009:2) recognizes that they did so with variable impact. Under the auspices of the Inter-American Development Bank, *Cultura Ciudadana* has also reached other corners of the region. In a study focusing on the relationship between culture and civic security, the think-tank Mockus set up after his second term as mayor of Bogotá addressed the regulatory power of culture on violence in the case of eight Latin American cities and the problematic interactions between legal, cultural and moral impunities. After carrying out a survey on *Cultura Ciudadana* in 2001 and 2003 during his second term, in 2004, Mockus started to apply it in twelve other Colombian cities, including Medellín, as well as in Caracas, Venezuela. Between 2009 and 2012, he applied it in Belo Horizonte, Mexico City, Quito, La Paz, and Monterrey. Some cities such as México City as well as Santa Marta in México, and Barranquilla and Barrancabermeja in Colombia, have carried out actions under the umbrella of *Cultura Ciudadana* (Mockus et al. 2012:255). Finally, over the years, the analytical framework that underpinned *Cultura Ciudadana* has been applied to other areas such as drug policy and cultural change in private sector organizations (Mockus 2008).

Given the impact that *Cultura Ciudadana* had in Bogotá, and given its potential applicability to a very broad spectrum of issues, it is surprising that it has not managed so far as to spread and become institutionalized throughout Latin America, and beyond. As scholars specializing in the study of processes of institutional diffusion have shown, many factors may play a role in that respect. Among them, a crucial one has to do with the epistemic legitimacy of a given framework. The more it is epistemically grounded and the greater its acceptance among the relevant communities of experts, the more apt it will be for replication beyond its context of origin. In turn, the quest for epistemic legitimacy is today a global one. To garner attention and ultimately gain global currency within relevant (global) epistemic communities, many elements are necessary. Surely, it is important to show that a given framework can have a major impact. Accordingly, that multilateral agencies recognize this fact is also important. For a number of years the Inter-American Development Bank and the United Nations Economic and Social Council have been headed by two Colombians who had the opportunity to witness the effects of Mockus's *Cultura Ciudadana* up close, and this may have helped with the initial attempts to project it within the region. Still, such recognition is not sufficient to motivate the buy-in of an idea on the part of epistemic communities. It is important to embed it more deeply within their networks.

Knowledge networks are generally quite hierarchical and therefore establishing close ties with their prominent centers may favor the exposure of an idea to the other members of the network. Such exposure, however, does not automatically translate into buy-in on their part. Furthermore, exposure cannot occur by mere contiguity with them. For example, appearing with them in a photo at the end of a seminar is not enough to prove that they have legitimized an idea. Knowledge networks make up communities of practice that share social norms, which in turn mark their collective identities. These norms include publishing work in certain journals or in specific book series of recognized publishers that every member of those communities will recognize as relevant for their own careers, as well as triggering an interlocution with such members to the point that they will not just refer to an idea casually or tangentially in their own work, but directly engage with its core and work both with it and from it. In other words, some contagion on the part of that idea must be apparent in their academic work.

For an idea to put down roots and gain legitimacy, it may have to take the form of an epistemic program. This means that its supporters must lay out a long-term intellectual agenda that manages to attract and compel a growing number of people— senior scholars, young scholars, and doctoral students—across a prolonged stretch of time. This, in turn, implies at least two things. Laying out such an agenda requires to systematically address what works about that idea and document it but, even more importantly, to systematically pin down what does not work, and under what circumstances the effectiveness of that idea rapidly decays. This latter line of exploration is crucial for the purpose of progressively extending the initial framework that underlies the idea and paving the way for its broader applicability.

On this front, Mockus has managed to adequately address a few issues, while on others there is still a significant margin for dramatic improvement. For example, Mockus (1994b:1) recognized that, to be relevant, Colombian academia would need to tie its work more closely to global processes of knowledge creation that take place in international research networks and to be more effective at articulating the local with the global. When Mockus (ibid.:31) further elaborates on what he means by better articulating the local with the global, he analogically applies Basil Bernstein's idea of the recontextualization of knowledge, and suggests that Colombian academia must contribute to the global process of knowledge circulation as a "conscious recontextualizer." Following Bernstein, Mockus (ibid.:32) thinks of recontextualization as a "process of selection, hierarchization, and adaptation of knowledge that comes from one context and is directed to another, by virtue of which that knowledge is reelaborated to make it significant and useful within the latter." On this basis, Colombian researchers should "select and circulate within the country a small fraction of the knowledge that is available around the world" (ibid.).

Such a top-down understanding of global knowledge production processes has implicitly oriented, for example, the seven international seminars that Mockus has organized since 2002 together with the National University of Colombia, which have brought an important number of internationally renowned scholars to Bogotá almost every other year. More precisely, by organizing these seminars for a decade, Mockus has sought to circulate or embed his ideas in a network that includes thirty-one foreign or foreign-based scholars and forty-four Colombian or Colombia-based participants, the majority of whom are scholars. The involvement of such an astounding group of people, however, has not translated into sustained collaborations and publications among them, which would have instead signaled some buy-in of Mockus's framework and its progressive transformation into an epistemic program. Mockus's practices have barely been noted in publications by foreign scholars. In very isolated cases has it resulted in passing mentions of his practice or something slightly more than that. It was only during the 2013 seminar that was possible to witness the emergence of a genuine intellectual dialogue between Mockus and one of the international scholars he has involved, Doris Sommer. At that event Mockus, Sommer, and a long-term fellow traveller of Mockus, Carlos Augusto Hernández, presented a joint paper that began to outline the relevance of Mockus's proposal for the public humanities. On the Colombian front then, there has not been a systematic buy-in of Mockus's framework. Scholars have maintained their own agendas and the attempt to intellectually seduce them has consistently failed.[5]

Thus far, Mockus's failure to translate his practices into a full-blown epistemic program that is regarded as sufficiently fertile to enroll a broad base of scholars who may actively engage with its development does not imply that it would not be possible to articulate a research agenda in that respect, and therefore identify a set of questions with a potential to attract not only contingent attention, but most importantly long-term intellectual commitment. By delving directly into Mockus's writings, it is possible to identify a number of fronts that appear quite worth systematically exploring.

For example, one conceptual pivot of Mockus's intellectual framework (worth discussing for the purpose of laying out a possible direction that an epistemic program based on his practices might take) has to do with the idea that a misalignment between law, morals, and culture within society is a source of social problems and that "intensified communication" is needed to bring them to light. I suggest that on this end we still need to lay out a more fine-grained theory of what "intensified communication" actually involves and why it appeared to work in the case of Mockus's practices.

To begin, Mockus (2000:1) argues that he was successful in aligning law, morals, and culture in the course of his actions because he resorted to "intensified communication." If communication gets intensified, Mockus (ibid.) says:

> Interlocutors will assume validity in what people say (understandability, sincerity, truth, rectitude) much more often and their pretensions will be accepted or problematized and defended. Possible disbelief on the part of some will lead the other under conditions of intensified communication to formulate more arguments. Criticism will gain more space and justification, as well. There will be more chances to accept the challenge of assessing one's own arguments and those of one's own counterpart. Rules will be assessed in terms of reasons and results and not just in terms of whom they benefit…Communication helps us decenter ourselves far enough to understand that our own rights are related with those of others. (P. 9)

Then, while addressing the topic of intensified communication, Mockus brings in a variety of correlated notions. "More private communication" among citizens, he says, may change their posture over specific issues that have to do with legal or social regulation. Intensified strategic interaction is also helpful to identify differences in interests and perspectives (ibid.). Sincerity, he insists, may deliver "a better result than traditional diplomacy." He then stresses the importance of honorability and openness, "radical frankness," and face-to-face interaction (ibid.:9–10; Mockus 2002:26).

Apart from the latter, the remaining part about "intensified communication" in Mockus's writings is fragmentary, vague, and confusing. Sincerity, honorability, radical frankness, and openness, after all, are anything but straightforward and cannot just be presented by the author or received by the reader at their face value as if they were unproblematic. Besides, the ideas of "intensified strategic interaction" and "private communication" are not self-explanatory either.

Take, for example, honorability, which Mockus recognizes as one of the ingredients of intensified communication. As in any process of social interaction, many elements come into play to define its meaning in a given pragmatic context. Some actors will try to project their understanding of honorability onto their audiences and they will articulate it in a script that will distill a broad set of relevant background collective representations. The mise-en-scène of that process of interaction will also influence the interaction. The same will happen with the means of symbolic production that the actor will tap into for the purpose of selling his own understanding of honorability to the audience (together with many other things). Social power will also play a role by pre-selecting, for example, the participants in that process of social interaction. When such elements fuse with one another, the idea of honorability that actors try to project on their audiences may come across as authentic and therefore convincing. If those elements do not fuse, on the other hand, the audience will start to doubt the content of the message and the intentions of the actor (Alexander 2006a; Alexander, Giesen, and Mast 2006). Besides, each process of social interaction is nested into or correlated with other processes. This, in turn, may influence the extent to which fusion is achieved in any single context. The fact that Mockus presents such concepts as sincerity, honorability, radical frankness, openness, or intensified communication as straightforward may signal the fact that, in his own experience, fusion was achieved in the pragmatic settings in which they came into play. Our job, however, is to explain how this fusion was possible.

To do so, it is useful to focus on the practices in which Mockus failed to achieve his goals. Under those circumstances, after all, it will be possible to spot whether defusion had something to do with the concrete ways in which either the actors, the audiences, the mise-en-scène, the script, the background collective representations, the means of symbolic production, or social power played out in that respect. Once we get a clear sense across all practices of what may have mattered most, it will be possible to reproduce those practices outside of their context of origin in a more controlled fashion, enabling us to anticipate the problems that may arise in these new settings and begin to formulate potential solutions.

In conclusion, without analytically grounding this notion of intense communication, which is so central to Mockus's pedagogic practices, on much firmer terrain, it will be difficult to argue in favor of its replicability outside its context of origin. It is not enough for an architect who managed to raise a skyscraper that appears to defy the laws of gravity, and the design of which has never been tried before, to say, "Hey, it worked just fine with me!" His example alone is not necessarily a selling point for those who are interested in importing and reproducing that design.

The critical edges of Mockus's intellectual framework identify a possible terrain on which an epistemic program might emerge that could keep a decent number of scholars occupied for some time. To move in that direction, however, it is necessary to depart from Mockus's understanding of the way local knowledge needs to be articulated with global knowledge generation circuits. For Mockus this is about recontextualizing bits and pieces of global knowledge within local contexts. In a way, Mockus understands the global process of knowledge creation as top-down, like the traditional diffusionist understanding which sees knowledge as flowing from the center to the periphery. To see opportunities for the launch of a new epistemic program that might back the practice of a given cultural agent, however, one cannot just enact the passive role of mere recipient of external knowledge who tweaks and adapts it to local contexts. To catalyze an epistemic program, Antanas Mockus, the cultural agent, must also think as an epistemic agent, who rejects his role as mere peripheral recontextualizer of knowledge and locates his practice straight on the cutting-edge frontier of global knowledge generation.

Critics might warn Mockus, at this point, against getting himself stuck in the quicksand of academic research and to instead keep to his policy practices. As long as he is around, this will be sufficient guarantee that they will prosper. There are three possible responses to this invitation.

First, other Latin American intellectuals have actively participated in the global process of knowledge generation, trusting the fact that intellectuals in the South are not doomed to be producers of peripheral knowledge, spearheading the emergence and diffusion of important epistemic programs, and using that capital to back their successful action in government. The case of Fernando Henrique Cardoso is one example.

Second, granting that cutting-edge research and effective policy practice need not be divorced, and acknowledging the fact that epistemic legitimacy can serve the purpose of sustaining effective practices over the long term, it is important to recognize that international academic communities have their own norms as to how to go about building legitimacy. Looking for easy shortcuts will not do. Anyone seeking to extend and sustain the benefits of *Cultura Ciudadana*—for Bogotá, for other corners of Colombia, and for other communities across Latin America and beyond—simply cannot afford to take shortcuts. The long march to a sustainable practice demands epistemic legitimacy, and epistemic legitimacy can only be achieved by generating an epistemic program that can consolidate right at the center of global processes of knowledge generation.

Finally, engaging the center of such processes not only meets the long-term needs of a policy practice. It also aligns it more closely with the new identity of a globalized Colombia that over the past two decades has progressively taken shape and that might increasingly influence the way in which future Colombians see themselves and project themselves before other societies. Perhaps today more than ever before, an increasing number of Colombians—and on certain occasions Colombia itself—have managed to be positively valued on the global scene, indicating that the country is finally reaching a critical threshold of capabilities that allow it to play assertively in multiple games opened up by globalization. Colombia is taking steps toward membership in the Organization for Economic Co-operation and Development (OECD). Within important foreign circles some have imagined the possibility that a Colombian president might win the Nobel Peace Prize, as it indeed happened in 2016. Until recently, a Colombian sat on the board of the world's largest and most powerful transnational mining company. Colombian scientists have joined the faculty of many prestigious universities in the United States and Europe and an increasing number of those who are in Colombia are intimately integrated into the center of global networks of knowledge generation. More and more Colombian artists are incorporated into important international circuits. Colombian cultural products circulate internationally, are successful, and inspire imitations. On the military front, Colombia has launched a series of operations that have entered the annals of world military history and have been compared to some of the most legendary operations carried out by Israel in its own history. The Colombian police have managed to inflict overwhelming damage on drug cartels and today their cutting-edge practices are exported from Colombia to Mexico, the United States, and even Afghanistan. A Colombian has been chosen by the UN Human Rights Council in Geneva to serve with four other members from around the world in the UN Working Group on Human Rights and Transnational Corporations and to lead the global diffusion of the UN Guiding Principles on Human Rights and Transnational Corporations. And *last but not least*, there are trade unionists and local community leaders in quite peripheral contexts of Colombia who would appear to be irremediably distant from the great games of globalization, and who, in spite of that, are not only capable of interacting with a very large spectrum of international cooperation agencies and transnationals of civil society, but also do so in a way that resists those troubling frames that promote relations of subordination between saviors and saved, recasting them instead within a new context of mere exchange with mutual benefit, that is, *nothing personal, just business*!

This new Colombia, which is made up of segments of society that may be ideologically very different among themselves and which today lurks just beyond the horizon, contains a new element with respect to the modern and democratic Colombia that came out of the 1991 Constitution. Before the difficulties and the manifest barriers that are being put on the path of lighter-weight players of globalization, this Colombia does not retreat and close into itself like a hedgehog, nor does it console itself by taking part in coalitions among the excluded. Faced with the dilemma of choosing, as Colombians say, between "being the head of a mouse or the tail of a lion," this new Colombia simply declines to consider the dilemma. The narrative about Colombia's participation in the game of globalization that underpins this new forming identity, in other words, no longer evokes the myth of Icarus, but rather appeals to the image of David against Goliath. This is a Colombia that does not share the belief that it is enough to simply participate in these games. This is a Colombia that has been accumulating over many decades the capabilities that today equip it to play better than ever before, more actively, and at greater advantage in the global economy and within global civil society. To realize the aspiration of this emerging identity, to be an integral part of the center, this Colombia is today mobilizing its capabilities to be part of the processes of global knowledge creation that feed directly into the epistemic structures underpinning the center.

Coupling Mockus's practices with an epistemic program that can sustain them in the long term therefore aligns it with an emerging collective identity that is shaping Colombia powerfully and promises to do so even more in the future, thereby securing another front of legitimacy—cultural legitimacy—that is only indirectly linked with epistemic legitimacy.

In the interview published in this book, Jon Elster points out that Mockus has been extremely creative and has put forward a variety of brilliant ideas, but has failed to properly develop any of them. However, he concludes, Mockus's creativity and his precarious follow-up on his intuitions come as a package deal; one cannot have one without the other. And since Mockus's practice depends on his charisma, Elster implies, one must accept the package as it is. If we want to reap the fruit of that practice, we need Antanas Mockus.

Here, I have distanced myself from this conclusion. The public value of Antanas Mockus demands that we scratch beneath the surface and account for the factors that actually contributed to his success. Charisma is a black box that prevents us from seeing into the fine mechanics of Mockus's practices and does away with the possibility of identifying ways to reproduce them without Mockus. To claim that Mockus is irreplaceable can only be acceptable after taking that analytical step and after gaining a much more fine-tuned understanding of his practices. Even more importantly, looking for the conditions that make it possible to replicate Mockus's practices without Mockus is imperative for those who live in the South or care for it. Observers in the North might get a kick out of Mockus's eccentric practices. In the South, however, that is a pleasure we cannot afford for long. In the South, society needs more solid institutions and demands steady and unwavering institution-builders. We cannot be content with the mere witnessing of brilliant policy practices. We must, instead, work to sustain them and to root them in society. This implies looking beyond the contributions of single outstanding actors, de-personalizing them, and paving the way for their institutionalization. Developing a research program that looks straight into the use of culture and communication in Mockus's practices may be one first step towards responding to this urgent demand.

Towards a Sturdier Cultural Agency

Insisting on the fact that cultural agents must be keenly concerned with the epistemic legitimacy of their own practices in order to be able to sustain them over time, and arguing that scholars should take notice of the epistemic base that underlies cultural agency is important for one further reason. There are cultural agents whose activities fit squarely into the theoretical framework that the former apply to make sense of the latter. In that case, scholars will contribute to setting cultural agents on a firm epistemic ground and to placing their creative activities onto a sustainable path. On the other hand, there are also cases in which the theoretical framework that cultural agents apply to their activities is not fitting. Under those circumstances scholars will fall short of grounding cultural agency on a solid epistemic base and will therefore miss the opportunity to contribute to its long-term sustainability. Cultural agents who overlook the culture-knowledge link cannot distinguish between the former and the latter cases, which is why they must necessarily address both the cultural practices above the surface and their epistemic grounding below.

Antanas Mockus is heuristically powerful. Unlike other cases of cultural agents that scholars have so far addressed, he puts forward a set of practices that wrestle with the theoretical framework that scholars have applied to the analysis of his case, as well as of other cultural agents. As a result, in the case of Mockus, the culture-knowledge link becomes more apparent because it is being cut.

Since her seminal book, Sommer (2006:2) has recognized Gramsci as "a patron saint of cultural agency," given his use of culture as a trigger for social change even under those adverse local circumstances that would appear to preclude it. Creative practices, Sommer (ibid.:3) says, may identify the existence of wiggle room for change within the interstices of social structure, something that social movements have clearly understood.

While recognizing the virtues of the Gramscian framework, however, Sommer also acknowledges, with Ernesto Laclau, an important weakness that undermines its applicability in the context of complex societies. Gramsci, she remarks, believes that social change can be achieved by replacing one national culture with another. This, in turn, will articulate an alternative hegemonic bloc with the capacity to redesign social structure. In complex societies, however, striving for one new national culture is no longer possible (ibid.:6). Based on that, and along with Laclau, Sommer (ibid.:7) recognizes that agents of social change must strive for "plural emancipations" that address structural asymmetries in their own local contexts of reference.

One might complement the line Sommer draws in connecting Gramsci to Laclau by also bringing into the picture Chantal Mouffe's (2007) reading of democracy as a site of inextinguishable agonistic conflict among collective groups that hold antagonistic interests and rationally irreconcilable discourses by which they articulate their diverse identities. This agonistic democracy, Mouffe (ibid.:552) insists, "endorses a politics of diverse social, cultural, and political movements organized around the values of cultural recognition, direct democracy, and performative resistance."

Again and again, we have had the opportunity to appreciate the fruitfulness of such a social theory to make sense of many cultural agents who, across Latin America and beyond, have struggled to promote the rights and liberties of marginal social groups that in many ways have challenged standard understandings of gender, sexuality, or ethnicity, to name just a few.

The intellectual encounter between Mockus and Sommer has been fruitful and has apparently enriched Sommer's perspective on cultural agency. For example, Sommer (2006:7) argued that "struggles for particular freedoms don't presume to destroy the state; they need it as an antagonist to struggle against in a contest for concessions. The object is to win ground in hegemonic arrangements that depend on popular consent. And the mechanism is to irritate the state in ways that stimulate concessions of more freedoms and resources." In light of Mockus's experience, however, Sommer (2014:23-24) has recently come to recognize in her latest work that "governments need not be eliminated, either by armed force or by cumulative cultural revolution; they can be reformed through the intrinsic dynamism of programs that coordinate active citizens with creative and transparent leadership."

That said, there are still some theoretically irritating aspects about Mockus's cultural practices that so far have been systematically eluded by all scholarship on cultural agency. First, Mockus's approach to social interaction focuses on individuals, not on members of social classes. Second, he focuses on duties as much as on rights. And third, which in a way is also linked to the second point, Mockus's insistence on the need to rely on a minimum common ground that can tie citizens together brings into the picture a preoccupation with integration that marks a clear departure from other forms of cultural agency that, instead, have traditionally emphasized dissent and conflict.

Gramsci, Laclau and Mouffe lay out a conflict social theory that does not make much of the issue of integration and that, as a result of its implicit collectivist bias, does not make much of individuals, either. Reading Mockus through such lenses, as a consequence, will result in a misalignment between the practice and the theory that interprets the practice. On one occasion, Mockus (2004:17) himself explicitly remarked that he feels like an outsider in regarding to "a supposedly self-critical neomarxism."

Such a misalignment, in turn, is problematic for a number of reasons. First, it does not capture Mockus's specificity with respect to other cultural agents who, instead, are quite well represented by Gramsci, Laclau and Mouffe. And second, it does not necessarily help build a coherent epistemic basis on which his cultural agency may be sustained in the long term and beyond its context of origin.

Acknowledging the culture-knowledge link in cultural agency does not only introduce a new analytical check that alerts us to the possibility of such misalignments. It also allows us to more effectively decenter the idea of cultural agency with which we started out our analysis of Mockus a few years ago. And as a result of such a move, we may still go south with our exploration of cultural agency, but we will add to it a commitment to expand the depth of our encounters with the creative practices we stumble upon during our search.

Such a decentering move and its consequent implications on the mode of our encounter with cultural agents in the field also provide an escape route from a thorny discussion. Some critics of Sommer (2006:9) have warned that "when Westernized intellectuals use indigenous informants, the dynamic ends in the familiar traps of vampirism and co-optation." Other scholars, however, have responded by reminding such critics that in spite of all asymmetries, we may still engage in mutually beneficial exchange. They have pointed out that "'using people is an effect of normal, healthy relationships as well as of mutually interested deals." And they have suggested that "vampires do drink other people's blood. There's no denying it. But the victims can get eternal life in exchange" (ibid.:6). Now, by decentering our understanding of cultural agency, we may come to realize why both threads of this discussion are dead ends.

If we approach Mockus merely from the perspective of change, the US public humanities surely stands to benefit from their end of the deal, because they will be able to count on a remarkable model that enhances their own cause. On the other side of the exchange, Mockus will benefit from the spotlight derived from such exposure, and scholars in the South writing about him will also have a exchange to gain their place in the sun.

Mere exchange, however, does not compel either side to spot and address the weak flanks in Mockus's practices or in our understanding of cultural agency. Here, I have shown that eluding a consideration of both issues has serious consequences. It prevents us from understanding the conditions under which Mockus's creative practices might be sustainable in the long term and could be institutionalized beyond their context of origin, and it prevents us from taking stock of an entire dimension of cultural agency, the culture-knowledge link, that has so far eluded the attention of scholars in this field. Demanding that we ask each other a series of irritating questions, thereby engaging in an exercise of mutual unveiling, compels us to move beyond the politeness of mere exchange and obliges us to take the risks that are inherent in a relation based on that mutual solidarity that can only arise from helping each other do better.

This departure from a logic of mere exchange to one of solidarity and the realization of the potential gains that might accrue as a result of it becomes clear, once we choose a different vantage point from which we can observe the phenomenon of cultural agency, or, more concretely, when we abandon a conflict social theory for a multi-dimensional theory of society that gives both conflict *and* integration their due.[6] Only the latter will put us in a position to recover that very impulse for integration that leads to solidarity on the terrain of social practices, on the terrain of knowledge creation, and, in the end, also on the terrain of our mutual engagements between North and South.

Seduction, and Not Only That

Any intellectual project is a collective enterprise that must involve, seduce, and motivate just the right spectrum of contributors necessary to fulfill its goals. At the time we started this book, it was not at all clear to many of us that a propitious vantage point from which to observe cultural agency would be at the edge of it: where cultural agency either fails to be faithful to its own creative impulse or where it is true to itself in ways it did not mean to be. Failing to see this, we did not realize, either, that melodrama and epic are not necessarily *the* genre to tell the story of cultural agency and that comedy, instead, might be fit for the purpose. After all, if a story of cultural agency gets to celebrate its accomplishments, it must do so against the backdrop of its instability and its fragility, always at risk of contradicting its own creative impulse or of being true to it in ways it did not intend. Those accomplishments, after all, become more apparent at the site of creativity, which is generally the site of the unobvious and the unexpected.

In *Scusate il ritardo* (Sorry for the Delay), the Italian actor Massimo Troisi, best known to international audiences for his main role in *The Postman*, is prompted to declare whether he would prefer to live one day as a lion or one hundred days as a sheep. He resolves that fifty days as a teddy bear would be best. If, along with Troisi, we get to tell the story of cultural agency in ways that resist stiffening into something all too powerful and all too foresighted, and if at the same time we avoid falling into cynical disbelief, maybe we will have a chance to successfully draw into the writing of our narration both those who stand on that side of the edge where creative practices have shone their light and those who stand on the opposite side where those practices have painfully failed to meet their promise. Together, by holding onto each other as they walk along the slippery edge of creative practices, which become all the more slippery when they are promoted from powerful positions, narrators from both sides have a chance to keep the narration of cultural agency right on the spot of that unstable and fragile site where creativity manifests itself.

This book is an invitation to readers, scholars and artists to complement our narration with their edge of the story, to show us the merits and cracks in Mockus's creative practices that so far have eluded our analysis, and hopefully to identify opportunities and tensions in our own understanding of cultural agency of which we still need to be urgently aware. The book consists of five parts. *Part One* includes my introduction. This part provides a general framework of discussion that makes it possible to understand why the practices and legacy of Antanas Mockus are significant, both for what they have achieved and for what they fail to achieve. *Part Two* features a visual essay that assembles images and information about a large number of policy programs that made up Mockus's *Cultura Ciudadana* during his two administrations as mayor of Bogotá. *Part Three* will include eleven essays that delve into different aspects of Mockus's practices. *Part Four* includes four interviews with some of Mockus's fellow travelers in Bogotá and with one of Mockus's major sources of intellectual inspiration, Jon Elster. The last part will feature a series of short comments on *Cultura Ciudadana* by seven additional authors and Mockus's response to the material presented in this book. Some of the authors and interviewees have been close associates of Antanas Mockus; either in his administrations, such as Paul Bromberg, Rocío Londoño, and Efraín Sánchez; or in his own think-tank, such as Henry Murraín, or within the Federici Group, such as Carlos Augusto Hernández. Contributors cut across a variety of fields and disciplines, such as sociology, urban studies, philosophy, history, literature, communication studies, the arts, psychology, and education. Some of the authors are academics, others are practitioners; and yet others have moved repeatedly across the fields of academia and practice. Some authors are based in Latin America, the majority of whom are currently in Colombia, and the others are based in the United States. Their approach to Mockus's experience also varies and reflects quite well the styles of engagement that Mockus has been able to spark within the Colombian academic community and internationally. In the case of the two essays written by Henry Murraín and Carlos Augusto Hernández, respectively, the elaboration of which Mockus followed closely, one may also gain an extremely valuable glimpse, however indirect, into the intellectual environment of Mockus's current inner circle.

Before laying out the eleven essays that reflect in depth on the thought and practice of Antanas Mockus, José Luis Falconi opens with a visual essay presenting the broad spectrum of programs that made up Antanas Mockus's *Cultura Ciudadana* during his two administrations as mayor of Bogotá. This essay not only summarizes important facts about each program, but perhaps, more importantly, captures one crucial dimension of *Cultura Ciudadana*: the visual, which today still vividly resonates in the memory of the Bogotanos who experienced it.

In the first essay, "'*Por Amor al Arte*': Haber-Mockus Plays with the Possible," Doris Sommer starts by introducing some of the creative interventions Mockus carried out during his administration that turned out to have a transformational impact on Bogotá and have commanded the attention, curiosity, and also admiration of many observers both within and outside of Colombia. Mockus, she observes, vindicated the positive role that pleasure and passion can play in social reform and in the establishment of the rule of law, an intuition that is already apparent in Friedrich Schiller's 1794 *Letters on the Aesthetic Education of Man*, in which he recognized that the arts could serve as a conduit to channel pleasure into civic experience. Mockus's administration's programs on *Cultura Ciudadana* did exactly that for the purpose of harmonizing some of the social, cultural and moral norms of Bogotanos, hence tackling some of the most pressing problems that plagued the city. Sommer dwells on the traditional opposition between reason and passion and discusses Mockus's approach through Kant, Schiller, Habermas, and Dewey. Finally, applying the arts to the solution of social issues, Sommer recalls, can be problematic for various artists, a point that Jesús Martín-Barbero also addresses in his chapter. Both Sommer and Martín-Barbero, however, conclude that Mockus's cultural agency had beneficial effects both on aesthetic and political ends.

In his essay titled "BOGOTÁ: Between the Violence of Chaos and Civic Creativity," Jesús Martín-Barbero opens by weaving together the threads of different narrations of past and recent life in Bogotá, in which fictional escapes are attempted to relax the grip on life of a city that has often come across as grey, dangerous, and violent. Martín-Barbero observes that television has played an important role in stabilizing such a perception. Bogotanos have been able to retreat into the private space of their living rooms and have accepted experiencing their city in that mediated fashion as a result of a systematic representation of the city as inhospitable, and unworthy of trust or attention. This, in turn, has progressively eroded the social fabric that would otherwise link citizens to one another and has paved the way for aggressiveness as a culturally legitimate form of relating to others. When Mockus began his term as mayor of Bogotá, he had to face such a situation. By intervening on representations of the city and on the self-representations of Bogotanos, Mockus was able to influence their behavior, and he did so by innovating on the cultural policy front and by systematically tapping into the arts, as a means of transforming the city on the one hand and politics on the other.

In "Transforming Expectations through *Cultura Ciudadana*," Henry Murraín further reflects on Mockus's idea about the tension between moral, social, and legal norms and its effects on anomie. His analysis, which originates directly from within Mockus's inner circle, is embedded within a broad literature about social norms that goes from Durkheim and Elias through Merton to Douglass North, Cristina Bicchieri and social norms analysis within social psychology, and insists on the effects that the representation of fellow-citizens as transgressors ultimately has on anomie.

In his essay titled "Effective Rule of Law Requires Construction of a Social Norm of Legal Obedience," Gerry Mackie places Mockus's exercise of cultural agency within the international debate on the establishment of effective rule of law. He observes that many have considered criminalization as the way to address and contain harmful social norms, although at times legal norms can inhibit the change of harmful social norms. Laws, however, need compliance, and legal obedience is difficult whenever social and moral norms pull in different directions. Various literatures, Mackie points out, have looked into the reasons why people obey the law, whether it is right to criminalize certain social norms, what to do about the absence of social norms of legal obedience, how to harmonize diverging norms, as well as how to cope when new legal norms are too distant from social norms. Mockus, Mackie concludes, has the merit to have realized very early that the lack of alignment between legal, social, and moral norms undermines the rule of law and has shown innovative ways of bringing them into alignment through the exercise of cultural agency.

In her essay entitled "Social Norms and the Cross-Border Citizen: From Adam Smith to Antanas Mockus," Fonna Forman establishes an interpretative parallel between Mockus's ideas on social regulation and those of Adam Smith, thereby adding one further classical theorist to the list of authors that scholars interested in the work of Mockus should take into account, in order to locate Mockus within the broader landscape of classical and contemporary social thought. In her essay, Forman also presents the first instance of the application of *Cultura Ciudadana* framework to a frontier context, that is, the San Diego-Tijuana border.

In his essay entitled "Social Reform and the Limits of Education," Jaime Ramos begins by recognizing the many good qualities of Mockus's practice. Nonetheless, after doing so, he rapidly comes to focus on the limits of his practices. First, he criticizes Mockus's framework, which takes law, morals, and culture as separate spheres, and its underlying rationalist understanding of normativity, which does not do justice to the social embeddedness of norms. Then, he turns to empirical data and argues that it does not support the extent to which Mockus and his supporters claim that *Cultura Ciudadana* actually contributed to the prevention of crime and the reduction of the homicide rate in Bogotá. Finally, building on Bourdieu's notion of *habitus*, he stresses the limits of educational campaigns and explicit teaching in general as triggers of social change.

In his essay entitled "Antanas Mockus, the Academic," Carlos Augusto Hernández offers a rather intimate account of Mockus's practice in the 1970s as a young faculty member in the Department of Mathematics at the National University of Colombia, of his interest in the public communication of science, his involvement since 1979 as a member and later as director of the Federici Group, of which Hernández was also a fellow-member and which, as Hernández explains, played an important role in the Colombian pedagogic movement throughout the

1980s, and finally his contributions as a vice-chancellor and then chancellor of the National University.

In their essay entitled "Law, Morality, and Culture at School," Enrique Chaux and Andrea Bustamante focus on the issue of harmonization among legal, social, and moral norms, but shift away from the urban turf and bring their exercise of cultural agency back to the realm of education in schools for the purpose of inspiring a novel approach to tackling aggression and violence in schools, theft, and fraud. The collective construction of rules in schools, the promotion of social regulation among the students, the development of moral emotions, and the prevention of moral justifications or moral shortcuts are some of the foci of intervention for which Mockus's experience may turn out to be inspiring.

After addressing the many fronts along which Mockus's exercise of cultural agency has been particularly fertile, Javier Sáenz Obregón and Paolo Vignolo attempt to push analysis to the edge, where Mockus's experience has been exposed to criticism. In his essay entitled "Antanas Mockus as Pedagogue: Communicative Action, Civility, and Freedom," Javier Sáenz Obregón credits Mockus for transforming the civic culture of Bogotá and for creating new, more democratic and legitimate forms of public power. Even so, Mockus's pedagogical discourse and practice, Sáenz continues, constitutes a sophisticated instance of a post-disciplinarian form of government, which strategically acts upon the sense of citizens' individual freedom to steer their behavior toward the ruler's desired orientation. Mockus's pedagogic practices, in other words, fell short of cultivating freedom among his fellow citizens and played instead with their illusion thereof. To make his argument, Sáenz begins by shedding light on the long engagement that Mockus has had with pedagogy and the Pedagogical Movement in Colombia. Then, he discusses how this escalated to a pedagogical experiment within the city of Bogotá when Mockus became mayor and undertook an extensive program of pedagogization of urban life. Finally, Sáenz focuses on the limits of that effort.

In his essay titled "Mockus the Artist, Mockus the Idiot," Lucas Ospina notices that in the course of his academic career, Mockus gradually lost the performative capacity he used so effectively during his two administrations as mayor of Bogotá. During the 2010 presidential campaign, Ospina insists, Mockus's creativity was stiffened by his advisors' more traditional understandings of political communication and his naïve authenticity lost much of its earlier appeal.

In his essay entitled "The Dark Side of Mooning: Antanas Mockus Between Norm and Transgression," Paolo Vignolo takes stock of Mockus's original response to physical violence through performance, first as chancellor of the National University of Colombia and then as mayor of Bogotá, in an effort to channel it into displays of milder symbolic violence. Mockus's proposal, Vignolo says, manages to make nonviolent struggle viable in a context of extreme violence. As he works through a series of performances that Mockus carried out, Vignolo discusses on how Mockus uses reflexive transgression as a way to boost the power of ritualized responses to violence. He then moves to adress the limits and latent contradictions in Mockus's action.

The book then features four interviews with Paul Bromberg and Rocío Londoño who led the District Institute of Culture and Tourism during the first and second Mockus administrations, respectively; with Efraín Sánchez, who was director of the Observatory of Urban Culture during the second administration; and with Jon Elster, whose intellectual work has inspired Mockus's practice over many years.

Fabio López de la Roche, Andrés Salcedo, Alejandra Jaramillo, Marta Zambrano, Marsha Henry, Francisco Thoumi, and Fabián Sanábria add a series of short comments on Mockus's *Cultura Ciudadana*. And the conclusive essay includes a reflection by Antanas Mockus that builds on the contributions featured in this book.

Endnotes

1 For example, after inviting him to speak in her "Democracy From Theory to Practice" class, Jane Mansbridge, Adams Professor of the Kennedy School, reacted in the following terms: "We found Mayor Mockus's presentation intensely interesting. Our reading had focused on the standard material incentive-based systems for reducing corruption. He focused on changing hearts and minds—not through preaching but through artistically creative strategies that employed the power of individual and community disapproval. He also spoke openly, with a lovely partial self-mockery, of his own failings, not suggesting that he was more moral than anyone else. His presentation made it clear that the most effective campaigns combine material incentives with normative change and participatory stake holding. He is a most engaging, almost pixyish math professor, not a stuffy 'mayor' at all. The students were enchanted, as was I" (Caballero 2004).

2 Tognato (2011) and Cuellar (2009) refer to the discourse of the *hacienda* as the horizon within which legitimacy is articulated within that culture.

3 "Comunicado: 43 Aniversario de las FARC-EP" [Communication: 43rd Anniversary of the FARC-EP], Secretariat of the Central Command of the FARC-EP, May 25, 2007, http: //www.redresistencia.org from www.farcep.org.

4 By going public, the humanities have looked for new scenarios within which they can do "serious work," thereby addressing the frustration that Stuart Hall once voiced in a piece about "The Emergence of Cultural Studies and the Crisis of the Humanities" where he stated that "most of us had to leave the humanities in order to do serious work in it" (Hall 1990:11-12; in Bartha 2010:85). The public humanities have made space for "serious work" by setting the stage for "critical and creative intellectual, political, and cultural work that makes a social difference" and meets the standards of rigorous scholarship (Bartha 2010:86).

5 Many scholars in Colombia and around the world have referred to Mockus's innovative approach to urban policy and to the changes that have ensued in Bogotá as a result. A very small minority has engaged at a deeper level with the intellectual framework that has oriented his practices. Almost regularly, though, such an encounter has not produced any particular effect on their intellectual trajectory. They have not pushed the interlocution with Mockus's intellectual work far enough to build on it for the purpose of testing the limits of their own, but rather they have used Mockus as a confirmatory sounding board of what they were already out pursuing. Mockus, for his part, has not drawn from them any concrete insights about what the critical limits might be of his own intellectual framework. Only rarely has the interaction resulted in a more

productive encounter. In the case of Doris Sommer, for example, the interlocution has moved beyond the threshold of a reassuringly safe exchange and has opened up to the possibility of an intellectual dialogue that might produce something potentially unexpected and definitely more promising. For example, see: Elster (2006a; 2006b), Dubreuil and Gregoire (2013), Petersen and Zukerman (2010), Bicchieri and Mercier (2014), Moncada (2009), Nogueira (2009), Cala Buendía (2010), Ardila (2013), Dundjerovic and Navarro Bateman (2006), Pasotti (2009), Rojas (2004), Salcedo and Zimmerman (2008), Greiner (2010), Sommer (2006, 2014), Hunt (2009), Ortiz (2009), Perez (2010), Saenz (2011), and Martín-Barbero (2008).

6 See: Alexander (1988), Alexander (2003), and Alexander (2006b).

References

Abers, Rebecca. 1998. "From Clientelism to Cooperation: Local Government, Participatory Policy, and Civic Organizing in Porto Alegre, Brazil." *Politics and Society* 26:511–523.

Alexander, Jeffrey, Bernhard Giesen and Jason Mast, eds. 2006. *Social Performance*. Cambridge: Cambridge University Press.

Alexander, Jeffrey, 2006a. "Cultural Pragmatics: Social Performance Between Ritual and Strategy." Pp. 29-90 in *Social Performance*, edited by Alexander Jeffrey, Giesen, Bernhard, and Jason Mast. Cambridge: Cambridge University Press.

———. 1988. *Action and its Environments*. New York: Columbia University Press.

———. 2003. *The Meaning of Social Life*. Oxford: Oxford University Press.

———. 2006b. *The Civil Sphere*. Oxford: Oxford University Press.

Ardila Pinto, Ana Marcela. 2013. "Visões compartilhadas, Visões divergentes do espaço *público*. Uma comparacão sobre a construcão da política de espaço *público* em Bogotá e no Rio de Janeiro (1992-2008)" [Shared Visions, Divergent Visions of Public Space. A Comparison on the Construction of a Policy of Public Space Policy in Bogotá and Rio de Janeiro]. *Anais: Encontros Nacionais de Anpur* [Anais: National Anpur Meetings] 15:1-17.

Bartha, Miriam. 2010. "Serious Work: Public Engagement in the Humanities." *Western Humanities Review* 54(3):85-104.

Beckett, Katherine and Angelina Godoy. 2010. "A Tale of Two Cities: A Comparative Analysis of Quality of Life Initiatives in New York and Bogotá." *Urban Studies* 47(2):277-301.

Bell, David. 2010. "Re-imagining the Humanities." *Dissent* 57(4):69-75.

Bicchieri, Cristina and Hugo Mercier. 2014. "Norms and Beliefs: How Change Occurs." *Iyyun: The Jerusalem Philosophical Quarterly* 63:60–82.

"Bogotá, el mejor ejemplo para capitales latinoamericanas" [Bogotá, the Best Example for Latin American Capitals], 2002. *El Tiempo*, December 2.

Bromberg Zilberstein, Paul. 2003. "Ingenieros y profetas, transformaciones dirigidas de comportamientos colectivos" [Engineers and Prophets, Transformations Resulting from Collective Behaviors]. Pp. 67-104 in *Reflexiones sobre Cultura Ciudadana en Bogotá* [Reflections on Civic Culture in Bogotá]. Bogota: Instituto Distrital de Cultura y Turismo [Institute of Culture and Tourism].

Buber, Martin. 1965. *The Knowledge of Man*. New York: Harper & Row Publishers.

Caballero, María Cristina. 2004. "Academic Turns City into a Social Experiment," *Harvard Gazette*, March 11.

Cala Buendía, Felipe. 2010. "More Carrots than Sticks: Antanas Mockus's Civic Culture Policy in Bogotá." *New Directions for Youth Development* 125:19-31, doi: 10.1002/yd.335.

Casas Dupuy, Pablo and Paola González Cepero. 2005. "Políticas de seguridad y reducción del homicidio en Bogotá: Mito y realidad" [Security Politics and the Reduction of Homicides in Bogotá: Myth and Reality]. In *Seguridad Urbana y Policía en Colombia* [Urban Security and Police in Colombia], edited by Pablo Casas Dupuy et al. Bogotá: Fundación Seguridad y Democracia [Foundation for Security and Democracy].

Cuellar, Sebastián. 2009. "Entre la hacienda y la sociedad civil: Lógicas culturales de la guerra en Colombia" [Between the Estate and Civil Society: Cultural Logics of War in Colombia]. Master Thesis, Department of Sociology, National University of Colombia, Bogotá.

Dubreuil, Benoît and Jean-François Grégoire. 2013. "Are Moral Norms Distinct from Social Norms? A Critical Assessment of Jon Elster and Cristina Bicchieri." *Theory and Decision* 75(1):137–152. doi: 10.1007/s11238-012-9342-3.

Dundjerovic, Aleksandar and Ilva Navarro Bateman. 2006. "Antanas Mockus's *Cultura Ciudadana*: Theatrical Acts for Cultural Change in Bogota, Colombia." *Contemporary Theatre Review* 16(4):457-467.

Ellison, Julie. 2009. "This American Life: How Are the Humanities Public?" *Humanities Indicators Prototype*, The American Academy of Arts and Sciences.

Elster, Jon. 2006a. "Fairness and Norms." *Social Research* 73(2):365-376.

———. 2006b. "Altruistic Behavior and Altruistic Motivations." In *Handbook of the Economics of Giving, Altruism, and Reciprocity* 1, edited by Serge-Christophe Kolm and Jean Mercier Ythier. Amsterdam and Oxford: Elsevier.

Estrada Gallego, F. 2004. *Las metáforas de una guerra perpetua. Estudios sobre pragmática del discurso en el conflicto armado colombiano* [Metaphors of a Perpetual War. Studies on the Pragmatics of Discourse in the Colombian Armed Conflic]. Medellín: EAFIT University Press.

Gilbert, Alan and Julio D. Dávila. 2002. "Bogotá: Progress within a Hostile Environment." In *Capital City Politics in Latin America: Democratization and Empowerment*, edited by Myers, D.J. and Dietz, H.A. Boulder, CO: Lynne Rienner.

Gilbert, Alan. 2006. "Good Urban Governance: Evidence from a Model City?" *Bulletin of Latin American Research* 25(3):392–419.

Greiner, Karen. 2010. "Exploring Dialogic Social Change." PhD Diss., Scripps College of Communication, Ohio University, Athens.

Gutiérrez de Pineda, Virginia. 1992. *Honor, familia y sociedad en la estructura patriarcal* [Honor, Family, and Society within Patriarchy]. Bogotá: National University of Colombia.

Hall, Stuart. 1990. "The Emergence of Cultural Studies and the Crisis of the Humanities." *October* (53):11-23.

Hoyos Vásquez, Guillermo. 2008. "La comunicación: la competencia ciudadana" [Communication: The Civil Competence]. Pp. 135-172 In *Ciudades en Formación* [Cities in Formation], edited by Hoyos Vásquez, Guillermo and Ruiz Silva, Alexander. Bogotá: Civitas y Magisterio.

Hunt, Stacey. 2009. "Citizenship's Place: The State's Creation of Public Space and Street Vendors' Culture of Informality in Bogotá, Colombia." *Environment and Planning D: Society and Space* 27:331-351.

Jay, Gregory. 2013. "The Engaged Humanities: Principles and Practices for Public Scholarship and Teaching." *Journal of Community Engagement and Scholarship* 3(1).

Kalandides, Ares. 2011. "City Marketing for Bogotá: A Case Study in Integrated Place Branding." *Journal of Place Management and Development* 4(3):282-291.

Martín Barbero, Jesús. 2008. "Lo público: experiencia urbana y metáfora ciudadana" [The Public: Urban Experience and Civic Metaphor]. *Cuadernos de Información y Comunicación* [Bulletins on Information and Communication] 13: 213-226.

Martin, Gerard. 2007. *Bogotá: El renacer de una ciudad* [Bogotá: The Rebirth of a City]. Bogotá: Grupo Editorial Planeta, S.A. Mundo Editores.

Martin, Gerard and Miguel Ceballos. 2005. *Bogotá, anatomía de una transformación: políticas de seguridad ciudadana, 1995-2003* [Bogotá, Anatomy of a Transformation: Policies of Citizen Security, 1995-2003]. Pontifica Javeriana University, Bogotá.

Mockus, Antanas, et al. 2012. "*Cultura Ciudadana*: En las Antípodas de la Violencia" [Civic Culture: At the Antipodes of Violence]. Pp. 253-276 in *Antípodas de la Violencia:* [Antipodes of Violence], edited by Antanas Mockus, Henry Murraín, and María Villa. Washington, D.C.: Inter-American Development Bank.

Mockus, Antanas. 2000. "Armonizar ley, moral, y cultura. *Cultura Ciudadana*, prioridad de gobierno con resultados en prevención y control de violencia en Bogotá, 1995-1997" [Harmonizing Law, Morals, and Culture. Civic Culture, Priority of the Government with Results on Prevention and Violence Control in Bogotá, 1995-1997]. Unpublished manuscript.

———. 1994a. "Anfibios culturales y divorcio entre ley, moral y cultura" [Cultural Amphibians and Divorce Between Law, Morals, and Culture]. *Análisis Político* [Political Analysis] 21:37-48.

———. 1994b. *Pertinencia: Futuro de la Universidad Colombiana* [Pertinence: Future of the Colombian University]. November 15, Bogotá.

———. 2002. "Co-existence as Harmonization of Law, Morality and Culture." *Prospects* 32(1):19-37.

———. 2004. "Ampliación de los modos de hacer política" [Broadening the Ways of Doing Politics]. Paper presented at the Colloque CERI, Paris, December 2-3. (https://www.researchgate.net/publication/267362347_AMPLIACION_DE_LOS_MODOS_DE_HACER_POLITICA).

———. 2008. "Hacia una política latinoamericana sobre drogas" [Towards a Latin American Drug Policy]. Bogotá: Corpovisionarios.

———. 2009. "Siete cartas para la convivencia" [Seven Letters on Coexistence]. *Revista Letral* 2:83-97.

Moncada, Eduardo. 2009. "Toward Democratic Policing in Colombia? Institutional Accountability through Lateral Reform." *Comparative Politics* 41(4):431-449.

Montaner, Carlos Alberto. 2010. "Presidentes e histriones" [Presidents and Buffoons], *El Tiempo*, May 11.

Morales, Jorge. 1998. "Mestizaje, malicia indígena y viveza en la construcción del carácter nacional" [Mestizaje, Indigenous Malice, and Shrewdness in the Construction of National Character]. *Revista de Estudios Sociales:* [Journal of Social Studies], 1:39-43.

Mouffe, Chantal. 2007. *En torno a lo político* [On Politics]. Fondo de Cultura Económica.

Narvaez-Goldstein, Michèle. 2002-2003. "L'éthique de la discussion au service d'une nouvelle politique de la ville: l'expérience de Antanas Mockus à la mairie de Bogotá (1995-1997)" [The Ethics of Discussion in the Service of a New City Policy: Antanas Mockus's Experience as Bogotá's Mayor]. *Quaderni: La revue de la communication:* [Notebooks: The Communication Review], 49:119-133.

Nogueira de Oliveira, Mario. 2009. "Ethics and Citizenship Culture in Bogotá's Urban Administration." *The University of Miami Inter-American Law Review* 41(1):1-17.

Nussbaum, Martha. 2010. *Not for Profit: Why Democracy Needs the Humanities*. Princeton: Princeton University Press.

Ortiz, Ismael. 2009. "Bogotá 1995-2005. Tecnología y cultura. (Modelos Esparta-Atenas para la transformación del comportamiento ciudadano)" [Bogotá 1995-2005.

Technology and Culture. (Sparta-Athens as Models for the Transformation of Citizen Behavior)]. Master Thesis in Cultural Studies, National University of Colombia.

Palacios, Marco. 1999. *Agenda para la democracia y negociación con las guerrillas* [Agenda for Democracy and Negotiation with Guerrillas]. In *Los laberintos de la guerra*: [The Labyrinth of War], edited by F. Leal Buitrago. Bogotá: Tercer Mundo Editores.

Pasotti, Eleonora. 2009. *Political Branding in Cities*. Cambridge: Cambridge University Press.

Pérez Fernández, Federico. 2010. "Laboratorios de reconstrucción urbana: hacia una antropología de la política urbana en Colombia" [Laboratories for Urban Reconstruction: Towards an Anthropology of Urban Policy in Colombia]. *Antípoda*: [Antipode], 10:51-84.

Petersen, Roger and Sarah Zukerman. 2010. "Anger, Violence, and Political Science." In *International Handbook of Anger: Constituent and Concomitant Biological, Psychological, and Social Processes*, edited by M. Potegal, G. Stemmler, and C. Spielberger. New York: Springer.

Rojas, Cristina. 2004. "Decentralization and the Culture of Citizenship in Bogotá, Colombia." Pp. 291-328 in *Citizens in Charge: Managing Local Budgets in East Asia and Latin America*, edited by Isabel Licha. Washington, D.C.: Inter-American Development Bank.

Sáenz Obregón, Javier. 2011. "La pedagogía ciudadana en Bogotá: ¿Un proyecto autoritario o el mínimo común necesario para la construcción de una democracia radical?" [Civic Pedagogy in Bogotá: An Authoritarian Project or the Common Minimum Necessary to Construct a Radical Democracy?] *Revista Educación y Pedagogía*: [Education and Pedagogy Journal], 23(60):137-145.

Said, Edward. 2004. *Humanism and Democratic Criticism*. New York: Columbia University Press.

Salcedo, Andrés and Austin Zeiderman. 2008. "Antropología y ciudad: un análisis crítico e histórico" [Anthropology and the City: A Critical and Historical Analysis]. *Antípoda*: [Antipode], 7:63-97.

Sandy, Marie. 2013. "Tracing the Liberal Arts Traditions in Support of Service-Learning and Public-Engaged Scholarship in the Humanities." *Humanity & Society* 37(4):306-326.

Skinner, Reinhard. 2004. "City Profile: Bogotá." *Cities* 21(1):73-81.

Sommer, Doris ed. 2006. *Cultural Agency in the Americas*. Durham and London: Duke University Press.

———. 2014. *The Work of Art in the World*. Durham and London: Duke University Press.

Souza, Celina. 2001. "Participatory Budgeting in Brazilian Cities: Limits and Possibilities in Building Democratic Institutions." *Environment and Urbanization* 13:159–184.

Tognato, Carlo. 2011. "Extending Trauma Across Cultural Divides: On Kidnapping and Solidarity in Colombia." In *Narrating Trauma: Studies in the Contingent Impact of Collective Suffering*, edited by Jeffrey Alexander, Ron Eyerman, and Elizabeth Butler Breese. Boulder: Paradigm Publishers.

Uribe Celis, Carlos. 2003. "El integrismo de Mockus. Una apreciación de la '*Cultura Ciudadana*'" [Mockus's Integralism. An Evaluation of Civic Culture]. *Revista Colombiana de Sociología:* [Colombian Journal of Sociology], 20:209-216.

Valenzuela Aguilera, Alfonso. 2008. "Spaces of Trust: Crime, Surveillance and the Social Control of Space in Latin American Megacities." Lecture at the Berlin Roundtables 2008, Urban Planet: Collective Identities, Governance and Empowerment in Megacities, Wissenschaftszentrum für Sozialforschung [Science Center for Social Research], Berlin, June 10-17.

PART TWO: VISUAL ESSAY

José Luis Falconi

2

MORAL COSTUMES

(What is the use of considering Antanas Mockus an artist?)

José Luis Falconi

Figure 1: Mockus characterizing Lincoln, 2013. Photo: Alberto Newton. Model: Catalina Londoño. Courtesy of *Publicaciones Semana* / SoHo Magazine.

The resemblance is certainly remarkable: Antanas Mockus makes a really good Abraham Lincoln.

An excellent one, actually—as the images published a few years ago in the Colombian magazine SOHO alongside famous actress and model Catalina Londoño can attest (Figure 1).[1] Of course, I am not only talking about a physical resemblance—copycat sideburns can only get you so far—but something closer to what we might call a "moral-stature" resemblance: a similarity the magazine's team picked up on for the tongue-in-cheek photographic production. Who else in Colombia could make a better Lincoln than Antanas Mockus? Or, more pointedly: who else could actually pull off such a stunt and not fail miserably?

In fact, the oversized Lincoln costume—always cartoonishly big on anyone else—acts less as a disguise for Mockus as that which exposes his true nature, highlighting Mockus's moral stature among his compatriots. The overt over-identification of Mockus as not merely a virtuous politician, but as a moral giant elevates him into a category virtually no other (active) Latin American politician can match, with the exception of former Uruguayan President, José "Pepe" Mujica. For Mockus to have worn such a costume so naturally might serve as a sign of his most crucial political victory: to have accumulated political capital from sources other than the usual mix of inherited privilege, legacy, charisma, and political expediency. In his case, as with Lincoln, his moral capital coalesces into the revered figure of a "statesman-teacher" who can guide us towards attaining an elevated version of ourselves.

Indeed, for Mockus, who has made a political career out of aiming to reduce the gap between normative stances and our system of beliefs—showing us for years that only substantive changes in customs and habits will yield any significant societal change—the identification with Lincoln might also suggest a subtle recognition of the way in which the crucial endurance of his legacy as Mayor and as runner up for the Presidency lives among Colombians: as a perennial promise.

Nonetheless, the latency of this promise should not be taken as a failure, and should be understood instead as the sign of a long-term project that might start as a political campaign but that strives to become a social one—the realm where his ideals can be ultimately developed and harvested. In fact, it is only through understanding the structure of promises—the mechanisms by which they work—that we might be able to appreciate why Antanas retains his strong political capital to this day, as well as how it ultimately might be linked to his cultivated persona. In other words, it is the very structure of promises that contains the mechanism through which the trustworthiness of his unclassifiable and challenging persona is transformed into unique political capital, allowing Antanas to maintain his presence in politics despite numerous public defeats.

Promises, as Austin and others remind us, do special things with words.[2] Promises do not describe the state of the world, but instead actually do something in the world. To utter a promise is the equivalent of making a contract, binding the utterer of the promise to those who receive and accept it. Promises, therefore, are the quintessential social binding, strengthening the fabric of a community of speakers in the face of uncertain futures. And they strengthen this fabric, not only because they depend on the truthfulness of the proposition uttered, but also on that of the one who has uttered it. In contrast with descriptions, which can be evaluated solely by their truth or falsehood, promises need to be evaluated not only by what has been promised, but also by the trust one places in the one who does the promising. Therefore, it requires assessing the character of the one who promises, in addition to the strength of the connection had with that person—assessing not just what has been offered, but how likely the offer is to be carried through to fruition.

It is at this juncture that the importance for Antanas of his persona as a pedagogue, as an educator becomes clear. In fact, if one takes into consideration the particular regard there is for the educator figure in Latin America—due to its still uneven modernization process and its strong Iberian "lettered" legacy—one would be able to understand the depth and robustness of the archetype, which encompasses versions that range from the dedicated teacher to the personalized mentor, to the brilliant and challenging professor, etc. What is particular about the pedagogue is that his or her position of authority stems from the knowledge he or she commands because it, supposedly, holds the key to progress.

Ultimately, at the basis of the authority of the pedagogue there is a promise of progress. Thus, insofar it holds the key for social improvement, such authority has been easily translated into political capital and clout in the region since the establishment of the republics across the continent in the early nineteenth century: from the "Maestro" Domingo Faustino Sarmiento in Argentina to Juan Bosch in the Dominican Republic, passing through Venezuelan Rómulo Gallegos and the vast number of Grammarian-Presidents of Colombia (Caro, Marroquín, and Abadía), what is clear is that their status as "lettered men" implied a pedagogic dimension in most cases which, in turn, was transformed into political capital.[3]

In the case of Antanas, this lineage is complemented by his particular capacity for appearing as what some commentators have labelled as a "deliberate amateur": someone capable of trying new paths, new careers, and new possibilities without being afraid of failing in the attempt.[4] And although this perceived "freedom" to enter into new terrains might be seen by some commentators as an irresponsible, cavalier attitude, it also brings a freshness to the character, allowing him to maintain a level of naiveté and innocence in the public eye. In other words: his repertoire as a "maestro" has features that allow him to temper the stuffiness, harshness and authority of the lettered man, as it includes a level of cultivated and calculated clumsiness that keeps him continuously fresh and daring. Thus, Antanas has been able to remain both cautious and a risk taker, an authority and a rebellious agent, a serious thinker and a playful trickster, all at the same time.

To wit, it is through a number of characteristics of his carefully crafted persona—which includes the archetype of pedagogue he embodies, and the different alter-egos into which he has morphed, albeit only temporarily—that we see how Antanas has been able to place his political capital in the terrain of "promises": opening up a future tense, a necessarily incomplete temporal mode that, requires, from a contractual standpoint, to work for its fulfillment. That is: it implies always a look to the future, setting up a necessarily incomplete scenario that needs to be worked out in order to be completed. In fact, this way might be the most useful for understanding Antanas as a utopian leader and thinker: insofar as utopia is defined as a place and a time which will never be reached, Mockus encourages us to continue working on the unfinished project of transforming society to its fullest potential.

This might sound vacuous as a way of measuring Mockus's legacy, but it is not, as it requires us to consider it in tandem with the lessons he presented for us during his two terms in office as Mayor of Bogotá and during his campaigns—lessons which this portfolio has tried to systematize to their fullest extent.

To rephrase, Mockus's legacy should not be measured only by the path he opened to us and has left open in the terrain of promises, but also considering the ways in which such paths should be achieved: intervening in the societal realm through the careful nudging of certain symbolic nodes. Such nudging, as we know, proved effective in Bogota, where he acted as a diligent cultural acupuncturist across the megalopolis, implementing an array of projects that hoped to be effective in the destabilization they meant to achieve. And it is precisely the nature of such nudging that makes Antanas interesting to the arts—and why, as this portfolio of projects tries to showcase, it might be useful to consider him accordingly.

The link not only deals with the symbolic but also with Mockus's deep appreciation for the effects that surprises can cause in a constituency, as well as the way in which he precisely uses such surprise to position his agenda. It is not only the decision to work on the symbolic realm which makes him closer to an artist as it is, foremost, his capacity to exploit the surprise element (and the level of pleasure it produces) to advance his political agenda that really makes him closer to espousing an artistic process—at least on some basic, important level.

Undoubtedly, there is a critical and unsolvable distance between the projects presented here and art, per se: art, by definition, cannot and does not have a function, but these campaigns, despite their careful and robust work on the symbolic, are expressly built on a purpose. So, why insist on considering him akin to an artist? What could be the use of such description in the way we view Mockus?

The answer is simple: because, just as any other artist, Mockus placed the effectiveness of his actions (and therefore of his political agenda) on the surprise factor they were capable of eliciting. That is: just like an artist, Mockus thought of his actions, events or campaigns as first and foremost *experiences*—a perceived event that is not only understood by the intellect but, most importantly, felt by our sensorial apparatus. Just as a painting, a novel or a song, Antanas's campaigns were conceived as experiences that the spectator should live and enjoy. From *Ladies' Night* (see pages 234-239) to *Serenade to Taxes* (see pages 116-125), a large number of his plans were conceived as spectacles in which the audience participated and enjoyed the sudden recasting of otherwise very familiar and unsurprising gatherings. If the mimes directing traffic (see *Mimes and Crosswalks*, pp. 82–87) worked, it was because they not only de-familiarized the most public space, but because they also invited rethinking, recasting the city as a whole. Even in the cases in which the campaign only had an image directly associated with Antanas—think of *Super Citizen* (pp. 94-99) or *Bulletproof Vest* (pp. 222-225)—it strove to produce such a de-familiarization of signs (i.e. a bulletproof vest with cut-out hole in the shape of a cartoonish heart which, despite rendering it useless, makes it more powerful symbolically) that it was capable of producing a space for wonderment and new possibilities by the mere fact of being surprising.

What is crucial for our analysis here is that the enjoyment of the public came directly from the subversion of signs the campaigns pulled off: it was the sudden, profound temporal de-familiarization with events otherwise already so lexicalized in society. The moment the campaign presented to people a new way of reading the same old event by simply subverting the signs, it opened new possibilities within the social realm, and the very feeling of the sudden unlocking of things becomes precisely the source of the enjoyment.[5]

At the center of Mockus's plan for the restoration of agency in Colombian society, thus, laid the *concerted use of the disconcerting*. The funny thing is that to produce a sensorial experience that bases its enjoyment (and pleasure) on its de-familiarizing effect and then impel reflection about it is pretty much the textbook formula for art; it is that which has made "art" art since the (re)foundation of aesthetics in modernity in the eighteenth century.[6] What might make Antanas akin to an artist is his mastery of the timely construction and deployment of a number of artifacts that achieve in their public or spectator the fleeting but important temporal disposition to *feel* that certain deep-seated categories (and problems, therefore) can be actually re-signified and changed, and that maybe, we might be able to dissolve (instead of solving) problems that have previously felt impossible to address.

It is the appeal to the pleasurable sensorial experience as tied to the consequent reflection which might actually make some of Mockus's actions considerable, by some of us, as some of the best conceptual art *avant la lettre* that has come out in the region in the last decades, as well as the most decisive political interventions through the arts and the symbolic since high modernist times. The compilation that follows attests to this fact, and so if it genuinely surprises the reader, it has truly done its job.

ENDNOTES

1. Other people from Colombian civil society recruited to shoot with model Catalina Londoño by photographer Alberto Newton in his editorial "Remakes a la Colombiana" (Colombian Remakes) included such notable figures as businessman Jean-Claude Bessudo, President of Aviatur, as Edward Lewis of *Pretty Woman*, renowned filmmaker Sergio Cabrera as Jack Dawson from *Titanic*, Senator Antonio Navarro Wolf as Jack Sparrow from *Pirates of the Caribbean* and Edward Niño (the smallest man in Colombia) as the eponymous *ET.* (Newton 2013:202-22).

2. J. L. Austin is widely recognized as having revolutionized the philosophy of language with his detailed studies of ordinary language and his contributions in the performative aspect of language, which included a thorough examination of the way promises and similar spoken constructions work. (Austin 1975).

3. For more information on Colombian Grammarian Presidents, see "Miguel Antonio Caro y Amigos: Gramática y Poder en Colombia" in Malcolm Deas, *Del Poder y la Gramática y otros ensayos sobre historia, política y literatura colombianas.* (Deas 2006:27-61).

4. As Harvard art historian Sarah Lewis has stated: "An amateur is unlike the novice bound by lack of experience and the expert trapped by having too much. Driven by impulse and desire, the amateur stays in the place of a 'constant now,' seeing possibilities to which the expert is blind and which the apprentice may not yet discern. [...] The term amateur is now pejorative: to lack in skill and knowledge, to be a dilettante, dabbler, fancier or hobbyist—all conceptual flirts. Yet centuries ago, the word amateur wasn't meant to disparage. It described a person undertaking an activity for sheer pleasure, not solely pursuing a goal for the sake of their profession. The French *amateur* is from the Latin *amator*—a lover, a devotee, a person who adores a particular endeavor." (Lewis 2015:151-52).

5. A lot could be said about the appeal and use of enjoyment as central to Mockus's actions—not only do they reveal his interest in promoting political change through *pleasure*, as a result, they might have more potential for success than changes that are felt as merely "sacrifices," but this is not the place for such discussion. Suffice it to say that this might be a notion that has been so little studied that even its superficial discussion feels disconcerting in its own right.

6. Although no major modern philosopher dealt with or found a place for aesthetics until Immanuel Kant produced his third critique, *The Critique of Power of Judgment* in 1790, it is widely considered that the foundations for the resurgence of aesthetics as the legitimate branch of philosophy can be traced to Joseph Addison's "Essays on the Imagination," which he contributed to the London based publication *Spectator* between 1711 and 1714, to the publication in 1713 of *Characteristics of Men, Manners, Opinions and Times* by the 3rd Earl of Shaftesbury and Francis Hutcheson's *Inquiry concerning Beauty, Order, Harmony and Design*, published in 1725 in Scotland. On the European continent, it is Alexander Baumgarten's 1750s *Aesthetica* which is considered the foundational text on aesthetics. For a more detailed discussion on the aesthetic militancy of Mockus see Doris Sommer's "Por Amor al Arte: Haber-Mockus Plays with the Possible" included in this same volume (pp. 251-276).

REFERENCES

Austin, J. L. 1975. *How to Do Things with Words*, Cambridge, MA: Harvard University Press.

Deas, Malcolm 2006. "Miguel Antonio Caro y amigos: Gramática y poder en Colombia" [Miguel Antonio Caro and Friends: Grammar and Power in Colombia]. *Del poder y la gramática: y otros ensayos sobre historia, política y literatura colombianas* [Power and Grammar: and Other Essays on Colombian History, Politics and Literature]. Bogotá, Colombia: Taurus: 27-61.

Lewis, Sarah. 2015. *The Rise: Creativity, the Gift of Failure, and the Search for Mastery.* New York, NY: Simon & Schuster: 151-52.

Newton, Alberto. 2013. "Catalina Londoño: Remakes a la Colombiana" [Catalina Londoño: Colombian Remakes]. *SoHo*, March, (157) 202-22.

0 NOMENCLATURE

(Nomenclatura)

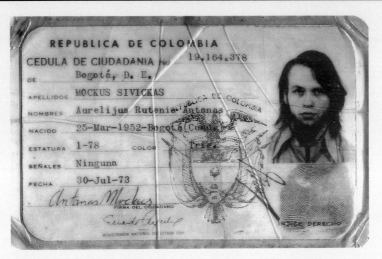

Figure 2: Antanas Mockus's ID.

The following "artist portfolio" should not be understood as comprehensive, but rather anthological, detailing what I believe to be Mockus's *Greatest Hits* during his time in office. Organized chronologically by the term in which they were enacted—during either Mockus's first or second term as mayor of Bogotá—each of these cases details not only the purpose of the campaign, but also its perceived result (an emphasis on measurable results as encouraged by Mockus himself). An additional effort was made to find and include the city edict by which his interventions were enacted, whenever they were carried out by the office of the Mayor. In the same fashion, we have also dug deep, especially in the Mockus–Córdoba family archive, to find little known images of each of the campaigns. I am grateful to the team of researchers, led by Laura Oliveros, who worked steadily and diligently for over two years mining a number of archives in Bogotá so we could compile the dossier presented here before you.

Note: The resolution of the included images represents the highest available quality, per the archives from which they were sourced. In some instances, the image may still be lacking in definition due to the quality of the analog source.

1 TOP

(Pirinola)

First term: 1995–1998

Figure 3: Top detail, ("Everyone Contributes, Everyone Benefits"), 2014. Courtesy of Futuro Moncada.

OBJECTIVE

The electoral campaign *"Todos Ponen y Todos Toman"* (Everyone Contributes and Everyone Benefits) was the driving force and main message behind Antanas Mockus's electoral campaign. With this toy, Mockus attempted to place both the individual player and the group in the ambiguous place between chance and strategy, where it would become clear that municipal government is something that should include everyone: "Everyone Contributes and Everyone Benefits."

"The top was perceived to be such an important part of the campaign that $6000 of the $12000 total USD spent on the first campaign was used to purchase tops" (Mockus 2014, pers. comm.)

DATE OF PRODUCTION

The tops were first produced during the registration of his candidacy in 1994 and then again during his second candidacy in 2001.

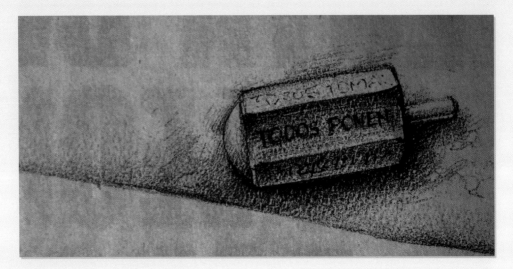

Figure 4: Top, 1996. Courtesy of *El Espectador*.

RESULTS

In both electoral campaigns, the toy demonstrated that what constituted good or bad behavior was established by the first few players' actions, and these norms were maintained until the end of the game. This demonstrated that good and bad behaviors are contagious.

For this reason, during the second term, the game was altered to add another face to the top, so that two options would appear at the same time. For example, *Todos ponen* (Everyone Contributes) and *Toma uno* (Take One) would appear together, giving the player the option to play as she sees fit, either favoring herself or the group and demonstrating that whoever starts the game determines the rules of play for the rest.

ORDINANCE / LAW / EDICT

Not applicable.

Figure 5: Top and Package, 2014. Courtesy of Futuro Moncada.
Figure 6: Top, 1994. Courtesy of *El Espectador*.

REFERENCES

Ávila, Fernando. 1994. "Sobre pirinolas y chances" [On Tops and Chances], *El Tiempo*, November 8 (http://www.eltiempo.com/archivo/documento/MAM-242695).

"Todos los empleados de la Alcaldía tienen pirinola" [All the Employees of the Mayor's Office Have a Top], 1995. *El Tiempo*, January 4 (http://www.eltiempo.com/archivo/documento/MAM-307525).

2 MIMES AND CROSSWALKS

(Mimos y cebras)

First term: 1995-1998

Figure 7: Mimes, 1995. Photo: Eduardo Sotomayor. Courtesy of the Mayor's Office of Bogotá, Secretary General, Central Archive, Photo Archive.

OBJECTIVE

This project sought to improve interactions between pedestrians and automobile drivers and to demonstrate the ease of establishing and observing rules that facilitate coexistence.

DATE OF PRODUCTION

May 1995

DESCRIPTION

The initiative focused on peaceful and mutually accepted interpersonal regulation—a new form of intervention that bases authority on education, communication, and signage.

"Can the mimes give fines?" asked a journalist.

"No," answered the mayor.

"Then they're not going to work," the journalist responded (Mockus 2014, pers. comm.).

The mayor began the program as a pedagogical move to change the behavior of Bogotanos when they crossed the street. Pedestrians were only permitted to cross streets and avenues

Figure 8: Mimes, 1995. Photo: Leonardo Castro. Courtesy of *El Espectador*.

Figure 9-10: Mimes Teaching People to Use the Crosswalks, 1995. Courtesy of *El Espectador.*

at corners and at crosswalks (*cebras*), and drivers would have to respect both traffic lights and pedestrians.

Mimes were placed along Avenida 19, especially at its intersection with Carrera 7, both of which are important arteries in the center of Bogotá. Citizens responded by whistling at drivers who, when faced with a red light, refused to respect conventions, and would instead stop within the crosswalk. If the driver did not respond to the friendly and playful cajoling of the mime, a traffic police officer would intervene. Pedestrians would applaud, as the police officer fined the driver. Following this protocol, police action was the last recourse in a pedagogically motivated sequence of actions. Thanks to the legibility of the situation and public support for the police sanction, the pedagogical effect was strengthened. Beginning in July 1995, and lasting for three months, following this protocol, young mimes taught Bogotanos—without words or shouting—how to respect the rules of pedestrian and vehicular traffic (no throwing trash in the street, helping the elderly to cross, respecting stop lights and crosswalks). They used shame as an educational tool in the hope that citizens themselves would begin to judge those who broke the rules. Afterwards, the mimes were posted in the nineteen urban zones of the city.

Intersections: An educational campaign was carried out at high-traffic intersections to teach

Figure 11: Mimes Correcting the Behavior of Pedestrians and Drivers, 1995. Photo: Rafael Guerrero. Courtesy of *El Tiempo*.

drivers to stop at crosswalks and to teach pedestrians to cross only in designated areas. Mimes and various factions of the police force, such as the traffic police, carried out the campaign.

Bus stops: By painting bus stop signs on the ground and the mobile signs that read *mal parados* (Stopped Incorrectly) to point out failure to comply with the norm, the campaign hoped to teach passengers and drivers to get on and off the bus only in designated areas.

Crosswalks: A campaign was undertaken to teach pedestrians to only cross the street in designated areas and to teach drivers to stop at these places to ensure pedestrians' safety. The campaign was carried out by mimes, volunteer drivers, Auxiliar de Policía Bachilleres (Auxiliary Police Forces), and students.

RESULTS

Although many were skeptical at first, this measure was hugely successful in uniting civil servants and citizens from different sectors to promote correct behavior on the street, transforming a state-driven educational program into a citizen-to-citizen process.

The educational campaign was carried out at 482 intersections with the participation of 425

Figure 12: Mimes Correcting the Behavior of Pedestrians and Drivers, 1995.
Photo: Rafael Guerrero. Courtesy of *El Tiempo*.

people (mimes, police officers, etc); 364 intersections were marked throughout the city. The positive results at bus stops were especially apparent on Calle 80, one of the most densely gridlocked streets in the city. The number of passengers who respected the bus stops grew from 26.2% in 1995 to 38% in 1996; between February and May of 1997, 43% of minibuses respected bus stops. The citizens themselves began to police rule–breakers. In 1996, 76.46% of drivers and 72.25% of pedestrians respected crosswalks. This campaign was distinctive in its playful and un-repressive nature, which encouraged citizens to follow traffic rules (Mockus 2001).

ORDINANCE / LAW / EDICT
Not applicable.

Figure 13: Mimes Teaching People to Use the Crosswalks, 1995. Courtesy of *El Espectador*.

REFERENCES

Mockus, Antanas. 2001. "Cultura ciudadana, programa contra la violencia en Santa Fe de Bogotá, Colombia, 1995-1997" [*Civic Culture*, Program Against Violence in Santa Fe de Bogotá, Colombia, 1995-1997], Washington, D.C.: Interamerican Development Bank, Social Development Division (http://es.calameo.com/read/00047752906c074dfce6b).

"Sin mimos, vuelve juego de las cebras" [Without Mines, It's a Zebra's Game]. 1995. *El Tiempo*, May 29 (http://www.eltiempo.com/archivo/documento/MAM-334805).

3 KNIGHTS OF THE CROSSWALK

(Caballeros de la cebra)

First term: 1995-1998

Figure 14: "Knights of the Crosswalk," 1995-1998. Courtesy of the Personal Archive of Antanas Mockus.

OBJECTIVE

This initiative aimed to improve relationships between drivers, passengers, and pedestrians.

DATE OF PRODUCTION

July 1996

DESCRIPTION

During the first term, in a clash between taxi divers, a driver accidentally shot and killed a passenger's baby. This painful event sparked the creation of a program to overhaul taxi services.

The "Knights of the Crosswalk" was a group of taxi drivers who engaged in good *cultura ciudadana* (civic culture) with their passengers. The group's actions were guided by the following four points:

1. The taxi driver and the passenger must greet each other, "because it costs nothing but carries great meaning." The agreement continues: "Then we should talk about where the passenger is going, agree upon a route and, if possible, talk about something else."
2. The second point says: "Charge and pay what the taximeter says." According to the document, "change should be available, and the price on the taxi meter should be paid. If change is not available, the price should be rounded to a mutually agreed upon price."
3. The third point refers to traffic jams: "We should remember that it is better to walk a few short meters than to waste valuable time in traffic jams."
4. The last point encourages the taxi driver and the passenger to collaboratively come up with the best route to avoid problems that could arise from a disagreement.

The passenger could register a complaint or a positive review by phone (*El Tiempo*, July 15, 2006).

RESULTS

The program saw significant improvements in traffic and mutual cooperation between passengers and drivers.

One hundred fifty model taxi drivers were easily identified by employees of the Mayor's Office and the Institute of Culture for their positive disposition (greeting passengers, not haggling) and for their honesty (giving correct change). They then easily identified more than one thousand other model drivers in a matter of days. In two years, by the end of 1997, the program grew to more than fifteen thousand drivers. It is common to hear taxi drivers in Bogotá say, "Antanas nos educó" (Antanas educated us) (Mockus 2004).

Despite this, or perhaps because of it, taxi drivers staged a strike in 2002, paralyzing the city. The strike was not only relatively peaceful, but was also accompanied by acts of citizen solidarity and trust. For instances, neighbors took in children trapped in their school buses for the night. The strike also had an unexpected outcome: a federal judge handed down a ruling that stopped the Mayor's Office's plan to intensify a system of mandatory driving shifts. In this case, a third unforeseen actor—aided by a writ of protection—was stronger than both the strike and the will of the Mayor. It served as a small lesson in Constitutional Law, as several months later the Constitutional Court overturned the judge's decision for overreaching. Nonetheless, having reestablished the legal competence of the Mayor's Office, neither the taxi drivers not the Mayor had any further interest in modifying the norm, which had already taken hold (Mockus 2014, pers. comm.).

Figure 15: "Knights of the Crosswalk," 1996. Courtesy of *El Espectador*.

Figure 16: Newspaper Classified by Mayor's Office, Bogotá, 1996. Courtesy of *El Tiempo*.

ORDINANCE / LAW / EDICT

Not applicable.

REFERENCES

Mockus, Antanas. 2004. "Ampliación de los modos de hacer política" [Amplifying the Ways of Doing Politics], Paper presented at the Colloque CERI, Paris, December 2-3 (http://www.revistaaleph.com.co/component/k2/item/50-ampliacion-de-los-modos-de-hacer-politica.html).

"Taxistas con título de caballeros…de la cebra" [Taxis Titled as Knights… of the Crosswalk]. 1996. *El Tiempo*, July 15 (http://www.eltiempo.com/archivo/documento/MAM-434055).

"Los caballeros de la cebra en carrera de observación" [The Knights of the Crosswalk Under Observation], 1996, *El Tiempo*, July 19 (http://www.eltiempo.com/archivo/documento/MAM-430029).

"Kit Zanahorio para taxistas" [Carrot Kit for Taxi Drivers], 1996. *El Tiempo*, June 20 (http://www.eltiempo.com/archivo/documento/MAM-430029).

4 SUPER CITIZEN:
SUPERHERO OF BOGOTÁ, ANECDOTAL ACTION OF THE MAYOR

(Súper cívico: Superhéroe Bogotano, acción anecdótica del Alcalde)

First term: 1995-1998

Figure 17: "Super Citizen," 1996. Photo: Juan Castañeda. Courtesy of the Personal Archive of Antanas Mockus.

OBJECTIVE

"Super Citizen" sought to strengthen *Cultura Ciudadana.*

DATE OF PRODUCTION

First term of 1995

DESCRIPTION

This character was developed for a campaign through a collaboration between the newspaper *El Espectador* and the Mayor's Office, in which readers were asked to find "Super Citizen" in a crowd (in an image similar to "Where's Waldo?"), engaging in five appropriate and inappropriate behaviors.

After the appearance of "Super Citizen" in *El Espectador*, the idea took off and was turned into a video for National Radio Network (RCN) in which Antanas appeared dressed as "Super Citizen." The next day he was asked to appear in photos for the national press, and by the third day he was an international news story. As a result, Antanas spent three days dressed up as "Super Citizen," appearing in various parts of the city. It's worth recounting that during these three days, a woman saw him stepping into a church in La Candelaria neighborhood and said to him, "Alcalde, trabaje" (Mayor, get to work) (Mockus 2014, pers. comm.).

RESULTS

From that moment on, Mockus has maintained that the great success of "Super Citizen" was to leave people wondering if the character of "Super Citizen" was the mayor or a citizen, sparking a debate about whether cultural change starts at the top or the bottom.

ORDINANCE / LAW / EDICT

Not applicable.

Figure 18: "Super Citizen," 1996. Photo: Fernando Vergara. Courtesy of *El Tiempo*.

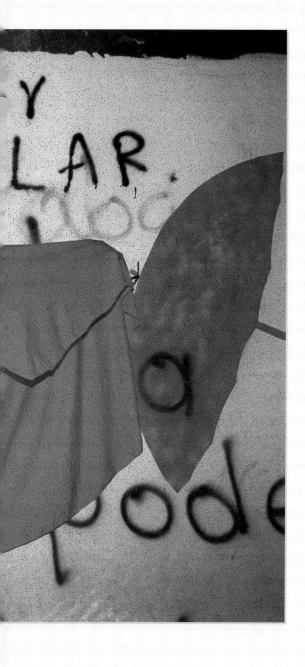

Figure 19: "Super Citizen," 1996. Photo: Fernando Vergara. Courtesy of *El Tiempo*.

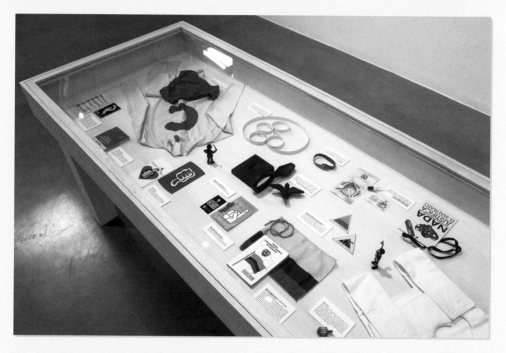

Figure 20: Exhibition Case *"Cultura Ciudadana:* Artists and Architects Give Shape to Public Politics," 2015. Santa Monica Museum of Art, California. Courtesy of Futuro Moncada.

5 CARROT KIT

(Kit zanahorio)

First term: 1995-1998

Figure 21: Still with Bugs Bunny, 1997. Courtesy of the Personal Archive of Antanas Mockus.

OBJECTIVE

The "Carrot Kit" was meant to encourage pedagogical acts among citizens and to articulate different points of the plan for civic education plan.

DATE OF PRODUCTION

1995

DESCRIPTION

The "Carrot Kit" contained:

–A condom: This was a small, fun step toward familiarizing Bogotanos with condoms in a playful way. It came with the instructions: "Inflate and pop." Besides this, the condom also came with a *carta bomba* (bomb letter)–a letter with an illustration of a bomb, on which people could write a false news item and give it to someone else.

–A coin: The orange and gray coin had a variety of functions. One suggestion was for children to give the coin to a homeless person, so as to eliminate the gap created by societal differences. Another potential use was to combine the coin with the local planning

Figure 22: Suggestion Slip "I Contribute My Idea," 2014.
Courtesy of Futuro Moncada.

suggestion slip, which could then be exchanged for an idea.

–A whistle: The idea was to encourage people to overcome their inhibitions and blow the whistle. The whistle was adopted as something positive that was necessary in emergencies, and it was considered a good substitute for fireworks because of the noise it made.

–Local planning suggestion slip: This was a sheet of paper on which citizens could write ideas about the local development plan. Once they had filled out the slip they could trade their idea with another person in exchange for the coin from the kit.

RESULTS

"...I think that if someone were to take the 'Carrot Kit' and look at it piece by piece, they could use it to come up with a sort of synthesis of my first year of government," said Mockus, the intellectual author of the idea, who proposed that six supermarket chains sponsor the idea. For him, this kit brings together symbols of all the main messages his administration had tried to communicate with people up to that point (*El Tiempo*, December 20, 1995).

ORDINANCE / LAW / EDICT

Not applicable.

Figure 23: "Carrot Kit," 2014. Courtesy of Futuro Moncada.

REFERENCES

"Kit Zanahorio para taxistas" ["Carrot Kit" for Taxi Drivers]. 1996. *El Tiempo*, June 20 (http://www.el-tiempo.com/archivo/documento/MAM-386679).

"El Kit sintetiza mi primer año: Mockus" [The Kit Synthesizes My First Year: Mockus]. 1995. *El Tiempo*, December 20 (http://www.eltiempo.com/archivo/documento/MAM-488180).

"Qué pasó con el Kit Zanahorio" [What Happened with the "Carrot Kit"], 1996, *El Tiempo*, January 23 (http://www.eltiempo.com/archivo/documento/MAM-374514).

Figure 24: "Carrot Kit," 2014. Courtesy of Futuro Moncada.

6 WATER CONSERVATION

(Ahorro de agua)

First term: 1995-1998

Figure 25: Press Conference, 1997. Photo: Luis Acosta. Courtesy of the Personal Archive of Antanas Mockus.

OBJECTIVE

This campaign sought to raise awareness about rules of coexistence and the importance of following them (Mockus 2002:23).

DATE OF PRODUCTION

1995

DESCRIPTION

The campaign was created to prevent water rationing in the city due to damages to tunnels of the Chingaza Dam, which supplies water to Bogotá.

Saint Rafael the Archangel was chosen as the emblem of the campaign, alluding to another name often given to the Dam. Stamps with pictures of the Saint and a text explaining how to reduce water consumption were distributed.

The campaign also gave practical advice on how citizens could put water conservation into practice:

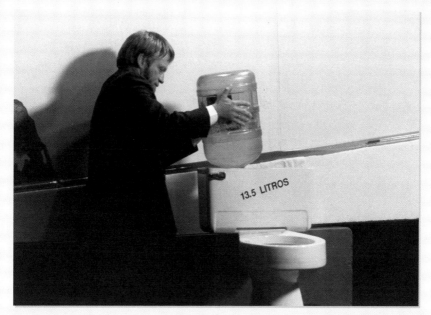

Figure 26: Press Conference, 1997. Photo: William Martínez. Courtesy of the Personal Archive of Antanas Mockus.

1. When doing laundry, use as little water as possible.

2. When showering, cut the water pressure by half for half the shower.

3. In the bathroom, flush only when necessary.

4. When washing dishes, close the tap until it is time to rinse.

A group called *Acuacívicos* (Aqua Civics) was also created, made up of four thousand children and young people who put these measures into practice.

In addition, a deal was made with the Empresa de Teléfonos de Bogotá* (Bogotá's telephone company) to promote these measures. The usual dial tone was replaced with the voice of the mayor saying: "Thank you for conserving water." Later on, the voice was changed to that of Shakira.

*This was the first time in the history of Santa Fe de Bogotá that telephone lines were used to spread messages of *Cultura Ciudadana* (ibid.).

Figure 27: Chingaza Dam, 1995. Photo: Francisco Carranza. Courtesy of *El Espectador*.

Figure 28: Chingaza Dam, 1995. Photo: Juan Castañeda. Courtesy of Personal Archive of Antanas Mockus.

Figure 29: Recording a Telephone Message, 1995. Courtesy of *El Espectador.*

RESULTS

The results were so positive that the city reduced its water consumption to historically low levels, rendering a decree for mandatory water rationing unnecessary.

"During an emergency, we made a commitment to take a risk and not shut off the water. After that, people began to discover (and the city began to promote) economic incentives that led to a continued decrease in water consumption. This decrease in water use continued, from an initial 14% to 40% in eight years. The water conservation initiative reduced familial consumption from 27 m³ to 23 m³ in 1995, during the emergency. Seven years later it had dropped to 16 m³" (Mockus 2004:13).

ORDINANCE / LAW / EDICT

National Decree put forth by the President of the Republic (Mayor's Office of Bogotá 1997).

Figure 30: Graphic Work, 2014. Courtesy of Futuro Moncada.

REFERENCES

Alcaldía de Bogotá [Mayor's Office of Bogotá]. 1997. "LEY 373 de 1997" [Law 373 of 1997]. June 6 (http://www.alcaldiabogota.gov.co/sisjur/normas/Norma1.jsp?i=342).

Mockus, Antanas. 2004. "Ampliación de los modos de hacer política." [Broadening of the Modes of Doing Politics]. Paper presented at the Colloque CERI, Paris, December 2-3 (https://www.researchgate.net/publication/267362347_AMPLIACION_DE_LOS_MODOS_DE_HACER_POLITICA).

———. 2002. "Bogotá: Camino a la igualdad: Avances en la *Cultura Ciudadana* y en la Construcción de lo Público" [Bogotá: On the Path to Equality: Advances in Civic Culture and Construction of the Public]. Bogotá: Alcaldía Mayor de Bogotá.

"Listas las sanciones para quienes desperdicien el agua; decreto será expedido al martes" [List of Sanctions for Wasting Water; Decree to be Issued Tuesday]. 2009. *El Tiempo,* December 26 (http://www.eltiempo.com/archivo/documento/CMS-6843269).

"Mockus dio clase de ahorro" [Mockus Gave a Class on Saving]. 1997. *El Tiempo*, February 7 (http://www.eltiempo.com/archivo/documento/MAM-534578).

**RECOMENDACIONES
PARA UN CONSUMO RACIONAL**

1. Mantenga en buen estado todas las llaves, grifos y cerciorese que los sanitarios, lavamanos, tanques, etc., no tengan escapes.

2. No deje llaves de agua abiertas cuando el suministro esté interrumpido. El aire a presión hace mover las agujas del control.

3. No permita que sus niños desperdicien agua.

4. No deje las llaves abiertas cuando lave utensilios de cocina o ropas, ni cuando se hace el aseo personal

5. Debe cambiar las tuberías interiores que por ser demasiado viejas se obstruyen o estallan, ocasionando fugas difíciles de detectar a simple vista.

6. Mantenga su contador libre de obstáculos que impidan su lectura.

**· No Tengamos Deudas con la Naturaleza ·
¡CUIDEMOS EL AGUA!**

**A PRENDA
CONTROLAR
SU CONSUMO
DE
AGUA**

Figure 31: Informative Flyer About Wasting Water, 1995-1998. Courtesy of the Mayor's Office of Bogotá, Secretary General, Central Archive, Photo Archive.

Figure 32: Informative Flyer About Wasting Water, 1995-1998. Courtesy of the Mayor's Office of Bogotá, Secretary General, Central Archive, Photo Archive.

7 FAMILY COMMISSARY

(Comisaría de familia)

First term: 1995-1998

Figure 33: "Family Commissary," 1995-1998. Courtesy of Personal Archive of Antanas Mockus.

OBJECTIVE

This initiative sought to address the multi-causal issue of family violence.

DATE OF PRODUCTION

1995-1998

DESCRIPTION

In order to increase the extension and potential benefits of the "Family Commissary" service, the mayor set the goal of establishing up one commissary in each area of the city (*localidad*), renovating those already in existence, and opening up new spaces so as to achieve wide coverage and address problems related to intrafamily violence, child abuse, and neglect.

The Family Commissaries program started in 1989 with six offices. In the last term of 1996, these centers handled 9,735 complaints, an average of 1,600 cases per Commissary.

Each Commissary had a team made up of a family commissioner, a doctor, a psychologist, a social worker, an officer in charge of reporting, and a secretary. (*El Tiempo*, October 19, 1996).

Figure 34: Solution to Park Conflicts, 2003. Photo: Ignacio Prieto. Courtesy of the Mayor's Office of Bogotá, Secretary General, Central Archive, Photo Archive.

This project was part of the Safety and Coexistence program that was meant to decrease high levels of violence in Bogotá. The program was a strategy that was articulated through various projects such as: "*Semilleros de Convivencia*" (Incubators of Coexistence), "*Jornadas de Vacunación contra la Violencia*" (Vaccination Days Against Violence), "*Centros de Conciliación*" (Reconciliation Centers) and the "*Plan de Desarme Voluntario*" (Plan of Voluntary Disarmament).

RESULTS

During Mockus's first term, the "Family Commissary" service was revamped and expanded in all locations. Six that were already in operation (Puente Aranda, Ciudad Bolívar, Usaquén, San Cristóbal, Barrios Unidos, and Tunjuelito) were revamped. Another seven were created (Kennedy, Engativá, Suba, Rafael Uribe, Candelaria, Teusaquillo, and Bosa). In conjunction with these Commissaries, Reconciliation Centers began to handle cases involving police, traffic, injuries, and theft.

ORDINANCE / LAW / EDICT

Decree 653 of 1996 (Mayor's Office of Bogotá).

Figure 35: Solution to Park Conflicts, 2003. Photo by: Ignacio Prieto. Courtesy of the Mayor's Office of Bogotá, Secretary General, Central Archive, Photo Archive.

REFERENCES

Alcaldía de Bogotá. 1996. "Decree 653 of 1996."

(http://www.alcaldiabogota.gov.co/sisjur/normas/Norma1.jsp?i=1657).

"Inauguración comisarías de familia" [Inauguration of Family Commissaries], 1996. *El Tiempo*, (http://www.eltiempo.com/archivo/documento/MAM-547716).

Figure 36-37: Solution to Park Conflicts, 2003. Photo: Ignacio Prieto. Courtesy of the Mayor's Office of Bogotá, Secretary General, Central Archive, Photo Archive.

8 COLLABORATING FOR PARTICIPATORY PLANNING—

PUBLIC RESOURCES, SACRED RESOURCES

(Concertar para planear con participación—recursos públicos, recursos sagrados)

First term: 1995-1998

Figure 38: "Tax Serenade," 2001. Photo: Eliseo Rúa. Courtesy of the Mayor's Office of Bogotá, Secretary General, Central Archive, Photo Archive.

OBJECTIVE

The goal of this program was to create legal, moral, and cultural harmony, promoting citizen participation in the planning of public investment projects through open debate.

DATE OF PRODUCTION

1996

DESCRIPTION

The project had two main tasks: to promote local planning and generating works with a pedagogical payoff.

LOCAL PLANNING

The citizens of all twenty regions of the Capital District were invited to actively participate in creating each "Local Development Plan." In the first meeting, in which the three-week process was introduced, citizens received a card and a plastic coin with the caption: "Public Resources, Sacred Resources." They were supposed to write an idea having to do with a need or an important project for their community on the card. Immediately upon doing so, they were asked to place the card and their coin in one of six transparent urns, representing the six priorities of the development plan, "*Formar Ciudad*" (To Form the City). Citizens had the option of depositing their card in one urn and their coin in another, if they wanted to indicate that they were proposing an idea, but preferred that resources be spent on something else. When everyone had voted, they were invited to participate in the tallying of the votes, and the results were made immediately public. In this way, all those present were aware of the results of the vote, since the process of tallying them gave them a clear indication of the relative importance of different priorities. When coins were missing, which was almost always the case, it was requested that they be returned. When more than half of the coins had been returned, the meeting was brought to a close with both the national and city anthems. Both in the meeting and through other forms of communication, the community was informed of the timetable for the project proposals to be approved and prioritized in public meetings. In the following days,

Figure 39: "Tax Serenade," 2001. Photo: Eliseo Rúa. Courtesy of the Mayor's Office of Bogotá, Secretary General, Central Archive, Photo Archive.

Figure 40: Construction of the Archive of Bogotá, 1995-2003. Photo: Ignacio Prieto. Courtesy of the Mayor's Office of Bogotá, Secretary General, Central Archive, Photo Archive.

working groups transformed these ideas into drafts of possible investment projects, which would be classified into six groups. Each group was given a priority, with the understanding that each list would later be cut in order to make the cost of each project compatible with the investment budget of each region. In each region, and in meetings that were supposed to be public (and almost always were), a technical committee preselected projects according to the priorities of the *"Formar Ciudad"* plan. In order to assign priority to different investments, the Index of Basic Needs (IBN) was taken into consideration, along with other criteria such as unfinished public works and the community that stood to benefit. (Mockus 2014, pers. comm.).

WORKS WITH "PEDAGOGICAL PAYOFF"

Members of the Community Action Groups received training in contracting and planning. Meanwhile, they also put forth a project that was intended to reflect the needs of their neighborhoods and that would benefit their communities. At the end of the training, the projects competed for funding with other selected projects.

Figure 41: "Tax Serenade," 2001. Photo: Eliseo Rúa. Courtesy of the Mayor's Office of Bogotá, Secretary General, Central Archive, Photo Archive.

Figure 42: Chiva Tax–Contributors Trip, 2001. Courtesy of the Mayor's Office of Bogotá, Secretary General, Central Archive, Photo Archive.

RESULTS

The project established a regulatory system for drafting project proposals and adopted a methodology for classifying projects proposed by communities or their representative organizations, within the framework of the six priorities of "*Formar Ciudad*"; financial support from the central administration was available for those projects that emphasized one of the six priorities. Projects were classified according to the "*Formar Ciudad*" plan and within one of its six priorities. Local administration groups, which were given the power to approve the plans, deviated only minimally from the collectively elaborated drafts and expressed great approval for the technical support that the mayor's office offered in the area of project design. Four hundred leaders were trained, and projects were completed (including their planning, contracting, and usage of resources) in more than 190 neighborhoods. This process is now recognized as helping to build a "culture of planning" (Mockus 2001:18). Midway through 1998, a civic contest was held called "*Iniciativas por una Bogotá Mejor*" (Initiatives for a Better Bogotá), established by the Corona Foundation and the *El Tiempo* publishing house. Mockus gave this statement of recognition following the contest (Mockus 2001:21):

> "...the community is using the tools that the State has provided for their benefit. The "*Obras con saldo pedagógico*" (Works with pedagogical payoff) program from the

Figure 43: Construction of the Archive of Bogotá, 2001. Photo: Ignacio Prieto. Courtesy of the Mayor's Office of Bogotá, Secretary General, Central Archive, Photo Archive.

District's Department of Community Action has played an important role in all these processes. Through this program, the community has learned to design projects, carry them out, oversee their execution, establish priorities, and to work in conjunction with the District."

This project was a precursor of the "*Priorizador*" (Prioritizer), a project that sought citizen participation by allowing them to choose democratically, which projects would be prioritized during Mockus's second term.

ORDINANCE / LAW / EDICT

Not applicable.

Figure 44: Chiva Tax–Contributors Trip, 2001. Courtesy of the Mayor's Office of Bogotá, Secretary General, Central Archive, Photo Archive.

REFERENCES

Alcaldía de Bogotá. 1996, *Informe formar ciudad: 371 logros a ½ camino* [Mid-term Report on To Form the City: 371 Accomplishments]. Bogotá: Imprenta Distrital.

Mockus, Antanas. 2001. "*Cultura Ciudadana*, programa contra la violencia en Santa Fe de Bogotá, Colombia, 1995-1997." [Civic Culture, a Program against Violence in Santa Fe de Bogotá, Colombia, 1995-1997], Washington, DC: Interamerican Development Bank, Social Development Division. http://es.calameo.com/read/00047752906c074dfce6b.

Mockus, Antanas. 2004. "Ampliación de los modos de hacer política" [Broadening the Ways of Doing Politics]. Paper presented at the Colloque CERI, Paris, December 2-3. https://www.researchgate.net/publication/267362347_AMPLIACION_DE_LOS_MODOS_DE_HACER_POLITICA.

Figure 45-46: Chiva Tax–Contributors Trip, 2001. Courtesy of the Mayor's Office of Bogotá, Secretary General, Central Archive, Photo Archive.

9 BOGOTÁ FLIRTS—

CITIZENSHIP CARDS

(Bogotá coqueta—tarjetas ciudadanas)

First and Second Term: 1995-1998 / 2001-2003

Figure 47: Launching "Bogotá Flirts" Citizenship Cards, 1995. Photo: Eduardo Sotomayor. Courtesy of the Mayor's Office of Bogotá, Secretary General, Central Archive, Photo Archive.

OBJECTIVE

"Bogotá Flirts" was intended to encourage positive interpersonal social control, encouraging citizens to regulate each other's behavior through peaceful means.

DATE OF PRODUCTION

1995–1997 and 2001–2003

DESCRIPTION

Cards with one white side and one red side were distributed to the masses. The white side showed a hand giving a "thumbs–up." The caption read: "*Bogotá Coqueta*" (Bogotá Flirts). The red side showed a hand giving a "thumbs–down," as a sign of disapproval. Initially, these cards were manufactured and distributed by the private sector. They were given out by the hundreds of thousands to pedestrians and drivers to help them identify both good and bad citizen behaviors (Mockus 2001:13).

This project emerged from images used during Mockus's election campaign: an eye and ear with the slogan, "I See You, and I Hear You." At the end of the campaign, the Instituto Distrital de Cultura (District Institute of Culture) turned them into the thumbs-up/thumbs-down campaign. Starting with just these two symbols, the campaign eventually grew to include eight symbols created by designer Marta Granados; it was extremely successful in its first iteration. The increasing number of symbols inspired the creation of other projects like the Black Star Campaign, which came from a symbol that asked, "*¿Qué nos pasa?*" (What's up with us?). Nonetheless, the increasing number of cards turned out to be impractical for daily use, as it resulted in too many to carry and to use at the right moment.

RESULTS

The campaign was successful in encouraging citizen-to-citizen education and improving traffic in Bogotá. Many drivers used the cards, and some of them went so far as to attach them to one of the windows of their vehicle. The red side (to denounce bad behavior on the part of pedes-

Figure 48: Press Conference, "No Car Day," 2003. Photo: Eduardo Sotomayor. Courtesy of the Mayor's Office of Bogotá, Secretary General, Central Archive, Photo Archive.

Figure 49: "Bogotá Flirts," 2005. Courtesy of *El Espectador*.

Figure 50: Newspaper Classified by the
Mayor's Office, Bogotá. 1996. Courtesy
of *El Espectador.*

trians or drivers) was used more than the white one. Those who wished to applaud good citizen behavior continued to use the white side with the "thumbs–up." In some tense situations, labor unions and communities expressed their disapproval with large "thumbs–down" cards.

It is important to clarify one key point about this project: it was never allowed to affect people's self-worth. No one said, "You are a bad citizen." The red and white cards were entirely situational, and never declared a behavior to be simply good or bad. The cards seem to have two sides, but they actually present four options. Depending on the severity of a situation, the Mockus administration encouraged people to use their discretion in how they were used. For example, a red card with the thumbs–up might signify a warning. Or in the case of a red card with the thumb–down, this might signify an expulsion.

EDUCATIONAL POSSIBILITIES

"...Let's just say that when we talk about these things with Europeans, people say: 'No, a European citizen would be extremely offended by someone pulling out a card in response to their behavior'; but that's just the magic of context." (Mockus 2014)

Figure 51: "Bogotá Flirts," Logo, 1995-1998.
Design by Martha Granados.

ORDINANCE / LAW / EDICT

Not applicable.

REFERENCES

"Bogotá le coqueteará a todo el mundo" [Bogotá Will Flirt with the World]. 1995. *El Tiempo,* November 30: (http://www.eltiempo.com/archivo/documento/MAM-469215).

Mockus, Antanas. 2001. "*Cultura ciudadana,* programa contra la violencia en Santa Fe de Bogotá, Colombia, 1995-1997." [Civic Culture, a Program against Violence in Santa Fe de Bogotá, Colombia, 1995-1997] Washington, DC: Interamerican Development Bank, Social Development Division: (http://es.calameo.com/read/00047752906c074dfce6b).

"Tarjeta roja de Mockus a estudiante de la UN 1994" [Mockus's Red Card to a Student of the UN 1994], 2012, YouTube video, 6:06, posted by "ombrablava76," March 30: (https://www.youtube.com/watch?v=FLWC2kubc44).

Figure 52: "Bogotá Flirts," 2006. Photo: Gabriel Aponte. Courtesy of *El Espectador*.

Figure 53: "Bogotá Flirts," 2006. Photo: Gabriel Aponte. Courtesy of *El Espectador*.

10 CARROT LAW

(Ley Zanahoria)

First and Second Term: 1995-1998 / 2001-2003

Figure 54: "Carrot Cocktail," 2003. Photo: Eduardo Sotomayor. Courtesy of the Mayor's Office of Bogotá, Secretary General, Central Archive, Photo Archive.

OBJECTIVE

The "Carrot Law" looked to confront social obstacles and cultures, eliminating aggression, and supporting peaceful coexistence and the negotiation of conflicts. It was meant to reduce the violent deaths that were linked to alcohol abuse, and the levels of violence, intolerance and insecurity in Bogotá. The restrictions imposed by the "Carrot Law" could be modified when there was justification.

DATE OF PRODUCTION

1995–1997 and 2001–2003

DESCRIPTION

The "Carrot Law" responded to the close relationship between the consumption of alcohol, especially during the weekends, and the number of violent deaths and traffic accidents. In 1995, 49% of deaths from traffic accidents, 33% of homicides from firearms, 49% of homicides from sharp weapons, 35% of suicides, and 10% of accidental deaths showed an association between elevated levels of blood alcohol concentration and people being injured. (Mockus 2001:11).

In response, a closing time of one A.M. for bars and other establishments that serve alcohol was imposed. This measure supported others that sought to promote cultural regulation, self-regulation, and sanction. Televised statements like "*Entregue las llaves*" (Hand Over the Keys) and "*El conductor elegido*" (Designated Driver) helped to strengthen the regulations practiced by the citizens. They also improved the control of thoroughfares at night and how sanctions were applied to drunk drivers. They believed that the pilot program persuaded citizens to "*Saber antes de beber, uso responsable del alcohol* "(Think Before You Drink and Consume Alcohol Responsibly). It educated people about the diverse consequences that come from drinking alcohol, from the biochemical effects to those on the environment and on society. This program was presented to 3,500 secondary students from tenth and eleventh grade and to one hundred fifty teachers (Mockus 2002:15).

Figure 55: "Carrot Law," 1995. Photo: Gabriel Aponte. Courtesy of *El Espectador*.

Figure 56: "Carrot Law," 1995. Photo: Luis García. Courtesy of *El Espectador.*

Figure 57-58: "Carrot Law," 1995. Photo: Gabriel Aponte. Courtesy of *El Espectador.*

ADDITIONAL INFORMATION

This campaign was framed by an initiative known as *"Diciembre Zanahorio"* (Carrot December). The objective was to make December, the month with the highest rates of traffic accidents and homicides, less violent. The campaign was launched with the slogan: *"Diciembre Zanahorio, Enero Seguro"*(Carrot December, Safe January). The "Carrot Law" was established for the first month and then indefinitely for the year of 1995. The measure lasted for many years, but during the government of Peñalosa it was suspended for weeks, during which the number of deaths rose (Mockus 2014).

RESULTS

In 1995, homicides resulting from high blood alcohol concentration were reduced by 9.5%. The number of deaths from traffic accidents in which some of the people involved were drunk was reduced by 24.2%. And the number of female victims from homicide went down by 30% in that period.

During the Christmas of 1996, homicides went down by 26.7%. And in 1997, in comparison with 1996, the level of common homicides was reduced by 15% and traffic deaths by 13%

Figure 59: Closing Hour of Public Establishments, "Carrot Law," 1995. Courtesy of *El Espectador.*

(Mockus 2002:16). Lowering the level of alcohol consumption in Bogotá, despite the city's growth in 1996, led to the least violent December of recent years (in relation to 1993), and helped people recognize the benefits of the measure and get used to it more each day, especially after some initial resistance during the first few weeks.

OTHER FIGURES

The homicide rates dropped by 40%; homicides from traffic accidents decreased by 75%, and personal injuries were reduced by 23%. Between 1995 and 1997, with the disarmament, the "Carrot Law," and good cooperation between the citizens and the police, 3.5 lives were saved in Bogotá each day (*El Espectador,* 2009).

ORDINANCE / LAW / EDICT

Decree 890 of 1995 (Mayor's Office of Bogotá).

Figure 60: Carrots, 2014. Courtesy of Futuro Moncada.

REFERENCES

Alcaldía de Bogotá, 1995, Decree 890:

(http://www.alcaldiabogota.gov.co/sisjur/normas/Norma1.jsp?i=5544).

"El fin de la zanahoria." [The End of the Carrot], 2014, *Semana*, July 26: (http://www.semana.com/enfoque/articulo/el-fin-de-la-zanahoria/397141-3).

"Ley Zanahoria" [Carrot Law], 1996: (http://www.eltiempo.com/archivo/documento/MAM-545342).

———. 2002. "Bogotá: Camino a la igualdad: Avances en la Cultura Ciudadana y en la Construcción de lo Público" [Bogotá: On the Path to Equality: Advances in Civic Culture and Construction of the Public]. Bogotá: Alcaldía Mayor de Bogotá.

Mockus, Antanas. 2001. "Cultura ciudadana, programa contra la violencia en Santa Fe de Bogotá, Colombia, 1995-1997," [Civic Culture, a Program against Violence in Santa Fe de Bogotá, Colombia, 1995-1997]. Washington, DC: Interamerican Development Bank, Social Development Division: (http://es.calameo.com/read/00047752906c074dfce6b).

Serrano Guzmán, Alejandra P. 2014. "Adiós a 20 años de 'ley zanahoria' en Bogotá," [Goodbye to 20 Years of the "Carrot Law" in Bogotá]. *El Tiempo*, July 26: (http://www.eltiempo.com/bogota/analisis-sobre-la-rumba-extendida-en-bogota/14305517).

Figure 61: Carrots, 2014. Courtesy of Futuro Moncada.

"Si con está medida se lograra salvar 1 sola vida humana" [If This Measure Can Save One Human Life], 1996, YouTube video, 0:10, posted by "Mauricio L," May 2, 2010: (https://www.youtube.com/watch?v=QSkDh-ok_8).

"Volvería la ley zanahoria a Bogotá." [I Would Bring Back the Carrot Law to Bogotá] 2009, *El Espectador*, January 23: (http://www.elespectador.com/noticias/bogota/articulo110966-volveria-ley-zanahoria-bogota).

11 POLICE CODE

(Código de Policía)

First and Second Term: 1995-1998 / 2001-2003

Figure 62: Launching the New "Police Code," 2003. Photo: Fernando Rodríguez. Courtesy of the Mayor's Office of Bogotá, Secretary General, Central Archive, Photo Archive.

OBJECTIVE

Legislation regarding offenses that affect the coexistence of citizens should be modified through participation of offenders, concerned citizens, and authorities. This action sought to generate a greater social consciousness around the laws of coexistence and the importance of complying with them, as well as the reform of the "Police Code" of Bogotá.

DATE OF PRODUCTION

1995-1998 ("Civility Charter") and 2001-2003 ("Police Code")

DESCRIPTION

FIRST STAGE: CIVILITY CHARTER

After reading the "Police Code" during his first day of office, Mockus decided that his administration would carry out a reform. He requested the sanctions listed in various articles in order to see which were the most repetitive, using them to create interest groups. Subsequently, he invited citizens to participate in these work sessions that centered on specific problems in order to develop their own "Civility Charter" as an alternative to the reform of the "Police Code." These sessions were called *"Semilleros de Convivencia"* (Incubator of Coexistence). For each problem (for example, the use of animal traction in city transport) they invited people commonly involved, such as the offenders or those directly affected, and the authorities who should or could intervene. They would act out various scenarios, distributing roles among the participants to arrive at a wide range of solutions. Children, young adults, and adults participated to solve different problems related to harmonious coexistence.

The process lasted for two years, resulting in a multitude of initiatives that were then organized in a new "Civility Charter" that was presented to the Council of Bogotá as a replacement for the "Police Code." However, the city council shelved the project.

Figure 63: Launching the New "Police Code," 2003. Photo: Carlos Julio Martínez. Courtesy of *El Tiempo*.

"Civility Charter" Preamble:

"When someone cares for us, the city is beautiful. When someone helps us, the city is kind. When someone offends us, the city is detestable. The city is charged with our affections and heartbreaks, and no one acts anonymously without impacting the rest of us who inhabit the city. Each one of us is represented in each action. Even those we do not know, who fill the streets, travel in the buses, cross the parks, and stand in line with us, they are part of our lives …Keep them in mind so that one day we can again walk in the streets without fear, watch without suspicion of who is near, and be able to be supportive without fearing the consequences of lending a hand.

We can coexist precariously in a daily city life that pits everyone against each other, but it is not sufficient. We need to change civility into a common and shared legacy. We must construct it, as it will not construct itself from the reality of the city. We must create a collective and lasting work, by facing the difficulties of a large number of people, including men and women of all ages, from diverse professions, with varying beliefs and customs, who live in a relatively small space, forming complex relationships that are shaped by beliefs and habits, values and interests, and needs and desires.

Figure 64: Launching the New "Police Code," 2003. Photo: Carlos Julio Martínez. Courtesy of *El Tiempo*.

Among millions of anonymous individuals, encounters tend to be only fleeting, superficial, and fragmentary. But, in spite of this, it is necessary for everyone to share the same rules of the game, in order to feel that the city is for all.

The rules of the 'Civility Charter' are intended as contributions to the collective effort of constructing *Cultura Ciudadana*. They refer to the matters that sometimes seem small, but are significant in people's lives...

...If the city is for everyone, each change will visibly transform the face of the city, and we are going to need to be filled with patience, with resolve, and happiness as well as put up with disagreements to enable a cohesive city of connections that will lead to a respect for the limits."

FIRST STAGE: POLICE CODE

In the second mandate in the program entitled "Holding the rules in esteem and admiring the good" emphasized the participatory consultation process leading to the "Police Code" and drew from the "Civility Charter" during the first mandate.

Figure 65: Children Participating in the Launching of the "Police Code," 2003. Photo: Fernando Rodrí-guez. Courtesy of the Mayor's Office of Bogotá, Secretary General, Central Archive, Photo Archive.

In 2003, the "Code" was issued by the Council of Bogotá, and both the process in which it was approved, as well as its content illustrate the type of practices that strengthen participative democracy and legitimize legal norms.

The code retains elements of reforms drafted by the two earlier administrations and institutio-nalizes the corner stone of *Cultura Ciudadana.* Nine hundred and seventeen districts and social organizations participated in enacting the code. It is an instrument for promoting coexistence and citizenship, establishing minimal rules that should be respected by the citizens. It also in-cludes some of the values and the central pillars of *Cultura Ciudadana,* such as self-regulation, the sharing of responsibility between of the state and its citizens, the development of a sense of belonging in the city, and the use of dialogue to resolve conflicts.

The "Code" stipulates the ways in which the police can exercise its power and meet its responsibilities. It additionally establishes the rights and duties of the citizens and the responsibilities of city police authorities who are performing public service to promote solidarity, tranquility, and neighborhood relations through the promotion of security; the conservation of public health. These authorities are entrusted with protecting vulnerable populations and public spaces, promoting mobility by maintaining mobility standards, protecting cultural heritage, enforcing basic rules guaranteeing the freedom of industry and commerce, and protecting consumers and their right to conduct raffles, games, competitions, and public events.

The "Code" also includes a series of corrective measures to stimulate *Cultura Ciudadana*. Corrective measures are characterized by the emphasis placed on the pedagogical dimension of the actions: in educating offenders about the rules of coexistence and the negative social effects of their violation, as well as the strategic progression of its implementation, which is meant to generate an understanding of coexistence. In ascending order, the sanctions applicable to citizens are as follows: private admonition, public admonition, exclusion from the scene of the violation, attending pedagogical programs about civic coexistence, working on public interest projects, and fines.

The "Code" also establishes stimuli to educate citizens so that they will act on the conviction that complying with the rules guarantees a better quality of life for everyone, more than out of a fear for the sanctions. This includes a civic educational campaign, as well as recognizing and encouraging people who comply with these duties and carry out activities promoting public interest. They also promote dialogue about conflicts among citizens and peaceful resolution. The 'Code' introduces the pledge card of coexistence in which it negotiates agreements between people to resolve their differences that have resulted from the anticompetitive behavior rules of coexistence (Mockus 2003a:24-25).

RESULTS

FIRST STAGE: CIVILITY CHARTER

About eighteen thousand people participated in sixteen workshops within the District, one hundred eighty-one local workshops, and twenty-nine workshops that helped resolve short-term or spontaneous problems, outside of government organizations. At the end of the two years about thirty thousand initiatives organized by a reform commission had been collected.

Figure 66: Launching the "Police Code," 2003. Photo: Fernando Rodríguez. Courtesy of the Mayor's Office of Bogotá, Secretary General, Central Archive, Photo Archive.

Despite the fact that offenders represented barely one third of attendees, the exchange of roles almost always guaranteed more arguments in defense of the transgression than adherence to the norm. The Council of Bogotá shelved the project, arguing that the Congress should first approve the law of reform of the national "Police Code." The district government distributed 1,300,000 copies of the summary of the "Civility Charter" project among citizens (Mockus 2001:15).

SECOND STAGE: POLICE CODE

The new "Code of Coexistence" highlights, on the one hand, the incorporation of the policy of *Cultura Ciudadana*, based on the principles of self-regulation and mutual regulation of citizens, and, on the other hand, a closer relation to the culture of Bogotanos, which was achieved through the consultation of a range of social leaders, academic institutions and other entities of civil society.

Apart from the new "Police Code," specific decrees like the *"Ley Zanahoria"* (Carrot Law) and the *"Horario Optimista"* (Optimist Hours) were issued, as well as restricting the use of

Figure 67: "Police Code," 1995-1998. Courtesy of *El Espectador.*

fireworks and the bearing of weapons, which significantly contributed to the improvement of coexistence indicators.

PREAMBLE OF THE POLICE CODE:

"The new 'Police Code' of Bogotá, then, is based on self-regulation because it looks to compliance with the norms as mainly a matter of conviction rather than of fear of punishment; as a question of shared responsibility, because the protection of coexistence is a shared responsibility between the citizens and the authorities; and as an issue of solidarity because it is based on the willingness to always think of others and take their rights into account" (Mockus 2003b:5-6).

ORDINANCE / LAW / EDICT

Decree 928 of 1997 by which it invites the revision of the "Civility Charter." (Mayor's Office of Bogotá)

Agreement 79 of 2003 (January 20), "Por el cual se expide el código de policía de Bogotá D.C." (By Which the "Police Code" of Bogotá D.C. is Issued) (Mayor's Office of Bogotá)

Figure 68: "Police Code," 1995-1998. Courtesy of *El Espectador.*

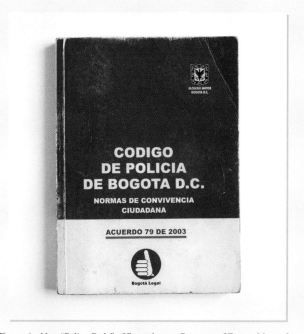

Figure 69: New "Police Code" of Bogotá, 2014. Courtesy of Futuro Moncada.

Figure 70: "Police Code." Courtesy of *El Espectador*.

REFERENCES

Alcaldía de Bogotá, 1993, "Decree 928 Civility Charter." (http://www.alcaldia- bogota.gov.co/sisjur/normas/Norma1.jsp?i=4881).

Alcaldía de Bogotá, 2003, "Agreement 79." (http://www.alcaldiabogota.gov.co/sisjur/normas/Norma1.jsp?i=6671).

"Código de Policía de Bogotá" [Bogotá's Police Code], 2003, Vimeo video, 0:40, posted by "pachomoreno," 2010, (https://vimeo.com/5121051).

———. 2003b. *Código de policía de Bogotá D.C.* [Police Code of Bogotá DC].

Bogotá: District Press.

Mockus, Antanas. 2003a. *Bogotá para vivir, 2001–2003* [To Live in Bogotá, 2001-2003], Bogotá, OP Graphic Group S.A. (http://www.sdp.gov.co/portal/page/portal/PortalSDP/ciudadania/PlanesDesarrollo/Bogotaparavivirtodosdelmismolado/2001_2004_BogotaparaVivirTodosdelMismoLado_c_InformeFin2.pdf).

Mockus, Antanas. 2001. "Cultura ciudadana, programa contra la violencia en Santa Fe de Bogotá, Colombia, 1995-1997," Washington, DC: Interamerican Development Bank, Social Development Division: (http://es.calameo.com/read/00047752906c074dfce6b).

Figure 71: Police Reading the New "Police Code," 2003. Courtesy of the Mayor's Office of Bogotá, Secretary General, Central Archive, Photo Archive.

12 SEAT BELT

(Cinturón de seguridad)

First and Second Term: 1995-1998 / 2001-2003

Figure 72: "Seat Belt," 1995-1998. Courtesy of *El Espectador.*

OBJECTIVE

To increase the use of seat belts as part of the program to save lives and reduce traffic accidents.

DATE OF PRODUCTION

April of 1995

DESCRIPTION

In order to increase the use of the seat belts, a number of measures were carried out that soon caught on among Bogotanos.

While the "Knights of the Crosswalk" focused on taxi-driving citizens, when it came to seat belts, it became necessary to address the mockery that citizens would make of drivers wearing a seat belt. During the first year of the program's implementation, drivers lied about wearing their belt and refer to the problems inherent in complying with this norm.

The "Seat Belt" intervention was necessary to address widespread avoidance of seat belts among drivers, including taxi drivers. During the first year, even taxi drivers who were part of the "Knights of the Crosswalk" would lie about using their seat belts, which was evidence of the difficulties people faced in internalizing these measures.

Figure 73: "Seat Belt," 1995-1998. Courtesy of *El Espectador.*

RESULTS

According to Mockus, "The great majority of Bogotanos used seat belts two months after the measures were established, thereby demonstrating the support that this good practice achieved among them. Seat belts were used by more than two-thirds of the drivers.

At the beginning, it gained validity as a norm because people feared being fined by the police so they would take precautions and wear the seat belt. But I think that now a great percentage of Bogotanos use the safety belt because the behavior has become customary; one feels uncomfortable to get in the car without using a seat belt." (Mockus 2014, pers. comm.).

ORDINANCE / LAW / EDICT

Not applicable.

REFERENCES

"Podra Mockus con Bogotá?" [What can Mockus do With Bogotá?], 1995, *Semana,* April 10:

(http://www.semana.com/especiales/articulo/podra-mockus-con-bogota/25203-3).

13 PLAN OF VOLUNTARY DISARMAMENT

(Plan de desarme voluntario)

First and Second Term: 1995-1998 / 2001-2003

Figure 74: Surrender of Weapons, 1996. Photo: Gabriel Aponte. Courtesy of *El Espectador.*

OBJECTIVE

The goal was to reduce the number of anger-driven or accidental homicides, and to resort to citizen engagement to control what epidemiologists call "risk factors."

DATE OF PRODUCTION

1995–1997 and 2001–2003

DESCRIPTION

In 1995 and 1996, 74% and 73% respectively, of documented homicides in Bogotá resulted from the possession of illegal or legal firearms. In the United States, a traditionally liberal country with regard to firearms, an investigation that examined the acquisition of firearms intended for self-defense was carried out. According to the results, the probability of causing death due to accidental or unplanned use of weapons is forty-two times more likely than the probability of doing so for self-defense (Mockus 2001:11).

Figure 75: Surrender of Weapons, 1996. Photo: Gabriel Aponte. Courtesy of *El Espectador.*

With the slogan *"Que las armas descansen en paz en esta Navidad"* (May the Weapons Rest in Peace This Christmas) mass media campaign was created urging citizens to voluntarily return the firearms and ammunition in their possession. They surrendered weapons, ammunition, explosives, and even hand grenades. With the help of private companies and local embassies that joined the campaign, they encouraged people to surrender weapons, ammunition, and explosives in exchange for vouchers to purchase Christmas presents, although some people asked for nothing in return.

"Armas a la basura vida más segura" (Trash Weapons for a Safer Life) is one of the slogans of the 2003 plan for voluntary disarmament. With the support from the Catholic Church, the mayor gave people vouchers for clothing and books. The vouchers could also be used in the market.

As part of the initiative for voluntary disarmament, weapons were transformed into objects such as spoons and birds that were mounted on pedestals and that stated: *"Arma Fui"* (I Was a

Figure 76: The Plan for Voluntary Disarmament was Supported by the Catholic Church, 1996. Photo: Humberto Pinto. Courtesy of *El Espectador*.

Figure 77: "Plan of Voluntary Disarmament," 1996. Photo: Humberto Pinto. Courtesy of *El Espectador.*

Weapon). And, in the case of the spoons, they were accompanied by a statement: "*Las armas sí están para cucharas"* (If Weapons Were for Spoons).

ANECDOTAL EVIDENCE:

In Mockus's words: It was announced in a press conference that we would ask the Ministry of Defense and the Minister to suspend the open use of weapons not only on the weekends but all of the time, encouraging safe conduct. Then a journalist asked President Samper: 'What do you think of the mayor's proposal?', to which the President responded: 'No, that is crazy! *El palo no está pa' cucharas** (The Gun Is Not for Making Spoons).' When we came to speak with the president, it was very strange since we were unfamiliar with his statement. He arrived and repeated the phrase '*El palo no está pa' cucharas*,' this is not the moment to speak of disarmament. After that, in a very deflated press conference, Monsignor Rubiano and I were powerless.

However, just two days later, we began organizing the program for voluntary disarmament, where guns were received in exchange for gifts, a program that had already worked well in New York and Central America.

With Monsignor Rubiano we invoked a biblical text, in which the metal that had been used to

Figure 78: Foundry with Bladed Weapons, 2003. Courtesy of the Mayor's Office of Bogotá, Secretary General, Central Archive, Photo Archive.

kill later was later used to protect human life by being made into ploughs. 'They forge their swords into ploughshares, and their spears into pruning shears. They do not raise a spear against the nation, nor will they train for war' (Proverb Isaiah 2:4).

But we realized that the plow is no longer a common tool. In those days, we were raising our first daughter Adriana, and so it occurred to us that a Gerber spoon would be a beautiful symbol, curved so that a child can't scratch their eyes, and so we realized that, *yes*, guns are for making spoons (more than 2,300 of them).

And why use the phrase: '*Arma Fui*' (I Was a Weapon)? It was an attempt to tell people that the spoon was made from the metal of weapons. Someone once suggested that the statement should be '*Arma Soy*' (I Am a Weapon), a new weapon, not '*Arma Fui*' (I Was a Weapon).

But why '*I Am a Weapon*'?

Because if the gun is telling its history, it continues to act as a weapon, but one with a different register…This is problematic in an argument for disarmament because I too can say: I don't want to abandon all of my weapons; leave me something." (Mockus 2014, pers. comm.)

Figure 79: Foundry with Bladed Weapons, 1997. Photo: Luis Acosta. Courtesy of the Mayor's Office, Bogotá. Secretary General, Central Archive, Photo Archive.

RESULTS

With citizens turning in 2,538 weapons, the administration then used a cast to produce baby spoons for feeding infants. The baby spoons, mounted on stands made of the same metal, had the inscription: '*Arma Fui*' (I Was a Weapon). The spoons and stands came together in nice wooden and acrylic gift boxes for residences and offices.

The homicide rate dropped by 397 in December of 1995 and by 291 in December of 1996. In the second term of 1997, after the total ban on carrying weapons, homicides dropped 30% in September, 23% in October, and 26% in November, in comparison to the same months in 1996. In 2001, twenty-six days of voluntary disarmament were established, during which more than five thousand firearms and homemade weapons were collected (Mockus 2001:12).

ORDINANCE / LAW / EDICT

Not applicable.

Figure 80: Foundry with Bladed Weapons, 1997. Photo: Luis Acosta. Courtesy of the Mayor's Office of Bogotá. Secretary General, Central Archive, Photo Archive.

REFERENCES

Mockus, Antanas. 2001. "Cultura ciudadana, programa contra la violencia en Santa Fe de Bogotá, Colombia, 1995-1997," [Civic Culture, a Program against Violence in Santa Fe de Bogotá, Colombia, 1995-1997] Washington, DC: Interamerican Development Bank, Social Development Division: (http://es.calameo.com/read/00047752906c074dfce6b).

"Mockus pide desarme total" [Mockus Asks for Total Disarmament], 2003, *El Tiempo*, July 16: (http://www.eltiempo.com/ archivo/documento/MAM-967395).

Figure 81-82: Spoon, Base, and Bird Transformed from Surrendered Weapons, 2014. Courtesy of Futuro Moncada.

Figure 83: Spoon, Base, and Bird Transformed from Surrendered Weapons, 2014. Courtesy of Futuro Moncada.

14 RESTRICTION ON THE BEARING OF ARMS

(Restricción al porte de armas)

First and Second Term: 1995-1998 / 2001-2003

Figure 84: "Restriction on the Bearing of Arms," 1997. Courtesy of *El Espectador*.

OBJECTIVE

This measure affirmed that a citizen should not take justice into her own hands, nor should she be a danger to other citizens. The measure was also meant to promote trust between strangers.

DATE OF PRODUCTION

January, February, March, and December of 1996

DESCRIPTION

The private possession of legal or illegal arms was a threat to citizens who do not carry them, and it posed a challenge to the principle of equality established by the National Constitution. Gun ownership had increased because many citizens saw it as something normal, justified by the unsafe conditions of a city like Bogotá.

The incidence of the use of firearms, legal or illegal, in the number of recorded homicides was high. In 1995, 74% of common homicides were committed with this type of weapon, and in 1996, 73%. In many cases, weapons that had been legally obtained were used, as demonstrated in the census of the arms confiscated in crimes committed in 1995 and in those committed in the first trimester of 1996. In the latter 126 crimes, fifty-one confiscated weapons were sold by the military industry of Colombia and thirty-seven had authorization (Mockus 2001:11).

On several occasions, the mayor of Santa Fe de Bogotá proposed that the national government suspend the granting of permits to private individuals to carry firearms for an indefinite period of time, pending periodic evaluations to analyze the results. This measure would not include security companies and departments or companies that transported valuables.

However, the general commander of the military and the Ministry of Defense not only refused to accept these reforms, but they also called to eliminate the restriction on carrying firearms during the weekends, which led to a progressive increase in homicide rates beginning in April of 1996 when the decision went into effect.

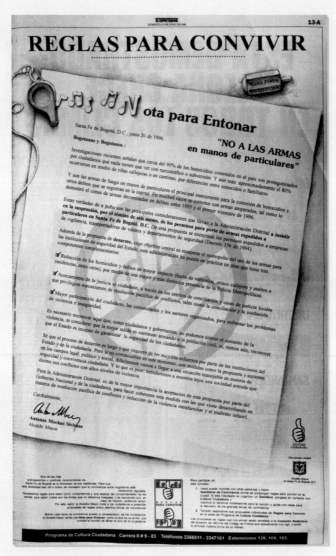

Figure 85: Rules for Coexistence by the Mayor's Office, Bogotá, 1996. Courtesy of *El Espectador*.

Figure 86: "Restriction on the Bearing of Arms," 1991. Courtesy of *El Espectador.*

Figure 87: "Restriction on the Bearing of Arms," 1991. Courtesy of *El Espectador*.

RESULTS

During the first quarter of 1996, when the restriction on carrying firearms during the weekend was upheld, the rate of homicides decreased by 12.11%. Between April and November, when no restrictions were in place, it increased by 5.49%. In the case of homicides caused by firearms, the measure decreased the rate of homicides caused by firearms by 6.74% in the first quarter, but then it increased by 6.3% between April and November (Mayor's Office of Bogotá 1996).

In December, when the mayor and the archbishop of Bogotá led the campaign "*Que las Armas Descansen en Paz*" (May the Weapons Rest in Peace) and restricted the bearing of firearms, the homicides decreased by 26.7% with respect to the rate in December of 1995. During the first term of 1998, when Peñalosa maintained the ban on carrying firearms, there was an average of 143 homicides per month, compared to the months prior to the restriction of December 1997, when the average was 182 homicides per month.

After the state council's decision to remove the restriction in the second half of 1998 and the first quarter of 1999, the rate of homicides by firearms continued to increase. In May of 2000, for instances, there were 161 homicides (León 2012).

ORDINANCE / LAW / EDICT

Decree 757 of 1996, "Por el cual se declara la temporada de navidad zanahoria en el Distrito Capital" (By Which Carrot Christmas is Temporarily Declared in the Capital District) (Mayor's Office of Bogotá).

REFERENCES

Alcaldía de Bogota. 1996. *Bogotá ciudad coqueta.* Bogotá: Imprenta Distrital.

Alcaldía de Bogotá, 1996, "Decree 757." (http:// www.alcaldiabogota.gov.co/sisjur/normas/Norma1. jsp?i=8640).

León, Juanita. 2012. "Los cinco mitos de la prohibición del porte de armas" [Five myths about the prohibition on bearing arms], La Silla Vacia [The empty chair], January 3: (http://lasillavacia.com/ historia/los-cinco-mitos-de-la-prohibicion-del-porte-de-armas-30546).

"Mockus pide desarme total" [Mockus Calls for Total Disarmament], 2003, *El Tiempo,* July 16: (http:// www.eltiempo.com/archivo/documento/MAM-967395).

"Prohibir el porte de armas: un viejo deseo fracasado." [Prohibiting the Carrying of Arms: an Old, Failed Desire], 2012, *Semana* [Week], January 2: (http://www.semana.com/politica/articulo/prohibir-porte-armas-viejo-deseo- fracasado/251461-3).

"¿Adiós a las armas?" [Goodbye to Guns?], 2012, *Semana* [Week], January 7: (http://www.semana.com/ nacion/articulo/adios-armas/251586-3).

15 PROHIBITION OF FIREWORKS

(Prohibición de la pólvora)

First and Second Term: 1995-1998 / 2001-2003

Figure 88: Voluntary Surrender of Fireworks, 1995. Photo: Humberto Pinto. Courtesy of *El Espectador.*

OBJECTIVE

To reduce the number of children burned or killed by fireworks.

DATE OF PRODUCTION

December 10, 1995

DESCRIPTION

On New Year's Eve, the burn units of various hospitals in Bogotá were overrun, and while the media reported on this situation, no one spoke out against the practice.

During Christmas in 1994, five children under the age of fourteen were killed, and one hundred twenty-seven suffered burns from the use of fireworks. (Mockus 2001:11).

During Christmas of 1995, only adults were allowed to use fireworks in limited and permitted locations. The local government had publicly announced that they would completely ban the use of fireworks upon receiving notification of the first case of a child who had been burned by fireworks in the city. The accident occurred, and the sanction was put into place as a pedagogical measure. The parents who had allowed their children to play with fireworks were assigned civic work. In the city, the illegal production of fireworks was common, periodically leading to tragic accidents. All of the manufacturers and distributors authorized their sale, but only during limited periods and in situations that were laid out by the government of the capital district.

For those who worked in the sale of firearms (many of whom had inherited the job), there were two solutions: the voluntary surrender of their products in exchange for economic compensation, as well as a path to labor retraining programs. Those who chose not to comply with the law would suffer not only the rigors of working underground but also the confiscation of pyrotechnic products and the resulting economic loss.

Figure 89: Voluntary Surrender of Fireworks, 1995. Photo: Humberto Pinto. Courtesy of *El Espectador.*

Figure 90: Decommission of Fireworks, 1995. Photo: Alejandro Rivera. Courtesy of *El Espectador*.

Figure 91: Sanction for Those Whom Use Fireworks, 1996. Photo: Luis Acosta. Courtesy of the Mayor's Office of Bogotá, Secretary General, Central 90Archive, Photo Archive.

The parents and adults who irresponsibly allowed their children to continue using fireworks received a pedagogical sanction, as well as mandatory civic work assignments, such as sweeping hospital floors or cleaning prison bathrooms. In addition, parallel measures were instituted such as the whistle in the "Carrot Kit," which provided an alternative way of creating a festive atmosphere by providing a comparable noise that could replace fireworks.

RESULTS

As a result of the sanction, fewer children were burned during Christmas festivities. Before this administration, there were no consolidated statistics on the number of burned children, although it was known that there were hundreds of victims. The Christmases of 1995 and 1996 showed how effective these measures were. During Christmas of 1995, no children were killed by fireworks, and the number of children injured decreased from one hundred twenty-seven injured in 1994, to forty-six. The next year, during Christmas of 1996, there were also no deaths, and the total number of children injured from fireworks was down to forty-one (Mockus 2001:12).

Communication between the district government and the manufacturers and distributors of

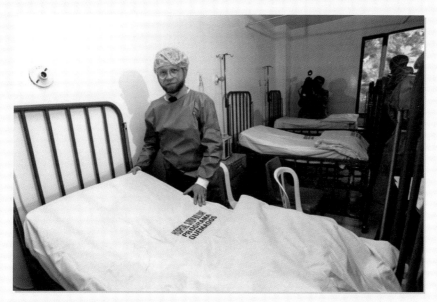

Figure 92: Press Conference for Burned Children, 2002. Courtesy of the Mayor's Office of Bogotá, Secretary General, Central Archive, Photo Archive.

fireworks, as well as with their institutional spokespersons and lawyers, played a crucial role in adapting to the prohibition and managing the consequences for its producers.

Over time, the number of burn victims in Bogotá declined, until the number was reduced to zero per year; this measure was repeated in the majority of Colombian cities, which were all able to achieve the same results (ibid.).

ORDINANCE / LAW / EDICT
Decree 791 of 1995 (December 10) (Mayor's Office of Bogotá).

REFERENCES
Alcaldía de Bogotá, 1995, "Decree 791."

(http://www.alcaldiabogota.gov.co/sisjur/normas/Norma1. jsp?i=1972!).

Mockus, Antanas. 2001. "Cultura ciudadana, programa contra la violencia en Santa Fe de Bogotá, Colombia, 1995-1997," [Civic Culture, a Program against Violence in Santa Fe de Bogotá, Colombia, 1995-1997] Washington, D.C.: Interamerican Development Bank, Social Development Division: (http://es.calameo.com/read/00047752906c074dfce6b).

Figure 93: Civic Work as Educational Sanction, 1996. Photo: Humberto Pinto. Courtesy of *El Espectador*.

Figure 94: Civic Work as Educational Sanction, 1996. Photo: Humberto Pinto. Courtesy of *El Espectador*.

16 VACCINE AGAINST VIOLENCE

(Vacuna contra la violencia)

First and Second Term: 1995-1998 / 2001-2003

Figure 95: "Vaccine Against Violence," 2002. Courtesy of the Mayor's Office, Bogotá. Secretary General, Central Archive.

OBJECTIVE

Reduce the level of abuse through quick, massive, effective actions.

DATE OF PRODUCTION

March 1996

DESCRIPTION

Fireworks were not the only thing causing children's burns. There were other factors in place that resulted in injury to children. Some children were being burned with cookware, and punished with lashes. Others suffered from other forms of violent abuse.

According to a study by Felicia Marie Kanaul of the Department of National Planning and UNICEF (1994), the percentage of mistreated children was 67.7% and of those, 23% were in a critical situation. The administration had to decrease this level of abuse with rapid, massive and effective change.

This study served as a basis for the action labelled "Vaccine Against Violence". This initiative sought to generate a space to explore the experience of violence, particularly on the part of children, and to begin to confront it by expressing their internalized pain or discomfort. The goal was to provide a framework for releasing anger and resentment, to heal these wounds, and break the cycle of becoming a future perpetrator of the same acts of violence. It is scientifically proven that having an outlet for these emotions can deactivate the charge of violence that is otherwise held internally (ibid.)

It is essential to recognize that there are beliefs, customs, and habits that lead to the continued abuse of children, and these risk factors begin during childhood. There are also cultural barriers that can lead to violence and compromise the physical safety of those who are weaker; children are the first to suffer violence. This has a circular structure: if you suffer from violence as

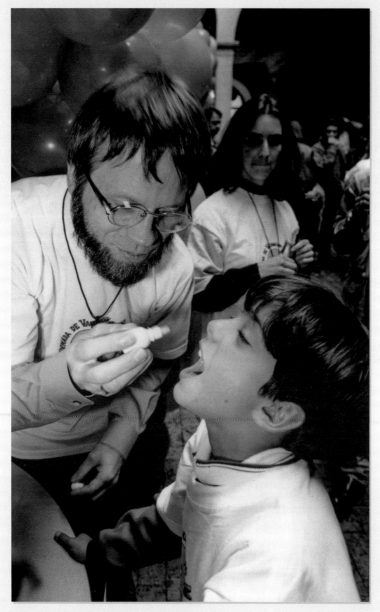

Figure 96: Second Day of "Vaccine Against Violence," 1996. Photo: Juan Castañeda. Courtesy of the Mayor's Office, Bogotá, Secretary General, Central Archive.

Figure 97: "Vaccine Against Violence," 1996. Courtesy of the Mayor's Office, Bogotá. Secretary General, Central Archive.

a child, it is very possible that it will lead to violent actions as an adult, especially under conditions of social and psychological stress or under the use of psychoactive substances or alcohol.

The symbol used during the Vaccination Day was a doll whose body and head were inflatable balloons, employed as a symbol to absorb the emotional impact on behalf of the person who was receiving the vaccine. Popping the balloon-doll (that represented the perpetrator) was the first step of the process.

The idea of using the doll drew from a holiday tradition that consists of making a doll out of old clothes that is then filled with fireworks and ignited on the evening of December 31.

The Vaccination Day ritual entailed four further steps. One featured the *"Arbol de los deseos"* (Tree of Desires), in which people expressed their yearnings by writing them on paper shaped as leaves from a tree; when knotted together, the leaves made up a network that was used as a symbol of people's unity against violence. The vaccination was another symbolic element, consisting of drops of water; individuals would receive a card "certifying" their vaccination

Figure 98: Mockus at the "Vaccine Against Violence" during his First Administration, 1995-1998. Photo: Jaime García. Courtesy of *El Tiempo*.

after it was complete. Furthermore, a hotline was also established to receive calls, and letters could be sent reporting abuse (Mayor's Office of Bogotá, 1996).

ANECDOTAL EVIDENCE

"...with the '*Vaccine Against Violence*' the traditional doll is re-contextualized...I used to make them in my apartment. I would take a pair of old pants, and fill them with foam (which would only create fantasies, you know, being surrounded by a bunch of mannequins' lower halves).

Stuffing the dolls, we had the idea of recreating the head of the perpetrator on the doll and to ask the person who was being vaccinated: Who is the person who abused you most in your life? Paint the characteristics of his or her face, and now say or do to him or her what you wish.

It was an attempt to relieve the footprint and the violence that one has suffered in a socially controlled setting, in an atmosphere that is calm but festive. For example, Andrea Echeverri, the singer of *Aterciopelados* (The Velvety Ones), accompanied us at the vaccination and said that she had not been abused as a child, but that this was the case for many; in *Bogotá Change* there is a scene that I remember, one of the three times I was vaccinated:

Figure 99: Mockus at the "Vaccine Against Violence" during his First Administration, 1995-1998. Courtesy of El Tiempo.

I remembered something that I had never told anyone. My mother's friend took me to the gallery one Sunday and said: I am going to teach you how to wrestle. Let's say that I was seven or eight years old and didn't have the vocabulary to understand the situation. I knew that it was bad, but why? Why is this man doing what he's doing? Why does he clearly have a hidden agenda? Somehow you suspect that it is not okay; when I understood the situation, I kicked him away and told him: 'if you like men, look for an adult, but not children! Not children!' I told him this forty-five years later when I had had the vaccine..." (Mockus 2014).

RESULTS

The authorities of the district administration participated in the events, alongside with other private and non-governmental organizations that primarily collaborated by providing specialized mental health professionals. The two vaccination days were organized in the city on March 3rd and June 2nd of 1996. More than forty thousand people attended, and of these, the critical cases were referred to mental health professionals. The program was extended to other places, such as correctional facilities, universities, schools, as well as public and private companies.

Figure 100: "*Vaccine Against Forgetfulness*". UNICEF, 2002. Photo: Ignacio Prieto. Courtesy of the Mayor's Office of Bogotá, Secretary General, Central Archive, Photo Archive.

The balance was very positive because there were a lot of people who changed their attitude, and among other things, began to overcome the fear of condemnation. For example, in Bosa, one of the twenty localities of the city, the complaints went from one hundred in February to nine hundred in March, proof of the changing attitude of the people (Mayor's Office of Bogotá 1996).

ORDINANCE / LAW / EDICT

Not applicable.

Figure 101: Certificate of Vaccination, "Vaccine Against Forgetfulness," 2014. Courtesy of Futuro Moncada.

REFERENCES

Alcaldía de Bogota. 1996. *Bogotá ciudad coqueta* [Bogotá Flirts]. Bogotá: District Press.

Knaul, Felicia Marie. 1993. "Menores en circunstancias especialmente difíciles: Su vinculación escolar" [Minors in Especially Difficult Circumstances: Their School Enrollment]. *Revista de planeación y desarrollo,* [Review of Planning and Development], 24:201-224.

"Vacuna oral contra la violencia - Fotonoticia," [Oral Vaccine Against Violence, Photo Essay], *El Tiempo*, February 28: (http://www.eltiempo.com/archivo/documento/MAM-353712).

"Vacuna contra la rabia," [Vaccine Against Anger], 1996, *El Tiempo*, March 4 (http://www.eltiempo.com/archivo/documento/MAM-345399).

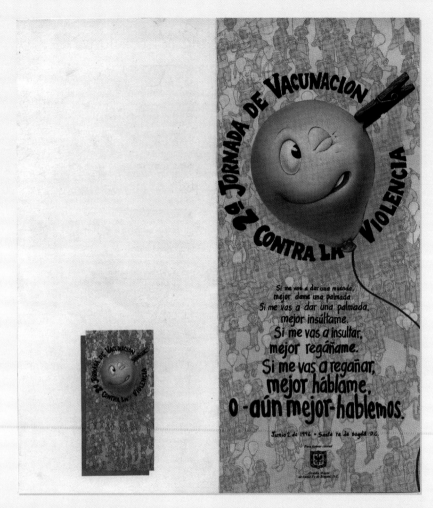

Figure 102: Exterior of Brochure, "Vaccine Against Forgetfulness," 2014. Courtesy of Futuro Moncada.

Te esperamos en los siguientes lugares :

USAQUEN
PLAZA PRINCIPAL USAQUEN Cra.6ª Calle 118
C.D.C. SIMON BOLIVAR Cra.7ª Calle 165

CHAPINERO
PARQUE LOURDES Cra.13 Calle 63
EDIFICIO SAN JOSE Cra. 7ª Calle 82

SANTA FE
C.D.C. LOURDES Cra. 2ª Calle 3ª
ESTACION TELEFERICO Monserrate

SAN CRISTOBAL
CAMI ALTAMIRA Cra12A Este Nº 89A-41 Sur
C.D.C. LA VICTORIA Diagonal 37 Cra.2ª Este
C.D.C. SAN BLAS (Alcaldía) Cra.3ª Nº 15-57 Sur

USME
COMPENSAR LA MARICHUELA
Cra.42A Este Nº 89A-41 Sur
C.D.C. TEJARES Calle 84B Este Nº 41-33 Sur

TUNJUELITO
PARQUE EL TUNAL Calle 47B sur Cra.24 Esquina
C.D.C. PABLO DE TARSO Diagonal 47A Nº 53-92 Sur
CASA VECINAL ISLA DEL SOL Cra.67B Nº 62-03 Sur

BOSA
ALCALDIA LOCAL Cra.14 Calle14
ESCUELA LA LIBERTAD Diagonal al CAI de La Libertad
C.D.C. BOSA Calle11 Sur Nº 19A-66

KENNEDY
PLAZOLETA LEY Parqueadero CAFAM
Cra. 75 Calle 35 Sur
COLEGIO RODRIGO TRIANA Cra.97A Nº 18-15
C.D.C. KENNEDY Transversal 86 Nº 43-43 Int.1
PALMITAS Calle 38A Sur Cra.119 Esquina

FONTIBON
C.D.C. LA GIRALDA Cra. 110 Nº 34-35
J.I. EL PORTAL Calle 22A Nº 118-25
ALCALDIA LOCAL Calle 25 Nº 99-02

ENGATIVA
ESCUELA REPUBLICA DE CHINA Cra.91 Nº 82-20
C.D.C. SANTA HELENITA Calle 70 Nº 78-07
CONCENTRACION GENERAL SANTANDER
Calle 13 Nº 11-32

SUBA
CENTRO COMERCIAL CENTRO SUBA
Calle 140 Nº 91-19
J.I. HELVETIA Calle129 Nº 47-05
ALCALDIA LOCAL Cra.91 Nº 143-15

BARRIOS UNIDOS
PARQUE BENJAMIN HERRERA Cra. 29 Nº 63C-60
J.I. SANTA SOFIA Cra.32 Nº 75-25
CENTRO OPERATIVO LOCAL Cra.47 Nº 69B-31

TEUSAQUILLO
PARK WAY Avenida 22 Calle 42
GALERIAS Parqueadero Oriental Cra. 24 Calle 53

LOS MARTIRES
C.U. RECEPCION DE NIÑOS Avda. 19 Nº 24C-10
PLAZA ESPAÑA Cra. 18 Calle 10

ANTONIO NARIÑO
BARRIO POLICARPA Salón Cultural Luis A. Morales
Calle 3ª Sur Nº 10- 25
PARQUE BARRIO SANTANDER Calle 29 Sur Cra. 29
PARQUE VILLA MAYOR Cra.34C Calle 34 Sur

PUENTE ARANDA
C.D.C. JOSE ANTONIO GALAN Calle 1ª B Nº 57-50
J.I. BOCHICA Calle 2ª Nº 34-50

LA CANDELARIA
PLAZA DE BOLIVAR Cra. 8ª Calle 10
Alcaldía Mayor de Santa Fe de Bogotá, D.C.

RAFAEL URIBE URIBE
C.D.C. MOLINOS Calle 48P Nº 5-86
J.I. SAN JORGE Diagonal 45 Nº 13-04
C.D.C. COLINAS Calle 32 Sur Nº 15C-10
J.I. SAMORE Calle 40 Sur Nº 31-77
J.I. MARCO A. IRIARTE Cra. 21 Nº 23-21 Sur
J.I. PIJAOS Cra. 10B Nº 35-02

CIUDAD BOLIVAR
CAMI VISTAHERMOSA Calle 70 Sur Nº 56-16
CASA VECINAL CARTAGENA DE INDIAS
Calle 70 Sur Nº 58-04
CENTRO OPERATIVO LOCAL ARBORIZADORA ALTA
Calle 70 Sur Nº 34-05 Sur
CAFAM GALICIA Cra.74Q Calle 69A Sur
J.I. SAN FRANCISCO Cra. 20A Nº 67-27 Sur
ALCALDIA LOCAL Calle 62 Sur Cra. 18A

SUMAPAZ
CENTRO DE SALUD San Juan de Sumapaz
HOSPITAL DE NAZARET San Juan de Sumapaz

* J.I. Jardín Infantil
* C.D.C. Centro de Desarrollo Comunitario

Figure 103: Interior of Brochure, "Vaccine Against Forgetfulness," 2014. Courtesy of Futuro Moncada.

17 BIKE PATH AND CYCLING ROUTES

(Ciclovía y Ciclorutas)

First and Second Term: 1995-1998 / 2001-2003

Figure 104: Bicycle Day, 1996. Photo: Eduardo Sotomayor. Courtesy of the Mayor's Office, Bogotá. Secretary General, Central Archive.

OBJECTIVE

The goal of this intervention was to create cultural actions to foster communication, enjoyment of the city, and to reduce cultural and socioeconomic gaps.

DATE OF PRODUCTION

1996-1998 and 2001-2003

DESCRIPTION

One of the principal innovations of the *Cultura Ciudadana* policy was democratizing the cultural, recreational, and sports services offered by the public institutions of the city.

This program sought not only to increase recreation opportunities but also to strengthen tolerance and appreciation for cultural diversity. It was also meant to prioritize artistic activities and to open recreational and leisure spaces in an attempt to weaken social and cultural barriers preventing or hindering communication between citizens (Londoño 2009:171).

Figure 105: "Bike Path," 1997. Photo: Felipe Caicedo. Courtesy of *El Tiempo*.

LA CICLOVÍA (BIKE PATH)

The widespread use of Bogotá's bike lanes illustrates the success of this intervention. The arterial system of the city, as in other places, is used less frequently on Sundays. Nearly twenty years ago, Mayor Augusto Ramírez Ocampo, had the idea. The first routes were only a few kilometers long, and they were isolated circuits separated along class lines: the elite class, the middle class, and the popular sector. Although it was initially met with some concern from the citizens, this program merged separate paths into one single circuit and extended the hours that the paths were open for use.

LAS CICLORUTAS (BICYCLE ROUTES)

"Formar Ciudad" (To Form the City) was one of the projects that prioritized public space. It was meant to create a system of permanent "Bike Paths" in the capital district that would join the city's water ways and the green metropolitan system that were the principal medium for recreation (IDU 2014).

Figure 106: Guardians of the "Bike Path," 2003. Photo: Eduardo Sotomayor. Courtesy of the Mayor's Office of Bogotá, Secretary General, Central Archive, Photo Archive.

ANECDOTAL EVIDENCE

"I recall the Japanese (JICA consulting) in the meetings that we held in my earlier administration to study the public transportation system. They arrived smiling from ear-to-ear and said: 'Mayor, here are your first bicycle routes,' and that became the reality. They were convinced that the whole team was a fan of the bicycle routes, and it was true; district planning and IDU were fundamentally for cycling. As a professor, I too used my bicycle as a means of transportation for fifteen years. The Japanese had a certain irony, as skeptics, but said: 'we respect your priority.' All of this was incorporated in our Master Plan for Transportation and then was developed in the IDU; the first bicycle path was constructed around a wetland in Suba (a neighborhood in the north of Bogotá). The current system was designed, financed, and constructed by the Peñalosa administration, giving the city a complete circuit of "Bike Paths" more quickly than I would have imagined. We had an extremely optimistic goal regarding the volume of bikers using the paths. I imagined the Japanese consultants' skeptic smiles, if we had said that we aspired for 30% of total commutes to be made by bicycle in the future, but our immediate objective was more modest, to raise the 4% of the city's population using the "Bike Path," to 15% or 16%. This would be a significant achievement and would relieve the city of the traffic congestion

Figure 107: Guardian Possession of the "Bike Path," 2003. Courtesy of the Mayor's Office, Bogotá. Secretary General, Central Archive.

that was afflicting the city at the time. Those results would place Bogotá at a different cultural level (Mockus 2001:12-13).

RESULTS

FIRST MANDATE

On March 17, 1996, the pact for two sections of eighty-one kilometers to be added to the "Bike Path" was put into effect.

During 1997, use of the "Bike Path" became the main recreation activity in the country. With the Bogotanos' approval, a jingle for the "Bike Path" was launched: "*Bogotá No Tiene Mar Pero Tiene Ciclovía*" (Bogotá Does Not Have the Sea, But it Has the "Bike Path"), and it was used in 70% of the city's localities. An inter-institutional team was set up to provide daily support on the part of different departments: Auxiliary agents within the Police, the Secretary of Health, the Secretary of Traffic and Transportation, and the Secretary of Education.

Figure 108-110: "No Car Day," 2003. Courtesy of the Mayor's Office, Bogotá. Secretary General, Central Archive.

Figure 111: "Bike Path," 1995-2003. Courtesy of the Mayor's Office of Bogotá, Secretary General, Central Archive, Photo Archive.

A system of radio communication throughout the entire network was also implemented. The first sponsor was *Brisa* (breeze), as part of the project to continue providing coverage for unserved areas (IDRD 2014).

SECOND MANDATE

In 2001, more that two million people took to the streets, in a great expression of increased equality and confidence in Bogotá. During the week many use the bus system *Transmilenio*, on Sunday, they take to the *Ciclovía*. It is there that an executive who rides in a chauffeured car during the week mixes with the common citizens, all on bikes (Mockus 2014, pers. comm.).

Today, both systems show their relevance, and more Bogotanos use the bicycle paths and lanes. Ten years after the first "Bike Path" was built, construction of these types of projects is still expanding. A great example is the creation of special bike lanes for different routes through the city, designated bike lanes, and the appearance of bicycle parking in some of the *Transmilenio* stations.

Figure 112: "Bike Path," 1995-2003. Courtesy of the Mayor's Office of Bogotá, Secretary General, Central Archive, Photo Archive.

ORDINANCE / LAW / EDICT

Not applicable.

REFERENCES

"Bogotá tendrá ciclovías permanentes, dice IDRD" [Bogotá Will Have Permanent Bike Lanes, Says IDRD]. 1995. *El Tiempo*. July 10 (http://www.eltiempo.com/archivo/documento/MAM-363098).

IDU (Instituto de Desarrollo Urbano de Bogotá) [Institute of Urban Development of Bogotá]. 2017. "Infraestructura cicloinclusiva" [Infrastructure for Inclusive Biking]. (https://www.idu.gov.co/atencion-al-ciudadano/infraestructura-cicloinclusiva).

IDRD (Instituto de Recreación y Deporte) [Institute of Sports and Recreation]. 1995. "Bogotá tendrá ciclovías permanentes, dice IDRD" [Bogotá Will Have Permanent Bike Lanes, Says IDRD]. (http://www.idrd.gov.co/sitio/idrd/?q=node/1606).

"La ciclovía se alista para celebrar sus 40 años" [The Bike Path Gets Ready to Celebrate Forty Years], *El Tiempo*, May 16 (http://www.eltiempo.com/bogota/la-ciclovia-cumple-40-anos/13999298).

Londoño, Rocío. 2009. "De la cortesía a la cultura ciudadana" [From Courtesy to Civic Culture], Pp. 162-182 in *Cultura Ciudadana en Bogotá: Nuevas persepectivas* [Civic Culture in Bogotá: New Perspectives], edited by Efraín Sánchez Cabra and Carolina Castro Osorio. Bogotá: Corprovisionarios.

18 BLACK STARS

(Estrellas negras)

First and Second Term: 1995-1998 / 2001-2003

Figure 113: Launching the "Black Stars," 2003. Photo: Fernando Rodríguez. Courtesy of the Mayor's Office, Bogotá, Secretary General, Central Archive, Photo Archive.

OBJECTIVE

To reduce the number of deaths caused by traffic accidents.

As part of the public policy for road safety in Bogotá in 2002, a very detailed process was executed, using information systems to identify victims and reduce the number of pedestrian deaths caused by traffic accidents. Accordingly, it focused on this population through persuasive pedagogical actions that promoted the use of crosswalks and pedestrian bridges, and also prevented people from committing reckless actions in the streets that put their lives in danger. In Colombia, many fatal accidents occur on intercity roads, so in a return to traditional practices, families and friends of the victim often erect an altar with a cross that marks the location where their loved ones died (Murraín 2009).

DATE OF PRODUCTION

2002

Figure 114-115: Launching the "Black Stars," 2003. Photo: Fernando Rodríguez. Courtesy of the Mayor's Office, Bogotá, Secretary General, Central Archive, Photo Archive.

Figure 116-118: "Black Stars." Courtesy of the Mayor's Office, Bogotá, Secretary General, Central Archive, Photo Archive.

DESCRIPTION

The campaign "*Bogotá, nos estamos acostumbrando: ¿Qué nos pasa?*" (Bogotá, We Are Getting Used to It: What Is Happening to Us?) was created within the program "*Apreciar la norma y admirar lo bueno*" (To Value the Rules and Appreciate the Good). As a part of this program, among other pedagogical actions, a star was painted with a hand in the form of a question mark. Each one was placed at a place on the roads where pedestrian deaths had occurred in previous years; 1,500 stars were painted throughout the city. Other presence-based practices were carried out in public spaces across educational, labor, commercial, community and re-creational contexts.

Civic guides, auxiliary agents, and school patrols would also regulate the behavior of drivers and pedestrians at critical points in the city. Bikers and taxi-drivers were enrolled in formal training that resorted to dialogic practices and moral dilemmas to foster moral reasoning on their part. Offenders also received pedagogical sanctions (Mockus 2003:28).

RESULTS

The decrease in the number of traffic accident deaths highlights the positive impact of the campaign, which reduced the number of pedestrian deaths by 34% between July and September of 2003, compared to the same period the previous year. Forty-five lives were saved (ibid.).

OTHER ACHIEVEMENTS

The campaign was so effective that the Road Safety Organization applied it nationally to the main highways and in eighteen Colombian cities. It was recognized as the best institutional campaign of the world at the Festival de Publicidad de Barcelona (Barcelona Advertising Festival) in 2005. With time, the campaign changed its slogan to: *"Tú decides: eres persona o eres estrella negra"* (You Decide: You Can Be a Person or a Black Star) and *"Lo que las estrellas te dicen"* (What the Stars Tell You).

Figure 119: "Black Stars," 2003. Courtesy of the
Mayor's Office of Bogotá, Secretary General,
Central Archive, Photo Archive.

ORDINANCE / LAW / EDICT

Not applicable.

REFERENCES

Castaño Beltrán, Carmen Lucía. 2006. "Lo que dicen las estrellas" [What the Stars Say], *Semana*,
February 12 (http://www.semana.com/on-line/articulo/lo-dicen-estrellas/76405-3).

"Estrellas negras/carreteras" [Black Stars/Highways]. 2010. Vimeo video, Advertisement by the Road
Safety Organization, posted by "pachomoreno." (https://vimeo.com/4957809).

Mockus, Antanas. 2003. Bogotá para vivir, 2001–2003 [To Live in Bogotá, 2001-2003].
Bogotá: Grupo OP Gráficas S.A.

Murraín, Henry. 2009. "Cultura ciudadana como política pública: entre indicadores y arte" [Civic Culture as Public Policy: Between Indicators and Art]. In *Cultura Ciudadana en Bogotá: nuevas perspectivas*, edited by Efraín Rueda, Juan Pablo. 2001.

"Estrellas en las Calles de Cali Piden Acabar con el Maltrato de Caballos Carretilleros" [Stars in Cali's
Streets Ask for an end to the Mistreatment of Horse-drawn Carts], *El Tiempo* (http://www.eltiempo.
com/multimedia/fotos/colombia1/estrellas-en-las-calles-de-cali/14295037).

Figure 120-121: Campaign Balance, 2003. Courtesy of the Mayor's Office of Bogotá, Secretary General, Central Archive, Photo Archive.

19 PRIORITIZER

(Priorizador)

Second Term: 2001-2003

Figure 122: "Prioritizer," 2001. Courtesy of Futuro Moncada.

OBJECTIVE

To democratize governmental decisions by incorporating citizen participation.

DATE OF PRODUCTION

Beginning of the second term of 2001

DESCRIPTION

The "*Priorizador*" (Prioritizer) was a tool developed by the Mayor's Office, to consult citizens about how they valued the following six themes, with an eye to defining the priorities of the new administration. The themes were the following:

1. Collective building of Bogotá
2. Inclusivity and fairness
3. Child-friendliness
4. Living in peace with one's conscience and the law
5. Dynamic and competitive economy
6. What is public should be treated as sacred

The idea was very simple; each person had three votes that could be distributed based on the preferences expressed in relation to the six options. The priority of each category was determined by the number of votes it received. The real difficulty with this model was to accept the results when it did not fit one's moral position or contradicted an individual's beliefs (Mockus 2014, pers. comm.).

RESULTS

This program defined priorities that the Mayor's office would deal with. The popular consultation was carried out in Corferias as well as in settings like the Council of Bogotá, among others (ibid.).

Figure 123: "Prioritizer," 2001. Courtesy of Futuro Moncada.

ORDINANCE / LAW / EDICT

Not applicable.

REFERENCES

"Cordial fogueo Mockus-Concejo" [Cordial Blank Mockus-Board]. 2001. *El Tiempo*, January 25 (http://www.eltiempo.com/archivo/documento/MAM-629653).

"Priorizador en la feria" [Prioritizer at the Fair]. 2001. *El Tiempo*, April 28 (http://www.eltiempo.com/archivo/documento/MAM-538796).

Figure 124: "Prioritizer," 2001. Courtesy of Futuro Moncada.

Figure 125: "Prioritizer," 2001. Courtesy of Futuro Moncada.

20 TAXES:110% FOR BOGOTÁ

(Impuestos: 110% con Bogotá)

Second Term: 2001-2003

Figure 126: First Ten Taxpayers, 2002. Courtesy of the Mayor's Office, Bogotá, Secretary General, Central Archive, Photo Archive.

OBJECTIVE

The "110% for Bogotá" program was framed under the program *"Aportar de buena gana"* (Contribute Willingly).

The general goals of the "Contribute Willingly" program were:

- Behaviors: Increase timely payments of district taxes.
- Expertise: Increase knowledge of district taxes.
- Attitudes: Increase positive attitudes about paying taxes and eliminating undeserved subsidies.
- Perceptions: Decrease the perception that tax evaders have the impunity and increase the confidence that district money is going to good use.

DATE OR PRODUCTION

2002

Figure 127: Taxes: "110% for Bogotá," 2001-2003. Courtesy of *El Tiempo*.

DESCRIPTION

The principle of co-responsibility between the state and the citizens was the core of principal of the "110% for Bogotá" initiative. Although it was not formally part of the development plan, the idea of a direct relationship between promoting the rights of citizens and emphasizing the duty to pay taxes was a central component the mayor's platform during his election campaign. The original idea was based on a proposal to increase the tax rate....failed to pass the tax reform for which Mockus's administration had called. Decree 040 of 2002 invited citizens to voluntarily pay an additional 10%, that would be deduced from their property, industry, and commerce taxes.

On 2002 tax declaration forms, the administration presented the projects that they considered to best represent their vision for the city, and they explained how resources would be invested. Taxpayers prioritized fifteen projects where their voluntary contribution would be allotted. The highest percentage of contributions (50%) was allotted for social justice projects, 16% went to education programs, and 15% was allocated to the *Cultura Ciudadana* projects. In 2003, the administration focused on the eight projects with the highest citizen support as expressed during the previous year (Mockus 2003:31-33).

Figure 128: Inauguration of Kindergarten in San Cristobal, 2002. Photo: Carlos Julio Martínez Courtesy of *El Tiempo*.

RESULTS

In terms of achievements, the high number of contributors should be underscored: 63,493 in 2002 and 45,753 in September of 2003, contributing $1.178 and $884 million pesos respectively. In fiscal terms, this figure may appear to be relatively insignificant, but in the context of a country with a high rate of tax evasion, it is a clear indicator of the high level of trust that the administration would properly use the resources (Mockus 2003:31-33).

Further important achievements included:

- The collection of district taxes was 32% higher than expected, and the Secretary of the Treasury raised property taxes by 89%.
- Health subsidies for 12,965 people who did not need them were waived.

- $24,869 million of outstanding debts were recovered by the Ministry of Traffic and Transportation (STT). A savings of $7.734 million was accomplished through 144 governmental contracts, maintenance, and economical use of public space (Mockus 2003:31-33).

Figure 129: "110% for Bogotá" Logo, 2001-2003. Courtesy of the Mayor's Office, Bogotá, Secretary General, Central Archive, Photo Archive.

ORDINANCE / LAW / EDICT

Decree 040 of 2002 (Mayor's Office of Bogotá).

REFERENCES

Alcadía de Bogotá. 2002. "Decree 040." (http://www.alcaldiabogota.gov.co/sisjur/normas/Norma1.jsp?i=4607).

Mockus, Antanas. 2003. Bogotá para vivir, 2001–2003. Bogotá: Grupo OP Gráficas S.A.

"110% con Bogotá" [110% for Bogotá]. 2013. YouTube video, 0:30, posted by "Idennto México," July 15. (https://www.youtube.com/watch?v=Y13H5bb4p9Y).

"Video institucional homenaje a los contribuyentes" [Institutional Video Tribute to the Taxpayers]. 2014. YouTube video, 35:22, posted by "Laura Oliveros," July 17 (http://youtu.be/F3ypxAoyacE).

21 MOEBIUS STRIP:
DEVELOPMENT PLAN "BOGOTÁ TO ALL LIVE ON THE SAME SIDE"

(Cinta Moebius: Plan de Desarrollo "Bogotá para Vivir Todos del Mismo Lado")

Second Term: 2001–2003

Figure 130: Presenting the Education Center for Homeless Children, 2001. Photo: Ignacio Prieto. Courtesy of the Mayor's Office, Bogotá, Secretary General, Central Archive, Photo Archive.

OBJECTIVE

The development plan's seven goals correspond to the broad categories used to analyze and classify the visions for the city's future: *Cultura Ciudadana,* productivity, social justice, education, environment, family, children, and admirable public action (Mockus 2003: "Introduction").

DATE OR PRODUCTION

2001–2003

DESCRIPTION

"Bogotá para Vivir Todos del Mismo Lado" (Bogotá, For All to Live On the Same Side) sought to emphasize elements that could unite Bogotanos: a common history, an increasingly shared vision, a commitment to fiscal security, and an understanding of the rules of the game as a condition for living pleasurably in the city. Believing that the universal brings people together and that the idea and co-creation of human rights exposes people to the radical experience of the universal, the administration was convinced that promoting human rights would place all citizens on the same side.

The vision of integration underpinning this plan was symbolized by the "Moebius Strip," which is a key structure in the Tucana culture: it appears to have two opposite sides and two borders at each point, but it actually features only one side and one border globally. In the same way, society may well exhibit difference and polarization locally but lives as a unit globally, thereby being all on the same side, sharing a context of general agreement over a shared vision of the city, and sharing the same search for solidarity.

RESULTS

The structure of the development plan "Bogotá, For All to Live On the Same Side" resulted from the vision laid out through the participation of two hundred groups of citizens, each one ranging from ten to forty-five members. In comparison to the former development plan "To

Figure 131: "We Are Going in the Right Direction," 2002. Photo: Arcesio Vega. Courtesy of the Mayor's Office, Bogotá, Secretary General, Central Archive, Photo Archive.

Figure 132: "We Are Going in the Right Direction," 2002. Photo: Arcesio Vega. Courtesy of the Mayor's Office, Bogotá, Secretary General, Central Archive, Photo Archive.

Figure 133: "Bogotá, For All to Live On the Same Side" Logo, 2001-2003. Courtesy of the Mayor's Office, Bogotá, Secretary General, Central Archive, Photo Archive.

Form the City, 1995-1998", in the proposed structure of the second plan greater emphasis was laid on collective creation and democratic validation of priorities."

ORDINANCE / LAW / EDICT

Not applicable.

REFERENCES

Alcaldía de Bogotá. 2003."Plan de Desarrollo Económico y Social de Obras Publicas" [Plan for the Economic and Social Development of Public Works]. Bogotá DC: District Press.

Gélvez, Germán. 2001. "No todos del mismo lado" [Not All On the Same Side], *El Tiempo,* August 9 (http://www.eltiempo.com/archivo/documento/MAM-458453).

Mockus, Antanas. 2003. Bogotá para vivir, 2001–2003. Bogotá: Grupo OP Gráficas S.A.

Quintero Arturo, Fernando. 2001. "Todos del mismo lado" [All On The Same Side], *El Tiempo,* May 4 (http://www.eltiempo.com/archivo/documento/MAM-529690).

Figure 134: "Moebius Strip," 2001-2003. Courtesy of Futuro Moncada.

Figure 135: Presenting the Education Center for Homeless Children, 2001. Photo: Ignacio Prieto. Courtesy of the Mayor's Office, Bogotá, Secretary General, Central Archive, Photo Archive.

Figure 136: "We Are Going in the Right Direction," 2002. Photo: Arcesio Vega. Courtesy of the Mayor's Office of Bogotá, Secretary General, Central Archive, Photo Archive.

22 BULLETPROOF VEST

(Chaleco antibalas)

Second Term 2001-2003

Figure 137: "Civil Resistance," 2002. Courtesy of the Mayor's Office, Bogotá, Secretary General, Central Archive, Photo Archive.

OBJECTIVE

An act of "Civil Resistance"against the threats by Fuerzas Armadas Revolucionarias de Colombia (FARC, Colombian Armed Revolutionary Forces).

DATE OF PRODUCTION

2002

DESCRIPTION

"Una bala no lo atraviesa, pero un cuchillo sí" (A Bullet Can't Get Through, But a Knife Can)

The history of the "Bulletproof Vest" began on April 19, 1991, when Mockus, then chancellor of the National University, met with a number of art faculty members up for promotion to full professorship, as they were exhibiting their work. During the conversation one asked: "If you had to wear a bulletproof vest, what would you do?" Mockus replied that he would sell the vest and donate the money to a student.

Figure 138: "Bulletproof Vest," 2001-2003. Courtesy of the Mayor's
Office of Bogotá, Secretary General, Central Archive, Photo Archive.

Many years later, mayor Mockus received a vest as a gift by the US embassy. Though tempted
to resell it, as it was not a commercial item, he ended up wearing it as an external armor, thereby explicitly denouncing the conditions of hardship that Colombian mayors had to put up
with as a result of the FARC's threats against them.

Later on, Mockus realized that, though the vest could not be penetrated by bullets, it could be
cut with a knife or scissors. So he carved a heart-shaped hole into it, challenging his potential
aggressors to recognize and respect his vulnerability.

The vest travelled with Mockus to different summits; one that is often evoked was his encounter with the King of Belgium, when Mockus states his armor made him feel like a bodyguard.

RESULTS

After a while the vest was auctioned off, and the collected money was donated to a good cause:
to guarantee the education of at least one child in Bogotá.

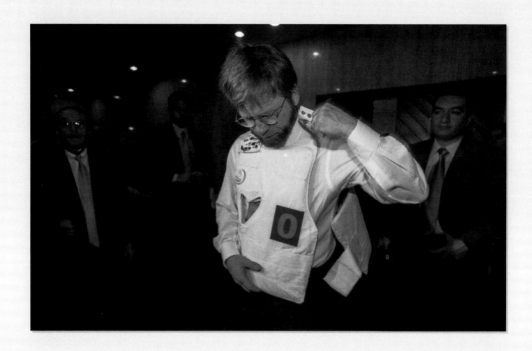

The "Bulletproof Vest" was an act of "Civil Resistance" and a peaceful form of denouncing the terrorism perpetrated by armed groups.

ORDINANCE / LAW / EDICT

Not applicable.

REFERENCES

"Mockus se quita hoy el chaleco" [Today Mockus Takes Off His Vest]. 2002. *Noticias*, November 1 (http://www.caracol.com.co/noticias/mockus-se-quita-hoy-el- chaleco/20021101/nota/109948.aspx).

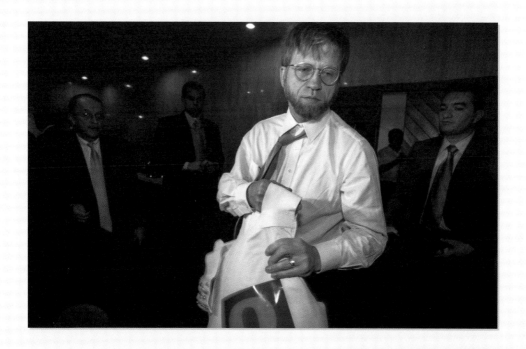

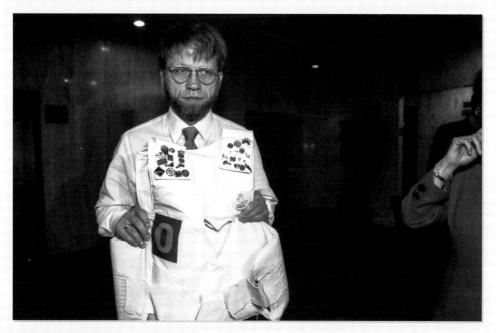

Figure 139-141: Mayor Removes "Bulletproof Vest" for Auction, 2002. Photo: Arcesio Vega. Courtesy of the Mayor's Office, Bogotá, Secretary General, Central Archive, Photo Archive.

23 CIVIL RESISTANCE

(Resistencia civil)

Second Term: 2001–2003

Figure 142: "Civil Resistance," 2001-2003. Courtesy of the Mayor's Office of Bogotá, Secretary General, Central Archive, Photo Archive.

OBJECTIVE

To encourage acts of "Civil Resistance" that protect citizens from terrorist acts.

DATE OF PRODUCTION

Beginning of the second term of 2001.

DESCRIPTION

Some observers consider that "Civil Resistance" only involves citizens against the state or an invader. Occasionally, it may be organized by the state (Mockus 2014, pers. Comm.).

During the second term civil servants working for the city would exhibit a button with the slogan "Contra la destrucción, construcción" (Against Destruction, Construction) at civil marches, protests, walks, dance workshops," and *cacerolazos* (a form of popular protest in which kitchenware is used to make noise), during the construction of an important tower* at the center of the Plaza de Bolivar, and at certain cemetery ceremonies, among others.

Figure 143-144: March for El Nogal, 2003. Photo: Ignacio Prieto.
Courtesy of the Mayor's Office of Bogotá, Secretary General,
Central Archive, Photo Archive.

Figure 145: March for El Nogal, 2003. Photo: Ignacio Prieto. Courtesy of the Mayor's Office of Bogotá, Secretary General, Central Archive, Photo Archive.

*A tower is often a target of attacks by armed groups, but it is also a symbol of resistance to such violent acts.

RESULTS

"The action in Bogotá began as a state initiative to promote 'Civil Resistence.'

"Civil Resistance" was a response to the Chingaza bombing and the bombing of the Club El Nogal. The day that I learned of Chingaza, I asked the employees to wear a button, stating 'Against Destruction, Construction.' Although the stickers were handmade, at lunch people were wondering why the employees wore the stickers, thereby starting a conversation about the cause.

In another important action, citizens painted symbols of international humanitarian law on the Suba water tanks and the Tominé Reservoir" (Mockus 2014, pers. comm.).

In addition to these outcomes, it should be highlighted that "Civil Resistance" was used in other cities in the country, where marches and protests were recreated to denounce violence and reject terrorism (ibid.).

Figure 146: Walk Against Terrorism, 2003. Photo: Ignacio Prieto. Courtesy of the Mayor's Office of Bogotá, Secretary General, Central Archive, Photo Archive.

Figure 147: March for El Nogal, 2003. Photo: Ignacio Prieto. Courtesy of the Mayor's Office of Bogotá, Secretary General, Central Archive, Photo Archive.

Figure 148: Aerobics, 2002. Photo: Ignacio Prieto. Courtesy of the Mayor's Office of Bogotá, Secretary General, Central Archive, Photo Archive.

Figure 149: "Civil Resistance," 2001-2003. Courtesy of the Mayor's Office, Bogotá, Secretary General, Central Archive, Photo Archive.

Visual Essay

Figure 150: Walk Against Terrorism, 2003. Photo: Ignacio Prieto. Courtesy of the Mayor's Office of Bogotá, Secretary General, Central Archive, Photo Archive.

ORDINANCE /LAW /EDICT

Not applicable.

REFERENCES

"Bogotá se resistió ante los violentos" [Bogotá Held Out Against Violence]. 2002. *El Tiempo,* February 18th (http://www.eltiempo.com/archivo/documento/MAM-1313626).

"Mockus llama a la resistencia." [Mockus Calls for Resistance] 2002. *El Tiempo*, February 6 (http://www.eltiempo.com/archivo/documento/MAM-1329917).

"Resistencia al atajismo propone Mockus" [Mockus Proposes Resistance to Attacks]. 2003. *El Tiempo*, August 14. (http://www.eltiempo.com/archivo/documento/MAM-1015986).

Figure 151: Walk Against Terrorism, 2003. Photo: Ignacio Prieto. Courtesy of the Mayor's Office of Bogotá, Secratary General, Central Archive, Photo Archive.

24 LADIES' NIGHT

(Noche de las mujeres)

Second Term: 2001-2003

Figure 152: Signatures for Credit Lines for Women, 2001. Photo: Carlos Martínez Courtesy of *El Tiempo*.

OBJECTIVE

To protect the lives of men and women in public places and to restore confidence in people's ability to protect their own lives and the lives of others in their charge. To promote an enjoyable city nightlife in solidarity with other citizens and with authorities, by reshaping both men and women's roles in public and private spaces and to reestablish the rights of children to enjoy the company of their parents.

DATE OF PRODUCTION

2001

DESCRIPTION

"Ladies' Night" is one of the actions with the greatest impact that the district government carried out. While it was not foreseen in the development plan, it was related to the program's goals. The "Ladies' Night" was held during each year of the three-year administration, as an experiment that had no precedent anywhere else in the world. It enabled women to take to the town for one night, promoting men's voluntary compliance to observe the restrictions on circulating on roads or in public places. Apart from men who had to circulate to provide

Figure 153: "Ladies' Night," 2001. Photo: Carlos Martínez Courtesy of *El Tiempo*.

essential services for the city, those who could not or did not want to adhere to the restriction had to carry a safe conduct pass authorizing them to circulate and explaining their reasons for doing so, which were subject to the objections and rebukes of women who dominated public spaces.

The design of this pedagogical experiment and the activities prompting self-reflection that came with it responded to the realization that in Bogotá murder was twice among men than women and that the majority of the crimes were committed by men.

RESULTS

"Women's Nights Out," which included artistic and cultural events and recognized women's social contributions, had the desired effect in terms of security. On the first night, only one homicide occurred—as opposed to the four deaths that occur on a typical day–and there was only one traffic accident. The other gain was that security for women increased—in 2002, 52% of participating women stated that they had felt safer. In the same year, 85% of the women who were questioned agreed that they would participate again (Mockus 2003:28).

Figure 154: "Ladies' night," 2001. Courtesy of the Mayor's Office, Bogotá, Secretary General, Central Archive, Photo Archive.
Figure 155-156: Celebration of "Ladies' night," 2001. Photo: José Barrera. Courtesy of the Mayor's Office, Bogotá, Secretary General, Central Archive, Photo Archive.

Figure 157: "Ladies' night," 2001. Courtesy of the Mayor's Office of Bogotá, Secretary General, Central Archive, Photo Archive.

ORDINANCE / LAW / EDICT

Decree 190 of 2001 (Mayor's Office of Bogotá).

REFERENCES

Alcadía de Bogotá, 2001. "Decree 190." (http://www.alcaldiabogota.gov.co/sisjur/normas/Norma1.jsp?i=3786).

Mockus, Antanas. 2003. *Bogotá para vivir, 2001–2003*. Bogotá: Grupo OP Gráficas S.A.

"Mockus llama a la resistencia". [Mockus Calls for Resistance] 2002. *El Tiempo*, February 6 (http://www. eltiempo. com/archivo/documento/MAM-1329917).

"Resistencia al atajismo propone Mockus" [Mockus Proposes Resistance to Attacks]. 2003. *El Tiempo*, August 14. (http://www.eltiempo.com/archivo/documento/MAM-1015986).

Figure 158-159: "Ladies' night," 2001. Photo: Carlos Martínez Courtesy of *El Tiempo.*

25 LIFE IS SACRED

(La vida es sagrada)

Second Term: 2001-2003

Figure 160: Cemetery of the South, 2002. Photo: Ignacio Prieto. Courtesy of the Mayor's Office of Bogotá, Secretary General, Central Archive, Photo Archive.

OBJECTIVE

The objective of the *"Vida Sagrada"* (Life is Sacred) program was: "To initiate disarmament and other actions to reduce violent deaths in the city, to promote healthy lifestyles and to generate trust, security, and tranquility for people to exercise their rights and liberties, to enjoy the city, to fulfill their duties, and to have confidence in the justice system and in the proper use of public force" (Mockus 2014, pers. comm.).

DATE OF PRODUCTION

2001–2003

DESCRIPTION

The following general goals were established:

1. Behaviors: Decrease the number of victims to violence crimes, increase the number of firearms relinquished, and reduce violence (homicides, traffic accidents, suicides, other accidental causes), injury as well as other crimes such as thefts, and kidnappings.

Figures 161: Columbariums, 2003. Photo: Ignacio Prieto. Courtesy of the Mayor's Office of Bogotá, Secretary General, Central Archive, Photo Archive.
Figure 162: Press Conference, 2002. Courtesy of the Mayor's Office of Bogotá, Secretary General, Central Archive, Photo Archive.

2. Perceptions: Improve the perception of security. Twenty-four of the twenty-six projects under the program were executed by the Secretary of Government via surveillance and security, two by the Road Safety Organization and one by the Secretary of Health and the Health Finance Fund. The projects had a number of functions: dissemination, education, investigation, participation, organization, agreement, management, monitoring, infrastructure, and funding. The project's budget placed importance on the goal of improving prisons and educations practices within them, the treatment of prisoners, the qualification of police detective work, prevention, and surveillance.

Furthermore, a significant proportion of resources were meant to promote citizen practices of self-regulation for coexistence such as security campaigns with civic participation, conflict resolution through police inspections, communication geared to foster peaceful coexistence, the development of healthy lifestyles, and voluntary compliance with traffic laws.

The majority of projects with a pedagogical component were geared towards promoting learning, to transform knowledge, behaviors, and attitudes. Face-to-face communication and dialogue were prioritized, with the use of pedagogical means of transmission and those centered

Figure 163: "Life is Sacred," 2002. Photo: Ignacio Prieto. Courtesy of the Mayor's Office, Bogotá, Secretary General, Central Archive, Photo Archive.

on public rationality. Due to the project's emphasis on strengthening the police intelligence, prevention, and surveillance capabilities, the law was meant to regulate citizens' behavior, while pedagogical interventions addressed the three systems of regulation: legal, moral, and cultural (Mockus 2003:26-27).

RESULTS

Various artistic actions that were part of the campaign saved lives, such as the 2002 *"Cementerio del Sur"* (Cemetery of the South) intervention, which represented the lives that had been saved by leaving empty tombs. Six hundred young men and women from IPIDRON participated.

Thanks to the work of the Observatorio de Violencia y Delincuencia (Observatory of Violence and Crime) and the Sistema de Información sobre Violencia y Delincuencia (Information System on Violence and Crime) the impact of the program was recorded, tracking practices and behaviors that were part of the central goals.

The following tables illustrate the gradual reduction in the rate of violent deaths, with the

Figure 164. "Life is Sacred," 2002. Photo: Ignacio Prieto. Courtesy of the Mayor's Office, Bogotá, Secretary General, Central Archive, Photo Archive.

Table 3. Violent Deaths

Year / Type	2001	2002	2003 (OCT. 31)
Homicides	2.037	1.902	1.316
Traffic Accident Deaths	750	697	489
Suicides	305	256	244
Accidental Deaths	262	281	223
TOTAL	3.354	3.136	2.272
Daily Average	9,19	8.59	

Table 4. Crimes of Social Impact

YEAR / TYPE	2000	2001	2002	2003 (OCT. 31)
Common Injuries	16.871	13.431	11.229	7.421
Vehicle Theft	6.178	6.993	5.969	4.305
Bicycle Theft	1.445	1.481	1.300	1.084
Personal Theft	12.447	10.327	8.083	4.112
Residential Theft	5.090	5.794	4.711	5.596
Commercial Theft	3.589	3.728	3.581	3.030
Bank Theft	169	55	36	25
TOTAL	45.789	41.809	34.909	25.573
Variation %			-8,7	-16,5

Figure 165-167: Press Conference, Report on the Violence, 2002. Courtesy of the Mayor's Office, Bogotá, Secretary General, Central Archive, Photo Archive.

exception of accidental deaths from any cause other than traffic accidents (ibid.:28).

ORDINANCES/LAW/EDICT

Not applicable.

REFERENCES

Alcaldía de Bogota. 1996. *Bogotá ciudad coqueta*. Bogotá: District Press.

———. 2003. "Plan de desarrollo económico y social de obras publicas" [Plan for the Economic and Social Development of Public Works]. Bogotá: District Press.

———. 1996. *Informe formar ciudad: 371 logros a ½ camino*. Bogotá: District Press, [Mid-term Report on To Form the City: 371 Accomplishments].

Mockus, Antanas. 2001. "Cultura ciudadana, programa contra la violencia en Santa Fe de Bogotá, Colombia, 1995-1997." [Civic Culture, a Program against Violence in Santa Fe de Bogotá, Colombia, 1995-1997] Washington, D.C.: Interamerican Development Bank, Social Development Division. (http://es.calameo.com/read/00047752906c074dfce6b).

———. 2002. *Bogotá camino a la igualdad: Avances en la cultura ciudadana y en la construcción de lo público* [Bogotá on the Path to Equality: Advances in Civic Culture and in Construction of the

Public]. Bogotá: Alcaldía Mayor de Bogotá.

———. 2003. *Código de Policía de Bogotá D.C.* [Police Code in Bogotá] Bogotá: District Press.

———. *2003. Bogotá para vivir, 2001–2003* [Living in Bogotá, 2001-2003] Bogotá: Grupo OP Gráficas S.A.

———. 2004. "Ampliación de los modos de hacer política." [Broadening the Modes of Doing Politics] Paper presented at the Colloque CERI, Paris, December 2-3. (https://www.researchgate.net/publication/267362347_AMPLIACION_DE_LOS_MODOS_DE_HACER_POLITICA).

Sánchez Cabra, Efraín and Carolina Castro Osorio. 2009. *Cultura Ciudadana en Bogotá: Nuevas Perspectivas.* [Civic Culture in Bogotá: New Perspectives] Bogotá: Tangrama.

Figure 168: Hands and Freedom, 2002. Photo: Ignacio Prieto. Courtesy of the Mayor's Office, Bogotá, Secretary General, Central Archive, Photo Archive.

PART THREE: ESSAYS

Doris Sommer

Jesús Martín-Barbero

Henry Murraín

Gerry Mackie

Fonna Forman

Jaime Ramos

Carlos Augusto Hernández

Enrique Chaux *and*

Andrea Bustamante

Javier Sáenz Obregón

Lucas Ospina

Paolo Vignolo

3

1. *"Por Amor al Arte"*: Haber-Mockus Plays with the Possible

Doris Sommer

> When I feel trapped, I ask myself, what would an artist do?
> –*Antanas Mockus*

Mime over Matter

"Professor Mockus, what gave you the idea to replace the traffic police with pantomime artists?" It was an obvious question for the recent mayor of Bogotá, but if the student hadn't asked, I might not have learned that one principle of the mayor's astounding success is his disarming sense of humor. He knows when to take a joke seriously and set off ripples of shared fun. Antanas Mockus and I were co-teaching a graduate course at Harvard University during that fall semester of 2004. "Foundational Fictions and Other Cultural Agents" framed his reflections on creativity during two terms in office (1995-1997 and 2001-2003) against the backdrop of nineteenth-century national novels. Those novels, written by political leaders to fan desire for national consolidation, were background cases for considering art's recent work in public life (Sommer 1991).

According to the US State Department advisory against travel to Colombia, before Bogotá elected Mockus in 1994, it was the most dangerous city in Latin America. At international airports, official warnings singled out Lagos, Nigeria, and Bogotá as places too troubled to traffic in tourism. On this count, Bogotanos themselves didn't question the North American advice to keep a safe distance from the city. Many had lost confidence altogether and emigrated if they could afford to, so that—for example—their children could attend school without personal body-guards. The city seemed hopelessly mired in a level of corruption that turned al-most any investment against itself, because conventional cures of money or more armed enforcement would have aggravated, not mitigated, the greed and the vio-lence. Stumped for a while, like the political scientists and economists (including Larry Summers) who admit defeat when I ask what they would have done, the new mayor took an unconventional turn towards art. Mockus had been reluctant to call his creativity by its common name. But by 2006, *"Por Amor al Arte"* (For the Love of Art) became the name of his political platform for winning the presidential elec-tions in Colombia.[1] His next, and nearly successful, 2010 presidential campaign was more cautious, but it was buoyed by citizens already primed to co-create proj-ects with Mockus.[2] Then an invitation from the curators of Berlin's 2012 Biennale confirmed his international reputation as a creative artist.[3]

The mimes were only one of the mayor's many arts-inspired interventions—or so-called "cultural acupunctures"—during his first administration. This therapeutic term customizes "urban acupuncture," coined by Mayor Jaime Lerner (2003) of Curitiba, Brazil, to highlight social practices that can be utilized for collective healing. If the acupuncture shows even modest relief, it signals the efficacy of collective action and encourages skeptics to join the first movers (Murraín 2009). For Mockus, these treatments included painting city streets with 1,500 fleeting stars and crosses that were 1.2 meters long to mark the points where people died in car accidents. It was a warning to pedestrians who were used to taking "shortcuts" (shorthand for all sorts of corruption in Colombia). Citywide contests for the best poster promoting condom use went along with distributing them by the hundreds of thousands. Gun shafts were sawn into rings, commemorating the violence that was thereby ritually relegated to the past. "Rock the Park" concerts every week gave youth a regular public stage to reclaim their space after dark. "Vaccine Against Violence" was a citywide performance-therapy against domestic aggression that had reached "epidemic" levels. To follow the medical metaphor, epidemics call for vaccines, those tiny doses of aggression that inoculate vulnerable victims against far greater violence. Over several weekends, nearly forty-five thousand citizens lined up holding balloons on which they painted the haunting image of the person who had abused them most. And then—upon reaching real and "acting" doctors—they expressed rage, burst the balloon, and either felt relief (catharsis) or were signed up for therapy programs. The mayor's team also printed 350,000 laminated cards with a "thumbs-up" on one side and red "thumbs-down" on the other, for citizens to flash in approval or disapproval of traffic behavior and mutually regulate a shared public sphere (Sáenz Obregón 2007). They discontinued the game after a season, however, when Mockus conceded to critics that disapproval might interfere with the development of self-esteem and self-efficacy.

Another interruption of the murderous routine was "Ladies' Night." Unlike the direct demands for women's rights in the Anglo-American "Take Back the Night," Bogotá's feminist project was indirect and playful. It encouraged sociability among women who took to the streets, bars, and dance clubs while men stayed home. Seven hundred thousand women went out on the first "Night Out." The men balked but mostly obeyed the order to stay indoors, probably reluctant to be taken for women. Those who insisted on coming out carried self-authorizing "Safe-conduct Passes" that had been printed in newspapers. The morning after, headlines reported in bold capital letters that, astonishingly for Bogotá, there was only one homicide and no traffic deaths.[4] Another initially unpopular measure among men was the time limit on selling alcohol. Bars closed by one a.m., at the time when things would have gotten lively and violent. But once the media regularly reported fewer homicides, resentments abated. For women, their night out showed that respect for life and for the law did not sacrifice fun, but instead made it possible, and the men too began to enjoy the liberating effects of renewed civility and improved domestic life.

One important lesson that we learn from Mockus is that without pleasure, social reform and political pragmatism shrivel into short-lived, self-defeating pretensions. Friedrich Schiller (1793/2006:127-154) had known this by 1793, even before his 1794 *Letters on the Aesthetic Education of Man* took single-minded reason to task: "In order that obedience to reason may become an object of inclination, it must represent for us the principle of pleasure, for pleasure and pain are the only springs which set the instincts in motion." Pain and fear of punishment are of course among the incentives for obedience, Mockus also admits, but they generate resentment, along with a destabilizing resistance to law. Unwilling compliance sours subjectivity with opposition to the world, while pleasurable observance sweetens social integration. Mockus doesn't entirely trust pleasure, and neither did Schiller, who called it "a very suspicious companion" for morality (ibid.:146). But, as Mockus taught in his seminar on "Hedonism and Pragmatism," the uneasy partnership can hardly be avoided: unhindered hedonism leads from precarious pleasure to lasting pain, as lawlessness provokes scarcity and violence, and pragmatism without pleasure breeds an equally self-defeating distaste for obligations.

Philosopher Mockus may once have overlooked this productive tension between reason and passion so familiar to artists, because the field of philosophy typically discounts Schiller and even abbreviates Kant, leaving out his *Critique of Aesthetic Judgment* (Beiser 2005). Nevertheless, several essays by *Professor* Mockus evoke something of Schiller's paean to creative play and to the counterfactual exercise of imagination (Mockus 1994, 2006a, 2006b). *Mayor* Mockus, however, never doubted the efficacy of art, and on reading Viktor Shklovsky's "Art as Technique" (1913), the formalist manifesto that identifies art as interruption of habit, Mockus conceded that yes, he is an artist too (Shklovsky 1917/1965). The Mayor's knack for interrupting quotidian corruption and cynicism animated his general platform of *Cultura Ciudadana* (Civic Culture.) "Civic Culture" combines pedagogy and persuasion to "harmonize" the competing norms of moral, legal, and cultural practices, first by demonstrating the costs of "divorce" among them and then by cajoling citizens to reconcile formal and informal codes of behavior (Mockus 2001).

"Antanas sees the city as a huge classroom," his Deputy Mayor, Alicia Eugenia Silva, used to say (Schapiro 2001). That classroom looked like a vaudeville theater when Mockus dressed up as "Civic Citizen" in tights and a cape to talk on TV, or when he'd perform civic messages in rap, or proudly wear a toy frog (equivalent to a stool pigeon) to celebrate informants for their courage to denounce a crime. This "croactivity" brought culture close to morality and in line with the law. Think of traffic in this framework of harmonizing formal and informal rules: it had long been legally wrong, sometimes morally indifferent, but culturally cool to cross the street in the middle of a block or at a red light (drug-traffic and related violence showed similar asymmetries of legal intolerance, moral ambivalence, and cultural acceptance). But the mimes who mocked infringements, and the fleeting commemorative stars that intercepted incautious pedestrians, raised moral support for traffic laws and cheapened the cultural caché of ignoring the law, bringing all three codes into closer agreement.

Governments will inevitably attempt to direct creativity towards "harmonization," and official preferences can come close to censorship, so artists typically resent these priorities and defend their freedom to dissent or to simply ignore official interest (Quinn 2008). Among these artists, Víctor Laignelet had kept his distance from government until Antanas Mockus made him think again:

I asked myself what would be gained and what lost by working with the new mayor in a desperate city. My conclusion was that Antanas was worth the gamble. He does not instrumentalize art for pre-defined ends, as standard politicians do, but rather engages debate and polysemic interpretation through art. In any case, full artistic freedom made little sense in a violent society that lacked freedom of movement and exploration.[5]

Mockus himself would joke about the illusion of uncluttered freedom in a country as chaotic as Colombia. "In the United States or Canada I'd probably be an anarchist. My ambition for Colombia is for my grandchildren to have the anarchist option because right now, and for the immediate future, no one here would notice." From this lawless condition, Mockus engaged Jean Francois Lyotard during his 1995 visit to Bogotá. The local philosopher asked the French guest for his opinion about which disposition best suited contemporary Colombia: one that favored obedience to the law or one that reserved judgment in order to preserve political flexibility. The pointed question from City Hall represented a risk to Mockus's campaign against "shortcuts" in everything from jaywalking to buying votes. Lyotard's book, *The Postmodern Condition* (1979), was a fashionable defense of contemporary skepticism: the book recommends the flexible and pragmatic scientific method to test hypotheses that last only as long as they are useful. Lyotard showed that scientists don't presume to establish fixed laws, and neither should anyone else. But, in the there and then of Colombia's borderline situation, as Mockus confronted it, Lyotard conceded that law was in order.[6]

Risks and Results

If you ask Antanas Mockus how he arrived at art for civic education he may modestly fail to mention the dissertation he wrote in philosophy, about the power of (art-ificial) representation to mediate between personal perception and interpersonal communication. Published in 1988, the thesis describes an arc from Descartes's achievement of conceptual clarity by using linguistic artifice/representation to Habermas's invitation to communicative action: through representation, conflicting positions can play and construct universally acceptable principles (Mockus 1988:72) (Augusto Boal [1995:13] treated all representation as theater; that is, to act and to know that one is acting).

Whether or not Mockus mentions his significant contribution to philosophy, he will not fail to attribute his initiation in art to his adored mother, a ceramic artist who raised two children on her own strength and talent after her husband's early death. Mrs. Nijole Šivickas Mockus is a Lithuanian immigrant of delicate proportions and solid determination who still produces massive and dynamic ceramic sculptures every day even though she is now in her eighties. Serving as her assistant from childhood through his young adult years, Mockus would be instructed, for example, to increase the dimensions of a work in progress by 10%. Years later, he launched a municipal tax-paying campaign called "110% for Bogotá" which encouraged citizens to pay a tithe in excess of the taxes they owed. The city needed the extra money to unclog and to rebuild itself, Mockus told voters in his first mayoral campaign. He actually promised—not threatened—to raise taxes in order to finance urgent public works, but an intransigent City Council refused to approve the increase. Mockus responded with a cleverly contradictory program: *Impuestos voluntarios* (Voluntary Impositions/Taxes). Almost unbelievably, in a city where corruption had for years dissuaded citizens from paying up, over sixty-three thousand families paid in excess of their obligation. They added 10% to fund particular projects: schools, parks, hospitals, transportation, etc., confident that this mayor would not steal the money.

From the time he took office to the time he left his second term, Bogotá's tax revenues had increased astronomically, almost 300%. The same period marked a sharp decline in homicides (67%) and in traffic deaths (51%). Independent studies corroborated the results of the mayor's Observatory of Urban Culture, established in 1995 to collect and analyze surveys of citizens' attitudes and behavior.[7] Programs were designed to address specific survey results, and new surveys provided feedback to determine if the programs should continue, change, or be discontinued (Murraín 2009). Regular reporting of even small incremental results had its own feedback effect, as citizens began to acknowledge a measurable trend, which encouraged them to participate more fully (ibid.). Along with the qualitative analyses prepared by sociologists, anthropologists, and political scientists, the Observatory's statisticians and economists produced quantitative reports that have cured me of a humanist's allergy to statistics. Numbers may be the Mayor's most eloquent evidence of the aesthetic effects he provoked (Figures 169-170).

The documented results of *Cultura Ciudadana* prove that positive change is possible, even in apparently intractable conditions. During a memorable moment of our co-taught course on cultural agents, Mockus made this point with aplomb

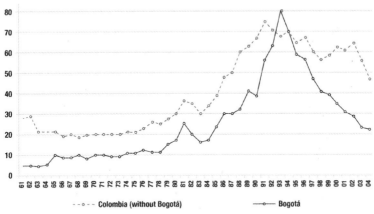

Figure 169: Homicides Drop. Graph by Sumona Chakravarty.

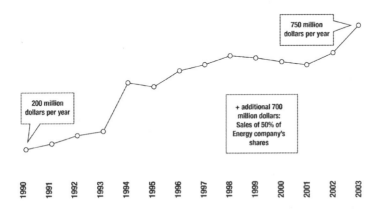

Figure 170: Income from Tax Increases. Graph by Sumona Chakravarty.

and understatement. We had invited Homi Bhabha to speak on Franz Fanon, about whom Bhabha has written brilliantly. The talk made references to Antonio Gramsci, who located opportunities for change at the margins of government, under its radar, in the cracks and contradictions that exist between government and oppositional forces. This was an apt figure for Gramsci's "war of position," waged in historical conditions always "rich with contradictions" in culture (Forgacs 2000). Mockus listened attentively, as he always does, and then made a single comment: "There are cracks and contradictions inside government too, where wars of position can gain ground through cultural persuasion and alternative practices." Here was a participating observer who had enough experience and imagination to ground Gramsci's hunches in reformist, rather than revolutionary, politics. Governments need not be eliminated, either by armed force or by cumulative cultural revolution; they can be reformed through the intrinsic dynamism of programs that coordinate active citizens with creative and transparent leadership.

After the icebreakers of artistic acupuncture, Bogotá's mood changed.[8] Citizens voluntarily collaborated with government and expected good results. The success surprised everyone, including the mayor. There were fiscal reforms (transparency and voluntary tithes), educational improvements (with arts and evaluation), better law enforcement (Mockus and his staff taught at the police academy), new public transportation (the *Transmilenio*), and water conservation (40% reductions that continue today). Despair turned out to be unrealistic or lazy, a failure of determination and creativity.

When admirers from other cities eagerly solicit his advice but remain shy about playing games, Mockus recommends more creativity. And when they simply copy an intervention, as the mimes were copied in more than one hundred Colombian cities without any measurable effect, he urges more serious analysis (Mockus 2004). *Cultura Ciudadana* is not a recipe but an approach, Mockus consistently tells them. It combines the ludic with the legal and relies on analyses of local conditions. In other cities, programs should be customized or replaced by new games (Murraín 2009). The *Transmilenio*, for example, is adapted from "Curitiba's rapid transit bus system, with its trademark clear tubes for same level pre-boarding... Bogotá and Seoul have borrowed from the concept. Los Angeles and Detroit envy it."[9] The point is to think adaptively and creatively.

Play assumes risks that depend on freedom, and therefore demands it, anticipating failures as cues for abandoning some experiments and designing new ones.

Play also admits to living the shadow-life of mere appearances, to being blatantly counterfactual. When critics accuse Mockus of thinking counterfactually, he agrees with them but adds, with playful self-evidence, that it is impossible to think of change without appealing to counterfactual flights of imagination. The equivalent term in Schiller for counterfactual thinking is *Schein* (appearance), and he defends it at length against both "extreme stupidity and extreme intelligence."[10] The one has no imagination, and the other refuses anything but ideal truth. They cannot—or will not—think outside the box of reality and consequently forfeit the freedom that appearance can exercise.

Deliberative Differences

Under-determined and available for imaginative explorations, appearance is precisely the feature that draws Habermas to Schiller's *Letters*. It had already drawn John Dewey, for ethical reasons. Dewey described ethical deliberation as "dramatic rehearsals" that take place in the imaginary space that Schiller had called *Schein* in Letter XXVI, where the artist can consider a variety of options to mold material before making a cut, a stroke, or a rhyme that commits to one option and cancels out others. "The instinct of play likes appearance, and directly it is awakened if it is followed by the formal imitative instinct which treats appearance as an independent thing." That mental theater of possibilities is also where deliberation can exercise freedom to play out a range of scenarios and their results without the irrevocable, possibly harmful, rush toward habitual or preconceived conclusions.

We are apt to describe this process as if it were a coldly intellectual one. As a matter of fact, it is a process of tentative action; we "try on" one or other of the ends, imagining ourselves actually doing them, going, indeed, in this make-believe action just as far as we can without actually doing them (Dewey, EW 4:251 in Fesmire 2003:74).

As an antidote to other reductionist formulae, Habermas also defends imaginative room to maneuver. For him, "extreme stupidity and intelligence" were the willfully naïve tendentiousness of surrealism on the one hand, and the withering intelligence of deconstruction on the other. In the 1920s and 1930s, surrealism had imagined that art—true to its unconventional nature—could dissolve the tensions built into modern life by plumbing a deep and irrational level of consciousness that dreamt away the distance between art and life (Habermas 1995:49). By the 1970s, deconstruction revived this oneiric campaign against reasonable distinctions in a more philosophical register: if meaning is constructed from words, and words are artificial abstractions that overshoot or underestimate the things or actions they signify, then words betray us; they mislead intentions and undermine communication (Habermas 1987:53). Presumptively real information unravels under this rigorous scrutiny and leads practically nowhere. Both surrealists and deconstructionists exposed the fragile distinctions between data and desire, hoping to finally unhinge the gate, already worn down from centuries of skepticism about reasonable communication that separated art from life and rhetoric from literal meaning.

But for Habermas the hinge between life and art is worth repairing, as he takes an "Excursus on Schiller's *Letters on the Aesthetic Education of Man*" to get from one lecture on Hegel to another in *The Philosophical Discourse of Modernity* (1987). By differentiating fact from fiction, the gate of consciousness safeguards a realm for imagination. It marks a border between the land of material and ideological conflicts—that run people aground—and the fresh air of counterfactual "appearances," which Schiller defended as the dimension for free speculation. Alongside the factual world of competition for limited resources and winning ideas, there is a creative, disinterested region for the inter-subjective communication that Schiller calls art and that Habermas (1987) claims as his own baseline for constructing collective agreements:

> If art is to be able to fulfill its historic task of reconciling a modernity at variance with itself, it must not merely impinge on individuals, but rather transform the forms of life that individuals share. Hence, Schiller stresses the community-building, solidarity-giving force of art; its *public character*. The point of his analysis of the present is that in the modern conditions of life, particular forces could be differentiated and developed only at the cost of the fragmentation of the totality (P. 46).

"*Totality* of character [of a society] must therefore be found in a people that is capable and worthy of exchanging the State of need for the State of freedom" (Schiller, Letter IV). And freedom issues from the joyous play of appearance, which is why Habermas defends play against the Surrealist blurring of the border between art and life, and also against Nietzschean deconstruction of their differences. These facile egalitarianisms collapse the imagination's room and stymie the dynamism on which democracy depends. This inter-play between politics and art distinguished democratic Greece from republican Rome, Arendt (1961) writes:

Athens [unlike Rome] never settled the conflict between politics and art un-equivocally in favor of one or the other—which incidentally may be one of the reasons for the extraordinary display of artistic genius in classical Greece—and she kept the conflict alive and did not level it out to indifference of the two realms with regard to each other (P. 17).

As a response to the often violent opposition between reason and desire that Habermas locates at the heart of modernity, art's sidestep from factual reality isn't exactly what to expect from the theorist of communicative action—unless, that is, we take him at his word about Schiller and allow that art should be understood as free communication that builds community. In fact, the genealogy of ideas from Kant to Schiller gives us good warrant to do so. It was Schiller's friendly amend-ment to Kant's *Third Critique* that taught Habermas to pick his way through mo-dernity's deadlock between impersonal pure reason and embodied subjective prac-tical reason. Kant himself gave art credit for developing inter-subjective common sense by communicating feelings and ideas that elude standard uses of language. Artistic genius can give voice to ineffable states of mind and make them "generally communicable." The faculty that guides this communicability is taste, and taste or judgment is not the privilege of genius.[11] This Kantian Bridge between actor and spectator—aesthetic judgment—as expanded by Schiller into a dynamic process of autonomous creativity, underwrites Habermas's long sessions of communicative action. Schiller's unpretentious process made good, Habermas saw, on Kant's en-lightened project to promote disinterested communication:

Kant's *Critique of Judgment* also provided an entry for speculative Idealism that could not rest content with the Kantian differentiations between understand-ing and sense, freedom and necessity, mind and nature, because it perceived in precisely these distinctions the expression of dichotomies inherent in modern life-conditions. But the mediating power of reflective judgment served Schell-ing and Hegel as the bridge to an intellectual intuition that was to assure itself of absolute identity. Schiller was more modest. He held on to the restricted significance of aesthetic judgment in order to make use of it for a philosophy of history. He thereby tacitly mixed the Kantian with the traditional concept of judgment, which in the Aristotelian tradition (down to Hannah Arendt) never completely lost its connection with the political concept of common sense. So he could conceive of art as primarily a form of communication and assign to it the task of bringing about 'harmony in society': 'All other forms of communication divide society, because they relate exclusively either to the private sensibility or to the private skillfulness of its individual members, that is, to what distinguishes between one man and another; only the communication of the Beautiful unites society, because it relates to what is common to them all' (Letter XXVII).[12]

I offer this fundamental connection between aesthetic education and discourse ethics as a tribute to Mayor Mockus and to other daring public figures who may feel disinclined to call their work "art," and yet who strive to adapt Habermas's communicative action in the service of local democracy.[13] When I first interviewed Mockus, he politely resisted my insistent line of questioning about the artistic cast of his administration, probably because the art label would somehow diminish, for some compatriots, the seriousness of his efforts and accomplishments. All the same, convinced as he is that communicative action or discourse ethics is the principle of his politics, Mockus does admit to thinking like an artist when nothing else works. "When I feel trapped," he explains, "I ask myself, 'What would an artist do?'"[14] Perhaps there is less contradiction between communicative action and free play of the imagination than he or I had assumed, and fewer "unbridgeable gaps" than the inflexible categorical imperatives would locate as obstacles to negotiation.

Defending the ever-changing and self-correcting explorations of art, in contrast to the heady ambition of Idealist philosophy, Habermas underlines the debt that Hegel owes to Schiller for conceiving history as an uneven process between the fits and starts of gradual progress through moments of aesthetic accomplishment. With Schiller's advance as a point of departure, Hegel will take on Kant's inflexible categorical ethics of abstract universals to advocate for a more deliberative process, and Habermas will follow up with an argument for communicative action. Thanks to the flexibility and stretch that he learns from Schiller, Hegel can level a critique against the short shrift that Kant gives to the procedure of judgment, and he can offer the remedy of expanding the moment into a working session of inter-subjective deliberation. "Discourse ethics replaces the Kantian categorical imperative by a procedure of moral argumentation" (Habermas 1990:197). It is as if Habermas's reading of Hegel was rounding off the circle that Kant had opened up when he dislodged "imperious reason" from its apparent self-sufficiency in the first two *Critiques*. The *Critique of Judgment* calls attention to reason's dependence on judgment in order to process information, and it shows that judgment is free of pre-existing categories and concepts. Judgment is precisely that faculty—necessary for both pure reason and for the practical reason of moral life—that brackets the categorical imperatives that Hegel had rejected and emerges instead from experience and disinterested contemplation. Kant dislodged the confidence in his own imperatives with his critique against imperiousness, giving Schiller the room to maneuver a defense of the realm of appearances, a space to experiment freely with possible resolutions of conflict without doing damage to the world. Hegel moves in with a backward glance to trace how freedom's development through time accounts for history's progress, and Habermas reads Hegel's particular objection to Kant's categorical imperatives as a re-dedication to an ethics of judgment, Kant's project tweaked by Schiller's praxis of play.

Play builds artful bridges, Habermas (1990) will say in the spirit of Schiller, across apparently unyielding drives or demands:

> The unbridgeable gap Kant saw between the intelligible (realm of duty and free will) and the empirical (realm of phenomena, inclinations, subjective motives, etc.) becomes, in discourse ethics, a mere tension manifesting itself in *everyday communication* as the factual force of counterfactual presuppositions" (P. 203).

Without counterfactual appearance and short of the free play that appearance allows—that is without Schiller—it would be difficult to follow Habermas's instructions for developing discourse ethics.

Seriously, Folks

Among the many imaginable games and the ones that Mockus pioneered, the mimes remain a special case of city-sponsored performance because they were the first experiment with government-generated art, and their engaging shows rehearsed an entire repertoire of possibilities. The effective antics of twenty artists—who had no authority to issue traffic citations but who did run after violators to mock and beguile them under the watch of an enchanted crowd—encouraged Mockus and his inspired staff to keep playing. Within ten years, traffic deaths decreased from 1,300 per year to six hundred. Each mime trained another twenty amateurs—gradually including the homeless among the eventual four hundred recruits—over two weeks' time; and soon the grid of urban space became a massive stage for daily fun poked at rule breakers at red lights and crosswalks. The spectacle created a public from the discreet and defensive citizens who, during years of lawlessness, mutual suspicion, and fear, had been avoiding eye contact with one another. A public is formed in response to a spectacle, as performance theory makes clear; it is not a natural formation or a pre-constituted body with a general will to see a show.[15] Even a public formed through previous spectacles counts on previews and publicity as incentives to re-convene. In Bogotá, the pantomime performances re-constituted a res publica of residents who had become too cynical to appreciate some pedestrian elements of the law. Now they came together in public to abide by the law, with pleasure. Active citizens are not spectators in the conventionally passive sense, nor are they disinterested observers—Kant's *Weltbetrachters*—whom Arendt (2006) also defended as non-partisan, truly free, political subjects. Instead, the jaywalkers, the laughing crowd, and the corrected crossers at crosswalks were all spect-actors, in Boal's deconstructed neologism that undoes the difference between the doers and the done to.

The idea to replace the traffic police with mimes didn't occur to Mayor Mockus immediately, as I said. In fact, he spent the first month in office practically paralyzed politically, worried along with everyone else about what to do in a city so hot with crime that applications of the law went up in smoke. Voters had taken a risk on the unlikely mayor. He was a distinguished professor of philosophy and mathematics, and recently the Chancellor of the National University, but hardly a career politician.[16] And now they wondered if they had not made yet another mistake, along with the increasingly desperate conclusion that staying put in Bogotá was in and of itself a major mistake. The new mayor had wanted to first address the high rate of traffic deaths to show some success before he tackled entrenched interests, and he commissioned a study of causes by the Japanese International Cooperation Agency. It turned out that at least 25% of those accidental deaths could be prevented by improving behavior among pedestrians and drivers. A follow-up study on the streets pinpointed a single target for his cultural acupuncture: the deadly crosswalks (Murraín 2009:17-20). With the troublesome nerve exposed, Mockus encouraged the Institute of Culture and Tourism to design cultural pressure that would incite *shame* for ignoring crosswalks, not fear of fines. (Culture and Tourism, by the way, had been an under-funded afterthought for city government before Mockus became mayor; under him it became the hub of *Cultura Ciudadana*.)

Each day for a month, the mayor asked for a good idea from the Institute's Director, Paul Bromberg. (Bromberg would become interim mayor when Mockus left office a year early to campaign for the presidency.) Finally ready to admit failure, Bromberg confided his discouragement to his aged father-in-law during dinner and asked for advice. Instead of help, Bromberg told Mockus the next morning, he got a sarcastic dismissal: "When there's nothing to be done," the ironic old man quipped, "it's time to bring out the clowns." After Bromberg's unhappy report, and a short pause in the conversation, Mockus lit up. "That's a great idea!" He would propose replacing the embarrassingly corrupt Traffic Police with a few funny, face-painted mimes poised to make people laugh at lawlessness. Citizens would learn to play together in public space and to love the props of striped crosswalks and red lights. The city would stop—for a time—giving traffic tickets to resentful drivers, and discontinue—for good—the predictable bribes demanded by uniformed imposters of law enforcement. As more mimes trained to take over for the Traffic Police, that unfriendly force faced dissolution, which happened nine (gestating) months after the experiment started.

Mockus had purposefully misinterpreted an old man's mockery as a marching order. A metaphor for defeat was realized into a program for advancing toward a war of position called "Civic Culture." With characteristic and almost impish innocence, like an artist, the mayor chose to hear a literal message on the surface of the familiar figure of speech. Instead of meaning disgrace and defeat, the tired figure of bringing out the clowns now meant graceful new maneuvers. This was not the only time that Mockus chose to listen badly, with intentional naiveté. He also solved the dilemma of where he would get married in 1996 by hearing a dead metaphor as if it were plain living language. Finding a spectacular venue for his wedding as the newly installed mayor would allow the public to participate in his change of civil status. There would be no list of special guests for the celebration but rather a general invitation extended to the city. Churches were out of the question, because the still devout groom had been excommunicated for marrying and divorcing a previous partner. Mockus asked his fiancée for a recommendation. To tease him she joked, "If you want a three-ring circus, why not get married there?" Antanas Mockus and Adriana Córdoba did just that—inside the tigers' cage the tamer whipped his wards away from the happy couple and from the terrified elephant they were riding.

By making the common expression unfamiliar, defamiliarized by an intentional mistake, Mockus made a work of relational art that engaged an entire city on the streets and at the circus. Sometimes, and probably often, creativity follows misunderstanding, either artlessly or on purpose. This is why bilingual and bicultural games are a source of endless fun as they track the artful failures of understanding and hint at the wisdom that comes from appreciating language as arbitrary and slippery material (Sommer 2004). Misunderstanding, intentional or not, is also why foreigners help to keep democracies dynamic when they ask for justification and explanation of procedures that are familiar to natives (Honig 2003).

Antanas Mockus, with his Lithuanian name and his Colombian patriotism, lives a cultural complexity that takes on several forms in his thinking about the condition of democracy today. One form is "learning to listen better," as when he honors literal meanings and also anticipates mistakes in multicultural settings (Mockus 2006a:15). In my reading, his essay "Cultural Amphibians" takes advantage of his own bi-cultural formation to reflect on subjects who can shuttle between systems and thereby promote the harmonizing of legal, moral, and cultural codes to create Civic Culture. Educators, he writes, are fundamentally amphibious, because they manage to communicate material from one register of language and experience into others; without this ease of movement and talent for translation, teachers could not teach. The same ability to interpret elements of one code in terms of another allows cultural amphibians to participate in legal, moral, and cultural expressions without violating their personal integrity. Amphibians help to bridge the dangerously divorced codes of behavior by translating the terms of one into others. "The idea of modern democracy is inseparable from the possibility that different reasons may back up the same rules" (Mockus 1994:38).

This is a significant departure from traditional Colombian politics, which advocated cultural coherence and consistency of legal reasoning. Intolerance for political and ethnic diversity went so far—according to at least one historian—as to practically sacrifice Panama to the United States in 1903, when the future canal was already predicting fantastic incomes. For conservative Colombia, it was apparently worth the price of the canal to be rid of the culturally inassimilable and politically radical population of Afro-Panamanians (Múnera 1998). Late nineteenth and early twentieth-century grammarian-statesmen reviled local particularities in language and politics, just as they denounced deviations from Catholic dogma; and well into the twentieth century, non-Catholic immigration was severely limited if not denied.[17] Bogotá was known as the "South American Athens" mostly because it defended its linguistic heritage of Castilian Spanish and Classical Latin to the letter (Deas 1993:31). By 1886, conservative Rafael Núñez (twice president between 1880 and 1888) had replaced the earlier liberal and secular constitution with a Church-centered document that would last for over a century and that acknowledged Spain as Colombia's mother country—while other Latin American states had come to consider her unnatural, castrating, or simply insignificant (Ospina 2009).

On this historical background of mono-cultural conservatism, Mockus advocated the pedagogical and developmental dynamism of amphibious cultures to mark a new procedural modernity for the country. It was at this moment when he and other intellectual leaders were also helping to draft Colombia's new Constitution of 1991. For the first time at the national level, Colombia recognized minority cultural rights and honored local levels of authority. Mockus would adapt this move toward decentralization to the city level, once he became the Mayor General for twenty self-administering locales—each with a locally elected board and mayor appointed by the *Alcalde Mayor* from the board's candidates—in the socially fragmented and sprawling capital of almost eight million residents. Local, as well as general, human rights would continue to inspire his subsequent political campaigns, including another successful bid as mayor of Bogotá in 2001 and two runs for the national Presidency, in 1998 and 2006, which he will hopefully repeat until he wins. Meanwhile he continues to direct Corpovisionarios, a consulting institute for public policy and idea generation.[18]

A Numbers Game

Theories about socially constructive art are still in stages of underdevelopment, given political skepticism about what art is good for, as well as humanistic defenses against usefulness. Grant Kester (2005) makes a significant contribution in "Dialogical Aesthetics: A Critical Framework for Littoral Art," proposing new criteria for collaborative projects that negotiate the boundaries between aesthetic and social values, but taking statesmen into account as "littoral" artists is a stretch (Rancière 2007). Either creative leaders seem too rare to generate principles, or they appear practically diabolical. More people have heard about Adolf Hitler, for example, than about Antanas Mockus. Hitler, we know, was a mediocre painter and then a devastatingly successful director and lead actor of a historical epic that he made sure to choreograph, decorate, broadcast, and film.[19] Maybe the Spanish conquerors will come to mind as exemplary administrative artists. They were consummate architects and city planners on lands that were already populated but that, as artists, they imagined to be empty canvases wiped clean. Add the pomp of Catholicism that dazzled believers and has dignified violent conversions from the Middle Ages into modern times and also the general taste for refinement and beauty that justifies privileged classes taking advantage of everyone else—not to mention the devious creativity of financial institutions that have sunk the global economy into a general depression—and you may conclude that the combination of art and power creates an unfair imbalance against civic decency.

But resistance to abuse also uses art: painters and poets in concentration camps defended their human dignity as creative agents; anti-fascist Red Army posters outdid Nazi propaganda in design and impact; indigenous New Christian artists smuggled old symbols of local cults to keep their chain of worship unbroken; and other popular arts, from slave songs to graffiti murals, shore up cultural autonomy and self-worth against dehumanizing force and indifference. Nevertheless, in powerful hands, art seems to support unjust advantages. After the Enlightenment—when creativity could get full credit for doing political work—artists have often distanced themselves from government projects even when they receive government support. Social commitment for artists more likely means opposition to political authorities than collaboration with them (Sommer 2014, chap. 3).

However, hoping to withhold art from government, or objecting to its use because governments have used art harmfully, is like condemning language because it can curse. Language arts, like others, are born of innate and hard-wired human faculties, so abstinence from art is a self-denying and self-cancelling caution against living. A more practical response to the dangers would distinguish art that does damage from art that does good. Are there family resemblances among cases? I think there are. Power-brokered art is most harmful when power is concentrated in political elites. An autocrat designs a personalized state that can be realized as long as the general population of non-artists executes the plan and dutifully rehearses the script. The roles, props, and symbols come from agreeable artists. "My idea of an agreeable person is a person who agrees with me," Benjamin Disraeli explained.[20] Improvisation or levity—not to mention contestation—is dangerously out of place in monolithic top-down art. It rejects Schiller's caution against violently molding human material into another's work (ibid.,chap. 5).

The contrast I want to suggest between this auteur model of political art and more democratic forms is in the numbers. It is a difference of participatory scale in art making, "a distribution of the sensible" in Rancière's (2004) formulation. To borrow Sir Frances Bacon's (1625) quip about money, art "is like muck, not good except it be spread." Brazil's Ministers of Culture Gilberto Gil (2003-2008) and Juca Ferreira (2008-2010) understood this principle when they fertilized networks of local artists with bottom-up programming.[21]

Claire Bishop (2006) worries that inclusiveness blunts art's provocative edge when consensus building matters more than aesthetic results. The danger, she says, is double (despite Kester's reassurances): either artists stay fixed on personal projects and merely use the collective to fill in the design, or artistic vision is lost to negotiations. But many distinguished artists hold out for a third possibility: participants are creative whether they stay with the collective project or ripple out into new works.

Artist-citizens become admirable to one another. No single artwork cancels out the value of many others, and each exercises a particular charm for other creators. Another lesson we learned from Mockus during his Harvard stay (along with the pragmatics of pleasure) is that admiration is the feeling that sustains democracy. A much stronger feeling than tolerance, admiration is an aesthetic response of surprise and wonder that Boal, for example, consciously coached on stage and on the street (Boal and Jackson 1995:XXIII). To merely tolerate is to continue to count on one's own opinions and simply wait until others stop talking. Tolerant citizens can feel themselves to be the real source of good judgment and imagine that the rights enjoyed by others apparently stem from one's own generosity. Paulo Freire hated this kind of self-celebrating munificence that confirms an imbalance of power between giver and receiver (Freire 2000).

Admiration shifts the balance of feeling; it favors others without sacrificing self-love. To admire one's fellow (artist) is to anticipate original contributions and to listen attentively. Mockus stimulated admiration by creating "The Order of the Zebra" (Knights of the Crosswalk). Identifying decent taxi drivers—decent despite the personal dangers and the general divorce of law and morality from culture—and honoring them with zebra-shaped lapel pins and car stickers. These insignia of "moral giants" gave admiration a multiplier effect. As business boomed for the "Knights of the Crosswalk," other drivers coveted membership and strove to earn it (Mockus 2004, slide 7).

Consider the difference between the chorus effects of fascism and the ripple effects of democracy. *Triumph of the Will* projects the same single voice as do Hitler's newsreels, whereas Bogotá's mimes and the traffic flashcards encouraged each citizen to improvise in games of mutual regulation. Nazi Germany did not promote general arts projects to stimulate debate and deliberation among youth through theater and writing, as Bogotá and Medellín have done with "Youth Weaving their Futures" (Pearl et al. 2010). Nor did the Nazis issue a call to all children aged six to sixteen, as did Mexico and Colombia, to create posters that bid "Good-bye to Tricks" to denounce corruption at every level.[22] Fascist games targeted uniform results. Hitler himself attacked creative education by closing the Waldorf Schools, which he called "a Jewish method to destroy the normal spiritual state of the people" (Salazar 1999:35).[23] It is worth wondering whether a country alive with artists—by definition non-conformists and risk-takers—is less likely to support dictatorship than a nation of dutiful followers. I've asked this almost rhetorical question to political scientists and political leaders; they generally concur that dictatorship frowns on creativity and embraces censorship (Nachmanovitch 2009:11). Schiller (1793/2006) put it this way:

> Art, like science, is emancipated from all that is positive, and all that is humanly conventional; both are completely independent of the arbitrary will of men. The political legislator may place their empire under an interdict, but he cannot reign there. (Letter IX).

The difference between dictatorial and democratic arts, then, is formal as much as ideological. Recognizing the citizen as artist promotes rhizomes or networks of civic effervescence, as opposed to a pyramid with the creator atop his creation. Logically, Mockus objects to being called a leader: "It is important to develop collective leadership... Millions of people contributed to the results that we achieved" (Mockus 2012:168; Caballero 2004). The political appeal of citizen-as-artist is similar to the checks and balances of democratic republics that hope to decentralize executive power but also to coordinate local autonomy with federal structures.

Endnotes

1 Antanas Mockus and colleagues, "'*Por Amor al Arte*': Lineamientos para la campaña presidencial para el gobierno de Colombia 2006-2010." [For the Love of Art: Guidelines for the Presidential Campaign for the Government of Colombia 2006-2010]. Powerpoint presentation sent to me on July 28, 2005.

2 See documentary film, *La Ola Verde: La ilusión de una generación* [The Green Wave: The Hope of a Generation] (*Antanas's Way*) by Margarita Martínez Escallón (2011).

3 Mockus (2012). His installation, "Blood Ties," aims to reduce drug-related deaths in Mexico by inviting visitors to pledge reduced consumption and to donate blood in empathy: (http://www.berlinbiennale.de/blog/projekte/%E2%80%9Eblood-ties%E2%80%9D-von-antanas-mockus-23032).

4 The first time was on March 9, 2001. See, for example, Hernández-Mora (2001).

5 Letter from Víctor Laignelet, October 30, 2009.

6 Conversation with Antanas Mockus and Amparo Vega, February 3, 2009.

7 Fundación Corona's series of publications, "Bogotá, ¿cómo vamos?" (Bogotá, How are We Doing?) was an important watchdog and measure of Mockus's success.

8 See the documentary *Bogotá Cambió* (Bogotá Changed) (2010) by Andreas Dalsgaard (Danish Film Institute), with footage of arts interventions: (http://www.youtube.com/watch?v=32aSCZbWslU).

9 Hinchberger (2006). See also Jaime Lerner's TED talk "A Song of the City" (2007): (https://www.ted.com/talks/jaime_lerner_sings_of_the_city).

10 Schiller, Letter XXVI: "Extreme stupidity and extreme intelligence have a certain affinity in only seeking the real and being completely insensible to mere appearance. The former is only drawn forth by the immediate presence of an object in the senses, and the second is reduced to a quiescent state only by referring conceptions to the facts of experience. In short, stupidity cannot rise above reality, nor the intelligence descend below truth."

11 Kant, *Third Critique of Aesthetic Judgment* (1790), SS 46, Arendt (2006:63).

12 Habermas (1995:48-49). After lecture 2, "Hegel's Concept of Modernity," is an "Excursus on Schiller's *Letters on the Aesthetic Education of Man.*"

13 Perhaps Dewey would deepen Habermas's approach by counting on experience as a ground for deliberation. See Kadlec (2007). She argues that Habermasian critical theory dismisses the life-world as saturated with ideology, abandoning the potential rich challenges of concrete experience.

14 Mockus, March 18, 2005. *Interview with Antanas Mockus/Interviewer: D. Sommer,*

Hemispheric Institute's 5th Encuentro, Belo Horizonte, Brazil. Video. (http://hemisphe-ricinstitute.org/hemi/enc05-interviews/item/1851-interview-with-antanas-mockus).

15 "Performance can be broadly construed as a public spectacle which, depending on what is being performed, draws in a citizen audience, allowing them possibilities to engage with its multiple elements in a manner of their own choosing" (Singhal and Greiner 2008:43).

16 1994 was apparently full of unconventional candidates in Colombia. See "La horas de los antipolíticos." [The Time for Anti-Politicians]. *Revista SEMANA*, November 21, 1994 (http://www.semana.com/nacion/articulo/la-hora-de-los-antipoliticos/24098-3).

17 Andrés Bello, cited by Deas (1993:46). For Deas (1993:47): "…la preocupación por el idioma no se derivaba del temor al aislamiento, aunque Colombia estuviera aislada, ni del menguante nivel de comunicación con los mexicanos, chilenos o argentinos, que le importaban poco. Me parece que el interés radicaba en que la lengua permitía la conexión con el pasado español, lo que definía la clase de república que estos humanistas querían." ("…the preocupation for language did not stem from the fear of isolation, although Colombia was isolated, nor from the dwindling level of communication with Mexicans, Chileans, or Argentinians, who cared little. It seems to me that the interest laid in the fact that the language allowed for a connection with the Spanish past, which defined the kind of republic that these humanists wanted." See also María Ospina, *Pre-textos*.

18 See Corpovisionarios: http://corpovisionarios.org/.

19 Syberberg (1977). See also Dreijmanis (2005).

20 Benjamin Disraeli's character Hugo Bohn in *Lothair* (1870, chap. 35).

21 See George Yudice's "Introduction" to Garcia Canclini (2012).

22 "Adiós a las trampas" [Goodbye to Tricks], Colombia, 2004:
   http://www.comminit.com/en/node/41025/348
   http://www.fas.harvard.edu/~cultagen/models.htm?adios.

23 See also Uhrmacher (1995).

References

Arendt, Hannah. 1961. "The Crisis in Culture: Its Social and Political Significance." In *Between Past and Future: Six Exercises in Political Thought*. New York: The Vikings Press.

———. 2006. *Lectures on Kant's Political Philosophy*. Palo Alto: Stanford University Press.

———. 2007. *Reflections on Literature and Culture*, edited and with an Introduction by Susannah Young-ah Gottlieb. Palo Alto: Stanford University Press.

Bacon, Sir Frances. 1625. "Of Seditions." (http://www.authorama.com/essays-of-francis-bacon-16.html).

Beiser, Frederick. 2005. "Introduction." Pp. 1-12 in *Schiller as Philosopher: A Re-Examination*. Oxford: Clarendon Press.

Bishop, Claire. 2006. "The Social Turn: Collaboration and its Discontents," *Artforum,* February (https://artforum.com/inprint/issue=200602&id=10274).

Boal, Augusto and Adrian Jackson, A. 1995. *The Rainbow of Desire: The Boal Method of Theatre and Therapy*. London and New York: Routledge.

Caballero, Maria Cristina. 2004. "Academic Turns City into a Social Experiment." *Harvard Gazette*, March 11.

Casas Dupuy, Pablo, and Paola Gonzáles Cepero. "Políticas de Seguridad y Reducción del Homicidio en Bogotá: Mito y Realidad" [Politics of Security and Reducing Homicide in Bogotá: Myth and Reality]. Bogotá: Fundación Seguridad & Democracia [Foundation for Security and Democracy]. (http://pdba.georgetown.edu/Security/citizensecurity/Colombia/evaluaciones/politicasBogota.pdf).

Deas, Malcolm. 1993. *Del poder y la gramática y otros ensayos sobre historia, política y literatura colombianas* [Of Power and Grammar and Other Essays on Colombian History, Politics, and Literature]. Bogotá: Tercer Mundo Editores.

Dreijmanis John. 2005. "A Portrait of the Artist as a Politician: The Case of Adolf Hitler." *The Social Science Journal* 42(2):115-127.

Fesmire, Steven. 2003. *John Dewey and Moral Imagination: Pragmatism in Ethics*. Bloomington: Indianapolis.

Freire, Paolo. 2000. *Pedagogy of the Oppressed,* translated by Myra Berman Ramos, 30th Anniversary Edition. New York: Continuum.

Garcia Canclini, Nestor. 2012. *Imagined Globalization*. Durham: Duke University Press.

Habermas, Jürgen. 1987. *The Philosophical Discourse of Modernity: Twelve Lectures*. Cambridge: MIT Press.

————. 1990. "Morality and Ethical Life: Does Hegel's Critique of Kant Apply to Discourse Ethics?" In *Moral Consciousness and Communicative Action*. Cambridge: MIT Press.

————.1995. *The Philosophical Discourse of Modernity: Twelve Lectures*, translated by Frederick Lawrence. Cambridge: Polity Press.

Hernández-Mora, Salud. 2001. "Bogotá organiza una noche «sólo para mujeres» para combatir la violencia" [Bogotá Organizes a Night 'Only for Women' to Fight Violence], *El Mundo*, March 11.

Hinchberger, Bill. 2006. "Curitiba: Jaime Lerner's Urban Acupuncture." *Brazilmax.com* February 18. (http://www.brazilmax.com/news.cfm/tborigem/pl_south/id/10).

Honig, Bonnie. 2003. *Foreigners and Democracy*. Princeton: Princeton University Press.

Forgacs, David, ed. 2000. *The Gramsci Reader: Selected Writings, 1916–1935*. New York: New York University Press.

Kadlec, Alison. 2007. *Dewey's Critical Pragmatism*. Lanham: Lexington Books.

Lerner, Jaime. 2003. *Acupuntura urbana* [Urban Acupuncture]. Rio de Janeiro: Record Publishers.

Kester, Grant. 2005. "Dialogical Aesthetics: A Critical Framework for Littoral Art," *Variant* 9.

Mockus, Antanas. 1988. *Representar y disponer: Un estudio de la noción de representación orientado hacia el examen de su papel en la comprensión previa del ser como disponibilidad* [Representation and Availability: A Study Examining the Notion of Representation and Its Role in the Prior Understanding of the Being as Availability]. Bogotá: National University of Colombia.

————. 1994. "Anfibios culturales y divorcio entre ley, moral y cultura" [Cultural Amphibians and the Divorce Between Law, Morals, and Culture]. *Análisis político* [Politica Analysis] 21:37-47.

————. 2001. "*Cultura Ciudadana*, programa contra la violencia en Santa Fe de Bogotá, Colombia, 1995-1997" [Civic Culture, Program Against Violence in Santa Fe de Bogotá, Colombia, 1995-1997]. 3:8. Washington, D.C.: Interamerican Development Bank. (https://publications.iadb.org/bitstream/handle/11319/5252/Cultura%20ciudadana%2c%20programa%20contra%20la%20violencia%20en%20Santa%20Fe%20de%20Bogot%C3%A1%2c%20Colombia%2c%20 1995-1997.pdf?sequence=1).

————. 2004. "América Latina, consensos y paz social." [Latin America, Agreements and Social Peace]. Speech delivered at the XXXIV Congreso Internacional de Conindustrias. June 30, Caracas.

———. 2006a. "Ampliación de los modos de hacer política" [Broadening the Ways of Doing Politics]. *Revista Aleph* 135:2-26.

———. 2006b. "La innovación y la extraña frontera que separa escuela y sociedad" [Innovations and the Strange Border that Separates School and Society]. *Revista Aleph*, 136:2-5.

———. 2012. "When I Am Trapped" Pp. 164-170 in *Forget Fear: 7ᵗʰ Biennale For Contemporary Art,* edited by Artur Zmijewski and Joanna Warsza. Berlin: KW Institute for Contemporary Art, Walther König Publishers.

Múnera, Alfonso. 1998. *El fracaso de la nación: región, clase y raza en el Caribe colombiano (1717-1821)* [The Failure of the Nation: Region, Class, and Race in the Colombian Caribbean (1717-1821)]. Bogotá: Banco de la República, Ancora Editores.

Murraín, Henry. 2009. *"Cultura Ciudadana* como política pública: entre indicadores y arte" [Civic Culture as Public Policy: Between Indicators and Art]. In *Cultura Ciudadana en Bogotá: nuevas perspectivas* [Civic Culture in Bogotá: New Perspectives], edited by Efraín Sánchez and Carolina Castro. Bogotá Chamber of Commerce, Ministry of Culture, Sports, and Recreation, Terpel Foundation, Corpovisionarios.

Nachmanovitch, Stephen. 2009. "This is Play." *New Literary History* 40(1).

Sáenz Obregón, Javier. 2007. *Desconfianza, civilidad y estética: las prácticas formativas estatales por fuera de la escuela en Bogotá, 1994-2003* [Distrust, Civility, and Aesthetics: Formative State Practices Outside of School in Bogotá, 1994-2003]. Bogotá: Institute for Educational Research and Pedagogic Development, National University of Colombia, Faculty of Human Sciences, Social Studies Center.

Ospina, María. 2009. "Prácticas de memoria o cómo resistir el acabóse: Violencia y representación en la narrativa colombiana" 1985–2005 [Memory Practices or How to Resist the Ending: Violence and Representation in the Colombian Narrative, 1985-2005]. Ph.D. Dissertation. Harvard University, Cambridge.

Pearl, Frank et al. 2010. "Tejer el camino, guía conceptual y metodológica componente de convivencia y reconciliación. Estrategia de reintegración basada en comunidades" [Weaving the Way, Conceptual and Methodological Guide Component for Coexistence and Reconciliation. Community Based Reintegration Strategy]. Project Bank of the High Presidential Council, May.

Quinn, Susan. 2008. *Furious Improvisation: How the WPA and a Cast of Thousands Made High Art out of Desperate Times.* New York: Walker Publishing Company.

Rancière, Jacques. 2004. *The Politics of Aesthetics: The Distribution of the Sensible,* translated with Introduction by Gabriel Rockhill, afterword by Slavoj Žižek. London, New York: Continuum.

———. 2007. "The Emancipated Spectator." *Artforum International* 45(7):270-281.

Salazar, Deborah. 1999. "What Every Jewish Parent Should Know about the Waldorf Philosophy." *Jewish Parenting*, Spring.

Schapiro, Mark. 2001. "All the City's a Stage." *Atlantic*, September.

Schiller, Friedrich. 1793/2006. "On Grace and Dignity." Pp. 127-154 in *Aesthetical and Philosophical Essays*. Middlesex: Echo Books.

Singhal, Arvind, and Karen Greiner. 2008. "Performance Activism and Civic Engagement Through Symbolic and Playful Actions." *Journal of Development Communication* 19(2):43-53.

Shklovsky, Victor. 1917/1965. "Art as Technique." Pp. 3-24 in *Russian Formalist Criticism, Four Essays*, translated by Lee T. Lemon and Marion J. Reis. Lincoln: University of Nebraska Press.

Sommer, Doris. 1991. *Foundational Fictions: The National Romances of Latin America*. Berkeley: University of California Press.

———. 2004. *Bilingual Aesthetics: A New Sentimental Education*. Durham: Duke University Press.

———. 2014. *The Work of Art in the World: Civic Agencies and Public Humanities*. Durham: Duke University Press.

Syberberg, Hans Jürgen. 2007. *Hitler, ein Film aus Deutschland* [Our Hitler, a Film from Germany]. Chicago: Distributed by Facets Video. www.imdb.com/title/tt0076147/.

Uhrmacher, Bruce. 1995. "Uncommon Schooling: A Historical Look at Rudolf Steiner, Anthroposophy and Waldorf Education." *Curriculum Inquiry* 25(4).

2. BOGOTÁ: Between the Violence of Chaos and Civic Creativity[1]

Jesús Martín-Barbero

Cities change faster than our hearts.
–*Charles Baudelaire, Le Cygne (*The Swan*)*

Bogotá, stop being so chauvinistic, so harsh. Halt the rush, halt fear, aggressiveness, cement, verticality, rationality and recover your emotions, the places for words, for differences: become more feminine!
–*Florence Thomas, Pensar la ciudad para que ella nos piense...Una mirada feminina sobre la ciudad* (Thinking the City so that It Thinks of Us...A Feminine Gaze on the City)

From Village Tales to Urban Chronicles

Perhaps the best way to approach Bogotá is through its narratives. Its opening narrative, *El carnero* (The Ram), was written by Juan Rodríguez Freyle in 1638. As the author tells, "it is a tale of its discovery, of some civil wars, of its customs and peoples, and from whence came this celebrated name: El Dorado" (Rodríguez Freyle 1994). With great irreverence, and in contrast to the ostentatious genealogies and deceiving heraldries that were common at the time, the story tells the daily lives of its inhabitants and of some sorcerers as well as of certain erotic miracles. Interpreters argue over the meaning of its title since *carnero* (ram) means both the animal with twisted horns that the pre-Christian tradition saw as a symbol of lust and fertility, and that the Christian tradition saw as the devil, and it also means a leather trunk for storing old, useless papers. In this sense "ram" would be synonymous with a "social tomb," a symbol then, of the falsity and presumption of a decaying society. Critics do agree, however, that this chronicle represents Bogotá's classic narrative style, weaving a plot that intertwines chronicle and literary invention. "Confronted with a pathetic village spectacle, the chronicler escapes it by ridiculing and satirizing it, by mixing in his caustic gaze historical fact and pleasurable occurrences" (Chaparro 1999).

All the chroniclers who followed Rodriguez Freyle—from Cordobez Moure to José Asunción Silva or Carrasquilla and Vargas Vila—wrote to escape from tediousness or the lack of opportunities, a practice that has continued until today. Faced with the visual, emotional, and literary *greyness* that has been associated with Bogotá, its writers react with a type of fascination that paradoxically translates into bitterness and flight.[2] From Osorio Lizarazo to Moreno-Durán, the eagerness to bear witness confronts the chaos of the city by transforming chronicle into fiction, from "the dark boiling of race-mixing bubbling with hunger and despair" in *De sobremesa* (After-Dinner Conversation), to the deterioration of the urban, literary, and historical body, which *El caballero de la invicta* (The Knight of the Unconquered) can only survive and be saved from by reinventing the city through words. Thus, he cannot understand Bogotá without *its stories,* "as if the city were made more of words and images than buildings, streetlights, and stores" (Botero 1999).

In the early 1980s in *Sin remedio* (Hopeless) its author, Antonio Caballero, ridicules a rainy, horrible, and dangerous city, whose geography condemns its inhabitants to isolation and leaves no other outlet but poetic imagination. This is the case of its protagonist, sick with an illness that keeps him alive in an atmosphere where only he can breathe, since only he knows that "things are the same as things" (Caballero 2004:119). And Bogotá is not an externality—the grey that some days clouds over an incomparable light, tirelessly interrupted by rain at four in the afternoon—but rather the inside of houses and people; that is why he composes verse after verse through which he exorcises the *ciudad sin remedio* (hopeless city). From another angle, in the 1990s, the young writer R. Chaparro in *Opio en la nubes* (Opium in the Clouds) describes the urban monster that Bogotá was becoming: the flow of masses, images, and sensations through which passersby *drifts*, because they are in a city that now not only is a sea, but that also has a sea! And turned into a carnival, Bogotá is the city where anything can happen, where streets extend into infinity, their names change, the limits are erased and through its labyrinths the nameless masses walk, run, lose themselves, find themselves, and un-find themselves again.

One of the latest key novels about Bogotá was written by a woman, Laura Restrepo, but it was yet another woman, Soledad Acosta de Samper who, at the end of the nineteenth century, wrote the story "Bogotá en el año 2000: una pesadilla" ("Bogotá in the Year 2000: A Nightmare"). She lived most of her life between Paris and Lima, and in this story she tells of the nightmare of a high class lady returning to Bogotá in the year 2000 to find that the servants have become university students—a cook-turned-philosopher, a chamber lady that has graduated from the Academy of Fine Arts, anarchists with dazzling dresses, and atheists-in a city that had just created the *Institute of Happiness* with the slogan "Long live emancipation and freedom." The novel by Laura Restrepo is entitled *Dulce compañía* (Sweet Company) and in it, the author, journalist, and novelist "replaces her attempt to achieve journalistic reports that explain the elusive worlds" in which she lives with a "fictional solution" (Ordoñez 2000:2): the appearance of an autistic angel in a working class neighborhood in the south of Bogotá, with whom a female journalist falls in love. In her search she crosses a wet and dirty, fragmented, dangerous, and demented city, but she is rewarded with the discovery of a mad love, and a voice that emmerges from marginal and marginalized knowledge, mystically illuminating the shredded and torn city.

There is another story that situates Bogotá in the nation, showing that Colombia is not the most violent country in the world—as it frequently appears in international news releases—but rather the country where the violence and fears at the threshold of the third millennium are most visibly interwoven with those at the end of the first. It is the book by George Duby (1995) entitled *Año 1000, año 2000. La huella de nuestros miedos* (Year 1000, Year 2000. The Footprint of Our Fears), weaves a tale faithfully characterizing the situation of Colombia:

At the close of the millennium *death mattered little;* the savagery of gentlemen *made everything permissible* and only *the church* was able to impose a few minimal rules for communal life. At that time, even *the gangs that laid waste along the roads did not wage war on Fridays or Sundays,* and respected women and monks— wouldn't we Colombians like to enjoy even that modicum of tolerance today! There was violence *everywhere,* and *when the military forces were not under the control of some political force,* the situation was devastating. The cavalry itself had become an *extortion business* against which the peasants resisted, but everything became more dangerous when *an uprising of rich peasants exasperated the brutality of the warriors*—it is not possible to express in fewer words what the confluence and brutality of guerrillas, para-military groups, and the army has meant in this country. The war had already lasted *fifty years* throughout the country! And if that was not enough, Duby rounds up the picture affirming that, in spite of it all, that society of the year one thousand was much less convoluted than that of the year two thousand, *less worked over by inner perturbation.*[3]

With his cynical and lucid expressivity, Jean Baudrillard (1993) has also described a situation that especially characterizes Colombia:

> Nothing that was thought to have been overcome in history has truly disap-peared; it is all waiting to spring to life again, all of the archaic, anachronistic forms, like a virus in the deepest crevice of a body. History has only let go of cyclical time to fall into the order of the recyclable (P. 21).

This is the operation carried out by thousands of media images that by feeding back into violence end up living from it, reinforcing the *inner perturbation* that interweave ancient forms of violence with today's fears.

The City of Mediating Fears

My first encounter with the question of the *visibility of urban fears* occurred with the assassination of Luis Carlos Galán, presidential candidate in the 1990 elec-tions. The constant threats against candidates upset the electoral campaign to the point that it almost ended their public appearances, depriving politics of its vital street theatricality and forcing it to take refuge, reducing it to a televised spectacle. It was then that I realized that *fear was feeding off fear*, and that this was not only happening during electoral campaigns. I then began to study the complicities, the secret partnerships between media and fear (Martin-Barbero 1991). We cannot understand the sense and the breadth of new fears by only referring to them in terms of an increase in criminality or insecurity in the streets, since fears are key to the new modes of living and communicating large cities today, nor can we really understand what the media does without studying how fear has become an essen-tial part of communication processes.

The Reason for Prejudice: Motives for Fear

Let us propose, then, the need to confront two equally tenacious prejudices: one that comes from the field of communication studies, and the other from experts on violence and fear.

The first prejudice consists in believing that communication processes can be understood by studying the media alone. However, what the media do, especially with people, can only be understood with reference to transformations in urban ways of communication: that is, in reference to changes to public space, in the relations between the public and the private that are produced by a fluid city, increasingly made up of circulating information, and less and less by face-to-face encounters and conversations. The possibility of understanding the attraction of television lies less in studying what TV does, than in studying those processes and situations that make people feel compelled to take refuge in the small space of the private, the domestic, and to project on it an imaginary of security and protection; if TV attracts, it is largely because the street repels. It is the absence of spaces—streets and squares—for communication that makes television something more than an instrument of leisure, a vicarious place of encounter with the world, with people, and even with the city we live in.

The second prejudice leads us to propose that we cannot understand the sense and breadth of new fears by referring to them only through an increase in violence, criminality, and insecurity in the streets, since fears are the key to the new ways in which we live and communicate. That which has turned some of our Latin American cities chaotic and insecure is not only the number of thefts or murders, but the *cultural angst* in which the majority of their inhabitants live. When people live in a city from which they feel estranged, it takes them to another vital plane: that of *not recognizing ourselves as from that place*, and that kind of insecurity makes even the most peaceful of people aggressive. A city inspires fear not only when there are thefts and murders—in what large city in the world do these things not happen?—but also when our own corporality becomes aggressive, which is what happens when the city's memory is destroyed, since that destruction robs its inhabitants of the referents of their identity. Having come to Bogotá in 1963, I have borne witness to the anguish produced in both the old downtown and the other town that until a few years ago was Chapinero, which is now spreading throughout the entire city. [4]

Of course, when delinquency grows and becomes professionalized, it is frightening. But if fear paralyzes us, it is distrust that makes us insecure and aggressive.

A large part of the aggressiveness that the city accumulates comes from our feeling of being lost, making us distrust everyone, and so we store up a deaf rage that does not allow us to hear even ourselves—a rage against everything around us that makes us explode, demolishing all urbanity and solidarity.

This anguish is derived from several factors. First, it comes from the loss of a sense of collective belonging in cities where a savage urbanism reigns, one that is related to the calculations of formal and commercial rationality. Secondly, it is an anguish produced by the way the city normalizes differences. We blame the media for homogenizing life, when the strongest and most subtle homogenizer is the city itself, by impeding the expression and growth of differences; by normalizing behaviors as well as buildings, the city erodes collective identities, it obstructs them, and that erosion robs us of our cultural foundation, thrusting us into a void. Lastly, it is an anguish that comes from the order imposed on us by the city. For the city imposes a precarious, vulnerable, yet effective order. What is this order made of and how does it work? Paradoxically, it is an order created by the uncertainties that the "other" creates in us, the unknown, which is the majority of the people I will come across. In the street, anybody making a gesture that cannot be deciphered in twenty seconds has become suspicious, and therefore intolerance builds: the difficulty of recognizing oneself in the other's thoughts and preferences, in what the other has as his/her vital, aesthetic, or political horizon.

We can state that in Colombia *the media draws life from fear*. Television is a parasite eating away the need for communication that is no longer taking place in the street. It is a flagrant paradox that, in a country with such huge structural gap in housing, health, and education, we have disproportionately developed communication media, both economically and technologically speaking. It is the *reality* of a country with a very weak civil society, long-term political polarization, and deep cultural schizophrenia. These factors strengthen the media's excessive capacity to represent. It is not that the amount of time or type of program seen does not matter. What I am proposing is that the political or cultural weight of television, as that of any other medium, is not *measurable* in terms of direct and immediate contact. It can only be evaluated in terms of the social mediation its images achieve, and in the case of violence this mediation is decisive.

Imagined Fears and Images of Violence

Until the mid-1990s, the fears of Bogotá were not only those of the city but those of the entire country. A country with *generalized violence*, in the sense that "violence is not experienced as a catastrophe, but as a banal process that offers opportunities, produces accommodations, and has norms and regulations" (Pécaut 1997:16). This can clearly be seen in three spheres: the professionalization of violence as a type of widespread *informal work*, in the context of *economy of violence* that has its own forms of inclusion and exclusion, and the passage from fear to terror that occurs when the "law of silence" intensifies to the point of paranoia: a distrust of everyone by everyone, experienced without any major rupture since it is not inscribed in the plot of our collective memory/narrative (Perea 1996; Sanchez and Peñaranda 1991).[5] But what causes terror to circulate across the length and breadth of the land is the staging done by some media, morbidly and obscenely exploiting terror, erasing the deep and dense diversity of violence contributing to the generalized feeling that collective action is impotent, while in turn promoting the individual's retreat to the domestic sphere.

A second look focuses on the *exhibitionist* character that violence has enjoyed, and its effects on speeches and social topographies: we are faced with a violence without a social subject, for "the social subjects and their activities remain masked behind the image of national malignity" (Jimeno 1998). The *repeated* presence of violent acts in the images the country constructs of itself points, on the one hand, to their banalization, and, on the other, to the psychological need to overcome the trauma allowing them to be assimilated as experience. This must be related to the fact that "85% of Colombians declare themselves to be distrustful, and 90% declare themselves to be courageous!" This means that in the act itself of *domestication* of violence, that is, of its psychological control and habituation, and of its transformation into *habitus*, Colombian society bears witness to a profound deterioration of the quality of civic life, since it legitimizes the *right to fear*, as well as its structural consequence: *distrust*.

In the mid-1990s, Bogotá was—according to a chronicler—a wet and dirty, fragmented, dangerous, and crazy city. It had a population of some seven million, that in the previous twenty years had lived through a process of rapid decrease in the number of native inhabitants and an accelerated *heterogenization* of its population due to a flood of people from all regions of the country, the greater part of which were the millions displaced by the war. In addition to the permanent *informality* of its urbanization processes—the precariousness of its streets, deficiencies in all services, and chaos in public transportation—there was *topographical discrimination*: divisions between the north "of" the rich and the south "for" the poor, between the territory of enclosed residential complexes and the half-built, poor neighborhoods full of immigrants and displaced persons; a city with a lack of collectively enjoyable public spaces and the presence of enormous "empty" spaces with a tremendous degree of social and physical deterioration. The narrative of chaos added another trait to this map: the greatest number of violent injuries were not from fights among strangers—in spite of the high indices of criminality and insecurity—but within neighborhoods where "debts" and revenge, domestic violence, and sexual crimes most commonly occurred. In addition, the most defining trait of all: "Its inhabitants walk from home to work as if they were in a tunnel" (Uribe 1996; Niño Murcia et al. 1998), clutching their handbags, attentive to any indication of danger and responding immediately and aggressively to any minimally undecipherable gesture.

Thinking about violence outside the dualist, essentialist framework that lies beneath the idea that the peculiarity of violence in Colombia relates to the precariousness of the state, which is in turn indebted to the absence of a strong *foundational myth* the country suffered—an absence due to the size, diversity, and isolation of the indigenous communities in the territory—Daniel Pécaut (2001) states that "what Colombia is missing is a *relato nacional* (national tale) more than a foundational myth." That is, a "multi-tale" that makes it possible for Colombians of all classes, races, ethnic origins, genders, regions, etc. to locate their daily experiences in a minimally shared fabric of griefs and dreams. It needs a tale that will weave a common memory that, like all social and cultural memory, will always be a conflictive but binding memory, to wrench violence away from this sub-history similar to that of natural catastrophes or cataclysms, the way violence has been made politically visible and explained: as brutal clashes between two tectonic plates or ferocious retaliations by factions moved by essentially antagonistic visions and interests.

The absence of an inclusive national tale is expressed in an image of Colombia that is as expressive as it is heart-rending: a country trapped between the yammering of its politicians and the silence of its warriors. Few images point so poignantly to the complicity and correspondence between these two traps: politicians are trapped in their babble, incapable of resolving complex conflicts and demands or meeting the country's demands, and they are also incapable of visualizing the ways in which the country yearns to be known and represented regionally, ethnically, and generationally. Along with this bellowing of so many empty words rises the *silence of the warriors*, made manifest by the fact that a great majority of the thousands who die each year are not recognizable, have no name, nor are deemed worthy of recognition. The corpses are thrown in fields, rivers, roadsides, or urban outskirts, and the closest there is to a tribute is the mute gesture of the marks of cruelty on the victims' bodies.

Silence is the other side of the coin of impunity, a wound inflicted on the social fabric, on communal life, perhaps deeper than the fact that the assassin is not judged. For how can we take on the responsibility of the errors and abuses, if we do not share a minimum discourse through which we can name them? And how do we share the grief, if we do not even share the *feeling-in-common*, without which no community can subsist? Thus, much of the thinking about the Colombian situation, from both within and outside academia, fragments society, paralyzing it, for these thinkers do not weave a tale, and are unable to name where the intolerable begins. Hence *the polarization* encouraged from positions of power over the last ten years has been reinforced by the *fragmentation* of critical discourse, incapable of providing citizens with a reading of the situation that can help them place their daily experience of humiliation and rage within a minimal tale containing some meaning that might spur their hopes.

Citizens' Supervision and New Urban Visibilities

In 1995, Bogotá elected as mayor the former chancellor of the National University, the mathematician and philosopher Antanas Mockus, with almost double the votes of his closest opponent and without the support of any political party. He brought independents and people from academia to his government, a decision that radically transformed the future of Bogotá. In late 1997, I had the good fortune to be invited to participate in evaluating a document prepared by the recently created Observatory of Urban Culture that was part of the city's Institute of Culture.

Only Citizens Can Shape the City

The slogan of Mockus's campaign was really the driving force behind his administration: "*Formar Ciudad*" (To Form the City) (Mockus 1995). This meant three things: first, what truly gives shape to a city is not its architecture and engineering, but its citizens; secondly, for this to happen, citizens must be able to recognize themselves in the city; and thirdly, both processes are implied in the other: to *make the city visible as a whole*, that is, with respect to everyone's space/project/task. If the city had been previously rendered invisible by its multiple disasters and the thousand failings that affected the citizens daily—defects in the water system, electricity, transportation, etc.—what it sought was to change the focus in order to perceive the deficiencies not as an isolated and inevitable fact but as the mark of a figure that is deformed as a whole—that is, de-formed—without shape.

The city began to become visible when a series of street-based communicative strategies drew inhabitants out of the "tunnel" in which they habitually moved, enticing them to look and see. The first action was strategically placing more than four hundred mimes and clowns in numerous places around the city, particularly in congested areas, who pointed to the crosswalks for pedestrians and who walked with them, in the face of a flurry of protests and bewilderment manifested by both drivers and passersby. What in the beginning was taken to be a "bad joke" by the mayor soon became a question of public space. This questioning was soon translated into gestures and behavior: the mayor's office distributed a card that on one side had a thumbs-up and on the other a thumbs-down to thousands of drivers, who quickly learned to use it to applaud conducts that were solidary and respectful of the norms, or to reproach infractions and violence. A few months later, the mayor created a contest to find an official anthem for Bogotá, since a city without an anthem *cannot hear itself.* Later came the appearance of the *carrot* as a sign of the very controversial imposition of a closing time for establishments serving alcohol. Then came the rituals of vaccination against violence, the installation in the poorest neighborhoods of *justice houses* where people could settle their conflicts locally and without the participation of any formal institutions, and the creation of "Ladies' Night," among others.

It was a rich and complex struggle against the explosive mix of conformity and the accumulation of rage and resentment, as well as the simultaneous reinvention of a political culture of belonging and of everyday life. There were two threads that wove together the multiple dimensions of this experience: a cultural policy whose objective was to promote the daily culture of the majorities, rather than specialized cultures, with one strategic objective: to strengthen to the maximum the communicative competence of individuals and groups as a way of solving conflicts in a civic-minded manner and to channel new ways of expressing inconformity as a replacement for physical violence.

A very heterodox idea underlay it all, that the cultural (the *we*) mediates and establishes a continuum between the moral (the *individual*) and the legal (the *others*), as can be seen in acts that, while they may be illegal or immoral, nevertheless, are culturally accepted by the community. To strengthen Civic Culture means, then, to increase our capacity to regulate the acts of others by increasing our own expressive capacity and that of the media, in order to understand what the other wants to say. Mockus calls this the "increase in the capacity to generate recognized public space" (Mockus 1998:18). Initially armed with such conceptual baggage, the city government of Bogotá carried out a complex survey on citizen contexts, sense of justice, and relationship to public space, among many other topics. He dedicated 1% of the city's investment budget to his "To Form the City" campaign, launching his strategy on two fronts—interaction among strangers and between marginalized communities—and on five strategic programs: respect for traffic regulations (mimes in the crosswalks); dissuasion from bearing arms (in exchange for symbolic goods); prohibition of the indiscriminate use of fireworks in popular festivities, the "Carrot Law" (setting 1AM. as closing hour for public establishments that sell liquor, as well as non-alcoholic beverages); and the "Vaccination Against Violence" (a public ritual of symbolic aggression especially among neighbors and relatives to combat child abuse).

A Heterodox Cultural Policy

The other common thread of the strategy was a *cultural policy* carried out by the city's Institute of Culture. The institute shifted away from promoting the arts to administering the diverse cultural programs under the umbrella of the "To Form the City" framework, which articulated the many cultural actions of the mayor's office, those of specialized cultural institutions and those of community associations.

The form of this *cultural policy* that articulated cultural programs and projects for Bogotá in the first administration of Antanas Mockus was clearly unorthodox. Until then, scholars of cultural policy in Latin America had held one principle: one could only talk strictly of *cultural policies* when dealing with specialized and institutionalized cultures such as theatre, dance, libraries, museums, cinema, or music (Canclini, Bruner and Miceli 1987). Nonetheless, what Mockus made possible was a clear and positive rupture with the academic conception of cultural policies. The axis of his cultural policy was what he called Civic Culture, which regulates social coexistence from promoting positive interactions with the bus driver to respecting traffic signals; and peaceful resolution of conflicts among neighbors, from the rules of the game among young gangs to the relationship to public space on sidewalks and in parks and plazas, and the highly disputed closing hour for bars. Based on these policies regarding the *cultural life* of citizens, other policies were developed drawing from the specialized cultures of the arts. This guideline permeated both the work of the institutions through their agents, and also that of artists, creators, and professionals of the arts who consented to the use of their work in civic projects.

For many artists this constituted a huge blasphemy, but it was in this way that *culture took the street*, introducing ruptures and decisive proposals to transform fear and aggression into creativity. This is what we were able to attest to during the evaluation of the tasks and programs of the city's Institute of Culture. Following the fall of the Berlin Wall and the disappearance of the socialist camp—which had led many artists to a profound and paralyzing demoralization—a good number of creators and cultural workers in Bogotá found new meaning for their artistic work within this new experience as citizens. In this way, some found political motivation in their work in the neighborhoods that seemed to have been lost in the ideological chaos the world was experiencing. To "do" art in the neighborhoods with the people, to recreate the memory of the communities, to experiment with aesthetic and expressive practices, enabled the reweaving of a social fabric of belonging to a territory and the re-creation of identities. The rediscovery of people as *neighbors* in their communicative and expressive capacity also gave new potential to both the oral narratives of the elders and the oral expressions and melodious cultures of the youth with their rock and rap.

A beautiful example that illustrates the connection between policies that touch on cultural life and specialized cultures is the meaning that public space began to acquire and the new uses given to it, by recovering the capacity to construct a mobile, cultural infrastructure for community enjoyment. Giving back public space to the people meant not only respect for norms, but also new possibilities for collective enjoyment that linked for the first time a sense of belonging with participation and creation.

He presented the theoretical challenge to me via the complex experience I had been tasked to evaluate, leading to a provocative discussion with the directors of the program and area coordinators in various localities of Bogotá. Some artists expressed their fears about the inherent dangers of inserting their work into a

Civic Culture program, because, by subsuming the specificity of their cultural work within a government program, they ran the risk of serving as a seal of approval for official policies and the partisan interests of its authorities. In other words, several artists wondered whether having participated in this experience could not be taken as an approval of the policies of the city's administration. Nevertheless, it was precisely that debate among artists and cultural promoters on the risks their work faced that ended up convincing me of the strategic importance of the new concept of cultural policy that had broken new ground in Bogotá. In fact, what became visible in the discussion was the deep maladjustment between the new cultural policy and *politics* as we had understood it, that is, conservative or liberal, from the right or the left. What we were discovering was that true politics, which deals with the needs, demands, and hopes of citizens, stepped completely outside the old institutional frameworks and outside the status of distinction and authority that it granted its traditional actors. The artists' confusion and perplexity made it patently visible that democracy had begun to enter into dimensions, positions, and practices that were no longer those of the politicians, but rather those of citizens.

Endnotes

1   Translated from Spanish by Sebastián Cuellar and Cathy Girvin. Final revision by Javier Sáenz Obregón.
2   In the sense of monotony.
3   See my editorial note to the Special Issue on "Fin de siglo" [Fin de Siècle] in *Revista de Estudios Sociales*, "Journal of Social Studies" No. 5, 2000.
4   An old shopping district.
5   For absence of a plot and its consequences see: Perea (1996); for historical context see: Sánchez and Peñaranda (1991).

References

Arocha, Jaime, Fernando Cubides, and Myriam Jimeno. 1999. *Las violencias: inclusión creciente* [Violence: Growing Inclusion]. Bogotá: CES/National University of Colombia.

Baudlaire, Charles. 1857. "Le Cygne" [The Swan]. In *Charles Baudlaire, Les Fleurs du Mal* [The Flowers of Evil]. Hachette: Paris.

Baudrillard, Jean. 1993. *La ilusión del fin* [The Illusion of the End]. Barcelona: Anagrama.

Botero, Beatriz L. 1999. "El exilio de los extraviados" [The Exile of the Lost]. *Número* [Number] 21:88.

Caballero, Antonio. 2004. *Sin remedio* [Hopeless]. Bogotá: Alfaguara.

Chaparro, H. 1999. "Sobre como huir de Bogotá escribiendo sobre ella" [On How to Flee From Bogotá by Writing About it]. *Número* [Number] 21:81.

Duby, Georges, ed. 1995. *Año 1000, año 2000. La huella de nuestros miedos* [Year 1000, Year 2000. The Footprint of Our Fears]. Santiago de Chile: Andrés Bello.

Garcia Canclini, Nestor, José J. Bruner, and Sergio Miceli. 1987. *Políticas culturales en América Latina* [Cultural Policy in Latin America]. Mexico City: Grijalbo.

Jimeno, Myriam. 1998. "Identidad y experiencias cotidianas de violencia." [Identity and Everyday Experiences of Violence]. Pp. 246-275 in *Cultura, política y modernidad*, [Culture, Politics, and Modernity], edited by Gabriel Restrepo et al. Bogotá: CES/National University of Colombia.

Martin-Barbero, Jesús. 1991. "Comunicación y ciudad entre medios y miedos" [Communication and City Between Media and Fears]. In VV. AA, *Imágenes y reflexiones de la cultura en Colombia*. [Images and Reflections of Culture in Colombia]. Bogotá: COLCULTURA.

Mockus, Antanas. 1998. "Cultura, ciudad y política" [Culture, City, and Politics], P. 18 in *La ciudad observada. Violencia, cultura y política* [The Observed City. Violence, Culture, and Politics], edited by Ismael Ortiz. Bogotá: Tercer Mundo Editores.

———. 1995. *Cultura ciudadana. Programa contra la violencia en Santa Fé de Bogotá, Colombia, 1995-1997* [Civic Culture. Program Against Violence in Santa Fé de Bogotá, Colombia, 1995-1997]. Bogotá: Mayor's Office of Bogotá.

Niño Murcia, Soledad et al. 1998. *Territorios del miedo en Santa Fé de Bogotá* [Territories of Fear in Santa Fé de Bogotá]. Bogotá: Tercer Mundo Editores.

Ordoñez, Montserrat. 2000. "Ángeles y prostitutas: dos novelas de Laura Restrepo" [Angels and Prostitutes: Two Novels by Laura Restrepo]. Paper presented at the international colloquium: Celebration of Female Contemporary Writing, Montreal, Concordia University, March 9-11.

Pécaut, Daniel. 1997. "De la violencia banalizada al terror: el caso colombiano" [From Banalized Violence to Terror: The Case of Colombia]. *Controversia* [Controversy] 171. 171:16.

———. 2001. *Guerra contra la sociedad* [War Against Society]. Bogotá: Espasa Hoy.

Perea, Carlos M. 1996. *Cuando la sangre es espíritu. Imaginario y discurso político en las elites capitalinas* [When Blood Is Spirit. Imaginary and Political Discourse in the Capital's Elite Class]. Bogotá: Aguilar/Institute for Political Studies and International Relations.

Rodríguez Freyle, Juan. 1994. *El carnero* [The Ram]. Madrid: Testimonio Compañía Editorial.

Sánchez, Gonzalo and Ricardo Peñaranda, eds. 1991. *Pasado y presente de la violencia en Colombia* [The Past and Present of Violence in Colombia]. Bogotá: Institute for Political Studies and International Relations, Cerec.

Thomas, Florence. 1996. "Pensar la ciudad para que ella nos piense... Una mirada femenina sobre la ciudad" [Thinking the City So that It Thinks of Us... A Feminine Gaze on the City] Pp. 409-414 in *Pensar la ciudad* [Thinking the City], edited by Fabio Giraldo and Fernando Viviescas. Bogotá: Tercer Mundo Editores.

Uribe, María T. 1996. "Bogotá en los noventa, un escenario de intervención." [Bogotá in the 90s, the Scene of an Intervention]. Pp. 391-408 in *Pensar la ciudad* [Thinking the City], edited by Fabio Giraldo and Fernando Viviescas. Bogotá: Tercer Mundo Editores, CENAC-FEDEVIVIENDA.

3. Transforming Expectations through
Cultura Ciudadana[1]

Henry Murraín

C olombian philosopher Antanas Mockus introduced his *Cultura Ciudadana* (Civic Culture) as a public policy strategy that could contribute to addressing problems of coexistence and systematic norm transgression experienced in many Latin American cities. According to Mockus, such issues depend on lack of harmony among the three systems that regulate people's behavior: legal, moral, and social norms. Building on that insight, I emphasize the dominant role played by social norms in achieving social harmony and question a traditional view on illegality traditionally held by many Latin American scholars who believe that norm transgression results exclusively from a lack of moral self-regulation.

Based on some of the main contemporary developments in social norm analysis and on the results of a series of empirical studies, I introduce an alternative approach to the study of illegality and systematic norm transgression in Latin American cities by taking a closer look at social norms and the way they influence people's behavior through the representations they hold. In particular, I argue that merely inculcating pro-norm attitudes in individuals is not enough for them to actually abide by the norms. People's expectations about one another's behavior, after all, deeply influence and shape their own behavior. This has practical implications, particularly with respect to policies, such as *Cultura Ciudadana*, that seek to mitigate systematic norm transgression and trigger cultural change. Policy programs that attempt to develop individual support for norms through communicational or training campaigns (such as workshops or courses) and that focus on inculcating support for norms in people may be insufficient if people persist in maintaining their representation of others as transgressors.

Norms and Transgression

In all societies, behavioral norms regulate the boundaries between what is acceptable and desirable on the one hand, and what is unacceptable and undesirable on the other. As Malinowski (1922/1986:28) showed, when anthropologists do ethnography by immersing themselves in communities, they engage in a detailed descriptive exercise that seeks to interpret behavior and to understand "the laws and norms implied in any cultural phenomenon." To a large extent, understanding societies is about understanding their norms.

Norms "provide the grounds for the predictability and regularity of social behavior" (Merton 1949/2002:239) and, as a result of their stabilizing role, they prevent "cultural chaos" (ibid.). Now, why do some individuals disobey them? Authors like Merton consider the analysis of norm-breaking and divergent behavior vital for the analysis of society. Traditionally, they used to regard it as an anomaly or as a deviation from social structural determinations of people's actions. Merton, however, questioned such an understanding of transgression as something abnormal and insisted instead that, to explain it, one would need to look into social dynamics. For such a purpose, he focused on two central elements in social and cultural structures, namely the *objectives* people try to reach and the *rules* by which they are supposed to attain these objectives (ibid.).

Merton's central hypothesis is that anomalous behavior constitutes the symptom of a dissociation between culturally assigned aspirations and socially validated means to reach them. Hence, anomalous behavior is the result of a tension between ends and means (ibid.). Objectives, goals, and aims make up the aspirational structure of society, which stipulates what pursuits are desirable within a given culture and what rules, means, and methods are legitimate to realize those aspirations. Objectives and norms therefore perform vital functions in the dynamics of everyday practices. Still, they are not always aligned. For example, some societies may highly reward success, but at the same time they may not provide equally strong emotional support of respect for the norms that regulate their attainment. As Merton (ibid.) puts it, whenever people seek to win irrespective of institutional rules, and when they see triumph just as "winning the game" instead of "winning according to the rules," then they will implicitly support effective means, however illegitimate. Whenever the intensity with which objectives are promoted is stronger than lending emotional support for norms, the desire to reach objectives "at any cost" will take a toll on norm vitality and will restrain individuals' emotional support for norms (ibid.). When this tendency is generalized, Merton continues, and therefore when the pressure towards the goals systematically weakens the respect for rules, society becomes unstable and experiences a lack of norms, or in Émilie Durkheim's terms, it falls into anomie (1893/2001:3).

Merton clarifies that his analysis is not moralist. He does not pretend to judge what is right or wrong. Instead, he explains transgression as part of the "natural" dynamics of social life. While he opposes the interpretation of anomalous behavior as an animal-like feature or uncontrolled instinct, his understanding of the way societies experience anomie does not explain transgression as mere lack of regulation but rather addresses the elements that produce it.

Law and Moral Regulation

For Durkheim, anomie is basically about lack of regulation. According to him, the desire for order and social stability can be carried out via in the law. If people's morals (i.e., internal regulation) were always solid and stable, there would be no need for the law. But since this is not the case, it is necessary to have an external point of view (the law) to guide us and bring about cohesion within society. Not all norms regulating our lives, though, are part of the law. Actually, most prescriptions describing what is right and wrong "lack any legal character; they are only sanctioned by opinion and not by the law" (ibid.), which is why the law cannot replace the vigor and the need for solid individual morals. As a consequence, to avoid anomie, a world without norms, it is necessary to have an external regulatory framework that performs as a permanent boundary for society as well as (and probably even more importantly) to educate the citizens.[2] This way, through reason and morals, people may internalize those constraints on behavior that may prevent them from undermining social cohesion.

Merton and Durkheim coincide on two aspects first, systematic transgression produces social chaos and second, the problem is ultimately related to society's moral regulatory capacity. In the case of Merton, though, moral regulation can be limited and overruled by culturally sanctioned incentives and objectives, whereas for Durkheim it boils down to a matter of a lack of moral restrictions.

Cultura Ciudadana: Coexistence as the Harmonization between Law, Morals, and Culture

Antanas Mockus builds on the idea that norms secure a minimum level of order in society, thereby preventing the "law of the strongest" from prevailing. The concept of *Cultura Ciudadana*, developed by Mockus (2002), is based on a description of human behavior as guided by three regulatory systems: the law, understood as the universe of formal norms determining what is allowed and what is not allowed in society; morals, viewed as the realm of informal norms that individuals have internalized as principles (usually referred to as "what my conscience tells me to do"); and finally, social norms, that is, the system of socially shared behavioral rules (for example, from the respect for the life of others to politeness through concern about what people say). According to this approach, the social chaos described by Durkheim and Merton results from the uncoupling of these regulatory systems. This entails a state of permanent tension in which formal rules imposed by society are not sufficiently accepted and respected by a significant group of individuals, whether this is because there is no moral support for the law, because of the existence of generalized social norms promoting unfulfillment, or because the degree of impunity cancels out the effect of legal sanctions (prison, fines, etc.).

In order to solve the above-mentioned uncoupling of these three regulatory systems and to develop coexistence, Mockus proposes a civic cultural policy that first acknowledges that individuals are simultaneously regulated by the law, morals, and social norms and therefore that people not only respond to the coercive power of the law but also to their own principles and to the need to fulfill social norms shared with others (Figure 171); and second, identifies powerful emotional mechanisms that can promote or restrain action and that can therefore be used to induce cultural change.

Legal Norms	Moral Norms	Social Norms
Admiration or respect of the law (Importance of compliance)	Conscious self-gratification (Peace with one's conscience)	Social admiration and recognition (Trust–reputation)
Fear of legal sanction	Fear of guilt	Fear of shame or social rejection

Figure 171: Behavior Regulation Mechanisms Proposed by Mockus.[3] Graph by Corpovisionarios.

At this point, it is important to stress that for Mockus governmental intervention in citizens' behavioral regulation is justifiable for the purpose of strengthening citizenship and coexistence. His *Cultura Ciudadana* is not a general policy that pursues some homogeneous "moralization" or "enlightening" of society, nor is it a totalizing project seeking (or at least wishing) that everyone falls under the same moral and social regulation framework. In fact, Mockus has shown his disagreement with any fundamentalist project (that is, one of moral homogenization). His idea of *Cultura Ciudadana* directs public policy towards the identification of minimum shared cultural elements, and the latter, he adds, is closely associated with the search for joy in diversity (Corzo and Mockus 2003). Inspired by the works of Rawls and Habermas, Mockus finds these minimum elements in the law.[4] Social consensus over the law, in turn, may yield a minimum regulatory framework capable of guaranteeing peaceful coexistence within a context of diversity.

In his *Introduction to Ethics*, Bernard Williams (1972/1998) describes three regulatory systems (legal requirements, moral norms, and social conventions). As his main concern is moral relativism, however, he does not register the regulatory force of social or cultural norms. Turning to economics, Douglass North (1990/2006) describes the lack of concordance between formal and informal institutions (in the current context, formal and informal norms) and the impact this has on the economic development of the nations. Yet he does not address the differences between moral and social norms in detail. In *The Civilization Process*, Norbert Elias (1939/2009) deals with the three types of norms, but he is mostly interested in the genetic relation between social and moral norms. Likewise, and mainly during his lectures at the Collège de France, which took place between 1978 and 1979, Michel Foucault described the internal and external dimensions of the regulation of behavior. However, his interest in highlighting the existence of an internal regulation "of governmental rationality" is meant to illustrate how sophisticated the modern exercise of power is on the part of public authority.

Unlike these authors, Mockus articulates the three regulatory systems under one single integrated framework. He does so with an eye to public policy, in relation to solving social problems that result from the uncoupling of legal, moral, and social norms. Furthermore, he not only addresses the punitive dimension of each system (fear, guilt, shame) but also shows the existence of positive regulatory mechanisms, thereby stressing that morals and social norms are powerfully sustained through recognition and moral self-gratification.

The Problem of Legalism

Antanas Mockus's strong interest in culture and education arose in the late 1980s, mostly in response to the persistent dependence within Colombian society on legalistic discourse to deal with large reforms and changes. Mockus (2012) questioned the pretension that implementing sophisticated formal regulatory frameworks could deliver such transformations, for example with regard to quality of higher education. These transformations, after all, would not mechanically result from legal reforms. Deep changes at the level of informal norms, (i.e., culture) would be needed. Nobel–Prize winning economist Douglass North (1990/2006) already saw this. The differential performance of formal institutions across societies crucially depends on differences in their underlying culture (morals and social norms). Specifically, North contrasts the United States with some Latin American countries.[5] As the performance of the law crucially depends on the articulation between formal and informal rules, we cannot therefore pretend to solve with the law what is totally absent in culture. As Herbert L.A. Hart (1961/2012) pointed out, any rule (even legal norms) needs interpretation.[6] Wittgenstein (1953/1988) had already shown that the actual meaning of "following the norm" can be worked out only in the light of a shared practice or custom.

The difference between legal norms on the one hand, and social and moral norms on the other, does not have to do with the fact that they are more precise nor with the fact that their content is different. What determines the legal, moral, or social character of a norm is not its content but the emotions and mechanisms acting upon individuals and supporting compliance. This is a point on which Mockus was clear when he reiterated the differences between fears associated with guilt, shame, and legal sanctions in relation to compliance with legal, moral, and social norms.

In summary, there is a clear difference between recognizing the law as a horizon (a guide for society, as described through minimum standards) and trying to solve all the problems of social life by introducing new legislation. This would rather constitute a vicious *legalism*. An excessive enthusiasm with the law may point to a society that lacks a minimum consensus in its practical life, a society that experiences fragmentation, anxiety, and paranoia about chaos. On a daily basis, the absence of a minimum agreement over informal norms is perceived as the chaos of anomie. The permanent hopelessness and fear from which everyone tries to escape are supposed to be mitigated by the implementation of new laws and stronger severity of enforcement on the part of institutions, as if the fear associated with legal sanctions could contain society's fearsome object. There is a desperate urge for the law to solve what does not exist in culture, and this is certainly impossible, just like the illusion of implementing *law without society*. No matter how sophisticated the legal regulatory framework is, if its content has no meaning in the light of social and moral norms, or receives no support from them, it will be useless.

Serendipity: A Controversial Finding (Social Versus Moral Norms)

The performance of the law depends on its cultural context. Hence the problem of social chaos (anomie) is not one of legal regulation. Based on Mockus's scheme about legal, social, and moral norms, we must look into the latter two in detail to determine if the problem, a lack of support leading to systematic norm transgression in Latin America, is moral or social in nature.

Let us start by asking what makes a human group deviate (sometimes in a very radical way) from the standards established by a given legal framework. At first sight, we might be tempted to think there is a moral disagreement or an unsupportive attitude towards the law, leading people to knowingly breach it. Mauricio García Villegas (2004) has followed this line of analysis. He argues that this attitude comes from the perception of the law as resulting from the illegitimate imposition on the part of some "alien and invading" political power—the Portuguese and Spanish empires in the case of Latin America—and therefore transgression in Latin America constitutes a rebellious reflex expressing lack of agreement with the social contract.

Others have proposed similar explanations by associating the phenomenon of legal non-compliance with moral considerations and by highlighting the individual and voluntarist character of transgression and even of corruption (Olivera 2001). According to this view, people carry out corrupted or illegal actions due to the social degradation that results from the lack of moral values or from a process of negative selection by which individuals with higher moral standards are weeded out of the economy, politics, and the public administration, thus paving the way for less honest citizens (Della Porta and Vanucci 2005; in Garay 2008:37).

It would seem that the problem of transgression and illegality in countries such as Colombia has to do with a general lack of support for the norms or, more precisely, a weakness in pro-norm attitudes. In this respect, many institutional efforts aimed at increasing legality and fighting corruption have focused on the issue of support for the laws governing society. As an example of this, to fight illegality and corruption in Colombia, a "Moralization Commission" was established by law in 2011. The Commission is composed of the president of Colombia, the attorney general, the heads of all control agencies, the presidents of the courts, the ministers of Justice and other high government officials.[7] The legal statute of the Commission insists on the need to work on morality and on "the other principles that must govern the public administration." It endows the Commission with a preventive character and calls on it to develop strategies to reduce corruption and illegality throughout Colombia.

As suggested by the "Moralization" project, the problem of norm transgression is associated with moral and personal attitudes, addressed by calling for pro-norm "moralization." The results produced by a recent survey on *Cultura Ciudadana*; however, seem to question this idea by showing that the purported generalized disagreement with norms is not so apparent, at least in the case of Colombia and some of the most important Latin American cities.[8] On the contrary, citizens tend to manifest a very positive valuation of normative and legal issues (Figure 172).

Merton (1949/2002) talks about serendipity when, in the course of an investigation, we find abnormal or unforeseen data that force us to propose new social theories or to expand previously existing ones. Such data inspires new analytical perspectives by compelling us to include aspects that had not been taken into consideration at the beginning of our research. In the present case, societies where stronger anomie is found report the highest levels of pro-norm attitudes in the survey.

Figure 172, for example, shows that Stockholm reports less enthusiasm for norms than the Latin American cities included in the survey. Establishing the comparison with this Scandinavian city is quite important because Sweden is recognizably one of the most honest countries in the world. In fact, it is usually ranked among the highest in terms of legality and transparency and lowest in corruption.[9]

Contemporary social science has repeatedly shown that individual preferences and moral convictions do not fully account for people's behavior. Specifically, the *social norms* literature produced over the last twenty years has been actively questioning this idea by showing how diverse human behaviors (probably most of them) can be understood by analyzing the role played by our beliefs about the behavior of others.

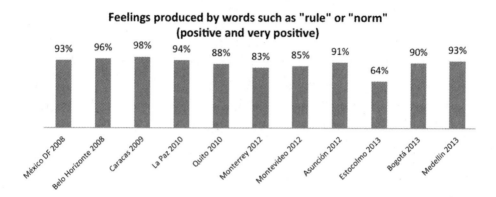

Figure 172: Answers to the question "Which feeling do the words 'rule' or 'norm' produce in you?" The figure presents "positive" and "very positive" answers. Graph by Corpovisionarios.

Social Norms and the Problem of Shared Expectations

In the last two decades the concept of social norms has attracted increasing attention even within disciplines in which it has not traditionally constituted a major topic of interest, such as economics. Even so, as Tena-Sánchez and Güel Sans (2011) point out, there is still no common agreement on what social norms actually are. Contributing to the debate, the philosopher Cristina Bicchieri has proposed a concept that broadly covers different perspectives on this issue. In her *Grammar of Society* (2006), Bicchieri proposes a definition of social norm that is both simple and widely recognized by social scientists working on this topic. Bicchieri distinguishes between *empirical* expectations that describe "what I believe others do" and *normative expectations* that stand for "what I believe others expect me to do, potentially leading to social rejection in the case of unfulfillment." The development of social norms, she argues, is associated with people's expectations about other people's behavior, and not with what they individually consider as desirable or preferable. Indeed, a person might have a particular attitude or moral stance toward a given behavior and expect that others will behave the opposite way. This is precisely what may shape the individual development of specific social norms.

Based on this, and considering the results presented in Figure 173, let us observe the opinion of the survey's respondents about their fellow-citizens' honesty.

They were simultaneously asked if they believe that *more than half* of the officers or *more than half* of the citizens are corrupt. The expression "more than half" makes it possible to observe if they consider corruption (i.e., transgression) to affect few or many people; in other words, if they consider it a rare or a generalized issue, respectively. As it appears in Figure 173, in this set of Latin American cities most people have a general perception of "the others" (e.g., of the rest of the people in their city) as cheating transgressors. This sets a contrast with the low perception of corruption observed in Stockholm (together with Belo Horizonte and Montevideo), both in relation to public officers and to other fellow citizens. In the remaining cities, people express their preference for norms and at the same time hold a generalized belief that they live in contexts whereby most people tend to be cheaters. If we are to take these opinions seriously, we may need to analyze their normative effects.

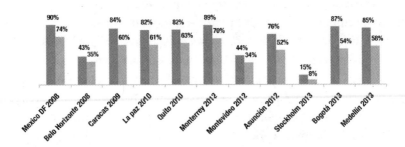

■ **Do you believe more than half of public officers are corrupt?**

■ **Do you believe more than half of the citizens are corrupt?**

Figure 173: Results of the survey about corruption opinion about both fellow citizens and public officers. Graph by Corpovisionarios.

The specific case of tension between proper attitudes (moral preferences) and expectations about others has been studied by a significant number of social scientists (particularly social psychologists), who have obtained quite relevant results to this article. In one of the most well-known works on social norms, Deborah Prentice and Dale T. Miller (1993) studied the relation between the personal attitudes of university students toward alcohol consumption on the one hand and their own perception of others' attitudes over the issue on the other. The results showed a clear divergence between the personal satisfaction experienced by the students with exaggerated alcohol consumption and their subjective estimation of the conformity of other students with such consumption practices.

Since beliefs and expectations about other people's behavior structure social norms, Prentice and Miller analyzed this specific case of divergence between personal attitudes (the moral stance of the individual) and the social norm. They found that average students are less willing to accept exaggerated consumption than (what he/she believes in relation to) the group. Inasmuch as they all have the same posture, one may observe a sort of "collective lie" or pluralistic ignorance. Most of them, in other words, do prefer something different from what they attribute to others.

What is most interesting about pluralistic ignorance is how students progressively align their position according to the social norm even though they perceive their attitudes to be different from those they attribute to the group. Prentice and Miller argue that this reorientation depends on the fact that the social norm has persuaded them or that they have internalized the feelings they had been expressing hypocritically. In any case, the ideas we have about other people's behavior are more than mere opinions, as they tend to build social norms, which in turn have a regulatory influence on our behavior.

Going back to Figures 172 and 173, we can observe how the most significant difference between Stockholm and the Latin American cities included in the study does not have to do with individual stances on rules and norms (the Swedish, indeed, are much less enthusiastic about them). The most outstanding contrast has to do with the expectation of probity on the part of fellow citizens, which is certainly more favorable in Sweden.

In conclusion, strictly legalist or moralist approaches to problems of social order are not enough to understand what might be happening in Latin American countries when it comes to explaining systematic norm transgression. Moral support for the law can be insufficient to explain non-compliance. According to Cristina Bicchieri (2006), the feeling of guilt, which might accompany law transgression, might reinforce our tendency to comply, but it is never the only nor the ultimate determinant of conformity to legal norms. The three regulatory system scheme (legal, moral, and social guidance) proposed by Mockus makes it possible to separately analyze the motivational mechanisms at stake in each case and to recognize that there are clear differences between the fears we experience in the face of guilt, social, and legal sanctions.

Social Genesis of Moral Norms

In his study of the social genesis of norms, Norbert Elias (1939/2009) shows how the moral norms we have internalized in the form of self-regulation or self-coercion must have necessarily passed through a social norm stage. According to him, if social norms associated with a specific behavior (or with a series of them) have not been developed, the corresponding moral norms can hardly be inculcated with a genuine self-coercive effect: "The behavioral precepts transmitted to the youth acquire their specific moral character under the progress of the feelings of shame" (ibid.:255).

A considerable part of the reflection proposed by Elias on the genesis of social behavioral norms, which are internalized as moral norms over time, is that it takes place in societies wherein the regulation of behavior or practices is marked by notions such as that of consideration or respect for others. This type of feeling manifests coercively in the form of shame, when we do not act according to expected standards. When shame is iteratively intensified and reproduced, it ultimately leads to a process of internalization known as moral support (guilt). For the German philosopher, there is a genetic relation between social and moral norms.

Although not highlighted in Elias's description of norm genesis, a positive and respectful valuation of others is important for us to experience shame, thus making it desirable to act the way that is expected from us. This idea is certainly important in the case of the Latin American cities in the above-mentioned survey, whereby such a positive valuation of others is quite scarce. Following Elias, in the case of Latin America the internalization of moral norms so that they act as self-regulatory mechanisms can only be possible if we transform the representations Latin Americans have of their own social context. It is necessary to start from a positive consideration of others, otherwise it becomes impossible to build appropriate social norms and the corresponding moral norms.

Mockus suggests that moral or self-regulation comes first, followed by social regulation, and then legal control. Occasionally, he has resorted to the metaphor of "three security rings" with reference to such a sequence: "The first security ring is your conscience; if it fails, the second ring corresponds to your neighbors, friends, and colleagues; in case self-regulation and mutual regulation are not enough, then there is the police and the tribunals. But precisely in that order" (Malaver 2012). Elias, however, shows that everything starts from social regulation. Moral regulation cannot be expected to play its role, if there has not been any social regulation. Moral norms, indeed, could not exist unless they were preceded by social norms.

Furthermore, the expectations and representations we have of other members of our society certainly play a leading role in the development of the latter.

In summary, Mockus assumes that social regulation fails as a consequence of moral regulation problems. Based on a socio-genetic approach, I would argue instead that social norms constitute a precondition for the moral norm to have some bite.

Cultura Ciudadana and the Transformation of Expectations

Mockus's *Cultura Ciudadana* approach, which seeks to harmonize the three earlier afore mentioned regulatory systems, has attracted international interest particularly in light of its impact in the city of Bogotá. To cite just a few examples, during Mockus's two terms as mayor, there was a substantial reduction in the murder rate, while traffic accident casualties declined by "75%, and household water consumption fell by half". Returning to the notion of the primacy of social norms, one may discuss at this point whether these behavioral changes resulted not only from a process of behavioral rule internalization, but also from the transformation of people's expectations in Bogotá about their fellow-citizens' behavior.

Through the civic games in which Mockus involved his fellow citizens, Bogotanos were given a chance to re-imagine (that is, to generate a new representation of) their fellow citizens. The *Cultura Ciudadana* interventions allowed people in Bogotá to build new representations of their neighbors, thus leading to the transformation of their expectations, and ultimately their behavior.

Although the concept of the social norm has been developed to explain the function of specific rules inducing specific behaviors, the statistical data presented seems to indicate that people's consideration of the "general" profile was attributed to others matters. More precisely, when others are represented as generally incapable of self-regulation and thus inclined to norm breaking, people behave below the expected standard.

In this context, *Cultura Ciudadana* actions appear as an antidote to a strange syndrome that exhibits the following features. As in any society, there are ideas about what is right and wrong, resulting in behavioral norms. Sometimes a generalized idea takes over the community, asserting that most people want or prefer to break morally validated behavioral parameters. In other words, the general opinion is that other members of society are morally "inferior" and have a marked propensity for transgression. Under such circumstances, that is, in the presence of asymmetrical representations of their fellow members of society, people behave undesirably (as evaluated in light of their own concept of correctness) in their daily lives. In the end, in societies manifesting such a syndrome, people tend to identify norm-breaking behavior as evidence of what people "essentially" are.

Conclusion

Although it is true that all societies develop rules that delimit what is right and wrong, the practical reproduction of these rules is not fully explained by the individual incorporation of norm-abiding feelings and ideas. The characterization of a social norm as a display of expectations about the behavior of others makes it possible to observe how these attributions have a molding effect on our behavior as well.

As already pointed out by Merton and Durkheim, anomie is a property of social and cultural structures. As such, it cannot be reduced to the sum of the attitudes of their individual members. In fact, the personal stances of most group members might not be coherent with the social result. In this context, transgression and illegality come to be a particular form of anomie resulting from pluralistic ignorance, that is, a situation in which the majority believes that sympathy for the norm is only their individual feeling, while the global tendency is different. Just as in the situation described by Prentice and Miller, we notice that people ground their estimations on the observed public behavior of their fellow citizens and wrongly assume that such behavior allows them to diagnose personal attitudes.

This asymmetric representation of others cannot be simply understood as a problem of pluralistic ignorance in relation to specific social norms. It has to do with the general understanding of others as morally childish or "inferior" from regarding their capacity to understand what is right or wrong and to behave accordingly. For this reason, describing the problem as a result of an expectation imbalance regarding specific behavior is insufficient, since we are dealing with the consideration of others as "always" prone to act below the standards of what "should" be done. Hence, we are dealing with a social norm system that also includes beliefs, attitudes, and practices aligned with this pejorative representation of others, that is, a cultural matrix that produces specific social norms.

Any *Cultura Ciudadana* policy trying to harmonize law, moral, and social norms should be mainly aimed at the transformation of shared expectations and at tuning into citizen preferences that, despite their similarities, may have not yet manifested and aligned in practice.

Endnotes

1 Text presented in May 2014 as part of the qualifying exams for the PhD program in Humanities and Social Sciences at the Universidad Nacional de Colombia.—NE

2 In this respect, the importance of education is fully developed in Durkheim (1902–1903/2002). For the French sociologist, moral education is the basis on which a cohesive society (i.e., one with an elevated degree of work division) can be attained. In this project, the educational system plays a central role. Education would provide individuals both with both the necessary intellectual development to serve society and with the moral formation leading to human dignity. These two elements are central to any social structure.

3 Mockus has described the three regulatory systems in question as "law, morals, and culture." In certain texts he associates culture with social norms. What differentiates the regulatory actions of the law, morals and culture is the type of emotions associated with transgression, namely fear of sanction (law), fear of guilt (morals), and shame (culture). For analytic purposes, in the present text, I shall use the concept of social norm that Mockus associates with culture in describing the third column.(Corzo and Mockus 2003:4).

4 "For Rawls and Habermas, the law basically expresses the minimum necessary morals upon which a society has managed to agree [...] The reference to the work of Turiel (2002) gives the possibility to characterize the specificity of morals and to show how children and adults recognize its superiority over conventional norms (i.e., those we simply agree upon, as if preparing a game)" (Corzo and Mockus 2003:7). Parentheses introduced by the author.

5 "The persistence of the institutional stamp initially imposed by Spain and Portugal played a fundamental role not only in the evolution of Latin American policies and perceptions, but in the differentiation of the history of this continent as well. In effect, after Independence, these countries adopted a similar set of norms to those of the British institutional tradition which, in turn, was also adopted in the United States" (North 1990/2006:135).

6 There is no doubt that tribunals structure their decisions in an effort to give the impression that they are the result of predetermined rules with clear and fixed meanings. In very simple cases this might be true; but the tribunals usually face situations in which neither the laws nor the precedents in which the norms are supposed to be contained lead to single results. In the most important cases there is always a choice. The judge has to choose among the different possible meanings of the words of a law, or between contrasting interpretations of what is "expressed" by a precedent (Hart 1961/2012:15).

7 Decree 4632 of 2011 partially defines the composition and functions of this commis-

sion, whose members, all from the national level, are: the president of the nation, the minister of the government, the minister of Law and Justice, the general attorney, the general controller, the general auditor, the president of Senate, the president of the Chamber of Representatives, the general prosecutor, the president of the Supreme Court of Justice, the president of the State Council, and the secretary of Transparency.

8   The survey on *Cultura Ciudadana* is a measuring instrument used to evaluate certain aspects of culture and citizen coexistence.

9   In this respect, see the *Corruption Perceptions Index* of Transparency International: (http://cpi.transparency.org/cpi2013/results/).

References

Bicchieri, C. 2006. *The Grammar of Society. The Nature and Dynamics of Social Norms.* New York: Cambridge University Press.

De Romilly, Jaqueline. 1971/2004. *La ley en la Grecia clásica* [Law in Classic Greece]. Translated by Gustavo Ponte. Buenos Aires: Biblos.

Durkheim, Émile. 1893/2001. *La división del trabajo social* [The Division of Social Work]. Madrid: Akal.

——.1902 – 1903/2002. *La educación moral* [Moral Education]. Madrid: Morata.

Elias, Norbert. 1939/2009. *El proceso de civilización: investigaciones sociogenéticas y psicogenéticas* [The Civilizing Process: Sociogenetic and Psychogenetic Investigations]. Mexico City: Fondo de Cultura Económica.

Elster, Jon. 1989/2006. *El cemento de la sociedad* [The Cement of Society]. Barcelona: Gedisa.

——.1999/2001. *Sobre las pasiones: emoción adicción y conducta humana.* [Strong Feelings: Emotion, Addiction, and Human Behavior]. Barcelona: Paidos.

Foucault, Michel. 2007. *Nacimiento de la biopolítica: curso en el Collège de France 1978-1979* [The Birth of Biopolitics: Lectures at the Collège de France, 1978-1979]. Translated by Horacio Pons. Mexico City: Fondo de Cultura Económica.

Garay, Luis Jorge. 2008. *La Captura y Reconfiguración Cooptada del Estado en Colombia* [The Capture and Coopted Reconfiguration of the State in Colombia]. Bogotá: Método Foundation, Avina Foundation, and Transparency for Colombia.

García Villegas, Mauricio, ed. 2010. *Normas de papel. La cultura del incumplimiento de reglas* [Norms on Paper. The Culture of Non-compliance with Rules]. Bogotá: Siglo del Hombre.

García Villegas, Mauricio. 2004. "No sólo de mercado vive la democracia. El fenómeno del (in) cumplimiento del derecho y su relación con el desarrollo, la justicia y la democracia" [Democracy Does not Live by Market Alone: The Phenomenon of (Non-)Compliance with the Law and its Relation to Development, Justice, and Democracy]. *Revista de Economía Institucional* 6 (10):95-134.

Hart, H. L. A. 1961/2012. *El concepto de derecho* [The Concept of Law]. Buenos Aires: Abeledo-Perrot.

Malaver, Carol. 2012. "Bogotanos enterraron en una década la *Cultura Ciudadana* de Mockus," [Bogotanos Buried Mockus's Decade Long Civic Culture], *El Tiempo*, September 16 (http://www.eltiempo.com/archivo/documento/CMS-12225158).

Malinowski, Bronislaw. 1922/1986. *Los argonautas del pacifico occidental* [The Argonauts of the Western Pacific]. Barcelona: Peninsula.

Merton, Robert K. 1949/2002. *Teorías y estructuras sociales* [Social Theory and Social Structure]. Mexico City: Fondo de Cultura Económica.

Mockus Antanas. 2002. "Convivencia como armonización de ley, moral y cultura" [Coexistence as Harmonization among Law, Morals, and Culture]. *Perspectivas:* [Perspectives] 32 (1):19-37.

———. 2012. *Pensar la Universidad* [Thinking the University]. Medellín: EAFIT University Press.

Mockus, Antanas and Jimmy Corzo. 2003. "Ley o moral: ¿Cuál prima?" [Law or Morals? Which Comes First?]. *Análisis Político* [Political Analysis] (54):3-17.

North, Douglas C. 1990/2006. *Instituciones, cambio institucional y desempeño económico* [Institutions, Institutional Change, and Economic Performance]. Mexico City: Fondo de Cultura Económica.

Olivera, Mario. 2001. "Hacia una Sociología del Derecho" [Towards a Sociology of Law]. *Revista Probidad:* [probity Journal] (16).

Platón. 2003. *Diálogos. Obra completa en 9 volúmenes.* Vol. 1, *Apología. Critón. Eutifrón. Ion. Lisis. Cármides. Hipias menor. Hipias mayor. Laques. Protágoras.* Madrid: Gredos.

Prentice, Deborah and Dale T Miller. 1993. "Pluralistic Ignorance and Alcohol Use on Campus: Some Consequences of Misperceiving the Social Norm." *Journal of Personality and Social Psychology* 64(2):243-256.

Tena-Sánchez, Jordi and Ariadna Güell-Sans. 2011. "¿Qué es una norma social? Una discusión de tres aproximaciones analíticas" [What is a social norm? A discussion of three analytical approaches]. *Revista Internacional de Sociología* [International Sociological Review] 69(3):561-583.

Turiel, Elliot. 2002. *The Culture of Morality: Social Development, Context and Conflict.* New York: Cambridge University Press.

Williams, Bernard. 1972/1998. *Introducción a la ética* [Morality: An Introduction to Ethics]. Madrid: Cátedra.

Wittgenstein L.1953/1988. *Investigaciones filosóficas* [Philosophical Investigations]. Barcelona: Instituto de Investigaciones Filosóficas UNAM.

4. Effective Rule of Law Requires Construction of a Social Norm of Legal Obedience[1]

Gerry Mackie

Introduction

Criminalization is a frequent remedy for harmful social practices. Often it fails. Imperial states in the past, and today's wealthy and powerful states, as well as the international organizations they influence, pressure and sometimes basically coerce weaker states into adopting the criminal prohibition of longstanding and widespread social norms. International human rights scorecards count enactment of a criminal prohibition as an achievement but, excepting regular laments about non-enforcement of the law, tend not to consider whether such prohibition has a beneficial effect. Using criminalization as the metric of success also creates the illusion that a difficult social challenge has been met, and thus inadvertently discourages allocation of resources to non-legal methods more likely to achieve the goal of harm reduction.

One could find hundreds of examples all around the world of legal failure in an attempt to change harmful social norms. The following is a perfunctory sample, only to illustrate a common pattern, and I do not mean to single out anyone for criticism.Female genital cutting is contrary to law or policy in almost all major practicing countries. Such laws are rarely enforced and have had little effect; in cross-national comparisons, there is no relationship between stricter laws or more rigorous enforcement on the one hand, or decreases in the practice on the other (Boyle and Corl 2010:199-201). Many such laws are enacted as a condition of receiving aid from national and international donors, including the United States, the International Monetary Fund (IMF), and the World Bank (Boyle 2002). Another example is caste discrimination, which has been illegal since the adoption of the Indian Constitution in 1950, and although there is progress, such discrimination is still common. The diagnosis for its persistence?: "The anti-discrimination efforts have been impotent through poor enforcement and a general lack of political will. The police and the low level judiciary have been at the center of the failure to prevent caste discrimination" (Sarkin and Koenig 2010:550). Prominent among proposed solutions: the international community, especially with bilateral pressure from other states, should "push" India towards compliance with international human rights norms (ibid.:575-576). In India, underage marriage has been illegal since the Child Marriage Restraint Act of 1929 (which set the legal age at fourteen for girls and eighteen for boys), the Hindu Marriage Act of 1955 (which set the legal age at eighteen for girls and twenty-one for boys), and the Prohibition of Child Marriage Act of 2006. Yet in 2002-2011, 47% of girls were married by age eighteen and 18% by age fifteen (UNICEF 2010). I suggest that eighty years of legal failure to deter underage marriage should prompt a reexamination of assumptions.

The main assumption at fault can be called the doctrine of *legal centralism* (criticized by Ellickson 1994; Galligan 2003; Williamson 1983): the belief that in most places most people obey most laws; hence, the law is always the best way to bring about social change and to reduce social harms. This belief is false. The law is often not obeyed, and the law is often not the best way to bring about beneficial social change. People are not objects that respond to written instructions; they are agents who act for reasons. As Robinson (2000) states:

> More than because of the threat of legal punishment, people obey the law because they fear the disapproval of their social group if they violate the law, and because they generally see themselves as moral beings who want to do the right thing, as they perceive it (P. 1861).

Legal centralism overlooks the moral—and especially the social—motivations for legal obedience.

The remainder of this essay explicates the strengths and weaknesses of legal and social methods of global development, expanding on the following points. Criminalization is an appropriate response to a criminal injustice (a deviation from accepted norms, its harmful consequences intended, knowingly committed by identifiable individuals whose wrongdoing should be punished). Nonetheless, criminalization is not an appropriate response to a structural injustice (in compliance with accepted norms, its harmful consequences are unintended and caused by everyone and no one). The proper remedy for a harmful social norm is organized social change, not fault, blame, nor punishment.

Effective rule of law requires a social norm of legal obedience in the population. Between Western Europe and Eastern Europe, for example, legal penalties and moral respect for the rule of law are equivalent. In the West, there are reciprocal expectations of legal obedience in the population, but in the East, there are reciprocal expectations of legal disobedience. Bribery and corruption in the East are morally condemned but socially necessary. They can only be changed by a shift in reciprocal expectations among a large enough portion of the population, a seemingly impossible task.

The *Cultura Ciudadana* (Civic Culture) program of the Mockus mayoral administrations (1995-1997, 2001-2003; now institutionalized in the Colombian non-governmental organization Corpovisionarios) invented and refined through practice successful methods to strengthen the social norm of legal obedience in Bogotá, thereby bringing about a more effective rule of law that greatly improved the lives of its citizens. How to establish the rule of law in the many settings where it is absent is an urgent question on the international development agenda, and progress is, at best, uncertain. *Cultura Ciudadana* is unique both in recognizing the necessity of the social norm of legal obedience and in showing how to construct it. Elsewhere, I have written about how Bogotá's revival is due more to pedagogical politics than to fashionable theories of democratic deliberation (G. Mackie 2015). The program requires meticulous analysis from the standpoint of social norms theory. The purpose of this essay, however, is to make known a sound theory and effective practice to strengthen the rule of law where it is weak—an issue of great interest to global policymakers.

Cultura Ciudadana's doctrine and civic practice is the harmonization of moral, social, and legal norms. Policy should rely first on moral regulation, next on social regulation and, only as a last resort, on legal regulation, and all three systems of regulation should be in harmony with one another.

Criminalization fails where there is no social norm of legal obedience, when a new legal norm is too far from a current social norm, or both. When a new legal norm is too far from a current social norm, law enforcement personnel have reasons not to enforce it, and citizens have reasons to disobey it. Extralegal sanctions, moral and social, in support of legal obedience are absent. A growing number of unenforceable laws can erode obedience to other laws and general legal obedience. It may be more effective to enact a new legal norm closer to the current social norm.

Then law enforcement personnel and citizens have more reasons to obey. Enacting enforceable laws, integrated with moral and social mobilizations, strengthens the social norm of legal obedience.

Liberal democracies hold the view that a reason to support the criminalization of an act is to reduce harm to others. However, criminalization is not justified if the benefit of the harm reduction intended by the law is outweighed by unintended harms done to other important values. Also, criminalization, which threatens deprivation of liberty, is only justified if it is significantly more effective than non-coercive methods of reducing harm, such as changes in moral and social norms. Many international campaigns to criminalize social norms would not survive application of standard liberal-democratic principles. Instead of assuming that law is automatically effective, policy design should consider whether and how a law hurts or helps on a topic of concern.

Why do People Obey the Law?

Tyler (2009) emphasizes legitimacy as a motivation to obey the law and urges that we should socialize citizens to internalize moral values so that we can rely on their voluntary cooperation with legal commands, rather than on punishment. In contrast, Becker's (1968) economic approach to crime and punishment emphasizes the material costs and benefits of the criminal act and predicts that a citizen would break the law whenever the expected value of the benefits exceeds the expected value of the costs. In other words, deterring crime increases its costs. A more nuanced view is that, across the diverse members of a population, both an acceptance of authority as legitimate and a fear of punishment are necessary for a state to achieve stable legal obedience. A study of German respondents (Kroneberg et al. 2010), for example, finds that the material costs and benefits of crime are irrelevant among the larger part of the population motivated by internalized norms. It is not that they weigh up normative costs and benefits with the material costs and benefits; rather, if normative considerations apply, material considerations do not. Thus, only a subgroup of the population is governed by material costs and benefits.

There is a tendency in several literatures to neglect the social norm of legal obedience. There are important exceptions to this tendency, notably the scholars of "legal pluralism" (Toomey 2010). Among legal philosophers, H. L. A. Hart (1994:86), for example, clearly states that internalized moral obligation, social pressure, and physical sanctions are among the motivations for legal obedience. Furthermore, consider that extralegal sanctions, moral and social, contribute to the reduction of harmful behavior, legal or illegal. American criminologists have found that the deterrent force of criminal law depends less on the legal sanctions themselves and more on the extralegal sanctions associated with the suspect's arrest, trial, conviction, or imprisonment:

> Studies investigating extralegal sanctions have shown that a belief that illicit conduct is wrong…and the fear of peer disapproval, embarrassment, or social stigma…discourage offending behavior. Further, several studies investigating the relative strength of both sanction forms find the conforming influence of extralegal sanctions to be far greater than that from legal sanctions…(Nagin and Pogarsky 2001:11)

These findings are appreciated by some legal theorists, notably Robinson (2000):

> The "normative" crime control mechanism, as it might be called, does not shape desires by threat of official sanction, as deterrence does, or through a coercive regime of official therapy or treatment, as traditional rehabilitation does. Nor does it simply give up on altering desire and simply detain or incapacitate the offender. Instead, it works through unofficial avenues to bring the potential offender to see the prohibited conduct as unattractive because it is inconsistent with the norms of family or friends and, even better, with the person's own internalized sense of what is acceptable.
>
> Not every potential offender is amenable to this normative pressure, but many non-offenders may obey the law because of it. Thus, code drafters must worry not only about controlling the hardest core amorals among us, but also about maintaining the criminal law's influence in keeping law-abiding that vast proportion of the population for which normative crime control is important, perhaps more important than coercive control (P. 1840).

Therefore, not only makers of the law but all those who design policies and programs should be mindful of the interplay among the moral, social, and legal aspects of community regulation.

Is it Right to Criminalize a Social Norm?

Iris Marion Young (2011) offered a social connection model of responsibility and community action in place of the liability model of responsibility that faults, blames, and punishes individuals. I shall illustrate her ideas by comparing the structural injustice of dowry to the criminal injustice of dowry deaths in India, borrowing from Brendan Mackie (2005).

Dowry is a practice wherein the bride's family is expected to make sizable, even lavish, gifts to the groom's family, both at marriage and thereafter. Since all families expect dowry for marriage, to forego it would make the daughter difficult to impossible to marry. It is a social norm, held in place by reciprocal expectations in the population. Because daughters will marry out and not contribute resources in the future to the natal household and because the natal family is additionally burdened with dowry obligations, the birth of a daughter is a loss compared to the birth of a son. The practice is a major cause of female inequality, incentivizing families to devalue the female child, to neglect her health, education, and welfare, and to commit female feticide and even infanticide.

Dowry death is practiced by a tiny minority of grooms' families, who systematically extort further payments from the brides' families by threat of abuse, murder, or forced suicide of the wife. Dowry death is a criminal injustice. It is ghastly but rare; the frequency seems to be about ten thousand deaths per year (Babu and Babu 2011), which is two orders of magnitude fewer than the number of dowry marriages initiated per year. Those who force dowry death are a minority who deviate from widely accepted social norms. The harmful consequences of their actions are fully intended. One or a few individuals are culpable in a dowry death. The remedy is backward looking: punishment of guilty individuals, for the purposes of retribution, deterrence, or both. Dowry itself, however, is a structural injustice. The prevalence of dowry in rural India from 1960 to 1995 was about 93% (Anderson 2007). Those who engage in the practice of dowry are in compliance with a widely practiced social norm, followed even by those who oppose it. The harmful consequences of the norm on the welfare of women are largely unintended byproducts. The practice exists as a matter of shared responsibility among all in the community of reciprocal expectation. It can change only if the reciprocal expectations among those in the community change. The remedy is forward looking: organized community change of the norm.

Legal centralism would apply the liability model of responsibility to dowry death, where the model's assumptions are appropriate and would probably reduce harm. Legal centralism would also unreflectively apply the liability model to a structural injustice such as dowry, where the model's assumptions are inappropriate, and could even increase overall harm. To threaten the vast majority of some population with the deprivation of liberty is harmful. It is more harmful if the law is ineffective because it is unenforceable, and is yet more harmful if the disobeyed law contributes to a weakening of the social norm of legal obedience. To criminalize a harmful social norm can be, on balance, a moral wrong.

Whether or not it is right to criminalize harmful social norms, is it effective to do so? Law often fails at this task. I suggest that such failure occurs in settings where there is a weak or absent social norm of legal obedience (or even where there is a social norm of legal disobedience), or when a new legal norm is too far from the current social norm, or both.

Where There is No Social Norm of Legal Obedience

The discord between legal norms and social norms is well documented in post-Soviet Europe. It is also a problem in some postcolonial regimes, for similar reasons. Galligan (2003) calls it a double pathology. For the Soviet regimes, and sometimes their imperial predecessors, law was purely instrumental, based only on threatened and actual punishment. Law was alien and external to the population; the state itself acted arbitrarily and was not constrained by law. Widespread social norms of getting around the law emerged in response, norms of bribery and corruption that would be pathological in better political circumstances.

A social norm is constructed from what one believes that others do (Bicchieri 2005 – empirical expectations; Cialdini and Trost 1998 – descriptive norm) and what one believes others think one is socially obliged to do (Bicchieri –normative expectations, Cialdini – injunctive norms). Empirical expectations and normative expectations are often aligned, but they can diverge: picture a table full of smokers sitting under a no smoking sign. When they diverge, people tend to do what they believe others do, rather than to do what they believe others think they have an obligation to do, according to one human-subject experiment (Bicchieri and Xiao 2009).

Reciprocal expectations of legal disobedience in a population are locked in: no few members of the population opt for obedience if others do not, even as the political regime that originally created such expectations vanishes from the scene. I know of no better illustration than the following remarks by Oleg Bocharov, chairman of the Legality and Security Commission of the Russian Duma, Moscow:

Ask any law-abiding citizen when corruption in Russia will diminish, and he will reply: when fines are made reasonable and the procedure of paying them simple. But he does not believe that the time will come when the inspector will stop soliciting bribes. The inspector on his part will tell you that he will stop soliciting bribes when he is paid a normal living wage. But he does not believe that the businessman will start paying taxes. The businessman says that he will start paying tax to the treasury and not to the inspector when taxes are reasonable and the state comes to show concern for him. But he does not trust the politicians and the bureaucrats. The politician tells you that he will agree to tax reform when the treasury gets enough revenue to pay decent salaries and social benefits. And then there will be growing social protest against bribery. But he does not believe that will happen (Kurkchiyan 2003:28)

Kurkchiyan contrasts a society whose members, I would put it, happen to be born into reciprocal expectations of legal obedience: "There is a strong belief that most of the people function most of the time according to the rule of law...and that to break the law, or even to bend it, is socially disgraceful" (ibid.:28); to a society whose members happen to be born into reciprocal expectations of legal disobedience: "People generally assume that everybody else is routinely disobeying the law. People are generally disrespectful, or believe that everyone else is, of all the agencies and agents of the law" (ibid.:29).

Legal disobedience, says Kurkchiyan, citing population surveys and systematic interviews, is contrary to the moral values of most post-Soviet citizens. They morally endorse the rule of law as much as do their Western European neighbors (Galligan 2003:1). If they expected that enough others would comply with the law, they would abandon bribery and corruption. They disobey, "not because they want to, but because they feel they must if they are to manage their lives and reach their personal goals under the conditions imposed on them by the society around them" (Kurkchiyan 2003:31). I add that it is a matter of luck, not of personal virtue, whether one is born into circumstances of legal obedience or of legal disobedience.

Thus, what is needed to overcome a "culture" of legal disobedience is probably not moral reform of the citizenry (and if such reform were needed and did succeed, it would still not be sufficient). What is needed is a shift from reciprocal expectations of disobedience in the community to reciprocal expectations of obedience to the law. One "does not believe that will happen," but Mockus's *Cultura Ciudadana* shows us how to help it happen.

The Harmonization of Norms

Mockus (N.d.:15) talks about a shortcut-culture among some Colombians, sometimes using means that are immoral or illegal, such as corruption or violence. Sometimes the harmful shortcut is forbidden by law but not by moral or social norms. Illegal shortcuts can even elicit social esteem, acceptance, and approval; there can be a social norm of legal disobedience. This leads Mockus to propose the doctrine and civic practice of harmonizing moral, social, and legal norms. By this, we mean neither the harmonization of all norms across society, nor their harmonization within the individual. Rather, in response to a particular harm, legitimate and effective regulation requires that the applicable moral, social, and legal norms be in harmony rather than discord. He distinguishes three regulatory systems and the main reasons to obey in each. His scheme posits emotions as motivators, which I think is mistaken: emotions properly interweave with beliefs to form judgments, but an emotion in isolation usually is not and should not be a sufficient reason to act (compare Hart 1994:180). Here is my amended version of the scheme.

	Legal Norms	**Moral Norms**	**Social Norms**
Positive Reasons	Respect for the law	Good conscience	Social approval
Negative Reasons	Legal penalties	Bad conscience	Social disapproval
A Typical Emotion in a Violator	Fear	Guilt	Shame

Figure 174: Regulatory Systems and Reasons to Obey. Table by Gerry Mackie, adapted from Mockus (N.d.).

Guillot (2012) of Corpovisionarios illustrates how the three regulatory systems apply to different actions. Helping a blind person cross the street is legally, morally, and socially permitted. In Colombia, to overpay taxes would be both legal and moral but would invite social ridicule. It is legal for a very Catholic woman to obtain an abortion in another country, although it would be morally and socially condemned.

Sometimes aggressive flirting is socially accepted, and legal, but it would also be considered immoral. In the past, bribing a police officer would be socially accepted or even expected in Bogotá, although illegal and immoral. Informal construction of neighborhoods was socially and morally condoned, although illegal. A destitute woman requiring an abortion might do so in good conscience, even though the act is socially and legally discouraged.

Corpovisionarios presents this scheme in its pedagogical engagements and surveys, and asks people to say what one reason moves them to obey the law, and what one reason moves others to obey the law. The typical modal responses in Colombia are that "I obey the law for moral reasons, but that others obey the law to avoid legal penalties" (Guillot 2012). This is consistent with a set of findings in social psychology that people tend to think of themselves as intrinsically motivated and of others as extrinsically motivated (Feldman 2011). Guillot suggests that people might mistakenly demand that the state apply harsh legal penalties, when in fact moral appeals would be more effective in the community.

In the shortcut-culture, says Mockus (N.d.), discord between harmful social norm and beneficial legal norm is frequent. The obeyed social norm trumps the disobeyed legal norm; people are more likely to do what others do than what others believe they are obligated to do. *Cultura Ciudadana* seeks to harmonize beneficial moral, social, and legal norms. Individual moral principles can be revised in individual and collective deliberations, the *concientización* (raising awareness) already practiced in Latin America. The greatest innovation in Bogotá was municipal efforts to change social norms in the city. Mockus proposed: since we don't obey legal norms, let's change social norms. The pedagogical politics advocated by Mockus can also promote public discussion of justifications for existing or proposed laws, and law enforcement can resort to pedagogy before force. New legislation and its legal enforcement should be accompanied by moral and social mobilization.

Municipal administration and law enforcement were reformed, and the state became more responsive. The city code was thoroughly revised to promote moral self-regulation first, mutual social regulation next, and law enforcement as the last resort. A core moral value appropriate to a pluralistic society was celebrated: human life is sacred. Controversial revisions of social and legal norms were justified in part by reference to that core moral norm. Homicide was reduced by harmonizing moral, social, and legal remedies, as were traffic fatalities. Tax collection was substantially increased by harmonizing remedies, including a request that citizens voluntarily pay 110% of municipal taxes due. The direct effect was that sixty-three thousand individuals from all social classes made the voluntary contribution; the attendant moral and social mobilization had the much larger indirect effect of a dramatic increase in tax compliance. Mockus (ibid.) says:

> Voluntary contributions are also the basis for a pedagogy by example. Social and moral norms of approval, admiration, and self-gratification come into play...There is a shift from a situation where paying taxes is a tiresome obligation to one where there are reasons to feel proud and to congratulate people who contribute. The strategy of mobilizing pride and social approval is a useful alternative to legal sanctions...In fact, a good part of the collection strategy in the Finance Secretary was based on persuasion, not coercion.

The state itself became more legal and respectful of citizens, inviting reciprocation from them. The social norm of legal obedience to particular firearm laws, traffic laws, tax-collection laws—an increasing number of individuals believing that an increasing number of individuals comply with the law—was strengthened with respect to each particular law. I propose that, just as multiple disobedience to particular laws can feed disobedience to law in general, multiple changes in obedience to particular laws can feed obedience to the law in general. That has been the subjective impression in Bogotá, which went from one of the most violent cities on earth to a better (yet imperfect) place.

For a group to escape the social trap of legal disobedience, enough people must believe that a significant amount of the population is becoming obedient to the law. This is the purpose of many of the superficially disparate and zany methods of *Cultura Ciudadana*. In this essay, because of its focus on the importance of the social norm of legal obedience to the rule of law, there is not space to report the content of those intriguing methods.

When the New Legal Norm is Too Far from the Current Social Norm

What happens if a law criminalizes a behavior supported as a social norm among most of the population or some insular part of it? The "criminal law's audience," says Stuntz (2000:1871), "is...law enforcers, not ordinary citizens...popular norms...regulate the conduct of the citizenry." Law enforcers do not enforce a new law too far from the current social norm (adapted from Kahan 2000). Police and prosecutors are usually granted discretion to selectively enforce the laws, and they are limited in resources. As a result, they will pursue crimes that enforcers and the local community most want to be punished. Additionally, judges and juries will be reluctant to punish if crimes that they think are worse are punished less, or not at all, by the courts. Recall the hypothesis reported in the introduction to this essay: that the failure of laws against caste discrimination in India is due to inaction by local police and courts. Finally, legal enforcement might even strengthen the harmful social norm by increasing public knowledge of the fact that many don't obey the law against it (Carbonara et al. 2008).

Citizens tend not to obey a law too far from local social norms. If the law is also too far from one's moral norms, then the law's legitimacy is weak, and although (on some accounts) the obligation to obey the law just because it is the law still applies, there is no further moral motivation arising from the content of the particular law. The citizen knows that law enforcers are unlikely to enforce this type of law. Social reasons to obey are weak or absent. The citizen knows that the new law is backed only by legal sanctions, not by extralegal sanctions of greater force. For all these reasons, the citizen knows that many others will not obey the law. The citizen, especially if he/she is disadvantaged by compliance may ask, "If others don't obey, then why should I?" Finally, a legal norm can be an outside option that works to increase the bargaining power of the weak living under local community social norms, a magnet pulling the social norm in the direction of the legal norm, but not if the legal norm is so far away that the threat to seek its enforcement is not credible to other members of the local community (Platteau et al. 2010).

Stuntz (2000) says that if there is pressure from above to enforce, it will likely be against the weaker parts of the community. He examines the prohibition of alcohol in the United States from 1920 to 1933. There was enough moral and social motivation to enact Prohibition, which added legal sanctions to existing moral and social sanctions. The legal norm, however, undermined moral and social regulation of alcohol consumption. Since vice is everywhere, enforcement is inevitably selective. Law enforcers are tempted to take the cheapest course of action, and thus enforced Prohibition in poor urban neighborhoods, and not among the middle and upper classes. Differential enforcement against the urban poor created a contempt for the law among them. According to Stuntz, Violations of laws associated with Prohibition and its enforcement were no longer socially stigmatized, collapsing the criminal pro-hibition's deterrent force, according to Stuntz.

The same counterdeterrent effects are reported today in poor urban neighborhoods in the United States that are exposed to differential enforcement of law, notably the enforcement of drug laws in (certain) African-American communities. The US incarceration rate is the highest in the world, and 25% of it is for drug violations. This has two effects, according to Fagan and Meares (2008). First, state budgets are limited, and increasing expenditure on formal legal controls means decreasing expenditure on activity that supports informal social controls in the community, such as health, education, and welfare. Second, "high rates of punishment produce 'stigma erosion'" (ibid.:170): the deterrent force of extralegal negative sanctions for law violation vanish, requiring ever-greater enforcement effort and harsher legal punishments. I add that this can even result in a new norm of pride and approval for having been imprisoned and an outlaw culture regulated by strong social norms including one of more general defiance of the law.

Thus, even if there were the political will to zealously enforce an unpopular legal norm, the results would likely be perverse. What can be done is to enact a new legal norm closer to the current social norm (Kahan 2000). For law enforcers, and for citizens too, their respect for the law in general is of greater weight than the moderate departure of the legal norm from the current social norm. The citizen expects that some citizens will comply voluntarily, that law enforcers will enforce, and that some would apply social pressure on the disobedient. An effective legal norm also works as an outside option strengthening the bargaining of the weak living under local community social norms (Platteau et al. 2010).

Here are some examples. In Bogotá, which suffered from high firearms mortality, it was politically and legally impractical to ban them. Yet Mockus was able to ban firearms on weekends (when, in association with alcoholic revelry, more shootings occurred). This was both practically enforceable and a prompt for many local discussions about the purposes and benefits of firearms regulation, thereby strengthening moral and social regulation of firearms in public. His administration also organized voluntary surrender of firearms, among several other elements of an integrated moral-social-legal mobilization to reduce violence. Gabon and Senegal, former French colonies, banned the practice of polygamy, with little effect. Each shifted to a more moderate—and effective—regime of monogamy or polygamy as a choice in the initial marriage contract (ibid.). In Ghana, a more moderate law bestowing inheritance rights on women and children was more effective than the previous extreme law (ibid.). Ostrom observed across many cultures that local community regulation of tragedy-of-the-commons dilemmas (use of common pasture, forest, or fishery) relies on negative sanctions that are initially mild and gradually increase (Cox et al. 2010).

Also, following Kahan (2000), we could turn what I call the legal-social-legal ratchet. Enact a moderate new legal norm. It is more respected, more enforced by legal and social sanctions, and more obeyed. As obedience increases, those motivated to do what others do obey as well. The effective law sparks discussions about its purposes, and if there are good reasons to believe that one is obligated to follow it, then they gain in salience. Changing moral and social attitudes lead politically to a moderately stronger new legal norm, which pulls the social norm further towards it. Later still, a stronger legal norm can be enacted and so on. Kahan traces the strengthening of legal and social norms in the US over thirty years regulating public smoking, domestic violence, and sexual harassment in the workplace. If one were to transplant strong antismoking regulation from a country with a long history of the ratchet, to a country with no history of the ratchet, the regulation would fail, as I am told happened in Albania. The US ratchets described by Kahan were not deliberately designed but were the result of the forces of change clashing with the forces of tradition. When the forces of change gain an extraordinary advantage, such as when a stronger power pressures a weaker one, ineffective law can result. Advocacy of the ratchet is not motivated by conservative sentiments but by a concern that law effectively obtains its intended results. Sometimes, of course, the situation requires that strong laws be enacted immediately.

Many international institutions have ongoing agendas of imposing laws on states, on the legal-centralist assumption that law reliably causes social change. A first-best alternative would be for these institutions instead to support harmonizing moral-social-legal engagements, carefully designed to respect autonomy and to minimize harm. There is some motion in this direction; for example, a bill pending before the U.S. Congress contemplates an array of programs to prevent underage marriage (including pressure for criminalization) which, with vision, *could* be implemented in an integrated fashion (H.R. 6087: International Protecting Girls by Preventing Child Marriage Act of 2012; 112th Congress, 2011–2012). Legal centralism is so firmly entrenched, however, that we should also consider second-best alternatives. If institutional imperatives continue to require criminalization of harmful social norms, then enforcement of the law often should be explicitly moderate. For example, the law can state that its penalties will begin to apply five years hence, or that they can increase gradually over time. Officials could convict violators but suspend penalties. By declared policy, the law would only be enforced in egregious circumstances or at the request of local communities or women's associations; or a violation would trigger official-local community consultations.

Whether moderation in substance, scope, penalties, or enforcement is appropriate depends on the context. For example, in Sudan and the Horn of Africa, some influential policy makers proposed the substitution of an intermediate form of female genital cutting for the extreme version. Those familiar with the practice and with successful abandonments elsewhere correctly opposed this attempt at moderation: research showed that there was widespread confusion about what would count as intermediate, whether an intermediate form were actually adopted would be impractical to verify, and the social effort required for successful abandonment of the practice altogether would be about the same as the social effort required for moving to an intermediate form.

Minimize Harm

What justifies coercively interfering with an individual's liberty by arrest, trial, fine, reparations, or imprisonment? For liberal democracies, it is usually justified by some version of John Stuart Mill's harm principle ("On Liberty," 1859, in Mill 1989). Which version is best is controversial, but let's focus on Feinberg's (1987) prominent formulation:

> It is always a good reason in support of penal legislation that it would probably be effective in preventing (eliminating, reducing) harm to persons other than the actor (the one prohibited from acting) *and* there is probably no other means that is equally effective at no greater cost to other values (P. 26).

Reducing harm to others is a good reason to support criminalization of an action. Not all harm to others is wrong; for example, J.S. Mill (1859/1989) argued that there are winners and losers in honest economic competition but that overall such competition is better for society. If an action that harms others is wrong overall, the question remains whether law and its enforcement do greater wrong to other values. Romantic betrayal is quite harmful, but for the state to criminalize it would be a cure worse than the disease; even if we would tolerate the police and courts poking their noses into intimate relations, the legal process is ill suited to discover the truth, if any, in such disputes.

Criminalization of a harmful social norm could result in greater harm, for example, to family relations, or to religious freedom, or to social peace. If, due to unpopular pressures from outside or within the country, unenforceable prohibitions are regularly enacted, then that will erode people's general respect for the law, doing greater harm in other realms. The harms that a law and its enforcement impose on citizens are not justified if that law is not actually effective in reducing the harms it purports to punish. Even if a law were effective, we must consider whether non-legal methods could be at least as effective and applied with less harm to other values. Many purportedly liberal international efforts to "push" and "pressure" weaker states into adopting criminal prohibition of harmful social norms would not survive application of the harm principle, would be illiberal.

The imposition of legal centralism is the most coercive form of the social-engineering approach to global development assistance that treats humans as objects. Non-coercive methods can also be objectionably paternalistic, supplying resources on the condition that the recipients perform particular actions, or supplying biased and one-sided information in order to "manipulate" the "behavior" of the "targets." The indirect, autonomy-respecting, capacity-enhancing approach to development aspires to engage humans as agents (Ellerman 2006). Would it be improperly paternalistic for a state to engage in a public pedagogy intended to alter moral and social norms among its citizens? Not necessarily. As we have seen, it can be justified to coerce in order to minimize harm to others, to protect the conditions of their autonomy. Deploying public pedagogy to minimize the same harms must be at least as justified as coercion. The liberal democratic state is obliged to refrain from coercively interfering with the right of free expression. Yet the state's expressive powers—as educator, speaker, spender—can, within limits, be legitimately deployed in support of basic rights such as life, liberty, and equality, which are presupposed by the liberal democratic state (Brettschneider 2012).

Law Can Retard or Hasten Change in a Harmful Social Norm

Ellickson (1994) studied how ranchers in Shasta County, California, settled cattle ranging disputes and found that they followed local social norms, not the applicable legal norms; indeed, there was a social norm against resorting to legal remedy. In face-to-face relations among equals, and assuming little harm to people outside the group, favoring social norms over legal norms could easily make most people better off. In populous anonymous settings undergoing change, however, a beneficial system of social norms is less likely to emerge and spontaneous correction of harmful social norms is even less likely. The state is needed to foster and coordinate a moral, social, and legal framework among pluralistic and anonymous citizens (Galligan 2003).

There are manifold relationships between legal norms and social norms (McAdams and Rasmusen 2007). Here are some of interest in this context. Independent of its regulatory purpose, a law can have expressive purpose (McAdams 2000): laws can indicate that society judges something as wrong, and thereby be a reason for people to morally reevaluate the prohibited action, as well as to socially regulate compliance. In contrast, an unpopular and ineffective law can drive harmful activity underground, perhaps carried out under more dangerous conditions. A law can do more harm than it prevents by foreclosing the possibility of honest public discussion, making more effective moral and social methods of regulation impossible to undertake. Laws against female genital cutting, for example, drive the practice underground and lead parents to cut their daughters at younger ages; the threat of prosecution can cause survey respondents to falsely report abandonment (Boyle and Corl 2010:200). Biased survey responses create the illusion of harm reduction.

The interplay between legal norm and social norm in any particular context requires careful study. Shell-Duncan et al. (2013), for example, scrutinize the relations between the legal norm and social norms regulating FGC in Senegal (I have added my personal knowledge about these events as well). In Senegal, shortly after the first organized community abandonments of FGC, the president unexpectedly rushed to enact legislation harshly criminalizing the practice. The communities that had acted socially to abandon FGC opposed the law on the grounds that other communities should, and would, voluntarily abandon it after due consideration. The new law did discourage public discussion and progress on voluntary approaches for some time. In response to popular outcry, the government indicated that the law was more aspirational, expressive in intent, and that it would only be enforced in quite narrow circumstances: a few were arrested but not prosecuted; later a few were prosecuted but given suspended sentences, and later some circumcisers were jailed but released early. As time went by, the law in its expressive aspect was sometimes offered as one reason for voluntary community abandonment, and the law became a resource in such communities. Potential transgressors could be warned that they would be taken to the police. The combination of social and legal sanction is potent (see also UNFPA-UNICEF N.d. on the insufficiency of law alone).

Conclusion

For those who would advance the realization of human rights, there are good moral and practical reasons to discard legal centralism and take up a contextually variable and integrated moral-social-legal approach to harm reduction. General legal disobedience can do great harm. Effective rule of law is absent in many settings. To bring it about requires construction of a social norm of legal obedience. Mockus's *Cultura Ciudadana* shows us how to do that. It is worthy of study, elaboration, refinement, and dissemination.

Endnotes

1 Acknowledgements: I am grateful for advice from students and staff in the summer course on organized social norms taught to UNICEF personnel by Cristina Bicchieri and me at the University of Pennsylvania where this material was first presented, especially the advice from Francesca Moneti (then at UNICEF) and Javier Guillot (then at Corpovisionarios). I'm also especially grateful to Bettina Shell-Duncan for inspiration and discussion on this topic over the years.

References

Anderson, Siwan. 2007. "The Economics of Dowry and Brideprice." *Journal of Economic Perspectives* 21(4):151-174.

Babu, Gopalan Retheesh, and Bontha Veerraju Babu. 2011. "Dowry Deaths: A Neglected Public Health Issue in India." *International Health* 3(1):35-43.

Becker, Gary. 1968. "Crime and Punishment: An Economic Approach." *Journal of Political Economy* 76(2):169-217.

Bicchieri, Cristina. 2005. *The Grammar of Society: The Nature and Dynamics of Social Norms*. Cambridge, UK: Cambridge University Press.

Bicchieri, Cristina, and Erte Xiao. 2009. "Do the Right Thing: But Only If Others Do So." *Journal of Behavioral Decision Making* 22(2):191-208.

Boyle, Elizabeth Heger. 2002. *Female Genital Cutting: Cultural Conflict in the Global Community*. Baltimore: Johns Hopkins University Press.

Boyle, Elizabeth Heger, and Amelia Cotton Corl. 2010. "Law and Culture in a Global Context: Interventions to Eradicate Female Genital Cutting." *Annual Review of Law and Social Science* 6:195-215.

Brettschneider, Corey. 2012. *When the State Speaks, What Should it Say?* Princeton: Princeton University Press.

Carbonara, Emanuela, Francesco Parisi, and Georg von Wangenheim. 2008. "Legal Innovation and the Compliance Paradox." *Minnesota Journal of Law, Science, and Technology* 9:837-860.

Cialdini, Robert, and Melanie Trost. 1998. "Social Influence: Social Norms, Conformity, and Compliance." Pp. 151-192 in *The Handbook of Social Psychology*, 4th edition, vol. 2, edited by Daniel T. Gilbert, Susan T. Fiske, and Gardner Lindzey. Oxford: Oxford University Press.

Cox, Michael, Gwen Arnold, and Sergio Villamayor Tomás. 2010. "A Review of Design Principles for Community-based Natural Resource Management." *Ecology and Society* 15(4):38.

Ellerman, David. 2006. *Helping People Help Themselves*. Ann Arbor: University of Michigan Press.

Ellickson, Robert C. 1994. *Order without Law: How Neighbors Settle Disputes*. Cambridge: Harvard University Press.

Fagan, Jeffrey, and Tracy L. Meares. 2008. "Punishment, Deterrence and Social Control: The Paradox of Punishment in Minority Communities." *Ohio Journal of Criminal Law* 6:173-229.

Feinberg, Joel. 1987. *Harm to Others.* Oxford: Oxford University Press.

Feldman, Yuval. 2011. "The Complexity of Disentangling Intrinsic and Extrinsic Compliance Motivations: Theoretical and Empirical Insights from the Behavioral Analysis of Law." *Journal of Law and Policy* 35:11-51.

Galligan, Denis. 2003. "Legal Failure: Law and Social Norms in post-communist Europe." Pp. 1-24 in *Law and Informal Practices: The Post-Communist Experience*, edited by Denis Galligan and Marina Kurkchiyan. Oxford: Oxford University Press.

Galligan, Denis, and Marina Kurkchiyan, eds. 2003. *Law and Informal Practices: The Post-Communist Experience.* Oxford: Oxford University Press.

Guillot, Javier. 2012. "Citizenship Culture as Public Policy." Slide show and oral presentation at Project Concern International, San Diego, February 6.

Hart, H. L. A. 1994. *The Concept of Law*, 2nd ed. Oxford: Clarendon Press.

Kahan, Dan M. 2000. "Sticky Norms: Gentle Nudges vs. Hard Shoves: Solving the Sticky Norms Problem." *The University of Chicago Law Review* 67:607-645.

Kroneberg, Clemens, Isolde Heintze, and Guido Mehlkop. 2010. "The Interplay of Moral Norms and Instrumental Incentives in Crime Causation." *Criminology* 48:259-294.

Kurkchiyan, Marina. 2003. "The Illegitimacy of Law in Post-Soviet Societies." Pp. 25-46 in *Law and Informal Practices: The Post-Communist Experience*, edited by Denis Galligan and Kurkchiyan. Oxford: Oxford University Press.

Mackie, Brendan. 2005. *Blame and Belief: Structural Female Inequality and Justice.* Manuscript.

Mackie, Gerry. 2015. "Traveling to the Village of Knowledge." Pp. 85-106 in Deliberation and Development, edited by Patrick Heller and Vijayendra Rao. Washington D.C.: The World Bank.

McAdams, Richard. 2000. "A Focal Point Theory of Expressive Law." *Virginia Law Review* 86:1649-1729.

McAdams, Richard, and Eric Rasmusen. 2007. "Norms in Law and Economics." Pp. 1573-1618 in *Handbook of Law and Economics*, vol. 2, edited by A. Mitchell Polinsky and Steven Shavell. Amsterdam: North Holland.

Mill, John Stuart. 1859/1989. *"On Liberty" and Other Writings*. Cambridge: Cambridge University Press.

Mockus, Antanas. N.d. "Bogota's Capacity for Self-Transformation" and "Citizenship Building." Manuscript.

Nagin, Daniel S. and Greg Pogarsky. 2001. "Integrating Celerity, Impulsivity, and Extralegal Sanction Threats Into a Model Of General Deterrence: Theory And Evidence." *Criminology* 39(4):865-892.

Platteau, Jean Phillipe, G. Aldashev, and Z. Wahhai. 2010. "Confronting Oppressive Customs: Reformism or Radicalism?" Working Pape of the Center for Research in Economic Development (CRED), University of Namur. Manuscript.

Robinson, Paul. 2000. "Why Does the Criminal Law Care What the Layperson Thinks is Just? Coercive Versus Normative Crime Control." *Virginia Law Review* 86(8):1839-1869.

Sarkin, Jeremy, and Mark Koenig. 2010. "Ending Caste Discrimination in India: Human Rights and the Responsibility to Protect (R2p) Individuals and Groups From Discrimination at the Domestic and International Levels." *The George Washington International Law Review* 41:541-576.

Shell-Duncan, Bettina, et al. 2013. "Legislating Change? How Social and Legal Norms Influence the Practice of Female Genital Cutting in Senegal." *Law & Society Review* 47(4):803-805.

Stuntz, William J. 2000. "Self-Defeating Crimes." *Virginia Law Review* 86:1871-1899.

Toomey, Leigh. 2010. "A Delicate Balance: Building Complementary Customary and State Legal Systems." *The Law and Development Review* 3(1):156-207.

Tyler, Tom. 2009. "Legitimacy and Criminal Justice: The Benefits of Social Regulation." *Ohio Journal of Criminal Law* 7:307-359.

UNICEF (United Nations International Children's Emergency Fund). 2010. "Statistics." (http://www.unicef.org/infobycountry/india_statistics.html).

UNFPA-UNICEF (United Nations Population Fund-United Nations International Children's Emergency Fund) Joint Program on FGM/C. N.d. "Senegal: Human Rights Key to Ending FGM/C; Legislation is Just One Aspect of an Effective Campaign."

Williamson, Oliver E. 1983. "Credible Commitments: Using Hostages to Support Exchange." *American Economic Review* 73:519-540.

Young, Iris Marion. 2011. *Responsibility for Justice.* Oxford: Oxford University Press.

5. Social Norms and the Cross-Border Citizen: From Adam Smith to Antanas Mockus

Fonna Forman[1]

As mayor of Bogotá, Antanas Mockus committed his administration to institutional integrity, transparency, collaboration, and social justice. He simultaneously deployed pedagogic strategies designed to disrupt civic dysfunction from the bottom-up, by changing the behavioral patterns of a violent and lawless city. He wrote: "As mayor I assumed a fascinating pedagogical task: learning and teaching in a community of seven million people. I decided to confront the culture of the city, its languages, perceptions, customs, clichés, and especially people's excuses" (Mockus 2012:128-9).

In this essay I will engage Mockus's pedagogical work as both a theoretical system with a long intellectual lineage in social theory as well as a practical model that can be, and has been, adapted to other contexts. First, I will situate Mockus's pedagogical interventions in what might seem an unlikely tradition of thought—an eighteenth-century European discourse about social norms that emerged from the Scottish Enlightenment. I will focus particularly on the social thought of Adam Smith, who exemplified the Scot's commitment to investigating human behavior empirically and contesting the predominant rationalism of British and Continental thought at the time. This eighteenth-century empirical tradition is the intellectual root of what eventually became modern social science, and I have argued elsewhere that Smith was the keenest observer of social behavior within this tradition (Forman 2010). He was also perhaps the most important eighteenth-century theorist of social norms. No thinker provided as complete a theoretical system and as rich an empirical portrait of the operation of social regulation as Adam Smith (Forman 2013).

The parallels between his formulations and the theories that ground Mockus's successes in turbulent late-modern Bogotá are striking and worth elaborating. Specifically, I will emphasize their essential agreement on the nature of human motivation, social coordination, and the dynamics of culture formation and culture shift, including important similarities in their thoughts on the relation between social norms and moral norms and the comparative ineffectiveness of the law in regulating human behavior.

After establishing these intellectual affinities, which I believe add considerable theoretical depth to the theory and practice of social norms, I will turn in the second part of the essay to engage Mockus's work in more practical ways, explaining why his pedagogical approach to urban transformation has inspired interventions in cities across Latin America and further afield, including most recently along the US-Mexico border region, where I live and work. I will describe the recent collaboration between Mockus (and his think-tank Corpovisionarios) and the Center on Global Justice at the University of California, San Diego to design a "Survey on Bi-National *Cultura Ciudadana* (Civic Culture)" for application in the cities of San Diego and Tijuana.

Antanas Mockus and the Legacy of Adam Smith

Some will dismiss any suggestion that an intellectual history of Antanas Mockus should begin with a figure conventionally understood (sometimes maligned, sometimes celebrated) as the father of free-market capitalism. It is an interpretation obviously not without basis. Smith's book *The Wealth of Nations*, published in 1776, is a manifesto of open markets and small states; where justice is "negative," confined to the protection of property; where humans are motivated primarily by self-interest; and where social bonds are a product of "enlightened selfishness"—in other words not intrinsic but instrumental, the result of cost-benefit calculation.

It would seem to border on insult, then, to link such a system to a figure like Mockus, who committed his mayoral administration to an "ideal of justice" grounded in "social equity" and the "redistribution of wealth." As Mockus (N.d.) described his mandate:

> Those who have come to the world at a disadvantage, those who live in extreme poverty and lack the means to have access to health services, or to adequate nutrition and education, have an inalienable right to a minimum standard of

living. These minimum conditions must be sufficient for each to be able to begin building their own life as they imagine and desire it (Pp. 6-7).

Before making my case, I should spend a moment salvaging Smith from the caricature that has been foisted on him by succeeding generations left and right, eager to deploy his legacy for ideological purposes. The conventional interpretation of Smith neglects what he actually said about human motivation, as well as the historical circumstances that provide context for what he wrote about the state and markets. Smith in fact was a moral philosopher by training, not an economist. While he wrote a major treatise on economy in 1776, he also wrote another book, an ethical treatise called the *Theory of Moral Sentiments*—which was revised five times over thirty-one years, between its first appearance in 1759 and its final, dramatically revised sixth edition in 1790, the year of Smith's death. In the *Moral Sentiments*, Smith presented an empirical portrait of human motivation that seems at odds with the utilitarian portrait conventionally attributed to him today. He opened the treatise as follows:

> However selfish soever man may be supposed, there are evidently some principles in his nature, which interest him in the fortune of others, and render their happiness necessary to him, though he derives nothing from it except the pleasure of seeing it (Smith 1759/1982:9).

The *Moral Sentiments* is an extended reflection on what this means. It is a settled fact among Smith scholars today that the ethical themes of the *Moral Sentiments* are the motivating center of Smith's intellectual life, though this more contextual reading of Smith has not yet worked its way into public knowledge, which has been dominated by paradigms of privatization and supply-side economics and a denigration of the welfare state.

In fact, the *Wealth of Nations* itself is a far more complex set of ideas than is often acknowledged. Without actually reading the book, one might not know that Smith was a vicious critic of greedy accumulation, of the commodification of human relationships, and of the degradation of the working poor in early industrial capitalism. Smith was also among the century's most vocal critics of European slavery and empire—indeed, his fear of the state was rooted primarily in this since state policy in the eighteenth century was too easily hijacked by the agendas of corrupt international trading companies like the East India Company (Muthu 2008). And perhaps most astonishing of all, Smith devoted an entire section of his seminal *Wealth of Nations*, indeed the longest section of this biblical economic treatise, to elaborating the state's provision of public goods and the necessity of cultivating a vibrant Civic Culture, producing citizens who are civically engaged with one another and aware enough to collectively constrain the vices and corruptions of their leaders.

These are dimensions of classical economic thought—the primacy of the ethical, the limits on accumulation, the degradations of the laboring poor, the virtues of an engaged citizenry, the importance of public goods, public space, public education, and public health—all the provisions that private entities do not have proper incentives to carry out well. These elements of Smith's thinking have lost currency in the last two centuries, as neoliberals have effectively severed capitalism from its classical roots.

So I hope I have alleviated at least some of the initial reaction against linking Mockus with Smith and perhaps even posed a provocative justification for doing so, oriented around a shared commitment to public goods. But this paper is not primarily about public goods, though this theme will re-emerge periodically. The intellectual lineage I wish to elaborate here teases out a particular strand of Smith's thought about the endogenous springs of social coordination. It is my claim here that an intellectual history of Antanas Mockus and his theory of Civic Culture must begin with the theories of human motivation and the empirical descriptions of modern social coordination and culture formation, first articulated as a coherent system by Adam Smith.

My discussion here will proceed in two parts. First, I will discuss the informal social processes through which modern societies cohere without the formal institutions of state coercion, law, or religion—how people regulate each other, according to Adam Smith, and collectively produce social norms.[2] I will note important similarities with Mockus's idea of mutual cultural regulation.

In the section that follows I will discuss how Smith conceived of the difference between social norms and moral norms, a distinction that is essential to Mockus's theories and techniques of urban intervention. We will see that the category of the moral emerged in Smith's thought, as in Mockus's, to provide an external vantage point and correction to social norms that had become corrupted.

Informal Social Coordination

Adam Smith insisted that modern societies cohered after the dissolution of traditional forms of formal authority (kings, churches, static feudal hierarchy) because our relationships with one another are regulated by the conventions and habits that emerge through informal social interface in shared spaces over time. His empirical account of informal social coordination was contained in his book *The Theory of Moral Sentiments* of 1759, which he wrote as a young man, and which more people should read today. There, Smith offered a brilliant account of human cooperation and culture formation as emergent social phenomena, a view that cognitive scientists and neuroscience researchers are confirming today with increasingly sophisticated diagnostic technologies in the lab.[3] But Smith, as an eighteenth–century Scottish empiricist, did not know what mirror neurons were; he had no fMRI to observe the function of our brains. He studied human behavior the only way he could—by observing and describing in rich detail the texture of social life among the people around him how cooperation actually seemed to work.

Smith's account of informal social coordination proceeds in two general "stages." The first describes a spectator observing the behavior of another person, arriving at a judgment about that behavior, and somehow communicating judgment—what Smith calls "sympathizing" with the other. One thinks of Mockus's use of the iconic "thumbs–up" and "thumbs–down" as a social technique to express approval and disapproval of another's behavior:

> … we distributed "Citizenship Cards" to drivers. These cards had a thumbs-up on one side and a thumbs-down on the other, and citizens could use them to express approval or disapproval for each other's behavior. This was an example of how mutual cultural regulation could change behavior and increase compliance with the law (Mockus 2012:131).

Smith's account helps us understand why the thumbs were such an effective regulatory tool. The second stage of social coordination for Smith describes the *disciplinary* impact that the spectator's surveillance—the thumb—has upon the other. Not only are we creatures who judge, we are also "approbative" creatures, who desire the love and approval of those around us. Indeed for Smith (1759/1982), we don't even know who we are without using the other as a mirror:

> Were it possible that a human creature could grow up to manhood in some solitary place, without any communication with his own species, he could no more think of his own character, of the propriety or demerit of his own sentiments and conduct, of the beauty or deformity of his own mind, than of the beauty or deformity of his own face. All these are objects which he cannot easily see, which naturally he does not look at, and with regard to which he is provided with no mirror which can present them to his view. Bring him into society, and he is immediately provided with the mirror which he wanted before. It is placed

in the countenance and behavior of those he lives with, which always mark
when they enter into, and when they disapprove of his sentiments… (P. 110).
The judgment of the other regulates our behavior, leads us to constrain ourselves,
to behave as we believe the spectator expects us to. Again:

We examine our persons limb by limb, and by placing ourselves before a look-
ing-glass, or by some such expedient, endeavour, as much as possible, to view
ourselves at the distance and with the eyes of other people (ibid.:112).

In the flows of ordinary social interaction, then, we are regularly confronted with
choices—to indulge in present, undisciplined gratification or to calmly pursue a
duller but more mature enjoyment of love, approval, and congenial relations with
those around us. We are always negotiating these ends, calculating how best to
bring our behavior into harmony and "concord" with the expectations of those
around us. Smith offers a developmental account of how a child becomes "master
of himself" as he enters school and discovers that his peers will not tolerate the
tantrums he once indulged in so freely at home. Maturity takes hold of the child
as he begins to use others as a mirror in which he learns the social norms of his
context and regulates the temper of his behavior (ibid.:145). This developmental
way of thinking about "mutual regulation" runs through Mockus's thought as well.
In the chaotic urban tangle of Bogotá in the 1990s, Mockus sought to uproot what
he called a "short-cut culture," a sort of embedded restlessness and social immatu-
rity, which too quickly tipped moral choice in the direction of the immediate. We
might say that he designed pedagogies that could elongate the moment of decision
and cultivate a more reflective culture of delayed gratification (Mockus N.d.:12-19).

Culture Formation and the Corruption of Social Norms

The dynamics of mutual regulation sustained Smith's faith in the spontaneous order of modern social life—that coordination could be achieved without exogenous
coercion or law. This is the story I have provided up to this point. But from the
perspective of *Cultura Ciudadana*, and in connection with Mockus's work on social
norms, the theory becomes even more interesting from this point forward.

Smith's description of social coordination is also an important theory of culture formation, indeed the most textured theory of culture formation in early modern European social theory. Smith used the language of "custom" rather than "cul-

ture" (Smith 1759/1982:201), but he provided a systematic, empirically nuanced account of the processes through which the self learns the tastes and values of the people with whom it lives and interacts, becomes a member of that particular moral culture, and then passes that culture on to others. We might think of this as the transmission of social norms, passed from each generation to the next through the infinite repetition of sympathetic interfaces, or in Mockus's language, infinite experiences of mutual regulation.

When compounded over time, disciplinary engagements with others progressively constrain our understanding of ourselves, of others, and of the world, and they serve to condition the moral criteria that we will use when we judge others. An individual in Smith's theory comes to know who she is, what she believes, and the standards by which she will judge herself and others through a lifetime gazing into what Smith called the "mirror of society," participating repetitively in sympathetic exchanges over time with those around her. For Smith, conscience is a synthesis of "habit and experience" (ibid.:135). An agent internalizes her experiences with actual spectators so that at a certain point in time she can turn her eyes inward and away from their gaze when evaluating herself and her world. This is the process through which we learn and teach others what it means to be "us," and what emerges is a normative culture that is particular to those who participate in it. Society's norms are internalized as we move through the social world, producing an internal regulatory system that some have compared to a Freudian superego, or what political theorist Sheldon Wolin (1960:344) at the dawn of the cultural revolution in the United States called "a socialized conscience."

The problem is that the social norms around which cultures cohere are not always beneficial; sometimes they are corrupt or "warpt" (Smith 1759/1982:200). If norms of legal obedience govern social behavior, if one lives in a society regulated by the norms of mutual respect and human dignity, then mutual regulation will reinforce those norms.[4] But if one lives in a society where slaveholding, racism, "short-cutting," criminality and gang violence, or cronyism are the norms, where chauvinism and violence against women is accepted, where paying one's taxes is understood as optional, where natural resources like water are understood as expendable, and so forth, then mutual regulation will not constrain these troubling behaviors but actually reinforce them. We see this in cases around the world, from genital cutting in West Africa, to honor killings in Afghanistan, to road rage and "boob jobs" in Los Angeles. The examples are obviously endless. Mutual regulation alone is insufficient for a healthy and just social order, since it will simply reinforce whatever norms happen to govern relations among people. In a corrupt, violent society, mutual regulation will reinforce corruption and violence. In an egalitarian society mutual regulation will serve to constrain disrespect.

In his discussion of "custom," Smith (ibid.:201) articulated the problem clearly: people "brought up amidst violence, licentiousness, falsehood, and injustice... have been familiarized with it from their infancy, custom has rendered it habitual to them, and they are very apt to regard it as, what is called, the way of the world..." Smith's examples were European slaveholding and the Greek practice of exposure, what he described as a "dreadful violation of humanity"—"can there be greater barbarity...than to hurt an infant?" Even Plato and Aristotle were "led away by the established custom" and "instead of censuring, supported the horrible abuse" (ibid.:209-10).

This is precisely where "moral norms" emerged in Adam Smith's otherwise thoroughly empirical account of social coordination: to provide an external vantage, an alternative source of value, to challenge social norms that had become "warpt." He referred specifically to the need to bring social norms in harmony with moral norms, which required that one make an additional theoretical move beyond culture—a move that necessarily embodies moral judgment. It is this very sort of "move" that remains at the center of debates about perspective and judgment in cultural theory today. I would argue that Smith was among the most perceptive cultural theorists of the eighteenth century, with the richest empirical narrative not only of the sociological processes that produce culture but also the difficulties of changing corruptions of culture endogenously and the need for an external vantage point.[5]

This issue of intervening into intransigent cultural patterns lies at the heart of what Mockus did during his administrations and what Corpovisionarios helps cities do now. Take again Mockus's (N.d.) campaign against "short-cut culture" in Bogotá, which he described as a sort of moral shortsightedness:

Colombians pride themselves on being very ingenious and creative, and on being able to get out of specific problems with great ease through their own capacities. This ability for innovation frequently leads us to assume costly consequences or to affect other people in undesirable ways. I define shortcut culture as the social acceptance and even promotion of actions that are mainly aimed at obtaining immediate results without taking into account future costs or negative effects on socio-culturally distant individuals or communities... According to Jon Elster's work in social sciences one could explain shortcut culture in the following way: in the first place, as the result of high discount rates when assessing future costs or benefits; then, as an inability to project, which is a kind of shortsightedness. (P. 12)

Mockus's campaign against "short-cut culture" deployed pedagogical interventions that would disrupt conventional behavioral patterns, opening spaces of reflection and opportunities for "self-binding" whereby citizens would pre-commit to healthier social norms. One of the greatest lessons of Mockus's administration was that harmful social norms needed to be replaced with moral norms that honored and respected human life. Improving the quality of urban life is not only about improving government, public infrastructure, and social services; these interventions must be accompanied by interventions into the social norms that maintain harmful urban habits. Meeting urban violence with stricter penalties will not work. Law and order solutions don't interiorize new values.

Moral Norms and a New Civic Imagination

But people have problems talking about morality in democracies. Morality is typically understood as a "universal" source of value and out of place in modern democracy, which is based on open contestation and agonistic accommodation to the views of others. Generations of post-war political thinkers, chilled by radical abuses of political power, have insisted that the role of politics must be constrained to providing a framework for public disagreement and debate and not a resolution to the tension. There is obviously much to agree with in this argument, since there will always be disagreement on fundamental moral principles. Democratic governments at every scale must do whatever they can to ensure open debate, to enable spaces of contestation, and to actively prevent diverse voices from being stifled. Nevertheless, a democratic government must also never lose sight of basic egalitarian moral norms and must never let these norms become subordinated to the private interests of a few. When this happens, democracy is undermined, becomes oligarchy, and even the open spaces of contestation risk becoming a "feel good" camouflage for power—like "public" spaces in shopping malls and the gentrification of our main streets.

This is precisely why only a particular kind of political leadership can be entrusted with articulating the content of moral norms and intervening into civil society to activate them. Power and private wealth masquerading as political morality is not a new danger—indeed it was Plato's greatest fear in the *Republic*. The conflation of politics with economic power needs to be scrupulously avoided. Morality is safe for democracy only when it is stewarded by political leadership committed to social equity—only when political leadership is combined with a tenacious commitment to eliminating political corruption and building a new public trust in government.

What Mockus's work demonstrates is that social norms, which emerge informally from the bottom-up, can only be re-oriented morally at the urban scale through top-down municipal intervention. As mayor of Bogotá, Mockus declared emphatically the moral norms that should regulate relations among citizens: that human life is sacred, that radical inequality is unjust, that adequate education and health and the capacity for aspiration are inalienable human rights, that gender violence is intolerable, that paying one's taxes and conserving natural resources are duties of citizenship, and so forth. And he developed a corresponding urban pedagogy that deployed sometimes outrageous performative interventions to demonstrate precisely what he meant, inspiring generations of civic actors, urbanists, and artists across Latin America and the world to think more creatively about disrupting behavioral conventions and transforming social behavior.

In 2013 we invited Antanas Mockus and Corpovisionarios to the San Diego-Tijuana border region to help us cultivate a new *Cultura Ciudadana*, driven by a moral claim: that human beings, regardless of formal legal citizenship, regardless of race and socio-economic privilege, have dignity, deserve equal respect and basic quality of life. In the next section, I will explore the distinctive challenges of our binational region and our collaboration with Mockus and Corpovisionarios to design a "Survey on Bi-National *Cultura Ciudadana* (Civic Culture)," which was just completed in February 2015.

The Cross-Border Citizen: Cultura Ciudadana in the Borderlands

I live and work in a territory of conflict and poverty that divides two cities, two countries, two continents, and two hemispheres. This region exemplifies the global phenomenon of uneven urban growth of the last decades, as some of the poorest, most marginalized informal settlements in Latin America sit just minutes away from the mega-wealthy suburban paradise of what is often called "America's finest city." The border cities of San Diego and Tijuana together comprise the largest binational metropolitan region in the world, with one hundred thousand border crossings every day. This border region is also a microcosm of all of the conflicts and deprivations that globalization has inflicted on the world's poorest people, intensified by two geo-political institutions: first, the North American Free Trade Agreement (NAFTA) that enables multi-national corporations to set up *maquila-doras* on the peripheries of Tijuana, where they generate massive profits freed from any restriction on labor practices, environmental protection, and urban zoning regulation; and second, an aggressively militarized political border that cuts across and radically disrupts the social, economic, and environmental flows that situate and give meaning to people's lives in this region.[6]

I am a political theorist by training. Much of my research has focused on recuperating the ethical, social, spatial, and public dimensions of Adam Smith's thought. My research has become increasingly practical in recent years, having established an academic center focused on global justice and development (the University of California, San Diego [UCSD] Center on Global Justice, which I direct with fellow political theorist Gerry Mackie) and another focused on theories and practices of equitable urbanization, with a particular emphasis on Latin American cities (the UCSD Cross-Border Initiative, which I direct with architect and urbanist Teddy Cruz). The projects I am describing in this essay have evolved through my partnership with Cruz, who is best known for his work on informal urbanization and border dynamics in cities across Latin America and particularly in the neighborhoods flanking the San Diego-Tijuana border (Cruz 2015).

Our collaboration fuses my work in social and political theory with Cruz's work in architecture and urbanization, and it has focused on the convergence of informal flows in twenty-first century cities (social, moral, economic, spatial, urban) and the investment by formal institutions in enabling and scaling up these bottom-up dynamics. Our work investigates the informal circulation of beliefs and norms among the co-habitants of space and how this generates patterns of group life, for both good and bad effects. We are also interested in the physical manifestation of social informality, particularly among people navigating conditions of scarcity, and the emergence of informal settlements, economic flows, and general strategies of collective survival.

Our work on informal urbanization in the Tijuana-San Diego border region sits at the threshold between Latin America and the United States, both physically and intellectually. We've discovered that the most compelling examples of progressive urban transformation do not come from American cities, or other cities of abundance, but have emerged primarily from Latin America in the last half century, as cities across the continent mobilized alternative strategies of development and emergent forms of grassroots participation and civic imagination to counter the effects of neoliberalism, most frequently aligned with Cold War dictators and oligarchy. There is no other continental region in the world with so many examples of inclusive urbanization, where municipalities invested political capital and economic and intellectual resources in the informal sectors of society and mobilized cross-sector networks to rethink public infrastructure and social service. The North has much to learn from the South when it comes to social justice in the city.

From Antanas Mockus we have learned specifically that intervening in the city at the behavioral level is the essential groundwork for infrastructural intervention when rethinking urbanization today.[7] His work in Bogotá was an entry point for us into a lineage of visionary Latin American urbanists in the second half of the twentieth century committed to the relationship of citizenship, urban pedagogy, cultural action, and equitable development. Situating Mockus in this tradition is not to diminish his originality, only to say that he was a receptacle as well as an iconoclastic producer of late-modern Latin American municipal culture. Several examples in the last half-century stand out, particularly in Brazil, from São Paulo's Serviço Social do Comércio (SESC, Social Service of Commerce)—privately run, non-profit institutions that emerged in the late 1970s to promote culture and healthy living in urban communities; to Mayor Jaime Lerner's interventions into the urban fabric of Curitiba with a series of low-tech acupunctural gestures designed to ignite civic participation, paving the way for the renowned Bus Rapid Transit system; and the emergence of participatory budgeting in Porto Alegre in 1989 that enabled citizens to decide deliberatively how a percentage of the city budget would be allocated.

Mockus absorbed these lessons, infusing them with a richer understanding of individual and social behavior and the power of performative artistic intervention to transform urban life. He first came into office in 1995 at a moment of intense violence and urban chaos in Bogotá; and while Bogotá's transformation has been "spotty" in the years since (in Mockus's [2012:131] own words: "originality has its costs and is difficult to sustain"), it is nevertheless hard to imagine that Enrique Peñalosa's celebrated infrastructural interventions—the *Transmilenio* bus rapid transit system and the *Ciclovía*—could have succeeded without the normative shifts that Mockus's behavioral interventions initiated and the public trust in institutions and culture of taxation that they enabled.[8] More recently, the celebrated "Social Urbanism"[9] of Medellín, Colombia, in which *Cultura Ciudadana* mobilized the dramatic infrastructural interventions led by Mayor Sergio Fajardo's administration, as well as more recent cases of participatory urbanization in Cali, La Paz, and Quito, were clearly inspired by what happened in Bogotá.

Justin McGuirk (2014) recently named this urban tradition in Latin America "radical cities," which embodies what Cruz and I have described as a new "civic imagination"—a way of thinking collectively and publicly about urban life that has lost its way. This is seen in the United States, which has denounced its own New Deal history and seems to have eliminated the very notion of "the public" from its dominant political discourses, and incrementally across Europe. During recent years of decline in public spending, we have seen a misguided faith in austerity and the demonization of the welfare state. It is from Latin America that we have learned most about designing municipal and civic processes that yield more equitable forms of urbanization in a neoliberal world of uneven growth. In recent years, we have been interested in translating these Latin American lessons and carrying them to the Tijuana-San Diego border region, where we are investigating informal urban dynamics and *Cultura Ciudadana* as tools to transform urban policy and improve quality of life for all in our region.

In late 2013, we discussed Mockus's work with the Democratic candidate for mayor in San Diego. After he was elected, we introduced him to Mockus at a dinner in Tijuana; soon after he summoned us to his office to support his "neighborhoods first" agenda by developing an agile unit to experiment with public space and strategies of civic engagement in neighborhoods long neglected by municipal investment.[10] The Southeastern quadrant of San Diego is comprised of ethnically diverse, largely immigrant communities who have internalized their own marginality, having for decades been sidelined from a political process beholden to downtown and suburban interests in this city of tourism and sprawl. Our agenda was to identify municipal projects that would push hard against the policies and processes of a deeply reactive, regulatory planning culture in the city and the developer interests that have historically dominated it. We were also determined to advance a new cross-border municipal agenda with our counterparts in Tijuana, to frame a new era of cooperation between the cities.

The Civic Innovation Lab became a cross-sector municipal think-tank that we modeled explicitly after examples in Bogotá and Medellín—particularly the administrations of Mockus (1995-1997; 2001-2003) and Sergio Fajardo (2003-2007). Indeed, when we presented our first (it would be our only) annual budget to a conservative San Diego City Council in the summer of 2013, our slide show began with an image of Mockus in a red cape as "Super Citizen", with the provocative claim that we needed a fresh approach to civic engagement in San Diego's most challenged neighborhoods, beyond conventional advocacy planning methods that are too often hijacked by people from *Not in My Back Yard* (NIMBY) and identitarian agendas.

Indeed, Bogotá and Medellín have been the most important political and civic models for us—Bogotá for Mockus's commitment to an open and collaborative model of governance and his strategies of infiltrating the behavioral patterns of civic dysfunction with performative gestures designed to penetrate and change social norms; and Medellín for Fajardo's commitment to municipal reorganization and civic ingenuity combined with dramatic infrastructural interventions to tackle violence and poverty. In recent years we have been partnering with the main actors in these now legendary stories of urban transformation to better understand and translate their best ideas. Cruz and I have written elsewhere about our work in Medellín (Forman and Cruz 2015).[11]

The Survey on Bi-National Cultura Ciudadana (Civic Culture)

In partnership with Mockus and Corpovisionarios, we produced the very first "Survey on Bi-National *Cultura Ciudadana* (Civic Culture)," an instrument to measure *Cultura Ciudadana* in the San Diego-Tijuana border region ("New San Diego-Tijuana Survey" 2015). We worked with the municipalities of San Diego and Tijuana as well as dozens of partners across sectors on both sides of the border—government agencies, cultural institutions, foundations, the private sector, university researchers, community-based and civic organizations across issues of public health, environment, immigration, arts and culture, and so forth. We spent nearly a year designing a survey that was responsive to the needs and challenges, as well as the resources and aspirations, of this distinctive binational region.

Corpovisionarios has applied (and frequently reapplied) its Survey on *Cultura Ciudadana* (SCC) in forty-five cities across Colombia, an additional ten cities across Latin America (México City, Belo Horizonte, Caracas, La Paz, Quito, Monterrey, Uruguay, Asunción, Panamá City, and Santo Domingo) and recently in Stockholm.

They have developed an impressive database of comparative urban research on issues of legal culture, behavior regulation systems, mobility, tolerance, tax culture, public safety, agreements, civic participation, mutual regulation, public trust, and victimization.

The San Diego-Tijuana survey produced entirely new challenges and opportunities for Corpovisionarios. This was their first survey of a US city, and particularly of a US border city, where citizenship means something very particular. In early conversations with Mockus, he was eager to explore *Cultura Ciudadana* in a context like ours where the designation "citizen" is frequently used as a divisive patriotic tool to separate and marginalize people, often wrapped in the flag of "us versus them," to defend private rights against the encroachment of the other—rather than its more aspirational usage in Latin American cities, where citizenship has been mobilized as a participatory tool to integrate what has been divided despite conflict and difference, and to emphasize public ends. In a press interview with Mockus just after the binational survey was completed, he discussed the difference between the United States and Latin American conceptions of citizenship, drawing on actual survey results to illustrate his point:

> Something that impressed me a lot is that defense of property as a justification for illegal behavior is much higher in San Diego than in the rest of Latin America… I believe the concept of citizenship in the US is behind the times as compared to Latin America (ibid.).

Perhaps this also explains why many people in the United States typically are not receptive to the door-to-door survey format that Corpovisionarios regularly performs in Latin American contexts, and which was ultimately performed in Tijuana by the highly regarded Mexico City–based firm, Consulta Mitofsky. We were advised that a door-to-door survey in San Diego would not work. San Diego needed an alternative method of convening a survey panel, which produced a set of complexities that took many months to unravel.[12] Corpovisionarios had designed an Internet-based survey for Stockholm, which had worked well. So we resolved to do an Internet-based survey and identified a reputable survey research company, GfK, that specializes in convening probability-based Internet panels in the United States. The survey was ultimately and successfully applied electronically, though the panel size was considerably smaller than the panel convened in Tijuana.

The San Diego-Tijuana survey was not a typical single-city study but Corpovisionarios's first study of two cities. But they were not parallel surveys intended mainly to compare the similarities and differences of the two cities—though they did do this—but a survey of two border cities that are intimately intertwined across a militarized border wall that has been fortified over time as a national bulwark against porosity. The challenge in our case was to design a survey that would convey the interpenetration and interdependence of these two cities with one another rather than rehearse the same old stereotypes that these cities have always held of one another. How useful would it be for us to know, for example, that victimization is higher in Tijuana? Or that public trust in institutions is higher in San Diego?

We decided to produce city-based surveys that would each stand independently as a resource to the individual cities as discrete entities and whose data would contribute to the Corpovisionarios's database for purposes of comparative urban analysis. But additionally, we resolved to develop an all-new "bi-national" module intended to measure the relationships and flows between these two cities, as a binational region. Our claim has always been that the border wall ultimately cannot disrupt the informal, normative, social, economic, and environmental flows that define our region. The purpose of the survey was to document these informal flows to compel a new era of public self-knowledge as well as cross-border municipal and cross-sector collaboration. And we envisioned that this new module might be adapted to other cities straddling the US-Mexico border, as well as other contested borders across the world. The survey advances the idea of a "cross-border citizen," whose conception of citizenship is organized around shared values and social norms, common interests, and a sense of mutual responsibility around which a new binational *Cultura Ciudadana* can be cultivated—beyond the formal jurisdictional boundaries that too rigidly define both cityhood and citizenship in the United States.

One final significant distinction is that Corpovisionarios's surveys on *Cultura Ciudadana* are typically commissioned by municipalities where mayors and their staffs lead the project. In our case, the project was housed at a university (at the Center on Global Justice at the UCSD) and led by two professors, Cruz and myself. This organizational structure obviously shifted the center of activity and commitment to outside the municipalities, although both mayoral offices remained partners throughout, participating in the survey design process, the public communication of results, and committing to participate in the binational prioritization exercises that will take place in the next stages. Housing the survey at the university also subjected our project to a lengthy review process by our campus

Institutional Review Board (IRB), which scrutinizes academic research on human subjects for ethical compliance. This review ultimately made it impossible for us to survey children under the age of eighteen. Corpovisionarios typically surveys youngsters, which means that any comparison between Tijuana and San Diego with the other cities in the database will need to be adjusted for age. However, despite these complications, housing the survey on campus was ultimately a great asset. For one thing, it enabled us to insulate—and likely save—the project from political volatility in San Diego over the past two years.[13] And our university base ultimately produced an exceptionally high quality survey, since an impressive team of social scientists and survey research experts (including renowned public opinion research consultant Barbara Lee and UC-San Diego political scientists Tom Wong and Gerry Mackie) collaborated with us and Corpovisionarios in the design of the survey instrument, the coordination of its application with survey research firms in both cities, and the current process of interpreting the data.

Over the years, a progression of mayors in San Diego and Tijuana have signed Memoranda of Understandings, promising to collaborate on shared concerns such as economy, research and development, and risk management. We want to believe that these MOUs are inspired by the noblest of intentions, but they have tended to be largely symbolic, lacking specificity and content.[14] One of the most important lessons of Antanas Mockus's views on achieving peace in Colombia is that it makes no sense to sign formal agreements at the top if citizens themselves do not *interiorize* a new civic consciousness. This is precisely how we see our work in the border region. While municipal agreements are essential—and indeed we have been working with the mayors to build new relations of trust and cooperation from the top-down, seeking to generate content for formal agreements to cooperate—we are interested primarily in identifying the existing informal dynamics that bind these two cities together, the cross-border urban flows through which a new regional civic consciousness can emerge from the bottom up (Forman and Cruz 2015a).

Conclusion

I conclude by returning to Adam Smith's (1759/1982:201) thoughts about the difficulty of uprooting cultural beliefs and habits: people "brought up amidst violence, licentiousness, falsehood, and injustice...have been familiarized with it from their infancy, custom has rendered it habitual to them, and they are very apt to regard it as, what is called, the way of the world..." We invited Corpovisionarios to San Diego-Tijuana to help us shake up "the way of the world"—to help cultivate a new regional *Cultura Ciudadana* where identity is place-based, organized by genuine affinity, shared interests, and a real sense of responsibility that is not oriented by the arbitrary jurisdictional markers set down by the nation-state.

The "Survey on Bi-National *Cultura Ciudadana*" was an opportunity to demonstrate that the region was, in fact, already halfway there. Border activists have always insisted that the region is defined by the informal flows that move back and forth across the border—economic, environmental, social, normative, ethical. We believed the survey could help make the invisible visible: that in fact a regional *Cultura Ciudadana* was already latent in our practices but unrecognized in our deeply entrenched culture of neglect, emblematized by the metal wall and surveillance infrastructure that separates us. Indeed the wall is as much a mental as a physical barrier, which of course works very differently on the mind depending on where fate has placed you.

For the majority of San Diegans without affective ties to Tijuana, it enables them to go about their daily lives with little thought to what goes on on the other side. My students are astonished when I tell them that there is a slum of eighty-five thousand people barely twenty miles from their classroom. They are surprised that waste from that slum flows under the wall through drainage tunnels constructed by Homeland Security, polluting San Diego's estuary and beaches. For San Diegans with affective ties to Mexico, the wall reinforces separation from home. The sense of alienation typically experienced by immigrants is reinforced in our region by the disruption of family life that the intensification of surveillance since 9-11 has inflicted on those who travel north in search of work. For the Tijuanense with wealth and privilege, the wall is a porous inconvenience that can be traversed; but to the majority of Tijuanenses and other Latin American immigrants and refugees who cluster near it, the wall reinforces inferiority and marginality and sets up an impenetrable barrier to hope.

In February 2015, Henry Murraín, Executive Director of Corpovisionarios, stood before a room of fifty bureaucrats, business leaders, community activists, academics, artists, and civic philanthropists who had convened in San Diego to witness the results of the "Survey on Bi-National *Cultura Ciudadana.*" A similar configuration that included Tijuana Mayor Jorge Astiazarán convened in Tijuana the day before. The city-based surveys contained information that reinforced what most of us already knew or suspected about ourselves: San Diegans tend to drive cars; Tijuanenses tend to mistrust public officials; San Diegans tend to keep to themselves; Tijuanenses have a more participatory Civic Culture. The city-based surveys presented a reality that was familiar to us—though there were some outliers, such as Tijuana's disturbing cultural acceptance of domestic violence and homophobia (both were more severe than any other Latin American city studied by Corpovisionarios). We were also intrigued that Tijuanenses are far more receptive to law and behavioral regulation than San Diegans, and particularly when it comes to protection of private property—a finding that surely reflects the liberal biases of US political culture.

As for the binational module, we learned very new things about our region regarding the presence of a binational *Cultura Ciudadana*, results that have potential to change the way these cities see each other, their identity as participants in a larger urban region with common interests and values, and their aspirations for a shared future. San Diegans, it turns out, overwhelmingly trust citizens of Mexico and respect Tijuanenses far more than we would have expected—far more than Tijuanenses trust and respect citizens of the United States and of San Diego, and sadly far more than Tijuanenses even seem to trust and respect themselves, no doubt a function of marginalization and pervasive corruption and economic insecurity.

There is much to say about Tijuana's challenges and the city-based results of Tijuana demonstrating low levels of *Cultura Ciudadana*. These results are not altogether surprising. Cultivating a new *Cultura Ciudadana* in Tijuana is an essential goal moving forward, as it has been in cities Corpovisionarios has surveyed across Latin America, and it has been encouraging to witness the commitment and interest of Mayor Astiazarán and his advisors in using the survey as a mirror to better understand Tijuana's challenges. But the San Diegan results have been surprising to all. This finding of trust in Mexicans and Tijuanenses undercuts deep assumptions about racial and socio-economic biases on the San Diego side, reinforced by immigration politics and the intensification of drug violence in the past decade. It reveals an arguably more tolerant and egalitarian sensibility in San Diego, and more readiness to collaborate than we would have expected. This readiness was confirmed by perhaps the most exciting result of all: that roughly 60-70% of San Diegans believed that the cities have an interest in, and should be collaborating on, issues ranging from border wait times and immigration to public health and environment. These findings are important tools in our goal of producing a more just and equitable urban region, but obviously the challenge remains: to translate the value of this data into cross-border urban policy and real change on the ground.

Endnotes

1 My great thanks to Carlo Tognato for welcoming my paper into this collection and for his excellent editorial advice; and to Gerry Mackie, for introducing me many years ago to the work of Antanas Mockus and the importance of "social norms change" as a strategy for improving quality of life in villages and cities. Gerry has also been an indispensable support in the development of the "Survey on Bi-National *Cultura Ciudadana* (Civic Culture)" that I discuss in this paper. I am grateful to Antanas Mockus for meaningful conversations over the last years about mayors, social behavior, and urban pedagogy; to Alejandro Echeverri for helping me understand the relation between civic culture and "social urbanism" through the case study of Medellín; and to Sergio Fajardo for his hand-written process diagrams (I still have the napkin). My thanks as well to Jim Tully, Darrel Moellendorf, Rainer Forst, and Ben Barber for important conversations about civic participation. Earlier versions of this paper were presented to audiences in Bogotá and Cartagena, and I particularly appreciated the reflections of Henry Murraín, Javier Guillot, and Pablo Abitbol. It was Teddy Cruz who first brought me "down" to the city, as Plato would say. I am grateful for his partnership as we advance the projects I explore in this paper and the ones still to come.

2 A more elaborated account can be found in Forman (2010).

3 For an overview see Kiesling (2012).

4 See Gerry Mackie's essay in this collection.

5 I explore this theme at length in Forman (2010).

6 *Maquiladoras* are factories for the assembly, processing, manufacturing and export of products.

7 For more on the convergence of our practices, see Cruz and Forman (2015).

8 The *Ciclovía* is an extensive "Bike Path" that crosses large areas of Bogotá. On Sundays and on national holidays, in addition, many major roads are closed to cars and transformed into "Bike Paths."

9 A term coined by Medellín's Director of Urban Projects, Alejandro Echeverri (2005-2008).

10 Civic Innovation Lab Pioneering Neighborhood Upgrades, *San Diego Union Tribune*, March 14, 2014, (http://www.utsandiego.com/news/2014/mar/14/innovation-lab-planners-/).

11 We have partnered in recent years with Sergio Fajardo and his director of urban projects, Alejandro Echeverri, who were responsible for many of the city's most important interventions. Together Cruz, Echeverri, and I, in collaboration with the Frankfurt-based

public interest graphic designer Matthias Goerlich, produced a pedagogical tool called the Medellín Diagram, a visual map of the political and civic processes that enabled the renowned infrastructural interventions in that city. The Diagram was first presented in April 2014 in the Medellín Museum of Modern Art on the occasion of the 7th UN-Habitat World Urban Forum, which was hosted in Medellín. See "La experiencia de Medellín es ahora una guía," *El Colombiano*, April 10, 2014. The first articulation of the Medellín Diagram can be found online, in both Spanish and English at: (www.medellin-diagram.com). "Later iterations of the Diagram appeared in Fall 2014 in the exhibition 'Citizen Culture', curated by Lucía Sanromán in the Santa Monica Museum of Art; in December 2015 in the Shenzhen Architectural Biennial exhibition Radical Urbanisms, curated by Alfredo Brillembourg and Herbert Klumpner; and most recently in March 2017 at Visualizing Citizenship, the Yerba Buena Center for the Arts, San Francisco, curated by Lucía Sanromán. See https://www.youtube.com/watch?v=z89ixMyyE1o"

12 We considered a telephone application, but Corpovisionarios advised against this since the existing questionnaire was too long to hold the attention of interviewees, and our survey was made even longer with the addition of the new binational module. We decided that we did not want to shorten the survey for telephone application, which would reduce its comparability with the Corpovisionarios database.

13 Soon after the Civic Innovation Lab was launched, the Democratic mayor who appointed us was forced to resign. He was replaced by an interim Democrat eager to distinguish himself from his predecessor, who kept us alive only to banish us to the planning department. A few months later, the Republican who was elected to office immediately cut our funding, and it was then that we withdrew our Lab projects from the municipality to the campus. For more on the emergence, evolution, and untimely demise of the San Diego Civic Innovation Lab, see: "One Mayor's Downfall Killed the Design Project that Could've Changed Everything: Public Interest Design's Wild Ride into City Hall," *Next City*, February 23, 2015. (http://nextcity.org/features/view/teddy-cruz-fonna-forman-civic-innovation-san-diego-public-interest-design).

14 In San Diego's current political climate, cross-border collaboration has focused primarily on economic development, drawing recent attention in the *Wall Street Journal*: "San Diego Mayor Forges New Relationship with Mexico," February 10, 2015. (http://www.wsj.com/video/san-diego-mayor-forges-new-relationship-with-mexico/7BC7A4D8-1A01-4C65-AA01-98E900CA3B50.html).

References

Cerda, Magdalena, Jeffrey D. Morenoff, Ben B. Hansen, Kimberly J. Tessari Hicks, Luis F. Duque, Alexandra Restrepo, and Ana V. Diez-Roux. 2012. "Reducing Violence by Transforming Neighborhoods: A Natural Experiment in Medellín, Colombia." *American Journal of Epidemiology* 175(10):1045-1053.

Cruz, Teddy. 2016. "Spatializing Citizenship: Marginal Neighborhoods as Sites of Production." In *Territories of Poverty*. Atlanta: University of Georgia Press.

Forman, Fonna. 2010. *Adam Smith and the Circles of Sympathy: Cosmopolitanism and Moral Theory*. Cambridge: Cambridge University Press.

———. 2013. "Adam Smith, Moral Portraiture and the Science of Man," *Adam Smith Review* 7:186-91.

Forman, Fonna and Teddy Cruz. 2015. "Changing Practice: Engaging Informal Public Demands." In *Other Markets: A Reader*, edited by Helge Mooshammer, Peter Mörtenböck, Teddy Cruz, and Fonna Forman. Rotterdam: nai010 Publishers.

———. 2018. "Global Justice at the Municipal Scale: The Case of Medellín, Colombia." In *Institutional Cosmopolitanism*, edited by Thomas Pogge and Luis Cabrera. New York: Oxford University Press.

Kiesling, L. Lynne. 2012. "Mirror Neuron Research and Adam Smith's Concept of Sympathy: Three Points of Correspondence." *Review of Austrian Economics*. February 28.

McGuirk Justin. 2014. *Radical Cities: Across Latin America in Search of a New Architecture*. London: Verso.

Mockus, Antanas. 2012. "Building 'Citizenship Culture' in Bogotá." *Journal of International Affairs*, 65(2):129-132.

———. N.d. "Bogotá's Capacity for Self-Transformation And Citizenship Building." Unpublished paper, 1:29.

———. 2003. "Do Constitutions Constrain? Legal, Moral and Cultural Self-bindings to Prevent Shortcuts." *Columbia 250 Symposium on Constitutions, Democracy and the Rule of Law*, October 16-17, Columbia University, New York, 1:21.

Muthu, Sankar. 2008. "Adam Smith's Critique of International Trading Companies: Theorizing 'Globalization' in the Age of Enlightenment." *Political Theory* 36(2):185-212.

"New San Diego-Tijuana Survey Holds Mirror Up to Border Cities." 2015. *Next City*, February 25. (http://nextcity.org/daily/entry/binational-survey-san-diego-tijuana-border-antanas-mockus).

Smith, Adam. 1776/1981. *An Inquiry into the Nature and Causes of the Wealth of Nations*, edited by R.H. Campbell and A.S. Skinner as vol. II of *The Glasgow Edition of the Works and Correspondence of Adam Smith*. Oxford: Oxford University Press; reprint ed. Indianapolis: Liberty Press.

Smith, Adam. 1759/1982. *The Theory of Moral Sentiments*. Edited by D.D. Raphael and A.L. Macfie as vol. I of *The Glasgow Edition of the Works and Correspondence of Adam Smith*. Oxford: Oxford University Press; reprinted. Indianapolis: Liberty Press.

Wolin, Sheldon. 1960. *Politics and Vision: Continuity and Innovation in Western Political Thought*. Boston: Little, Brown and Company.

6. Social Reform and the Limits of Education[1]

Jaime Ramos

> For men are not born fit for citizenship, but must be made so.
> —*Baruch Spinoza, A Political Treatise, Vol. 2*

Antanas Mockus is a most unlikely character in Colombian politics. In a country where most politicians are mediocre, ill–prepared, entirely self–interested, and often dishonest, he is deeply intelligent, well–learned, absolutely honest, and genuinely interested in the well-being of his fellow citizens. He left an important mark on the history of Bogotá, as one of the best mayors the city has seen. Moreover, he could have had an impact on national politics if the spontaneous "green wave" that accompanied his presidential campaign in 2010 had not evaporated so abruptly, partly due to his own mistakes. I am not a political analyst, and I will not try to explain here why Mockus failed to consolidate a movement of popular discontent against the government of President Álvaro Uribe, which many people perceived as a militarist and corrupt regime (he was defeated by Uribe's Minister of Defense, Juan M. Santos).

I have some profound ideological differences with Professor Mockus, and some of them will become apparent in my discussion of his program of *Cultura Ciudadana* (Civic Culture), which is the main subject of this brief essay. In the first, more philosophical section, I discuss Mockus's understanding of norms (moral, social, and legal) and his Kantian interpretation of morality as a sphere independent of cultural norms and practices. I criticize his rationalism and what I regard as a moralist approach towards upholding the law. I argue that all normativity is grounded in social practices and, following Spinoza, I claim that politics belongs to the domain of opinion, not of reason. In the second, more "empirically" oriented section, I examine the data that allegedly support Mockus's claim that the citizenship campaign he led as mayor of Bogotá was effective in preventing crime and that it was responsible, to a large extent, for the reduction of homicides in the city. I argue that it is unlikely that the campaign had any major impact on violence and that other social processes that were taking place in the country at the same time may better explain the phenomenon. Following Bourdieu's notion of *habitus*, I conclude by arguing that there are significant limits to what can be achieved through educational campaigns and explicit teaching in general.

The Alleged Distinction between a Private Moral Sphere and a Public Social/Legal Sphere

Mockus distinguishes moral norms from cultural and legal norms. Moral rules are viewed as having an internal source in the subject's conscience and their violation is sanctioned by guilt. Cultural norms, on the other hand, root their source of authority in the traditions of a community; they have an external sanction and they are incorporated in the attitudes and behavior of community members (Mockus 2001; Mockus and Corzo 2005).[2] What Mockus means by "cultural norms" amounts approximately to what some authors call "social norms" (e. g., Jon Elster). Social norms are rules shared by a group of people, in some cases perhaps implicitly, that prescribe or forbid certain behaviors. They are not enforced by a special body such as the judicial system as legal norms are but rather by the approval or condemnation of the community (social exclusion, disrepute, etc.). Social norms include norms of reciprocity (gifts, invitations), norms of retribution (punishing someone who has harmed us), norms of cooperation (helping friends and neighbors), and so on. Mockus (2001) and Elster (1996) claim that one of the characteristic differences between moral norms and social norms is that the former are enforced by guilt, while the latter are sustained by shame.[3]

Mockus follows Kant in regarding moral law as a product of the autonomous reason of the individual as opposed to a heteronomous doxa that derives from public opinion. The moral law is framed in the personal sphere: it has an inner source and it regulates an individual's life. Morality, he believes, following Kant, cannot be assimilated to custom or cultural practices. This can be inferred from the fact that moral law must be absolutely universal, but cultural practices vary widely. This point led Kant (1785/1981:442) to regard the foundation of morality as an *a priori* enterprise (independent of experience) and to disregard history and custom as guides to a moral life. The moral subject only needs to follow the dictates of practical reason. I believe this sort of rationalism has long been discredited, and Mockus ought to think twice about going down that dead end.[4]

Moreover, I find a sharp distinction between moral norms and cultural norms somewhat problematic. It is not plausible to regard moral norms as having originated in the private moral conscience of the subject. All normativity is originally founded on social practices.

Wittgenstein (1953/2001) persuasively suggested a social view of norms:

Is what we call "obeying a rule" something that would be possible for only *one* man to do and to do only *once* in his life?—This is of course a note on the grammar of the expression to "obey a rule." It is not possible that there should have been only one occasion on which someone obeyed a rule. It is not possible that there should have been only one occasion on which a report was made, an order given or understood; and so on.—To obey a rule, to make a report, to give an order, to play a game of chess, are *customs* (uses, institutions)... (§ 199).

Wittgenstein (1978) compares the idea of a solitary person following rules to the idea of an individual carrying out trade alone.[5]

The concept of a rule presupposes a communal practice, a regular way of carrying out actions and applying techniques. Thus the ground of normativity lies on actions, not on abstract principles. When we talk of "a practice," that is already a normative notion. Practices are not externally regulated, from the outside, so to speak; for that would imply that we could conceive of the practice as unregulated or without the norm (and that we could conceive of the norm independently of the practice).

Such considerations lead us to regard moral rules as essentially grounded in social practices. The very idea of someone actually building her own moral code is preposterous. How could morality be entirely private? How could such a make-believe normative system be truly binding? Rather, one gradually internalizes socially prevailing principles.[6] Freud's (1930/1988) persuasive story showing that a civilized person is the one who has internalized social principles, which are then enforced by his conscience (guilt), is too well known to be restated here. In any case, even if one accepted Kant's notion of the moral law as legislated by the individual subject following his own reason, only a tiny minority of wise individuals would ever attain that level. Granted that, Kant conceived the "kingdom of ends" (where everyone acts according to a maxim that treats humanity, in oneself and in every other person, as an end in itself and not merely as a means for something else) as a merely regulative idea, but he believed such a will has causal power in the world.[7] Thus, even if rare, it is at least possible, according to Kant, to overcome every inclination and act on purely rational grounds. In contrast, I side with Spinoza (1677/1982:IV 4, Cor.) in concluding that human beings are necessarily subject to passions, and that as mere modes of beings of nature (we are neither autonomous substances nor ends in ourselves), we are subject to the "common order of nature." However, even if we prefer to remain neutral with regard to the ontological dispute between Spinoza and Kant on the nature of human beings, we may find it preferable to choose Spinoza's political realism over Kant's (and Mockus's) extremely optimistic view that a society of rational, autonomous, enlightened individuals is possible. Spinoza (ibid.:IV 54 Sch.), much savvier than Kant on psychological matters, rightly pointed out:

> As men seldom live according to the dictates of reason, these two emotions humility and repentance, and also hope and fear, bring more advantage than harm;…For if men of weak spirit should all equally be subject to pride, and should be ashamed of nothing and afraid of nothing, by what bonds could they be held together and bound? The mob is fearsome if it does not fear.[8]

I do not mean to assert that everybody follows social rules blindly. I agree with Mockus's suggestion that there is room for reflection and argumentation. But while it is individuals who participate in the debate on moral issues, morality itself is in the social sphere. Morality can be no more private than thought, language, and aesthetic values; they are all rooted in social practices.[9] For these reasons, it should be evident that Kant's dream of a society of enlightened individuals proves to be illusory.[10] As Spinoza suggested, politics is in the sphere of the imagination, not of reason.[11]

Certainly not all cultural norms have a moral nature. There is a sort of loose hierarchy of social norms dealing with deep sentiments, vital needs, and so on, to more banal issues of everyday life. For instance, in most and perhaps in all cultures, there are implicit norms regulating the exchange of gifts and favors: one should return favors (but not too quickly though, or else you make it look like a business transaction) and there must be some equivalence between favors done and received, and so on. However, we would not deem it immoral, only embarrassing, not to have invited to dinner a colleague who has invited us several times. In any case, some behaviors have a more fuzzy nature. Consider homosexuality. In a quite liberal society, it is an entirely natural sexual option; in some more conservative quarters, it is regarded as something deviant, somewhat embarrassing (hence the expression "coming out of the closet"), and in some other cultures or even for some people in our own culture, it should be regarded as an immoral behavior (moreover, it is illegal in some countries). Thus, are the implicit rules that condemn homosexuality in many countries moral or social? I do not believe there is a clear borderline between them. Elster (1989:100) describes norms prohibiting behavior "contrary to nature" as examples of social norms. But certainly, many people would regard rules proscribing incest and cannibalism as moral principles. Something similar could be said of rules of reciprocity, which Elster mentions as examples of social norms. (However, in contrast, many people would regard it as a moral obligation to help those who help us.)

The crucial issue here, however, is Mockus's (2001; 2002:23; Mockus and Corzo 2005:7) thesis that the main cause of crime and violence is the lack of consistency between the legal regulation of behavior and its cultural and moral regulations. He believes that crime and violence are often morally and/or culturally justified in Colombia and other Latin American countries.[12] Conducts that are proscribed by the law are culturally tolerated, such as giving and receiving bribes, evading taxes, and smuggling merchandise across borders. In some other cases, people justify their crimes on moral grounds, arguing, for example, that stealing was the only way to help their kin. It is well known in Colombia, and in other places where a mafia culture has prospered, that some of the coldest hit men follow the highest moral standards concerning their behavior towards other members of their gang and their family. Mockus (2001) thus describes the dangers of this gap between moral, cultural, and legal norms:

> In an ideal society, culture is stricter than law, and morality is even stricter than culture. The 'divorce' among the three of them has led to a surge of violence, delinquency, and corruption in Colombia. It has led to the disrepute of [public] institutions, to the weakening of many cultural traditions, and to a crisis of individual's morality. (P. 3)

I find this vision of an ideal democratic society quite moralistic. Mockus believes that everything that is morally acceptable should also be culturally acceptable and everything that is culturally acceptable should be legally permitted. Thus every type of conduct that is outlawed must be culturally censured, and every type of conduct that is culturally forbidden should be morally proscribed. Of course, this state of affairs would avoid the situation where some conduct (such as dumping garbage in a public area) that is proscribed by the law could be culturally or morally acceptable. But then, one should feel that it is morally repugnant to drop an ice cream wrapper on the street, and one should regard it as somewhat sinful not to buckle up one's seat belt when driving. I believe that people in most cultures have a more sensible way of organizing their systems of norms. Even in Babylon, ancient Rome, and Victorian England, people paid their taxes without feeling it was their moral duty to do so (they knew better). However, to be fair to Mockus (1994:3), he has something different in mind when he defends a "moral rigorism." He is concerned about saving one's moral integrity and rigor while at the same time being open to different systems of cultural norms. Moreover, he encourages our ability to adapt to such different regulatory systems (someone who achieves this is described as a "cultural amphibian"). I find the idea of cultivating abilities so that people are able to manage pluralistic cultural systems very appealing, but I doubt that moral rigorism is the right key to achieving such a postmodern aim. His moralistic inclination is reflected in Mockus's unusual attempt to read Kant as a forerunner of multiculturalism, as he seeks to somehow both preserve a strict moral law and at the same time create an opening for the diversity of cultural traditions.

I find the thesis that an imbalance between morality, culture, and law is a major cause of crime and violence to be an ambiguous claim. According to one reading, it is trivially true, but under another, it is false. If the thesis just means that when someone breaks the law, he or she does not have enough regard for the law to prevent him/her from breaking it, then the statement is obviously true; otherwise, the person would not have violated the law. However, if the thesis means that the main cause of crime and violence is to do with people's conscience, that it is, so to speak, an ideological cause, then I believe that the thesis is false. Indeed, some people may justify their violations of the law appealing to what appear to be culturally accepted beliefs, but it may well be the case that such justifications are *post-hoc*.[13] Furthermore, such justifications are not restricted to countries where there is a widespread "crime culture"; rather, they are common among law breakers around the world. In fact, Mockus appears somewhat naive when he uncritically accepts people's justifications for their crimes. He appears to be confusing the reasons and justifications someone gives for his conduct with what would be the "true" motivations for it. Defending the claim that the law in Colombia is often violated on moral grounds makes the traffickers, kidnappers, assassins, and petty criminals (all of them abundant in Colombia) appear as moral champions willing to break the law to protect their moral principles.

It would be interesting to inquire more deeply into the philosophical presuppositions of the thesis that crime has a preponderant ideological cause. I cannot expand on this now, but let me point out that such a thesis is grounded in the old individualistic principles that society is composed of autonomous individuals—each with his/her own beliefs, principles, and goals who form society (through a social contract) because it is in their best self-interest to develop a division of functions (division of labor) and to engage in some common projects that they could not advance by themselves (defense against common aggressors, projects of infrastructure, and so on). But there are no such autonomous individuals outside society and culture. When individuals are such (as opposed to merely stereotypical minds closely resembling one another), they are formed through social structures such as economic relations that enable individual growth, laws that protect an individual's rights, and a cultural milieu (not just formal education), all of which promote autonomous thinking and so on. This means that the way to go is not to transform individuals' minds, one by one, to achieve a more healthy society, but to transform the societal structures that shape individuals' minds. Hence, the main instrument for the transformation of a society cannot be educational campaigns to promote respect for the law, to promote cooperation, and whatever other values one deems necessary for coexistence and social harmony.

We must keep in mind that Professor Mockus not only endorses the hypothesis that crime and violence are mainly the product of this imbalance among morality, culture, and the legal system, but he also asserts that it can be remedied by a program that promotes *Cultura Ciudadana*.[14] Let us now focus on that claim.

Attempting to Transform Society Through Education

Antanas Mockus has not only theorized on *Cultura Ciudadana*, he has had the opportunity to put his ideas into practice, serving twice as mayor of Bogotá (1995-1997 and 2001-2003), a rare opportunity for a theoretician. Bogotá is a difficult city to manage by anybody's standards. Not only is it very large and densely populated (around eight million inhabitants today), it has the typical problems of a third-world metropolis, including high crime and violence, which were even worse when Mockus became mayor. Overall, Mockus's tenure, and that of Enrique Peñalosa (1998-2000), were quite successful and transformed the city substantially.

Mockus (2001) made *Cultura Ciudadana* the core of his program of government. It is worth noting that this was the priority of his plan for government, not something subsidiary, for this makes clear his philosophical position regarding the role education should take in politics and the transformation of society.

Let me briefly sketch some of the elements of the *Cultura Ciudadana* campaign and their results.

Mockus (2001:7) defines *Cultura Ciudadana* as "the minimal set of shared customs, actions, and rules that generate a sense of belonging, facilitate urban co-existence, lead to respect for the common patrimony, and the acknowledgement of citizens' rights and duties."[15]

Promoting a *Cultura Ciudadana* means promoting a set of shared customs and rules, cultivating a sense of belonging to a community, strengthening the capacity to forge agreements and solutions to conflicts, and promoting the active participation of citizens in enforcing other people's duties and the defense of other people's rights. Enforcement of the law cannot be up to the authorities alone: they showed themselves to be unable to handle it by themselves; hence there must be a mutual regulation among members of the community.

Mockus argued that the divorce among law, culture, and morality can be remedied through alternative modes of communication, what he described as "intensified interaction." Often, people resort to violence when they cannot communicate in any other way; in this sense, violence is a distorted way of expressing oneself. When communication is intensified and face-to-face interaction among participants in a conflict of interest is secured, people must present arguments in favor of their position. This exchange forces one to revise more carefully one's reasons and those of the other participants; this, in turn, takes one beyond the exclusive consideration of one's own interests (Mockus 2001:6). This somewhat idealized version of human interaction appears to owe much to Habermas and Rawls, both of whom influenced Mockus's thinking.

Let us briefly examine the citizenship campaign itself. Bogotá invested $130 million dollars during three years (1995-1997) in the implementation of the *Cultura Ciudadana* program (3.7% of the budget) (Mockus 2001:7). Among other things, the city hired four hundred mimes to amicably remind people to respect the traffic signs (e.g., using the "zebra" crossings) (Mockus 2001:10); hundreds of thousands of cards were handed to people to be used as congratulatory signs for those cooperating with traffic control (thumbs–up) or else as a sign of censure (red card) for traffic violations. The city government adopted a widespread campaign to avoid drunk driving, and ordered the closing of bars at one a.m. to lower alcohol-related crimes. A campaign was initiated to prevent children from using pyrotechnic devices and to restrict the sale of fireworks. The city prohibited people from carrying handguns (even if they had a permit for owning them) and promoted the voluntary decommission of weapons (in exchange for Christmas gifts). There was a vast campaign in the media to reduce water consumption, which was scarce due to a severe drought at the time (the mayor himself was shown on television turning off the water while soaping himself up—not that he minds being in the spotlight). Forty-five thousand people participated in a symbolic vaccination campaign against domestic violence. Four thousand seven hundred and fifty police officers received training in mediation and conflict resolution, citizens' rights, and *Cultura Ciudadana* in general. A campaign was developed to suggest that citizens voluntarily pay an extra 10% in their city taxes.

Given my skepticism about the power of education (I am a teacher after all), I was amazed by the positive, though limited, results obtained by Mockus's campaigns. Thanks to the campaign against drunk driving, deaths in traffic accidents went down 20%, a significant decline. There was an impressive 75% reduction in children burned by pyrotechnic devices. A significant 2,538 firearms were voluntarily handed over to the authorities (Mockus 2001:13), although he himself estimated that this was only 1% of the total number of firearms circulating (Mockus 2002). Bogotá's rate of homicides decreased from 82 per 100,000 people in 1993 to 35 per 100,000 in 2000. Mockus estimates that about 14% of that reduction is due to the campaigns of voluntary disarmament. The role that the Cultural Ciudadana campaign actually played in the reduction of homicides and of crime in general is a controversial issue, and I will come back to it in a moment. The 1997 campaign for the reduction in the consumption of water led to a 11-14% reduction (varying by month). The campaign encouraging water conservation was accompanied by a differential fare that charged less for each one of the first 20 m^3, as compared to additional consumption (this economic incentive probably played as large a role as the educational campaign). In 2001, sixty-three thousand people voluntarily paid a 10% excess over their municipal taxes (Mockus 2003). That is impressive, because it was an entirely voluntary donation to an abstract entity such as the city. Still, I would estimate this was less than 5% of the total taxpayers who paid the city tax. Thus, the proportion of collaborators was rather low.

I do not mean to minimize the importance of these results. The campaigns did have some impact on citizens' behavior. But I believe Mockus and his followers tended to exaggerate their scope. It often happened that the transformations the Colombian philosopher-king attempted to achieve through education were later obtained through punitive laws. Mockus was the first, I believe, to promote the use of seat belts while driving, and he achieved some results, but their use only became universal when there was a law to make it compulsory nationwide. The use and sale of pyrotechnic devices was afterwards entirely forbidden in Bogotá and some other major cities. The rate of deaths in car accidents in Bogotá has been decreasing steadily since 1999 (from 19.5/100,000 to about 8/100,000).[16] This is due partly to educational campaigns but also to increased police control and much tougher laws. In fact at the end of 2013, Congress approved—what seem to me—disproportionate sanctions.[17]

I now want to focus on the role played by the *Cultura Ciudadana* program in the reduction of homicides. Mockus himself acknowledges that the reduction obtained in 1996 through the education campaign and decommission of firearms was substantially superseded by the reduction in 1997 when a complete prohibition of carrying arms was imposed (Mockus 2001:12). That was not an educational measure but pure coercion. As I mentioned before, Mockus estimates that 14% of the reduction in the rate of homicides, which went from 82/100,000 in 1993 to 35/100,000 in 2000, was due to the voluntary disarmament campaigns (Mockus 2003:70); I have no idea how he can know that. First of all, the reduction in homicides started two years previous to his first tenure as mayor in 1995. Moreover, the handover of arms started around Christmas of 1995, so it should have had effects starting in 1996. This shows that there was already a trend for the reduction of homicides when the campaign began having any effect. To understand what happened in Bogotá, however, it is necessary to have some idea of what was going on in Colombia as a whole. The period between 1946 and 1960 (roughly) is known in Colombia as *La violencia* (the Violence), when a bloody war was waged between liberals and conservatives, particularly in the rural areas.

At its worst moment, in the late 1950s, the rate of homicides was about 100/100,000. In 1958, the elites of the parties negotiated an agreement (*El frente nacional*, or The National Front) to share political power, rotating the presidency between the two parties every four years. In the following decades violence decreased significantly, and many guerrilla groups were dismantled. However, some liberal guerrillas, feeling betrayed by the political elite who negotiated behind their backs, continued their rebellion in the countryside, later joining the communists to form the powerful guerrilla group FARC. During the subsequent period between 1960 and 1984, Colombia had a rate of homicides that oscillated between 20 and 30/100,000 and Bogotá had rates oscillating between 10 and 20/100,000. Though things were much better than during *La violencia*, Colombia still had a homicide rate five times higher than the United States (Gaitán 1995:212). Then in 1984, both in Bogotá and in Colombia as a whole, the rate of homicides started rising sharply, largely due to the so-called "drug wars" (E. Sánchez 2012; F. Sánchez 2007; Casas and González 2005) and to a surge in political violence (in fact, both were intermixed). The terrible bloodshed can be explained not only by the presence of the powerful and ruthless drug cartels (associated with paramilitary groups and in many cases with the government's own military and police forces) but also the presence of powerful guerrilla groups that effectively controlled vast territories of rural Colombia.[18]

The rate of homicides in Colombia reached a peak of 81/100,000 in 1991 and then of 80/100,000 in Bogotá in 1993. Colombia was then the most violent country in the world by far, except for those openly at war and some African countries for which we have no reliable data. I should stress that the trends of violence in Colombia and Bogotá between 1961 and 2009 are more or less symmetrical: though the rate in Bogotá is lower than in the country as a whole, they show the same tendencies (F. Sánchez 2007:304; E. Sánchez 2012:24). In the early 1990s, homicides started to decline, probably due in part to the aggressive war by the government against the drug cartels and to the strengthening of the military. Bogotá's reduction of homicides was even superseded by the reduction in Medellín (Colombia's second largest city and the one most permeated by drug traffic) of the homicide rate by 43% between 1989 and 1993. Cali's homicide rate dropped by 37% between 1991 and 1995. The number of homicides went down 29% in the country as a whole between 1991 and 1998 (Casas and González 2005:246). Obviously, the *Cultura Ciudadana* campaigns had nothing to do with these crime reductions parallel to the one in Bogotá. This by itself does not prove that the *Cultura Ciudadana* campaign played no role in crime prevention in Bogotá, but it does suggest that another causal mechanism played an important role in that process. The aggressive war of the government against the drug cartels in the early 1990s certainly played a role in bringing down the rate of homicides back to their "normal" level previous to 1984.

I am not suggesting that most of the homicides in Bogotá at the time can be directly explained by drug trafficking or by political warfare. Probably the majority of them can be attributed to assaults, quarrels involving alcohol, domestic violence, and so on. However, the country had seen the growth of a drug culture that permeated society in every aspect. Nobody knows for sure how much drug trafficking was worth in the mid-1980s (the economists Steiner [1997] and Rocha [2000] diverge enormously about its value for the period 1983-1987), but the net annual income certainly reached 2.5 billion dollars in 1990, about 6% of the Colombian GNP. Until then many "respectable" businessmen, bankers, and ranchers associated with the drug lords acquired legal businesses and huge tracts of land. Drug dealers befriended the political elites, controlled local governments, and had an important influence in the Colombian Congress. The sort of *familismo* that Mockus blames as a standard justification for crime is usually extended in social groups where a mafia and gang culture flourishes.[19] Thus, one cannot ignore the climate of criminality that was prevalent in many large cities in the country at that time. Bogotá was not isolated from the prevailing conditions of a country on the verge of collapse. The gap between morality, culture, and law that Mockus blamed as the culprit of crime was in turn the result of very material and economic conditions.

The putative role of the *Cultura Ciudadana* campaign in reducing homicides can be questioned if we take into account other crimes such as criminal battery (*lesiones personales*). Although Bogotá has a lower rate of homicides than the national average, its rate of criminal battery is about 80% higher than the national average and has been rising since 2004 (E. Sánchez 2012:30). One may wonder why, if an educational campaign promoting citizen values did have some impact on homicidal behavior, it did not impact the rates of criminal battery at all. A similar analysis could be made with regard to other types of crimes.

Corpovisionarios, an NGO founded by Mockus, conducted an extensive survey on *Cultura Ciudadana* in more than twenty Latin American cities. Mockus et al. (2012) presents the results for the surveys in eight cities between 2008 and 2010: Belo Horizonte, Bogotá, México City, Caracas, Medellin, La Paz, Quito, and Monterrey. The survey covers the five factors that Mockus and his group now regard as essential for *Cultura Ciudadana*. These are: (1) the willingness to build agreements and pacts, (2) mutual regulation of behavior among citizens, (3) respect for the norms, (4) honesty of public officials, and (5) legal security offered by the state and the state's monopoly on the use of force. Medellín got the highest grade in *Cultura Ciudadana* followed closely by Belo Horizonte and Bogotá, leaving far behind the other five cities (Mockus et al. 2012:264). However, Medellin had the second highest rate of homicides at the time (topped only by Caracas), 94/100,000 inhabitants in 2009 (four times higher than the next on the list), and Bogotá had the third highest rate of homicides (23/100,000) in 2009 (almost doubling La Paz, the next on the list) (Aldana and Ramírez 2012:94). Thus, there was no positive correlation whatsoever between high *Cultura Ciudadana*, as assessed by Corpovisionarios itself, and a low homicide rate. There is also no clear correlation between *Cultura Ciudadana* and low criminal battery in those eight cities (Mockus et al. 2012:264; Aldana and Ramírez 2012:99).

Let me summarize these results and offer some suggestions. I am not saying that there is no correlation at all between *Cultura Ciudadana* and the reduction of criminality. Probably there is, but both criminality and *Cultura Ciudadana* are complex phenomena with multiple facets (in fact, the names may well stand for very different phenomena that we crudely subsume under broad categories), and it is hopeless to attempt directly to explain one through the other. The available data do not offer conclusive evidence about the positive role played by the *Cultura Ciudadana* campaign in lowering the rates of homicides in Bogotá. On the contrary, they suggest it played a minor role.

I will close by sketching a hypothesis with both a psychological (or perhaps "sociological," as will become apparent) and philosophical aspect. This conclusion is by no means supported but only suggested by what I have said so far. First, on the psychological side, there is a significant limitation to what can be taught through civic campaigns and formal methods of education, including the direct use of punishment/reward techniques. This is due to the fact that people's behavior cannot be explained entirely through their conscious beliefs and choices. Our conscious decisions to act in this or that way are severely biased by the way we interpret the situation at hand and the possible alternatives. The way we "see" things and value them depends on psychological structures shaped by our experiences, which in turn depend on the condition of interaction with the surrounding world.

It is particularly useful to take notice here of Pierre Bourdieu's (1990) notion of *habitus*—understood as a system of dispositions structured by our material conditions of living particularly in early infancy, structuring our modes of thinking, perceiving, and interpreting the world.[20] The *habitus* shapes, to a large extent, our tastes regarding music, food, clothing, sceneries, and so on, but also our capacity to make certain discriminations (seeing something as elegant, vulgar, old-fashioned, dangerous, interesting, difficult, etc.). Our body language, posture, accent, table manners, linguistic idioms, and so on are unconsciously structured by our *habitus*. This explains why we fit so naturally and effortlessly in our social milieu: why *that* sort of people, of games, or of furniture seems so familiar and appropriate to us; why we find certain options entirely obvious, while there are other things we would not consider doing (even if at the present we have, e.g., the economic capacity to do it; one does not suddenly change one's preferences and old habits just because one has suddenly become rich by winning the lottery. What this shows is that the habitus may have been structured in a setting that has changed with respect to our present circumstances). To a large extent, we' share structuring dispositions with other people (close kin, for instance) who grew up in similar conditions—eating similar types of food, playing in the same alleys, and so on. It is thus possible to construct a much more refined notion of social class than the one found in orthodox Marxism, because it not only takes into account economic capital but also symbolic and social capital. We can now see clearly the difference between those conducts we perform under the influence of the *habitus* and those that, being alien to it, are taught explicitly through formal education, at home and at school. We can never achieve a complete mastery of a technique or practice that we only learned later in life through explicit teaching (something that is perhaps evident when reading this poorly written piece, despite the many years I have spent reading in English!).

On a more philosophical note, Professor Mockus may be seen as a liberal reformist (more or less in the spirit of early liberal thinkers such as Jeremy Bentham) with a profound faith in the power of education to transform society.[21] His motto could be something like: "Transform the mind of many individuals and you will change society." I believe, however, that Mockus underestimates the importance of socioeconomic structures and the people's way of life in the structuring of their minds. As Marx (1845) forcefully argued against German idealist philosophers, "life is not determined by consciousness, but consciousness by life." Vygotsky, Wittgenstein, Elias, Geertz, and many others have built on that principle, establishing an indissoluble bond between the structure of the mind and the structure of the social world a person inhabits. As I remarked before (Endnote 2) Mockus (2001:5) himself mentions in passing that cultural norms are "incorporated" in people's attitudes and behavior, yet he does not seem to realize that they are literally embodied in our actions. As Bourdieu (1990) points out:

> Practical belief is not 'a state of mind,' still less a kind of arbitrary adherence to a set of instituted dogmas and doctrines ('beliefs'), but rather a state of the body. [On the following page he adds] Every social order systematically takes

advantage of the disposition of the body and language to function as depositories of deferred thoughts that can be triggered at a distance in space and time by the simple effect of re-placing the body in an overall posture which *recalls* the associated thoughts and feelings, in one of the inductive states of the body which, as actors know, give rise to states of mind. (Pp. 68-69)

It certainly does not follow from these considerations that education is useless. On the contrary, there is a lot that can be attained through education, particularly in early infancy. What I question about Mockus's programs is the large extent to which they are grounded on the possibility of teaching values later in life. I am skeptical about the efficacy of the explicit teaching of values, and I rather believe that there is a very tight connection between compliance with the norms and a certain form of life. Civility must be a "second nature," a byproduct of determinate forms of life.

Perhaps we should not concentrate on changing people's ideas but on changing people's living conditions and practices. It seems to me that educational campaigns can have only a limited impact in a country with deep structural problems and an ingrained tradition of violence and crime. I believe only a substantial transformation of economic and social relations in Colombia (the state regaining the monopoly of force, reforming land ownership, reducing income inequalities, securing basic public services, guaranteeing a functioning judicial system, and so on) can bring a significant change to our country's pain. But, of course, just saying this is of little use; one would have to show in detail how to achieve these things. At any rate, there are no recipes for mending social problems; perhaps there aren't even good diagnoses of what the malady really is. However, the politician may not have to be concerned with this; he does not have to carefully evaluate the arguments and the theories. He cannot expect to solve everything in order to solve *something*. Only the theoretician can remain perplexed and skeptical. The man of action must adjust to the urgent needs of real life. Surprisingly, Antanas Mockus was an excellent mayor; perhaps he was even a better politician than theoretician, after all.

Endnotes

1   I want to thank my friends Louis Sass, Garrett Thomson, and Carlo Tognato for making many grammatical corrections and useful suggestions to an earlier draft of this paper.

2   This is an important aspect of cultural norms that Mockus mentions incidentally, but that he never fully pursues (Mockus 2001:5). I will come back to this when discussing the role of education in promoting *Cultura Ciudadana*.

3   I do not believe there is an intrinsic difference between moral and social norms. Associating guilt with the violation of certain norms is itself a historical phenomenon; presumably, it was not always like that. Nonetheless I will not argue in favor of this here.

4   The categorical imperative turns out to be either entirely formal, thus useless to guide our actions, or it ends up appealing to empirical considerations such as utility.

5   Certainly, a sort of Robinson Crusoe can follow norms because he carries with him a whole culture. The question is if it would be conceivable, not to mention empirically feasible, that a "wild child" could guide his conduct by norms. One can make rules for one's own private use, because one lives in a world with normative practices.

6   From the fact that different people who live in the same society may have diverging moral codes, it does not follow that moral codes are individual and private. One would have to go into the details of a person's history to see how her aesthetic and moral values are developed. At any rate, the whole process is carried out within a social milieu and it is not separated from it.

7   Kant asserts: "Teleology considers nature as a kingdom of ends; morals regard a possible kingdom of ends as a kingdom of nature. In the former the kingdom of ends is a theoretical idea that explains what exists. In the latter it is a practical idea that brings about what does not exist but can be made actual by our conduct, that is, what can be actualized in accordance with this very idea" (Kant 1785/1981:42). A rational will, therefore, can actually change the world according to Kant.

8   Spinoza does not regard humility and repentance as virtues. Both are forms of pain caused when a man observes his own weakness (Spinoza 1677/1982:IV, 53–54), and pain is never good. A man who acted only guided by his reason would not experience those feelings, but ordinary people in Colombia and in Sweden need such constraints.

9   As Vygotsky (1934/1986) persuasively argued against Piaget (and the dominant modern tradition) that language does not open up to the world; it does not progressively become social. It is social right from the beginning. It is rather the other way around. Language and thought are gradually internalized and personal mental structures are built from interpersonal relations.

10 I was astounded by the uselessness of seventy-four years of teaching socialist values in the Soviet Union. When the Soviet Union dissolved in December of 1991, most of the population had been born under the revolution. However, the principles of social solidarity, the ideals of the proletariat, and the teaching of philosophical materialism evaporated to be succeeded by a surge of consumerism and shallowness.

11 Perception and imagination (opinion) are the lowest forms of knowledge for Spinoza. They present us the world in a fragmentary and confused way. Thus, action grounded on them can never be adequate (and hence autonomous). Appeals to coercion, incentives, and the vagaries of the imagination (eternal punishment and so on) are legitimate and even necessary in the political sphere.

12 "Colombian society has paid a very high price because some Colombians have repeatedly put moral considerations on top of legal ones (attempting to morally justify outlawed actions and even organizations)" (Corzo and Mockus 2005:8). I have translated this quotation and others from papers originally in Spanish that appear in the bibliography.

13 Someone may, for example, justify drug trafficking to the United States and Europe by arguing that it is the free decision of consumers that drives the trade. Moreover, she may argue that those countries have traditionally exploited our people and it is about time we got something in return. Justifications, however, are cheap. It is likely that whenever someone breaks the law, or any other social normative system, she constructs some justification that makes her conduct appear acceptable.

14 "In summary, the strategy of *Cultura Ciudadana* sought to strengthen cultural and moral regulation. It purported to increase the congruence of these regulations with the law and achieve a complementary efficacy. It aimed at weakening the moral or cultural legitimacy of actions contrary to the law, and in many cases it did achieve it" (Mockus 2002:27)

15 Mockus, Murraín, and Villa (2012) developed what appears to be a more complete notion of *Cultura Ciudadana*, but it incorporates many elements of a different nature, so the very core of *Cultura Ciudadana* is lost.

16 See: (http://camara.ccb.org.co/documentos/4954_muertes_por_millon_de_habitantes.pdf).

17 For first time offenders, the penalties include the suspension of the driver's license for one year and a fine equivalent to three months of minimum wage, just for having 20 mg of alcohol per 100 ml of blood (0.02% in USA) or drinking one glass of wine. The law contravenes a universal legal principal, that of the due proportionality between the offense and the punishment. Moreover, in a country with a highly corrupt police force, such sanctions actually encourage bribery.

18 The guerrillas targeted some kingpins and their wealthy families through kidnapping and extortions. The cartels reacted forming the group *Muerte a secuestradores* (MAS

or Death to Kidnappers). There was also the deadly war between the Medellín cartel and the Cali cartel in the early 1990s. Moreover, between 1986 and 1994 paramilitary groups associated with the cartels and right–wing ranchers exterminated approximately five thousand members of the leftist political party Unión Patriótica. The killings included the assassination of two popular presidential candidates, Jaime Pardo and Bernardo Jaramillo, eight congressmen, and many regional deputies and town mayors. To make things even worse, the allegedly communist guerrilla got itself involved in drug trafficking (supposedly, it was legitimate to use every means at their disposal for the sake of the revolution).

19 *Familismo* is a cultural and moral code grounded in family ties that only recognizes obligations towards family members and close friends. That sort of family isolation weakens social bonds, but what else could be expected of a people literally surrounded by crime and violence? Many Colombians, including myself, had close family members kidnapped and/or assassinated. I wonder if the world had ever seen the extent of kidnapping Colombians faced in the last two decades of the twentieth century. Precise figures are hard to come by (families often negotiate secretly with kidnappers), but in 2000 there were around 3,600 kidnappings in the country.

20 The notion has antecedents, for instance, in the phenomenological tradition and the work of Norbert Elias.

21 Just as Bentham intended to reform the entire prison system through the construction of the "Panopticon," Mockus intended to end crime by turning the whole city into a huge classroom. "I now have a 6.5 million student class," he once said.

References

Aldana, Sayra and Gabriela Ramírez. 2012. "Seguridad ciudadana: viejos problemas, nuevas miradas" [Civic Security: Old Problems, New Vision]. In *Antípodas de la Violencia* [Antipodes of Violence], edited by Antanas Mockus, Henry Murraín, and María Villa. Washington, D.C.: Inter-American Development Bank.

Bourdieu, Pierre. 1990. *The Logic of Practice*. Stanford: Stanford University Press.

Casas, Pablo and Paola González. 2005. "Políticas de seguridad y reducción del homicidio en Bogotá: mito y realidad" [Security and Homicide Reduction Policies in Bogotá: Myth and Reality]. Pp. 242 - 289 in *Seguridad Urbana y Policía en Colombia* [Urban Security and Police in Colombia] edited by Casas, Pablo et al. Bogotá: Fundación Seguridad & Democracia [Foundation for Security and Democracy].

Corzo, Jimmy and Antanas Mockus. 2005. "Ley o moral: ¿cuál prima?" [Law or Morals? Which Comes First?]. *Análisis político* [Political Analysis] 54:3-17.

Elster, Jon. 1996. "Rationality and the Emotions." *The Economic Journal* 106 (438): 1386-1397.

———. 1989. "Social Norms and Economic Theory." *Journal of Economic Perspectives* 3 (4):99-117.

Freud, Sigmund. 1930/1988. *El malestar en la cultura* [Civilization and Its Discontents]. Bogotá: Alianza.

Gaitán, Fernando. 1995. "Una indagación sobre las causas de la violencia en Colombia" [An Inquiry over the Causes of Violence in Colombia]. Pp. 89-415 in *Dos ensayos especulativos sobre la violencia en Colombia* [Two Speculative Essays About Violence in Colombia] edited by Malcolm Deas and Fernando Gaitán. Bogotá: Fonade, National Planning Department.

Kant, Immanuel. 1785/1981. *Grounding for the Metaphysics of Morals*. Indianapolis: Hackett Publishing Co.

Marx, Karl. 1845. *The German Ideology*. (http://www.marxists.org/archive/marx/works/1845).

Mockus, Antanas. 1994. "Anfibios culturales y divorcio entre ley, moral y cultura" [Cultural Amphibians and Divorce Between Law, Morals, and Culture]. *Análisis Político*, [Political Analysis] 21:37-48.

———. 2001. "*Cultura Ciudadana*, programa contra la violencia en Santa Fe de Bogotá, Colombia 1995-1997" [Civic Culture, Program Against Violence in Santa Fe de Bogotá Colombia 1995-1997]. Washington, D.C.: Interamerican Development Bank.

————. 2002. "Convivencia como armonización de ley, moral y cultura" [Coexistence as Harmonization of Law, Morals, and Culture]. *Perspectivas* [Perspectives] 32 (1):19-37.

Mockus, Antanas, Henry Murraín, and Maria Villa, eds. 2012. *Antípodas de la violencia* [Antipodes of Violence]. Washington, D.C.: Inter-American Development Bank, Corpovisionarios.

Rocha, Ricardo. 2000. *La economía colombiana tras 25 años de narcotráfico* [The Colombian Economy After 25 Years of Drug Trafficking]. Bogotá: Siglo del Hombre.

Sánchez, Efraín. 2012. "Bogotá: de la vigilancia y el control a la resolución pacífica de conflictos" [Bogotá: From Vigilance and Control to Peaceful Conflict Resolution]. In *Antípodas de la Violencia* [Antipodes of Violence], edited by Antanas Mockus, Henry Murraín, and María Villa. Washington, D.C.: Inter-American Development Bank.

Sánchez, Fabio. 2007. *Las cuentas de la violencia* [The Numbers of Violence]. Bogotá: Norma.

Spinoza, Baruch. 1677/1982. *The Ethics and Selected Letters*. Indianapolis: Hackett Publishing Co.

————. 1951. *A Theological-Political Treatise. A Political Treatise*. New York: Dover Publications.

Steiner, Roberto. 1997. *Los dólares del narcotráfico*. [The Drug-Trafficking Dollars] Bogotá: Tercer Mundo Editores, Fedesarrollo.

Wittgenstein, Ludwig. 1978. *Remarks in the Foundations of Mathematics*. Oxford: Basil Blackwell.

————. 2001/1953 *Philosophical Investigations*. Oxford: Blackwell Publishing.

Vygotsky, Lev. 1934/1986. *Thought and Language*. Cambridge: MIT Press.

7. Antanas Mockus, The Academic

Carlos Augusto Hernández

Before his two successful terms as mayor of Bogotá, which transformed him into a renowned figure of contemporary politics, Antanas Mockus was a university professor who went from being an exuberant, radical critic of the arbitrary exercise of power to acting as the *chancellor* of the principal university of the country. From there, without previous administrative experience, he produced great changes that launched the National University of Colombia on a path of research and radical engagement with academic culture. We know the works and ideas of Mockus, the mayor of Bogotá; as for Mockus, the university professor, there is still much to be said.

The Young Professor, Friend of Students

In 1976, the Faculty of Sciences buzzed with the surprising news that the young professor Antanas Mockus had completed the entirety of his professional studies in mathematics, including his master's degree, in just three years. At that time, it was not unusual for a mathematician to take five years to finish his degree, and at least three more years to obtain a master's. The news of Mockus's vertiginous career, however, was not a simple exaggeration on the part of colleagues fascinated by his enormous talent; after graduating with his Bachelor's degree in 1969, Mockus obtained his master's in mathematics from the University of Dijon in 1972, with excellent scores. But Professor Mockus was not an intellectual convinced of his own superiority and confined to his area of study, as one might imagine considering his academic achievements. Rather, he kept a certain critical distance from the formalities of academia. He was not neutral towards the cultural proposals of the end of the 1960s and early 1970s. His relationship with the students was much friendlier and less hierarchical than many of his colleagues. He knew that literature, art, philosophy, and politics represented a marvelous world that even mathematicians should not miss out on, and he was aware that he lived in a time of transition and hope that allowed students to dream. He even had a few students with whom he established a relationship good enough to form a group of academic and political discussion, forging friendships, and sharing time together in work and leisure.

Despite the radicalization of the student movements, and in good part because of it, the 1970s were "marvelous years" for Latin American universities. Mockus was not a Marxist but, along with the majority of students during that decade, he felt as if he were the protagonist of a time when myths and boundaries were being overturned and a new world opened up, in which academics believed and wanted to be freer and more unified. Those who, early in their lives, felt the excitement of the student movements of 1968 continued to find in the student protests of the 1970s expressions of collective vitality similar to what had emerged in France as "empowered imagination." Just like Herbert Marcuse (1969), they recognized in the expressions of the opposing youth the manifestation of a new sensibility that could save human beings from the one-dimensionality of consumerist society.

At the beginning of the 1980s, Delfín Avendaño, an engineering student, tried to give a name to the group of students enthralled by philosophy, the university, and imagination, which included the young professor Antanas Mockus, and he called it "Butterfly Brigade Number 40." At the end of the 1970s, Mockus had created a newspaper, which is unrecoverable today, called *The Bucket*. To highlight such desire to come up with new forms of expression that would come to characterize the newspaper, it is enough to remember the slogan: "Don't spit on the floor, spit it out in *The Bucket*." One might conjecture that those words foreshadowed an attempt at creativity in service of criticism and simultaneously of *Cultura Ciudadana* (Civic Culture). What is now clear, in light of Mockus's current concerns, is that he had the intuition from early on that, in order to change attitudes, he needed to explore the different possible meanings of words and to find new ways of naming things.

Scientific Attitude and Scientism

Thanks to the recognition of his academic achievements, Mockus had gained the right to do work outside the ordinary bearings of a math professor. In 1978 he offered an extraordinary course on the representation of science in mainstream media. In this course, students read accounts in magazines and newspapers about the achievements of science and its applications, and they discovered how these references, far from teaching science, instead propagated uncritical admiration for scientific knowledge and its uses. Science, which guaranteed technological advancement and rationalized the quality of market products, appeared in mainstream media as unquestionable truth, accessible to only those of exceptional intelligence. This method of dissemination and the use of scientific achievements excluded common readers from the world of learning and remained, instead, in the realm of inaccessible "magic." In the media there was no critical rigor, no attempt to make observations understandable, no interest in increasing the decision-making capacity of the readers or their understanding of the subject, no effort to produce an informed opinion. It was simply about disseminating novelties and allusions in keeping with the formation of a submissive attitude towards a world of powerful and unquestionable concepts ultimately employed in the service of the market. Mockus called this passive attitude "scientism," meaning submission to and distance from science. Such a scientistic attitude was the opposite of the will to critically understand science through the appropriation of rational content, of the rules of the field, the dynamics of scientific production, and science's own limitations.

Mockus and his colleague Jorge Charum read and discussed other texts in their course that showed how mathematics miraculously managed to persuade those who did not succeed in school early on that their exclusion, as they had been taught to believe, depended on their lack of intelligence.[1] Soon, the suspicion that exclusion in school was more than lack of capacity would be corroborated by the work of Basil Bernstein, who demonstrated the correlation between the social codes of school, daily life, and social class. The "elaborated codes" of school, as Bernstein (1974) showed, are close to the ones that the upper classes use in daily life and far from the "restricted codes" of the lower class segments of society. School features a certain inclusive linguistic continuity with upper class families (who also have private libraries at home and easy access to information) and an exclusionary discontinuity with respect to the language used within families that have been traditionally separated from the valuable products of universal culture.

Later on, this phenomenon would become clearer in light of such notions as that of "cultural capital" by Pierre Bourdieu (1970).

The Federici Group

In 1979 Professor Carlo Federici brought together a research group to discuss training in the sciences. The group was comprised of Carlo Federici (mathematician and physicist), Antanas Mockus (mathematician), José Granés (physicist), Jorge Charum (mathematician), and Carlos Augusto Hernández (physicist); they were later joined by Berenice Guerrero (mathematician) and María Clemencia Castro (psychologist). For a brief time, the Uruguayan researcher Araceli de Tezanos also participated. Only María Clemencia belonged to the Faculty of Human Sciences; the other members came from hard science backgrounds. However, everyone shared interests in philosophy and social studies and were thus motivated to focus their work on education and society. Professor Federici was open about his interest in anthropology, art, literature, and music; at the beginning of the 1980s, Mockus and three other members of the group were among the first students of the master program in philosophy. The Federici Group's first research topic focused on cultivating a scientific attitude in children through the teaching of mathematics and natural sciences in primary school. In particular, the group was interested in contrasting scientific attitudes with scientistic ones, an issue that greatly interested Mockus.

It is enough to look at the concurrence of the objective of the research group and the theme of Mockus's course to get an idea of the role he took within that group of researchers. Mockus contributed some of the most important and novel ideas that the group discussed. He also contributed the most time, imagination, and effort to what was later recognized as collective work. His ideas ended up being those of the whole group because he assumed the double task of both conceiving and then convincing his colleagues of the value of the ideas. From the group's beginning, all the members recognized the immense generosity with which Mockus shared his knowledge, his initiatives, and the merits of his conceptual work. In truth, that generosity was a shared feature and a source of great strength for the Federici Group.

The group had two leaders. One was Professor Federici, who happily contributed his knowledge and experience and who praised the novelties that arose in conversation. The other was Mockus, who more often than the othe suggested new ideas that came from his reflections and readings. He was the one who defined *scientism* as the intention of reducing a plural experience of the world to a certain objectivist and generalist perspective, eschewing not only the diversity of potential relationships between subjects and the world that they live in but also the differences between the projects inherent in various sciences. He also proposed a definition of "the scientific attitude" as the capacity to study science while recognizing its limitations, its characteristics, and the role of consciousness in the construction of its objectives.[2]

The work of the Federici Group was productive and intriguing. On occasions, the group would have long conversations about the meaning and legitimacy of a single word. Through these prolonged discussions, the richness of language became clearer and more precious to everyone involved. They recognized the resonances, connotations, history, and musicality of words. Federici and Mockus were passionate about philology and explored the original meanings of important terms. There was an almost aesthetic pleasure that went along with a shared desire for the members to express themselves with the utmost clarity and precision.

Instructional Design, Taylorism, and the Autonomy of the Educator

Beginning in 1978, the Ministry of Education initiated the reform of the curriculum based on a meticulous instructional design that attempted to convert teaching into a sequence of planned, repeatable actions. It was inevitable that the Group found out about this proposal and opposed it, as it began to circulate to the general public at the beginning of the 1980s. Habermas, whose school of thought had just been introduced to Colombia, thanks to Professor Guillermo Hoyos, distinguishes between "instrumental action" (an action that follows the logic of technical control of natural processes), "strategic action" (a social action that proposes to effectively influence the actions of someone else), and "communicative action" (the social action that seeks understanding between subjects capable of self-recognition).[3] In consideration of Habermas's distinctions, Mockus synthesized and clarified the essential difference between the position of the Federici Group and that of the Ministry: pedagogical relationships could not be understood as instrumental action because they are an interaction between subjects, and that interaction should not be purely strategic action either. What education is, and should be, is the relationship between teacher and student as a communicative interaction.

The distinction between instrumental action and communicative interaction, which Mockus examined in his critique, rescued the communicative nature of the pedagogical relationship, a relationship that implies complex processes of recognition and mutual acceptance. On the other hand, this distinction made apparent the danger of reducing the work of the teacher (with his art and experience) to an application of techniques conceived outside of his know-how, his history, and his own understanding. Although education may have objectives that are more or less defined and although it is possible and legitimate to plan these educational actions and to define curricular organization, what will happen in a classroom cannot be defined beforehand if one accepts that the student is a subject, that professors have gathered different knowledge and experiences, and that knowledge is collectively constructed (just like the very documents that propelled the reforms). Communicative processes are, by nature, unpredictable. One cannot know beforehand how an interlocutor will respond.

Mockus had recognized the hegemony of instrumental action in the Ministry's proposed curricular reform, but he also highlighted other essential aspects that "educational engineering"—understood in the Ministry's proposal as instructional design in which the process of teaching was exhaustively planned out as a series of predetermined activities, accompanied by an objective and evaluation—had in common with the Taylorist organization of work. This system departed from rigorous analysis of times and movements and charted the process of production as a chain of actions determined in advance for maximum efficiency.[4] The analogy with Taylorism illustrated how the Ministry's proposal could convert teachers, managers, and local leaders, enriched by their personal experiences, into executors of a curriculum designed by an office of experts. The sequence of objective activity-evaluation was presented as a "proposal" to the teachers, but it covered and thoroughly overshadowed the act of teaching, transforming the teacher into an administrator of the curriculum. This technical approach to teaching denied the autonomy of the educator.

This minute planning of activities, which completely prefigured the process of teaching/learning as if it were a process of planned production, implicitly suggested something impossible: that all teachers teach the same way and all students learn the same way. Moreover, given the separation between the producers of the curriculum, the logistics planners, and the teachers in the classroom, the conceptual coherence of those choosing the curriculum content was lost due to a fragmenting of the units of activities whose hierarchy and articulation were not clear for those tasked with carrying them out in the classroom. Mockus (1982) collected the fruits of these reflections in his book *Tecnología Educativa y Taylorización de la Educación* (Educational technology and Taylorization of education).

At the beginning of the 1980s, unveiling the planning and control mechanisms that prevent teachers from fully understanding the interaction-creation process in which their action is fundamental turned out to be an essential quality of the work of the researcher in his/her capacity as educational intellectual committed to changing the school system. Still today, this critical exercise, which in the words of Habermas (1965/1984) followed an emancipatory interest, could expand our shared understanding of the meaning and complexity of teachers' pedagogical actions; and it could help teachers recognize the forms of negation, hierarchy, and exclusion associated with different methods of conceiving and organizing the practice of teaching. The theoretical understanding of the work of a teacher is directly political and as such, it is not surprising that pedagogical reflection was viewed by teachers and the majority of education researchers as a form of resistance and a source of ideas for reform. The Federici Group's critique of the 1978 reform reached the public for the first time in 1981, during the First National Symposium on the Teaching of Sciences and through Antanas Mockus's (1981) article, "The Autonomy of the Educator."

The Pedagogical Movement

If earlier primary and secondary education teachers emphasized wage claims, they realized that their entire identity was placed in danger. The ministerial reform denied, as Mockus pointed out, the educator's autonomy: the right to organize work based on the individual educator's own knowledge and experience. The educational reform disregarded and attempted to generalize the individual knowledge of the teacher and the nature of pedagogy as communicative interaction. Educators do not work as well-trained technicians of inert material; they are "qualified workers in the field of socialization and culture" (Mockus 1981:11). The ministerial reform disregarded the specificity and complexity of pedagogy. As such, teachers took part in a massive mobilization, a great Pedagogical Movement, against the reform. In the words of Mockus (2002):

> The Pedagogical Movement emerged from the convergence of two problems: the rejection of instructional design as a strategy for qualitative improvement,

> which entails the degradation of the job of the educator and the limitation of intellectual and professional autonomy, and the will to rescue—and for the first time to make known—the Colombian educator's identity as a *cultural worker*, intellectually and practically engaged with his historical context.(P. 294)

Teachers and researchers united in defense of individual knowledge and the autonomy of the educator. The national organization of teachers, the Colombian Federation of Educators (FECODE), directed by the exceptionally intelligent and sensible Abel Rodríguez, understood the specificity of the moment and the nature of the problem associated with the reform. Rodríguez led the Pedagogical Movement, which started in 1982 at the Bucaramanga Conference. It was not very common for a union to commit, beyond pushing for salary reform, to the defense of the identity of teachers, which displaced the fight into the realm of the symbolic. However, FECODE had recently obtained a Teacher's Statute that fulfilled the material needs of teachers and thus had sufficient legitimacy to support and empower a movement that focused on the dignity of the teaching profession. It was inevitable that Mockus would become the leader of this movement since he had most clearly stated the possible implications of the reform. It was Mockus who had constructed the strongest links between research, on the one hand, and the defense of knowledge and the autonomy of the educator on the other. And he had provided the most comprehensive and thorough conceptualization of the communicative dimension of teaching. As a result, Mockus played a definitive part in defining the direction of the Pedagogical Movement and the foundation and direction of FECODE's magazine *Education and Culture*, which offered a foundation for the teachers' cultural grievances and presented their achievements.

The Pedagogical Movement was an extraordinary experience that displayed the political dimension of pedagogy and denounced the practice of separating the "intellectual field" of educational researchers from the "pedagogical field" of teachers, as defined by Mario Díaz (1993). Many teachers recognized themselves as intellectual, cultural workers, as subjects capable of reflecting on their work practice and of producing knowledge about their field. The Federici Group, for its part, had begun its work by examining the teaching of science, but the focus of that work drove it to tackle problems of language and culture and to examine the boundaries between school and society, a topic that concerned many teachers. The Federici Group quickly became active in the Pedagogical Movement. Similarly, other research groups that studied pedagogical practices became linked to the great mobilization of teachers.

The Pedagogical Movement grew quickly, defeating the Ministry's proposed reform and exciting teachers from different regions of Colombia. At the Bucaramanga Conference in 1982, those who supported pedagogy and protecting the identity of teachers easily overwhelmed those who thought that the movement betrayed the central interests of the Colombian Federation of Educators. To bring about the union between educational research and practice, they founded the national *Centro de Investigaciones Docentes* (CEID, Center for Teaching Research) and regional groups that were responsible for research on education and led by the teachers themselves. The CEID-FECODE's magazine, *Education and Culture*, where Mockus served on the editorial team, was launched with ten thousand initial copies and soon reached thirty thousand copies. The magazine published texts that were most representative of the Pedagogical Movement. Between 1981 and 1982, FECODE shifted its orientation from union politics towards cultural politics, without weakening its position as a teachers' union. And Mockus, the mathematician-turned-education-researcher, became a political leader, without foregoing his role as a researcher.

Philosophy Lessons

The beginning of the 1980s was rife with events that, on top of strengthening the union between pedagogy and politics, demonstrated the power of philosophical reflection. Philosophy was central to the identity and work of both the Federici Group and Mockus. Without a doubt, José Granés, a prominent member of the group, was correct in insisting that scientific training is the formation of a perspective, a way of understanding a plethora of phenomena, and a rationality that extends beyond this universe. But if this could be said of the sciences, it can also apply, perhaps with even more force, to philosophy. The master's degree in philosophy, recently established at the National University, covered the theories of the great philosophers (Plato, Aristotle, Descartes, the English empiricists, Kant, Hegel, Marx, Nietzsche, Husserl, Heidegger, Wittgenstein, Gadamer, and Habermas). The professors at that time had studied at top universities in Europe that were heavily influenced by the German school of thought. Perhaps because of this, the German-style seminar was the predominant model. Guillermo Hoyos Vásquez, Rubén Jaramillo Vélez, Ramón Pérez Mantilla, Rubén Sierra Mejía, Carlos B. Gutiérrez Alemán, and José Lorite Mena, professors of the master's program, were, and are, recognized as masters in the field. Each one, in his particular style, favored discussion and rigorous critique, understanding critique not as an attempt to destroy an argument but rather to highlight what deserved to be brought out. Each professor was adroit in the field and infected the students with a passion for philosophy and for the authors to whom the professors had dedicated years of study and reflection. Although the members of the Federici Group, who participated in the study of philosophy, continued in their original academic niches in the Faculty of Sciences (only Mockus kept a foot within both the Faculty of Sciences and that of Human Sciences), the master's program changed their identities from scientific inquirers to students of philosophy.

Mockus learned from Kant rigor of argumentation, the critical perspective of epistemology, and the aspiration to accept a universal ethic based on responsibility; from Hegel he understood the dialectic of knowledge and history; from Marx the necessity to overcome alienation of work, production, and gender; from Heidegger the concern for the hegemony of the technical gaze; from Husserl the intentionality in action on a plane of meaning; from Gadamer the hermeneutic perspective that recognized the vital importance of language in relation to the Other and the world; and from Habermas the respect for communication and democracy. Kant's (1788/1951:35) categorical imperative—"Act as if the maxim of your own could always become, at the same time, a principle of universal law," which has been considered utopian for good reason—is in fact a clear guide to Mockus's actions. Mockus's defense of teachers' autonomy can be considered a struggle against work alienated from the field of pedagogy; his exploration of scientific attitudes and scientism, as Mockus saw it, from the perspective of modes of relating to science and to the world through the sciences owes much to Husserl's phenomenological orientation; his analysis of schooling and the sciences successfully stemmed from Wittgenstein and Gadamer. Philosophy, epistemology (Bachelard and Kuhn), and the critique of social sciences (Bernstein, Bourdieu, Gouldner) served as conceptual sources that the Federici Group, with Mockus at its head, tapped into to advance their own take on pedagogy and its problems.

At the same time of the boom of the Pedagogical Movement, the *Comité Amplio* (Extended Committee) of professors at the National University was established. The committee defended the autonomy of the university and advocated the need to draw from the most worthy elements in the institution's tradition. The philosopher Guillermo Hoyos, professor and friend of Mockus, became the representative of this professorial movement, actively supported by other remarkable professors, including Mockus. The entire Federici Group joined the ranks of professors defending the very meaning of academia. For Mockus, who at the time attended Professor Hoyos's classes in philosophy and allied with the movement both inside and outside the university, the connection between the political action of professors, the grievances of university professors, and the proposal to understand politics and pedagogy as spaces of communicative interaction was apparent.

Academic Culture and Pedagogy as a Reconstructive Discipline

By the time the surge of enthusiasm for the Pedagogical Movement began to subside and the number of conferences and meetings declined, the Federici Group had successfully conceptualized academic culture and characterized pedagogy as a "reconstructive discipline." It was Mockus who, picking up on a Habermasian concept, defined pedagogy as a reconstruction of "knowing what" as well as "knowing how," to make the job of teaching more effective. Mockus also proposed the idea "academic culture" that would later be converted into one of the most interesting conclusions of the group. For Mockus (and later for the whole Federici Group), academic culture is the combination of three elements: the written tradition that allows us to access an accumulation of culture; rational discussion that seeks consensus through argumentation; and prefiguration and reorganization of action that allows for planning a sequence of actions, representing possible outcomes and reorienting actions that correspond to knowledge derived from written tradition and rational discussion.

Towards the end of the 1980s, Professor Mockus offered a conference at the Department of Engineering entitled "The Mission of the University." This conference was transcribed and converted into required reading to think about the problems and specificities of the university; even today this text is studied as a part of the general education courses that are offered to students across the Faculty of Sciences. In his presentation, Mockus insisted on the autonomy of the university, characterized academic culture, and defended the right of the institution to "serve its own demons," along with his engagement with knowledge and research, enabling his effective study of the great problems of society. The governing board of the university took interest in Mockus's ideas and, in general, in the work of this mathematician-philosopher. In 1989 Mockus was appointed vice-chancellor of the National University.

Academic Reform of the National University

The university professor who had stood out as a critic of the Curricular Reform of 1978, the member of the Extended Committee who had consistently criticized university policies, the professor who shared his concerns with students and who had achieved solid friendships with some of the most fervent critics of the *status quo*, in 1989 took upon himself the responsibility of working towards academic transformation as a member of the university senior management. And he sure did! In a short time, the new vice-chancellor launched a proposal for a broad academic reform that took on the challenge of establishing a research university without weakening teaching or integrated education that was open to interdisciplinary work, through early exposure of students to the construction of knowledge and that increased—through general education courses and the possibility of taking courses in different fields—the abundance of possible learning experiences in an institution that offered undergraduate and graduate degrees in the sciences, arts, humanities, and engineering.

The pillars of the reform were: (1) the integration of research, teaching, and outreach and (2) the increased flexibility of the curriculum. This second pillar increased students' ability to plan their own academic careers and freed schedules and spaces in order to increase contact among professors and students from different fields, to reflect on the epistemological and social meaning of varieties of knowledge, and to allow students towards the end of their degrees to gain some deeper exposure to problems alongside researchers.[5] At the same time, Mockus developed the idea of "intensive pedagogy," according to which professors should simulate the dynamics of the work and communication that research required. This meant that interactions between students and professors had to become more meaningful and effective, heightening communication so that every minute counted and every word was important. The ideal of this model of communication becomes apparent when a project director recommends reading or suggests a method that removes the obstacle paralyzing an investigation. This kind of communication is possible when the professor works with the student, when classes offer the tools for independent work, and when a professor's suggestion becomes the key to subsequent steps.

Later during the 1990s, curricular flexibility became, in Colombia and the rest of the world, a hegemonic academic policy in higher education. However, in contrast with flexibility as conceived by other institutions as a strategy to deal with mobility and lack of employment, Mockus based his concept of flexibility on the necessity to increase students' autonomy, fully aware that students could better take advantage of the academic richness and cultural diversity of the National University of Colombia.[6]

It was only natural that the vice-chancellor who had imagined and propelled this important reform would be appointed chancellor of the university when the new governing board was elected in 1991. Mockus's term heralded a period of extraordinary change for the National University. Although even before his appointment the university had been active on research, the reform gave a phenomenal boost to this function of the university. The university established salary bonuses that rewarded academic production later followed by all public universities. This stimulated the creation of research groups and strengthened institutional support for such groups. In addition, the university launched special conferences for young researchers. The number of publications in renowned journals increased exponentially. The University initiated interdisciplinary courses, open to all students, and offered lectures open even to students from other universities, where well-known and respected professors from specific fields could be heard and recognized by a broader public. During Mockus's tenure, Law 30 was passed in 1992, which is still regulating higher education in Colombia, as well as the National University's own "*Ley Orgánica*" (Organic Law), which is still valid twenty years later. Mockus's participation was instrumental in the creation of both laws, particularly in the case of the "Organic Law."

Antanas, the Chancellor: Responsibility and Imagination

This chancellor, gifted with great imagination and the capability of using symbols in an unexpected and radical way, turned out to be an effective and absolutely transparent administrator; his unconditional honesty was just as notable as the effectiveness and appropriateness of his decisions. He was a chancellor who spoke to the students directly and without pretext, who moved calmly amongst them in moments of great agitation, and who never made concessions nor evaded an argument. Mockus was committed to tirelessly promoting rational agreements and transforming physical violence into symbolic violence when consensus was impossible. The students bought into the game. As such, Mockus could enter into the building occupied by students on strike without bodyguards or go inside to speak with those who had built a dump, as a sign of protest, in the central square of the university.

From infancy, with his mother Nijole, a sculptor, Antanas Mockus had been surrounded by art and had learned to love metaphor. During his bachelor's degree, Mockus was enticed by literature and wrote his own plays. As such, it was no surprise that on a few occasions, as a vice-chancellor and as a chancellor, Mockus relied on the political force of images. For the most part, he was interested in truthful, comprehensible, sincere, and direct communication (the four valuable aspirations that according to Habermas (1965/1984) should satisfy communicative action), but this did not exclude his passion for expressive actions, unexpected gestures, or unusual metaphors whose deeper meanings would later be revealed. So Chancellor Mockus spoke of "living fossils," alluding to the way professors gathered and delivered written tradition, the historical cumulation of the most valuable there is in culture; he spoke of "midwives of the future" to refer to the work of those who taught the new generation that would lead the country and "cultural amphibians," referring to graduates capable of living in the cultural context of their professional posts without giving up the principles of academic culture. "Cultural amphibians" were the practitioners of what would later be referred to as "generalized pedagogy;" the graduates of the National University would be honest and effective professionals, capable of learning and teaching, which is to say, capable of transforming the context of their work into opportunities to act responsibly and impart to people and communities, along with the required solutions, the necessary knowledge to solve their own problems autonomously. Thus it was not only about "learning for the sake of learning," as the popular mantra dictates, but rather "learning to teach" in order to spread the knowledge required to cultivate autonomy of the self and of others. As engineers, architects, or economists, "cultural amphibians" must be able to explain their decisions and the outcomes; social scientists must provide communities with the tools to understand and manage their own problems, and doctors should increase patients' understanding of their own body and health risks.

Mockus introduced radical innovations to undermine barriers between disciplines and to overcome the tensions between research, teaching, and outreach. He then explained coherently and consistently that these were valid strategies to make academia into all it should be. He effectively communicated his intentions, motives, and reasoning to professors and students and went about infecting his interlocutors with his own passion for knowledge and study as academic reform moved forward. To achieve the changes, Mockus worked tirelessly, as he always had, and as he continues to do.

The Pedagogical Movement represented an enrapturing experience of change in the very image of teachers. Similarly, academic staff from different faculties experienced the academic reform as raising greater awareness about the meaning of training and, more fundamentally, as a process of materialization of a shared idea of the university. Both cases harkened to an experience of collective construction, the fruits of solidarity.

For those unaware of the essential differences between the ambition to design an interaction beforehand and the will to promote students' autonomy, it might seem like a paradox that the radical critic of the 1978 reform of primary and secondary school education would become the author and representative of the academic reform of the National University that began in 1990. However, the latter reform focused on what the Reform of 1978 denied: the capacity of the professors from different fields to choose, order, and reorder their knowledge.[7] The academic reform proposed by Mockus demanded that the teaching staff assume a role in constructing pedagogic discourse that, through university training, would allow students access to academic knowledge. Choosing the fundamentals that define the "core" of a profession or discipline and realize "intensive pedagogy" implied a process of collective reflection that, instead of reducing professors' work to the implementation of what had been previously identified, demanded instead that they think about their work both in terms of the more general process of educating new professionals within the context of a complex institution, rich in opportunities for accessing different levels of knowledge and developing a diversity of talents.

In his career as vice-chancellor and chancellor of the National University, Mockus was clear that his work required models of organization and action to realize truthful communication and increase freedom of choice. He exercised his authority with efficiency and with great legitimacy based on his absolute honesty, his fame as an intellectual, his intelligence and responsibility as an administrator, and his conviction that the more aware each individual was of his/her own identity and role in the context of collective actions, the better the chances of tightening bonds and achieving common goals. Mockus believed in modern rationality and criticized the reductionism of instrumental rationality. Thus, he proposed that all students of the university attended courses in the humanities. He believed in the value of communication and trusted that each faculty and each department of the university could arrive at a consensus over the manner of implementing the academic reform, heeding the specificity of the shared formative project.

This turned out to be easier said than done. The habit of encyclopedism and the fear of losing status on the part of professors who taught compulsory topics made it very difficult to arrange and select content. When certain topics became optional, some of the teaching staff felt that they would become inferior to the professors teaching the core curriculum; they felt that they would lose recognition, which according to Bourdieu is true scientific capital. In the university there are "tribes" and "territories," hierarchies and traditions that were difficult to remove (Becher 1989/2001). Fortunately, at that time there emerged academic leaders from practically all the departments and programs who were convinced of the good will of the proposal, and the process offered everyone a larger perspective on their work as teachers and researchers.

In any case, all programs were in need of reform, and indeed some of the proposed reforms were superficial or denied, in practice, flexible orientation. Chancellor Mockus, who participated in the Academic Council and was charged with evaluating them, took advantage of moments of disagreement and converted the council's meetings into spaces of academic debate and effective pedagogy. Not only did he defend the intentions of the reform, but he also showed, for example, that it is impossible to cover all the possible applications of knowledge in each academic field. To successfully confront the new challenges of professional life, it was more essential for students to gain a grasp on the rules of the game and learn the languages of each field than to try to cover the whole universe of possible problems. Moments of potential conflict frequently turned into opportunities for reflection on the purpose of academia, reaffirming the legitimacy of the reform.

The successes of Mockus's administration increasingly legitimized his proposals for change, but the well-known incident at the meeting with students from the Faculty of Arts changed history for this scholar dedicated to academia and transformation. The chancellor, confronted with an auditorium of artists who refused to let him speak, knowing that the youth who admired and loved him were in the majority, and feeling that he was in an environment where acts and symbols produce more impact than words, executed the "performance" of dropping his pants and mooning the students who would not let him talk. Someone was filming. The act left the stage where it was understandable and could bear aesthetic meaning and reached mainstream media.

Mockus was forced to step down from his position as chancellor. However, from then on he was not only recognized for his grasp of symbols, but rather he himself turned into a symbol of integrity, intelligence, and effectiveness in administration. He was already a public figure admired outside the university for his perceptiveness. As such, in spite of being forced out of the space in which he had earned recognition through hard work and unshakable morals, he was invited to participate in the race for mayor of Bogotá. Soon the chancellor, who had been overthrown by the scandal, found himself running a campaign for mayor that seemed impossible—without money, without endorsements by powerful leaders, and without corruption or lies. As a candidate, Mockus was still convinced of the power of communication based on an inalienable commitment to the truth. He spoke more like a professor than a politician, and the citizens recognized his sincerity and integrity. Although not everyone understood everything he said, they understood enough to trust him.

Those who trusted Mockus were not wrong. Surprisingly, the chancellor-philosopher secured a sweeping victory in the election and became a mayor who would change the city, who would increase its resources and achievements, and who would make the city beautiful and pleasant in the eyes of those who had previously perceived it as ugly and hard to live in. Those who elected Mockus knew that he would not betray the city or himself. Many simply trusted his sincerity and the testimonies of those who knew him from his time as a university professor, knowing that he would be faithful to the work that he had started in the Pedagogical Movement and continued at the National University: the work of converting all citizens into a community of teachers and pupils, the work of changing culture and changing perspectives to bring out the collective capacity to transform the world we live in.

Endnotes

1   According to Mockus, Jorge Charum, his respected colleague in mathematics who had similar concerns, gave Mockus key reading recommendations. Some of these readings were important first to Mockus and later to the entire Federici Group.

2   At that time, Mockus was excited by phenomenology, which Guillermo Hoyos promoted within the Department of Philosophy at the National University. This is why the scientific attitude is defined phenomenologically as "conscious ability to deliberately adopt the specific posturing of a science, and while in that project and the particular world, to maintain parallel awareness of the limitations of the field of comprehension determined by that project"(Mockus et al. 1984:105).

3   There is also "symbolic action," which is expressive, aesthetic in nature and drives the production of works of art and, in general, symbols (Habermas 1984/1993).

4   Soon there emerged a community of principles between this proposal and what was called in other contexts "Teacher-proof curriculum," a strategy that would ideally guarantee quality education by fulfilling precise instructions, regardless of teacher training.

5   Curricular flexibility, in the reforms put forth by Antanas Mockus, was conceived of as a distinction between the "professional core," which comprised between 55% and 75% of total hours in each degree and included the basic subjects required for the degree and demonstrated the social expectations of any graduate in each discipline or profession, and a "flexible program," which filled the remaining time—between 25% and 45% of the required hours—and included basic requirements in the humanities or art, a "context course" that provided basic tools for assuming a critical perspective on the student's concentration and social standing inside his/her discipline or profession, and a specialization course to be chosen from several options. As for the courses of the flexible program, these could be core curriculum classes in other departments, specialty classes in other departments, specialty classes offered jointly with other departments, and context courses that covered, among other things, contemporary issues and topics of philosophy, history, sciences, or engineering.

6   Autonomy, and the responsibility that it implies, are basic assumptions of "grown-ups" in the Kantian sense. Autonomy is a vital and unavoidable skill to master in modernity. Mockus had recognized the importance of this principle from the Enlightenment, upon which both he and his colleague philosopher Rubén Jaramillo insisted.

7   Bernstein (1990) demonstrated that learning content was the result of a process of "recontextualization" that transforms knowledge by taking it from the general education

of its construction within research and placing it in the context of appropriation in the classroom. "The pedagogical discourse is, then, a principle that transfers (dislocates) a discourse of practice and substantive context, and relocates it in accordance with its own principles of reordering and selective focus" (Bernstein 1990:127). This transfer implies a combination of three processes: selection, hierarchization, and reorganization of contents.

References

Becher, Tony. 1989/2001. *Tribus y Territorios académicos. La indagación intelectual y las culturad de las disciplinas* [Academic Tribes and Territories. Intellectual Inquiry and Disciplinary Cultures]. Barcelona: Gedisa.

Bernstein, Basil. 1974. "Social Classes, Language and Socialization." Pp. 170-189 in *Class, Codes and Control*, edited by Basil Bernstein, Vol. 1, 2nd ed. London: Routledge. Iin Spanish in Basil Bernstein, "Clases Sociales, Lenguaje y Socialización." *Revista Colombiana de Educación* 15 (1974):17-34.

———. 1990. "Sobre el discurso pedagógico" [On Pedagogic Discourse]. Pp. 119-164 in *La construcción social del Discurso Pedagógico* [The Social Construction of Pedagogic Discourse], edited by Basil Berstein. Bogotá: El Griot.

Bourdieu, Pierre and Jean-Claude Passeron. 1970. *La reproduction: eléments pour une théorie du système d'enseignement* [Reproduction: Elements for a Theory of the Education System]. Paris: Minuit.

Díaz, Mario. 1993. *El campo intelectual de la educación.* [The Intellectual Field of Education]. Cali: University Texts, Universidad del Valle.

Habermas, Jürgen. 1984/1993. "¿Qué significa pragmática universal?" [What is Universal Pragmatics?] Pp. 299-368 in *Teoría de la Acción Comunicativa: complementos y estudios previos* [Theory of Communicative Action: Complements and Prior Studies]. Mexico: Rei.

———. 1965/1984. "Conocimiento e interés" [Knowledge and Interests]. Pp. 159-181 in *Ciencia y Técnica como Ideología* [Science and Technique as Ideology]. Madrid: Tecnos.

Kant, Inmanuel. [1788] 1951. *Crítica de la Razón Práctica* [Critique of Practical Reason]. Buenos Aires: El Ateneo.

Marcuse, Herbert. 1969. *Un ensayo sobre la liberación* [An Essay on Liberation]. Mexico City: Joaquín Moritz Press.

Mockus, Antanas. 1981. "Autonomía del educador" [Autonomy of the Educator]. *Revista Naturaleza* [Nature Review] 1:11-16.

———. 1982. *Tecnología educativa y Taylorización de la Educación* [Educational Technology and Taylorization of Education]. Bogotá: National University of Colombia.

———. 1995a. "La misión de la universidad" [The Mission of the University]. Pp. 15-61 in *Reforma Académica. Documentos* [Academic Reform. Documents]. Bogotá: National University of Colombia.

———. 1995b. *Las fronteras de la escuela* [The Frontier of the School]. Bogotá. Magisterio.

———. 2002. "Movimiento Pedagógico y defensa de la calidad de la educación pública"

[The Pedagogic Movement and the Defense of the Quality of Public Education]. Pp. 281-301 in *Veinte años del Movimiento Pedagógico 1982-2002. Entre mitos y realidades*, [Twenty Years of the Pedagogic Movement 1982-2002. Between Myths and Realities], edited by Abel Rodríguez et al. Bogotá: Magisterio.

Mockus, Antanas, et al. 1984. *El problema de la formación de una actitud científica en el niño a través de la enseñanza de las matemáticas y de las ciencias naturales en la escuela primaria* [The Problem with Forming a Scientific Attitude in Children Via Math and Natural Science Education in Primary School]. Bogotá: National University of Colombia.

8. Law, Morality, and Culture at School[1]

Enrique Chaux and Andrea Bustamante

Legal, Moral, and Cultural Regulation

One of the pillars of Antanas Mockus's *Cultura Ciudadana* (Civic Culture) proposal is the search for harmony between three regulatory systems: law, morality, and culture. For Mockus (N.d.), legal regulation refers to taking certain actions and avoiding others out of fear of punishment because following laws or rules is deemed correct or out of admiration and respect for the legal system. Moral regulation is the internal control each person has over their own actions, based on what they consider right or wrong, driven by emotions such as guilt for acting against their moral conceptions or pride in acting coherently with those conceptions. Cultural regulation refers to the effect that other's reaction has on one's own behavior, which is related to the fear of social sanctions or the search for social recognition.

Mockus (1994) has shown that many of the problems in our societies are related to the lack of alignment among these three systems. Something may be illegal but not be considered immoral by a person or not socially rejected by those around him or her. For example, tax evasion may be illegal, but those who evade taxes may feel proud of their actions and may be admired by others. Mockus suggests that to overcome problems such as violence or corruption these three systems must be aligned. In the evasion example, it would require that whoever considers evading taxes feels fear for the legal sanctions he or she may receive (law), guilt for doing something that goes against ethical principles (moral), or shame caused by disapproval of those around them (culture). In contrast, those who decide not to evade taxes may feel pride for their coherence with their principles, avoiding the fear of legal punishment, and receiving admiration of those around them. If this happens, fewer people would seriously consider these behaviors as an option.

Aligning these three systems inspired many of the actions implemented by Mockus and his team during his two terms as mayor of Bogotá. For example, to increase compliance with traffic regulations, the office of the mayor handed out 350,000 cards that had a "thumbs-up" on one side, as a sign of approval, and a "thumbs-down" on the other with a red background, as a sign of rejection, to pedestrians and vehicle drivers. Through this intervention, citizens began to socially regulate their behavior, aligning culture with morals and the law. This also generated situations where not only police officers were in charge of controlling drivers or pedestrians but also where citizens themselves were exercising control.

However, these citizen-education actions focused almost exclusively on informal settings; that is, they were staged outside formal education institutions. As explained by Sáenz (2007), the citizen education actions of Mockus's terms as mayor favored actions outside of schools.

During Mockus's terms as mayor, several citizen education actions were coordinated by the Office of the Secretary of Education. For example, several massive surveys on *Cultura Ciudadana* were conducted (e.g., Secretaría de Educación Distrital 2001; 2003) and programs such as *"Cultura de la Legalidad"* (Culture of Legality) were piloted in a small number of schools (Bustamante 2008). However, these initiatives did not have the reach and visibility of actions that took place outside of schools. This suggests that a valuable opportunity might have been lost, since schools are a privileged place to impart civic education. In addition, some of the serious problems present in schools today may also be caused by a separation of law, morality, and culture, so that similar strategies that seek harmony among the three systems could also be useful to schools.

In this essay, we aim to show how the proposal of aligning law, morality, and culture can be extremely useful in facing the serious problems that many schools are currently facing. Through this we seek to define possible areas of research and interventions that could be rigorously implemented and evaluated.

The Divorce Among Law, Morality, and Culture at School

Among the most serious problems facing education today are high levels of aggression and school violence. International reports on school violence are concerning. For example, the World Health Organization (Craig and Harel 2004) studied children in forty-one countries and found that on average 16% of students above age eleven (and 25% of boys) have had at least three physical fights in the last year. Also, 15% of eleven-year-old students report they have been subjected to some form of bullying at least twice in recent months.

Extensive studies in specific countries also confirm the existence of high levels of school violence. In Mexico, a study based on surveys of one hundred thousand students showed that 17% of primary school students and 14% of secondary school students have been physically hurt by classmates in the last school year. In addition, 24% of primary students and 14% of secondary students report that their classmates have mocked them constantly in the last school year (Aguilera, Muñoz, and Orozco 2007). In a study of eighty-seven thousand students in Bogotá, we found that one in every three students had been physically attacked by a classmate through punching, slapping, shoving, or pinching in the last month (Chaux and Velazquez 2008). In the same study, two out of every five students had been insulted by a classmate during the last week, and one in every five students reported having been bullied in the last month. All this indicates that aggression is very frequent in schools, a concerning fact given that today we know that frequent and systematic aggression increases the risk of severe problems in life, such as anxiety, depression, dropping out of school, delinquency, violence between romantic partners, and domestic violence, among others (e.g., DeLuca, Pigott, and Rosenbaum 2002; Farrington 2003; Forero et al. 1999; Gladstone, Malhi 2006; Olweus 1993; Pepler et al. 2006; U.S. Department of Education 1998).

School violence levels are high despite the existence of school rules against aggression and in favor of peaceful relationships. When schools set rules and regulations that govern relationships within the school community, they frequently refer to their mission to educate people who can contribute constructively to life in society, inside and outside of the institution. In other words, there seems to be a large distance between school rules and school reality.

On the other hand, laws and rules do not seem to be in harmony with morality, as understood by Mockus. In several studies, we have found that many students approve of aggression and consider it legitimate in various situations. For example, in a study with 1,235 students in seven public schools in Bogotá (Chaux, Arboleda, and Rincón 2012), we found that:

- 71% of students consider that "it is alright to attack those who say bad things about one's mother."
- 57% consider that "it is alright to fight to defend a friend."
- 51% agree that "you have to stop those who offend you the hard way so that they won't do it again."
- 50% think that "people who get hit usually deserve it."

In the same study we found that 40% of students consider that "seeing fights between classmates is fun" (Chaux et al. 2012). This is coherent with studies of conflicts where we have seen that those surrounding the conflict incite aggression by serving as an audience, cheering, or taking sides. Only in 25% of the conflicts do bystanders is one word intervene to de-escalate or curb aggression (Chaux 2005). In other words, many of those who could play a social regulation role in stopping aggression seem, on the contrary, to promote it.

Additionally, in some contexts, the most aggressive children seem to be socially recognized and valued, while non-aggressive children may be undervalued. For example, in the study of seven schools in Bogotá (Chaux et al. 2012), we found that:

- 39% of students consider that "those who are most aggressive are the most respected."
- 28% think that "you have to fight so that people don't think you are a coward."

These results are consistent with studies done in the United States that have shown that some aggressive adolescents can also be popular in their schools (Rodkin et al. 2000). This suggests that assignment of social value and social regulation, which are at the core of what Mockus calls culture, are also contrary to laws and rules. In other words, there seems to be a split between law, morality, and culture behind the high aggression levels in schools.

If school violence is related to a break among law, morality, and culture, finding harmony between these three regulatory systems could contribute to promoting peaceful relationships. This suggests at least two paths of complementary intervention:

(1) interventions that lead students to stop considering that aggression is acceptable or legitimate (moral regulation); (2) interventions that promote willingness to, and knowledge of how to, intervene in order to stop aggressive situations taking place around them (social regulation).

Similar fractures between laws, morality, and culture may be present in other problems in schools, such as theft and fraud. In our studies we have found that 56% of the students in Bogotá and 47% in El Salvador report having been victims of theft at their school in the last year and month, respectively (Chaux and Velásquez 2008). This prevalence is very high, particularly compared with the results of a similar study in the United States where only 4% of the students reported having had something stolen from them at school in the last six months (DeVoe et al. 2004). To better understand the phenomenon of school theft we implemented a qualitative study in a public school located in a neighborhood in Bogotá with serious delinquency problems (Bolívar et al. 2010). First we applied surveys to measure the attitudes of the students towards theft. Of the responses, 54% classified theft as very serious, 39% as slightly serious, and only 7% as not serious at all. In other words, despite most students considering theft very serious, a large number seem to justify it or at least consider it only slightly serious.

In the second phase of the study we interviewed the twenty students with the most lenient attitudes towards theft. During the interviews, several of them spoke freely of their participation in thefts. They explained that there are student networks dedicated to stealing at school, with division of labor: some identify what can be stolen, others serve as lookouts for anyone passing by, others search and take the objects, and others hide and take the objects out of the school to be sold. In addition, several mentioned that stealing gave them status within their group of friends (ibid.). Instead of there being a social regulation mechanism against theft, there seems to be an incentive in the form of social praise from the group. Maybe this is why those interviewed did not seem to feel shame but instead showed pride when narrating the thefts they had committed.

Finally, the study showed that there are rules regarding theft, but that they are seldom applied. Most recognized that there is little teacher supervision, that the thieves are rarely caught, and that when they are caught the disciplinary consequences are not applied or are minor; for example, a few days of suspension or taking some extra-curricular workshops (ibid.).

The results of this study suggest that, if the high levels of school theft are to be reduced, interventions focused on the three regulatory systems may be required:

(1) regarding the regulation of law, rules should be widely and consistently applied and should really play a dissuasive function; (2) regarding moral regulation, it is necessary to reduce the legitimacy of theft and promote the understanding that theft is reprehensible because it negatively affects the victims; (3) regarding cultural regulation, it is necessary to prevent those who steal from being socially admired. Interventions seeking to align legal, moral, and cultural regulations may be key in reducing the problem of school theft in itself. In addition, it could be an opportunity to promote caring for the property of others and even to prevent corruption in the future.

Academic fraud also seems to be very common in schools. In a study done with 440 students from four public schools in Bogotá, we found that 51% of students admit to having copied off a classmate's exam in the last thirty days, and 25% admit to having offered money to someone to complete an assignment in the last month. Both conducts are against the rules set by the schools. Thus these behaviors happen despite only 11% of the students considering that it is alright to cheat when teachers write very difficult exams, and only 8% considering that it is alright to cheat when they need a good grade (Chaux et al. 2006). It is possible that social recognition plays an important role here, if those who commit academic fraud are admired instead of rejected by their classmates. This could help explain why this happens so frequently despite there being so few who state that it is alright to do so. If this is the case, what Mockus calls culture seems to be distanced from laws and morality, which would suggest that interventions focused on changing the social appraisal of fraud could reduce it. This could be an opportunity to change, beginning at school, the social appraisal that those who obtain personal benefits through deceit and cheating frequently receive in our society what Mockus terms the culture of "shortcut culture" (Corzo and Mockus 2003).

In the above paragraphs we have attempted to show how some of the relationship problems in schools may be related to a split among the three regulatory systems identified by Mockus. If this hypothesis holds, the idea of aligning the three systems may inspire interventions that promote peaceful relationships and provide citizenship education within schools. In the rest of the essay we present some aspects that could be taken into account if this alignment of law, morality, and culture were sought after in schools.

Classroom and School Norms

Participating in the process of constructing norms is fundamental for people to understand the meaning of laws, make them their own, and be willing to follow them. To achieve this internal understanding of the law, it is important that the rules that guide relationships in the classroom and at school be built collectively, guaranteeing the active participation of students and teachers. In addition to allowing them a better understanding of the reasons behind the rules and their importance for peaceful relationships, this also reduces the number of arbitrary rules decided upon by a small group but having an impact on many. In other words, the collective construction of rules both helps the members of the community to share and commit to their enforcement (bringing morality and culture closer to law) and also helps the rules come closer to what the members of the community consider just (bringing law closer to morality and culture).

There are two useful dimensions in classifying the way teachers lead their classes. One of them is their level of structure, or how much they promote the establishment and constant application of rules. The other dimension refers to caring, or how much teachers are concerned for the wellbeing of their students, and how much their relationship is based on communication and kindness. Depending on how much teachers gravitate or not towards one or both dimensions (Hughes 2002), their style may be classified into one of these four categories: (1) the authoritarian style, which privileges structure over care. Authoritarian teachers usually define and modify rules arbitrarily and unilaterally without asking their students. They frequently use harsh disciplinary methods such as punishments, yelling, and nagging, and they have few effective communication channels with their students; (2) the permissive style, where teachers privilege care over structure and maintain close, friendly relationships with their students but leave aside limits and rules. Because of this, their classrooms are usually disorganized and there is little enforcement of rules; (3) the negligent style, where teachers do not care for the wellbeing of their students nor do they set limits and rules so that students are usually left alone and without much supervision; (4) the democratic style, where teachers focus both on caring for their students and on maintaining the structure of their classroom. This style allows for permanent student-teacher communication and warm relationships within the classroom, while giving importance to the participative construction of agreements and their constant and consequent enforcement.

When teachers employ a democratic style and students participate in the process of constructing norms through collective discussions, rules—and the benefits these provide to the group or the school community—are generally better understood and internalized. In addition, when they fail to meet any of the norms, it is useful that sanctions or consequences be targeted at repairing the damage instead of punishments that have no relation to the inappropriate behavior. Inspired by restorative justice, this approach helps students understand why what they did was harmful to others, themselves, or the community and propose reparative alternatives (Charney 2002; Elias and Schwab 2006; Nelsen 1998). All of this makes it easier to comprehend the meaning of existing norms and, therefore, could help reduce the distance between law and the other two regulatory systems.

Promoting Social Regulation

As explained above, some of the most problematic behaviors in schools, such as aggression or theft, are sometimes valued among classmates. This social appraisal has a strong impact on individuals due to: (1) the status achieved within the social group by behaving according to the expectations of the group; (2) the difficulty of resisting peer pressure when making decisions; (3) the shame generated by the disapproval received when not behaving according to what the group expects. The magnitude of the social appraisal effect has been verified by classical studies in social psychology. In fact, some experiments have shown that the worst actions of humans against other humans may be explained by pressure from those around them (Zimbardo 2007). For example, Stanley Milgram (1974) simulated a situation in which he told the subjects that the effects of punishment on learning and memory would be observed. The subjects were instructed to administer increasingly strong electric shocks to another person every time they made a mistake in repeating a series of word pairs. What was really being measured was the intensity of electric shocks the subjects were capable of administering under pressure from the instructions given by the experimenter. The victims were not real, but instead actors who pretended to be receiving the shocks. Milgram (ibid.) found that most subjects (63%) administered shocks high enough that the supposed "victim" could have died if the situation had been real. Milgram made several variations to the original experiment and found that the most effective way to make the subjects back out of the experiment was to have peers around them (who were in fact actors following a script) who would refuse to continue administering electric shocks. In this case, only 10% administered high shock levels to the victim. On the other hand, when the group of actors actively celebrated the shocks, laughing and undervaluing the victim, 92.5% of the subjects reached the highest shock levels (ibid.). In summary, the actions of others made over 90% of the subjects participate in what could mean the death of an innocent subject or made over 90% avoid doing so.

The strong effect of actions or appraisals of others (what Mockus calls cultural regulation) could have a strong impact on strategies aimed at promoting citizen education at schools. In the specific case of bullying, there are studies indicating that the role of those around the victims and aggressors determine which way situations go. For example, Hawkins, Pepler, and Craig (2001) found by observing school recesses that when bystanders laughed or showed acceptance towards bullying, aggression got worse. However, if those around the situation jointly intervened to stop the aggression, it stopped in an average of less than ten seconds. In other words, social regulation can be a fundamental aspect in preventing bullying at school. Some experiences have shown the effectiveness of this approach. For example, KiVa, the world's most successful program in curbing bullying, is based on empowerment and the intervention of bystanders (Kärnä et al. 2011; Salmivalli, Kärnä, and Poskiparta 2009).

In our own *"Aulas en Paz"* (Classrooms in Peace) program, we have also focused our prevention work on bystander intervention strategies: (1) holding activities that allow students to see the many ways in which they can intervene to stop the aggressive behavior they see; (2) showing them that if they do not somehow act when someone is being mistreated, they are passively contributing to such mistreatment; (3) teaching them strategies to socially punish aggressive situations, for example by expressing their disapproval in an assertive, firm, and non-aggressive way; (4) teaching them ways to collectively intervene because when a group acts together to stop mistreatment, the probability of success increases, and the risk of getting attacked themselves is reduced (Chaux 2007; Chaux 2012; Chaux et al. 2009).

This suggests that the great power of social regulation may be used by schools to promote peaceful relationships and prevent aggression, bullying, and delinquency, in the same way it was used in Mockus's terms as mayor to encourage citizens themselves to regulate the behavior of others.

Developing Moral Emotions

According to Nico Frijda (1988), every emotion is associated with an action tendency or, in other words, with motivation towards specific behaviors. Some emotions are considered moral because their tendencies towards action can be linked to moral behaviors such as taking prosocial actions that benefit others or avoiding antisocial actions that harm others (Eisenberg 2000). Research in the neurosciences has also shown that emotions are essential when making decisions, particularly moral decisions (Damasio 1994). In this sense, moral emotions are required to bring moral regulation closer to the other regulatory systems. We will briefly refer here to three moral emotions that exemplify this: shame, guilt, and empathy.

According to Elster (1999), shame, understood as the unpleasant sensation that arises when we know others disapprove of our behavior, is the support for social rules. Thus the anticipation of shame can be a strong regulator of human behavior (ibid.). Although we recognize the importance of shame as a behavior regulator, we do not believe that educational programs should promote stronger feelings of shame among students. In fact, this could be risky because some studies have shown that extreme violence is sometimes driven by shame (Gilligan 2001). Instead, it may be relevant to try to alter what the group as a whole values, so that antisocial behavior could provoke rejection and not admiration. In this scenario, when one person harms another, it would be more likely that he or she would feel shame instead of pride.

Guilt, understood as the unpleasant sensation that arises when we break a principle that we consider valuable, has also been defined as a conduct self-regulating emotion (Elster 1999). As presented by Bandura (1999), in the earlier phases of development, conduct is basically guided by external regulatory systems (such as social sanctions), but as time goes by, moral standards are adopted that become the basis for one's own regulatory system. We are not referring to guilt felt for something we have not done (like original sin) or for something that really does no harm (such as most sexual behaviors) but to the discomfort that appears when one has hurt others, when one has not done something that would benefit others, or even when one considers doing something to hurt others. As Mockus (1994:45) states: "A close relationship among morality, culture, and law contributes to linking illegal behavior to feelings of shame and guilt."

In addition, several studies have pointed out the importance of empathy for moral action. Empathy has been defined as the ability to feel what others feel, or at least feel something that is more related to the situation of others than to one's own

(Hoffman 2000). Several studies have shown that empathy is linked to prosocial actions (e.g., Eisenberg 2000) while others have shown that lack of empathy is linked to antisocial actions (Blair 2007; Decety et al. 2009; Endresen and Olweus 2001).

Thus taking moral emotions into account in the classroom may be another effective way of working on the moral regulation system. For example, empathy development can begin at early ages by teaching children to interpret and feel what others are feeling in a specific situation. In Classrooms in Peace, we have used various strategies that lead students to ask themselves what the other person is feeling, what they feel towards their situation, and what they would feel if they were in that position. For example, reading stories where the characters are victims of aggression and asking these thought-provoking questions are exercises that may contribute to developing empathy (Chaux 2010; Chaux et al. 2008).

Another example of how to approach moral emotions in the classroom is the development of strategies that promote considering consequences. In Classrooms for Peace, for example, we encourage students to identify different options to solve a specific conflict and then consider the consequences of each option in terms of: (1) emotions of those involved (e.g., How would X feel? How would Y feel?); (2) implications for their relationship (e.g., What would happen to the relationship between X and Y if they chose this option?) (Chaux et al. 2008). With strategies such as these, students learn to identify their own emotions and those of others as a consequence of their own actions.

As we have shown, moral action (whether prosocial actions that benefit others or inhibition of antisocial actions that may hurt others) is largely motivated by moral emotions, and for this reason, the development of moral action may be essential in bringing morality closer to law and culture. However, the relationship between moral emotion and action is not always direct. This point will be described next.

Preventing Moral Justifications or Moral Shortcuts

There are times when moral emotions such as guilt or shame seem not to be directly linked to behavior. Other times, these emotions are not even generated in people acting against their own ethical principles or against what is socially accepted. Bandura (1999) has suggested that this happens because of what he calls a process of "moral disengagement." This process consists of neutralizing the negative emotions that are generated by acting against one's own value system or against what is socially accepted by using various psychological maneuvers to justify or make the behavior seem reasonable. For example, justifying an action that breaks the law (such as drunk driving) because everyone also does it, neutralizes the effect that guilt could have on our conduct.

Bandura defines eight types of moral disengagement: (1) moral justification, in which "pernicious conduct is made personally and socially acceptable by portraying it as serving socially worthy or moral purposes" (ibid.:103) (e.g., stating that by buying a pirated CD we are helping the seller who has many needs); (2) euphemistic labeling, which takes place when inhumane acts are labeled with words that do not sound that negative (e.g., when civilians injured by bombs are referred to as collateral damage); (3) advantageous comparison, which allows the person to see an action as "not so bad" when compared to another which is much worse (e.g., when claiming that stealing is not as bad when compared with worse things that some people do); (4) displacement of responsibility, which allows people to justify their behavior by showing it as a result of orders of authorities rather than being personally responsible for it (e.g., in Milgram's experiment, some subjects stated that they had not acted freely but were following orders of the experimenter); (5) diffusion of responsibility, which refers to how, when an inhuman act is committed by a group, no one feels individually responsible (e.g., stating that a behavior is legitimate "because everyone does it"); (6) distortion or minimization of consequences, which occurs when the consequences of inhuman acts are disregarded or minimized, particularly when "destructive actions are physically and temporally remote from their injurious effects" (ibid.:108) (e.g., stating that cheating on a test doesn't hurt anyone); (7) dehumanization, which refers to the act of seeing the victims as objects or non-human animals (e.g., referring to the victim as "animal," "dog," or "rat"); (8) attribution of guilt, which consists of "blaming one's adversaries or circumstances" (ibid.:110) (e.g., stating that it is the other person's fault because "he/she started the fight").

Although Bandura's proposals are centered on guilt, other authors such as Elster (1999) mention the importance of shame in similar processes. Elster describes a process in which people unconsciously transform or "twist" the motivations for their actions after feeling guilty but also after feeling ashamed. For example, they make others see that their actions are morally acceptable and can support their justification to the extent that they believe it themselves.

What Bandura defines as a moral disengagement process comes close to the concept of "shortcut culture" mentioned by Corzo and Mockus (2003). The difference, however, is that Corzo and Mockus describe how this process can go beyond the individual and become a culture-wide phenomenon. Thus these disengagement mechanisms, or "shortcuts," become part of the discourse of a whole community, discouraging the harmony not only between moral regulation and law but also between social regulation and legal regulation. In the end, all these justifications are obstacles in bringing law, morality, and culture closer together.

Some interventions exemplify possible educational strategies to prevent moral disengagement. For example, McAlister (2001) reduced moral disengagement towards military actions against Iraq and Yugoslavia through an intervention based on presenting persuasive information in mass media. Similarly, McAlister et al. (2000) reduced moral disengagement related to intolerance and violence between ethnic groups by presenting adolescents with a newspaper that narrated how some students had managed to reject moral disengagement and overcome prejudice.

We also designed and evaluated two short interventions that sought to prevent moral disengagement among ninth-graders. The first intervention was based on social regulation and critical thinking strategies, in which students learned to identify the mechanisms and uncover them in distant or fictional characters, in people closer to them, and in themselves. Finally, students generated alternatives to disengaging (e.g., repairing the damage caused). The second intervention was based on strategies similar to those used by McAlister. In this case students created a newspaper with stories where they, or others close to them, had resorted to moral disengagement mechanisms. Afterwards, they presented the newspaper to seventh grade students and tried to convince them that moral disengagement was not a valid option. Results so far have shown significant reductions in moral disengagement in the first intervention but not in the latter (Bustamante and Chaux 2014).

Inspiring Research and Interventions

This essay has shown that Antanas Mockus's idea of generating a greater harmony among the moral, legal, and cultural regulatory systems is as valid within schools as it is outside schools. Aligning these systems may become a valuable contribution to civic education strategies that seek to prevent later problems such as violence or corruption. This essay has also given certain indications regarding aspects that must be taken into account when designing these actions.

This analysis can open promising areas of research and can help generate school interventions. The innovative actions executed during Mockus's terms as mayor may serve as inspiration for the design of these interventions. For example, the use of cards to socially regulate the conduct of drivers and pedestrians inspired us to include cards with a pirate symbol in one of the interventions we designed to stop moral disengagement. Seeing students use them to show their partners that they were turning to moral disengagement showed us that they were making this symbol their own and that it was working as a stepping stone to socially regulate themselves in a fun and non-aggressive way.

However, although the specific symbols and strategies implemented during Mockus's terms as mayor may serve as inspiration, our proposal is that it is necessary to continue being creative in developing other actions. The specific actions implemented in Mockus's office will not necessarily work within schools. Nonetheless, the general concept of harmonizing the three regulatory systems can be very valuable when combined with a high dose of imagination and creativity. In any case, any initiative must be accompanied by rigorous evaluations. Only then will we know if schools can really contribute to closing the gap among law, morality, and culture that exists within them as well as in society.

Endnotes

1   Acknowledgements: We would like to thank all those who gave us feedback and valuable insights for this essay, especially Sayra Aldana and the group of authors of this book. We are deeply grateful to Carlo Tognato, who patiently led and supported the whole process. We thank Felipe Estrada for translating the chapter. Our gratitude also goes to the editors of Harvard University's Cultural Agents and Fondo de Cultura Económica (Economic Cultural Fund). The final editing of the essay was made possible by a Georg Forster Fellowship granted to the first author by the Alexander von Humboldt Foundation, Germany.

2   Also called authoritative (not to be confused with authoritarian).

References

Aguilera, Antonieta, Gustavo Muñoz, and Adriana Orozco. 2007. *Disciplina, violencia y consumo de sustancias nocivas a la salud en primarias y secundarias* [Discipline, Violence, and the Consumption of Noxious Substances in Primary and Secondary School]. Mexico City: Instituto Nacional para la Evaluación de la Educación [National Institute for the Evaluation of Education].

Chaux, Enrique, Juliana Arboleda, and Claudia Rincón. 2012. "Community violence and reactive and proactive aggression: The mediating role of cognitive and emotional variables". *Revista Colombiana de Psicología* 21: 233-251."

Bandura, Albert. 1999. "Moral Disengagement in the Perpetration of Inhumanities." *Personality and Social Psychology Review* 3:193-209.

Blair, R.J.R. 2007. "The Amygdala and Ventromedial Prefrontal Cortex in Morality and Psychopathy." *Trends in Cognitive Sciences* 11:387-392.

Bolívar, Claudia, Julián Contreras, Manuela Jiménez, and Enrique Chaux. 2010. "Desentendimiento moral y dinámicas del robo escolar" [Moral Indifference and Dynamics of School Robberies]. *Revista Criminalidad* 52:243-261.

Bustamante, Andrea. 2008. *"Toda la sociedad sufre, por uno pagan todos... entonces por eso son las leyes": Análisis del programa cultura de la legalidad* [The Entire Society Suffers, Everyone Pays on the Behalf of an Individual... That's What Laws Are For. Analysis of the Culture of Lawfulness Program] (Documento CESO, No. 143). Bogotá: Uniandes.

Bustamante, Andrea, and Enrique Chaux. 2014. "Reducing Moral Disengagement Mechanisms: A Comparison of Two Interventions." *Journal of Latino-Latin American Studies.*

Bustamante, Andrea, Enrique Chaux, Melisa Castellanos, Manuela Jiménez, Ana M. Nieto, Gloria I. Rodríguez, Robert Blair, Andrés Molano, Cecilia Ramos, and Ana M. Velásquez. 2008. "Aulas en Paz: Estrategias pedagógicas" [Classrooms In Peace: Pedagogical Strategies]. *Revista Interamericana de Educación para la Democracia* [International Review of Education for Democracy] 1(2):123-145.

Charney, Ruth S. 2002. *Teaching Children to Care: Classroom Management for Ethical and Academic Growth, K-8.* Greenfield: Northeast Foundation for Children.

Chaux, Enrique. 2005. "The Role of Third Parties in Conflicts among Colombian Children and Early Adolescents." *Aggressive Behavior* 31:40-55.

———. 2007. "Aulas en Paz: A Multi-component Program for the Promotion of Peaceful Relationships and Citizenship Competencies." *Conflict Resolution Quarterly* 25:79-86.

———. 2010. "Empathy: Pedagogical Strategies to Promote Empathy." Pp. 143-158 in *Indirect and Direct Aggression,* edited by Karin Österman. Frankfurt: Peter Lang.

———. 2012. *Educación, Convivencia y Agresión Escolar* [Education, Peaceful Relationships, and Aggression in Schools] Bogotá: Taurus, Santillana, Uniandes.

Chaux, Enrique, Andrea Bustamante, Melisa Castellanos, María P. Chaparro, and Manuela Jiménez. 2009. "Intimidación escolar y el rol de los testigos" [Bullying and the Role of Bystanders]. Pp. 83-98 in *Educación en valores y ciudadanía desde una perspectiva cotidiana* [Education in Values and Citizenship From a Daily Perspective], edited by Gloria I. Rodríguez. Bogotá: Organización de Estados Iberoamericanos [Organization of Ibero-American States], Santa María Press.

Chaux, Enrique, Andrea Bustamante, Melisa Castellanos, and Laura Restrepo. 2008. "¿Una moralidad o varias moralidades? Desentendimiento moral y acción moral en el contexto educativo" [One Morality or Various Moralities? Moral Indifference and Moral Action in the Educational Context]. Bogotá: University of the Andes. Unpublished Manuscript.

Chaux, Enrique, Andrés Molano, and Paola Podlesky. 2009. "Socio-economic, Socio-political and Socio-emotional Variables Explaining School Bullying: A Country-wide Multilevel Analysis." *Aggressive Behavior* 35:520-529.

Chaux, Enrique, and Ana M. Velásquez. 2008. "Violencia en los colegios de Bogotá: Contraste internacional y algunas recomendaciones" [Violence in Bogotá's Middle Schools: International Comparisons and Some Recommendations]. *Revista Colombiana de Educación.* 55:13-37.

Corzo, Jimmy, and Antanas Mockus. 2003. *Cumplir para convivir: Factores de convivencia y tipos de jóvenes por su relación con normas y acuerdos* [Checklist for Coexistence: Factors for Coexistence and Types of Young People According to their Relationship with Norms and Agreements]. Bogotá: National University of Colombia.

Craig, Wendy M., and Yossi Harel. 2004. "Bullying, Physical Fighting and Victimization." Pp. 133-144 in *Young People's Health in Context. Health Behaviour in School-aged Children (HBSC) Study: International Report from the 2001/2002 Survey,* edited by Candace Currie, Chris Roberts, Antony Morgan, Rebecca Smith, Wolfgang Settertobulte, Oddrun Samdal, y Vivian Barnekow-Rasmussen. Copenhagen: World Health Organization.

Damasio Antonio. 1994. *Descartes' Error: Emotion, Reason, and the Human Brain.* New York: Puntam.

Decety, Jean, Kalina J. Michalska, Yuko Akitsuki, and Benjamin B. Lahey. 2009. "Atypical Empathic Responses in Adolescents with Aggressive Conduct Disorder: A Functional MRI Investigation." *Biological Psychology* 80:203-211.

DeLuca, Stefanie, Terri Pigott, and James E. Rosenbaum. 2002. "Are Dropout Decisions Related to Peer Threats, Social Isolation, and Teacher Disparagement across Schools? A Multilevel Approach to Social Climate and Dropout." Presented at AERA Conference, April, New Orleans, LA.

DeVoe, Jill, Katharin Peter, Phillip Kaufman, Amanda Miller, Margaret Noonan, Thomas Snyder, and Katrina Baum. 2004. *Indicators of School Crime and Safety: 2004* (NCES 2005–002/NCJ 205290). U.S. Departments of Education and Justice. Washington, D.C.: Government Printing Office.

Eisenberg, Nancy. 2000. "Emotion, Regulation, and Moral Development." *Annual Review of Psychology* 51:665-697.

Elias, Maurice J., and Yoni Schwab. 2006. "From Compliance to Responsibility: Social and Emotional Learning and Classroom Management." Pp. 309-341 in *Handbook of Classroom Management: Research, Practice, and Contemporary Issues*, edited by Caroline M. Evertson, and Carol S. Weinstein. Mahwah: Lawrence Erlbaum Associates.

Elster, Jon. 1999. *Alchemies of the Mind. Rationality and the Emotions.* Cambridge: Cambridge University Press.

Endresen, Inger, and Dan Olweus. 2001. "Self-reported Empathy in Norwegian Adolescents: Sex Differences, Age Trends, and Relationship to Bullying." Pp. 147-165 in *Constructive and Destructive Behavior: Implications for Family, School, and Society*, edited by Arthur Bohart, and Deborah Stipek. Washington, D.C.: American Psychological Association.

Farmer, Thomas W., Philip C. Rodkin, Ruth Pearl, and Richars Van Acker. 2000. "Heterogeneity of Popular Boys: Antisocial and Prosocial Configurations." *Developmental Psychology* 36:14-24.

Farrington, David P. 1993. "Understanding and Preventing Bullying." *Crime and Justice* 17:381-458.

Forero, Roberto, Lyndall McLellan, Chris Rissel, and Adrian Bauman. 1999. "Bullying Behaviour and Psychosocial Health among School Students in New South Wales, Australia: Cross Sectional Survey." *British Medical Journal* 319:344-348.

Frijda, Nico H. 1988. "The Laws of Emotion." *American Psychologist* 43:349-358.

Gilligan, James. 2001. *Preventing Violence.* New York: Thames & Hudson.

Gladstone, Gemma L., Gordon B. Parker, and Gin S. Malhi. 2006. "Do Bullied Children Become Anxious and Depressed Adults? A Cross-sectional Investigation of the Correlates of Bullying and Anxious Depression." *The Journal of Nervous and Mental Disease* 194:201-208.

Harris, Judith R. 1999. *The Nurture Assumption*. New York: Touchstone.

Hawkins, D. Lynn, Debra J. Pepler, and Wendy M. Craig. 2001. "Naturalistic Observations in Bullying." *Social Development* 10:512-526.

Hoffman, Martin L. 2000. *Empathy and Moral Development: Implications for Caring and Justice*. New York: Cambridge University Press.

Hughes, Jan N. 2002. "Authoritative Teaching: Tipping the Balance in Favor of School versus Peer Effects." *Journal of School Psychology* 40:485-492.

Little, Todd D., Antti Kärnä, Marinus Voeten, Elisa Poskiparta, Anne Kaljonen, and Christina Salmivalli. 2011. "A Multilevel Evaluation of the KiVa Anti-bullying Program." *Child Development* 82(1):311-330.

McAlister, Alfred L., Enomoyi Ama, Cristina Barroso, Ronald J. Peters, and Steven Kelder. 2000. "Promoting Tolerance and Moral Engagement through Peer Modeling." *Cultural Diversity and Ethnic Minority Psychology* 6(4):363-373.

McAlister, Alfred L. 2001. "Moral Disengagement: Measurement and Modification." *Journal of Peace Research* 38(1):87-99.

Milgram, Stanley. 1974. *Obedience to Authority. An Experimental View*. New York: Harper & Row.

Mockus, Antanas. 1994. "Anfibios culturales y divorcio entre ley, moral y cultura" [Cultural Amphibians and Divorce Between Law, Morality, and Culture]. *Análisis político* [Political Analysis] 21:37-48.

———. N.d. *Armonizar ley, moral y cultura. Cultura ciudadana, prioridad de gobierno con resultados en prevención y control de violencia en Bogotá, 1995-1997* [Harmonizing Law, Morality, and Culture. Citizen Culture, Government Priority with Results in Violence Prevention and Control in Bogotá, 1995-1997]. Retrieved February 10, 2007 (http://www3.iadb.org/sds/doc/2102spa.rtf).

Nelsen, Jane. 1998. *Disciplina positiva* [Positive Discipline]. Bogotá: Planeta.

Olweus, Dan. 1993. *Conductas de acoso y amenaza entre escolares* [Conducts of Harrassment and Threats Among Students]. Madrid: Morata.

Pepler, Debra J., Wendy M. Craig, Jennifer A. Connolly, Amy Yuile, Loren McMaster, and Depeng Jiang. 2006. "A Developmental Perspective on Bullying." *Aggressive Behavior* 32:376-384.

Sáenz, Javier. 2007. *Desconfianza, civilidad y estética: las prácticas formativas estatales por fuera de la escuela en Bogotá, 1994-2003* [Mistrust, Civility, and Aesthetics: Formative State Practices Outside the School in Bogotá, 1994-2003]. Bogotá: National University of Colombia.

Salmivalli, Christina, Antti Kärnä, and Elisa Poskiparta. 2009. "From Peer Putdowns to Peer Support: A Theoretical Model and How it Translated into a National Anti-bullying Program." Pp. 441-454 in *Handbook of School Bullying: An International Perspective*, edited by Shane R. Jimerson, Susan M. Swearer, and Dorothy L. Espelage. New York: Routledge.

District Secretary of Education of Bogotá. 2001. *Prueba de Sensibilidad, Comprensión y Convivencia Ciudadana.* [Quiz of Sensibility, Understanding, and Citizen Coexistence] Bogotá: Secretary of District Education, Mayor's Office of Bogotá.

———. 2003. *Evaluación de Competencias y Valores para la Convivencia Ciudadana.* [Evaluation of Competencies and Values for Promoting Citizen Coexistence]. Bogotá: Secretary of District Education, Mayor's Office of Bogotá.

Slaby, Ronald G., and Nancy G. Guerra. 1988. "Cognitive Mediators of Aggression in Adolescent Offenders: 1. Assessment." *Developmental Psychology* 24:580-588.

Tangney June P., and Ronda L. Dearing. 2002. *Shame and Guilt.* New York: Guilford Press.

U.S. Department of Education. 1998. *Preventing Bullying: A Manual for Schools and Communities.* Washington, D.C.: Department of Education.

Zimbardo, Philip G. 2007. *The Lucifer Effect: Understanding How Good People Turn Evil.* New York: Random House.

9. Antanas Mockus as Pedagogue: Communicative Action, Civility, and Freedom

Javier Sáenz Obregón

Introduction

Antanas Mockus (pedagogue, philosopher, former chancellor of the National University of Colombia, two-time mayor of the city of Bogotá [1995-1997, 2001-2003], vice-presidential and presidential candidate, and cultural agent of theoretical and practical significance) can be viewed as a cosmopolitan thinker and as a practical reasoner at the local level. His two administrations transformed the civic culture of Bogotá, creating new, more democratic and legitimate forms of exercising state power. Drawing from Mockus's conceptual reflections and, in part, from two studies (Sáenz 2004, 2007a) in which I scrutinized in detail the out-of-school pedagogical practices of his two administrations, I will examine the reaches and limits of Mockus's pedagogy. I will attempt to show that it constituted a creative and visionary pedagogical experiment with significant and positive effects in the creation of a more democratic culture in the city of Bogotá and in the collective ethical, pedagogical, and political imagination of the country's population.

From a Deweyan pragmatic point of view, the pedagogical practices of Mockus's two administrations positively transformed and adequately assessed, from a contextual perspective, the main problem of the civic culture of the city and the role of the local government in dealing with it: the problem of creating the "minimum commonality" required in a fragmented culture and society.

Furthermore, by bypassing conservative conceptions of a common *a priori* that would unite humanity around a common human nature, thereby narrowly fixing its possibilities, Mockus envisioned–following John Rawls–an *a posteriori* commonality as an effect of practices through which different cultural groups could agree on common norms *for different reasons* (Mockus 1997). In this sense, his vision was quite close to Dewey's radical conception of a democratic pedagogical experiment, but to my mind, there were problems in envisioning the city and its population as a "pedagogical situation," that is, as a formative "field of forces."

Viewed from the perspective of Foucault's later works (2006, 2007), Mockus's pedagogical discourse and practice can be viewed as one of the most sophisticated instances of liberal, regulatory, post-disciplinarian forms of government, founded on what I would term the "strategic uses of liberty." The pedagogical discourse and practices of his two administrations can be clearly understood as high modern ideals in their emphasis on the defense of life and their distrust of the sole use of the State's juridical and punitive force through their emphasis on "free persuasion" of the population and *voluntary* individual and social regulations.

The effectiveness of these liberal forms of governing depends on the perception that these regulations are carried out freely or, in Mockus's pedagogical terms, voluntarily. The problem with this is that freedom is not, as Christianity would have us believe, a natural spiritual dimension of human beings. Relative autonomy is something to be gained, always within relations of power. In this sense, one of the most problematic issues of Mockus's discourse and practice was that of believing that a governmental strategy can be placed on an equal playing field with that of civil society, in terms of the possibility of creating cultural and pedagogical situations characterized by reasonable rather than strategic forms of conversation.

I will begin with some conceptualizations of pedagogy and an examination of Mockus's pedagogical reflections in the context of his participation in Colombia's Pedagogical Movement, highlighting their recurrences and discontinuities with the pedagogical practices of his two administrations. I will then analyze in some detail the pedagogical discourse and practices of his two terms as mayor of Bogotá in order to understand their reach and limitations in terms of cultural agency. Finally, I will present some concluding reflections on Mockus as a state pedagogue-cultural agent.

Mockus, Pedagogy, and the Pedagogical Movement

In the mid-1980s, pedagogy entered the Colombian public sphere with enormous force, becoming the central discourse in two of the most significant cultural events in the country over the last century, and in which Mockus played a central role: the Pedagogical Movement and the pedagogical practices of his two terms as mayor of Bogotá. Since then, pedagogy has acquired very specific and intense resonances in the country: that of political and cultural mobilization, meaningful interactions, intellectual autonomy, and legitimate actions on the part of the state. In this context, Mockus is remembered and viewed by many in the country more as a pedagogue than as a philosopher or politician.

Pedagogy erupted on the public stage in Colombia at a moment in which, possibly with the single exception of German educational thought, it had become a subordinate knowledge internationally.[1] This subordination resulted, in part, from a process initiated in the first three decades of the last century through which pedagogy came to be seen as an unscientific and unsystematic knowledge from the past to be replaced by the "Sciences of Education" (psychology, sociology, educational administration, among others) which had become the dominant and "modern" educational discourse.[2] Until then, and since the birth of the school as an institution in the fifteenth century, pedagogy had been consolidated as a discipline that was formed through the pedagogical treatises of Vives, Comenius, Pestalozzi, Herbart, and Dewey, amongst many others.

Building upon Olga Lucía Zuluaga's (1987) groundbreaking conceptualizations, pedagogy, as it has historically existed, can be defined as a discipline that conceptualizes on, applies and experiments with, knowledge relative to formation in schools. The field of pedagogy has historically been one of tensions and struggles. It has been constituted as a complex and liminal knowledge that encompasses conceptual and prescriptive dimensions, as well as that of the goals of life and education. Therefore, it appears in the dualist borders of modern thought and practices, highlighting key problematic dimensions of social practices such as the relationships between the individual and society, between morality and knowledge, between words and things, and between means and ends.[3]

Furthermore, it can be argued that pedagogical discourse and school practices have been two of the main forces in the constitution of the modern subject and culture, as well as key scenarios for the production of social commonality.[4] In this sense, pedagogues and teachers can be viewed as the principal cultural agents of modernity, as agents of what can be called the "pedagogical obsession of modernity," through which the post-Enlightenment tribe has been led to believe that its individual and collective happiness, freedom, morality, and truth depend—almost exclusively—on how they are formed by others.[5]

Since the 1960s, following an international wave, pedagogy in Colombia increasingly became a term that encompassed out-of-school intentional educational practices, which was later amplified during Mockus's first term as mayor of Bogotá. The significant diffusion of these practices was a complex event. On the one hand, as part of the discourse and strategies for the *development* of peripheral nations, international agencies such as the World Bank and the United Nations Educational, Scientific, and Cultural Organization (UNESCO) pointed out the limits and failures of schooling in terms of their contribution to sustainable economic development and prescribed out-of-school policies such as non-formal and permanent education.[6] On the other hand, Marxist and Neomarxist sociologists such as Bowles and Gintis (1976) and Bourdieu and Passeron (1977) criticized the effects of schooling in the reproduction of cultural and economic differences. Simultaneously, especially in Latin America, an out-of-school popular education movement emerged, inspired among others, by the writings of Paulo Freire, and characterized by practices of literacy and political conscientization of workers.[7] In the 1990s, out-of-school pedagogy brought to the public scene new themes and concepts, such as the urgency of forming a "knowledge society."[8] There was also a concern for developing social capital and turning cities into educative scenarios.[9] In Colombia, it contributed to the crystallization of a new type of participatory and democratic citizen envisioned by the new Constitution of 1991—one who should contribute to solving the country's social problems, its violence, and the illegitimacy of the state.[10]

In the second half of the 1980s, as a member of the Federici Group, Mockus became a public figure who wrote and spoke extensively on pedagogy and educational policy.[11] This group was one of the main academic groups that were part of the National Pedagogical Movement, a cultural movement for the transformation of teaching and schools that in its years of greatest intensity (1984-1987) and, under the leadership of the Colombian Teachers' Federation (FECODE), had enormous impact on teachers' discourse and practices, on academia, and on educational policies.[12] Mockus and the group spearheaded the critique of the detailed design of teaching practices in the government's *Curricular Reform* that had begun to be implemented in 1978 and envisioned a "teacher-proof curriculum" (Mockus et al.

1985a, 1985b). The reform was ultimately withdrawn after strong opposition from the Pedagogical Movement.

As a pedagogue and cultural agent, Mockus's performances have been renewed periodically: he has chosen new scenarios, new scripts, new co-actors, new props, and new dramatic devices; but there have also been elements of continuity. Within the Pedagogical Movement there were two main themes in his writings that illustrate the pedagogical transformations and continuities between this period and his two terms as mayor of Bogotá.[13]

In the first place, Mockus and the Federici Group defined pedagogy as a primarily communicative competence to be developed through argued reorientations of classroom interactions. Following Habermas, this communicative competence was understood as the capacity of individuals to "reciprocally adjust their actions in the search of a mutual understanding and a free agreement that is subjectively perceived as such" (Mockus et al. 1995:19).[14] This made possible forms of communication that would exist outside relations of domination and the attainment of non-coactive consensus (Mockus et al. 1986, 1995). This idea of a free, non-coercive, open-ended, and dialogical communication, rather than its strategic disposition in order to influence the decisions of others in pursuit of specific ends, would be at the heart of the pedagogical discourse of his two administrations. It was problematic, as already noted, due to the asymmetrical power relations between state agents—who were the primary pedagogical subjects of his administrations—and the general population. Such an asymmetry becomes intensified in political cultures such as Colombia's where, historically, state agents represent a form of power that is extremely distant from having been constituted by processes viewed as legitimate by significant sectors of the population. Furthermore, this idealized conception of pedagogy was diffused during Mockus's two administrations and even used as an adjective. A "pedagogical" action or interaction was one that often referred to action that was intrinsically virtuous, democratic, entertaining, and intelligent.

In the second place, Mockus and the group proposed a transformation of traditional school practices, which they defined as "ascetic pedagogies" founded on the discontinuity and opposition between will and desire, into "hedonistic pedagogies" that would enable the formation of a will that would be a continuation of desire (Mockus et al. 1995:50). They conceived the formation of a "hedonistic morality" through the mediations of knowledge and through processes of intensified communication, expression, and interpretation (ibid.:52). This radical pedagogical transformation was, to their minds, something that required a change in the moral basis of social life and therefore "a step that probably transcends schools" (ibid.:62). The group also highlighted Habermas's conception of "symbolic actions" as non-propositional expressive actions, exemplified in artistic practices (ibid.:93) that, as we shall see, had a central place in some of the more hedonistic pedagogical practices of his two administrations.

Thirdly, Mockus reflected on the problems of schooling in terms that can be seen as conducive to the emphasis of his two administrations on out-of-school pedagogical practices. In his critique on the evaluation of quality of education in the country through standardized tests, Mockus pointed out a number of dimensions that these criteria left out and that would be central to his pedagogical strategies as mayor: the ethical-political dimension in terms of democratic coexistence (living well together), a truthful and sincere use of language, and the cultivation of an internal morality (Mockus 1984).[15]

Drawing from Basil Bernstein, the Federici Group also criticized the discontinuities between school and everyday knowledge, arguing that a more intense relationship between school culture and ordinary cultural practices would favor the weakening of schooling mechanisms such as social differentiation and segregation, as well as facilitate pedagogical innovations (Mockus et al., 1995).[16] What Mockus and the group sought was a meaningful articulation between the universalistic and "common" culture and *elaborated* linguistic codes characteristic of school knowledge and the diverse cultures and *restricted* codes of students' everyday knowledge: "it should be possible to relate in a mutually clarifying way, the 'epistemological' characteristics of school knowledge with its 'sociolinguistic' features" (Mockus et al. 1986:26).

For the Group, in Habermas' terms, the specificity of the communicative competence that should characterize school pedagogy would be that its statements relate to three dimensions: the external reality of what is held as the existing state of affairs; the internal reality that the speaker would like to express in terms of his/her intentions; and the normative reality of that which is recognized inter-subjectively as a legitimate interpersonal relation. This conception is quite close, in pedagogical terms, to the aim of Mockus's second administration, which was the harmonization of culture, morality, and the law that in practical terms was especially problematic given the population's existing cultural practices, norms, and values. It is in this cultural dimension that radical discontinuities took place. Rather than designing strategies to weaken the isolation of schools from everyday life, Mockus's two administrations undertook a pedagogization of city life, targeting the out-of-school population, without a sufficiently explicit and extended effort to relate the State's pedagogical strategies to the existing cultures of the city's population.

Mockus's critique of the limits and problems of school pedagogy helps explain the change of the pedagogical scenario: the achievement of the goal of his two administrations of radical and rapid transformation of the population's civic culture required scenarios closer to everyday life and where the population as a whole could be engaged in a host of strategic issues in the life of the city that are not part of the central concerns of schools. Along these lines, the development plan of his first administration states: "Civic culture can be acquired partly in schools, but without rapid changes in everyday culture, the schools' efforts will be cruelly destroyed by the everyday experiences of the city" (Mayor's Office of Bogotá 1997:3).[17]

This is the general scenario in which Mockus moved from being, as an academic, one of the main voices of resistance against the state's educational reforms for schools to becoming an out-of-school state pedagogue. In contrast to those who see him as a prophet, highlighting exclusively his innovations as pedagogue and cultural agent, I believe he can be best viewed as an innovator and as an empowerer of pedagogical discourses and practices of his time and also as an innovator in terms of pedagogical practices.

Pedagogy and Cultura Ciudadana in Mockus's Two Administrations

Mockus's two pedagogical administrations were extremely surprising and innovative events for the state's political and educational policies in the country—and probably in the world—in terms of their grounding in a rigorous and complex discourse that integrated pedagogical, philosophical, and human science conceptions. It would be hard to find another example in modern democracies of such a dynamic relationship between knowledge and power in state practices; of the use of concepts for the design and implementation of public policy; and of the examination of governmental experiences for the modification of the initial conceptual system. The two administrations also radically extended the formative reach of democratic forms of governance by redefining the central purpose of the State as the formation of the population in almost all places and times.

The Formation of a Cultura Ciudadana

Mockus's change of scenario and audience as mayor of Bogotá also brought a change in co-actors—none of the members of the Federici Group participated in his two administrations—and in the language that was used, which became more colloquial and used symbols intensively. The pedagogical core of the strategies of his two administrations was the formation of *Cultura Ciudadana* (Civic Culture), a term that since then has been appropriated extensively by the central state, other local governments, and social organizations. In general terms, Mockus's two administrations used the definition of *Cultura Ciudadana* that was incorporated in the development plan of the first administration:

> the minimum set of shared customs, actions, and norms that generate a sense of belonging, facilitate urban coexistence, and lead to the respect of the common heritage and to the recognition of citizens' rights and duties. Its purpose is the promotion and coordination of public and private actions that directly affect the way citizens perceive, recognize, and use social and urban milieus and how they relate to each other ... (Mayor's Office of Bogotá 1995).

In a series of reflections in the year before his first administration, Mockus (1994a, 1994b) established the central characteristics of this *Cultura Ciudadana*. He specified the individual and collective dimensions that it was to form: the common conducts, aptitudes, and customs necessary for social coexistence and the strengthening of social cohesion. He also specified the pedagogical strategies to be privileged: actions carried out in non-institutional settings for intensified face-to-face interactions through practices of cultural regulation between anonymous citizens. The idea here was that citizens would learn to regulate each other's conduct *voluntarily*, without the intervention of state authorities, thereby reducing the conflictive and impulsive behaviors that were deemed to be prevalent in the Colombian population.

Again, in the years between his two administrations, Mockus (2001, 2002) reflected on the strategies and results of his first term as mayor of the city, which led to changes in the pedagogical emphasis for the formation of *Cultura Ciudadana* in his second term. The central idea of these reflections was that unlike "stable industrialized societies," in Colombia there was a great divorce among legal, moral (individual), and cultural (collective) forms of regulation of conduct that weakened each one of them. He held that this fragmentation of regulatory systems in the country explained the "increase of violence, crime, and corruption, in the, illegitimacy of institutions, in the weakening of many cultural traditions, and in the crisis or weakness of individual morality" (Mockus 2001:6). For Mockus, this situation required the design of simultaneous and balanced actions on these three regulatory systems in order to produce greater harmony in what the individual considers to be morally valid, in that which is approved by the social group's cultural codes, and that which is sanctioned by state law. Each of these regulatory systems was to be transformed through the production of positive and negative feelings in terms of their civic adequacy or inadequacy: admiration for the law or fear of legal sanctions, self-satisfaction, or feelings of guilt in the case of moral regulations, and social admiration or fear of social censorship in cultural regulations.

The goal of harmonizing these regulatory systems was to "eliminate (or reduce) the moral and cultural approval of illegal actions" (Mockus 2001:6) and increase the approval of upholding the law. Although, as it stands, this could be read as yet another defense of the authoritative force and sanctity of the law—as some of Mockus's critics have pointed out, to my mind, erroneously—in Mockus's conceptions and in the pedagogical strategies of his second government, the law was not conceived as static but as something to be transformed through democratic processes so that it too could be adjusted, if necessary, to moral and cultural rules. Mockus's pedagogical and cultural project can be viewed as an attempt to go beyond communitarian perspectives that exclusively validate the cultural practices of specific groups, as well as universalistic ones—such as Lawrence Kohlberg's (1992)—that reify the autonomous universalistic moral rationality of the individual, conceived as capable of post-conventional (that is post-cultural) moral reasoning.

Mockus sought a commonality that can be best understood, to my mind, in the light of John Dewey's radical conception of democracy as the maximum possible of shared experience: a commonality not fragmented, neither by the irreducible differences amongst cultural groups, nor by the actions of heroic individuals impervious to shared communal experience.[18] It was an attempt to resolve the opposition between a practical and contextualized rationality—Aristotle's *phronesis* as delineated in his *The Nicomachean Ethics* (1998)—and moral universals, via the idea that the law should embody the common minimum agreements of a specific society. In a democratic society, it would be a plastic conception of the law that would best articulate the relative dynamism and contingency of modern cultural and individual practices with the relative stability and abstraction of shared principles and norms.[19]

The Pedagogization of City Life

The practices of Mockus's two administrations were disposed towards the pedago-gization of city life to the point that his two development plans read more like pedagogical manuals than traditional technocratic documents. Their central idea was that all the government's actions would lead to "civic formation, where we all learn from each other." (Mayor's Office of Bogotá 1997). In the first government's plan, this purpose emphasized state practices that would help "people to learn how to use their city well," (ibid.) through citizens' self-regulation, social regulation of others, and their regulation of the government's actions through participation. The general ends of this civic formation were very ambitious. In the first administra-tion they included the modification of conducts contrary to democratic life, the collective construction of a shared image of the city, the development of under-standing and observance of civic rules, and the generation of feelings of belonging to the city. More specifically, the plan contemplated a radical transformation in the conduct of the population regarding peaceful interactions; arguing for agreement on common ends; enriched forms of expression, communication, and interpreta-tion (that included the arts); an increase in the knowledge and understanding of environmental issues; the defense and adequate use of public spaces; the training of public servants in order to strengthen the credibility of state institutions; the development of citizens' consciousness of their duties and rights as taxpayers; and the rational use of public goods and services.

The development plan of Mockus's second administration (Mayor's Office of Bogotá 2001) introduced new objectives and, in comparison with the first administration—which had emphasized cultural regulations among individuals in its implementation—it sought to give equal force to pedagogical strategies for strengthening legal regulations as well as moral regulations that appealed directly to the individual's conscience. It focused the education of public officials and the population on a series of values and principles that were deemed to be especially weak in order to harmonize the law, morality, and culture.[20] The new goals introduced for the formation of a civic culture placed a greater emphasis on legal and political dimensions, with the purpose of making the population understand the democratic foundation of the law, the social benefits gained by observing it, and the democratic process through which laws can be changed. The population was to be educated in *voluntary* obedience of the law, in their knowledge and promotion of human rights, in the design and observance of mutual agreements, and in public debate and political participation. In discontinuity with the first administration, social organizations became specific targets of the government's pedagogical strategy; they were to be strengthened in their capacity to create ties of solidarity and to represent citizens in public decisions.[21] Through the program "Life is Sacred," the plan also introduced educational practices for protecting life, referring to the voluntary disarmament of the population, promoting healthy lifestyles, and decreasing violent crimes, accidents, and suicides.

Most of the state institutions of Bogotá and the investment projects implemented in Mockus's two administrations incorporated a pedagogical component, through which, in an almost omni-comprehensive way, the different scenarios of urban life became pedagogized: individuals' moral intimacy, family life, work places, social organizations, and state institutions; jails, bars, and places of entertainment; cultural and sporting events; private and public transportation; and public spaces. The content of their formative practices included the arts, culture, tourism, recreation, transportation, public utilities, the environment, taxation, commerce, security, health and nutrition, childhood and youth, emergencies and disasters, and housing. They also encompassed specific formative issues such as recycling, the use of free time, economic production, personal development, the consumption of alcohol and illegal drugs, violence against children and women, literacy, the use of fireworks, and technical education. Finally, they carried out a series of formation practices that were at the core of their central purpose of creating a *Cultura Ciudadana*, such as those regarding citizens' rights and duties, laws and norms of coexistence, the sense of belonging to the city, gender equity, peaceful conflict resolution, and the formation of democratic values and practices.

Formative practices were primarily carried out by state officials and were clearly focused on the poorest, although a good number were also directed at the general population as well as at specific groups, such as street-dwellers, sex workers, recyclers, unemployed youth, police, cyclists, pedestrians, and bus and taxi drivers. They used both face-to-face and deterritorialized pedagogical media such as television and radio programs and commercials, videos, street banners, the printed press, and other printed materials; and they put in practice different pedagogical methods: from dialogical ones to those founded on the punitive authority of the state. As far as this last dimension is concerned, there was a prevalence of formative practices founded on dialogical methods with open ends and as practices founded on public rationality; that is, practices of argumentation seeking to convince the population about the government's legitimacy at attempting to further public welfare and interest.

In this scenario of pedagogization, Mockus himself became a central character through the direct dialogue he established with the population and intensive media attention.[22] As a state pedagogue, he viewed himself as a bridge between academic and technical discourses and people's everyday experiences and as someone whose central role was that of communicating with the population: "Many people believe that a government is only a political or financial affair, but governing is serving the people...and to a great extent it is communicating with the governed" (Mockus 2002:25). His morally appealing trajectory (he was elected as part of an independent movement and spent very little money on his campaign) and his eccentric, courageous, and playful performances were central in focusing the city's attention on his pedagogical messages and strategies.

Commonality and Diversity

In line with the conception of a *Cultura Ciudadana* and a pragmatic valuation of the dominant Colombian culture, the overall goal of these pedagogical practices was creating the minimum common norms and conducts deemed necessary for civilized collective life, rather than the celebration or promotion of cultural differences. In Mockus's (2001) words:

> Colombia represents, probably, an extreme case...of the implications of pluralism without a common ground. With the actions organized around the idea of *Cultura Ciudadana* we tried to identify some common ground, that set of basic, shared, and minimum rules that would make possible the enjoyment of moral and cultural diversity. (P. 10)

Since his first administration, drawing from the work of John Rawls, Mockus (1997) had argued that the search for a common minimum was not opposed to cultural diversity:

> The same rules can be respected by different cultural traditions, many times for different reasons. In a democracy we all play the same game, or at least we play with the same rules, although if we are asked 'Why do you observe a rule?' there can be radically different answers...In a way, democracy is neutral in respect to people's reasons for following its rules. (P. 7)

In the text of his second administration's development plan, this core concept of commonality was expressed in very precise terms to explain of the plan's name and the symbol chosen to represent it:

> *Bogotá, For a Life All on the Same Side* seeks to highlight those elements that can unite the people of Bogotá: a common history, a growing shared vision … shared rules of play…as a symbol of this vision, the "Moebius Strip" that has been recognized as a key structure of the tucano culture emphasizes integration: it seems to have two opposite sides[23]…when in reality it has only one. Locally it has two sides and two borders; globally it has only one side and one border. Similarly, society, locally differentiated and polarized, is and must be lived as globally united (Mayor's Office of Bogotá 2001:78).

Figure 175: "Moebius Strip." 2001-2003. Courtesy of the Mayor's Office, Bogotá, Secretary General, Central Archive, Photo Archive.

Mockus's idea, which Dewey repeatedly advances in his writings, that a dynamic, contingent, and common ground is the best guarantee in a democratic society for the celebration and respect of individual and cultural differences, and for the intensification of dialogue between those who are different, is very compelling. From the perspective of cultural diversity, the limitations of the pedagogical practices of Mockus's two administrations lie elsewhere. In the first place, in a one-dimensional distrustful depiction of the culture of the city's population: the exhaustive description of the negative characteristics of knowledge, values, and practices that need to be transformed; and, besides some very specific appropriations of popular terms, the almost total invisibility of any positive traits that can be strengthened or built upon by the state's formative practices. Thus the development plan of his first administration only mentions the population's problems:

> a low capacity to solve conflicts amicably, weakness in the recognition of the duties of citizenship, and the limited willpower and capacity of the community to exercise adequate social pressure that end up expressing themselves in high degrees of intolerance, threats, and violence (ibid.).

A second limitation of these practices is their very weak pedagogical relation with the cultural practices of the city's population—something which he had prescribed in his writings with the *Federici Group*—and this was in spite of the fact that since the first administration local authorities had undertaken and promoted research on many aspects of the culture of the city.

Indirect Education: A Regulatory Form of Governing

As a paradigmatically post-disciplinarian, regulatory, liberal form of state power, some of the key pedagogical practices in Mockus's two administrations were, to use Dewey's (1904) term, forms of "indirect education." Together with their practices of "free persuasion" through communicative actions and the formation of self-regulatory actions, they constituted a form of power that *uses* freedom in the sense of forming subjects who perceive that they are free and that they are acting *voluntarily*. It is a form of power that, as Foucault (2007:84) stated, "consumes freedom, that is[,] it is forced to produce it…to organize it" offering that "which is needed to be free."

The purpose of educating the population *indirectly* was included in the first administration's development plan through the idea that the actions of construction, adaptation, cleansing, and embellishment of public spaces would form, in themselves, desirable attitudes and practices and prevent undesirable ones. They would benefit the population in an impersonal way, without their necessarily being aware of this. Adapting these urban contexts, together with the auto-regulation of the population and the use of authority were the three central strategies of the government's pedagogical approach.[24] The strategy of transforming zones of urban "disorder" and high crime rates, and other public spaces such as parks, was continued in the second administration. Another example of indirect education was staging a wide range of artistic, cultural, and recreational activities in public spaces with the explicit purpose of further enabling a part of the population to take ownership of the city, simultaneously intensifying interactions between different groups who rarely met otherwise due to the cultural and socioeconomic segregation of city life.

One of the most effective of these practices was *"Rock al Parque"* (Rock the Park), created during Mockus's first administration. It was a free and massive annual music festival, carried out in one of the city's major parks, that presented non-commercial rock bands of many genres. The event had indirect formative purposes: creating a positive image of the city, strengthening a sense of identity with the city, and strategically designing its spaces and times in order to form practices of tolerance amongst rival rock fans. To attain this last goal, the city's administration devised a plan so that different groups of audiences would coincide, such as *rappers* and *rockers*. The audacious nature of Mockus's initiative can be assessed by the reaction of the city's police force in its first version: they initially refused to sanction it, warning that there would be problems with violence. The impasse was solved when youth groups proposed the creation of a "Peace Force" in order to guarantee order through negotiations among rival groups, a strategy that was maintained during Mockus's second administration.[25]

Dramaturgical Formative Practices

In Mockus's two terms as city mayor, state institutions staged a series of actions characterized by their innovative aesthetic, dramatic, and playful traits. These actions sought to break the normal flows of city life, constituted a clear discontinuity with traditional school-like educational practices, and were widely publicized by the media. These actions shared a number of traits, firstly, in that they acted upon and in different ways sought to connect with the everyday scenarios, cycles, and rhythms of the population. Secondly, they made use of very specific elements of the knowledge, sensibility, and language of popular culture. Finally, they staged a series of poetic and dramatic devices: images, symbols, signs, grotesque theatrical characters, artistic performances, and unusual, metaphoric, local, comic, exaggerated speech-acts in order to emotionally move the population, creating intimacy. Their spectacular aesthetic found enormous resonance in the media.

These types of practices were particularly intensive in the first administration, which was particularly creative in staging educational performances in public spaces and transforming them onto dramatic stages where an especially effective collaboration was achieved between the formative purposes of the government and the everyday flows of the population. Much of their impact was due to the use of relatively flexible pedagogical strategies that engaged the population. Three of these practices had the greatest impact in their capacity to captivate the population, produce a lasting effect, and obtain free press: the actions of mimes and other dramatic characters regulating the conduct of pedestrians and drivers; the use of a "Citizenship Card" to approve or disapprove of driving behavior; and *acciones zanahorias* (Carrot-actions) to protect life.[26]

In terms of their dramatic and playful traits, these educational actions combined, as we shall see, two quite different perspectives. On the one hand, they included Mockus's ascetic conception of games or formalized types of play as a means of voluntary social discipline through which individuals learnt how to observe norms.[27] In Mockus's view, there was a close relation between games and democracy, in that they both imply clear rules for all that are intrinsic to the logic of the game and not imposed by an external authority and that have to be observed by all players. On the other hand, the more hedonistic conception of Enrique Velásquez, one of the members of the administration's *Cultura Ciudadana* team, emphasized the open-ended, pleasurable, contingent, and affective dimensions of play.[28]

One of the most intense car and pedestrian flows of the city, located along ten blocks of 19th Street, was the site of the first scenario of these types of actions and was marked by the dramatic entrance of a group of mimes. Through playful performances in twenty crosswalks, the mimes made drivers and pedestrians look at each other, playfully pushed those cars that had stopped on a crosswalk, incited pedestrians to hold hands, and interrupted their normal routines by asking them where they were going, what they did in life, and how they viewed the city. Mockus's (2000) description of these performances is revealing:

> Citizens enjoyed responding with whistles to pedestrians and drivers who did not abide by transit norms...If a driver did not take corrective actions, a mime appeared to try and persuade him to respect the pedestrian crossing; if this friendly invitation did not make him back up, the traffic police intervened. People were seen applauding the imposition of traffic tickets. Thus, police repression became part of an orderly pedagogical sequence and the pedagogical effect was amplified due to clarity in the interpretation of the situation and the social support of the sanction (P. 18)

In addition to mimes, whose performances would be reenacted throughout the city with the purpose of imaginatively creating a different space and time to the one in which the population lived, the performances on 19th Street also staged theatrical characters on bicycles dressed in nineteenth century garments. In addition, women on stilts dressed as brides interacted with pedestrians, telling them they were looking for a groom and asking them if they wanted Bogotá as a bride and what they would offer her. Rather than the direct literal transmission of specific messages, the idea behind these actions was to disrupt the frantic flow of urban life, so that drivers and pedestrians experienced, probably for the first time, where they were, who was around them, and how they were behaving.[29] While the performances of these theatrical characters were relatively free form, leaving ample room for improvisation— and thereby for the public's reactions—the general pedagogical strategy, especially in terms of its purposes, was carefully designed in order to achieve radical transformations in the flow of vehicles and pedestrians, in the use of public spaces, and in "some of the forms of public interactions, especially in incidental conflict resolution and practices of solidarity among pedestrians" (Velásquez 1995c).

Mockus used a forerunner of the "Citizenship Card" in a public debate during his campaign for mayor of 1994, when he showed a pink card as a symbol of a playful sanction to one of his electoral opponents. The card also had a similar meaning to those used by referees in soccer matches, in which yellow or red cards are used to punish players for conduct against the rules of the game. On one side, the card depicted a hand with a thumbs–up, and featured a thumbs–down on the other side. In 1995, the government distributed the card massively—more than a million and a half—to be used by the city's population in order to convey approval

Figure 176: "Citizenship Card." Courtesy of the Mayor's Office, Bogotá, Secretary General, Central Archive, Photo Archive.

or disapproval of other people's actions in public scenarios.[30] Its purpose, which became quite widespread among drivers, was the peaceful regulation of conducts in order to break "the psychological and social barriers that repress the expression of approval or disapproval" (Mockus 2000:18).[31] The card's widespread impact can be tied to its cultural resonance: it appropriated gestures that were already part of popular expressive practices.

As already noted, educational "Carrot-Actions" played with the popular meaning of the vegetable's name in Colombia: to be carrot-like is to be prudent, to play it safe. The government's media strategy managed to transform its ordinary negative usage, indicative of someone who is shy and afraid of taking risks, into a symbol of the wisdom of protecting one's life and that of others. These practices were directed at the self-regulation of the population in terms of conducts considered to be unhealthy or unsafe.[32]

The first "Carrot Christmas" was in 1995. Educational actions were geared towards incorporating *zanahoria* (safe) conducts in the population in relation to the use of fireworks, alcohol consumption, healthy entertainment, safe sex, and the beautification of the city. The government designed "Carrot Kits" and gift baskets that could be bought in some supermarkets. The kit included a whistle, a sticker of a carrot, and a condom, which was banned in certain supermarkets. The gift basket invited the population to decorate sidewalks, front gardens, and green areas, and included an instruction manual, grass to be planted, a mortar, and garden tools.

The strategy for alcohol prevention combined punitive and pedagogical measures. It began with the compulsory closure of night venues that sold alcohol after the legal time limit and was followed by media campaigns to prevent drunk driving. It also staged public, face-to-face, meetings between law-breakers and police agents through which "spectators could see in the same scenario the law-breaker and the upholder of the law making moral arguments" (Mockus 2000:21). Once more, the strategy had a great impact: the reduction of alcohol-related homicides and traffic accidents (Mockus 2000:1).

The campaign against the use of fireworks was a response to the death of five children under fourteen who suffered burns in the Christmas festivities in 1994.[33] During their first year in office, in 1995, the administration announced that if a single child was burnt by fireworks, they would be outlawed. On December 7th, the first accident occurred, and the government outlawed the fabrication, sale, and use of fireworks. This legal measure was followed by educational actions, which make it impossible to establish the relative impact of the campaign's persuasive and punitive actions.[34] In the first place, there was a "pedagogical sanction" for parents who allowed their children to play with fireworks. In the second place, a communicational strategy emphasized that children's use of fireworks was their parents' responsibility. The campaign had a clear impact: between 1994 and 1997 burns from firework accidents were reduced from 264 to 38 (Niño 1998).

As part of the *zanahoria* strategy, in 1996 the administration began a campaign for voluntary disarmament that, through intensive use of the mass media, encouraged citizens to give up their weapons and ammunition (Mockus 2000). Those who relinquished them to state authorities received a coupon for Christmas gifts. The campaign ended with a ritual act of symbolic transformation of the weapons: "The 2,538 weapons handed in, were melted and transformed into baby-spoons. These were mounted on pedestals made with the same metal, with the following inscription: *Arma Fui* (I Was a Weapon)" (Mockus 2000:24).[35]

At the same time as the disarmament campaign, in 1996 the government on two occasions staged, what it called the "Day of Vaccination Against Violence" in order to decrease violence against children. Those who wished to be inoculated had to follow a previously determined series of steps: 1) draw the head of someone who had mistreated them in their childhood on a balloon; 2) carry the balloon into a booth and place it on a headless body; 3) say or do to the body whatever they wanted, venting their aggression; 4) write a text that would allow them to pass from physical aggression to dialogue; 5) pin text onto a "tree of hope;" 6) knot together some hanging to represent the weaving of the social tapestry; and 7) ingest two drops of water as inoculations against violence. Some forty-five thousand people participated in this "rite," and a telephone line was created so that the population could express themselves on the subject. Unlike the relatively open-ended performances on 19th Street, the inoculation rite was closer to Mockus's conception of play: individuals had to enter into a "closed" game that was highly formalized with rules that had to be strictly upheld. What was voluntary in the game was the decision to play, the attitude towards it, and what was done and said to the offender but not the steps to be followed once play started.[36]

During Mockus's second administration, there were also dramaturgical formative practices, such as innovative, colloquial, and poetic uses of language and symbols, especially in the images and names that represented the programs. There were a host of actions intended to prevent violence against women and against children that sought to form an ethics of care for others.[37] There was also a program of self-care to prevent domestic violence and promote democratic family interactions. It also included campaigns of co-responsibility with the administration, such as a successful appeal for voluntary tax payments. Some of the most visible of these formative strategies were those of "Civil Resistance" and *Croactividad*, which exemplified the second administration's more explicit purpose of educating the population politically.[38]

The "Civil Resistance" strategy began as a response to the attack by the Revolutionary Armed Forces of Colombia (FARC), the oldest and strongest Marxist guerrilla group in the country, on the city's main water reservoir in Chingaza in January 2002. This bomb attack took place in the context of increased terrorist attacks in the city, which rose from 51 in 2001 to 131 in 2002. The administration defined "Civil Resistance" as "a direct protest, with political and public argumentation, expressed through protests and denunciations, in order to produce changes" (Secretaría General 2002). It implied a movement on the part of civil society in order to form political attitudes and conducts that would demonstrate the efficacy of democratic means vis–à–vis violent ones. As it was characteristic of Mockus's second administration, the diverse actions proposed sought to politicize the private sphere: public rejection of violence in private and public life, acting in nonviolent and constructive ways when confronted with violence and destruction, resisting extortion and kidnapping, and rejecting silent complicity. During the campaign, Mockus and Freddy Cante (2002) wrote a piece on its conceptual foundations that concluded by highlighting "Civil Resistance" as a form of collective action, as a moral duty, and as a means of increasing social cohesion and trust. They also specified that citizens could acknowledge the legitimacy of the ends of illegal armed groups, while opposing their methods.

The campaign used diverse signs to communicate its message: the flags of Bogotá and Colombia that were placed as visible signs of support for the state, a personal button of commitment to the campaign, and various signs placed in settings to be protected from violent acts, such as educational institutions and places that could endanger the population or those of vital public importance.[39]

The *Croactividad* campaign was related to that of "Civil Resistance" by its purpose of promoting collaboration with state authorities as a civic duty. The mayor made an appeal "for solidarity. We should be proactive and break the silence that facilitates terrorist actions and other criminal activities…" (Mockus 2003:2). The name of the campaign alludes to the characteristic sound of the frog (a croak), which has a very negative connotation in the country's extended subcultures of crime and illegality.[40] In colloquial terms, "to be a frog" is to rat on one's own friends or accomplices. The idea was to achieve an extreme makeover of this lowly creature, transforming him into a prince of civility and political correctness, while warning, at the same time, that the idea was not to "rat on controversial, but legally protected aspects of people's private lives" (ibid.). As part of the campaign, citizens could denounce a wide range of illegal activities that included terrorism, homicide, sexual violence, children who were not attending school, violations of public spaces, and problems with neighbors through a special telephone line (Jaramillo 2003).

Final Reflections

I will conclude this essay with two brief reflections. In the first place, I will reflect on the complex issue of the cultural impact of the pedagogical practices of Mockus's two administrations, and in the second place, I will contextualize and engage with some of the national critiques against his discourses and practices as a state pedagogue.

The pedagogical practices of Mockus's two administrations were staged in a complex field of formative forces, characteristic of a large, culturally globalized Latin American city. They competed with a dense and intense web of divergent messages in a culturally hybrid and fragmented scenario in which diverse temporalities, senses of space, life-projects, political cultures, cultural practices, and subjectivities coexist. Despite its one-sidedness, his government's depiction of the great weaknesses of Bogotá's civic and democratic culture was accurate. If we add the years of Enrique Peñalosa's administration, which in its civic dimension continued some of the formative practices of Mockus's administration, we have nine years of uninterrupted change until the administration of Luis Garzón (2004-2007), which ended the pedagogical experiment of fostering *Cultura Ciudadana*.

What can be said then of the long-term transformations of the city's *Cultura Ciudadana* and how Mockus transformed city life, beyond the anecdotes and positive recollections of taxi drivers and other citizens? Using an imaginative, non-technocratic vision, one can say that the more dramaturgical pedagogical practices affected and moved large sectors of the population permanently in marking their subjectivity profoundly—and they did so because they brought together individual and social dimensions that were fragmented: commonality and diversity, rationality and emotion, will and desire, impersonality and subjectivity, norm and freedom, private and public.

Therefore, the central issue here is whether these changes have been sustained over time, and on this we do not have solid empirical data. What we do have is significant evidence of the changes during his administrations. The specific polls carried out during the first administration and the comprehensive "Survey on Cultural Citizenship" applied during his second administration show dramatic advances on almost all dimensions of civic culture. Furthermore, they indicate a coincidence between the biggest advances and those dimensions of *Cultura Ciudadana's* objectives with the highest concentration of pedagogical practices. This was especially evident during the second administration: when virtually all the government's initiatives yielded highly positive results and privileged pedagogical practices: decrease in infant and maternal mortality, decrease in traffic accidents, decrease in homicides and burglary, increase in voluntary payment of taxes and increase in the establishment of voluntary agreements to solve disputes.

Although some of its discourses and practices have been appropriated by local governments both nationally and internationally, national academics have not given Mockus's two administrations the attention they deserve as central historical events in terms of creative public policy and out-of-school pedagogical practices.[41] Nevertheless, he became and remains a symbolic figure for the popular imagination and for the mass media. In the mass media, his administrations have tended to be valued in the characteristically dualist way in which it tends to portray novelty in the country: he has been portrayed either as a "savior" capable of correcting the evils of Colombian society or as someone to be deeply distrusted. Paradoxically, conservative critics who are wary of political audacity and communicative creativity and many leftist leaders and journalists who attack these practices as "authoritarian" have converged in this distrust of the pedagogical practices of his two administrations.

As I have pointed out, the local administration of Bogotá that followed Mockus's second term in office, that of Luis Garzón (a former trade union leader), ended the pedagogical experiment of *Cultura Ciudadana*, and the two administrations that followed (also left-wing) did not take it up again. Garzón did not publicly present any arguments in favor of his decision, but some officials of his administration argued that it was due to Mockus's "authoritarianism," an accusation that, as I have pointed out, has been recurrent on the part of leftist critics. In the arguments I heard from some of these state officials, Mockus's administrations had been "authoritarian" due to their emphasis, especially in his second administration, on the need to legitimate and promote the upholding of state law. This must sound puzzling for an international audience; to my mind, it derives from a state-demonizing discourse that many of left-wing militants in the country did not abandon even when appointed as representatives of the state.

Some academic critics have followed a similar route. For example, Ismael Ortiz (2009) has argued that the end goal of Mockus's administrations was to "homogenize" and "normalize" the behaviors of the population, thereby creating "docile" individuals. Furthermore, he points out that this was due to their emphasis on making individuals compliant with state law. For Ortiz, the practices of *Cultura Ciudadana* equated culture with a specific post-disciplinarian "technology of power," going as far as to depict it as a process of "Taylorization of culture, by its reorganization through homogenizing processes and procedures, which were founded on the written law designed in scenarios of power" (Ortiz 2009:4).

I can think of a host of arguments against these critics, but I will only put forward a rather obvious, pragmatic one: they seem to believe that in the ethical, political, and cultural "field of forces" of the country, the state is the only force of power: that is, it is the only agent seeking to direct the conduct of the population; and since they seem to think that all exercise of power—that is any technology used for directing the conduct of others—is per se, negative, then Mockus's administrations can be righteously accused of exercising power! In the scenario they depict, the state would be the only agent limiting individual and collective freedoms. Evidently a more complex and realistic reading of the field of forces is required, one that contrasts the practices of Mockus's two administrations with the other major forces of power at play in Colombian society who were concurrently trying to direct the conduct of the population: market forces including those of the mass media; traditional political parties riddled with corruption, patronage and an anti-democratic ethos; the Catholic Church and its intense symbolic and ethical power in the country; groups of organized delinquency; drug mafias; and illegal armed groups disdainful of the basic rights of the population.

Endnotes

1 Unlike the French, English, and American traditions, in Germany, pedagogy (and not the Sciences of Education or Educational Foundations) has been the central object of education policies and teacher education since the nineteenth century.

2 On this, see Zuluaga (1987). The dominance of these Sciences of Education in educational policy was to be replaced later by that of economic rationality.

3 For a fuller account of these characteristics of pedagogy, see Sáenz (2003) and Sáenz et al. (2010).

4 On this, see Sáenz (2007b).

5 My argument is based on a comparison with other cultures and historical eras in the "West" where practices of self-formation are considered of equal importance, if not more, than those through which individuals are formed by others (Sáenz 2010).

6 For an account of this event, see the analysis of Martínez Boom et al. (1994). For an example of a paradigmatic discourse on relations between schooling, non-formal education, and development, see Coombs (1985). The principle of "permanent education" was included in the Political Constitution of Colombia of 1991.

7 The writings of the Brazilian pedagogue Paulo Freire (1921-1997), especially *Educação como prática da liberdade* (Education As a Practice of Liberty 1967) and *Pedagogia do oprimido* (Pedagogy of the Oppressed 1970), both published in Spanish shortly after their first Portuguese editions, had a wide and profound impact throughout Latin America in the context of mobilizing grassroots social movements.

8 This concept points at the way in which, increasingly, individuals and institutions depend on more information, communication, and knowledge in order to function effectively. See McQuail (1988).

9 Social capital is understood as "an amalgam of certain characteristics of social organization, such as trust, norms, networks of contracts, and more generally, the long-term relations that can increase the collective efficiency of a community, facilitating not only coordinated actions but also making possible cooperative actions of mutual benefit" (Puntam 1993:167).

10 In the late 1980s, before Mockus's first administration, many progressive NGOs and worker's, women's, and farmer's social movements in the country developed innovative out-of-school pedagogical practices for the formation of a "democratic culture" in the country.

11 The group, based at the National University of Colombia, was named after Carlo Federici, mathematician and professor at the university who was its first director. When Federici retired, Mockus became its director. Other members of the group were

Carlos Augusto Hernández, María Clemencia Castro, Berenice Guerrero, José Granés, and Jorge Charum. Its main conceptual appropriations were from Habermas, Basil Bernstein, and the epistemological writings of Bachelard.

12 For a critical valuation of the Pedagogical Movement, see Suárez (2002). The Pedagogical Movement went beyond FECODE and included the participation of grassroots groups of teachers engaged in pedagogical reflection and experimentation, university research groups, and NGOs. In political terms, the movement was the result of the redefinitions, since the end of the 1970s, of many left-wing sectors that resulted in their rejection of Leninist forms of organization, of armed struggle, and of agendas for the "takeover" of the state. The movement's greatest impact was in identifying the teacher as an intellectual of pedagogy; consolidating schools as settings of pedagogical, cultural, and political transformation; and placing public education as a key issue in the political agenda.

13 The main articles of Mockus and the Federici Group in this period, most of which were published in *Educación y Cultura*, the journal of FECODE, are: Federici et al. 1984, Mockus 1984, Mockus et al. 1985a, 1985b, 1986, and 1987. In 1995, the group published a book with a synthesis of its reflections on school pedagogy.

14 All quotes originally in Spanish have been translated into English by the author of this chapter.

15 The term "coexistence" that is central to Mockus's discourse and in the practices of his two administrations is a rather literal translation of the Spanish *convivencia*, but there is no other single term in English that conveys the meaning Mockus gave it. In everyday language it means simply "living together," but Mockus amplified its meaning in order to convey a sense of living "well" together: that is peacefully, productively, and in intensified and meaningful interactions through practices of dialogue.

16 A similar idea had been part of UNESCO's policies since the 1980s. UNESCO recommended the adaptation of curriculum content to the cultural "reality" of the community (UNESCO 1980). Basing pedagogy on the cultural knowledge of workers was also at the core of Paulo Freire's popular pedagogy, and that of a number of social movements and NGOs in Colombia throughout the 1980s.

17 Regarding this, I asked Mockus why, simultaneously with the out-of-school pedagogical strategies, his two administrations did not carry out a policy to weaken the separation of schools and everyday life. Mockus answered that it was because during his first administration, the General Law of Education had just been passed, in which, due to the pressure of the Pedagogical Movement, schools had been granted great autonomy in the definition of their pedagogical projects and study plans, and out of respect for this

autonomy, his educational policy had been directed towards the strengthening of this process. See: Antanas Mockus, interview by email, November 2003.

18 After many decades in which his thought was mostly dismissed, John Dewey (1859-1952), pragmatist, philosopher, and pedagogue, has reemerged in the past two decades as a central theoretical referent in philosophy and education. My uses of Dewey's discourse in order to shed light on Mockus's pedagogy are based on Dewey (1963, 1977, 1980, 1984a, 1984b and 1997).

19 Mockus wrote that he felt understood in the ideas of the previous two paragraphs that synthesize the text I had sent to him.

20 These values and principles included: respect for others, the passion to achieve, honesty, transparency, equity, solidarity, mutual trust, and dialogue through open communication.

21 Other pedagogical aims of the plan included the increased use of public spaces, development of creative capacities, increasing the collective enjoyment of the city, forming necessary knowledge and habits of productive processes, increasing the participation of children and youth in family life, and the formation of a series of conducts for increased solidarity with the most vulnerable members of the population.

22 For accounts on media coverage of Mockus, see: Ismael Ortiz (state official in Mockus's two administrations in the Instituto Distrital de Recreación y Cultura [District Institute of Recreation and Culture]), July 27, 2004; López (2003).

23 A Colombian indigenous group.

24 For this, see Gómez (1998), Arturo et al. (1998), López (2003). The "three As" were an appropriation of the "three Es" model of transportation engineering: Engineering, Education, and Enforcement.

25 For more elaborate analysis of *Rock al Parque* see: López (2003) and Cante (2004).

26 In the popular speech of Bogotá, *zanahoria* (carrot) is an adjective that means healthy or prudent, as it is phonetically close to *sano* (healthy). Mockus's administration resignified the term, in order to celebrate and promote self-care and care of others, specifically in relation to alcohol consumption and driving.

27 A conception similar to Dewey's (1963).

28 On Velázquez's perspective which drew from the psychoanalyst D.W Winnicott, Paul Virilio, Gilles Deleuze, and Johan Huizinga, among others; see Velásquez (1995a, 1995b).

29 Enrique Velásquez (pedagogue and member of the group of *Cultura Ciudadana* in the first year of the first Mockus administration), interview, August 12, 2004.

30 Gabriel Gómez (Director of Communications, *Cultura Ciudadana*, first Mockus administration), interview by M. F. Rojas Mantilla, July 15, 2004.

31 In a survey conducted by an international private firm on August 1995, 71.3% of the population believed that the card was useful in improving the traffic situation of the city (Yankelovich and associates; quoted in López 2003:57).

32 Before the carrot campaign, 49% of deaths from traffic accidents, 33% of firearm homicides, 49% of knife homicides, 35% of suicides and 10% of accidental deaths were related to alcohol consumption.

33 I base my description on López (2003) and Mockus (2000).

34 For a reader from countries where the law has strong effects, this might be incomprehensible because the reader might think that it was the fear of juridical punishment that worked. This is not that evident in Colombia, where the upholding of the law by state agents is very weak.

35 The campaign had an important impact: in December 1996 there were 291 homicides, in comparison with 397 in the same month the previous year.

36 For accounts of carrot practices in Mockus's first administration, see Uribe (1996), Mockus (2000), and Gómez interview (2004).

37 That appropriated Carol Gilligan's (1982) conception on an ethic of care for others in everyday interactions that constituted a critique of Lawrence Kohlberg's conception of a morality based on the abstract principle of justice.

38 I explain the meaning of this term later, which is a play on words, or rather a play with the sound of frogs and the representation in Colombian culture of the word "frog."

39 I base my account of "Civil Resistance" on Londoño (N.d.) and Observatorio de Cultura Urbana (Observatory of Urban Culture 2002).

40 But not only in these subcultures; to be called a frog in a Colombian school is to be marked negatively.

41 In this respect, it can be said that Mockus has been more of a "prophet" in international academic scenarios, as can be attested to by the chapters in this book by international academics and by his constant invitations to international forums.

References

Alcaldía Mayor de Bogotá [Mayor's Office of Bogotá.] 1997. *Formar Ciudad: 1995-1997* [To Form the City: 1995-1997].

———. 2001. *Plan de desarrollo de Bogotá para Vivir Todos del Mismo Lado* [Bogotá's Development Plan For All to Live On the Same Side].

Aristotle. 1998. *The Nicomachean Ethics.* Oxford: Oxford University Press.

Arturo, Jorge and Mauricio Díaz. 1998. *Memoria y evaluación institucional del Instituto Distrital de Cultura y Turismo: el programa de Cultura Ciudadana. Análisis del impacto en la ciudadanía* [Institutional Memory and Evaluation of the District Institute of Culture and Tourism: The Civic Culture Program. Analysis of Impact on Civic Culture]. Center of Social Studies, National University of Colombia, Bogotá. Unpublished document.

Bourdieu, Pierre and Jean-Claude Passeron. 1977. *Reproduction in Education, Society and Culture.* Beverly Hills: Sage.

Bowles, Samuel and Herbert Gintis. 1976. *Schooling in Capitalist America.* New York: Basic Books.

Cante, M.I. 2005. *Aproximación a la experiencia del Rock en la ciudad: Rock al Parque 1995-2003* [Approximation to the Experience of Rock in the City: Rock the Park 1995-2003]. Undergraduate thesis. Sociology Department, National University of Colombia, Bogotá.

Cante, Freddy, and Antanas. Mockus. 2002. *Hacia una acción colectiva de resistencia civil* [Towards a Collective Action of Civil Resistance]. Unpublished document.

Coombs, Philip. 1985. *The World Crisis in Education. The View from the Eighties.* New York, Oxford: Oxford University Press.

Dewey, John. 1977. "Education, Direct and Indirect." Pp. 240-248 in *The Middle Works.* Vol. 3: 1903-1906, edited by J. Dewey. Carbondale: Southern Illinois Press.

———. 1997. *Democracy and Education. An Introduction to the Philosophy of Education.* New York: The Free Press.

———. 1984a. "Affective Thought." Pp. 104-110 in *The Later Works. Vol. 2:* 1925-1927, edited by J. Dewey. Carbondale: Southern Illinois Press.

———. 1984b. "Context and Thought." Pp. 3-21 in *The Later Works, Vol. 6:* 1931-1932, edited by J. Dewey. Carbondale: Southern Illinois Press.

———. 1980. *Art as Experience.* New York: Perigree Books.

————. 1963. *Experience and Education*. New York: Collier Books.

Federici, Carlo, Antanas Mockus, J. Charum, J. Granés, M.C. Castro, B. Guerrero, and C.A. Hernandez.1984. "Límites del cientificismo en educación" [The Limits of Scientism in Education]. *Revista Colombiana de Educación* [Colombian Education Review]. 14:69-89.

Foucault, Michel. 2006. *Seguridad, territorio, población. Curso en el Collège de France 1977-1978* [Security, Territory, Population. Class in the Collège de France 1977-1978]. Mexico: Fondo de Cultura Económica.

————. 2007. *Nacimiento de la biopolítica. Curso en el Collège de France 1978-1979* [Birth of Bio-politics. Course in the Collège de France 1978-1979]. Mexico: Fondo de Cultura Económica.

Gilligan, Carol. 1982. *In a Different Voice. Psychological Theory and Women's Development*. Cambridge: Harvard University Press.

Gómez Mejía, Gabriel. 1998. "Comunicación entre extraños" [Communication Among Strangers]. Pp. 131-154 in *La ciudad observada. Violencia, cultura y política* [The Observed City. Violence, Culture, and Politics], edited by Y. Campos and I. Ortiz. Bogotá: Tercer Mundo Editores, [Observatory of Urban Culture].

Jaramillo, Alejandra. 2003. *Informe final. Contrato de servicios 20048* [Final Report. Contract of Services 20048]. [District Institute of Culture and Tourism, Bogotá]. Unpublished document.

Kohlberg, Lawrence. 1992. *Psicología del desarrollo moral* [Psychology of Moral Development]. Bilbao: Desclée de Brouwer.

Londoño, Rocío. N.d. *Experiencias de resistencia civil en Bogotá* [Experience of Civil Resistance in Bogotá]. Bogotá: Instituto Distrital de Cultura y Turismo. Unpublished document.

López Borbón, Liliana. 2003. "Políticas culturales orientadas al plano de la vida cotidiana. Evaluación de las estrategias de comunicación del programa de *Cultura Ciudadana* (Bogotá 1995-1997) "[Cultural Politics Oriented Towards Daily Life. Evaluation of Communication Strategies of Civic Culture (Bogotá 1995-1997)]." Master's thesis in communication, National Autonomous University of Mexico, Mexico City.

Martínez Boom, Alberto, Carlos E. Noguera, and Jorge Orlando Castro. 1994. *Currículo y modernización* [Curriculum and Modernization]. Bogotá: National Forum for Colombia.

McQuail, Denis. 1998. *La acción de los medios. Los medios de comunicación y el interés público* [The Actions of Media. The Media and Public Interest]. Buenos Aires: Amorrortu.

Mockus, Antanas. 1984. "Movimiento Pedagógico y defensa de la calidad de la educación" [The Pedagogical Movement and Defense of the Quality of Education]. *Educación y Cultura* [Education and Culture] 2:27-34.

———. 1994a. "Anfibios culturales y divorcio entre ley, moral y cultura" [Cultural Amphibians and Divorce Between Law, Morals, and Culture]. *Análisis Político* [Political Analysis] 21:4-18.

———. 1994b. "Anfibios culturales, moral y productividad" [Cultural Amphibians, Morality and Productivity]. *Revista Colombiana de Psicología* [Colombian Journal] 3:125-135.

———. 1997. "Balance pedagógico" [Pedagogical Balance]. *Letra Capital* [Capital Letter] 1(2):14-19.

———. 1998b. "*Cultura Ciudadana.* Un programa con buenos resultados en seguridad ciudadana adelantado en Bogotá de 1995 a 1997" [Civic Culture. A Program with Positive Results in Civic Security in Bogotá from 1995-1997]. *Seminario internacional. Participación ciudadana, gobernabilidad y cultura de paz* [International Seminar. Civic Participation, Governability, and Peace Culture]. Mexico City: Federal Government of Mexico, UNESCO.

———. 2000. "Armonizar ley, moral y cultura. *Cultura Ciudadana*, prioridad de gobierno con resultados en prevención y control de violencia en Bogotá 1995-1997" [Harmonizing Law, Morals, and Culture. Civic Culture, Government Priority with Results in Violence Prevention and Control in Bogotá 1995-1997]. Unpublished document.

———. 2001. "Divorcio entre ley, moral y cultura" [Divorce Between Law, Morals, and Culture]. Unpublished document.

———. 2002. *Importancia de la comunicación. Aprender a echar el cuento. Palabras del Alcalde Mayor de Bogotá.* [The Importance of Communication. Learning to Tell the Tale. Words of the Mayor of Bogotá]. Edited by Mayor's Office of Bogotá. Bogotá: Alcaldía Mayor de Bogotá

———. 2003. "Invitación a la Croactividad."[Invitation for Croactivity] *De Ciudad* [Of the City] 14. Bogotá: Instituto Distrital de Cultura y Turismo.

Mockus, Antanas., Carlo Federici, José Granés, Carlos Augusto Hernández, María Clemencia Castro, and Jorge Charum. 1985a. "Puntualizaciones a la Reforma Curricular." [Clarifications on the Curriculum Reform] *Educación y Cultura*

Education and Culture] 4:6-10.

Mockus, Antanas, Carlo Federici, José Granés, Carlos Augusto Hernández, María Clemencia Castro, Jorge Charum, and Berenice Guerrero. 1985b. "La Reforma Curricular y el magisterio."." [The Curriculum Reform and Teachers] *Educación y Cultura* [Education and Culture] 4:65-88.

Mockus, A., C. Federici, J. Granés, and J. Charum. 1986. "Conocimiento y comunicación en las ciencias y en la escuela." [Knowledge and Communication in the Sciences and in the Schools] *Educación y Cultura* [Education and Culture] 8:22-29.

Mockus, A., J. Granés, C.A. Hernández, M.C. Castro, and J. Charum. 1987. "Lenguaje, voluntad de saber y calidad de la educación." [Language, Will to Know, and Quality of Education] *Educación y Cultura* 12:60-70.

Mockus, Antanas, C.A. Hernández, José. Granés, Jorge Charum, and María Clemencia Castro. 1995. *Las fronteras de la escuela. Articulaciones entre conocimiento escolar y conocimiento extraescolar* [Borders of the School. Articulations Between School Knowledge and Out-of-School Knowledge]. Bogotá, Cooperativa Editorial del Magisterio.

Niño, E.D. January 1998. "Seguimiento y evaluación del impacto de la prohibición del uso de la pólvora en Bogotá" [Tracking and evaluation of the prohibition of the use of gunpowder in Bogotá]. Alcaldía Mayor de Bogotá, Instituto Distrital de Cultura y Turismo, Observatorio de Cultura Urbana. Unpublished document.

Observatorio de Cultura Urbana de Bogotá. [Urban Culture Observatory of Bogotá] 2002. "Sondeo de opinión sobre Resistencia Civil en Bogotá, septiembre 5-6 de 2002." [Opinion Poll on the Civil Resistance in Bogotá, September 5-6 2002] Unpublished document.

Puntam, Robert D. (with Robert Leonardi and Raffaella Nanetti). 1993. *Making Democracy Work: Civic Traditions in Modern Italy*. Princeton: Princeton University Press.

Sáenz Obregón, Javier. 2003. "Pedagogical Discourse and the Constitution of the Self." London: Institute of Education. Doctoral thesis.

———. 2004. *Cultura ciudadana y pedagogización de la práctica estatal*. [Civic Culture and the Pedagogization of State Practice] Bogotá: Instituto para la Investigación Educativa y el Desarrollo Pedagógico [Bogotá: Institute for the Investigation of Pedagogical Development].

———. 2007a. *Desconfianza, civilidad y estética: las prácticas formativas estatales por fuera de la escuela en Bogotá, 1994-2003* [Distrust, Civility, and Aesthetics: The State's Formative Practices Outside Schools, 1994-2003] Bogotá: Centro de Estudios

Sociales, Universidad Nacional de Colombia - Instituto para la Investigación Educativa y el Desarrollo Pedagógico.

——. 2007b. "La escuela como dispositivo estético." [The School as Aestetic Device] Pp. 73-86 in *Educar (sobre)impresiones estéticas,* [To Educate on (Over)Printed Aestetics] edited by G. Frigerio and G. Diker. Buenos Aires: Del Estante Editorial.

Sáenz Obregón, Javier, Olga Lucía Zuluaga, Rafael Ríos, Humberto Quiceno, Sandra Milena Herrera. 2010a. "La pedagogía en Francia: precariedad, fragmentación e ilegitimidad" [Pedagogy in France: Precariousness, Fragmentation, and Illegitimacy]. Pp. 14-84 in Pedagogía, saber y ciencias, [Pedagogy, Knowledge, and Science] edited by J. Sáenz. Bogotá: Centro de Estudios Sociales – Universidad Nacional de Colombia, Facultad de Educación – Universidad de Antioquia.

Sáenz Obregón, J. 2010b. "Notas para una genealogía de las practicas de sí." [Notes for a Genealogy of the Practices of the Self] Universidad Nacional de Colombia. Unpublished document.

Secretaría General de la Alcaldía Mayor de Bogotá. 2002. "Compromisos de resistencia civil. Civismo para superar la violencia. Está en sus manos." [Commitments of Civil Resistance. Civics to Overcome Violence. It Is In Your Hands] Unpublished document.

Suárez, Hernán. 2002. *Veinte años del Movimiento Pedagógico 1982-2002. Entre mitos y realidades* [Twenty Years of the Pedagogical Movement 1982-2002. Between Myths and Realities]. Bogotá: Corporación Tercer Milenio – Cooperativa Editorial del Magisterio.

UNESCO. 1980. *Programa Principal para América Latina y el Caribe 1980-2000.* [Principal Program for Latin America and the Caribbean 1980-2000] Paris: UNESCO.

Uribe, María Victoria. 1996. "Bogotá en los noventa: un escenario de intervención." [Bogotá in the Nineties: An Intervention Scenario] Pp. 391-408 in *Pensar la ciudad,* [Think of the City] edited by F. Giraldo and F. Viviescas. Bogotá: Tercer Mundo Editores, CENAC, FEDEVIVIENDA.

Velásquez, Enrique A. 1995a. "Muñecas, frazaditas y tarjetas." [Dolls, Baby Blankets, and Cards] *Práctica barrial* [Local Practice] 8 (16).

——. 1995b. "Jugar, tiempo y espacio." [To Play, Time and Space]. *Lámpara* 33 (16).

——. 1995c. "Animación Calle 19. Plan de acción." [Street 19 Animation. Plan of Action]. Bogotá: IDCT. Unpublished document.

Zuluaga, Olga Lucía. 1987. *Pedagogía e historia.* [Pedagogy and History] Bogotá: Foro Nacional por Colombia.

10. Mockus the Artist, Mockus the Idiot

Lucas Ospina

Antanas Mockus's artistic career officially started in 1993 at a national convention of arts at the National University where he was chancellor. Mockus tried to speak, but was jeered by a minority; so he turned his back to the audience, dropped his pants, and opened his butt cheeks with his hands. The saint's behind performed the miracle. A video recording reached a news channel and the entire country saw it. The newspaper *El Tiempo* and the Chancellor of the Universidad de los Andes[1] asked the President of Colombia to destroy the video. The long-time Director of the Museum of Modern Art deemed it "vulgar" and "unnecessary," and the Director of the Colombian Security Agency (DAS) called for a psychiatric evaluation. Mockus responded with a tearful resignation, but not before he flashed a newscaster smile and explained his artistic act away with an analysis bordering on formalism: his behind "was the color of peace," "white," like the Caucasian skin he inherited from his mother, a Lithuanian artist. Two years later, Mockus won the election to become Mayor of Bogotá.

In 2012, Mockus was invited to participate in the Seventh Biennial of Art in Berlin. The event, proposed as an intersection of art and politics, was a small but radical collection, and Mockus, as the politician-artist, seemed more real than many of the political artists there. Mockus was asked to comment on a piece, and he chose the work of the Mexican artist Teresa Margolles: the annual compendium of 313 covers of *PM*, a sensationalist tabloid from Juárez that always opened with a photo of drug crime, along with an image of a girl taken from the endless annals of soft-core porn. As it often happens with art on top of art, Mockus's commentary turned into more art: the installation piece *"Lazos de Sangre"* (Blood Ties). The Mexican flag hung over a pool of acid and lowered every time someone was killed in Mexico. The attendees of the Biennial could stop the flag's fall if they donated blood or promised to decrease their cocaine intake. The work included its own bibliography and exhibited two books: one on philosophy, *How to Do Things with Words* by John Austin; another on sociology, *The City that Killed its Women* by Marc Fernandez and Jean-Christophe Rampal.

One might think that Mockus is, as many others, in transit between the uncertain world of politics and a peaceful retreat into the condominium of fine arts; and that he has gone from building policies to making "conceptual art." The perpetual presidential candidate Álvaro Gómez painted horses until his death, and former presidents Belisario Betancur and César Gaviria take refuge in culture, do paintings, or collect works of "contemporary art." It would be unjust to lock Mockus away in the same bestiary. Mockus has not had to use art as aesthetic surgery to hide the havoc of politicking. On the contrary, Mockus came to politics from art and philosophy.

Discussions about Mockus as a politician linger on the ideological nature of his administrations, and opinions vary; while some define him as a guardian of neoliberal policies, others see him as capable of building on the foundations laid by others. For some, he is an austere administrator; for others, he is a bad executor. He is considered an ethical animal incapable of fighting corruption, or a candid leader surrounded by a technocratic, pragmatic, and obstinate team.

Politically, Mockus positioned himself under the banner of the "anti-politician", a label that became his sword. Once he was elected mayor, he continued wielding this weapon and, when he was invited to meet with the warmongering president of the time, he arrived at the presidential palace armed: from his belt proudly hung a plastic sword. Perhaps one day the National Museum of Colombia will have a cabinet of Mockus's curiosities: the glass of water he spewed at two competing candidates during the election debates, the burlap suit he wore when he got married riding an elephant under a circus tent, the red cards used by his army of mimes against drivers who didn't respect traffic laws, the comical lycra costume that transformed Mockus into "Super Citizen", or the "Bulletproof Vest" with a heart-shaped hole where an assassin's bullet could pierce. This is his arsenal of symbols, of images that could be cliché, but that in the solemn and repetitive scene of political representation became, paradoxically, pure, honest, genius, symbols of reflection, icons capable of drawing attention to what Mockus and his people called "Civic Culture."

After serving two terms as mayor of Bogotá and campaigning as a presidential candidate, the irony that defined Mockus as an "anti-politician" became disconcerting, and with time Mockus's performances as a political actor became scarcer. This was evident in the 2010 presidential campaign. In the debates, declarations, and public events, Mockus didn't have the same performative capacity as before (perhaps the only symbol that he and his party successfully introduced was a sunflower that looked more like an advertisement for cooking oil than an image from the candidate's former arsenal). However, the documentary *La Ola Verde* (The Green Wave), made by a group of followers about the boom and debacle of his presidential campaign, records two sequences of inconclusive actions, and two failed performances that, since his defeat, portray the best of Mockus the artist and recall the brilliant improvisational skill that launched his artistic career.

The first image occurs on a makeshift recording set on the eve of the first round of voting. The *Partido Verde* (Green Party) candidate's campaign advisors are anxious. In this first phase, they consider the possibility of losing by a small margin, but in the second round they plan to go all-in and emerge triumphant. This tempered optimism translates into conservatism at a time when they should be taking action. A movie director and an actor coach Mockus on what he should say and how he should behave in front of the camera. There's an ornate seat where the candidate will sit to give his speech. Mockus makes fun of the piece of furniture, saying that it is "old-fashioned," and he kindly questions the seriousness of his image consultants. He reminds them of the current president's histrionics, his use of the camera—"that machine"—and his tendency to stage boastful televised acts that say, "I am a strong president." Mockus proposes a variation, reminding them that his strength lies in "inviting society to look into a certain direction," and suggests the image of an "anarchist utopia": an empty seat. Mockus says that the real politicians are "more on the side of the camera: editing, transforming images, and not there," and he points to the visible center of power. Mockus expresses his doubts about the presidential chair where they want him to sit: "That is a little fake. That is where Belisario sat powerless while they burned the Palace of Justice."[2] An Argentine producer, who seems to think that the problem is the green set or the chair itself, sticks up for the shot. Mockus then proposes two other ways of creating the image. His first proposal is a backlit shot that shows a hazy, almost invisible candidate. His second proposal is to find a rocking chair to go along with the sway of the speech–a rocker from which the candidate would give his address; the movement would correspond to the natural oscillation of intelligence.

The second performative image of *The Green Wave* occurs after the grind of the first round, that period of dead calm when it became clear that virtual enthusiasm in social networks can do little in the face of the *real-politik* of the country. Mockus, almost alone, argues with two advisors and proposes that they "campaign for Santos," his opponent and antagonist. Seeing that overwhelming defeat is imminent, he suggests turning the debacle into a win: "Defeat the abstention, achieve monumental support for Santos." His advisors, again, seem unconvinced. Somewhere between bothered and perplexed, one advisor calls Mockus's proposal a "Machiavellian trick," and the other says that it "gives him the chills." Mockus says that "the good thing would be to make something authentic: communicative action disguised as strategic action."

In both scenes no one appears to listen to Mockus, or at least no one takes the time to think about what he proposes to do with the image; the documentary camera appears to be the only witness. In speeches and televised appearances we see a man seated in a chair who fluently recites a text without conviction, an actor tied to a rigid and agonizing script that leaves no room for improvisation: a frustrated performance. The ephemeral variations proposed by Mockus demonstrate his best self, his pure potentiality as someone who risks and intuits, someone who creates. His image of an empty throne instigates us into living behind the messianic illusion of a king; his initiative to defeat abstention is a rational move that demonstrates the ultimate consequences of the logical progression of the democratic game.

None better than Mockus (2012:167) to describe himself: "My idea of the artist is someone who, in a prison cell, takes a piece of chalk and draws a border to define his space, a person who has more restrictions than those normally apparent. But upon defining those restrictions himself, he liberates himself."

Mockus, the Idiot

The movie *Being There* (1979) is about a middle-aged man named Chance, played by Peter Sellers, who has never—and never means never—left the four walls of the modest palace where he works as gardener of an elder gentleman from Washington.

One day his employer dies, and Chance, who knows only the world of his garden and what he has seen on television, has to leave. By pure luck, chance, or distraction, Chance is lightly hit by a millionairess's car, who, fearing a lawsuit, takes him back to her mansion and hands him over to the medical team that looks after her sick husband. On the road, she christens him with noble lineage; Chance, who is not given to speak or show signs of understanding what is being said, tells her his name and occupation: "Chance, the gardener." She does what everyone else in the movie does and hears only what she wants to hear: "Chauncey Gardiner," assuming that he is one of the Gardiners of noble blood. She is the wife of Benjamin Rand (a surname that parodies the powerful Rand Corporation), a big shot to whom presidents—even the president of the United States—owe his positions and who recognize Rand's favors with regular visits to demonstrate their gratitude and loyalty.

During the 2010 presidential campaign in Colombia, Luis Fernando Vélez, a blogger for the online publication "La Silla Vacía" (The Empty Chair), posted "A revealing debate" where he excerpted a dialogue from the movie with the idea of comparing Mockus to Chance. Vélez (2010) sustains that in the scene "you laugh at this exchange because you know that Chance is an idiot and by responding with metaphors he amazes everyone with his wisdom and intelligence, including the president of the country." To make his point, the blogger (ibid.) transcribed this dialogue:

President 'Bobby': Mr. Gardiner, do you agree with Ben, or do you think that we can stimulate growth through temporary incentives?

[Long pause]

Chance the Gardener: As long as the roots are not severed, all is well. And all will be well in the garden.

President 'Bobby': In the garden.

Chance the Gardener: Yes. In the garden, growth has its seasons. First comes spring and summer, but then we have fall and winter. And then we get spring and summer again.

President 'Bobby': Spring and summer.

Chance the Gardener: Yes.

Benjamin Rand: I think what our insightful young friend is saying is that we welcome the inevitable seasons of nature, but we're upset by the seasons of our economy.

Chance the Gardener: Yes! There will be growth in the spring!

Benjamin Rand: Hmm!

Chance the Gardener: Hmm!
President 'Bobby': Hm. Well, Mr. Gardiner, I must admit that this is one of the most refreshing and optimistic statements I've heard in a very, very long time. [Benjamin Rand applauds]
President 'Bobby': I admire your good, solid sense. That's precisely what we lack on Capitol Hill."

Using this conversation as a starting point, the blogger (ibid.) pulled some phrases from speeches given by Mockus and concludes:

Now is the time that "democratic legality," "with education for all," "not everything counts," "Constitutional Court guide us" really mean something and don't just become, as in the case of Chance the Gardener, pretty phrases that camouflage the ignorance of those who repeat them.

With this dramatic finale, the blogger concluded his composition, ergo, the Mockus of the presidential debates was ignorant, an idiot who by pure chance became the chancellor of the National University and served two terms as mayor of Bogotá, an imbecile whose acts didn't mean "anything really;" in short, a danger to the country.

However, the blogger used the example of Chance the Gardener—or Chauncey Gardiner—with bias, and with the clear intention of attacking one candidate in favor of, without naming him, the official candidate of his choice: Santos, who gave him an important post in his government after he was elected president.

But to return to the movie, if the point is to analyze politics in light of "Being There," the blogger left the penultimate scene of the movie out of his comparison. A group of big shots carry Benjamin Rand's coffin to his tomb, a memorial in the immense garden of his property crowned by a symbol carved in stone of the same image that appears on the US dollar: the pyramid capped by the eye-sees-all, the symbol of the Illuminati, a sect whose goal was to rule all nations under a new world order. The distinguished gentlemen discuss who will be the next president of the United States, given that the current one isn't up for reelection. They consider options, and after weighing the pros and cons, one man suggests Chauncey Gardiner, a man without a dirty past, a guy with strange ideas but who is a media symbol of acceptance, a person capable of inspiring hope (not fear), a sincere fellow who responds "I only watch television" when asked if he reads newspapers—and this strange act of honesty brings him up in the polls—a common, ordinary man who appears to be an astute politician but all he does is respond with the plain truth and leaves everyone else to freely delude themselves.

The blogger's comparison between Mockus, the politician, and Chance, the gardener, could even go as far as the last scene of the movie. Chance steps away from the funeral ceremony and goes into the woods. He lifts a fallen bush and then arrives at a lake. He turns his back to the camera, walks on the surface of the water, pauses, submerges his umbrella beneath his feet, testing the depth, and then continues walking on water while the audio plays the president's funeral speech and quotes celebrated lines by Rand. One final quote coincides with the miraculous image of Chance: "Life is a state of mind."

This final scene may be the movie director's (Hal Ashby) interpretation, or it may come from the author of the original book, Jerzy Kosiski, but it is here where the staging is at its finest and most convincing: the person we thought of as an idiot is now a savior, and if he is, is he Christ, or an impostor? The political metaphor does not refer only to the elected official, but also hits us with force, rebounds, and asks the voters, "Why do we need a leader-savior?" "Where does the need for redemption come from?" In terms of art and performance, the portrayal goes further: art as mental, cerebral, and the body of this strange man as the willing and propitious receptacle of whatever meaning we wish to give him. Art does not mean anything; we have to give it meaning. So we write texts about Mockus the politician, the performer, the unfinished work; we grind over theories and use them as vehicles for more verisimilitudes and crazy associations of a political, artistic nature.

The movie doesn't end there. The credits roll, and when the letters fade, we see Sellers repeating again and again the same scene, having to act like an idiot and recite inane, mechanical, half-witted dialogue. But parsimony is difficult and so, every time Sellers messes up, he laughs, they cut, and do another take. Perhaps the character of Chance the Gardener or Mockus the candidate hide something more, something that was left out of the movie. Something, in the case of Mockus, that couldn't be seen in his last campaign because the excess of consulting caused him to lose spontaneity and converted his serious game into simple and plain solemnity, or because during the campaign he was out of shape and his acting, which had begun degrading with time, was never as good as his initial performances. Mockus, the actor, never succeeded in embodying the character of the presidential candidate, and his attempts seemed more like self-destructive impulses than moves that promised radical development. His art wasn't fully realized; it went from a promise of happiness to an inconclusive promise. But what more can you expect from art or an artist? Perhaps his defeat has been his ultimate and greatest triumph.

Endnotes

1   The Universidad de los Andes is Colombia's top private university.

2   Belisario Betancur was president of Colombia in 1985, when the urban guerrilla group M19, entered the Palace of Justice where the Supreme Court was housed in the central square of Bogotá (located in front of Congress and very close to the presidential palace). The Army took control of the situation, apparently overruling the President, and ordered the tanks and its squads into the Palace. The fire burnt it down. All the judges of the Court were found dead. Recently, a video of a judge circulated in Colombian media showing him as he was being extracted injured but alive from the palace held by military personnel. The judge was later found in the ruins of the Palace executed. Various civilians, who were working in the Palace, disappeared and were never found. Many Colombians remember this event as the Holocaust of the Palace of Justice.

References

Mockus, Antanas. 2012. "When I am Trapped, I Do What an Artist Would Do. Antanas Mockus in Conversation with Johanna Warsza." In *Forget Fear: 7th Berlin Biennale for Contemporary Art*, edited by Artur Zmijewski and Johanna Warsza. Köln: König.

Vélez, Luís Guillermo. 2010. "Un revelador debate." [A Revealing Debate] *La Silla Vacía*, May 19. (http://lasillavacia.com/elblogueo/lgvelez/13764/un-revelador-debate).

11. The Dark Side of Mooning: Antanas Mockus, between Norm and Transgression

Paolo Vignolo[1]

I n October 1993, Antanas Mockus, then Chancellor of the National University of Colombia (UNAL), dropped his pants and mooned an auditorium full of students after a group of *encapuchados* (hooded militants of the extreme left) had burst into the hall shouting raucously.

If it hadn't been for an amateur videotape that fell into the hands of the country's major TV networks,[2] this would have been just another episode in an interminable series of confrontations in the struggle between academic authorities and student movements that has raged since the founding of the University in the nineteenth century. That night, national news programs broadcasted images of the Chancellor of the University displaying his buttocks to the entire country. Scandalous! Shameful! Disgraceful! Prominent voices at the high levels of the ruling class rang out demanding his resignation for having profaned his sacred mission (Ronderos 2002:148).

The Chancellor had no choice but to resign. Not many weeks later, however, a poll of voters in Bogotá reported that if Mockus decided to stand as a candidate in the upcoming municipal elections, the majority would vote for him; no sooner said than done. In the following year, October of 1994, Mockus was elected mayor of Bogotá after the most outlandish political campaign ever held in Colombia. He was elected with no alliance or connection with either of the traditional parties, and with no ties to any clientelist network or economic interest group, with practically no budget, and without promising anything to the electorate other than a commitment to raise taxes (Yes, to raise taxes!) in order to address the city government's extreme fiscal imbalance.

Antanas Mockus's famous mooning of students at the UNAL was the foundational performance of an extraordinary career that even today keeps him among the most visible protagonists of political life in Colombia. More than just ridiculous, his gesture was symptomatic of a new political dynamic emerging in the country. In this simple act we can make out the embryonic state of all of Mockus's potential and all his contradictions and ambiguities. Antanas Mockus is the principal exponent and the visible face of this political change. His is the face of a man, however, who will forever be associated with his own naked keister.

Nonviolent Action as a Response to Violence: Expose Your Buttocks to Those Who Hide Their Faces

The Chancellor's provocative act relates above all to his unusual approach to the question of violence, which in Colombia is the central issue of public discourse and debate. It must be remembered that Colombia is still embroiled in a decades-long armed conflict from which its universities are not exempt. They have been the scene of dirty war tactics including death threats, arbitrary detention, assassinations, and forced disappearances.

The phenomenon of the so-called *encapuchados* (hoodlums) would be incomprehensible outside of this context. After enduring a period of police repression and paramilitary threats against leftist students, some militant groups adopted the tactic of concealing their faces when participating in public meetings, political marches, and disturbances. Throughout the 1980s and the beginning of the 1990s, these *encapuchados*, sometimes infiltrated by guerrilla groups, carried out ever more extreme actions, going beyond throwing rocks at police to intimidating students and professors with different political positions and physically preventing some academic activities from taking place, often by brandishing weapons.[3]

In the context of systematic violence by riot police, paramilitary groups and pro-guerrilla factions, Mockus had visibly engaged in certain irreverent behaviors often inconsistent with his position of prestige. He was known to bicycle around campus without bodyguards, to show up late at night at the houses of student leaders, and to enter occupied academic buildings for face-to-face negotiations when things were at a stalemate. "I really enjoyed being Chancellor," said Mockus (2009:448), "because it was understood that we wouldn't kill each other."

In fact this was never stated anywhere, or maybe it was implicit in the theory of symbolic rather than physical violence:

> Some students would be occupying a building and I'd come in with my laptop, which was new-fangled at the time, and I'd say "Hey, let's write a statement. Say if you want me to resign and we can produce an agreement or write a poem," and they'd say, "Chancellor, let us sleep."

In perhaps the most representative action of this kind, because it entails the question of recognizing the other in a context of violence, Mockus went to the city of Manizales to negotiate with a group of *encapuchados* who had taken over a university building on the campus there. When the occupiers refused to talk with their faces exposed, Mockus agreed to sit at the same table with them only if he could face in the other direction. "He told the *encapuchados* that he refused to talk to people who wouldn't show their faces," reported María Teresa Ronderos (2002:167):

> He announced that he would go into the occupied office with two other University administrators and they would dialogue facing away from each other, that they wouldn't look at them, so as "not to know" that they were *encapuchados*. And that's what he did. Mockus explained to them that their demands were just, but not their methods. As they spoke they moved toward each other, always facing in the opposite direction, until one of the *encapuchados* gave Antanas his hood. Mockus put it on to show his understanding of the protest and left. That night they ended the occupation.

Ironically, face-to-face dialogue was reinitiated not by demanding the unilateral unmasking of his adversaries, but by engaging in reciprocal masking.

Mockus advocated and practiced symbolic violence rather than "crushing protest" or "doing away with violent troublemakers" in the name of law and order–practices advocated and systematically carried out by rightists in positions of power–or "combining all forms of struggle"–the approach adopted with disastrous results by FARC and ELN guerrillas. "When I was a boy," recalls Mockus (2009:443):

> I was the smallest in my class, so if things came to a fistfight I would lose. That's why the use of symbolic violence has been advantageous for me since I was small… When I was the University Chancellor I proposed to student groups that we engage in more symbolic violence and less physical violence… Symbolic violence like chaining yourself to the Chancellor's door or when

I refused to talk to *encapuchados* and I showed up with a hooded goat. From the time I started as Chancellor the slogans of some of the students were things like "*Antanas, hippie recién bañado: con tu reforma a otro lado*" (Hippie Antanas, call it a day, take your reforms, and go away!") Somehow symbolic violence leaves room for tenderness, while physical violence set as harsher space.

Symbolic violence is sometimes an antidote to physical violence, a kind of cultural acupuncture, a metaphor for this kind of response; small homeopathic doses of playful aggression can cure society of the systematic use of brute force to solve conflicts. Another medical metaphor even became a source of inspiration for public action during Mockus's first term as mayor:

> Outside a makeshift ambulance in downtown Bogotá, thousands of young Colombians line up to receive their "vaccination against violence." Inside the vehicle, fourteen-year-old Álvaro paints the face of his enemy on a balloon and pops it, pins a wish on a tree of desires and then he receives his symbolic inoculation–a drop of water on his tongue. Some forty thousand Bogotá residents have received similar treatment in the last two months (Lennard 1997:41).

This was only the beginning of a long series of performative acts aiming to establish the discourse against physical violence and plant the seeds for a less stilted public debate on the conflict.

During the 1998 presidential campaign, for example, in the middle of a televised debate against his opponent Horacio Serpa, Mockus said, "I'm probably very similar to people in the guerrillas or in the paramilitaries. The only difference is that for one reason or another I decided to brandish different things. I decided to do aggressive things, brash things." And with that, he threw a glass of water right in the face of Serpa, who was seated next to him. "This is the new form of violence," he continued to the shocked audience:

> That's what we need in Colombia. We need a Colombia where people accept this kind of war so there will be no loss of life and there will still be a way to ask for forgiveness of the person who was used to set the example.[4]

Mockus (1998) immediately sent a letter to the leading national daily *El Tiempo* to justify himself:

> Symbolic violence can either stimulate physical violence or substitute for it. Suspending negotiations [in Tlaxcala, Mexico],[5] calling a political adversary

a senile old man,[6] ignoring others' proposals, or silencing a rowdy auditorium by displaying your genitals and your rear end, inducing duplicitous behavior, showing images of physical violence, or throwing a glass of water in someone's face: these are forms of symbolic violence. I consider them successful if they achieve their objective (to insult, disturb, provoke, to make your target and other people think), if they don't cause any physical harm, if they don't unleash physical violence and if they have a positive pedagogical effect... My social project is no physical violence at all and very little symbolic violence to be carefully practiced by everyone, including parents, educators, and leaders. I think the transition will entail a great deal of symbolic violence to supplant physical violence and to respond to it. If the opposing parties accept the idea of saving lives and they're able to do so by using less physical violence and more symbolic violence, mission accomplished.

Years later, when the FARC declared all the mayors in the country as "military targets," Mockus responded with another gesture of peaceful resistance. Instead of unobtrusively wearing the "Bulletproof Vest" he'd been given for his personal safety, he wore it over his shirt to be more visible, and had a heart carved like a bull's-eye on his chest to add a touch of dark humor. Exposing the hidden practices of personal protection that Colombians resort to in the face of death threats became a way to publicly denounce these threats and a way to spread the idea of a nonviolent response.

From that time on, his initiatives with respect to symbolic violence were developed in the context of a campaign called "Life is Sacred," which sought to reaffirm the inviolability of the lives of others in a country where in many social sectors human life has little or no value, and the rate of homicides and forced disappearances continues to be among the highest in the world. In the central cemetery in downtown Bogotá there are large structures called *columbaria* that contain rows of empty funerary niches. At one time they were used to hold the remains of humble people, but they now sit empty. What was to be done with these evocative and ghostly structures? Mockus decided to transform them into a symbol of his program to reduce the city's homicide rate.

The transformation of these structures was simple. Signs saying "Life is Sacred" were hung on them along with floral arrangements, and these gloomy monuments to the deceased were transformed overnight into an artistic installation (Vignolo 2013:136). Once the space was transformed in this way, Mockus began to use it to hold events celebrating civic resistance. For example, he called on citizens to gather in solidarity with victims of the FARC's bombing of the Club del Nogal on February 9, 2002 (36 dead and over 200 wounded) as well as the International Day Against the Death Penalty on December 5 of the same year. (Mockus, 2005:371-390). This was a rare example of civil society initiatives systematically promoted from the top down by municipal authorities anywhere in the world (Sommer 2005:2). Mockus (2009) explains his relation to nonviolent action like this:

> Gandhi's civil disobedience was much more powerful. When they established a monopoly and prohibited salt mining, he took a handful of salt from the sea and went to the judge and said, "Look, I've just violated the law. Arrest me." Of course he was not alone. It was a public act, open defiance. I disobey the law accepting the consequences of my actions. Of course you need an extremely legalistic context for civil disobedience to have a very great impact.

As Carlo Tognato (2009) argues, there is a problem when there isn't a legal, cultural, and moral framework for recognizing the other:

> One wonders if this kind of tactic, if nonviolent action as a means of legal pressure—the kind that Gandhi practiced—could really ever work in a country like Colombia, where the discourse of political legitimacy is based on what I call *discurso de la hacienda* (estate discourse), a country where people aren't equal, where they aren't even included as potential citizens, where in fact they are categorized as either estate owners or peons, and where the peons may end up living in extreme poverty and even be considered *desechables* (disposable). If this is the discourse that structures politics and legitimacy, then the question is if nonviolent actors who use the tactic of open disobedience to the law aren't engaging in suicidal activities.

In fact, one of the most striking aspects of Mockus's reflections is that he is able to formulate nonviolent proposals in extraordinarily violent contexts, where the risk of retaliation comes not only from the State, but also from illegal armed groups, mafias, gangs, and other criminal organizations. His is not an abstract moral condemnation of violence itself, but an artistic re-elaboration that can be applied in what may be called a "friend-enemy" dynamic, transforming its destructive potential into creative energy. The irreverence of displaying his "private parts and rear end," according to Mockus himself, had a very clear meaning: symbolic violence is legitimate when one is faced with violent actors, and when confronted by those unwilling to reveal their own faces (the *encapuchados*), it is legitimate to show them your rear end.

Transgressions, Rituals, and Political Performativity: Don't Bare Your Butt if You Can't Face the Music

When the Chancellor of the UNAL bent over and showed his butt in the middle of a solemn public event, it was not to ridicule an academic ritual, but to reclaim it as a sacred space. In fact, Mockus has always shown himself to be strongly drawn to ritual. For example, he reclaimed the disused hymn of Bogotá as well as its traditional flag and map, and he has faithfully observed the solemnities of public ceremony in his positions of leadership, both political and academic.

It is said that as valedictorian of his high school, young Antanas was to give an address marking the end of the academic year. When he had the attention of everyone in the hall, Mockus turned to the Colombian flag and denounced it as though it were the person responsible for all the well-known outrages committed in the country. He thus displayed his outstanding rhetorical capabilities by thoroughly enraging his audience. After a calculated silence, however, he again addressed his audience, which had fallen silent in the face of his unsettling behavior, and proceeded to insult them for not having shouted him down or defended the honor of the flag (Dundjerovic and Navarro Bateman 2006:5). This anecdote illustrates his early attraction to solemn public acts where the moral, legal, and cultural norms that orient our social behavior come most explicitly into play.

In 2002 Mockus organized a rather bizarre neo-indigenist act in which he publicly asked Bogotá's voters for forgiveness for resigning from his job as mayor in order to run in an ultimately unsuccessful presidential bid. The ceremony was both an act of contrition and a platform for him to once again announce his candidacy for mayor, the post to which he was subsequently re-elected by a wide margin.

Furthermore, in his last campaign, which was for president in 2010, the Green Party produced a television commercial in which candidate Mockus walked along the streets of the country as if he were proselytizing for a Christian denomination. Under his arm, though, he carried a copy of the Colombian Constitution instead of a Bible. "What unites us?" he would ask the pedestrians that he encountered. "All that unites us as Colombians is this text, the Constitution."

With this gesture, Mockus almost literally put into action the theory of John Rawls, one of his philosophical heroes. In Taylor's (1996) words:

> What would it mean to come to a genuine, unforced international consensus on human rights? I suppose it would be something like what John Rawls describes in his Political Liberalism as an "overlapping consensus." That is,

different groups, countries, religious communities, civilizations, while holding incompatible fundamental views on theology, metaphysics, human nature, and so on, would come to an agreement on certain norms that ought to govern human behavior. Each would have one's own way of justifying this based on one's own profound background conception. We would agree on the norms, while disagreeing on why they are the right norms. And we would be content to live with this consensus, undisturbed by the differences in profound underlying beliefs. (P. 15)

The attention that Mockus pays to seemingly stale symbolism and received ritual confounds the customary and expected divisions between leftist and rightist politicians across the Colombian political spectrum. Wedded as rightists are to ritual, even if reduced to an empty simulacrum of what was once meaningful, they do not dare to embrace his transgressions. Their approach to ritual is above all a rigid adherence to rules with no room for questions about their nature or applicability to modern times. To leftists, on the other hand, Mockus's transgressions are seen as media manipulations that only mask his superficiality, and that do not address the country's fundamental problems or undermine the system in a meaningful way.

From Mockus's point of view on the other hand, the most effective way to illustrate the function of certain rituals in daily life is their transgression through performative acts, frequently carried out in the first person at the risk of one's own body, social status, and personal life. While President Samper was embroiled in a corruption scandal and faced with the open hostility of the United States, Colombians were entertained by the Mayor of their capital city riding on the back of an elephant at his own wedding ceremony, which was held at a circus and officiated by clergy subscribing to a wide variety of religions (Vignolo 2006; Lennard 1997:45).

In some cases these kinds of activities went no further than provocative media sensations, missed their target, or failed resoundingly. For example, there was an attempt to replace the traditional Christmas iconography of a comet in the nighttime sky on Montserrate, the most prominent mountain overlooking Bogotá, with a huge representation of a "thumbs-up" gesture, the symbol of the mayor's campaign for Cultura Ciudadana (Civic Culture). This proposal triggered a clamor of loud protests and was withdrawn. In another case, Mockus and his entire team in the 2008 presidential election campaign appeared on bicycles wearing ridiculous looking orange cones on their heads, a performance that was universally held to be bizarre, incomprehensible, and ultimately counterproductive.

Some of Mockus's proposals have caught on, though, and even influenced popular language and daily customs in Bogotá. For example, in his first electoral campaign he popularized the phrase *"Todos ponen"* (Everyone Contributes) to refer to his promise to increase taxes if elected. The phrase is used in a popular game of chance called *"Pirinola"* (Top); likewise the expression *"No todo se vale"* (Not Anything Goes), meaning that some political practices are unethical and beyond the pale, as well as *"Plata pública, plata sagrada"* (Public Money is Sacred Money) in a country where people seem to be anesthetized in the face of widespread social anomie and official corruption.

Throughout his career, Mockus has treated Catholic, patriotic, indigenous, and civic rituals with a mixture of irreverence and irony. He transgresses not by condemning rituals but by interpreting them actively as part of a conscious exercise of citizenship. His declared goal is to restore dignity to the image of public officials by changing the relationship between authority and citizenry, thereby meeting with it one of the priorities in both of his administrations, which was to build institutional legitimacy. In his words:

> Within three years, we need government representatives in Bogotá to be rec-
> ognized as honest, efficient public servants, just as the Constitution demands.
> We must make it clear and everyone should understand that public institu-
> tions exist to work for the long-term common good, not to provide special
> favors. Special favors make slaves out of people, while their legitimate rights
> liberate them (Mockus 2001a).

Mockus has also introduced innovative approaches to media and innovative electoral strategies in Colombia that have influenced others in Latin America and even
elsewhere. For example, the short-lived success of the so-called *Ola Verde* (Green
Wave) in the 2010 presidential campaign was due to the systematic use of communication techniques pioneered in the campaign of Barack Obama in the United
States (Martínez 2011). However, these techniques turned out to be disconcerting
in the context of traditional Colombian political culture.

There were even some innovative actions using the idea of the flashmob as
practiced by performance artists.[7] Aware that the heart of public life and public
manifestations of political expression are no longer churches and squares, Mockus's
supporters sought to burst onto the scene in the new metropolitan agoras, today's
temples of consumption (i.e. shopping malls) where political demonstrations are

generally prohibited. By sending text messages to sympathizers, a call would go out to meet at an urban mall. The only other instruction was to dress in green and bring signs to express the positive and negative emotions behind their wish to participate in politics, things like "indignation," "pride," "social transformation," "justice," etc. The rapidly assembled group would walk silently among the display windows and escalators and disperse just a few minutes later.

In this way, performative acts become an important tool in creating new and contemporary rituals (Schechner 1993). According to Paul Bromberg and Manuel Espinel (1995), two prominent figures in the Institute of Culture during Mockus's first term as mayor, this is an important tenet of the *Cultura Ciudadana* program. Due to the accelerating pace of transformation in urban life, citizens are unable to interiorize new urban meanings in a way that is coherent with their own socio-cultural traditions. "This leads to the development of lifestyles in which tradition mixes up in a disorganized and unsystematic way with 'modern' ways of living in the city" (ibid.:28). That is the reason why it is so crucial to generate strategic interventions based on new cultural dynamics that promote changes or modifications in citizen actions or behaviors that produce and reproduce these traditions, and facilitate the development of a less contradictory civic culture that is more in tune with the dynamism that characterizes urban life. In their analysis, Bogotá is a metropolis inhabited by a population that has arrived from all around the country to seek greater opportunities or that has been displaced by the waves of political violence and economic crisis that plague the country. To a great extent they are of peasant origin and do not yet have a sense of belonging or rootedness in the city. In order to symbolically and practically appropriate this urban space, the new population must adapt to it and learn to live together. In this sense, it is necessary to promote urban civility and mutual respect in the public sphere. This cultural and artistic expression has a role to play in meeting these goals. It is necessary to remind that *Cultura Ciudadana* arises from classical dichotomies: rural and urban, tradition and modernity, ancestral ritual and new practices. Faced with two discourses (opposite but mirroring each other) of the nostalgic evocation of an irremediably lost Bogotá of days gone by, and the exaltation of uncontrollable change and unreflexive and voracious urban transformation, Mockus opted for the systematic reinvention of popular tradition.

Fabián Sanabria (2009) also come close to Mockus, underlying the importance of transforming rural morality into an ethic of citizenship. The debate over

Cultura Ciudadana can thus be read as an attempt to reweave the social fabric through the construction and institutionalization of an innovative public rituality. In the words of Mockus (2001b:5), the starting point is "the hypothesis that there is a discontinuity among law, morality, and culture, that the three systems that regulate human behavior are 'divorced' from each other..." This hypothesis led the city administration to prioritize the initiative called *Cultura Ciudadana*:

> A set of programs and projects set forth in order to promote citizen *convivencia* (living together with tolerance and mutual respect) through conscious changes in behavior... And the actions of the city government did lead to improvements in citizen behavior that have improve the discontinuity between law, morality, and culture (ibid.).

This first experiment with "government generated art," as Doris Sommer (2005:261-276) described *Cultura Ciudadana*, had two fundamental goals: to improve social behavior and improve Bogotá's image. "I believe that if people know the rules and are sensitized by art, humor and creativity, they are more likely to accept change," said Mockus in an interview with Jeremy Lennard (1997:41). What is impressive and particularly innovative about the initiative is its method, which would have to be described with a kind of oxymoron like "directed drift" or "situational behaviorism," which in essence refers to the relationship between norms and their transgression. Its approach to cultural agency requires us to reconsider the boundary between the idea of the game and the act of playing (Vignolo 1997). Responding to normalizing interpretations of the social game, which above all emphasize the rule of law and the strategies of social actors such as game theories, rational choice, and others, Mockus counterposes the right to artistic expression and to a subjective reinterpretation of the game itself. He complements calculation with emotion and interests with passions, exploring imperfect, problematic, and complex suppressions of rationality along the lines set out by authors such as Jon Elster (1979 and 1989) and Albert Hirschmann (1977), as well as others studying play, theater, and performativity. Rather than an objectified rule of law, it opens the way to subjective transgression, if this is accompanied by a corresponding sense of responsibility. Acts like insulting the flag or throwing a glass of water in the face of a political opponent certainly violate norms. They are justified, however, by the existence of an emergent inconformity that must be heard. In the end, the purpose of this kind of transgression is to challenge existing norms in order to strengthen them on a deeper conceptual level, to challenge the law so that it may ultimately be respected.

Likewise, one of the conceptual pillars of Mockus's administrations was the idea of undermining the common practice of playing fast and loose with the law when doing so was considered the easiest way to achieve a goal, a practice embedded in the *cultura del atajo* (the culture of the shortcut). To Mockus, violating the law was extremely damaging to the citizenry as a whole, particularly if accompanied by moral indifference and if met with a degree of culturally approved tolerance. Legality must be maintained through some form of social control and its violation must be rejected on the basis of ethical principles.

The well-known example of mimes being sent to direct traffic is emblematic in this sense. In 1995-1996, the promoters of *Cultura Ciudadana* mobilized street performers to act out responses to certain problematic behaviors in public spaces.

> For example, a mime artist would imitate a driver who had stopped in a pedestrian crossing, obstructing it, enticing the public to mock him. Individuals throwing garbage on the streets would be singled out by a mime artist who would follow and ridicule their action. Or when a good action was spotted, for example, a pedestrian helping an elderly person cross the street, the mime would shadow the person and entice the public to applaud his/her action. Due to the success of the initial campaign in 1997 the number of mimes in the streets was increased in 2001 from 20 to 400. These theatrical acts became a popular form of theatrical street entertainment. Captured on television and broadcast to the whole nation they also became a national talking point (Dundjerovic and Navarro Bateman 2006:9).

It was not only the media's impact that made this a very unusual game. At first glance, it was structured over a playing field (an urban intersection with traffic signals), some players (the drivers), the public (citizen witnesses), and a referee (the mime). The winners were those drivers who successfully drove through the intersection and respect the traffic signal, while the losers were those who got stuck in the middle of the intersection blocking traffic and pedestrians. Winners were rewarded with public approval and admiration while the losers were punished with jeers and catcalls. Social control through of the mime took the place of police officers representing the law, and the moral sanction of public shaming replaced monetary sanctions through fines.

Bromberg and Espinel (1995:13) comment: "The game and other aesthetic expressions thus become powerful *devices* to energize the public culture of the city and promote positive attitudes and behaviors that define it." From a theoretical perspective of play, however, one essential requirement is missing: voluntary acceptance of the player, who ends up as an object of derision without ever having agreed to take part in the game. Thus, it is a pseudo-game that, putting all its emphasis on the performative nature of the situation (play), manages to be transgressive by violating the rules of the game, only to see them reaffirmed when the police later re-established control over the intersection.[8] The term "device," as Foucault employs it, betrays a search for governability by a hegemonic power, interested above all in implementing an ingenious set of mechanisms aimed at increasing security not by disciplining or repressing desires, but by regulating them and controlling their circulation (Castro-Gómez 2010).

Rather than adopt the reformist approach of changing social rules exclusively through codified devices, or the revolutionary goal of subverting and replacing them, Mockus proposes responsible transgression as a way to mediate between what is and what should be, between social practices and established law. The potential of the game is manifested above all in players' variable interpretations of the initial rules. The city government must determine how to apply a normative system while leaving space for transgressive performativity: a situation where it is socially unacceptable to violate established norms but acceptable to transgress them if done to question them as part of a process of changing them. The outrageous act that made Mockus famous can be understood in this light: if one must display one's buttocks to the *encapuchados* because they refuse to show their faces, it is also true that—unlike them—a person showing them his or her buttocks must face up to his or her own actions.

Celebratory Participation and Political Representation: The Face of the Mayor, the Buttocks of the Buffoon

If anything has characterized Antanas Mockus throughout his public life, it is that he does not hesitate to put himself on the line. He gives his ideas a physical shape, that of his own body, and puts a face on them, his own very recognizable visage. In this sense, Mockus is a performance artist who draws inspiration from festivity and from the carnivalesque.[9] Throughout his administrations, however, celebratory expressions were treated with a great deal of caution, more worrisome as potential challenges to law and order than appreciated as the free expression of collective subjects. How should we interpret this apparent contradiction? What were its political implications?

Let's examine, for example, Mockus's use of masks and costumes. He takes full advantage of their potential. He has impersonated a rapper, gone out onto the street with a pink cardboard sword, and dressed as the Lone Ranger and Jiminy Cricket. He began his first term as mayor going on TV dressed as "*Super Cívico*" (Super Citizen), a parody superhero dedicated to teaching the rules of responsible civic behavior in public spaces and shopping malls (Dundjerovic and Navarro Bateman 2006; Shingal and Greiner 2008). These appearances attracted so much attention that a mask of Mockus's face was mass-produced and it became popular to dress up as him on Halloween and at carnivals throughout Colombia.

Although this kind of public behavior incorporates aspects of celebrity culture with an electoral calculus, it would be wrong to underestimate it as nothing more than calculated media exposure in search of popularity. Mockus finds an original way to reinterpret phenomena already well known in other countries. In Ecuador, for example, President Abdala Bucaram, who called himself "*El Loco*" (The Madman) had at the very same time taken to wearing a Batman suit to struggle against crime and injustice. Bucaram's reference point was the world of classic comic superheroes, originally situated in New York City, but with imitators around the world. They had always been portrayed as avenging heroes and fighters for justice who stepped in to struggle against criminality in ways that police and corrupt politicians could not or would not. It was an individualistic and privatizing approach to the use of force.

In Mexico City, on the other hand, the forebear of "*Super Cívico*" could be identified as "*Superbarrio*" (Super Neighbor), a celebrated figure who emerged in the aftermath of a 1985 earthquake to symbolize self-help efforts to rebuild working–class neighborhoods, and as a spokes-hero in community conflicts with municipal authorities. "*Superbarrio*" was the latest in a long series of masked heroes in Mexican history from Zorro to parody superhero Chapulín Colorado on TV, popular figures in professional wrestling, and Zapatista Subcomandante Marcos (Restrepo 2009). All of them were rebels, if not openly revolutionary, icons of resistance who emerged from below and from popular culture.

These models had little to do with the clowning of Mockus, however. He was not a figure seeking private justice as a substitute for inept forces of law and order (an idea that in Colombia would inevitably be associated with the paramilitaries who were then devastating the country and its institutions), nor with the icons of popular uprisings promoted by leftist movements (often associated with guerrilla figures, and thus conflated with terrorists in the hegemonic discourse). Mockus opted instead for a top down logic: he was not an alter ego of established authority who would reestablish order and bring about justice, but the face of authority itself who, by comporting himself as he did in public and for the cameras, created his own alter ego.

His style of governing transformed classic opposites like king and jester, the solemnity of power and the belly laugh of the common folk. This philosopher in power was at the same time a jester. Law and transgression were presented in tandem; they reinforced each other and were understood together, sharing the media space normally separately assigned to each. Mockus was an oxymoron in the flesh incarnating at once the rational philosopher and the clownish joker, the power wielded by authority and the challenge posed by transgression. The countenance concealed and the rear-end revealed.

The mayor's attitude towards *la fiesta* (public celebrations and cultural events) was also fundamentally ambiguous. For the first time in the city's history, the municipal administration promoted a wide variety of mass events and recreational activities in public spaces. The traditional *Ciclovía* (the Sunday closing of the city's major avenues to automotive traffic allowing their use by cyclists, joggers, skaters, and walkers) was expanded to include music and entertainment, and it was even extended to overnight hours. To celebrate the anniversary of Bogotá's founding, the municipality organized a parade of music, dance, and theater groups representing every part of the city (Vignolo 2006). In the mayor's words:

Our boulevards, public spaces, *Ciclovías*, "Bike Paths," pedestrian areas, outdoor concerts, and parks have become spaces for social integration where every citizen has the same right to come with his or her family and friends and where differences of property or work category are suspended. In these last few years we have learned to include ourselves in being included and to help others to become incorporated (Mockus 2001a).

The paradigmatic example of this development is *"Rock al Parque"* (Rock the Park), which may now be the largest free, open-air activity of its type in Latin America.[10] At first the idea of bringing multiple rock groups together for a large public event caused a great deal of concern among officials in the mayor's office and absolute panic among some "right thinking" (traditionalist) sectors. According to many commentators, a concert that brought together hundreds of local rock bands would have the effect of concentrating in one space all of the many gangs that contested turf and effective control in the rougher parts of the city. It would have probably led to a rash of illegal and undesirable behaviors and would have been followed by an outbreak of vandalism in the center of the city. In fact the concert had the opposite effect. Young people peacefully appropriated spaces to which they had access for the very first time as protagonists, in which to perform and celebrate their own music, lyrics, dances, and rituals (Vignolo 2006).

Fans and members of Bogotá's lively rock culture did not hesitate to answer the call to active citizenship. They participated massively in the competitive "battles of the bands" that were held to select *Rock al Parque* performers, as they did in the festival itself. With its success, *Rock al Parque* (1995) quickly became a reference point for the wider Colombian music scene and generated a series of spinoffs in other musical genres such as *Rap al Parque*—later called *Hip-hop al Parque* (1996), *Jazz al Parque* (1996), *Salsa al Parque* (1997), *Opera al Parque* (1998), and *Colombia al Parque* (2002)—for regional folk music and dance from around the country, and others.

The mass media publicized what had been a lesser-known cultural activity in the city and the recording industry went into high gear, making Colombian music an exportable product. Instead of a hotbed of creative micro-experiences spread throughout the urban space that were often in conflict or unaware of each other's existence, these projects established a system for identifying and judging the best performers while also developing a cadre of experts in organized cultural activities and project proposals, such as researchers, writers, and evaluators. What was *play*, became *game*.

In addition to the apparently liberating spirit of the mayor-philosopher, however, Mockus also instituted a series of prohibitionist measures, and did so in a top-down fashion. These measures would have a profound influence on nightlife in the capital city. In a regulation known as the "*Ley Zanahoria*" (Carrot Law) bars and nightclubs were required to close at one in the morning. The traditional use of fireworks was prohibited, and it was forbidden to consume alcohol on the street (Lennard 1997:41). All of these changes were intended to reduce the number of violent deaths in Bogotá, though at the price of drastically limiting personal freedom and the active use of public space.

The most interesting and dramatic initiative to change the culture of leisure and festivity was the institution of "Ladies' Night." City Hall decreed that, "on the night of March 9th, 2001, only women may be present on public streets and in public spaces between 7:30 p.m. and 1:00 a.m. of the following day" (Decree 190 of 2001). This measure certainly illustrates the innovative aspect of what Mockus and his team intended to implement, but also suggests a dark side to the measures, ambiguities in their effect on the citizens, and unresolved contradictions.

In the introduction to a book that the city administration dedicated to the initiative, then director of the Institute of Culture and Tourism, Rocío Londoño reflects on the goals of this bold experiment:

> In the first place [the goal was] to better protect the lives of men by responding to a cultural phenomenon little known to the citizenry of Bogotá: men often act or react more violently or aggressively than women, and as a result they are more susceptible to accidents and violent deaths (Mockus, Londoño, and Sanchez 2002:7).

The same book presents a set of statistics broken down by gender, demonstrating the instrumental approach of the city and its use of the classic carnival transgression, i.e. the inversion of gender roles between men and women. "Ladies' Night" was conceived above all as a way to lower the homicide rate, not as an end in itself.

The unusual proposal to feminize the night in order to reduce violence was announced with great fanfare and immediately attracted attention throughout Colombia and the world, generating headlines such as: "Dads, Watch the Kids!" (*El Espacio*, January 19, 2001); "They'll Stay at Home" (*El Tiempo*, March 4, 2001); "The High-Wire Act of the City Hall Matriarchy" (*El Espectador*, March 8, 2001); "Mockus's Babysitters" (*El Espectador*, March 9, 2001); "Gender Night: Another of Antanas's Stunts?" (*El Espectador*, March 9, 2001); "If You're So Macho Don't Go Out" (*El Tiempo*, March 9, 2001); "Butt Out, Mayor" (alluding at the same time to his having dropped his pants, *El Espectador*, March 14, 2001); "Women's Rule: 'Ladies' Night' in Bogota" (*The Economist*, March 17, 2001). A statistical analysis of "Ladies' Night" revealed that 23% of women and 14% of men went out. So for the first time on a Friday night there were twice as many women as men on the street (Centro Nacional de Consultoria 2002:122).

Disagreement centered primarily on the risks inherent in limiting individual freedom:

The mayor of Bogotá is euphoric because that night… there were fewer violent incidents…History shows that authoritarianism can produce these kinds of results, at least at first… Many dictatorships can produce rosy crime reports, since they themselves have a monopoly on crime. If everyone in Bogotá were required to stay home after 6:00 p.m., nobody would die on the street and there wouldn't be any accidents… It is important not only to reduce crime, but to do so without further compromising the already precarious rights of citizens… These nights for his or her partying depending on whose turn it is… seem more like senseless little carnivals designed to entertain academics, but a foolish and costly pedagogy (*El Tiempo*, March 14, 2001).

Many argued that, even if the measure was well intentioned, it would be legally inadmissible (because it's unconstitutional), morally questionable (because it's discriminatory) and of dubious cultural value.

Armando Morales Ocampo (Mockus et al. 2002), on the other hand, defended the initiative:

The curfew has always been a repressive measure…In Colombia curfews are linked to the repression of popular protest after the perpetration of certain perverse frauds associated with our political system, events such as that of April 9th, 1948,[11] the presidential election between Rojas and Pastrana, the 1977 strike. The curfew proposed now, though, it would be the first of its kind, applied not to obstruct equality but to promote it, not to punish protest, but to extend it, not to detain men at police stations while their wives or partners think that they've been disappeared, but to liberate women while their husbands or partners will [supposedly] come to see that they've finally rediscovered themselves. (P. 30)

The tension between a liberating proposal (to open spaces for women's emancipation at home and in public) put into practice by restricting freedoms (prohibiting men to go out at night) was resolved with a legal balancing act typical of Mockus:

Those people who cannot or do not wish to participate in this pedagogical exercise will be exempted from the measures described above. The mayor's office will distribute a pedagogical safe conduct form that these persons will fill out, specifying the factors that impede their participation in the exercise (Decree 190 of 2001).

However, the most interesting aspect of this initiative may have had to do with what Doris Sommer calls ripple effects associated with its symbolic value. Penélope Rodríguez Sehk underlines the importance of the lasting transformation in gender relations of such a macro experiment in social psychology (Mockus et al. 2002:57). Likewise, Mónica Tobón describes her participation in this way:

> It seems to me that the response was very good for a first attempt. There was a lot of joy on that evening, a lot of playfulness, a lot of laughter and adventure. For women it was a collective exploration, a new and different kind of event (ibid.:36).

Public discussion of this inversion of spaces and values was unprecedented. On the street and in homes, buses, schools, and workplaces, the proposal dominated conversation to such an extent that everyone's daily life was affected. In the words of Ángela María Robledo Gómez, director of the city's Administrative Department of Social Welfare:

> Another goal of "Ladies' Night" was for men and women to inhabit the city differently, to feel and interact with it in ways that contrast with normal daily life, which by imposing a set of customs and prejudices becomes routine and repetitive. That's what makes it important to subvert the customary in the street and in the home, outside and inside, in public and private, in the culture and in nature, as dichotomies that have defined our models of masculinity and femininity for thousands of years (ibid.:126).

In this case we also see a sudden change of perspective. The international feminist movement of the 1970s took to the streets chanting, "Tremble, tremble, the witches are back!"[12] and sought to bring about change by mobilizing from below. In this case, however, it was city authorities who issue a decree inviting women to demonstrate. In the now classic debate between those who see mass celebrations as an escape valve for repressed social tensions and those who see them as spontaneous and liberating expressions of popular culture (Eco, Ivanov, and Rector 1984), Mockus has an original point of view based on his reflections on symbolic violence. In both his intellectual activities and his actions, Mockus aims to construct spaces for confrontation, where conflicts can be expressed without compromising mutual respect and legality. Without a doubt, one of these spaces is the celebratory space, as illustrated by his administration's many initiatives in the area.

Rather than exalt irony as transformative within the limits permitted by the status quo—the "cold carnival" proposed by Umberto Eco (ibid.)—or defend the popular festival as a moment with potential for social transformation—the "revolutionary" carnival of Mikhail Bakhtin and his followers—Mockus seems prone to another characterization, which to paraphrase him can be called a "reflexive carnival." "Let's modify," Mockus (Mockus et al. 2002) says:

> Let's adapt this in order to better understand, then maybe go back to behaviors similar to those of the past, but we'll have reflexibility [sic] and they'll seem less natural to us. We want to explore gender roles and vulnerabilities in the home and the city. The great vulnerability in public life is man's and in the home it is woman's…this happens a bit with carnivals, but this may be the exception that proves the rule. That night [Ladies' Night] isn't going to be a pure carnival, however, but an event accompanied by reflection and with lessons to be learned, and I suspect that the opposite will happen. Whatever happens that night can be expanded, and on more than one occasion. (Pp. 14, 17).

While sharing Eco's skepticism of the masses, the crowd, *communitas* and other collective subjects of social action, Mockus also distances himself from the disillusioned irony of the Italian intellectual. He privileges a kind of performative action in which citizens participate actively, putting their bodies and names on the line. But aware of the inherent risks of populism when managing popular celebrations, he seems to opt for something like a "carnivalization of daily life" targeted at a middle class anxious for self-expression and for that self-expression to be recognized as public opinion.

In some sense, it is as though Mockus had found a way to transform political into poetic representation. By assuming the role of artistic demiurge of social change, he deprived citizen participation of its political and poetic potential. His media overexposure filled the TV screens and pushed social movements and collective action out of camera range. The soliloquy of the televised ventriloquist replaced the polyphony of the public square, emptied now of carnival-goers in masquerade and their potential transgressions. Mockus's approach to festival goes beyond both the impotent irony of the intellectual (who shows his face and covers his ass) and the buffoon's rhetoric of collective spontaneity (he who exposes his butt and hides his face). No, he aspires to incarnate both power and its discontents, law and transgression, the face of the chancellor and the buttocks of the buffoon.

Open Questions: Antanas, Don't Mock-us!

> Antanas, Don't Mock-us!
> —*Graffiti on a Bogotá street, 1995*

There is no doubt that the appearance of Antanas Mockus on the public scene in Colombia disrupted the existing clientelist logic of electoral politics, opening the door to new kinds of political action, and altering relationships between officials and those they govern, in both theoretical and practical terms. I have tried to illustrate three innovative elements in particular. One is associated with the introduction of the notion of symbolic violence into the Colombian debate, another with the reinterpretation of civic rituals to relegitimize established authority, and the third with the management of festive and celebratory events in terms of representation and participation. However, the particular articulation that Mockus establishes between norms and their transgression in each of these areas also suggests a series of questions whose problematic character should be addressed.

First, the question of violence: Mockus promoted symbolic acts with the idea that individual behaviors among the citizenry could be altered if authorities were to adopt a pedagogical attitude toward society. This assumed that the problem of violence in Colombia is primarily due to the ignorance of a majority that is unable to behave "correctly." The mayor-philosopher was presumably the ideal figure to teach the masses how to best behave themselves in the public arena, albeit through rather peculiar practices in which the flatulence of the jester complemented the eructation of the esteemed public official.

No mention is made of structural violence produced through historical processes and perpetuated by specific social actors. Take the case of mass transit, for example. Isn't it simplistic and ultimately misleading to attribute the dismal condition of urban transit for the majority in Bogotá to their own bad citizenship and behavior? What about the oligopoly of a small number of operators, the privatization of public services, and the closed and self-interested groups that impede desperately needed change, the so-called *mafias del transporte* (transportation mafias)? Why should the city government focus on the behavior of individual private motorists when it is impotent in the face of powerful forces, when it is unable to end *la guerra del centavo* (the war of the penny) that has buses careening dangerously through the streets as they vie to pick up more passengers than their competitors? Why is there no interest in subsidized fares for those in economic distress, nor even in establishing something as simple as bus stops? As former Mayor Juan Martín Caicedo Ferrer (1996) pointed out some years ago:

> As a result of the economic opening and the massive increase in automobile imports that followed, the number of motor vehicles is growing at 10-12% per year while our road infrastructure can only grow at an annual rate of 2-3% if we are lucky...This being the case, it's worth asking if the mimes, while of course are amusing attention-grabbers, whether they constitute an effective response...The city can't be managed by applying a kind of collective hypnosis...In all of this there seems to be a kind of behaviorism: "Let's codify people's behavior and not change the conditions from which their behaviors spring" (P. 4).[13]

Policy toward street vendors was even more repressive. Rather than conducting an analysis of the use of public space in all its complexity, full responsibility for the privatization of urban space was laid at the feet of street vendors, the most vulnerable people in the supply chain. In the name of an abstract normativity, the city government ordered the violent removal of people whose only offense was trying to make a living through honest work. The second mayoralty of Mockus ended with the spectacle of police pursuing street vendors through the streets. It is a sad paradox that a mayor who had launched his political project in the name of symbolic violence to promote civility and the *"Ley Zanahoria"* to provide a "carrot," or incentive for healthy living, ended his term with sticks: an operation by the forces of physical repression armed with billy clubs.

The same can be said about the interpretation of political violence in the country. One of the most important achievements of Mockus's administrations was a sudden decrease in the number of homicides in Bogotá, but statistical trends by themselves don't tell us anything about the structures of power, mafia infiltration, the relations of coercive forces, or the exploitation present in a society. The recent history of Colombia demonstrates that the absence of killings may reflect forced pacification by illegal groups rather than increased social peace, no matter how fervently this is hoped for. Mockus's approach to political violence does not seem to provide any kind of interpretive insight that would help reconstruct the country's historical memory.

One of Colombia's urgent needs is to find a path to the collective reconstruction of divergent and conflicting narratives about the country's history that can somehow coexist in a common normative framework that is accepted as legitimate across the entire political spectrum. But in his nearly twenty years of political life, Mockus has never expressed a strategy for reconstructing or reconciling historical memory or for introducing any policy for the public use of history. This is a silence that speaks volumes. The lamentations of the mayor and the chortling of the jester evoke a collective emotional reaction to the violence that afflicts the country, but their sobs and guffaws drown out the bellowing of the perpetrators and the wailing of the victims, which are reduced to background noise.

This leads to another consideration that we might apply to the event that originally attracted so much attention to Mockus: the lowering of his trousers. The media storm that followed completely decontextualized Mockus's transgression, radically transforming its meaning and implications. Instead of an assertive but indirect mocking gesture in the context of university conflicts, it was tinged with populism as a pure television spectacle. In the words of María Teresa Ronderos (2002:148), "The meaning of Mockus's gesture was lost when it was presented to the public. It was seen as nothing more than an outrage." With this understanding, there can be no doubt that the election of a clown as mayor was more an expression of discontent among much of the voting public than support for a set of policy proposals.

Almost without knowing it, Mockus catalyzed the frustrations and the desire for change felt by countless people exasperated with clientelist networks, bad governance, the waste of public resources, and the crime and corruption that had characterized the city government over the course of decades. The newly introduced direct election of mayors changed the face of local politics and opened the door to new personalities in the political landscape, just as it had in Barranquilla a few months earlier in 1995. At the same time, it opened the electoral arena to populist proposals, often backed up not by organized political parties or medium to long-term visions for improved governance, but by charismatic personalities with a highly visible media presence. To put it in other terms, the former Chancellor was a pop phenomenon, both popular and populist, from the time he burst onto the scene. Through the celebration of his comedic character, Mockus ended up masking the serious intentions of his administration, and vice versa. The populism of the dramatic character of Mockus could only succeed when protected by the popularity of Antanas the comedian. One tangible sign of Mockus's success during his first administration was the widespread sale by street vendors of small dolls depicting the mayor pulling down his pants. The face of the popular politician was inseparable from the buttocks of the populist.

Mockus has not been able to consolidate his media exploits as public policy, and the many people who have worked with his administration—such as supporters, collaborators, and city officials—have been unable to form a stable party. As his own alter ego and dramatic counterpart, no one seems able to replace him. Condemned to campaigning permanently to regain the position to which he once acceded almost effortlessly, Mockus runs the risk of becoming a caricature of himself. A caricature of a caricature, since his initial pose had been a caricature of a traditional political figure. A square caricature, then. His last way out, brilliant as most of his moves, is to shift his place of enunciation, presenting himself as an artist (Ospina 2012). Mockus today doesn't act anymore as a man of power playing the fool, but as a fool who could anytime strike back as a man of power.

Finally, a review of Antanas Mockus's outstanding public career brings up a serious question. In effect, it seems that his political positions/impositions continue to be shrouded in a fundamental ambiguity. On the one hand, it seems that the former mayor has achieved the 1960s dream of bringing "the imagination to power," as demanded in a famous graffito seen in Paris in 1968. His discursive practices, to use Foucauldian terminology, promise an escape from the systematic militarization of daily life in Colombia that disciplines bodies and indoctrinates minds. His own body politics and creative use of media seem to challenge both the authoritarian conservatism that employs "estate discourse" (Tognato 2009:426) and the impositions of what's left of revolutionary ideology reduced to criminal trafficking. He acts both as a "stoic" government official, as he defines himself, and a cynical rebel who—like the dog philosophers of ancient Greece (in Greek *kynikos* literally means "dog-like")—challenges prevailing social conventions.

Mockus seems to be a reference point for liberating society from subjugation to norms perceived as unjust and asphyxiating. His proposals seem to have a strongly emancipatory component since they provide agency to those engaged in active citizenship and promise to develop the heuristic potential of the art of governing. Thus it is not an accident that they are often compared to Augusto Boal's "Theater of the Oppressed" (Sommer 2005; Dundjerovic and Navarro Bateman 2006).[14] Nonetheless, the eccentric and liberatory Mockus, personifying a peculiarly Latin American permutation of the protests and rebellions of the 1960s, seems to be overshadowed by a centralizing and neoliberal Mockus, a local expression of what Deleuze (1990:240-247) calls societies of control, which would, according to him, gradually replace the disciplinary societies theorized by Foucault.

Santiago Castro-Gómez (2010) synthesizes Deleuze's text in this way: Domination no longer operates by confining individuals in order to normalize subjectivity, but by modulating their desires in open spaces. The human-as-mole of disciplinary societies has given way to the human-as-snake of control societies…While in disciplinary societies human subjects are like moles moving from one closed space to another in a linear and progressive fashion (from school to army, from army to factory), no one in control societies ever comes to the end of their training. Subjects are like snakes who continually "surf" [across institutions] to acquire competencies, but while their movements seem to be free, they are in fact controlled by the services that they purchase on the market and by their consumption habits. (Pp. 215-216)

Mockus's proposal that we become *cultural amphibians* seems to confirm the analogy between the governing techniques described by Deleuze and those that made up his *Cultura Ciudadana* program. As Foucault (2008) put it:

On the horizon of this analysis we see instead the image, idea, or theme-program of a society in which there is an optimization of systems of difference, in which the field is left open to fluctuating processes, in which minority individuals and practices are tolerated, in which action is brought to bear on the rules of the game rather than on the players, and finally in which there is an environmental type of intervention instead of the internal subjugation of individuals. (Pp. 259-260)

This might be the source of the obsession of the Mockus's administrations with metaphors of play rather than work. If disciplinary societies sought to normalize behavior by enclosing bodies and regimenting practices, contemporary control societies are interested in influencing individual and collective behavior by taking actions to create contexts (environments) while letting subjects self-regulate. "Of course," continues Gómez-Castro (2010):

This situation does not mean that we now have a kind of "open" or "liberating" society, as is claimed by apologists for neoliberalism, but a society whose paradox is that control is imposed by providing a certain kind of freedom. The relaxation of disciplinary and punitive mechanisms in contemporary democratic societies does not reflect the triumph of liberating humanitarianism. It is the product of a governmental technology of controlling behavior by controlling the environment. (Pp. 216-217).

In Article 7 of "*Formar Ciudad*" (To Form the City), the 1995–1998 Development Plan of Mockus's first administration, we find language almost identical to that just detailed above to describe the "Strategy for *Cultura Ciudadana*":

> This strategy consists of carrying out and coordinating public and private actions that directly affect how citizens perceive, recognize, and use social and urban environments and how they relate to each other in each environment. To belong to a city is to recognize contexts and in each context respect the corresponding rules…. To modify certain individual and collective behaviors that are extremely detrimental to the social life of the city by means of citizen self-regulation.(P. 4)

In short, Antanas Mockus can be said to have acted like someone who wanted to teach traditional social graces as defined in a book of etiquette written by Groucho Marx, or an urban code of conduct as interpreted by Charlie Chaplin. A graffiti that appeared on a wall in downtown Bogotá several weeks after Mockus's first election as mayor expressed the contrast tellingly: "Antanas, Don't Mock-us!" it said. But behind this plea was the sentiment "Antanas don't [become] Mockus." Antanas, a desirous subject and at the same time the object of desire, an eccentric artist whose strange foreign name reflected his distance from traditional political rules; and on the other hand, Mockus, a harsh name whose etymology evokes the monk, a professor, and a prophet who descends from his ivory tower to teach the masses to desire and to manage their desires. Once more we confront the dilemma posed by his first media appearance, when like a two-faced Janus, Antanas's rear-end masked Mockus's face.

Endnotes

1 Translation from Spanish by Andrew Klatt, Professor of the Department of Romances Languages, Tufts University.

2 See: "Antanas Mockus se baja los pantalones y muestra su trasero al publico" [Antanas Mockus lowers his pants and shows his butt to the public]: (http://www.youtube.com/watch?feature=fvwp&v=kIc1g89iZlg&NR=1).

3 For example, several months prior to this, they burst into an auditorium where the famous French philosopher Jean-François Lyotard was speaking, terrifying the people there and prematurely ending the session. In April 1994, another group of *encapuchados* interrupted a debate between Mockus and fellow politician Enrique Peñalosa, throwing manure on the table and forcibly preventing both men from speaking. Mockus's response was to stand motionless in front of his attackers holding up a red card like a soccer official calling a foul. Both the attackers and the public were so taken aback by this reaction that Mockus effectively achieved his goal of confronting physical violence with symbolic violence.

4 See "Mockus y Serpa, El vaso con agua, lección de tolerancia" [Mockus and Serpa, the Water Glass, Lesson on Tolerance]: (http://www.youtube.com/watch?v=iIiZ90IZy5o).

5 The reference is to the 1992 peace negotiations involving three guerrilla groups: the FARC, the ELN, and the Popular Liberation Army (EPL).

6 This is what Horacio Serpa, Minister of the Interior for President Samper at that time, called businessman Hernán Echavarría Olózaga, who had previously called Serpa a *serpiente venenosa* (venomous snake), a play on the sound of Serpa's last name.

7 In an article entitled "Después de la euforia," (After the Euphoria), Jerónimo Duarte went so far as to characterize the entire phenomenon of the Green Wave as an extended flashmob. See: www.revistaarcadia.com/periodismo-cultural-revista-arcadia/ideas/articulo/despues-euforia/22868.

8 The invention of the "moving crosswalk" and other *Cultura Ciudadana* initiatives may be seen in a similar light. Moving crosswalks were long carpets printed with zebra striped pedestrian crossing patterns that groups of actors would roll out at intersections to help pedestrians open their way among vehicles to get across the street.

9 See the keynote address by Antanas Mockus, introduced by Doris Sommer: http://hidvl.nyu.edu/video/000516050.html.

10 See the *Rock al Parque* "Rock the Park" website: http://www.rockalparque.gov.co.

11 This was the day when the hugely popular political leader Jorge Eliécer Gaitán was assassinated and Bogotá broke out in massive, widespread, and destructive violence.

12 *Tremate, tremate, le streghe son tornate* (Shake, tremble; the witches are back!) is a slogan used by Italian feminists in the 1970s, whose translation spread beyond Italy.

13 This article also provided some other significant statistics applicable at that time: "Eight hundred thousand private vehicles that transport only 10% of the people and occupy 80% of the streets. Seventy thousand buses and taxis that transport 90% of the people but to which only 20% of road space is available...Bogotá has not been decentralized. Nearly seven hundred thousand people travel to the old historical and administrative area every day" (Caicedo Ferrer 1996:4).

14 "What Mockus's *Cultura Ciudadana* and Boal's theatre techniques unquestioningly have in common is the influence of Paulo Freire's educational philosophy defined in his *Pedagogy of the Oppressed*. Both Boal and Mockus reflect Freire's basic premise that through personal experience based on action, dialogue, and community involvement, individuals can instigate a new consciousness and therefore a cultural change...In Mockus's theatrical acts, both the public and private spaces are performance arenas and everybody in the community can become a spect-actor. By being spect-actors, the community takes an active involvement in re-writing and re-ordering their social narrative" (Dundjerovic and Navarro Bateman 2006:5-8).

References

Bakhtin, Mikhail. 1993. *Rabelais and His World.* Translated by Hélène Iswolsky. Bloomington: Indiana University Press.

Bromberg Zilberstein, Paul and Manuel Espinel. 1995. "La *Cultura Ciudadana* como eje del plan y los principales proyectos prioritarios a cargo del Instituto Distrital de Cultura y Turismo" [Civic Culture as the Axis of the Plan and the First Prioritized Projects Undertaken by the District Institute of Culture and Tourism]. In *Antanas: Del mito al rito* [Antanas. From Myth to Ritual], edited by Dario Bustamante. Bogotá: Mayor's Office of Bogotá.

Caicedo Ferrer, Juan Martín. 1996. "La hipnosis de los bogotanos" [Bogotanos Under Hypnosis], *El Tiempo*, September 29. Retrieved October 25, 2012 (http://www.eltiempo.com/archivo/documento/MAM-510221).

Castro-Gómez, Santiago. 2010. *Historia de la Gubernamentalidad.* [History of Governmentality] Bogotá: Siglo del Hombre, Javeriana University, Santo Tomás University.

Centro Nacional de Consultoria. 2002. *Survey and Analysis.* Bogotá, March 9-10.

Deleuze, Gilles. 1990. *Pourparlers.* Paris: Minuit.

Duarte, Jerónimo. 2010. "Después de la euforia" [After the Euphoria], *Arcadia*, July 21. Retrieved October 25, 2012 (www.revistaarcadia.com/periodismo-cultural-revista-arcadia/ideas/articulo/ despues-euforia/22868).

Dundjerovic, Aleksandar and Ilva Navarro Bateman. 2006. "Antanas Mockus's Theatre for Social Change: Creating Civic Culture in Bogotá, Colombia." *Research Paper Series.* University of Liverpool. Retrieved October 25, 2012 (http://www.liv.ac.uk/managementschool/research/working%20papers/wp200628.pdf).

Eco, Umberto, V. V. Ivanov, and Monica Rector. 1984. *Carnival!* Berlin and New York: Mouton Publishers.

Elster, Jon. 1979. *Ulysses and the Sirens: Studies in Rationality and Irrationality.* Cambridge and New York: Cambridge University Press.

———. 1989. *Solomonic Judgments: Studies in the Limitations of Rationality.* Cambridge, New York, and Paris: Cambridge University Press, Éditions de la Maison des sciences de l'homme.

Hirschmann, Albert. 1977. *The Passions and the Interests: Political Arguments for Capitalism Before Its Triumph.* Princeton: Princeton University Press.

Foucault, Michel. 2008. *The Birth of Biopolitics: Lectures at the Collège de France.* Edited by Michel Senellart and translated by Graham Burchell. New York: Palgrave Macmillan.

Lennard, Jeremy. 1997. "Mayor of a Different Mold." *Americas* (English Edition) 49(2):40-45.

Martínez, Margarita. 2011. *La ola verde, la ilusión de una generación* [The Green Wave, the Hope of a Generation]. Colombia: Documentary.

Mockus, Antanas. 2001a. "Discurso de Posesión del Alcalde Mayor 2001-2003" [Mayor's Inaugural Speech 2001-2003]. Retrieved on October 25, 2012. (www.bogota. gov.co/portel/libreria/php/frame_detalle_w3c.php?patron=01.0109020104&h_ id=392).

———. 2001b. "*Cultura Ciudadana*, programa contra la violencia en Santa Fe de Bogotá, Colombia, 1995-1997" [Civic Culture, Program Against Violence in Santa Fe de Bogotá, Colombia, 1995-1997]. Washington, D.C.: Inter-American Development Bank. Retrieved on October 25, 2012 (http://es.scribd.com/doc/63048/ Colombia-Cultura-Ciudadana-Experiencia-Bogota).

———. 2004. "Ampliación de los modos de hacer política" [Broadening the Modes of Doing Politics]. *La démocratie en Amérique Latine: un renouvellement du personnel politique?*. [Democracy in Latin America: A renewal of Political Personnel?] Colloque CERI, December 2-3. Retrieved on October 25th, 2010. (http://www. ceri-sciences-po.org/archive/mai05/artam.pdf).

———. 2005. "Resistencia Civil en Bogotá 2002-2003" [Civil Resistance in Bogotá 2002-2003]. Pp. 371-390 in *Acción política no-violenta, una opción para Colombia* [Non-violence Political Action, an Option for Colombia], edited by Freddy Cante, Freddy and Luisa Ortiz. Rosario University, the Center for Political and International Studies. Retrieved October 25, 2012. (http://www.lalibreriadelau. com/lu/pageflip2/UROS_accion_politica_no_violenta_70/).

———. 2005. "Keynote Address." In Hemispheric Institute Meeting. Performing Heritage: Contemporary Indigenous and Community-Based Practices, Belo Horizonte, Brazil. Retrieved March 2005. (http://hidvl.nyu.edu/video/000516050. html).

———. 2009. "Intereses, razones, emociones" [Interests, Reasons, and Emotions]. P. 443-451 in C*iudadanías en escena. Performance y derechos culturales en Colombia* [Citizenship On the Stage. Performance and Cultural Rights in Colombia], edited by Paolo Vignolo. Bogotá: National University of Colombia.

Mockus, Antanas, Rocío Londoño, and Efraín Sánchez Cabra. 2002. *Noche de las mujeres 2001: memorias* [Ladies' Night 2001: Memories]. Bogotá: Mayor's Office of Bogotá.

Ospina, Lucas. 2012. "Mockus, el artista" [Mockus, the Artist], *Arcadia*, July 19. Retrieved October 25, 2012. (http://www.revistaarcadia.com/opinion/columnas/articulo/mockus-artista/29039).

Restrepo, Laura. 2009. "Enmascarados en el mito y en la literatura" [Masked with Myth and Literature]. Conference. Retrieved October 25, 2012. (http://www.youtube.com/watch?v=LsXtshMRc9U).

Ronderos, María Teresa. 2002. *Retratos del poder: vidas extremas en la Colombia contemporánea* [Portraits of Power: Extreme Lives in Contemporary Colombia]. Bogotá: Planeta.

Sanabria, Fabián. 2009. "De tramoyeros a tramoyistas: compromisos cívicos contra la para-institucionalidad en Colombia" [From Stretchers to Stage-hands: Civic Commitments Against Para-institutionality in Colombia]. Pp. 427-440 in *Ciudadanías en escena. Performance y derechos culturales en Colombia* [Citizenship On the Stage. Performance and Cultural Rights in Colombia], edited by Paolo Vignolo. Bogotá: National University of Colombia.

Schechner, Richard. 1993. *The Future of Ritual: Writings on Culture and Performance.* London and New York: Routledge.

Shingal, Arvind and Karen Greiner. 2008. "Performance Activism and Civic Engagement Through Symbolic and Playful Actions." *Journal of Development Communication* 19(2):43-53.

Sommer, Doris, ed. 2005. *Cultural Agency in the Americas.* Durham: Duke University Press.

Taylor, Charles. 1996. "A World Consensus on Human Rights?" *Dissent* (Summer): 15–21.

Tognato, Carlo. 2009. "Introducción a Protestas no violentas en contextos violentos" [Introduction to Non-violent Protests in Violent Contexts]. Pp. 425-426 in *Ciudadanías en escena. Performance y derechos culturales en Colombia* [Citizenship On Stage. Performance and Cultural Rights in Colombia], edited by Paolo Vignolo. Bogotá: National University of Colombia.

Vignolo, Paolo. 1997. *La experiencia lúdica en una sociedad de mercado.* [The Ludic Experience in a Market Society.] Bogotá: Tercer Mundo Editores.

———. 2006. "La prise de la rue: carnaval et conflit à Bogotá" [Taking the Sreets: Carnaval and Conflict in Bogotá]. *Vie des Idées* [Route of Ideas] (April:71-82).

———. 2013. "¿Quién gobierna la ciudad de los muertos? Políticas de la memoria y desarrollo urbano en Bogotá" [Who Governs the City of the Dead? Politics of Memory and Urban Development in Bogotá]. *Memoria y sociedad* [Memory and Society] 17(35):125-142

PART FOUR: INTERVIEWS

Carlo Tognato *with*

Paul Bromberg

Rocío Londoño

Efraín Sánchez

Jon Elster

4

1. Interview with Paul Bromberg

Carlo Tognato

Carlo Tognato (CT): When did you start with the Instituto Distrital de Cultura y Turismo (District Institute of Culture and Tourism)?

Paul Bromberg (PB): Antanas asked me to be in charge of the *Cultura Ciudadana* (Civic Culture) program four days after winning the elections. He told me: "You are going to be responsible for *Cultura Ciudadana*." And I asked him: "What is that?" He gave me a piece of paper with a couple of ideas, and based on that I started to work. I was appointed director of the Institute of Culture and Tourism in 1995, the very first day Antanas took office as mayor.

CT: What was your relationship with Antanas and how did you come to be appointed to that position?

PB: I got to know Antanas in relation to the debate on the teaching of science. He was also my sister's fellow math student. So, my first contact with him dates back to 1980. I later attended an event in which he presented his point of view in November of 1980. I objected to it and received a loud applause from the traditional educators in the audience. That led to the development of our relationship.

A few months later, I called him to work with other people on educational issues for a magazine about the popularization of science and came to respect him a lot. I always learned a lot from our discussions, which were fantastic. I thought he was very clever. And when he became vice-chancellor for Academic Affairs at the Universidad Nacional de Colombia (National University of Colombia), he asked me to join his administration. Then he became the chancellor, and when I got back from my graduate studies, he asked me to work with him. So, the joke between us at the time was that he had the habit of using me to fill any vacancy that needed to be filled. Once a colleague begged the *Jefe de Vigilancia* (Head of Security) not to resign because then I would be asked to replace him! This happened again when Antanas resigned as mayor and had to choose among a number of potential successors. I was the one who filled in for him.

CT: How was the Institute of Culture and Tourism organized? What was inherited from the previous administration? What changes did you make?

PB: The Institute carried out the classic activities of any entity of this type. It had previously financed different artistic practices. Antanas decided that it was from there that they would coordinate and finance the actions of the *Cultura Ciudadana* program. That was why I was appointed director of the Institute. The page that I mentioned earlier, which he gave me during our first interview after the elections, referred to civic games. When the press came to me and asked what the *Cultura Ciudadana* program was about, I mentioned the games. The next day a title on the front page of a national newspaper (in January there is a great shortage of news) stated: "Mockus will educate citizens by playing" (*El Tiempo*, January 1995), which generated great expectations and compelled us to respond to them.

CT: How would you characterize the interaction between you and Antanas Mockus during the administration? To what extent did Mockus intervene in the work of the Institute? How did that work?

PB: At the Institute I brought in several people with the same level of experience as me, but from other disciplines. Among them was a cultural sociologist, Manuel Espinel—who was then pursuing his M.Sc in the sociology of culture at the National University in Bogotá (he later got his Ph.D. at the Universidad Complutense in Madrid [Complutense University]). With the help of Gabriel Gómez, a theoretically–minded communication specialist, we began to try to understand the issue, that is, how to carry out non-authoritarian actions from state institutions to prompt citizens to adopt behaviors that do not result in collective disasters. We prepared a list of actions that we thought should be carried out. Since the beginning it was clear to me, even without much administrative experience, that we needed to institute some compelling programs. This posed a very complex challenge in a city of six million inhabitants, which was also considered the worst in the world. We ended up dividing the issue into six fields. After we had developed the first draft, I spoke to him. He kind of said that it was okay. Nonetheless, throughout all our interactions with Antanas, it always happened this way: Antanas promoted on his own, directly from the mayor's office, those things that he considered important, relevant, and interesting. Sometimes he didn't even call us. But each thing we did was discussed with him: "we are going to do such thing" or "let's start this way," "it is going to be done this way," "there must be an event in which you may explain it," "let's do it this way: do you agree?"…and this is how we worked for almost two years.

CT: Were there any campaigns that were generated and developed outside the Institute?

PB: Yes, very relevant ones. Perhaps the most important was the one that sought to reduce the homicide rate in 1995. It hadn't been included in the *Plan de Desarrollo* (Development Plan). It was an issue that the *Consejero de Seguridad* (Security Adviser), Álvaro Camacho, brought in, and Antanas took it as a priority outside the plan of activities scheduled at the Institute.

Child abuse was not part of it, either. *Cultura Ciudadana* referred to social behavior out in public space, whereas intra-family abuse occurs in private spaces, at home. Therefore, when people working on a proposal on child abuse came to me, I replied: "No, sorry, it is important, but you have to turn to others," because I had been told that we had to focus our work *outside* homes. As a result, they turned to Antanas. Antanas was captivated by the problem and began to work on it on his own. The Institute "lent out" its communication specialist, and parts of the actions were financed by the Institute. Child abuse is another topic of great relevance that was developed outside of the Institute, by direct initiative of the mayor.

CT: Was the interaction between you and Antanas Mockus formal or informal?

PB: Antanas wasn't really a good team coordinator. He did well in selecting his team. That's why the administration functioned well. He built up a team that was loyal to the program, and had no hidden agendas. But interactions with him did not resolve the problems that arose from those programs and required a lot of institutional coordination.

In the complex administration of a complex city there are always conflicts because of the blurring of competences, and those conflicts were not resolved by Antanas. The message was: solve your issues amongst yourselves. Since I had lived under these precepts, in the first meeting with my team, [when I succeeded Antanas] I announced a change in this approach. The new policy was that, if they had problems amongst themselves, they should come to me so that I could solve them myself. After a couple of conflicts, and replacing very few people on the team, the administration began to work because the issues were solved. This differed enormously from Antanas's approach because Antanas did not resolve conflicts within the administration. Antanas used to say, "Don't bother me with those problems." Nonetheless, Antanas was very good in one aspect; he always responded to our calls. Antanas responded to us every time we would turn up to discuss the programs we had designed.

Most mayors were impossible to find. Luis Garzón and Samuel Moreno were impossible to find. No one had access to them. Antanas, on the other hand, was always available. So every time we were going to start a program, we always consulted with him. We made appointments, we showed up, and we discussed what we had. This is what used to happen all the time: a program would begin with an announcement on the part of the mayor that he would be introducing an issue in a press conference in an hour. I would arrive an hour earlier with the slides of the conference that summarized the approach we had agreed upon in our previous meetings. Nonetheless, at the time of the presentation, Antanas was no longer convinced about the slides that we had agreed on. So he would start by saying things such as "Well, I do not agree with this. I don't know. . .this is what the Institute says, but I'm not that sure. . ." Many times we had discussions during the press conference as though we were in an academic seminar.

CT: And the reactions?

PB: People seemed to like the relationship between two academics. We appeared as if we were in the midst of a deliberation at an academic meeting. Each one presented his point of view and discussed. That happened several times.

CT: Were there any programs in which the two of you held significantly different positions?

PB: I will tell you two stories. The first story occurred during the implementation of the program with the mimes. Antanas called the Institute to reprimand me. The Traffic Secretary had called him to complain about the immense traffic jam they had generated, and therefore he passed the complaint on to me. I replied that the traffic jam showed that the program had been successful because we had broken the routine. A few hours later, he conceded that we were right. The second story has to do with the civic cards with the thumb pointing up or down. A few days before their release, Antanas commented in a television program that he knew of a card that the Institute was about to release, and that he was probably going to give the order to recall them because he disagreed with them.

CT: In what other ways did such differences emerge?

PB: On the issue of the program against child abuse there were differences between the actions Antanas undertook and what we tried to do during the last months of 1997. The issue of child abuse was not very relevant in Colombia at the time. None-theless, Antanas embraced it, and invented the "Days of Vaccination Against Child Abuse." They were a success. On the first Vaccination Day, fifteen thousand people attended while during the second intervention, some months later, forty thousand people came. He raised awareness about the problem. But after the second instance, we could not continue with a third one. People returned after the second event, saying that the vaccine had not cured them. In other words, the symbolism was very strong for people from lower social strata who were not accustomed to such indirect language. It was now necessary to think how to trigger cultural change. What could a government do as a "cultural agent" beyond recognizing that child abuse was a problem instead of a neutral cultural behavior?

Another one of Antanas's ideas in 1996 and 1997, the "*Cruces escolares*" (School Pedestrian Crossings), is also worth commenting. Streets in Bogotá were dangerous for children to cross on their way in and out of school. We tried to make the rights of children visible, and it was important to do so in the public realm. Therefore, we designed a campaign called "*Por una ciudad al alcance de los niños*" (For a City Within the Reach of Children), along with García Márquez's dictum: "*Por un país al alcance de los niños*" (For a Country Within the Reach of Children). As the image of children is deeply evocative in Colombians' imagination, even though they are subject to abuse, we pursued a strategy of massification for the purpose of accelerating cultural change. And this required some cultural engineering. To achieve widespread change, we could not rely just on a charismatic prophet (i.e. Mockus) who would admonish everyone, "Thou shalt not hit any children." It was necessary to produce all the images in the public realm so that people would realize that children are more important than dogs in parks. Other strategies were also pursued, which required continuity on the part of subsequent administrations. But then came Peñalosa, and everything was discontinued. Even after the return of Antanas three years later, the program was not resurrected in spite of all the emphasis on children's rights.

CT: Many talk about the strengths of *Cultura Ciudadana*. What were its weaknesses?

PB: Well, there's a very big weakness: the lack of continuity. I have insisted on several occasions on the fact that *Cultura Ciudadana* instituted during Mockus's second administration was very different from the one instituted during the first administration. A careful analysis of the results the second administration produced shows that they are problematic. Some are within the range of uncertainty; others depend on errors in the surveys.

Now, *Cultura Ciudadana* encouraged people to feel solidarity towards others and to accept it from others. That was its greatest impact. That's why after it was discontinued as a policy in 2003, *Cultura Ciudadana* ended up fading away. All that is left is its story.

CT: Some critics object to *Cultura Ciudadana* on the grounds that its civilizing intent plainly overlooked the fact that people may hold worthy knowledge that should instead be recognized.

PB: This is false. Our first inquiry in 1995 was a survey that asked citizens about desirable behaviors in the contingencies identified by the "Police Code". We were surprised by the utter homogeneity of the behaviors respondents wished for. It was at that stage that we uncovered the problems inherent in collective behavior. We developed many programs based on ample cultural research.

CT: Was that research open enough to capture gender differences, ethical differences, and more?

PB: Of course. For example, in the research about rap fans and rock fans we learned about the conflicts between the two, and we staged events for the purpose of bringing them together. Also, in order to investigate social behavior on rubbish and waste, we engaged in a fifteen-day observation of the way people threw garbage onto the streets. We designed our actions based on those results.

CT: Some critics argue that *Cultura Ciudadana* turned out to be a form of post-disciplinarian government that exercised control over its own citizens by giving them the illusion of being free.

PB: I wonder what it means to them, "to be free"? Does one become less free if one controls one's sphincters? Do you become less free if you are prosecuted because you killed someone? Do you cease to be free when through family and community interaction you are taught your own language, which in turn determines, for example, nothing less than what you can name? Over the vast majority of the written rules governing the life of a city there is a huge consensus—not total, of course. There are always *Pablo Escobares* in all societies. That is, individuals who freely choose to engage in big crime, and what people are asking, almost crying for, in our cities is that authorities fulfill their function of regulating others because the majority says that others are those who do not want to comply with the standards. The type of argument I see in your question immediately evokes that of anguished philosophers who speak of the "anguish of man," while those in anguish are actually themselves.

CT: Would you do anything differently today?

PB: I see now where the errors lie. I would not spend so much money on advertising—I spent a lot on that—and Antanas always complained about that. At that time,

I justified it. Today, I wouldn't. Now that *Cultura Ciudadana* is fashionable, it tends to be confused with advertising campaigns, with a call to behave well. It is believed that the call *per se* can do wonders, a *miracle gel* that can lead any segment of society to act against the individual interests of its own members. We never saw *Cultura Ciudadana* that way.

CT: In your opinion, how much of *Cultura Ciudadana* is technique and how much is it charisma or biography?

PB: It is very difficult to know. I have talked about it in my (2003) article "Engineers and Prophets." It's hard to envisage a *Cultura Ciudadana* without a prophet.

CT: With Antanas, art enters government. At that point, the artist must also act as administrator, politician, and manager. To what extent can these dimensions coexist in the same person?

PB: How did we solve that puzzle? Well, Antanas had some very good ideas. I also had my creative group, which was very good. But yes, we did the engineering, which was not Antanas's strength.

CT: Do you think that it would be possible to imagine a site where managers and leaders could be trained to articulate art with politics?

PB: I don't know, because nothing like that has been tested. We've thought several times about offering a course on *Cultura Ciudadana*, which would include a component of engineering, and one of art. However, sooner or later we would have to test whether political commitment is sufficient on the part of the mayor, or whether it is also necessary to resort to all the symbolism that Antanas tapped into.

2. Interview with Rocío Londoño

Carlo Tognato

Carlo Tognato (CT): When did you join the Instituto Distrital de Cultura y Turismo (District Institute of Culture and Tourism)?

Rocío Londoño (RL): I joined the Institute on January 1st, 2001, when Antanas took office, and I left on December 31st, 2003. I served for the three years of Mockus's second administration.

CT: What relationship did you have with Antanas back then?

RL: I have known Antanas for many years. I met him at the National University of Colombia (UNAL) in a seminar that a group of academics organized called the "Permanent Professorial Seminar." The seminar was held in the 1980s, during one of the university's many crises. Then, by chance, while Antanas was the vice-chancellor for Academic Affairs of the University, we met one day, and I don't know why because I had never been his friend, he decided he would like me to work with him. I was appointed Deputy Director of the Comité de Investigaciones Científicas (CINDEC, Committee for Scientific Research). The director was José Luis Villaveces, a chemistry professor. When Antanas was appointed chancellor, he appointed me as the dean of the Faculty of Human Sciences against my will. This was my prior relation with Antanas. His term as the university's chancellor was very complicated due to the academic reform. Politically, it was very difficult. I had many problems. Antanas's chancellorship was quite singular not only in terms of his management style, but also in the way he analyzed and solved problems.

CT: Did you have any relation with him during his first administration?

RL: I participated very actively in his electoral campaign. Along with Fabio Chaparro,[1] I helped to organize the programmatic groups,[2] which were received extraordinarily well. I also served as Antanas's secretary because there was no money to hire one. We raised the first one million pesos through a party we organized at a bar in Bogotá called Salomé. But at some point towards the end of the campaign, I had a strong disagreement with him, and I dropped out of the campaign. He called me to be part of the cabinet, but at that time I had decided to do a PhD in history in order to finish research that I had begun years before. So I did not accept. I worked in the Institute of Culture and Tourism *ad honorem*: I served on the Board of Directors, and with the Consejero de Seguridad (Security Adviser), Álvaro Camacho, and Paul Bromberg we put together the Observatorio de Cultura Urbana (Observatory of Urban Culture). [3] Therefore, yes, I was quite close to his first administration on a voluntary basis.

CT: What was the relationship between the Institute and the Observatory of Urban Culture?

RL: The Observatory of Urban Culture was born within the Institute and was very important because it started systematic studies and measurements of homicides and other crimes in Bogotá. At that time, the District Security Council did not have unified and reliable statistics to support decisions; the data the police had did not square with the information from the Coroner's Office or with that of the Secretary of Government. Due to these discrepancies, the Institute of Culture and Tourism built up a data system on violence and crime, which is a pride for Bogotá up to this day. This is how the Observatory of Urban Culture was born. In addition, when Bromberg was in charge, the Institute did a lot of work on surveys and opinion polls so we had a better empirical base to support our decisions in relation to the campaigns on *Cultura Ciudadana*. Among the many studies carried out by the Observatory of Urban Culture, it is worth referring to the first published series of these studies, which sold out, and which bears witness to the impressive support on the part of the Institute in advancing research and knowledge about Bogotá.

CT: How was the Institute organized? What activities did it carry out, and how did they eventually change under your leadership?

RL: It is worth emphasizing that Antanas gave the Institute a new role. Before Antanas's first term in office, the Institute of Culture and Tourism had engaged in traditional programs such as cultural initiatives sponsored by City Hall, financial support for cultural organizations, and some promotion of tourism (tourism had always been a marginal activity within the institute). Antanas gave the Institute a primary role in his administration. In addition to its traditional functions and activities, he entrusted it with the management of his *Cultura Ciudadana* (Civic Culture) policy, which was the flagship program of his administration. This was reflected in its impressive budget increase. If I remember well, the Institute's budget was multiplied by six. The effort was not simply about designing and implementing programs as part of *Cultura Ciudadana*. Cultural activities were also meant to contribute to strengthening the sense of belonging and coexistence among citizens, and this was achieved not only by increasing the number of cultural activities, but also by investing considerable resources to expand public spaces in the city and to improve their use and quality. Thinking about how cultural activities could enhance culture, the quality of life, security, and peaceful coexistence among citizens was very innovative and extremely important.

CT: Would continuity or change best represent the Institute under your leadership?

RL: There were continuities and changes. In the first place, there was an interruption when Mayor Enrique Peñalosa, elected in 1997, dismantled the *Cultura Ciudadana* program. When we were appointed, we had to dig for the files from the program dating back to Antanas's first administration. When Antanas appointed me as director of the Institute of Culture and Tourism, I was given the task of coordinating the commission that would be responsible for guiding *Cultura Ciudadana* within the new administration. Therefore, it was essential to recover what he had done in his first administration. Before working on new programs, it was necessary to observe what had been done and what results it had yielded. Once the Plan de Desarrollo—*Bogotá para Vivir Todos del Mismo Lado* (Development Plans—Bogotá, Living All On the Same Side)—was approved, the team at the Institute and those responsible for *Cultura Ciudadana* undertook the task of defining the goals and the programs.

Among the programs carried out during Antanas's two administrations, there are some interesting debates that Bromberg has referred to in some of his writings. In addition, they appear in the books that have been published on *Cultura Ciudadana*. Bromberg, for example, suggests that there are some important differences between Antanas's conceptual approach and what was actually done as part of *Cultura Ciudadana*. I agree with Bromberg on some points. For example, the intention to change citizens' moral values —based on Antanas's idea that coexistence requires some harmony among law, morality, and culture— is not only debatable in terms of public policy, but also on a theoretical level. Perhaps Bromberg is right that a policy of *Cultura Ciudadana* should pursue above all changes in habits and routines in order to improve coexistence or, as he puts it, it is more a work of cultural engineering than a philosophical matter. However, I think that Antanas was right to highlight that in Colombia noncompliance with laws was a very marked cultural problem.

My role as the coordinator of *Cultura Ciudadana* during Mockus's second administration focused on ascertaining the practical feasibility of that policy and of Antanas's sometimes quite abstract ideas. An important innovation, which sought to boost the empirical solidity of that policy and of its programs was the design and implementation of the survey on *Cultura Ciudadana*, which continued in the administrations that followed—those of the Mayors Luis Eduardo Garzón (2004-2007) and Samuel Moreno (2008-2011)—though with certain variations. An important precursor to this survey was the opinion poll conducted by the Institute of Culture and Tourism during Mockus's first administration, when Bromberg was the director. Moreover, in 1997, at the end of that administration, a survey or opinion poll evaluated the administration, and showed a very positive opinion on the part of Bogotanos about *Cultura Ciudadana*.[4] It is worth remembering that the press initially reacted very negatively to these campaigns. It mocked and disparaged them. Several columnists wrote that the mayor was naïve or crazy to believe that mimes could increase the public's compliance with transit rules in the city. That survey also showed that at the end of his administration the police had much better approval ratings from the citizens. There were remarkable accomplishments along with the decline in the homicide rate. How much the *Cultura Ciudadana* programs did contribute to the decline in the murder rate is very difficult to know. However, the overall climate in the city and the willingness on the part of Bogotanos to respect fundamental norms of coexistence surely changed, and that was recognized and continues to be recognized by people.

The survey on *Cultura Ciudadana* was the result of a debate within the city council over the Development Plan. When we presented the goals of *Cultura Ciudadana* and the six programs that were intended to fulfill these goals, a member of the City Council asked us to quantify our goals. The presentation contained a diagnosis, but it lacked a solid empirical basis that would establish the baselines and set quantitative goals. As a result, we made a compromise before the Council to establish indicators, baselines, and targets in our goals for *Cultura Ciudadana*. This was how the survey came about. It was a very difficult exercise in which Antanas actively participated. We worked on it with Antanas between ten p.m. and one or two a.m., following the template of the survey he had made with Jimmy Corso called *Colcordia*, which was about violence and peaceful coexistence in school environments. It is from that work that Antanas developed the idea of *Cultura Ciudadana*. It wasn't some brilliant improvisation that he developed on the occasion of his first electoral campaign. Rather, he had been studying the problem of violence in schools for a long time. As a result, some of the indicators and questions in the 2001 survey on *Cultura Ciudadana* were taken from the *Colcordia* survey. The development of the forms for this survey built on the hard work done by the team of the Observatory of Urban Culture, particularly by Alberto Maldonado, Efraín Sánchez, and Carolina Castro, which defined the indicators needed to measure attitudes and perceptions related to social regulation, individual self-regulation, and ideas such as the harmonization among law, morality, and culture.[5] We included, in addition, a module on political culture since one of the programs of *Cultura Ciudadana* sought to strengthen the democratic culture of Bogotanos. Mockus's first administration had not dealt with such a challenge. This was a new gamble, and it yielded lasting results.

For us it was a very important tool that forced us to be much more precise in formulating actions that were part of *Cultura Ciudadana* and in measuring its impact on the population. In my opinion, it also allowed us to further rationalize the resources invested in the implementation of the programs. Another new thing we introduced, since the Development Plan was formulated not on the basis of administrative areas, but rather by objectives, was the involvement of the nineteen entities of the city district in the programs of *Cultura Ciudadana*. The heads of those nineteen entities constituted the "*Comisión de Coordinación*" (Coordination Commission). We presented monthly accounts of our work before the mayor which turned out to be very effective.

CT: Were the initiatives undertaken under the umbrella of *Cultura Ciudadana* led by the Commission or by the Institute? What was the relationship between them?

RL: The Institute did two things: it was in charge of coordinating the Commission, and it served as the technical secretariat (i.e. it monitored the programs and actions of *Cultura Ciudadana*). The Observatory of Urban Culture was in charge of this task. Efraín Sánchez was its director. When the Commission met, it was not to speculate, but rather to assess results and make adjustments as considered suitable. In the Development Plan, programs and projects were formulated and then translated into concrete actions. The job of translating is not easy. I think we did some good planning and achieved some good inter-sectorial coordination in spite of the tensions with senior officials from the previous administration who initially resisted Antanas's ideas as well as his attempt to work together. The achievements of *Cultura Ciudadana* in that period emerged from the evaluation of programs carried out by Javier Sáenz Obregón, who contributed to it as an external advisor.

CT: How was the interaction between Antanas Mockus and the Institute?

RL: Antanas has one virtue as a boss: he is very respectful of the autonomy of those who work with him. He is not a boss who gives orders, but one with whom you can discuss and even disagree. We created and discussed the forms of the *Cultura Ciudadana* survey. We regularly met to discuss the program's results. Moreover, some of his ideas were subject to tremendous political discussion within his cabinet. Thanks to those discussions, important changes were made to the proposals that Antanas wanted to pass at all costs.

I remember two particularly controversial actions: *"Noche de las Mujeres"* (Ladies' Night) and another called *"Croactividad"* (Croactivity)—from croaking—which sought to invert the stigma of the *sapo* (literally, toad; meaning snitch). "Ladies' Night" was controversial since it initially sought to prevent men from going out on one night. That curious proposal, which sought to spark a debate over the respect for life, triggered a huge controversy in the media. The discussion turned very aggressive. As a result, the idea was complemented by seminars on gender differences related to violence and aggression. The decree of the mayor was also modified and requested that any men intending to go out would need to issue to themselves a permit explaining the reasons why they would not comply with the measure. This is a good example of the way argumentation and discussion could alter or even invalidate Antanas's initiatives that were too bold or inconvenient from a political standpoint. In a publication of the Institute on "Ladies' Night," we included the polemic in the media and the results of a women's survey on that action.

The idea of *croactivity*, whose objective was to improve the cooperation of citizens in crime reporting, sparked a strong discussion within the cabinet. This issue, for me personally, was particularly difficult because the idea of the *sapo*, which in Colombia has a negative connotation associated with the snitch, or those who accuse each other of misdeeds, is very complicated as a result of the burden of violence and abuses committed by the security forces and the intelligence services. In fact, I was the victim of an unfair imprisonment. So for me it was very difficult to accept an idea like that, even on a theoretical level.

In addition, Antanas's idea, which introduced the possibility that neighbors might be allowed to kindly inspect each other's houses, neglected, in my opinion, the anonymity of the city's inhabitants and their respect for privacy and intimacy. Although he sought the voluntary collaboration of people with the police, the way that this idea was initially presented to the public seemed highly dubious and dangerous. Luckily, the discussion within the Cabinet led to the modification of the original idea. Instead of proposing mutual surveillance among neighbors, a public event was organized in several parks of the city in which the heads of the branches of the city government would receive complaints from people who, for various reasons, did not dare go to court or to other authorities. The challenge was tremendous because it wasn't simply about receiving the complaint but also making sure it would be addressed, for which it was necessary not only to verify the authenticity of the complaint, but also to take care not to violate any citizens' rights. I remember that a good part of the allegations were made by women, children, and elderly people who would write on little slips of paper about the instances of familial violence that they had not reported to the authorities, either because they did not know how or because they were afraid to do so.

CT: Were there any campaigns or actions coming from the Institute that were not supported by Mockus?

RL: No. We always had his support. Rather, it was more about the difficulties in finding ways to implement Antanas's initiatives. We could not always do it. For example, the entire campaign on "Civil Resistance" was very innovative— "Civil Resistance" had never been promoted by the state—and we had all the mayor's support, in addition to his active participation. Some of Antanas's initiatives were very difficult to implement. Antanas came up with the idea that for the days of "Civil Resistance" he would use PVC pipes. If I remember correctly, Antanas chose that material because, besides being very resistant, its initials could be read as *pacífica vida colectiva* (peaceful collective life). The campaign was staged for several days in defense of hospitals and educational institutions in response to an attack on the Chingaza Dam.[6] We used the symbols for the protection of the civilian population according to the Geneva Protocols. We met with representatives of the International Red Cross to learn how to use some of the symbols of international humanitarian law, but curiously we lodged our request for permission with the headquarters of the Red Cross in Switzerland, which delayed the process to the point that we ended up abandoning the use of international symbols. We opted to invent Bogotá's version of the triangles and circles to mark water and energy sources, as well as educational institutions, from scratch. With Antanas, we painted the symbols in several places in Bogotá and assembled a huge electrical tower in the Plaza Bolívar to raise awareness of the importance of protecting public goods from terrorist acts.

The only time we could not implement Antanas's idea, because it was not legally possible due to the location's status as a National Heritage Site, was when he sought to place a tile commemorating the adoption of Bogotá's new "Police Code" into the ground of the Plaza Bolívar. I told Antanas: "The Plaza Bolívar is untouchable because it's a protected heritage site. We cannot install the tile without the approval of the Ministry of Culture and the National Heritage Council. They are not going to give us that permission." Antanas insisted, but in the end he accepted that this was not possible when I showed him the relevant articles about the laws protecting heritage sites.

CT: The great strengths of *Cultura Ciudadana* are well known abroad. Focusing on your term in office, what would you reckon to be its greatest weaknesses and strengths?

RL: It's very clear to me that something that has not been recognized is that *Cultura Ciudadana* would not have had the social impact that it did if it had not been coupled with strong social investment. The actions of *Cultura Ciudadana* by themselves, without the increase in social investment that changed the city, would have had little impact. You cannot see *Cultura Ciudadana* as isolated from everything else that had been implemented for more than a decade before to improve safety, peaceful coexistence, and the quality of life of the inhabitants of Bogotá. During Mockus's two administrations, and even during Peñalosa's, citizens had greater incentive to comply with the law because they saw material and cultural results in the city.

CT: Did Mockus address the great structural issues of Colombia, or did he omit them (violence, memory, etc.)? Some authors claim that his approach to social issues is quite superficial and does not address deep factors.

RL: There is clearly a difference between Mockus's approach and that of *El Polo* (The Pole), the major Colombian leftist coalition party, which focused, during both Garzón's and Moreno's administrations, on reducing poverty and expanding the coverage of education and other goods or public services.[7] In Garzón's administration there was a considerable increase in investment in food for children in public schools. His top program was "Bogotá Without Hunger," which also resulted in a notable increase in *comedores comunitarios* (community diners). I remember a discussion with the Ministry of Finance, during Mockus's second administration, about the cost of the district's schools upgrading from a snack to a full lunch. That step, which occurred under Garzón, was important because of its impact on children. However, the Secretary of the Treasury at the time felt that a considerable increase in resources for that purpose was not sustainable. I think Antanas is sometimes too rigid with technical matters. In my opinion, it was necessary to go even further because of problems like abject poverty that were pervasive in the city at that time. For example, in the survey on quality of life conducted at the end of Mockus's second administration, it was observed that about 6% of households skipped two or three meals every week, a situation that in my opinion could not wait until new jobs were created. That does not mean that in Antanas's two administrations there was no significant increase in social investment. In education and health it is apparent that there were improvements. He also strengthened the Departamento Administrativo de Bienestar Social (Administrative Department of Social Welfare), which is now the Secretaría Distrital de Integración Social (District Secretary for Social Integration). Assistance programs for the homeless were very important, but there wasn't much emphasis on poverty.

That said, there is no doubt that the problem of compliance with the law, the rules of coexistence, and citizens' rights and duties are crucial issues in Colombia, not a secondary problems. Had that not been the case, Antanas would not have gained the recognition he has, not only on a national, but also on an international level. The issue of public transportation was also approached from an equity perspective. We know that Antanas is not a leftist, but that does not mean he is not sensitive to equality and social inclusion. The efforts made in the area of tax culture were also important because without new resources, redistribution cannot be achieved. On this front, on which I agree with Antanas, he was attacked. Paradoxically, in Colombia the left has been traditionally very opposed to taxes. The campaigns on tax culture sought precisely to modify this aversion to taxes, which moreover is universal in the country. In Colombia the justification of tax evasion is particularly marked, both in the upper and lower classes. The point is that addressing the issue of taxes meant dealing with the problem of redistributive justice. Many people could not explain how Antanas achieved the famous program "*110% con Bogotá*" (110% for Bogotá), which consisted of citizens, even those of the lower strata, giving a voluntary contribution. Relatively few people contributed the extra 10%. Even so, it was an achievement. Garzón maintained this campaign, although the extra contribution fell dramatically. I believe this was due to the fact that people did not see enough results in the city. A campaign of this nature must not be merely rhetorical, or merely seek to change citizens' attitudes. It must be based on objective or visible results for people.

The weakness of *Cultura Ciudadana* for me is that one administration is not long enough to achieve lasting results. The results of the surveys conducted every two years have shown a progressive decline in some indicators of *Cultura Ciudadana* and citizenship because they require some continuity over time. They should be institutionalized as general policy because of the ongoing turnover of the population in Bogotá, new dynamics, new migrants, and many other factors. For example, in Europe this type of campaign has gained strength given that immigration and multiculturalism have exposed generational and cultural problems with regard to compliance with or respect for the norms of social coexistence.

CT: Some critics complain that *Cultura Ciudadana* is an attempt to "civilize" Bogotanos that does not necessarily recognize the value of common people's knowledge. Do you agree?

RL: This is a very interesting discussion. I encountered this issue in relation to the national "Police Code" project. The problem was that every article of the first draft of this code affected the interests of specific groups such as indigenous groups and Afro-Colombians, whose cultures must be respected. Therefore, a pressing question came up: what do all Colombians have in common? There has to be a common basis among us, otherwise we would need to have many "Police Codes" or norms of co-existence. How do we ensure the peaceful coexistence of eight million inhabitants, without a minimum set of standards for everyone? To what extent can we find a common basis across cultural, ethnic, and religious diversity, while respecting knowledge, customs, and different moral principles? That is the effort made by the 1991 Constitution: to create common rules for all of society despite our differences. However, it is not easy to determine what is common to all citizens at a specific time. Yet that answer is not only essential to social harmony, but is also quintessential with regard to the possibility of managing a city or a country. It requires, of course, knowledge of the social norms of each group or community, and making sure that legal norms do not contradict the moral and social standards of different communities or groups. "Bogotá's Police Code" is a "handbook written for angels," as someone said, in comparison to the 1886 Constitution: it includes ethnic, gender, and sex considerations, as well as an emphasis on the care of women, children, and so on. What's more, is that its critics and opponents have discarded it as inapplicable.

CT: Some observers have suggested that in his administration, Mockus practiced a post-disciplinarian form of government. Citizens operated under the illusion of being free, but in the end they behaved the way their government planned and designed.

RL: Well, there has been persistent academic criticism of *Cultura Ciudadana's* approach, which stems from the belief that any emphasis on the respect of the law amounts to a kind of authoritarianism. I think that, if there is any kind of authoritarianism in Antanas's approach, it has to do with the fact that one must comply with the law beyond any personal or social consideration, whether one agrees with it or not. It could even be said that in Antanas's approach there is a kind of sacralization of the law and the state. But this is understandable because the contempt for the law in Colombia is deeply rooted in people, and even socially justified. It must be said, however, that thanks to the academic and political discussion of *Cultura Ciudadana's* approach, in his second administration there was an effort to correct the absolute value given to formal standards, which resulted in a program that was meant to strengthen democratic culture among Bogotá's population. This program was proposed to promote citizens' participation, not only along the lines determined by the law, but also in the reform of the laws and rules that for different reasons had lost their legitimacy—for instance, the "Police Code" or the regulations of the district system of cultural administration. One of the program's pillars was the democratic principle stated in our Constitution according to which, if citizens do not agree with a law, they have the right to express their disagreement and propose new laws or reforms.[8] This is the way that people can voice their opposition to the laws they consider unjust or absurd. This is particularly relevant in Colombia because there are many absurd laws that are difficult to implement. For that reason, citizens' reflection on their willingness to respect or comply with the law is crucial for the legitimacy of authorities. Neglecting space for such reflection, and even of opposition to a given law, is undoubtedly authoritarianism.

Although it is true that we achieved our goals in the programs of *Cultura Ciudadana*, including those of democratic culture, modifying habits, routines, and attitudes unfavorable to social coexistence, public policy requires time and continuity. In three years it is not possible to sustainably address the disrespect of the law by some or the deficit of democratic culture of others. These shortcomings or limitations are seen in people of all social strata. It must be said, however, that citizens' ignorance and disregard for democratic rules is particularly marked in the higher class, and more troublingly, among civil servants who paradoxically use their privileged position as a justification to violate the law, and even believe that they do not deserve to be punished. Such situations are common, for example, in the transgression of traffic rules. High tax evasion is also practiced by people with high incomes. With regard to democratic culture, it is worth noting that in a recent study of teachers in Bogotá's public schools, which we did at the National University, we gathered evidence that a significant proportion of teachers do not understand some of the basic rules of our democratic system—for example, the requirements set by the Constitution for anyone to run in an election.[9]

One of the goals was to strengthen the channels for citizen participation. The reform of the "Police Code" was one main avenue to achieve that, as the project of 2003 entailed the participation of very different sectors of Bogotá's population. Mockus's first administration attempted to pass that reform, but the District Council did not approve it. Therefore, an extensive popular consultation was carried out through the creation of the "*Semilleros de convivencia pacífica*" (Incubators of Peaceful Coexistence), which were undoubtedly an exceptional experience. Another effort to support democratic culture, which we made at the Institute of Culture and Tourism, was the change in the participatory model of the District System of Culture together with different representatives of this sector. Even so, we went further. In 2002, we established new rules to collaboratively determine a portion of the budget dedicated to culture, together with the Councils of Art and Culture.[10]

CT: What would you have done differently regarding *Cultura Ciudadana*?

RL: I can think of three things. First, I would have liked to go deeper into the analysis of the divorce between law, morality, and culture in Colombia in order to contribute to the design of public policies more in line with our reality from the side of the state. I think that the transgression of legal norms, in Bogotá and throughout the country, is partially due to the proliferation of laws and official regulations that citizens can hardly comply with. We still know too little about the reasons why many people resist complying with the law. The surveys on *Cultura Ciudadana* show that a significant percentage of Bogotanos older than twelve justify violations of the law when their own interests are affected or to protect their families. The statistical data that we gathered is not sufficient to explain such justifications. In this respect, it would be worth carrying out a detailed analysis of the tension and even contradiction between Colombian formalism and citizens' behavior. Or to put it in Antanas's words, the divorce of morals, law, and culture. The other two fronts on which I would like to dig deeper, if I had the chance, are democratic culture and culture in schools.

CT: How much of *Cultura Ciudadana* is based on technique and how much on charisma or biography?

RL: Well, I worked with the governor of Casanare and the mayor of Pereira, and I must say that the charisma of Antanas and his "biography" have affected the credibility and legitimacy that *Cultura Ciudadana* developed during his two administrations.[11] But I would also say that, in addition to these personal factors, the fact that Mockus became a moral example for Bogotanos was essential. Many people see him as a fair and transparent person, and this is relevant to the programs of *Cultura Ciudadana*. That said, as I've shown in this interview, in such programs what matters is not only the technical design of cultural and social interventions, but also the effort to maintain reliable and systematic information and analysis of those interventions.

CT: So does this mean that *Cultura Ciudadana* had a performative dimension and that the actors who performed such techniques needed to appear authentic?

RL: I have no doubt that the example set by senior officials was crucial for the development of a policy of *Cultura Ciudadana*. Good technical design is not enough. For example, in Casanare we found it hard to get people to believe in *Cultura Ciudadana*. During the workshops we conducted to explain the concept and the approach behind the intervention, people would object: "Do you see where public officials park their cars?" People did not believe in the program because senior officials in the regional government were the first to violate the rules. We called on senior officials to publicly pledge their commitment to abide by the rules, but we did not succeed in getting them to do so. So, more than charisma, authorities must set the example and exhibit coherence with what they preach and do. Institutional coordination is also fundamental, and it was not easy to achieve even in Bogotá, where *Cultura Ciudadana* was a central goal of the Development Plan. However, unlike many municipalities in Colombia, where every secretary has his or her own political agenda, in Bogotá effective interagency coordination was possible. Moreover, there were other elements, besides the legitimacy and the charisma that Mockus had in Bogotá, that were not easy to reproduce—elements such as an adequate technical team and financial resources commensurate with the goals. Mayors seeking to carry out programs of *Cultura Ciudadana* without knowing very well what it was about, sought to follow the example of Bogotá and ended up carrying out campaigns on traffic norms that lasted only a month and, of course, did not change the habits and attitudes that are very deeply rooted in people.

CT: Do you think that the experience with *Cultura Ciudadana* is exportable out-side of Latin America? What are the potential limits?

R.L: During my term in Mockus's administration we advised the Dominican Re-public in that respect, which was very interesting. We were a group of ten officials from the administration in Bogotá. The first thing we did was to gather informa-tion about the problems of coexistence in Santo Domingo, and when we arrived, we visited the critical spots and held workshops with officials and citizens. After a few days together, we managed to identify a few problems that required physical and cultural intervention in public spaces. Shortly thereafter, bike routes were cre-ated in the *malecón* (promenade), accompanied by a campaign called, if I remember well, "*Ciudadanos en el Malecón*" (Citizens on the Pier). I had another experience in Brazil with the United Nations Development Program (UNDP). I did a workshop on civic culture with officials from Rio de Janeiro and several nearby municipalities, including the chiefs of police. Despite our efforts to implement *Cultura Ciudadana*, I realized the enormous gap between what we did in the workshop and what would need to be done to adapt those programs in a society so different from ours. It would be worth taking a look at the experience of Corpovisionarios, which Antanas leads, in the application of the survey on *Cultura Ciudadana* in several cities across Latin America, including Mexico City.[12] I do not know, though, the results of those con-sulting projects Antanas has carried out there.

What I could say, based on my own experience, is that you should not export the idea of *Cultura Ciudadana* mechanically. One needs some minimum knowledge of the national and local context. We did so with the teams I led at the UNAL when we advised the mayor of Pereira and the governor of Casanare. In addition to diagnosing of the problems of coexistence, we read about municipal and regional history. We ran into problems with some of the questions on the survey on *Cultura Ciudadana* because both local officials and citizens with whom we discussed the forms told us that they did not understand words and expressions, especially those from Antanas's lexicon. Still, it was important to keep the language the same so as to be able to compare it with the survey used in Bogotá in 2001. However, in the end, the tests we did on the survey showed us that it was necessary to change some words and expressions that people didn't really understand due to local linguistic variations. For example, many people did not understand what *celebrar un acuerdo* (finalize an agree-ment) meant because the verb *celebrar* (to celebrate) is usually associated with holiday events. To culturally understand a community, even within the same country, is a great challenge; imagine trying to extend that understanding to another country.

I am now reading some chronicles from Valledupar, and the first thing that surprised me was that smuggling there has been a normal and socially accepted activity for many years.[13] Finding ways to modify behavior is a tremendous challenge. In the plains of Casanare, where people are used to carrying weapons, if you do not understand these cultural codes, and try to implement a program like those that were carried out in Bogotá, failure is inevitable.

CT: This brings me back to the question about the possibility of transferring these experiences to industrialized countries where political leaders are conceived in a more rational and controlled way than in Colombia. Antanas does not seem to be very rational...

RL: Paul Bromberg's approach is more technical. Antanas's ideas do not work in the field of public policy without *cultural engineering,* as Bromberg (2003) would say. If they are not viable, the brilliant ideas of a leader do not lead anywhere. However, it must be said that Antanas is not only very imaginative, but he can also have a great impact not only on people, but also in the media. There is no doubt that his personal intervention into the design and implementation of the campaigns on *Cultura Ciudadana* significantly contributed to their success.

CT: So all power to the imagination, and to engineering as well. . .

RL: In the development of government programs, the quality of the engineering (and the architecture) is essential. "Ladies' Night," for example, shows the importance of imagination as well as that of engineering. The event triggered a strong public controversy in Colombia, but at the same time it was praised for its audacity and originality in several recognizably prestigious publications, such as *The Economist* (2001).[14] But what was its legacy? Some remember it as an act by a genial mayor, and others remember it as the mayor's peculiar acts or an instance of authoritarianism. In any case, that original idea made sense within the programs oriented to alter behavioral routines and habits in family life, in the public space, and so on.

CT: With Antanas, we have a case of "empowered imagination," to paraphrase a notorious slogan of the 1968 French student movement. At the same time, he was also asked to manage a sophisticated bureaucratic machinery. To what extent can these two dimensions coexist within the same subject?

RL: Several elements enabled Antanas to bring them together. He is a mathematician and, culturally speaking, he has an artistic sensibility and even training. Thanks to his academic training, his work as a teacher, and his mother—sculptor Nijole Sivickas—I think that Antanas reconciles these two qualities quite well. I witnessed his knowledge and skill in the management of such technical matters as Bogotá's budget and the public transportation company *Transmilenio*, or the telephone company *Empresa de Telecomunicaciones de Bogotá S.A., ETB* (Bogotá Telecommunications Industry). He was flawless in his argumentation and technical analysis. The problem I see with Antanas is political. I think that he could not resolve the tension between the scientific and the political, as Weber would say. That tension has tormented him. However, I sensed no contradictions between his sensibility and wit to present issues from unusual perspectives, and in finding innovative formulas to deal with public affairs. Although his acts may surprise, and even trigger rejection, because they go against common sense, he generally comes out unscathed. In my opinion, Antanas has an important quality as a leader: he trusts and empowers those who work with him. He is slow to decide. He hesitates a lot, ponders a lot, examines all angles, and can even temporarily paralyze an action. But his long-term thinking and his willingness to delegate important decisions to his team, and not merely follow bureaucracy, make it possible to balance his weaknesses.

CT: Would it be possible to train administrators or politicians to systematically bring together art and government? And what would be the training sites for that?

RL: I don't think that a school of *Mockusism* is possible. I would say that one of the best legacies of Antanas in public administration was to show the importance of culture in society and that it can be carried out in many ways, not just in a *Mockusian* style. But unfortunately that legacy has not been assimilated enough in Bogotá and even less in the rest of the country, although the idea of *Cultura Ciudadana* has born some interesting and important developments in other cities such as Medellín. To the extent that our leaders are more aware of the importance of culture in general, and of *Cultura Ciudadana* in particular, they will give it more importance in public policy and will assign more funding to it.

Endnotes

1   Fabio Chaparro is a Colombian physicist and former vice-president of the Colombian Association for the Development of Science". He served as head of the Empresa de Energía de Bogotá (Energy Company of Bogotá) during the first administration of Antanas Mockus (1995-1997).

2   These were the groups that built the content of Mockus's campaign on each relevant issue.

3   Álvaro Camacho is a renowned Colombian sociologist, specializing in the study of violence and criminality in the country. He was the mind behind the *"Plan Integral de Seguridad y Convivencia"* (Integral Plan of Security and Coexistence) as he directed the Consejería Distrital para la Seguridad (District Council for Security) in Bogotá in 1995.

4   This poll, requested by the Observatory of Urban Culture, was carried out by Napoleón Franco's firm in 1998. It asked citizens about their perceptions of: the projects developed during Mockus's first administration; authorities' treatment of citizens and the conflicts between them; drivers' attitudes toward pedestrians; the city's appearance and the role of Bogotanos contributing to keep it tidy; and their attitudes about laws and rules of coexistence. An analysis of the results can be found in: Paul Bromberg Zilberstein (N.d.), "¿Son perdurables los cambios en comportamientos dirigidos desde el Estado? Las huellas de la *Cultura Ciudadana*" (Are the Chances in Behavior Directed from the State Lasting? The Footprints of Civic Culture). Available online: (http://institutodeestudiosurbanos.info/dmdocuments/cendocieu/1_Docencia/Profesores/Bromberg_Paul/Productos/Son_Perdurables_Cambios-Bromberg_Paul.pdf). The survey on *Cultura Ciudadana*—implemented for the first time in Bogotá, in 2001—built on the the 1998 poll and other studies on the topics of civil culture, security and coexistence, mobility, and public space. The survey probed the habits, attitudes, and beliefs of citizens in order to get an overview of the several dimensions relevant to *Cultura Ciudadana*. In response to the request of the Bogotá Council to measure the progress of the city in *Cultura Ciudadana*, six specific fields were evaluated: knowledge, attitudes, and perceptions of basic coexistence rules; security (perception, victimization, reasons to use violence); attitudes and perceptions about security and coexistence in Bogotá; tax culture; democratic culture; the District's cultural, sports, and recreational activities.

5   Alberto Maldonado is a Colombian economist and a consultant on the fields of urban and regional development, territorial decentralization, institutional development, local planning, and information systems. Efraín Sánchez is a Colombian sociologist and was head of the Observatory of Urban Culture during the second administration of Antanas Mockus (2001-2003). Carolina Castro is a professional in Government and International

Relations, specializing in urban sociology and a researcher on cultural public policy. Maldonado, Sánchez, and Castro—as members of the Observatory of Urban Culture—played an important role in formulating the indicators to measure Civic Culture in Bogotá the second time the survey on *Cultura Ciudadana* was conducted in 2003.

6   The Chingaza Dam is located in the central region of Cundinamarca, Colombia. It has a capacity of two hundred million cubic meters, and supplies water to 80% of the population in Bogotá. On January 20th, 2002, a terrorist attack, allegedly perpetrated by the FARC, destroyed one of the main valves of the system.

7   The *Polo Democrático Alternativo* (PDA) is a Colombian left-wing party, officially founded in 2005 as the result of an alliance between two political groups: *Polo Democrático Independiente* (PDI) and *Alternativa Democrática* (Alternative Democracy). Their most important political victory dates back to 2003 when Luis Eduardo Garzón, candidate of the PDI, won the elections for mayor in Bogotá to succeed Antanas Mockus. From 2004 to 2007, Garzón focused on social programs, aiming to tackle hunger and intolerance amongst citizens through education and an affordable food supply for the vulnerable population in the city. The PDA party came under the spotlight after the scandal that implicated Samuel Moreno Rojas—their candidate elected as the city's mayor for the 2008-2011 term—as responsible for signing contracts to develop the third phase of *Transmilenio* (the rapid bus transit system of Bogotá) without following the right process, favoring only a couple companies owned by some of his close business partners.

8   Article 40 of the Constitution of Colombia guarantees the fundamental right of its citizens to participate in the formation, practice, and control of political power. It enables Colombians to: elect and be elected for public office; engage in elections, plebiscites, referenda, popular consultations, and other forms of democratic participation; constitute parties, movements, and political associations without restrictions, be part of them freely and spread their programs and ideas; revoke the mandate of those elected for public office in the cases and the ways established by the law.

9   The study "Characterization of Public School Teachers in Bogotá – 2009" was carried out by the Center for Social Studies, ascribed to the Faculty of Humanities of the National University of Colombia. Published in 2010, it had as its goals: first, to give an integral characterization of public school teachers; second, to establish the level of satisfaction of teachers with their profession; third, to understand the difficulties teachers face in practicing their profession and in the renewal of their teaching practices; and fourth, to serve as material for new lines of research about the problems detected in this study as well as to provide the criteria for formulating policies about teachers' training and update processes.

10 The rules mentioned refer to those regulating Bogotá's District System of Culture, amended by Decree number 221 of 2002. This process involved not only the city's government but also representatives of artists, ethnic communities, and cultural managers. By creating the District System of Culture, the Local Systems of Culture, the District Council of Culture, and the District Councils of Artistic Areas, fostered negotiations between the District's authorities and the community regarding policies, plans, programs, cultural projects, and their budgets in order to develop and promote culture in Bogotá.

11 Casanare is a region located in the central eastern region of Colombia. Pereira is the capital city of the region of Risaralda, located in the west of Colombia.

12 Corpovisionarios is a non-profit organization that researches, advises, designs, and implements actions to achieve voluntary changes in collective behavior. Based on the tenets of *Cultura Ciudadana*, Corpovisionarios promotes citizen participation, the conclusion of agreements, and co-responsibility for the enhancement of social, economic, and political development. Their work has gone beyond Bogotá and Colombia, to countries such as Brazil, Mexico, Venezuela, Bolivia, Ecuador, Paraguay, Uruguay, and Sweden.

13 Valledupar is a city and municipality in northeastern Colombia, the capital of the Cesar Department.

14 Under the headline "Women's Rule," *The Economist* (March 15, 2001) reported about "a social experiment that has never before been tried in a capital city": it referred to the "Ladies' Night" (March 9, 2001) declared by the then Mayor, Antanas Mockus. The purpose was to examine whether men caused most of Bogotá's violence. According to the magazine, "the city's murder rate and road accidents both fell by 80% and other serious crimes by 30%." Available online: (http://www.economist.com/node/532970).

References

Bromberg Zilberstein, Paul. 2003. "Ingenieros y profetas, transformaciones dirigidas de comportamientos colectivos" [Engineers and Prophets, Directed Transformations of Collective Behavior]. Pp. 67-104 in *Reflexiones sobre la Cultura Ciudadana en Bogotá* [Reflections on Civic Culture in Bogotá]. Bogotá: District Institute of Culture and Tourism. (http://institutodeestudiosurbanos.info/dmdocuments/cendocieu/1_Docencia/Profesores/Bromberg_Paul/Productos/Ingenieros_Profetas-Bromberg_Paul-1.pdf).

3. Interview with Efraín Sánchez

Carlo Tognato

Carlo Tognato (CT): When did you take office at the Instituto Distrital de Cultura y Turismo (District Institute of Culture and Tourism)?

Efraín Sánchez (ES): I started as the director of the Observatorio de Cultura Urbana (Observatory of Urban Culture) in December of 2001 and left in February or March of 2004.

CT: What was your previous relationship with Antanas Mockus and how did you end up in that position?

ES: I didn't have a direct relationship with Antanas prior to 2001. I met him in London during his first administration as mayor of Bogotá. I was working with the British Petroleum at the time and they requested that I assisted Antanas during his visit. I think that Antanas does not remember that. Obviously, the visit was quite peculiar for me because that was a time, around 1998 or 1999, when Antanas was still engaging in his symbolic actions. He was still throwing glasses of water at people. For instance, he did so in an Oxford library with some scholars.[1] I recall that the faculty was furious because the water landed on some very old books. It was terrible.

I developed a close relationship with Rocío Londoño when she worked in England with Professor Eric Hobsbawm on her doctoral thesis. I had already finished my doctorate in 1995. She stayed at my house in Oxford for several days, and we became very good friends.

At that time, I visited Colombia frequently. By chance, during one of those visits in 2001, Rocío contacted me to see whether I was interested in working with the Observatory. I didn't know what it was about, because the idea of an observatory is a French thing, isn't it? In English, observatories have to do with stars, a completely different thing. That was how I got the job. I had never had any previous links with the administration of Bogotá. I had only worked at the Ministry of Foreign Affairs as a cultural attaché at the Embassy of Colombia in London.

CT: How did Antanas participate in the activities of the Observatory?

ES: Antanas participated in numerous ways. At that time, the priority for the Observatory, and one of the major priorities for the mayor's office, and for Antanas personally, was the implementation of the survey on *Cultura Ciudadana* (Civic Culture), which was the first project to be conducted.

That was one of my tasks. Since I started to work on the elaboration of the indicators on *Cultura Ciudadana*, the development of the survey, and its application, Antanas was constantly asking me how the survey was progressing and being implemented. He was very engaged with the details of absolutely everything, and we worked closely with him throughout 2002.

CT: Was the interaction informal or formal?

ES: Both. Antanas was going far beyond his own institutional commitment. He had a personal interest in the survey, which was largely inspired by the survey that he had run with students in Bogotá years earlier. Hence, he knew very well what was required to implement a survey and therefore wanted to know everything about our process. After conducting the survey, our main task was to define the goals of *Cultura Ciudadana*. That required very intense work sessions that sometimes lasted until two or three in the morning in Antanas's office in City Hall.

CT: What other activities did the Observatory carry out?

ES: The Observatory also promoted research about the city. We started some research programs on *Cultura Ciudadana*, on political culture, and on various other aspects. The idea was that at the end of Antanas's administration we would have built an information system on *Cultura Ciudadana* in Bogotá.

CT: This was crucial for the institutionalization of *Cultura Ciudadana*, wasn't it?

ES: Yes, of course, it was essential to rely on systematic and targeted knowledge about the city instead of shooting randomly here and there as it seems to me that Peñalosa's administration did. Peñalosa also had an office that researched the city.[2] The Observatory was discontinued during Peñalosa's administration because he opened the Urban Research Advisory Office that sought to achieve almost the same thing; nevertheless, my impression was that their research lacked focus. They did many things, including publishing many books, but there was no path, no strategy. In contrast, under Antanas and Rocío we always had a clear direction.

CT: And what was the relationship between the Observatory and the Institute?

ES: The Observatory was part of the Institute of Culture and Tourism. Rocío was my boss, and the Institute was divided into a few large divisions or branches. Formally, I wasn't the deputy director of the Institute, but rather the director of the Observatory, and I had my own budget.

CT: Were the other divisions in charge of the design and the application of the campaigns?

ES: Yes. However, we also worked on that front too. For example, I worked a lot on the campaigns addressing "Civil Resistance". It is a very demanding area of work. It called for a lot of contact with the media, with public opinion, and with local institutions. It was also about the creation of symbols.

CT: Was the Observatory in charge of the creation of the symbols of Cultura Ciudadana?

ES: The great inventor of the symbols was Antanas, but he always consulted with his team. I think that the results of that process were very impressive. *Cultura Ciudadana* involved approximately twenty-five institutions from the greater metropolitan area that had a seat on the Comisión de *Cultura Ciudadana* (Commission on Civic Culture), which was led by the director of the Institute of Culture and Tourism. I served as the technical secretary. As such, I was not only I supposed to record the meetings but also do many other things. The Institute of Culture and Tourism was also in charge of the "Civil Resistance" campaign, and I even invented the symbol. We came up with three triangles to mark the sites we considered protected.

CT: During your term as director of the Observatory, were you always in agreement with Antanas, or do you remember any disagreements?

ES: There were many differences in opinion, but never on fundamental issues. I am firmly convinced that culture should be a cornerstone in addressing urban problems. I am absolutely convinced of that. Antanas is someone with whom I could talk, even if we disagreed.

For example, on one occasion Antanas wanted to place a marker in Plaza Bolívar, to lay a symbol there, but legally it could not be done, so he accepted it. The great advantage of Antanas was that he did not impose things as mayor, as an authority figure. I never felt that Antanas was an authority figure, but rather a colleague.

CT: What were the weaknesses of that process?

ES: From the point of view of the Observatory of Urban Culture, the major weakness was our limited knowledge about the city. The other problem rose from the actual degree of massification of the very idea of *Cultura Ciudadana*. I believe people never had a clear understanding of what it was. People thought that *Cultura Ciudadana* had to do with the fact that the mayor was educating them. People associated it with the mimes and the campaign to save water, but *Cultura Ciudadana* is not only about that. They did not understand where *Cultura Ciudadana* was going where the city should go. I think that another weakness has to do with the need to strengthen the conceptualization from a theoretical standpoint.

CT: Give me an example.

ES: We may find fifty definitions of *Cultura Ciudadana*: Medellín's definition, Cali's definition, etc. People understand *Cultura Ciudadana* to mean different things.

There isn't a developed conceptual basis for it, and that is a job that still needs to be done. It is one of the challenges for *Cultura Ciudadana*.

CT: There are some who criticize Antanas Mockus's *Cultura Ciudadana* because it appears to start from the civilizing ideal of an enlightened elite group tasked with educating an ignorant multitude that behaves unacceptably, and which does not acknowledge that the very same multitude might also be the source of worthy knowledge.

ES: Culture is not a possession of the educated; culture is a social thing. It is a construction, a social creation, and it has positive and negative dimensions. In my opinion, one of the mistakes of *Cultura Ciudadana* is thinking that it is positive, that it is about being educated, about complying with rules, etc. For me, what does not comply with social standards is citizens' culture as well. It is negative, but still citizens' culture is part of the culture. The issue is whether the state has the capacity to intervene in it.

CT: What do you mean when you talk about a negative *Cultura Ciudadana*?
ES: By negative, I refer to negative social behaviors such as, for example, not stopping at a red light, throwing trash on the street, etc.

CT: For *Cultura Ciudadana*, how much is it about technique, and how much about charisma or biography?

ES: In Bogotá, much of it had to do with Antanas. Its success was based on his charisma and his biography, but also on people's willingness to accept new ideas. Other mayors could also be the forefront of *Cultura Ciudadana*.

CT: So this is an exportable technique, isn't it?

ES: Yes, but you have to be careful with the context of application. Medellín has its Secretariat for *Cultura Ciudadana*, but they have been able to develop *Cultura Ciudadana* there in accordance with Medellín's culture, with Antioquia's culture.[3] This is how it should work. Elsewhere it has not worked.

CT: What limits does art face in politics?

ES: There are legal limits, budgetary limits, and technical limits. There are things that simply can't be done because technically they don't work. There are also limits imposed by culture itself because there are symbols that cannot be fully understood.

CT: **Antanas Mockus managed to integrate art with politics. How can you train public administrators and leaders to do the same?**

ES: You only get a Mockus once every so many years. On the political scene of Bogotá, he brought something totally new. I do not think that the Escuela Superior de Administración Pública (School of Higher Public Administration) could ever train people to have an artistic sensibility. However, the university environment could do something along those lines. It allows the freedom for that. The problem is how to channel those energies and those creative forces within the university environment into public administration. It doesn't necessarily have to be someone who has studied political science. It could be an anthropologist, for instance.

CT: Or, a mathematician?

ES: Yes. Anyone who is crazy enough to come up with weird ideas, but also has a vision, would do. That is the peculiarity of Antanas. I would say that even more than training someone to do this job, someone needs to be discovered.

Endnotes

1 In August 1997, during the campaign for the presidential election, Antanas Mockus threw a glass of water at another candidate during a debate before two hundred executives of the Colombian Chambers of Commerce. Mockus explained that his symbolic action conveyed the need to replace physical violence with symbolic violence in Colombia.

2 The Oficina Asesora de Investigaciones de Ciudad (Urban Research Advisory Office) was the name the Observatory of Urban Culture adopted during Enrique Peñalosa's administration (1998-2000). Given the main goals of that administration—to recover public space and design the new massive transport system *Transmilenio*—the *Cultura Ciudadana* program was discontinued, and the office only worked to measure public opinion on Peñalosa's policies and the effects of some programs led by the Institute of Culture and Tourism.

3 The Secretariat for *Cultura Ciudadana* in Medellín was created by Decree No. 151 on February 20th, 2002, which modified the administrative structure and the central functioning of the Municipality of Medellín. The main goal was to oblige the municipality to cultivate a civic culture that would result in better ways of living. Social harmony, education, urban development, and public space were the cornerstones on which a civic culture.

4. Interview with Jon Elster

Carlo Tognato

Carlo Tognato (CT): Professor Elster, I will start by asking when and how you met Antanas Mockus, and what your relationship has been with him throughout the years.

Jon Elster (JE): I think it was in the spring of 2003 when someone called from Antanas's office saying that he was coming to New York City (NYC), where I was at the time, to speak to the chief of police on how to fight terrorism. Antanas had read my book and he wanted to meet me. So we met at the Four Seasons in NYC, and it turned out that Antanas wanted me to come to Bogotá to discuss issues relating to collective action and bargaining with his team. It must have been at the end of his second term as mayor. So I made my first visit to Bogotá in the fall of 2003. I talked to his team, and I presented various ideas from my books about these issues to see how they could be useful in Bogotá. Of course, all of this took place in a very, very violent period in the country. I think in 2003, when I came, there had just been a bombing of a nightclub, and I don't know how many killings there had been, sixty I think.

CT: ...well, more than a nightclub, it was the bombing of a major elite club in Bogotá, El Nogal.

JE: Yeah, I still remember a policeman following me on a motorbike around the city. So it was a very tense situation. Of course, we started talking about violence more generally, not just in Bogotá, but also around the country. Exactly at the same time, I got involved in a ten-year project organized by the Peace Institute in Oslo, doing research on civil wars. So for ten years I led a research group on the microfoundations of civil wars. In other words, what the motivations are that drive participants on all sides, what their emotions are, everything sort of micro-oriented. Then with Antanas and also, at the beginning, with Vice-President Santos, we organized a series of conferences on transitional justice in civil war situations, sort of anticipating what would happen right now. But it was from a comparative perspective. We compared transitional justice in civil war situations in the former Yugoslavia and in various African countries, keeping in mind the possibility of something similar happening here. Then, at one point, one idea struck me—and I *have* discussed this with Antanas many times—which is the following: to (end political violence) let's not call it civil war; it is necessary to somehow bring the perpetrators of violence to justice, to some extent, so that you have to address the injustices that caused the conflict. At one point we organized several conferences on land reform and on the interaction between transitional justice and distributive justice, and whether scarce national resources should be given to those who were entitled to restitution or to those who were in need of support, for instance, the landless without entitlements.

We had some conferences that were mainly theoretical. We had a conference on social norms in 2007, and which I will discuss in a minute, with Gloria Origgi and Gerry Mackie, and this one in 2013 about "Obscurantisms in the Social Sciences." Some conferences addressed urgent issues for political analysis and others focused on theory. I think Antanas's main contribution is, first, his distinction between legal norms, social norms, and moral norms. And second, his investigation of these norms when they are out of line with each other, which, I think, is a crucial issue. He researched these issues in a very imaginative way. For instance, most people, when asked, would say that they respect legal norms more than social norms, but others respect social norms more than legal norms. I do not think this is the first time this kind of asymmetry has been observed, but Antanas does it with great inventiveness and ingenuity. You know, at the same time I was having these discussions with

Antanas, I was asking and observing what Antanas had done as a politician, and maybe we could call him the first postmodern politician, the first postmodern mayor in the world, because the things he did were so unorthodox and so effective. The results speak for themselves.

I will never forget my first trip to Bogotá in October 2003, when, as I said, the conditions where more tense than they are today, and Antanas walked around with this "Bulletproof Vest"—the vest with the heart-shaped hole that says, "I am invulnerable, but I am also vulnerable."

So I got to meet the man, and Adriana, his wife, and I came to respect his immense integrity, his paradoxical flashes of insight that are almost close to poetry, and his actual commitment to public interest. When he ran for president for the second time, I organized an international campaign for signatures, and I got Jürgen Habermas to sign, among others. But he lost. We don't need a guy who is just supported by foreign academics... ah, I am just kidding...

Well, I don't think I am going to get into the question on why he actually lost the elections because you probably know more about it. Everyone knows about it. I don't know whether it was good for the country that he lost, whether he would have been as capable as President Santos seems to be in organizing a credible peace process. I don't know whether Antanas would have accepted all the compromises that have been made and will be made. Maybe he would, but, you know, integrity has its costs.

CT: Professor Elster, to you and possibly to international audiences, what is the most striking dimension of Antanas Mockus? Mockus as a thinker, as a practitioner, or as an artist? What do you think are the elements that make Mockus quite special and that are worth emphasizing to an audience that doesn't know him?

JE: I think that the thinker and the politician cannot be separated because the things he has done and what he has written have been based on the same counter-intuitive paradoxical ideas that somehow work. To be frank, though, what Antanas is lacking is discipline. You know, his ideas are all over the place, like rabbits. I've said that to him many times in public, and he has told me he is trying to improve. I think he should slow down and take one thing at a time, exhaust that topic, and move on to the next. But his mind is so fertile and his association machinery is so well oiled and full of ideas that it would be asking too much.

CT: Do you think that a person like Antanas Mockus could be replicated or routinized?

JE: No, because he is a paradigmatic case of a charismatic person. During the presidential campaign, before the televised debate, I was interviewed by a radio broadcasting station in Bogotá, and they asked me a question that helped me come up with a good answer: "So Professor, do you think Mr. Mockus is trying to be different?" And I answered: "No, he *is* different." He is not something he is trying to be. He is that way. That's why we cannot teach him not to be that way.

In Iceland there is this former stand-up comedian who shares some of Antanas's features. I believe they know each other. You know, these are events like being hit by a meteorite, things that you can't anticipate, but when they happen are wonderful. However, I think he is sometimes a bit impatient in the way he talks. I have noticed, though, that he is often amazingly far-sighted and he sees the consequences of the action that could be taken three or four steps ahead, so he is very far from a populist politician, though he is extremely popular. I remember when I walked around the streets with Antanas that every third person would stop him, say "Hello, Antanas," or take a picture with him. So, I think he is literally adored by the people of Bogotá. I don't know about the rest of the country. He has many, many wonderful qualities.

CT: Why, in your opinion, should audiences in Europe and the United States take a look at a book reflecting on Mockus's experience? Could it be a resource to export that experience elsewhere?

JE: Well, maybe I disagree on this point because I think the book should enable people to learn about this unique person and not enable people to learn the conditions under which something similar might be created. That's a different perspective. Is it possible that this uncanny combination of the political and artistic/aesthetic can or could be institutionalized? I don't know whether there is something called "institutionalization of charisma" or whether it ever works.

CT: Do you see anything problematic in Mockus's conceptual framework or practice? Or to put it another way, what might be the frontier of his conceptual framework?

JE: I don't think I know enough about Colombian politics or politics in Bogotá to really be able to identify that…Antanas himself often talks about the mistakes he has made.

All politicians make mistakes, and any politician who says he hasn't made any is a liar. Obviously a politician always has to take risks. Antanas has been willing to do that and sometimes he has indeed failed. A politician obsessed with never failing would get nothing done. And as I have said several times, his main problem is, in a sense, his own creativity. There are so many ideas coming out and stepping on their own feet sometimes when he is talking. But he comes as a package. His creativity has its upsides and its downsides, and we could not realistically take out the downsides without also taking out the upsides.

PART FIVE: COMMENTARIES

Fabio López de la Roche

Andrés Salcedo

Alejandra Jaramillo

Marta Zambrano

Marsha Henry

Francisco Thoumi

Fabián Sanabria

5

1. On the Significance of Antanas Mockus

Fabio López de la Roche

A few weeks ago in Cartagena, I decided to spend Sunday at the Manzanillo del Mar beaches—a nice, clean beach where one can eat some great fish. There wasn't a list of prices for the food or the drinks in the kiosk I visited. The waiter who was taking care of the tents sheltering the beachgoers seemed to decide on the price according to the client, or as we say in Colombia, *según marrano* (according to the pig). He changed the prices, tacitly imposing an inflated price, the remainder of which he would keep for himself. Whenever someone tried to nail down the prices, he always avoided giving a direct answer, saying something like: "Don't worry, we'll settle up later." In the middle of the afternoon, when I decided to head back to the city, the waiter charged me forty thousand pesos for renting the tent (which in Bocagrande costs twelve thousand). I had to firmly insist on the abusiveness of charging me such price and threaten to call the police to defend my right as a consumer to pay a fair amount. Minor conflicts of this nature in Colombia often end in death or injury. On the one hand, the conflict is caused by the absence of clear rules of the game, which in this case would have to do with prior and public knowledge of the prices of services.

The figure of the abusive and opportunistic waiter allows us to see the problems in the institutionalization of tourist services. It also brings up the role of morality and culture, since it's likely that they come into play in this conduct (in which, needless to say, there isn't a shred of empathy or consideration for others): the self-perception of excluded individuals and an implicit will to take revenge for that situation against the person considered to be wealthy. Social inequality and exclusion probably don't help us relate with empathy toward, and recognize, another person and his or her rights. Situations like this one that involve articulations and tensions between the law, morality, and culture, as Mockus proposed in the analysis of civic culture, constantly happen in Colombian life, feeding into the perception of precariousness of our legal-institutional, moral, and cultural constructions.

Personally and as a cultural analyst, I recognize the role played by Antanas Mockus in promoting the use of artistic and symbolic resources in the regulation of interpersonal relationships and in changing cultural norms and behavior in urban contexts. Despite the lack of continuity of *Cultura Ciudadana* (Civic Culture) in the post-Mockus administrations in Bogotá, several of the standards promoted by his *Cultura Ciudadana* sinked in and left a mark that remains to this day; for example, to take turns yielding the right of way as an attitude of social respect and consideration for others.

That recognition of culture and symbolic intervention as key resources in public policy is very important in contrast to traditional Marxist superstructural understandings of culture, which grant culture no autonomy or capacity for agency. It is also important in contrast to certain positivist or economicist models, which dismiss the relevance of the symbolic. This can be seen in the often scornful expression: "That's just symbolic," meaning that it has no real effect.

In the face of the expansion of the neoliberal model and the cutbacks in funding for public education and research in the social sciences, arts, and humanities, I think we share similar concerns with public humanists in the United States about the "what is" and "what should be" of those disciplines and fields in terms of strengthening a tradition of societal criticism and of looking for relationships of justice and respect for difference and dissidence (Burawoy 2013).

That being said, with all the importance of the cultural and the symbolic in social life that we are herein recognizing, it is true that Mockus's model has not included a redistributive policy or a clear proposal for economic and social justice in a country with marked inequality in income distribution. While the emphasis Mockus placed on civic duties and virtues is important, the perspective of social and economic rights as a substantial dimension of citizenship is no less important.

Regarding the role of the law in constructing citizenship, and distancing myself from those who see an authoritarian position in Mockus's thinking in this respect, I think we have to recognize the role that the law plays in the construction of a democratic culture. Beyond Mockus, the Constitutional Court has set important precedents in its rulings on forced displacement and the rights of the displaced, and these precedents have had an impact on significant processes of civic appropriation of this jurisprudence. I find it significant that in the debate on Caracol Television with presidential pre-candidates Lucho Garzón and Enrique Peñalosa that took place on February 28th, 2010, when faced with the question, "What would each of you do on the front of 'democratic security?'"[1] Mockus responded: "I would have people salute judges as they do with the military." In that same debate, faced with Juanita León's question of whether he "might have entered Ecuador to capture Raúl Reyes," Antanas's answer was a resounding "No!," while he showed the text of the 1991 Constitution. And when asked whether he "might have removed the Defense Minister [Santos] due to the 'false positives' scandal," he gave a resounding "Yes!"[2]

In a time of peace talks and *ad portas* of initiating the post-conflict, I consider Mockus's slogan "Life is Sacred" to be important. In this sense we can note the bravery of Mockus's campaign and that of former-Minister Rudolf Hommes in December 2008, who showed solidarity with the mothers in Soacha whose mentally handicapped or simply excluded children were disappeared by members of the Armed Forces, later found dead, and counted as guerrilla fighters killed in combat.[3]

With regard to the symbolic actions in which Mockus himself, as a public personality, acts as a cultural agent, I agree with Carlo Tognato and other critics who insist on the need of depersonalizing them, thereby separating them from the centrality of Antanas's figure as a charismatic leader, as they reflect on the sustainability and replicability of his *Cultura Ciudadana* model in other national and even regional contexts. The production of other forms of cultural agency, linked with community, is apparent, for example, in the experiment analyzed by Edwin Cubillos in his master's thesis in cultural studies entitled *"Agentes fotográficos. La fotografía participativa en la construcción de ciudadanías por parte de niñas y niños y jóvenes en Altos de Cazucá, Soacha"* (Photographic Agents. Participative Photography in the Construction of Citizenship by Girls and Boys and Youths in Altos de Cazucá, Soacha). Cubillos shows how, through creative social photography, children and youths rethink their lives as well as both their individual and collective roles; move past their identity as "displaced people" and as "victims" with which non-governmental and state organizations constantly label them; and transcend those notions, managing to imagine themselves as cultural agents in processes other than "populations on the edge."

I would also like to add that Mockus's idea of "cultural amphibians" who are able to recontextualize knowledge from certain national, territorial, cultural, and class contexts to others, and the necessity of these "translators" or "recontextualizers" of knowledge, is very important in the appropriation of experiences of cultural and symbolic intervention, not only based on a North-South logic. The experiences of library-parks in Medellín—another case of cultural and symbolic policy that should establish a dialogue with Mockus's *Cultura Ciudadana*—have been studied by European and North American researchers, and the experiment of the Metrocable gondola lift system has been studied by Brazilian city planners in order to consider the model's replicability in Rio de Janeiro. A photograph by Iwan Baan of Medellín's Biblioteca España (Spain Library), designed by the Colombian architect Giancarlo Mazzanti, was part of the experiences collected in a 2013 exposition at New York's Museum of Modern Art MoMA entitled: *POLITICAL. 50 Years of Political Stances in Architecture and Urban Design*.

Finally, I would like to say that I agree with Carlo Tognato regarding the role played by Antanas Mockus in transcending and bridging the liberal, conservative, and leftist points of view that are hegemonic in Colombian political culture. I believe that Colombia is facing a series of historical challenges that must be taken on by all Colombians, and that cannot be taken on and resolved by any of these points of view individually. In that sense, it becomes necessary today to transcend those political views and sensibilities to achieve basic agreements over the country that we want, fundamental consensuses that must also imply respect for difference and dissidence.

Endnotes

1   "Democratic Security" was a defense policy framework that President Álvaro Uribe laid out during his two presidential terms in the first decade of 2000.

2   Juanita León is a recognized Colombian journalist. It is important to remember the discrediting and persecution of judges during President Uribe Vélez's government along with the justification of extraterritoriality in the "Democratic Security" policy, which went against the non-interventionist tradition of Colombian foreign policy regarding neighboring countries.

3   This is a poor area on the outskirts of the city of Bogotá.

References

Burawoy, Michael. 2013. "La gran universidad norteamericana" [The Great North American University]. Series *¿Qué universidad queremos* [What University Do We Want?] 3 (July-December). Cali: Universidad del Valle

2. A Comment on *Cultural Agents Reloaded*

Andrés Salcedo

The following ideas are a commentary on the contributions of Carlo Togna-to, Paolo Vignolo, Javier Sáenz Obregón, and Gerry Mackie on the trans-formative potential of Antanas Mockus's thinking for political culture, both locally and globally. They comprise a discussion and critique of how a combination of sociological and philosophical approaches from the academic sphere was useful in creating an applied, culturally transformative social project, replicable and effective in restoring some sense of ethics to politics and public behavior, but problematic insofar as it put aside structural issues that are crucial for this model to endure.

First, I would like to discuss the reception of Mockus's political program by Colombian audiences; I believe this topic explains the wide range of distances and points of encounter that Mockus had with various sectors of the public both as mayor and as presidential candidate. The son of Lithuanian parents who survived German Nazism as well as Soviet invasion, Mockus trained himself to confront war and violence both spiritually and through politics. As a philosopher, he be-lieved in the power of reason, work ethic, justice, and pacifism as guiding principles and counterpoints to the fear, distrust, and unreasonable cycles of violence that in-fused social relationships in large Colombian cities and other contexts of political violence throughout the twentieth century (Salcedo 1996).

Both his first and second administrations as mayor of Bogotá (1995-1997, 2001-2003) were examples of transparency in the use of public resources amid a context of drug trafficking, clientelism, and dirty politics. Many young Colombians grew to greatly appreciate this new figure, brave enough to take politics out of a *patrón-peón* framework (with its traditional cultural scripts of an authoritarian father or powerful *patrón*; see Tognato's "Introduction" in this volume) and earn popular support by talking about legality, instead. By reviving the past respect populations had once had for the teacher figure, in 1995 Mockus proposed to change harmful behaviors using exemplary pedagogical devices. Instead of calling for weapons to defeat armed insurgency, he proposed argumentative dialogue, pedagogy, and an effective use of symbolism to promote collective participation. In lieu of the anti-intellectualism that has characterized recent Colombian politics, he encouraged deep immersion in literature and the arts. He championed solidarity, hard work, and vigorous citizen participation over individualism and the pursuit of material success through easy money.

Mockus's ideas were compelling to those with low tolerance for corruption and illegality, who were uninvolved in traditional political practices. This explains in part why he garnered incredible support from thousands of followers during the first round of the 2010 presidential elections, although his arguments were not convincing enough to win on important structural issues such as unemployment, health, and security.

Rarely did the Mockus movement address social inequality, class, or racial discrimination as structural forces feeding violence. Rather than attempt direct structural change, his team chose behaviorist, pedagogical communication strategies within a program of cultural transformation to eradicate habits considered uncivil or "bad" by the majority, such as: disrespect for norms, carelessness in the public sphere, individualism, and opportunism.

The first Mockus mayoral administration invented and defined *Cultura Ciudadana* (Civic Culture) as customs, actions, and rules that would instill a greater sense of belonging to the city, respect for public goods, observance of norms, and the peaceful coexistence among strangers. This culture aimed to decrease a long tradition of bribes, distribution of political favors through jobs, extremely high homicide rates, and widespread lack of respect for human life. The strategy was based on the assumption that Colombian society was in need of redressing and guidance, and that decency should be recovered in the city's governance practices. By promoting simple techniques of respect and solidarity among pedestrians and drivers,

Mockus and his staff were successful at turning cities into educational scenarios, as Sáenz (Essay 9 of this volume) would put it. It was an innovative device that broke with decades of what the Mockus team considered improper behavior by the majority (as Vignolo points out in Essay 11 of this volume).

From a behaviorist point of view, the Mockus administration posited that the disorganization of Bogotá was the result of a confluence of the rapid pace of transformation in urban life, the blending of different cultural codes and traditions, and incoherent aims, interests, and emotions. All this created the need for common cultural and legal ground based on general ethical principles. By transforming politics into an artistic demiurge of social change (Vignolo Essay 11), Mockus's program taught others how to behave in public and how to take care of public property.

Very often Mockus's government program alluded to an abstract notion of law as if conventions and norms were ahistorical, universal, and devoid of power relations. Law was presented as a "government device" (Sáenz Essay 9) to maintain social order and cohesion. Mockus and his staff were not critical of a liberal conception of law within its colonial history: a Western, modern device imposed as a universal truth worldwide for the betterment of individuals. Nor were they critical of the different ways in which law may become hegemonic: legitimizing itself as the appropriate and moral way of doing things, used to accomplish personal and private goals, dictating what is official and legal and what is chaotic and lawless. Mackie (Essay 4 of this volume) develops this critique when he refers to an excess of legal centralism in Mockus's thinking. Such focus, Mackie argues, prevents us from seeing the cultural and social mechanisms of legal disapproval or acceptance, which carry embedded codes of honor, solidarity, and reciprocity. This universal and abstract definition of law to which Mockus subscribed, while very conscious of social and moral norms, does not take into account the social mechanisms that negotiate citizens' distrust, obedience, or disobedience of the law for reasons not necessarily grounded in justice, but rather related to an authority founded on a mystical power (Derrida 1992:12). Sáenz (Essay 9) calls into question John Rawls's minimum common sense of collective responsibility as a process that takes place on an egalitarian playing field. Again, Mockus's assumptions lack critical thinking insofar as they express legality placating social conflict, while everyday life involves unequal, hierarchical, irreplaceable groups and lives as well as very concrete and diverse situations (Derrida 1992:17).

Mockus's ideas and political movement were socially powerful in forging and communicating notions of civility and good politics. They were also assertive in understanding that cultural processes involve law, state policies, and public institutions. What I find questionable, echoing Sáenz's, Mackie's, and Vignolo's pieces in this volume, is the Mockus team's attempt to "liberate" a mass of urban citizens from the burden of "bad" customs through an allegedly neutral civic program. His program was uninterested in understanding or addressing the historical sedimentation of cultural processes in Colombia involving differentials of power, class, race, and gender. Instead, the Mockus movement limited itself to the implementation of a universal ethical awakening of citizen consciousness and a model of virtuous public behavior.

References

Derrida, Jean. 1992. "Force of Law. The Mystical Foundation of Authority." In *Decon-struction and the Possibility of Justice*. London: Routledge.

Salcedo, Andrés. 1996. "La cultura del miedo: la violencia en la ciudad" [The Culture of Fear: Violence in the City]. *Controversia* [Controversy] 169:99-116.

3. Power and Culture: A Pair to Cut Down to Size

Alejandra Jaramillo

I n *Cultural Agents Reloaded: The Legacy of Antanas Mockus*, Carlo Tognato brings forward various issues that are necessary for a discussion of Mockus's contribution as a cultural agent. I salute this book, which assembles a variety of perspectives on Mockus by different thinkers. I believe it is relevant to reflect on the reasons that led a university professor in Colombia to draw so much media and political attention, and explore Mockus's actions and assess his importance, in spite of the concerns this may generate in various contexts.[1] I also salute Carlo Tognato's critical reflection in this volume and some of the controversial issues discussed within.

Having worked with Mockus during his second administration as mayor of Bogotá, and thus possessing a certain personal knowledge of it, I have decided to focus on two points that were touched upon in the "Introduction." On the one hand, I will set out to open up the horizon of analysis of the impact of Mockus's actions, and on the other I will complicate Tognato's critique.

First, I would like to refer to Tognato's claim that Mockus's actions and thought have not managed to gel into a solid epistemic field. I think it is necessary to take into consideration, as mentioned by Tognato, that many of Mockus's actions as a cultural agent have been part of an individual project and, in my opinion, happened by chance, having an ultimately isolating effect. Additionally, as a thinker and as a cultural agent, Mockus has not shown a marked interest in building collective processes, which might have resulted in a greater articulation and cohesion of his thought. Perhaps, in a society such as Colombia, so authoritarian and so messianic (two attributes that always come together), this may have been a virtue, because it has allowed him to maintain his personal image in the face of all the difficulties that come along with the building of political groups and groups of thinkers. Still, those who believe in collective political projects will still be doubtful about Mockus's individualistic behavior. Now, Tognato's critique is very much on point. However, I would like to emphasize that Mockus's appearance on the public stage as a mayor and as a politician has triggered a change in the conception of politics in Colombian culture, as he brought together the symbolic with culture and politics, and perhaps his impact has not been sufficiently recognized. This has often been boiled down to a matter of pulling out the mimes on street corners or to the variety of actions under the umbrella of his *Cultura Ciudadana* (Civic Culture) that were meant to translate a much more complex and solid thought process into cultural actions that sought to establish contact with Bogotanos. Politics, culture, and communication go together. This is the message that Mockus's actions and thought conveyed.

That said, I would like to refer to the triad "law, morals, and culture" upon which Antanas Mockus has worked over the years, and address the phenomenon of cultural anomie that is common in Colombia. I agree with Tognato about the fragility of this perspective insofar as it often forgets that laws are built upon specific interests, and hence one cannot buy into the illusion that the law is the supreme order, as Mockus would rather seem to believe. Additionally, and I think that this is Mockus's greatest mistake in his approach to the *Cultura Ciudadana*. In light of this triad, we cannot study compliance and noncompliance with norms, or the behavior that leads to them, without factoring in power. It is not sufficient to think that the only way to change the laws is by political action through democratic institutions without taking into account how power mediates this action. Not just any citizen has access to the legislature, and if she does, not just anyone will really have a chance to trigger change. This feeds into the stabilization of the status quo that is, of existing laws. Even so, I would like to emphasize that Mockus's work with his research on law, morals, and culture has been an important step forward toward understanding the way Colombian society organizes itself, takes up its civic duties, and deals with the laws, which is no small contribution.

I would like to conclude with an example of the results that have come from applying the law-morals-culture framework. In Colombia, many believe that they themselves act based on conscience while others do so under pressure or do not comply with the law. This way of thinking is probably one of the reasons for our difficulty with collective organizing; lose your trust in the other, and you'll never be able to organize with her. This is one of the examples that the application of Mockus's triad yields, and which has allowed Mockus to reach an understanding of our culture that is relevant for rethinking cultural and political action in Colombia. Following Tognato's line of thought, only by enriching that framework with different theories of power will it be possible to set Mockus's contribution on firmer ground.

Endnotes

1 Antanas Mockus is still a controversial figure in Colombian politics and many worry that a book about him, however critical, may serve the political purpose of his canonization, thereby contributing to the whitewashing of all the problems inherent in his practices.

4. Rethinking Antanas Mockus

Marta Zambrano

Perhaps because I am not an expert on Antanas Mockus's career, or because Carlo Tognato does a very good job of introducing Mockus's *Cultura Ciudadana* (Civic Culture), while situating the former mayor as a cultural agent, I learned a great deal from the "Introduction." I consider it an evocative and complex piece, as well as a provocative invitation to read this book.

I was captivated by Tognato's approach, which stands apart from both Mockus's band of loyal fans and his harshest critics. He chooses instead to explore the success and failure of the former mayor's agendas and policies, focusing on the legacies that might contribute to the Cultural Agents Initiative.

I note in particular the suggestion that Mockus's success relied on his ability to articulate key aspects of the three rival political cultures that have shaped Colombia's political culture: the liberal, the radical, and the conservative. I believe that from this approach we can extract critical lessons that permit a rethinking of Mockus and other charismatic figures. For example, it would be worthwhile to revisit from this perspective the success of our former president, Álvaro Uribe, who personified *el embrujo autoritario* (the authoritarian spell) that enchanted our nation for eight long years. On Mockus, however, I would have liked to hear more; especially about the dosages and procedures that contributed to the success of his peculiar recipe. I wish Tognato had delved deeper into the leader's intricate mix of authoritarianism and liberalism during his two terms in office; for example, the combination of what Mockus termed "The Carrot" (pedagogical campaigns) with "The Stick" (control and surveillance programs) (Salcedo and Zeiderman 2008; Sáenz 2011).

The analysis of the radical component left me particularly hungry for more. How is culture both the cause of and the solution for the disarray between law, morality, and culture in Mockus's viewpoint? I gather that this point of view entails the existence of two cultures: one legal, good, and moral; the other illegal, immoral, and bad. The bad culture is that of the others, often subordinates, such as street vendors, for example. Mayor Mockus believed this bad culture needed to be corrected, educated, seduced, and compelled, since it provoked precisely the ethical disarray he intended to remedy. It was, therefore, to be effaced and replaced by a "good" culture, the mayor´s (the professor's? the boss's?) culture. In this sense, the bad culture should be replaced precisely by the pedagogical, playful, yet tremendously modernist, Western, and correct culture. This good culture had everything to teach and little to learn.

From a related perspective, it is worth taking into account the case studies about Mockus's cultural pedagogy. Among others, his campaign in defense of public space comes to mind. Aiming at recovering and preserving public space, Mockus linked it to citizenship, a crucial and significant stake for political transformation. Nonetheless, he also linked it to *el buen comportamiento ciudadano* (well-behaved citizenship) (Mayor's Office of Bogotá 1998:466; cited by Pérez 2010:67), and street vendors were the main misbehavers that polluted what Mockus enthroned as "sacred public space." Drawing on academics who have studied the subject, I wonder whether street vendors can really be blamed for ruining citizen mobility by invading public space when they are but a very small part of the problem (only 10% according to official data) (Hunt 2009). Likewise, the role of the major contributors to this problem—private automobiles—is hushed up, thus confirming the class blindness that Tognato points to in Mockus's policies and conceptual foundations. Or could it be instead the result of the class bias (not to mention gender, ethnic, or sexuality omissions) implicit in the perspective of the two cultures mentioned earlier? (cf. Pérez 2010).

Moreover, as I already suggested, Tognato's text situates Mockus's relevance for the Cultural Agency project. To do so, he reviews the public humanities program advanced by a group of academics from the United States, comparing it summarily with the public configuration of the social sciences and humanities in Latin America, and contrasting it with the achievements and failures of Mockus's public policy initiatives. He also analyzes where Mockus and the US public humanities meet and depart. The main point of disjunction springs from the question of epistemic legitimacy.

Tognato suggests that Mockus advocates a top/down conception of knowledge in that he views himself and other academics from the periphery as contextualizers of what flows out of the metropolis (Granés and Caicedo 1999). Therefore, except in the case of Doris Sommer, this conception, which refuses to build an original program of knowledge, has prevented or limited peer dialogue between representatives of the public humanities in the United States and Mockus, who consequently has been relegated to the footnotes in the works by these scholars. Even more critical, it may have curtailed the successful and sustainable reproduction of cultural policies that have depended on Mockus's charismatic presence in order to endure. In other words, according to Tognato, Mockus ignores the link between culture and knowledge. Moreover, that absence poses incisive and irritating questions to the Cultural Agency program.

One way of reading Tognato's analysis is that all public policy programs depend on epistemological legitimacy for their success and in order to endure and be replicable. But, obviously, not all successful or replicable public policy requires a solid epistemological foundation. On the contrary, and while we await publication of the book, we are witnessing the media success and international marketing of several Colombian public policies that have shaky theoretical foundation such as democratic security, multiculturalism, and the country's LGBT policy. Paradoxically, too, even the street vendor approach to understanding and governing issues of public space has survived after Mockus's departure. As I understand it, Tognato's proposal is that the public humanities and social sciences program do need epistemic legitimacy to endure and have public impact. Therefore, it makes no sense to excuse Mockus's public policy making's lack of epistemic import by separating the academic Mockus from the policy-making Mockus (or even from the anti-political Mockus, a dimension I found lacking in the text). If my reading resonates with the author and those who have read the text, I would vote for a slight change in the book's title and, consequently, its focus: from *Cultural Agents Reloaded through Antanas Mockus* to *Antanas Mockus Reloaded through Cultural Agents*.[1]

Endnotes

1   This statement is a reflection of an earlier working title of the volume. Since the time of writing of this essay, the book's title was changed from *Cultural Agents Reloaded Through Antanas Mockus* to *Cultural Agents Reloaded: The Legacy of Antanas Mockus.* -Ed.

References

Granés, José and Luz M. Caicedo. 1999. "Del contexto de la producción de conocimientos al contexto de la enseñanza. Análisis de una experiencia pedagógica" [From the Context of Knowledge Production to the Context of Teaching. Analysis of a Pedagogic Experience]. Pp. 17-25 in *Libro de actas* [Book of Minutes], edited by José I. Benavides et al., 2.

Hunt, Stacey. 2009. "Citizenship's Place: The State's Creation of Public Space and Street Vendors' Culture of Informality in Bogotá, Colombia." *Environment and Planning D: Society and Space* 7(2):331–351.

Pérez, Federico. 2010. "Laboratorios de reconstrucción urbana: Hacia una antropología de la política urbana en Colombia" [Laboratories of Urban Reconstruction: Towards an Anthropology of Urban Politics in Colombia]. *Antípoda* [Antipode] 10:51-84.

Sáenz, Javier. 2011. "La pedagogía ciudadana en Bogotá: ¿Un proyecto autoritario, o el mínimo común necesario para la construcción de una democracia radical?" [Cultural Pedagogy in Bogotá: An Authoritarian Project or the Common Minimum Necessary for the Construction of a Radical Democracy?] *Revista Educación y Pedagogía* [Education and Pedagogy Review] 23(60):137-145.

Salcedo, Andrés and Austin Zeiderman. 2008. "Antropología y ciudad: hacia un análisis crítico e histórico" [Anthropology and the City: Towards a Critical and Historical Analysis]. *Antípoda* [Antipode] 7:63-97.

5. Engendering Responses to the Work of Antanas Mockus

Marsha Henry

An important figure in Bogotá and Colombian history, Antanas Mockus's life and work provide a rich tapestry for thinking about the political transformations of the past twenty years in Colombia, in Latin America more generally, and within interdisciplinary fields of academic study. Carlo Tognato ("Introduction") has outlined "key" moments in Mockus's intervention into what might have seemed to the international community to be a political lockdown in Bogotá and Colombia. It was here, and centrally as a result of Mockus, that innovative politics took form in acts of humor and defiance that stemmed not from the experience of the elite but from the mundane and ordinary aspects of the quotidian. On one famous occasion, for example, a group of protestors would not let him speak, and "Mockus mooned his audience to shock [them] into silence" (ibid.:27). While some might think that Mockus's shock tactics are fleeting, his ideas on culture have influenced activists' work in Bogotá to alter the fabric of everyday life and inject energy into citizens' sense of self. His ideas were premised on a pedagogy informed by everyday life and an appreciation of art as an embodied and lived experience. This approach has been highly praised (as well as criticized) for what it has contributed to social transformation in Bogotá. There is no doubt that Mockus and much of his contribution to the growth of public humanities and cultural agency in the Americas has been significant, no matter the final political measures of "impact."

However, to date, there has been virtually no gender analysis of Mockus's theoretical, epistemic, or practical contributions. What reviewers and critics have failed to consider is that while Mockus's work has been pedagogically innovative and some of his campaigns have been particularly gender-sensitive, much of his body of work has been based on a masculinist model of protest. His "mooning" tactics are a good example of the way in which he could use certain protest techniques in a way that a female agent might not so readily adopt.[1] By drawing on masculinist traditions of revolt, Mockus's call for cultural agency relies upon the idea of the human subject and agent being essentially male in nature. While Tognato pays homage to Mockus's influence on Sommer's (ibid.:28) fleshing out of the concept of cultural agency as a "range of social contributions through creative practices," agency itself remains an assumed and universal attribute of the human condition. Yet studies have long shown that knowledge—let alone cultural knowledge—in any given society is not something to which all human beings have equal access, nor are social subjects created through cultural discourses in uniform ways. Cultural practices involving art have often been the purview of those in positions of privilege, and even in Mockus's attempt to recognize daily art forms, there is a failure to acknowledge the very ways in which multiple forms of difference and discrimination cut through the idealistic world of politics by means of artistic expression.

Thus, while Mockus's work was a "series of pedagogic initiatives that tapped into symbolism and performance for the purpose of promoting peaceful coexistence and free debate" (ibid.:27), his work also (perhaps unintentionally) maintained many existing situations of inequality. As such, while much of his work "[helped to] bridge the dramatically deep divides that visibly partition the Colombian public sphere" (ibid.:29), it did not always recognize the very patriarchal roots from which such pedagogical strategies and ideas originated.

Importantly, Tognato points out how "in relation to Mockus's experience and legacy, there seems to be consensus over the idea that with him the creative practices have become so central to the exercise of government as to blur the border between art and government" (ibid.:28). This may signal some of the importance of Mockus's contribution despite the residues of patriarchy that are so stark in the depictions of Mockus as a charismatic trickster figure. Inadvertently, scholars focussing on his charisma have maintained a masculinist and superficial image of Mockus as more of a celebrity, rather than that of a political leader and subject who could transform politics.

Tognato warns of too idealistic a celebration of Mockus's life and work. Iron-ically, Mockus's ideas have often appealed both to conservative and an excessively progressive thinkers and politicians. His place then in the political spectrum sug-gests that he was less transgressive than he himself expected. Here, it might be pertinent to think of what the late Audre Lorde (1984:114) once famously said: "The Master's tools will never dismantle the Master's House." Thinking along these lines suggests that Mockus's model of working challenged some boundaries, but still accepted many of the structures and institutions of modern life which have been found to be responsible for the oppression of marginalized groups. In partic-ular, the mode of protest, while different and creative, still reflected male bias, and a male standpoint on hierarchy and power. Adding to the gender baggage was the way in which Mockus developed himself as an individual, and a lone charismatic figure. In many ways he became the unique, exceptional artist, pioneering new ways of being in a public and cultural world.

One of the reasons why Mockus failed to challenge the patriarchal baggage that accompanied him was that his political vision was founded on a grand narra-tive. Influenced by socialist ideas, Mockus often acted in contradictory ways. He was the charismatic individualist, while at the same time emphasising connected-ness—community, belonging, and mutuality. He wanted to challenge inequalities, but did not always approach this task by focussing on the structures of inequality. As such, paying attention to gender is a challenge to such a macro-political ap-proach, especially when it is understood as a singular identity or issue. In protest and revolution more generally, gender has had to take its place alongside with all the other identities jostling for attention in an era of identity politics; and in this way the promise that all such identity-based inequalities will subside once the macro social structures are altered has never been successfully realized, not even in Bogotá. Gender experts demonstrate that everyday life and art in Bogotá remains particularly unequal.

Finally, Mockus and his supporters could have benefitted from one more feminist theory that might have influenced the adoption of his work beyond Colombia. Mockus was very much interested in the everyday, yet he did not turn to the work of the (mainly) feminists who championed standpoint theory. It was Dorothy Smith who argued that a different view of the world arose out of not only the everyday, but the perspective of those marginalized within society. Women— Smith and others, such as Nancy Hartsock and Sandra Harding suggested— were often relegated to the domestic sphere, had a different trajectory into the production of knowledge, and might offer a different perspective of the means of social transformation. Thus, feminist standpoint theory offers a view from the margins and reveals the ways in which different forms of knowledge are valued or devalued in societies. Since Mockus and his advocates are interested in "…doing 'serious work' in the public humanities along the North-South axis" with an eye to "intervening in the global circuit of knowledge generation and reassembling the institutional resources put together by northern and southern partners to allow the emergence of new knowledge that can sustain a given practice in the long term" (Tognato "Introduction":38), it is somewhat surprising that Mockus did not directly engage with the work of key feminists who advocated looking away from the center and toward the periphery. While this work grew out of a gender critique, it was also highly relevant to global and geopolitical divisions.

Innovations within academia to incorporate everyday art practices might not directly challenge structural forms of inequality, including that of gendered discrimination. In this way then, Mockus's ideas were not all easily transferable or adaptable because they did not always account for the fact that the "everyday" is itself contingent on time and place, even more so because his model of cultural agency required a certain spontaneity and interpersonal connection that cannot always be replicated by others. As each individual is uniquely situated within global and geopolitical power relations, his inspired actions cannot be taken up in a uniform way and may have very detrimental effects on individuals not placed in the same privileged position as Mockus himself. Mockus's politics, like those of many others, also assumes a "full" human subject to act. But we know that the human subject is differently situated in the world along lines of differences such as "race," gender, age, ethnicity, religion, sexuality, and so on. Each individual then comes to be seen as a human subject in radically different ways (some may not be seen as fully human at all) and therefore experiences different levels of risk, security, or vulnerability when engaging in acts of resistance, protest, or marginality. Similarly, Tognato draws attention to Sommer's point that "agents of social change must strive for 'plural emancipations' that address structural asymmetries in their own local contexts of reference" (Sommer 2006:7; Tognato "Introduction":50). Agents must take care then, not to adopt Mockus in straightforward mimicry.

Endnotes

1 Having said this, there is a longstanding tradition of women in West Africa bearing their bodies in protest against male-dominated peace processes in the post-conflict period of the 2000s.

References

Lorde, Audre. 1984. "The Master's Tools Will Never Dismantle the Master's House." Pp.110-114 in *Sister Outsider: Essays and Speeches*. Berkeley: Crossing Press.

6. Antanas Mockus, Insider/Outsider

Francisco Thoumi

In a country that has had very little immigration, Antanas Mockus is a member of a very small group of "inside outsiders," analytically inclined Colombians of foreign ancestry who care deeply about their country. They grew up with a more worldly view than most Colombians and have had fewer epistemological obstacles in confronting the country's reality. Other members of this group might include Salomón Kalmanovitz, Emilio Yunis, Herbert "Tico" Braun, John Sudarsky, and Moisés Wasserman. They all have sought new ways to look at the Colombian conundrum and to understand it.

Colombia has struggled to establish a state that reflects a consensus among the great majority of its citizens. Not surprisingly, this has led to a very weak capacity for law enforcement on the part of the state. Most Colombians have accepted this fact as "natural" or "normal" and learned to live with it, even though it has led to a low-intensity conflict lasting more than sixty years, high levels of violence, corruption, human displacement, and the development of guerrilla, paramilitary, and organized criminal groups, among other social ills. It is no coincidence that the "inside outsiders" have not accepted these conditions as a normal way of life and have explored ways to harmonize law, morals, and culture as Antanas Mockus has asserted.

This goal requires significant changes in the world view of most Colombians, dominated by pre-modern social concepts such as: "society is always highly stratified and unequal, and I should strive to be on top" (there are hierarchies even in heaven); "wealth is based on natural resources and on privilege" (the conquest of Colombia has not finished); and "State laws are used to discriminate against the poor and those without power." Pre-modern values and economic and social instability have produced significant upward and downward social mobility but relatively little social change. The system tends to co-opt those who rise, and thus it reproduces itself.

Mockus's administration in Bogotá followed the successful mayoralty of Jaime Castro, who balanced the city's accounts and modernized the administrative structure of the city's government. Mockus then sought to change many of the behaviors of the city's residents, aiming to promote modern civil ethics. His methods were unconventional and appealed to histrionic techniques to attract attention and to illustrate the need for, and benefits of, a modern civil culture. His zeal for protecting public funds (which he labeled as "sacred") slowed the implementation of many infrastructural and other projects, but also paved the way for both the very successful administration of Enrique Peñalosa, his successor and an excellent manager, and his own reelection after Peñalosa's term.

Mockus's approach showed Bogotanos that it was possible to improve everyone's quality of life by making small behavioral changes and gave hope to the small but growing segment of the population that rejected pre-modern values; this was the reason why his 2010 presidential campaign received unexpected support, particularly among youth. I am afraid that Mockus was not prepared to debate many of the national issues required in a presidential campaign: monetary policy, national public finance, international relations, international trade, regional development, and rural and industrial development policies, among others. His main focus on altering behaviors did not resonate nationally, and he failed in his presidential quest.

Despite this failure, Mockus's contribution to Colombian society has been remarkable. He has shown that the harmony between law, morals, and culture is a strong contributing factor to the quality of life in a society. The subsequent three administrations of Bogotá led by left-leaning politicians have resulted in some improvements in the standard of living of some of the poor, but have misspent huge amounts of resources, witnessed some of the most dramatic cases of white–collar corruption, and have failed to cope with many of the main challenges of a growing urban metropolis. This clientelistic, pork barrel, unaccountable approach to the city's government has been an unqualified disaster.

Mockus failed in his quest for the presidency, and some may argue that he also failed when he resigned from his position as mayor to pursue the presidency. Despite these criticisms Mockus has achieved a lot. There is a struggle going on between the old and the potentially new "Colombias." He has shown that it is possible to change deep-rooted behaviors and that there may be hope for new generations. Mockus's achievement is based on the power of ideas, not on his ability to implement them. Antanas has been a much better teacher than a politician. After all, he is a trained academic and an amateur politician.

7. Breaking out of the Ivory Tower...

Fabián Sanabria

In May 1991, an academic of Lithuanian origin, who had been appointed Chancellor of the National University of Colombia, launched an institutional plan that he enigmatically labeled "Living Fossils, Cultural Amphibians, and Midwives of the Future." *Cultural Agents Reloaded* sets out on an exercise that essentially focuses on the second element of that title. Based on Basil Bernstein, Mockus's idea of *cultural amphibians* refers to social agents capable of moving across different spheres without being *chameleons*, while exhibiting the ability to interpret and translate the modes of feeling, thinking, and acting of the diverse worlds across which they move; they are recontextualizers that foster the circulation of knowledge, thereby sustaining society's strength and dynamism, both internally and externally.

This type of agent, who emerged under certain heteronomic conditions within the field of cultural production, and particularly of academia, overcomes the false Weberian dilemma between the scientist and the politician and invites a deconstruction of other false oppositions, such as that of theory vs. practice, North vs. South, autonomy vs. heteronomy.

During the past decades in US academia, various thinkers have established an epistemological framework that allows for the institutionalization of the possibility that knowledge may have a relevant impact on public life by fostering its projection into, and its interaction with, society and vice versa. In South America, and particularly in Colombia, it would seem that the prevalent form of cultural agency, which encompasses the practices and accomplishments of Antanas Mockus, involves some kind of charismatic prophecy coupled with political *caudillismo*.[1]

Still, given that in the contemporary world there are no longer *producers of total theories of society* such as Pierre Bourdieu, it is necessary to live, both in the North and in the South, with charismatic prophets and at the same time with spaces that produce theories in movement. The idea of the *total intellectual* à la Sartre is no longer viable. It is imperative to *extend the right of entry* into academia as well as to *facilitate the duty to exit* for the purpose of interacting with society and overcoming the pretension that all knowledge is concentrated in an ivory tower that does not exist.

One of Mockus's obsessions as an embodiment of the cultural amphibian he theorized was its contribution to the harmonization of three dimensions of social life: law, morals, and culture. Mockus took as his starting point the profound misalignment among these three spheres in Colombian society: the rupture between what has to be (the law); what it is said one does (moral); and what is really done (culture). The main legacy of Mockus's agency has focused on looking for the cultural minima that may bring the three dimensions into line without the pretension of triggering any revolution or structural change among social classes. Rather, Mockus has moved from a notion of cultural equality and tried to introduce regulatory elements that might apply to a fragmented university, a fragmented city, and a fragmented country.

As it has been remarked in *Cultural Agents Reloaded*, this attitude has not been sufficiently understood by some critics. Some, radicalizing their stance from theory, see in Mockus's practice a kind of servilism towards the state, cuing the typical controls in place in post-disciplinarian societies. Others, adopting a fundamentalist posture towards politics, perceive his gestures as those of a postmodern demagogue, as their revolutionary nostalgias prevent them from seeing Mockus's accomplishments on the front of *Cultura Ciudadana* (Civic Culture).

It is important to stress the national and international impact that Mockus's perspective has had in other Colombian cities as well as around the world. Not only have his performative gestures been recognized but so have his accomplishments as a politician, as an administrator of the *polis*, and as a public leader, bearing an impact on the everyday life and even on the intimate lives of his citizens. Beyond certain sociological reductions by those who regard Mockus as a *petit bourgeois* leader of the middle class, for Mockus, no statistics make sense without anecdotes. Cultural equality, in turn, is more viable and effective for him than any outmoded class struggle.

The overview that *Cultural Agents Reloaded* presents of Antanas Mockus pushes the analysis beyond those interpretations of him that exalt his commitment between reason and passion, *"Por Amor al Arte"* (For the Love of Art), as well as beyond the lamentations of those who see a decline in his performative capacity along his career. Readers outside Colombia will have the opportunity to learn about the concepts applied by Mockus, to recognize his legacy ("living fossil"), and to further it within other scenarios, thereby allowing that Socratic exercise par excellence that leads to the social appropriation of knowledge.

Some significant elements about Mockus's cultural agency still beg for more extensive discussion, particularly as far as the perfecting of democracy is concerned. In particular, this applies to conjuring violence through the will-belief-vision of escaping it through ritual and play.

The legacy of Mockus's cultural impulse instigates us to inevitably project ourselves into public life, being inscribed as it is in a humanism associated with art that does not content itself with the ivory tower of academia or with the museum that exhibits the pieces that constitute the pride of a culture.

Over the past few years, between his multiple attempts and his best failures in politics, his actions have established him as an inevitable prophet: the most constructive way to establish the "Thou shall not kill" in post-conflict Colombia is still to proclaim with deeds that "Life is Sacred," as he has done throughout his career.

Finally, between the child and the genius, the prophet and the fool, the academic and the politician, Mockus's play not only questions Colombian society but also other societies. By way of his multiple gestures, his agency paraphrases without intending to say what, according to Sartre, characterizes all culture and what has also inspired the literary fiction of one of Mockus's disciples: it does not save anybody, it does not justify. Still, it is a human product by which people project and recognize themselves, a critical mirror that makes their image transparent since it is possible to do away with a neurosis but never to cure themselves of their own.

Endnotes

1   *Caudillismo* refers to charismatic rule supported by masses.

PART SIX: CONCLUSION

Antanas Mockus

6

Peaceful Play as a Basis for Pleasurable Government

Antanas Mockus

Certainties

I found people and things, ideas and words exactly where I needed them. What I had learned was there, at hand. In that dizzying world even the most obvious enemies appeared mysteriously transformed into the best allies. I wish to say that I lived a long time in a very fluid manner, without fear, not very attached to previous roles, recognizing the potential of each moment, and appreciating the value of every instant. More than transforming individuals, which are not and should not be considered raw material, we could playfully transform some language games. But no one changes language without consequences. In order not to constrain people or things, we learned to constrain ideas; we learned to constrain words. Let's be fair: many times it was not a matter of constraining but rather of finding grounds where it would be possible and fruitful to tussle. To tussle is to recognize that one is on equal footing with others. Tussling is about opposing without knowing the denouement. It is about contradicting, about dealing with diverse initiatives and resistances, without foreseeing the results or taking them for granted. Many times the journey is more important than the destination, the path more important than the point of arrival, the process more important than the result; and yet in Bogotá, surprisingly, for nine years (January 1995–December 2003), including the three years of the dizzying Enrique Peñalosa administration, we eluded the dilemma.

There were many good games and many good results but also some monumental technical disasters, such as the landslide at the Doña Juana garbage dump or the breaking of most of the concrete tiles used in the *Transmilenio* bus system.

Although many of the traces of this period have been recorded and analyzed in theses, books, and articles, it seems fitting to present the international public with this book, which addresses the close relationships between *Cultura Ciudadana* (Civic Culture) and cultural agency, and which saves us from systematic doubt as to people's capacity to act with culture and on culture. We hope that this exercise will shed light on the manifold attempts, by artists and non-artists, to inspire us in art, in play, and in other manifestations of culture, to give us a happier and more meaningful life.

Before the Certainties, a Lot of Learning Backwards

Our world is easily polarized. Those of us who work with culture or in favor of culture often fall into the blind reproduction of prejudices. Prejudices freeze over, and knowledge becomes mere classifying. The use of labels greatly simplifies cognition, but at the end of the day it does a great deal of harm to political life and democracy. In Colombia and elsewhere, labeling hinders the transition towards peace, especially when it becomes a code uncritically shared by experts and citizens. Labels lead to postponing, sometimes for good, the careful exchange of arguments and emotions. In Colombia, such labels as *godo* and *mamerto* (radical conservative and left-winger, respectively) can be used for anything: as terms of contempt or insults, to express strong feelings, or to trigger shootings and stabbings.

The label becomes a black box, and we tend to make do with the first superficial evidence. Add a bit of intimidation, and labels will spare us from having to think and feel. They are codes that save us the trouble of knowing and understanding. So we create routines for thinking and acting (for example, for acting without thinking), and then we blindly reproduce the beliefs that support our prejudices. At times, it would seem that our only answer to prejudice is more prejudice. This gives rise to black-and-white oppositions. One of the goals of this book is to make us better able to resist such approaches.

In this book, the authors, the interviewees, and the editor have all made an admirable effort to avoid trivialization, and they have honestly asked themselves about the ultimate meaning of our action during my two terms as mayor of Bogotá and also about the limits of this action. The articles included in the book are rich in ideas, and cautious and/or generous in their judgments, suggestions, and conclusions. I shall address only a fraction of the issues raised by them.

I feel somewhat surprised and overwhelmed by this volume, by the diversity of the material produced, and by the great number of viewpoints the book has assembled. Thus I must take the risk of not doing full justice to each contribution. Only in a post-modern context would it be possible to bring together in a single space the government's intentions, the citizen's desires, and the book's own aspirations. This book seeks to record and acknowledge the value of actions and messages belonging to the past. In that sense, it could be seen as inappropriate as the beginning of an autopsy of what we have called *Cultura Ciudadana*. This autopsy would be performed in a new context, one which is gradually establishing itself: that of cultural agency. What if something that began as a set of creative actions, a friendly, pedagogically oriented *enforcement*, should come to be better understood as an imaginative game and the expression of a new territory for art? What if the government's intentions were serious and took the citizens' most serious desires seriously? Then we would inevitably have to ask ourselves about the intentions of this book. In simpler terms, what is it aiming at?

The editor, Carlo Tognato, as well as several of the contributors, sought to provide a more solid academic foundation and greater sustainability for two innovations which mutually shed light on each other: cultural agency and *Cultura Ciudadana*. The idea is to acquire a better understanding both of what was done in Bogotá between 1995 and 1997, and between 2001 and 2003, and what Doris Sommer has been recognizing and promoting in various areas of the world under the name of the Cultural Agents Initiative, based on the concepts of cultural agency and agents. According to the editor, once we have depersonalized the experiences recorded here and integrated them into a research agenda, they are worth presenting to a new generation of professors, students, and researchers who may study and use them.

In the following pages, I am at risk of falling into several temptations. First, I may find myself recounting irrelevant episodes. Second, I may be tempted to exaggerate in my defense of our administration and its results. The third temptation will be to exaggerate even more in my self-criticism (if only by saying that no one can ever overdo that…). And the fourth will be to swamp the reader with personal allusions, such as connecting the most important year of my life, 1985, with Orwell's novel, or recalling a course on "Society and Language" at the Universidad del Valle.

The Autobiographical Temptation

This is not the right place to tell the story of my life. However, I cannot help but devote a few paragraphs to certain autobiographical details possessing great illustrative force and associated with uncalled–for feelings that sometimes assail me, and which at other times I myself deliberately evoke. I believe that familiarity with these details may shed light on my conceptual preferences. For example, as the son of an artist who graduated with honors from the Academy of Fine Arts, and of a self-educated engineer who would have been very successful had he not lost his life very young, I could not but rebel against Taylorism, against the rule of "do not think, execute."

My second father was a classical philologist with a doctoral degree from Lovain University, who taught Greek and Latin in Bogotá and Soacha, a very poor municipality on the outskirts of Bogotá. Even though his job as a teacher was often monotonous, he endeavoured to make each class a singular event.

Like any other human being, I have learned from action and reflection. Certain readings, as well as certain actions, have changed the course of my life. Somewhat unwillingly, I studied Popper, Durkheim, Frederick W. Taylor, and Husserl; with a certain ambivalent anxiety, I brought together at the same table three unequal teachers: Stanley Milgram, Basil Bernstein, and Alvin W. Gouldner; with great pleasure I invited Wittgenstein, Habermas, Lakatos, Kuhn, and Feyerabend to stay. I also heard with enthusiasm the voices of less well-known authors such as Archier and Sérieyx (1984) who acquainted us with recent (and somewhat unorthodox) trends in administrative studies.

And there were small, medium, and great opportunities for actions that were as eye opening as the authors I read, or more so. People interested me more than things, and their actions interested me more than the people themselves.

When one is on a mission or some practical task, reading becomes passionate, and passionate reading brings many new opportunities for action. The dispute between those who celebrate structure and those who stress agency somehow clashes with the opportunities that life has given me. I have gone from reflection to action and from action to reflection dozens of times. The harmony and joy arising from this are unbeatable.

Once I finished my master's in mathematics, I spent a year and a half looking for my path in life (for example, I directed a Lithuanian choir and dance group). Luckily, several professors from the National University encouraged me to apply for an opening (out of forty-two candidates, two of us were selected). After one semester I was so enthusiastic that I became full-time faculty. I taught topology to a group of math undergraduates, to another group of students preparing for admission to a graduate program, and to a group mainly composed of primary school teachers training for promotion to high-school teaching.

I was surprised by the disparities among these groups and their professional futures. Soon I became interested in exploring the roots of students' success or failure in mathematics. At seventeen I had read the first part of *Reproduction* by Pierre Bourdieu and Jean-Claude Passeron (1970). At the French Bookstore in Bogotá I was lucky enough to find a book by Stella Baruk (1977), a very successful math re-educator. The title of the book neatly sums up the problem: *Échec et maths* may be understood either as *Checkmate* or as *Failure and Mathematics*. The first three articles I wrote in those early years are a good indication of the direction I was starting to take: "Indecent Mathematics," "Implicit Functions of the Educational System," and "Failure at Mathematics as a Breakdown in Communication."

At that time the National University had shut down its teacher-training programs in science and mathematics. Such programs, it was argued, were better suited for the National Pedagogic University. By 1979 the disappearance of the Pedagogy Department at the National University was a fact. However, the university undertook promoting research in pedagogy and in specialized didactics and twelve groups were created. Increasingly, and this trend was evident in France as well, teacher training was being separated from training in the scientific disciplines.

Starting-points (Collective and Individual)

Let us now turn from a critique of science and mathematics teaching to a critique and a transformation of society, without falling into over-seriousness.

The main collective starting-point was the Federici Group. Working in a meaningful community whose members shared a common ethics changed our lives. We met, we recognized each other, and we started to work together. We held that learning science and mathematics should not be a source of suffering but of pleasure. Our watchwords were pedagogical hedonism, criticism of scientism, and educational inequality, and of its official interpretation, which attributes failure to the student.

While the Federici Group defended pedagogical hedonism, in Colombian universities and teacher-training centers, pedagogy was being replaced by psychology, and the latter was being reduced to behaviorist psychology.

A more personal starting-point for me was the critique of instructional design, a pedagogical trend that approached the educational process as if it were an industrial process that could benefit from the advances in planning arising from Taylorism and from the detailed design of military training associated with the introduction of new weapons in the postwar era. Colombia, with its highly centralized public education system (in contrast with the decentralized character of education in North America), saw the advantages of economies of scale. In particular, there was an interest in strategies for improving quality that would not imply increasing costs. This kind of Taylorization would not diminish children's suffering but rather increase it.

From very early on I have been fascinated by science's capacity for self-criticism. I learned about Stanley Milgram's experiments at Yale University from a review of his book *Obedience to Authority* (1974). In my opinion, this book showed the great contemporary power of scientism. The first course I taught outside the field of mathematics was on Milgram's experiments. During the following semester our group, which included Jorge Charum and Carlos Augusto Hernández, read Jürgen Habermas's essay "Science and Technique as Ideology" which had come out in Spanish in the 127th issue of the Colombian journal *ECO* (Echo).

By 1982, my radical criticism of Taylorism had distanced me from the Leninist Left. During the attack by the M-19 guerrilla on the Palace of Justice in 1985, one of my best students and a very dear friend, Héctor Lozano, was killed. He was a brilliant mathematician with an unmistakable laugh. On the day of the attack, as I fled the sensationalist media coverage, I ended up at the university movie club, watching Herzog's *Aguirre, the Wrath of God*, a movie which in its own way describes another equally insane and costly conquest. Sometimes, reality and art help each other explore the excesses of human voluntarism.

Despite the great progress we had made over five or six years with the Colombian pedagogic movement, I then decided to concentrate on finishing my master's thesis in philosophy. A few months later, I accepted an offer from the recently appointed chancellor of the National University, Ricardo Mosquera, who invited me to join his team. He said to me, "You're so good at tearing things down, why don't you help me build something?" The fact is, at that point in my life, my three greatest achievements had all been negative: I had helped to stop the curricular reform of primary education in Colombia, I had helped to prevent the purchase of an Argentinian nuclear reactor, and I had contributed to blocking the so-called *puntímetro* (point-meter), an instrument designed to improve faculty income, but which ended up rewarding practically any academic activity with points leading to salary increases.

The Federici Group

My encounter with the team we eventually called the Federici Group was very important for me. The group was named after the man who encouraged us to create it, an Italian professor who arrived in Colombia in 1948, the day before the great riots of April 9. He set out to modernize the teaching of logic and mathematics in Colombia, and he succeeded. I still remember someone pointing him out to me many years later at a distance, as if he were a "relic": "There goes a humanist."

Carlos Augusto Hernández was the colleague who introduced me to the history and philosophy of science, to the criticism of behaviorism, and to the choice of new fields of interest within the wealth of options offered by the university's various faculties. Furthermore, at a university where people vied with each other in radicalism, Carlos Augusto taught me to admire the radicals without getting involved in their organizations. For many years, he and I, another physicist who was also interested in the history and philosophy of science (José Granés) and another mathematician (Jorge Charum), held together in our refusal to sign communiqués saying, "We condemn terrorist actions provided they have nothing to do with the masses." In the Federici Group seminar we discovered with Bernstein that, in a way, the four of us were artisans descending from artisans, members of a middle class that practiced professions in the process of being transformed with the strengthening of the market economy.

Federici was of great assistance in steering our non-conformist spirit and rebellious energy towards rigorous study and writing. We were even rash enough to found a Colombian Society of Epistemology and to present a paper at an International Congress co-organized by the French academic Michel Paty, the Italian Galileo Violini and the Colombian Carlos Vasco. The Federici Group's paper, titled "Limits of Scientism in Education," was well received and was subsequently published in Spanish (in the *Revista Colombiana de Educación*) and in French (in the French-Brazilian journal, *Fundamenta Scientiae* [Science Foundations]) (Federici et al. 1985). If teachers did not want the Ministry of Education to think for them and impose a "teacher-proof curriculum" on them, then they must stand up for their own profession and its autonomy, and consolidate the incipient pedagogic movement, its journal, and its research center (of whose board of directors I was a member during that first stage).

This movement published and distributed more than thirty thousand quarterly issues of the journal *Education and Culture*, which has now reached its 105th issue, and which for a time was the most important journal being read in Colombian faculties of education.

The Federici Group held very broad views, and only very late did we become aware of the responsibilities we had acquired. As we played at criticizing, we not only made a place for ourselves in the internal debates among the experts on these topics, we also acquired very high-profile commitments, which carried with them enormous responsibilities: I was appointed vice-chancellor for academic affairs and later chancellor of the National University of Colombia. This five-year experience, between 1988 and 1993, enabled us to broaden our perspective on administration and public management.

Playing to Rule or Ruling to Play?

Let us return to my two terms in office as mayor of Bogotá and to the most urgent question: Did we play with the power to form better citizens while carrying out a merely cosmetic operation of "admirable public management" (as the seventh and last objective of my second administration was called)? Or, rather, did we achieve "admirable public management" precisely by better applying technical rationality in the service of the citizens and the construction of citizenship?

To my knowledge no one has ever complained that the *Cultura Ciudadana* programs were intended as a distraction, a handy smokescreen for a modernization agenda. Nor, on the other hand, has anyone ever accused us of using rationalization to play, as no one had ever done before, with the symbols of power, with languages and roles. One way or the other, we will never know. Perhaps it was a bit of both, as Professor Federici used to say with his surprising moderation. And quite frankly, we did both relatively well.

Some higher-level officials, whom we nicknamed "pilots," because they held a knowledge that made them indispensable, and who had worked for years in the town hall and the various municipal agencies, were highly surprised by the seriousness with which we pursued our objectives and stuck to the letter of the law. They were surprised by our way of doing things: "you guys really are strange," "you're from outer space," "you respect bureaucracy." Years later, a journalist, Juanita León, compared our team with mayor Peñalosa's: Peñalosa had a team of managers and engineers she argued, while Mockus had a therapy group. And it was true: more than once I told my team that the improvement of the city depended, just like magic, on healthy communication among us.

Learning with Pleasure from the Left and the Right

I would like to state this emphatically and with pride: in all the teams I have ever worked with, I have learned how to learn from everyone, whether they were on the Left or on the Right. From the Left we learned outrage in the face of inequality. Risking my election on the two occasions when I was elected mayor, I promised more taxes while defending the principle of universal taxation ("Everyone Contributes"), that is, the principle of solidarity whereby everybody gives something but the rich give more; I also defended the principle of shared welfare ("Everybody Gets Something"), whereby the provision of public goods is progressive and benefits every member of society. It was very pleasant to turn an electoral campaign into a process of fiscal education.

Furthermore, by refusing to make promises or return favors, I participated in the most radical undertaking any left-wing movement in Colombia could possibly have taken on: opposing (I wish that had meant definitively ending) the clientelistic politics which scandalously jeopardize the citizens' rights, substituting them for favors which function as a kind of moral mortgage: not only are the citizens' rights not recognized as such, but they end up owing favors which have all been paid for with State money.

Let me give another example. From the Right I learned fiscal orthodoxy. Every expenditure must be supported by actual income. Policies were approved when their financing was ensured in the context of mid-term budgetary projections. Money and ideas had to be in tune. The management of the city's assets was strict. One example: if the Bogotá Electricity Company urgently needed an injection of capital, the money had to be found. And it was obtained by restructuring and subsequently capitalizing EEB (the Bogotá Electricity Company), which led to the separation between generation and distribution and a considerable increase in the value of the company (thanks to the transparency of the process, we obtained two billion two hundred million dollars instead of one billion dollars). This allowed successive reductions of capital, which provided the city with the equivalent of more than a year's tax income, which was invested over nearly five years. That we could use these funds freely largely explains the "miracle" of Bogotá.

As the director of the National Planning Department and the then Minister of Finances have acknowledged, thanks to this re-structuring and capitalizing of the Bogotá Electricity Company, the city and the company not only helped the national government to save the country from a crisis in the external debt service, they also helped the government to carry out its policy of breaking down vertical integration in the electrical sector and inducing competition in the two markets: distribution and generation. The aim was to secure the country's access to electricity by encouraging private investment.

When they call me a neoliberal, I answer: "I have learned from many sources, even from neoliberalism. But it's a pretty odd neoliberal who goes around preaching that 'public funds are sacred funds' and winning elections by proposing more taxes."

In 1985, a week-long intensive seminar at the Universidad del Valle, with Basil Bernstein coincided with the presentation of Pablo Neruda's *Canto General* (General Song) in the Colón Theater, directed by Mikis Theodorakis.[1] This was perhaps the broadest and most generous gesture the Colombian elite has ever displayed towards a left-wing work of art.

During this same period, at the opening of an exhibition, my mother surprisingly introduced me to President Belisario Betancourt, with the comment (referring to me): "I'd like you to meet this guy, I don't know if he is left-wing or right-wing." Yes, she was right and so are the authors of several essays in this generous book, when they identify my political leanings. I might say that I have borrowed shamelessly and joyfully ideas, principles, and criteria from both sides.

In 1984, I read Orwell's *1984*. In Colombia, in 1985, the occupation of the Palace of Justice closed certain doors and opened others. This began the debacle of the M-19 guerrilla group, which had succeeded in reproducing the Tupac Amaru group's practice of "revolution as spectacle," in the words of a professor from the Universidad del Valle. I sometimes imagined an extension of the concept: government as spectacle.

After the Constituent Assembly of 1991, as chancellor of the National University, I contributed to keeping liberals, conservatives and left-wingers connected (and, occasionally, amused). Carlo Tognato is surprised and intrigued by my (relative) closeness to these three traditional sectors, which make up the Colombian political spectrum. I myself hope that this book will help the reader to understand how this closeness came about. Sometimes I think I have a special interest in trios, lists of three: triangles, triangulations, triads, triptychs, and chords of three notes. I like the complexity that arises from any relationship among more than two units.

But in all of this my personal presence is weaker than it seems. Let me insist on this: something that has given and continues to give me great strength (and freedom to act) has been the choosing and knitting together of technically strong teams, while remaining entirely ignorant of—and indifferent to—their political loyalties. This has made it easier to substitute a political agenda with a pedagogic agenda, and it has enabled a daring combination of offices: that of the public servant, and that of the academic and that of the politician (who was blessed by life from childhood with a color-blindness extending to the political field as well). We treated Council Members with respect, as qualified interlocutors who would be receptive to arguments. We requested that, when asking for an appointment, they specify the topic of the meeting in writing, so that we could prepare it better. During the appointment, when the topic had been dealt with and they wished to raise another one, we would ask them to request another appointment. It was like a game that was played according to strict rules.

Towards Pedagogic Utopia, 2010

Young supporters would sometimes tell me that I was able to bring out the best in them, which is why at political meetings they would shout, not "My President, My Professor," but "My Professor, My President." This means that (1) they wanted a teacher for president and, in that sense, that (2) they already recognized pedagogical authority in their candidate, who had already exercised it. Many of us shared that pedagogical illusion and this probably explains the high participation among young supporters overseas. For any traditional politician, talking about pedagogy is just a waste of time.

Perhaps this highly unusual process led us to blur not only, or not so much, the boundary between art and government (or between art and politics). Maybe all together we succeeded in blurring, at least at times, the traditionally hermetic boundary between pedagogy and politics, subordinating politics to pedagogy and thereby reinterpreting our mandate and our office. The goal was not to stay in power. The goal was to prove to ourselves and to the world that a government without a party was possible, one that could listen to arguments, irrespective of their origin and intentions. When I asked a graffiti writer who had become a teacher of other graffiti writers what, in his life, had aroused the most wonder in him, he replied: "The day I understood that with education everything is possible."

It was as though the call of the 1960s and early 1970s ("Knock Down that Wire Fence!") had been temporarily replaced for a few days or even a few hours by the call, "Let's Get Educated Now!" In a way, what happened was a clear display of a pedagogical utopia and an illustration of this utopia thanks to the power of the media, with long-term effects: people were able to see the difference between unfulfillable promises and the responsible approach, which sought to promote a tax-paying culture. Subsequently, Sergio Fajardo's acceptance of the vice-presidential ticket strengthened our educational proposal.[2]

We thus succeeded in defeating, for a few hours, the mixture of skepticism and contempt that pedagogy arouses in our societies. However, let's face it: whether in the Northern or in the Southern Hemisphere, pedagogy is almost always boring, and art is almost always moving. One answer to this could be, "With Pedagogy, Play, and Art We Can Go Anywhere!"

TV Individualism

Some twenty years ago, I gave Nijole, my mother, a book about Dalí. She read some of it and, when I went back to visit her, she commented, with great assurance: "You're like Dalí. You can turn anything into an artwork, for example that coffee cup…" Then she added: "But you need to have cameras recording the transformation. Without what the cameras record, you would be nothing. And you would have done nothing. Truly, you have done nothing."

Television has technical and rhetorical limitations. It was a great help, and had an unsuspected multiplying power, especially during my first administration when there were no local channels. But in each of the three following stages—the end of the first administration, the campaign, and the second administration—it made invisible the quality and intensity of the teamwork that accompanied and supported me during each of these stages.

I acknowledge television's contribution. Still, I blame the TV cameras for paying too much attention to me and unfairly ignoring the extraordinary efforts and capacity for teamwork of the people whom, fortunately, I was able to hire with complete freedom. Thus, the two people who were mainly in charge of the *Cultura Ciudadana* programs—Paul Bromberg and Rocio Londoño, my colleagues from the Science and the Humanities Faculty—were able to leave their personal mark on these programs. Without Alejandro Deeb's technical competence as manager of the Bogotá Water Company we would not have broken free of the Performance Plan the World Bank had imposed on the company; but neither would we have promoted voluntary saving of water without the enthusiastic awareness that we were faced with a marvelous opportunity: circumstances and Alejandro Deeb's enthusiastic support gave us the chance to experiment with demand management—a relatively new approach in public utilities.

The Teams

Fifty percent of a mayor's success depends on choosing the right team and doing the job of learning what the city's, the mayor's, and the citizens' priorities are, what his predecessors did before him/her, and what benefited the city, in the context of global trends. The idea is to "build on what was built before." Not only was I twice a candidate and twice a mayor but also on these four occasions, I chose rather different teams. All the people on them were highly trained academically. Paul Bromberg, for example, several years before, had written a master's thesis at the University of British Columbia in Vancouver on the role of metaphor in physics.

His "engineer's" attitude drove Paul to methodically explore many possibilities, leading to many small victories at the pragmatic level, which constituted big steps towards the formation of citizens: the citizen's card, the use of seatbelts, the use of mimes, fewer people burnt by fireworks, better behavior among taxi drivers, more confidence among the citizens and towards public officials. By the end of the first year, such victories had made it clear to us that we had done a lot and that it was worth understanding that we could do more and know more. And we did, in fact, manage to bring together the conditions for continuing. How was it possible, with relatively little money, to bring about changes on such a scale? Certainly this team succeeded in interpreting the general interest accurately, though, on some occasions, acting for the sake of the general interest led us to contradict the popular will. These tensions, at least in part, were expressed, understood and assimilated by means of reasons and emotions, so we were right when we decided to explicitly work towards "increasing the capacity of the citizens to express themselves and interpret each other's expressions through art, culture, recreation and sports."

All the teams that participated in the *Cultura Ciudadana* programs, all those groups, were the people who ensured that the real work got done, while I was doing what I do best: re-contextualizing. I was almost forgetting the role of television, which brought me the closeness and surprisingly lasting affection of thousands of people, even while it cast me in the role of a Lone Ranger.

Television does not favor teamwork (except in the case of soccer, for which it has created very well-adapted technical devices, a specialized language, a trained audience, etc.). I sincerely think that television is what makes me look like a Lone Ranger or a rock star. We were actually a choir, and often times a good one. Sometimes, when the journalists did not understand us, Alicia or Paul would explain things—patiently, affectionately.

What Brought us Together?: Empathy, Rebelliousness, and Admirable Public Administration

Teams need to discover what brings them together. For example, during my two administrations in Bogotá, what brought us together was our epidemiologists' approach to the study of violence. What brought us together was the suspicion, and later on the evidence, that most of the violence occurring in Bogotá and in Colombia was due to intolerance, organized crime, and common delinquency. We also came together on the need to measure the results of our actions.

Let us return to Paolo Vignolo's criticism, in this volume. According to him, as mayor, I declared myself trapped between transgression and the norm. Perhaps, as the buffoon of the mimes and the sensationalist gesture, I simply cover up the decisions of the administrator. But the opposite can happen too. Perhaps the systematic search for excellence in management is what led us to make explicit the sixth objective of my second administration, which I baptized "Admirable Public Management;" and perhaps this is what made possible the well-deserved luxury of inviting the citizens to play a little. This is also what made the magic fade: there are gazes and judgments that break the spell. Sometimes it is painful, but necessary, to remember that the game can go too far and be taken too seriously.[3] About half of our successful actions were invented and carried out to attend to sudden, unforeseen agendas.

Decentralizing

We were able to hold government councils in each of Bogotá's boroughs jointly with the democratically-elected Local Board of Administration, and we ensured participative planning procedures for the preparation of the local development plan in each of Bogotá's twenty boroughs, which ended up assigning funds on the basis of hearings to select the competing projects. Lucho Ramirez (RIP) promoted two successful programs: "Works with a Pedagogic Balance" and "Weavers of Society."

The first program trained groups of ten young people to select, each one within his or her own community, a project that would cost approximately US $30. The project could be about building access stairs to the steeper part of the neighborhood, about carrying out repair work in eroded torrent beds, about building community halls, playgrounds, public toilets, etc. The process had a long-lasting impact throughout the following decade on the formulation of projects for public works and on cooperation among community organizations and between them and state agencies. This is how the idea of works with "a pedagogic balance" developed. Young people who in each group had prepared ten projects were supposed to choose only one of them. Thus, in each group of ten participants, the members had to reach, by debate, an agreement on reasonable criteria for selecting a single project. Later on, Peñalosa delegated this decision to a jury, a decision that we did not correct during our second administration (Isabel Londoño gave priority to the development of eco-neighborhoods, and Clemencia Escandón ran for congress in another region).

The second program consisted of two or three months of vocational training for high-school dropouts. This brief contact with high-quality education in a field of their interest was often enough to motivate them to return to school. One example was the course on videography offered by one of Colombia's best film directors. This program, which we called "Weavers of Society," was expensive but effective.

Intensified Communication

Academia usually dissociates the creation of knowledge from its re-contextualization and assigns a higher value to the former. Curiously enough, however, I have often engaged in re-contextualizing my own work in philosophy, pedagogy, and philosophy of law. For example, I acted as advisor for Clara Carrillo (1991) in the writing of her undergraduate thesis for the Philosophy Department. Guillermo Hoyos was amongst the examiners. I took on the task on the express condition that I might exercise an active influence in formulating the problem and reaching a tentative solution. This led to a very simple representation, in the form of a Venn diagram, of the various possible situations of harmony and divergence between law, morals, and culture. On the basis of the most general situation, four basic series can be identified: the universe of all actions, the subset of legally acceptable actions, that of morally acceptable actions, and that of culturally acceptable actions. That left the possibility for actions that were possible but unacceptable within the three regulatory systems. The intersections between the three subsets were not empty, and there were overlaps between two of them and sometimes between all three. We were looking at a very synthetic representation of the universe of actions and for any possible or imaginable action we could see where it stood in the Venn diagram that lay before us. As the cases in parentheses indicate, there are examples for each of the eight possibilities:

1. An action that is legally, morally, and culturally unacceptable (the rape and murder of a two-year-old girl);

2. An action that is legally and morally acceptable, but culturally unacceptable (the chancellor of the University, in an unpremeditated gesture and for pedagogic purposes, pulls his pants down and moons the audience in an Aula Magna [large lecture hall] full of shouting and catcalling art students—and, in another unpremeditated gesture, the action is filmed by one of the students and aired with very little premeditation by a TV news channel);

3. An action that is legal, but morally and culturally unacceptable (an abortion performed in Miami in the 1990s on a woman from a Catholic family whose personal beliefs and moral principles are Catholic);

4. An action that is legal, while being both morally unacceptable and culturally acceptable (someone phones, and you have someone else tell the caller you are not at home);

5. An action that is illegal and morally unacceptable, but culturally acceptable (selling a product without an invoice in order to evade the sales tax);

6. An action that is illegal, but morally and culturally acceptable (carefully driving through a red light in the middle of the night);

7. An action that is illegal and culturally unacceptable, but morally acceptable (an abortion after a rape in Catholic circles in Colombia in the 1970s);
8. An action that is legally, morally, and culturally acceptable (helping a blind man to cross the street).

In academic terms, the originality of the operation consisted of conceiving that a fairly broad set of actions could be classified as legal or illegal, morally, and/or culturally acceptable or unacceptable within the framework of three regulatory systems. In other words, different types of rules influence similar behavior (multi-regulation). As we can see from the eight examples, and in contrast with what common sense suggests, *the three regulatory systems are independent.* Not everything that is legal is morally acceptable, nor is everything that is morally accepted legal. It is precisely because the three systems are independent that it becomes conceivable to bring them into harmony: obeying the law (not committing illegal actions) becomes easier if these actions are acceptable, both culturally and morally. This is the be-all and end-all of what we call harmonizing law, morals, and culture: that compliance with moral and social norms should support compliance with legal norms, nothing more and nothing less.

How is this to be achieved? My initial hypothesis was that it could be achieved by means of an intensified Habermasian communication. Around that time I literally ran to show the diagram to Liliana Caballero, a lawyer and then secretary general of the National University. She liked it, and kept the document for several years. As for Clara Carrillo, her careful work on the subject and the pressure of a Fulbright fellowship to study at the New School for Social Research, led her to differ from my practical hypothesis. What she found was that it was not enough to intensify communication, not even the discursive communicative action that makes it possible to discuss problematized pretensions to validity while preserving a cooperative attitude and seeking an agreement exempt from any pressure other than that of the argument. Clara found good reasons to recommend something much broader: an intensification of interaction. Her monograph argues that all forms of interaction should be encouraged and intensified in Colombia. Obviously, communicative action and discursive communicative action should be strengthened but also covert or overt strategic interaction (as long as it is legal) as well as symbolic action (a form of communicative action that has abandoned all claim to truth while preserving the other three: intelligibility, sincerity, and integrity). This type of action, which is very important in Clara's text, includes expressive action, which, as it deals with the inner world, only aspires to sincerity. We relied throughout on

Habermas's (1989) typology of action, but we also used Ury and Fischer from the Harvard Negotiation Project. Ury and Fischer made it possible to conceive of principle-based negotiation as an alternative to the excessive division in Habermas between negotiation seen as strategic action and as communicative action. On Clara's recommendation, I read Ury and Fischer's (1983) classic *Getting to Yes, Negotiating Agreement Without Giving In*, which left me a little better equipped for my subsequent responsibilities. Clara graduated with honors from the National University in time to travel to New York where she became a student of Agnes Heller.

Learning from Basil Bernstein

One of Basil Bernstein's most original theses is that knowledge flows thanks to its re-contextualization. This flow, inevitably selective and transformative when it makes available certain knowledge to certain individuals, configures (or helps to configure) identities as well as work and professional categories. This is not a passive process. It is selective, and the principles that orient the selection, the organization, and, in general, the adjustment of what flows are not explicit. For knowledge to flow in any direction it has to be re-contextualized. To re-contextualize is to search in a given context (A), for relevant knowledge, which must then be selected, hierarchically organized, and adapted so it has meaning and application in a new context (B).

Teachers, publishing houses, Ministries of Education, professional organizations, the cultural industry, churches, etc., they all re-contextualize. Re-contextualization does not spring from the scientific communities of the Northern countries alone. In the educational utopia—what we call generalized pedagogy, which is starting to be visible—where everyone learns from everyone else, we are or we become re-contextualizers. In my opinion, cultural agents are re-contextualizers.

At first sight, re-contextualization would seem to be a subordinate function in relation to the creation of new knowledge. But this is not the case. Whoever re-contextualizes must, in order to do it well, discover the original and unrepeatable dimension of the other in the other person who inhabits context B. Of all kinds of re-contextualization, the kind that would appear to be the most harmless—but is indeed the boldest—is the one that operates again and again in art.

Politics also re-contextualizes, for example when it transforms complex facts into iconic images. Written facts are better grasped in writing. Our government used images so intensively that more than once, without intending to, we covered up what we wanted to show.

Bernstein was the first person we ever saw fluently combining what in the Federici Group we called the *objectifying attitude* and the *performative attitude*. Bernstein could shift from one to the other without a hitch. The knowledge that the *objectifying attitude* makes possible (education science, behaviorist psychology) cannot be immediately transformed into imperatives for technical action: some mediations are necessary. Whoever teaches, performs and leads his students to perform (and they, in turn, as early as possible, learn to promote and to correct the performance of others who are even more inexperienced than they are).

Discovering the Power of Social Rules

In countries with a relatively feeble state (with weak institutions easily captured by private interests), we require from the law what the law is unable to give us. Thus the law tends to become what is both most available and most fragile, and issues as critical as honesty or non-violence cease to be matters for informal regulation and become issues of formal regulation subject to a conscious transformation of the same. Issues formerly regulated by culture are now regulated by law. But the transition between the two is not guaranteed. For example, today there is awareness that respect for the rights of women and children cannot be achieved by legal or by social pressure alone; both are necessary.

According to Bicchieri, Mackie, Guillot, and Murraín, the normative expectation (the belief that most of the people in the reference group should obey the rules—a belief accompanied by the individual's own conviction that if he does not obey the rules, he will be ostracized) is exclusively associated with the application of social sanctions. I suspect that this aspect of their theory is easily questioned. I am firmly convinced that the real deterrent is often the combination of fear of the law, fear of recriminations from one's own conscience, and, finally, fear of social censure. If I transgress the law, moral principles, or cultural norms, and my transgressions are visible to those who are close to me and/or to more distant acquaintances, I will feel not only shame but also guilt and perhaps even some fear of legal consequences.

Fonna Forman has studied Adam Smith, and in her essay she shows the striking similarities between the conception of human motivations that Adam Smith constructs in his theory of moral feelings and the one that we have been using.

Social standards may perhaps be classified as harmful and harmless, but such a classification for Forman (and for Adam Smith) is precarious unless certain moral standards already exist, or can be constructed or selected, which can be made to harmonize with the social standards. Can there be a cultural reform without any previous moral judgment? Forman argues that there cannot, although she is well aware that this is one of the most contested areas of contemporary debate.

Clearly there are at least two lines of thought in tension here: one which argues that social rules come first and are more powerful than the legal and moral ones (Norbert Elias, Bicchieri and Murraín); and another position which argues that moral rules are more likely to provide guidance in an environment where social norms reveal their arbitrary nature and the laws have been losing the theocratic or natural foundation they once had (Smith, Kant, Mockus).

A very interesting feature of this book is that none of the twenty-five contributors proposed resorting exclusively to legislation or legal sanctions. From this perspective, perhaps the greatest practical contribution comes from Chaux and Bustamante when they explore how to incorporate the strengthening of the three regulatory systems into schools and how to prevent the separation of these systems within the formal educational process. For these authors, there is no doubt that people must be educated in the direction that Mackie defends: in the rule of law. If there is no rule of law, if the whim of the ruler or the official prevails, there is no democracy. In Colombia, we have great abstract respect for the law (see Murraín's essay in this book), but it is very often considered illegitimate, and this becomes the justification for outrageously high levels of lawlessness and violence.[4]

Agency and Cultural Agents

Doris Sommer is the person mainly responsible for the prevalence of an aesthetic approach in the American and Latin American reception of *Cultura Ciudadana*. After trying to accept only the borrowing of some techniques, I gave in to calling it "sub-art" (art unburdened by the claim of being art). She has been promoting a process of progressive clarification of what we might call, following her intuition and invitation, "cultural agents."

Like Sommer, I believe that any human being can be a cultural agent, and to be one you need only intervene in the course of human actions in such a way as to create meaning and leave a mark, to make people think and lead them to act. A cultural agent is someone who is not content to accept the current state of things; someone who takes sides, who sets an example and follows examples; someone who learns to surprise others and be surprised herself by her immediate results; but also someone who, whether one succeeds or fails, is always willing to play again.

I agree with Doris Sommer when she generously invites everyone to become a cultural agent. In fact, each of us can become one. And we can do so in different ways. For example, the most critical work at the moment is being carried out by Carlo Tognato, in preparing this book, and by Sommer, when she acknowledges in her Pre-Texts workshops the enormous importance of reading, writing, and literature, and their connection with the visual and performing arts. To refer life, training, and education to the living connection between texts, works, and life is perhaps the best way to achieve a thoughtful existence and remedy in many cases the mismatch between life in school and life outside. We may see a similar foundational gesture in the move from narration to the collective preparation of a bill intended to put an end to a collective problem.[5]

Six Fields of Agency

The cultural agent, in the games and other activities in which she participates, contributes a certain know-how and certain skills (in Amartya Sen's and Martha Nussbaum's terms) which may be identified and made explicit. Agency gives participants the possibility to advance in six mayor fields:

- *Agency:* The cultural agent is not content to accept the current state of affairs; she must be able to intervene by recreating and generating meaning (Mockus 1994a, 1994b); she must leave a mark, by acting and leading others to act (Mockus 1994a, 1994b); she must be capable of assuming risks (Sommer 2014); she should know how to generate unpredictable chain reactions (ibid.).
- *Inclusion:* Any human being can be a cultural agent (Mockus 1994a, 1994b; Sommer 2014); however, teachers, artists, booksellers, translators, interpreters, etc., are more able to assume this role (ibid.). The cultural agent can belong to the left or to the right (ibid.), and the innovations she proposes may proceed either from the bottom upwards (involving everyone) or from the top downwards (Mockus 1994a, 1994b; Sommer 2014).

- *The artistic dimension*: The cultural agent creates, and by creating surprises people; she invites them to judge, thus generating audiences; she offers role models, shows people that the institutions could be very different, and inspires innovations in close or distant fields (Shklovsky 2004; Sommer 2014).

- *The political dimension*: Examples like those of Edi Rama, Augusto Boal, and Antanas Mockus show that the cultural agent may blur the boundary between art and government (Mockus 1994a; Sommer 2014; Tognato 2015) and between art and politics (Mockus and his teams). The political dimension is assumed to be a privileged ground for discursive communicative action, and there is self-limitation in the use of overt or covert strategic action.

- *The pedagogical dimension:* It promotes a generalized pedagogy where we all learn from each other, and every interaction becomes an opportunity to teach and learn. In every move made by herself or by others, whether successful or not, the cultural agent re-contextualizes fragments of knowledge or fragments of morality (Bernstein 1984; Mockus 1994a), thus finding opportunities to learn. A central obstacle for this utopia to come into existence is paranoia, the fear that my openness to be educated will be strategically exploited.

- *The playful dimension*: The cultural agent promotes play because she sees it as the bridge between sensibility and reason, feelings, and concepts. Borrowing from Wittgenstein, we might play at saying that language games have always existed.

- Some cultural agents can perform adequately in the six fields. Others cannot. This is why many require teams.

Five Features of Art

With Doris Sommer, we have worked with five features of art that could be highly relevant in any process of cultural agency. These five features honor the individual who wants to surprise and be surprised, judge and judge himself or herself, give and assume models, identify alternate solutions and enjoy them, and finally acquire the certainty that what is real is only a tiny fraction of what is possible. Becoming acquainted with these five features of art facilitates the diffusion of art as an unexpected language; and a certain taste for surprise helps prevent everything from turning the same shade of gray. Increasingly, education—and especially aesthetic education—is geared towards enjoyment.

These are the five features we worked with:

1. Surprise. What has become excessively familiar has to become unfamiliar (Shklovsky). Some zebra crossings had been there for many years, but only a few citizens respected them. The same thing happened with pedestrian traffic lights.

2. Making opportunities to exercise judgment and thus create an audience (Arendt 1993 2003). "Citizenship Cards," for example, invited people to make a judgment. Mimes could be evaluated by citizens.

3. Creating role models. We imagined that the military parade on Independence Day (July 20th in Colombia) might include a battalion of judges and teachers, each of them bearing, instead of a weapon, a copy of the Constitution.

4. Showing that social structures and institutions could be very different, that there is something of historical contingency in their being what they are. Dreaming and experiencing possible worlds different from the one we find ourselves living in. Strategic planning promoted in Colombia by the National Planning Council and by multilateral agencies has revealed surprises that are deliberate results of cultural agency.

5. Inspiring innovations in close or distant fields. It was proposed to Teotonio Vilela Filho, the Governor of the State of Allagoas (Brasil), that he encourage massive attendance at funerals of young people who had died violently, and there were actually some timid attempts to implement the proposal in Maceió. The governor transformed the innovation proposed into an invitation to his mayors to attend the funeral of any newborn baby who should die in their jurisdiction. Even though a strict causal connection cannot be asserted, during the first semester of 2009, infant mortality decreased by 161 deaths in relation to the same period in 2008.

The Problem of Validation

The validation of academic-based innovations is a thorny issue. Carlo Tognato reproaches us for not having implemented a parallel research process that should by now have made the Bogotá experience into a source of highly relevant knowledge for mainstream contemporary social sciences. Tognato does not underestimate the international seminar that the National University has been organizing around the Norwegian social scientist, Jon Elster (seven seminars have already taken place). I think, however, that Tognato does slightly underestimate the impact of this initiative.

If innovation is not rigorously positioned before the scientific community, it runs the risk of not being taken seriously. Our innovations were received with prudence and curiosity, as can be seen from the hundreds of publications of various kinds on *Cultura Ciudadana* and the more than fifty theses submitted and defended on the subject, both within the country and abroad.

In a workshop held at the Oxfam headquarters in Oxford in 2005, Rosemary Thorp summed up our methodology in the following terms:

- Adopt explicit priorities for change, but seek snowball effects.
- Attack defeatism (with examples and indicators). Give information about behavior change. Use positive indicators.
- Use lateral analysis, with practical applications; take advantage of the impact (epidemiology).
- Attack different facets of the same problem.
- Use visual shocks (cards, stars on the roads).
- Identify simple tasks for people (blowing the whistle).
- Be seen as reliable (this could be the basis for everything).

Most of the actions of *Cultura Ciudadana* involved behavior that was embedded in daily life and had a very strong visual component. City Hall's communications team went on taking photographs and filming the mayor as if nothing was happening, which is why the visual memory of the process had to be reconstructed (this becomes apparent in the essay prepared by José Luis Falconi for this book).

Validating innovations may differ somewhat from validating knowledge that claims to be scientific. When can it be suspected that an innovation is going well?

When people who experience the innovation feel it to be relevant and when it withstands academic debate and, in spite of vigorous discussion, is not crucified in the media. If the innovation works, we feel all the emotions of success. Only later do the questions arise as to why it worked, and whether this success could be repeated.

Somehow I embody an uncomfortable separation/articulation of roles between the innovator, the scientist, and the politician. I deliberately refrained from developing my brand of anti-politics. Anti-politics is dangerously anti-democratic.

If there is little division of labor, there is more science than innovation; if there is a high level of division of labor, there might be more innovation than science. The ambiguity of my role sometimes leads me into a dangerous game, seeking approval from two very different audiences. When it comes to innovation, convincing the person who is going to use the innovation is more important than the approval of the academics or the quality seal.

The general recommendation, when faced with innovations like those that took place in Bogotá, would be to evaluate very early on whether they are worth documenting and whether they need "epistemic" support. Since public resources are sacred, it might be inappropriate to use any sizeable portion of them for carrying out detailed academic research, which in any case cannot replace the political assessment.

Some of our greatest successes, as far as security is concerned, took place just a few hours after measures such as the voluntary surrender of firearms were announced (December ceased to be the most violent month of the year). Tax income rose thanks to the program of voluntary tax payment, which we called "110% for Bogotá." We made the country familiar with expressions such as "Life is Sacred," "build on what was built before," "public resources, sacred resources," "the end does not justify the means," and "shortcut culture."

An Invitation to Build

Obviously, a few months after Chancellor Mosquera's offer, I had had a taste of how wonderful it is to build. Those two and a half years as academic vice-chancellor and two and a half years as chancellor were among the best in my life. I understood and assumed in practice that if your aim is to achieve a reasonable degree of harmony among the law, morals, and culture in societies overwhelmed by violence and illegality, you must intensify all forms of interaction, not just Habermasian communicative action.

For my change(s) of direction to be fully intelligible, two things would need to be added to those I have already mentioned: (1) The peremptory pressure from a businessman who also had a Lithuanian background: "If you are going to do research, get out of here and go to Boston, London, New York, or Paris. But if you stay here, do something for this country." This reproof made me decide to concentrate henceforth on reflections and studies that would be highly relevant for the Colombian environment. (2) Another point would be the impact and traces left by the seminar with Basil Bernstein at the Universidad del Valle. This seminar led me to confront my reading of Habermas. It was as if my stomach had become the arena in which Habermas and Bernstein were, and still are, struggling.

For Habermas, each communicative act (or more precisely, each communicative action) builds social bonds; for Bernstein, it is society that selects and considers legitimate certain expressions and not others. For the former, language enables the collective construction of a shared agenda; for the latter, only exceptionally are speech acts produced that illustrate human agency in most human gestures. Actually, in the chancellor's office, our never-officially-declared watchword for more than two years was "teachers: living fossils, cultural amphibians, and midwives of the future." We professionals in the field of education come from a tradition of long-term learning: we carry knowledge and fragments of morality from one context to the other; and we discover that the motor of human history is knowledge, not violence, as Marx once believed.

Why Leaders Are Afraid of Continuity

Why did *Cultura Ciudadana* take root? And why was it subsequently forgotten by governments and missed by the citizens?

Instead of celebrating the collective construction of the city, at the end of each period of government there is a kind of scramble to get hold of whatever legitimacy is left. Institutions lose a lot when they omit the elemental principle of communication. An external validator has much more authority than the operator or proprietor.

In my double role (at the university and in the city), my only option was to evade disjunction through a conjunction, strengthening the two poles of the conjunction, adopting both the performative and the objectifying attitudes without worrying too much about what would happen. Occasionally I would describe my internal conflict as a fight between cat and dog, between what I had understood in

Habermas and what I had understood in Bernstein.

In a nutshell: structure and agency are not the one thing or the other. It is the one thing *and* the other. The way in which we say things has an effect (along with many other things) on what we do and how we do it, and what we get and how we evaluate and share what we learn individually.

My Master's in Philosophy

In my master's thesis, I studied the philosophical, rhetorical, and literary roots of the notion of representation, and I ended up constructing a notion of representation that attempts to avoid the dualism of the theories that oppose language and reality. Following Richard Rorty (1980), I found it unacceptable that one should put things on one side and words on another and then try to connect them. It made no sense. Representing was just playing at changing the game. The only two conditions for turning a game into a new one (a new representation) are that this game should be comparable to one or several previous games, and that it should be more productive in deductive or organizational terms.

You do not simply change language and ways of saying things arbitrarily and gratuitously. Whether an awareness of innovation accompanies deliberate changes, or whether such changes are beyond our control and even our consciousness, in either case we have to recognize that neither we, nor the government, nor the citizens are the ones acting on language: it is language that acts on us. We start out from the dream of playing very freely with ways of saying things, and all at once, some of the proposed changes "stick," "take," make a way for themselves within the already existing language games and transform them.

Bogotá in the Early 1990

In the early 1990s, Bogotá was a nightmare. Despite the surge of hope that came in 1991 with the writing of a new constitution, consolidating the popular election of mayors (a measure first proposed by the FARC and adopted in 1988), and introducing the programmatic vote and the possibility of revoking a mayor's election, the Constituent Assembly gave the Congress and/or the national government the authority to establish a special regime for the capital city. As the Congress was not able to use the powers it had been granted, Mayor Jaime Castro, with the support of President Cesar Gaviria, drew up the reform of the Organic Law of the city, increasing the capital's autonomy in terms of taxation, mobility, and mass transportation. It also introduced mechanisms aimed at overcoming clientelist practices and took firm steps towards greater decentralization.

The insecurity in the capital took the form of terrorist acts such as the blowing up of an airplane that had just taken off with all its passengers or the bloody attack on the Departamento Administrativo de Seguridad (DAS, Administrative Department of Security), the main state intelligence agency.

The strongest interpellation is that of Doris Sommer. Her enthusiasm for the mayor-artist contrasts with the healthy skepticism of Jaime Ramos. While she tells me, "accept yourself as a cultural agent and an artist; you can do it without destroying your Habermasian political project," Habermas himself turns to Schiller to overcome Kant's rigidity. Doris places my actions as mayor of Bogotá half-way between art and politics: I am an artist and a politician—an artist who takes advantage of the scenarios and the demands of politics, and a politician who explores and exploits the transformative possibilities of art. I am caught between different extremes of academic classifications: the elitism of art, the prose of pedagogy, with an occasional stopover in the despicable depths of politics, amidst the more enveloping thrills of the most ambitious philosophy (Hegel, Heidegger, and Nietzsche), allowing myself on the way some closeness to the most modest and self-demanding philosophy (Wittgenstein and Elster).

As Sommer (2014) emphasizes, following Schiller's example, the necessary tension between hedonism and pragmatism may be reached in play. That is, play in both senses: as a self-rewarding playful activity, and as the representation, interpretation, and acting involved in a theatrical performance. As Sommer mentions, play relies on risk, freedom, and counterfactual thinking, which is why it has such power to imagine and create change. The need to generate consensus and shared rules within the city administration, which grows out of our reading of Habermas and is partly achieved via technical argument, can also be achieved through the playful creativity of art.

While other forms of communication divide society, Schiller argues that art unites society and creates harmony because it refers to what everyone has in common. This fundamental connection between aesthetic education and the discourse of ethics is what, according to Sommer, allows our work to be called "art." The art of play or the play of art makes it possible to build consensus among apparently irreconcilable positions: democracy allows different people to have different reasons for obeying the same rules. If all citizens are to some extent artists, then all citizens can become objects of admiration for others, and mutual admiration is the best emotion for sustaining democracy. To see the citizen as an artist also cures us, to some degree, of the effects of a single, vertical leadership and makes us commit ourselves to the "civic effervescence" that comes from collective leadership: indeed, this has allowed us to say that millions of people contributed to the results achieved during my terms in City Hall. For citizens there is great pleasure in completing the unexpected sentence, the proposed history. If it were not for the openness to diverse ends that persists throughout, the risks for all concerned would be unbearable: "What has created mankind is narrative" (Pierre Janet; cited in de Certeau 1990:170). There is art when the claim to truth is suspended. The declared suspension of truth prevents the use of lying that is characteristic of politics. We cannot tell lies when we do not claim to tell the truth. That's the game: the explanation and exaggeration characteristic of pedagogy are accompanied by a shift towards shared emotions. To be moved together is a good step towards sharing truths, especially when there are interests involved. There the citizen emerges.

Jaime Ramos is very careful in preferring Spinoza to Kant and Habermas. I totally agree with him when he says that no one is born a citizen: on the contrary, it takes considerable pedagogical effort to turn someone into a citizen. The fear of being led into illusions by philosophical idealism could end up in the carrying over of illusions from the field of pedagogy to that of "structural change." Between the two of them, a contest could be held to choose which is the greatest victim of illusions: the pedagogic reformer or the promoter of great changes. It should be clear to everyone that, at least sometimes, the reformer who takes one step at a time may go further than he who calls for one sweeping transformation in everything. It is a fact that *Cultura Ciudadana* explicitly assumed the mission to change very few things at a time and to do it gradually. This reforming spirit produced enough results to encourage us to persist. The collapse of socialism and Popper's warnings should tell us something about people who try to make too many changes at once. *Chi va piano, va sano e va lontano* (he who takes it slow, will safely go far). The sum of small reforms, agreed upon in good time and properly completed, can produce very respectable results.

How Bogotá Defeated Fear

Jesús Martín-Barbero shows that our management helped to mitigate the fear and chaos the city was experiencing and to go beyond the media's exploitation of that fear. According to the author, our administration contributed to reorienting and re-contextualizing cultural consumption by situating it in part within a pedagogy directed at creating peaceful coexistence and guided by four very precise objectives. Thus, culture could be understood ever more comprehensively, to the point of becoming the object of deliberate action (with some difficulties which, fortunately, have persisted). *Cultura Ciudadana* is seen as a "political culture of belonging and a cultural politics of the everyday," which takes art into the streets to increase people's ability to regulate their own and others' behavior by also increasing their ability to express themselves and understand what others are trying to express. For this, there are two necessary conditions, according to Martin-Barbero: citizen participation and the legitimacy of the teams in charge.

Jesus Martin-Barbero acknowledges that much was done to surprise, question, and improve our ways of expressing and interpreting ourselves. All of these actions challenged people, attracted gazes, got people out of the tunnel, and made it possible to radically alter certain beliefs and habits. Thus a new way of understanding cultural politics was born in Bogotá and became both an effective means of renewing politics and a way of transforming the city.

Javier Sáenz Obregón is the researcher who has devoted most rigor and enthusiasm to reconstructing both our contribution to the Colombian educational movement and our debt to it. He is also the best apologist and the one who harbored and still harbors the most hopes. Furthermore, he remembers at the end, as if it were an inescapable duty, to sow a few seeds of the Foucaultian nettle.

Sáenz rightly shows that the *Cultura Ciudadana* program weakens the extreme separation that exists between school life and daily life. This means that, as never before, extra-curricular knowledge took over the classrooms; but also, the knowledge of the classrooms and the experts took over the city. Bogotá could be seen as a large classroom. This made it possible to develop (partially) some of the ideas of the Pedagogic Movement. The main obstacle was a certain shyness when it came to fully involving the educational institutions in the *Cultura Ciudadana* processes.

Sáenz takes the participation of the Federici Group (formed in 1979) in the Pedagogic Movement in the mid-1980s as the starting point from which to monitor how, over a few years, pedagogy gained considerable ground in Colombia.

The trigger was the Pedagogic Movement's opposition to the curriculum reform that was being proposed at the time, a reform of eight thousand pages. It was supposed to center the educational process on the student, whereas it actually centered it on a curriculum that assimilated education as an industrial process. The Taylorization of the education system, whose application had been prevented in the United States due to the liberal ideals of Dewey, was tried out in Colombia. Either the teachers rethought their classroom practices or the state would do it for them.

In Sáenz's text, pedagogy is a recurring concern arising from the academic context and from the times of the pedagogic movement and establishing itself in the State via the City Hall as a discourse and practice giving shape to the "pedagogization of life in the city" that Sáenz sees as characteristic of my two terms in office.[6] This continuity is based on the conceptualization of pedagogy as a communicative practice and, following Habermas, a practice that should allow us to achieve democratic consensus and reach mutual understanding and free agreements experienced as such: a pedagogy, as Sáenz shows, that should focus (in and out of school) on the ethical-political aspects of democratic coexistence, which may arise from the development of an internal morality and the honest use of language. The dramatic and pedagogic practices that were implemented during my two terms in office, as Sáenz stresses, appealed to the population because they managed to reconcile previously fragmented areas: diversity and community, reason and pleasure, rules and freedom, the public and the private. How long lasting these changes will be is the main question remaining from this experience. What will determine this continuity?

One criticism Sáenz and some of the other commentators have made is that we described popular culture as homogeneous and primarily displayed its flaws and deficiencies, as if it had no redeeming features.

The Bogotá of Paul Bromberg, Rocio Londoño, and Efraín Sánchez

With Paul Bromberg, Rocio Londoño, and Efraín Sánchez *(Engineers and Prophets)*, we gradually built up a fast-reaction quintet. Moreover, in the Escuela Nacional de Minas (National Mining School) in Medellín, a new definition of "engineer" had been coined: "An engineer is someone who does for one peso what anyone else would do for two." I added my own twist to the phrase, in a conversation with Paul

Bromberg: "And a prophet is someone who does for one peso what anyone else would do for ten." Bromberg's humor and lucidity completed the caricature. And from then on he has always addressed me as the prophet.

The team's training in physics, history, and anthropology was useful for achieving a proper balance between the performative and the objectifying attitude.

It is interesting to compare Paul Bromberg's and Rocío Londoño's respective testimonies in their interviews with Carlo Tognato. Paul insists on his cultural engineering, and he is positive that he greatly improved teamwork after my departure in April 1997. Meanwhile, Rocío Londoño and Efraín Sánchez devoted considerable work to the cultural consumption surveys and, above all, to the *Cultura Ciudadana* survey. Rocío was very concerned about treating citizens with the greatest respect, as well as sticking strictly to the Constitution. Those of us who came from Science Faculties were sometimes less sensitive, more direct, and naive (admittedly, people helped us to apologize by accepting our apologies). Efraín Sánchez succeeded in institutionalizing *Cultura Ciudadana* with the national government, which led to the publication of two documents that define indicators and targets in an ambitious planning process intended to culminate in 2019. He is also right to emphasize the freedoms and innovations generated by the presence of a cultural agent in a field like the political one.

Rocío's democratic ideals were put to the test by her attempt to allocate resources for cultural activities in the city in a radically transparent, participatory, and democratic way. Paul was much more interested than Rocío in the subject that attracts Tognato: the academic validation, the systematic evaluation via surveys, the possible predictability of results, and the institutionalization of the *Cultura Ciudadana* program. At the end of the day, Paul is a physicist with a background in the philosophy of science, while Rocío and Efraín are historians, and therefore more accustomed to a posteriori explanations.

Paolo Vignolo and Lucas Ospina: Two Gazes, Two Halves

Paolo Vignolo's article about the administration of the city conceived as festivity suggests an interesting path by which a city could escape the paralysis caused by fear and aggression. Behind his rude, and witty title, Vignolo conceals a playful argument: according to him, my transgressions, more than being a desperate educational resource, respond to the Colombian taste for the festive.[7] The collective action par excellence would thus be the party. According to this argument, public policies (especially those intended to coordinate changes in social rules) need this reproductive, facilitating, and coordinating element for change.

If we are to substitute symbolic violence for physical violence, Vignolo insists, then there must be a framework (legal, cultural, and moral) allowing us to recognize others. In part, this framework is provided by the festive and carnivalesque nature that his text attributes to our administrations. Festivity is based on the transgression of rituals and even norms (in the first person and "putting one's own body at stake") in order to display and explore the functions they fulfill: transgression of everyday practices and discourses in order to return to them and make them stronger, while retaining the reflexive posture made possible by such a transgression or playful interpretation. This is not to deny the ritual but rather to reinterpret it and use it as an exercise for constructing citizenship and legality.

Contrary to what Vignolo argues, I believe that during both my terms in office, citizen participation grew and diversified with the help of the media, involving many more people than in the usual manifestations of social movements. Without an understanding and a practical mastery of the overlap between collective action and interpersonal communication processes, social movements are no longer viable. In our times, neither social movements nor the great advances in citizenship (such as the civil rights movement or tolerance for the LGBT population) can be conceived without the multiplying and catalyzing role of the press and other mass media, which were very important in amplifying the dissemination and pedagogic effects of initiatives such as the mimes and water saving. The desired changes (overcoming urban disorder, more peaceful coexistence among citizens via mutual regulation, a greater sense of belonging, development of citizenship as the capacity for critical and self-critical detachment) all had to be translated into tangible behavioral changes. In this sense, epidemiology instructs on the need to act upon risk factors, especially when we do not know or cannot control the real causes.

Vignolo discovered with some irritation that I never clarified whether I was playing a mischievous game with my office as part of a strategy to position myself politically and symbolically, or whether I was struggling to acquire technical prestige by "doing a good job" so that I could afford to question the office (whether the play served the interests of the game, or the game those of the play). His irritation flatters me. It places both of us back on the "Moebius Strip," adopted as a symbol of my second administration.

In this book, I most enjoyed the articles that, in my opinion, intensified the ambivalence. It may have bothered some analysts that I must have been some kind of *lucky man*.

Vignolo perceives the party and its institutional framework, Lucas Ospina, the omnipresence of levitation and the force of ingenuity. Alejandra Jaramillo has suspicion, which I share. And a list of chivalrous gentlemen express themselves in the tone that this effort deserves: Fabio López de la Roche, Francisco Thoumi, Fabian Sanabria. I admit that the ones who challenged me the most were Carlo Tognato, Doris Sommer, Javier Sáenz Obregón, and Paolo Vignolo; and the ones who made me understand my task best were Doris Sommer, Henry Murraín, Gerry Mackie, Enrique Chaux, Andrea Bustamante, Carlos Augusto Hernández, and Jaime Ramos.

Jon Elster, of whom I am very fond, praises me like no one else, but he also accuses me of inconstancy and regrets the fact that I do not finish many of the tasks that I undertake.

The Colombia of Hernández and His World

Hernández is an unconditional friend and colleague. Of all the people I know, he is the most committed to the real, flesh-and-blood teachers, and also to the utopia we call "general pedagogy." We eagerly imagine a society where everyone learns from everyone virtually all the time. *Only thus will we be able to bear the disenchantment that comes with secularization.*

Enrique Chaux and Andrea Bustamante, based on their research into school violence and civic skills, propose and explore ways to work from within the educational institution to reduce the separation between moral law and culture: specifically, they explore ways of reducing the moral and cultural approval of illegalities and increasing moral and cultural support to legal constraints.

Chaux and Bustamante explore the importance of aligning law, morality, and culture to address some of the worst problems that schools face today such as the high levels of aggression and violence, theft, and cheating. While Saenz highlights the fact that many of the actions carried out during our administrations can be understood as the application of pedagogic ideas directed outside schools and addressed to all the city's inhabitants, Chaux and Bustamante stress the importance of taking these ideas and the same style of intervention into the schools. The authors point out that a change in these behaviors and their social and cultural appraisal in schools might greatly contribute to creating intolerance towards similar harmful behaviors in the whole society (indeed, the chaos in Bogotá included extreme tolerance for dishonest behavior). To weaken the shortcut culture, which encourages violence and corruption, we need to avoid inhibiting moral conflict and the tension between shame and recognition.

Productive Ambiguities

Lyotard and Paolo Vignolo observe that all reflection inevitably bears the trace of the language in which it is carried out. Paolo Vignolo stresses that by using the same word (*juego*) to translate *game* and *play*, we are undeniably sacrificing something. I learned, often at a high personal cost, that if society is to let you play in the playful sense (*play*), it demands that you first play a lot in the competitive sense (*game*). Sometimes we manage an action that is well interpreted and appreciated on both levels (we somehow manage to be creative without losing effectiveness and to be effective without banishing creativity). With some immodesty, I will confess that in the chancellor's office and in City Hall I worked long hours in favor of instrumental rationality (clarification of goals, optimizing the use of resources, monitoring, attention to unwanted effects, planning cycles, execution and control, adjustments in planning, etc.), something one should not too hastily identify with neoliberalism. Using the media properly is an essential requirement for achieving one's objectives.

In the documentary *Bogotá Change*, one of the city councilors, who had been re-elected several times and who usually represented the private education sector, calls me a "neo-anarchist." Another one claimed around 1995 that I embodied a "pedagogic authoritarianism." I do not think we need to go that far. I hope this book will show the reader that in some powerful sense I am a pupil of Jürgen Habermas and Jon Elster, of Doris Sommer and Basil Bernstein. I have also learned a great deal from Guillermo Hoyos and Carlos B. Gutiérrez, from Jon Landaburu and Yvon Lebot, from Jean-Luc Batude and Robert Moussu, from Carlo Federici, Carlos Augusto Hernández, Jorge Charum and José Granés, Berenice Guerrero and María Clemencia Castro, and Juan Camilo Cárdenas and Enrique Chaux. Carlos Vasco taught me a lot during our discussions. And I also learned a great deal as the teammate, teacher, boss, or friend of Maria Isabel Patiño, Liliana Caballero, and Alicia Eugenia Silva. Henry Murraín, Amparo Vega, and Diego Cancino helped me to survive moments of withering pessimism. Cutting ninety pages down to forty-five was a feat on the part of the editor which helped clarify many ideas. With Diego Cancino I discussed many details and some challenges and problems. I also received great support and understanding from Danute Slotkus, Sofia Mantilla, Luz Marina Caicedo, Cielo Montiel, Nancy Carrillo, and Martha Stella Castaño. And of course I've learned from Adriana Córdoba, who came up with the humorous idea of getting married in the circus nineteen years ago. I was honored to take the idea seriously. I keep learning from her. We feel very close when the same human action makes us vibrate together with either admiration or disgust.

Innovations Disturb

When it comes to transforming nature, we often achieve completely repeatable models. That is the yardstick by which such inventions are measured. When it comes to transforming communities and relationships between people, or habits and beliefs, repeatability is more difficult to achieve. Of course, there are replicable social innovations (the multilateral agencies are always chasing after those). And there are innovations that depend on narratives (part of their strength comes from their originality, their ability to attract attention and create surprise). In extreme cases they work only once, though sometimes a single innovation can open out into multiple related options. There are also innovations that are clearly tied to certain personal traits of those who invent or promote them (in pedagogy, see Montessori, Freinet, Neil, Freire, Illich). And any innovation can depend on implicit assumptions sometimes tied to one person.

Innovations demand assimilation. This includes giving oneself some explanations but also experiencing some kind of feelings. Sometimes it also involves evaluations from the viewpoint of the various interests involved.

An innovation that has not been understood or explored is a scandal for countries with a developed university system (especially the North American one). We might say, with some exaggeration, that not understanding a technological innovation—whether hard or soft—properly and in good time can become a source of vulnerability for humanity (and most of all for a society as overwhelmed by its global responsibilities as North American society is).

From this point of view, it is crucial for the North American university system to reduce the new to what is already known as much as possible and to limit as much as possible whatever (if anything) is original about the innovation. Here's an example: appreciative communication has been received at Harvard only as an interview technique, although elsewhere (as Peter Lang has remarked) it is a comprehensive approach for transforming communities, businesses, and institutions.

Various Fears

Confessing fears sometimes means exorcizing risks. Wars can greatly delay processes of spontaneous cultural change. In Colombia the dozen years (1948-1960) of war between godless liberals and ultra-religious conservatives hindered the transition to a more clearly materialistic and hedonistic society.

North American hedonism and Latin American Catholicism should be given a chance to become acquainted and build alliances. They are undoubtedly very complementary. We Latin Americans are constructing our own asceticism. Indeed, without pleasures and especially without the pleasures that come with admiration, coexistence can become a sad life; rationality and individualism can form an oppressive iron cage (Max Weber's "iron cage").

To sum up, this essay, especially the part about Doris Sommer, manages to suggest the possible construction of a healthy life, an attempted synthesis between hedonism and pragmatism.

Bogotá was ugly. We found Bogotá ugly. We said so hundreds of times. In 1996 we asked the graphic designer Marta Granados to redesign the citizen's card to include the motto "Bogotá Flirts." She intensified the *pop* aesthetics already present in the two previous versions, which were distributed in 1995. Our playful thesis was that all of us were acquainted with ugly men or women who were very attractive and who were attractive because of their behavior. So it was our job to make Bogotá an attractive city and to position it in the world for its behavior, not (or not yet) for its infrastructure. If you cannot change your *hardware*, maybe you can improve your *software*. This is a clear invitation to play.

The *Cultura Ciudadana* survey has been applied more than sixty times and has enabled comparisons between different cities and between different periods for the same city. Bogotá and Medellín are the cities where the most numerous, most frequent, and most fully-analyzed measurements were carried out. The most important role of surveys is to contribute in constructing a common language, sharing representations that facilitate the identification of priorities, and building an agenda of actions.

For more than ten years, in Corpovisionarios, Henry Murraín has been promoting and following up the implementation of the *Cultura Ciudadana* surveys. They have been applied in approximately fifty cities. In more than half the cases involved, the diagnosis has given rise to a plan of action following up on a process of prioritizing problems or proposals for action derived from the diagnosis (a process usually carried out hand in hand with the communities).

Murraín has participated very actively in the creation of options for action. The anti-jealousy help-line in Barranca, or the pilot actions with shopkeepers and taxi drivers in Barranquilla, bear his mark. Art has become a word used frequently, and in this context we can use it to name what we do when we play, when we play so tenaciously, madly, and rashly that it is no longer just a game, but cultural agency.

Forgotten

The central concern of the editor, Carlo Tognato and the authors of this book is to draw the lessons to be derived from a period rich in innovations, which took place in politics and public administration in Bogotá between 1994 and 2003, a period whose echoes could be clearly heard in the *Ola Verde* (Green Wave) during the June 2010 presidential election process in which I was defeated in the second round by Juan Manuel Santos.

This book aims to satisfy the academic interest in the period and provide the key tools for others to appropriate what we, from very early on in the process, intended to keep a record of: the pedagogic balance of our actions, which should include understanding the academic foundations of our "rashness." Indeed, for us it was clear that this rashness, unless it is explained and understood in its genesis and effects, would lose its relevance and become a more or less arbitrary sequence of witticisms and humorous gestures.

Multiple Bets

When I fail as a cultural agent or as a politician, the unborn philosopher I still carry inside me gets a breath of fresh air and, undoubtedly, rejoices. But I must also admit that being able to move and modify culture—albeit in very limited ways—produces an unparalleled pedagogical pleasure; and to do this by borrowing elements from art can generate even greater satisfaction. Here too we have a festive gathering of images and other forms of representation, not to mention the happiness I feel when philosophy and cultural agency display political effectiveness, and this effectiveness makes it possible to solve pressing problems. There is something Faustian in all of this, which I would like to understand and discuss. I am not the only artist around. I want to share with many people the transformation of politics into art and the transformation of the political actor into a cultural agent. I am both happy and scared that we can go around inventing rituals, as if rites could just be pulled out of a hat. How rash! Sometimes I tell my colleagues (or I feel like telling them): be careful, we are walking in a minefield; or, one day we will be struck by lightning; don't be surprised when that happens. An overly instrumental vocabulary may be unnecessarily irritating.

It is important to somehow overcome the problem of claiming to make art (it is the art critic's job, or rather the cultural agent's, to recognize when a work is a work of art). With Marcel Duchamp, art becomes what the artist offers as art and what is eventually accepted as such. As with Duchamp's urinal, my mooning which had no artistic intention, had the good fortune of being read as art after being filmed (again without premeditation).

One can imagine a possible world where only involuntary art exists. Involuntary art is sub-art, art which makes no claim to be art, art without an author, art acknowledged only by third parties.

Endnotes

1   Basil Bernstein was Karl Mannheim Professor at London University, and chair of the Research Department in Sociology.

2   He had been a mathematical logics professor for many years and former mayor of Medellín. Today, as governor of Antioquia, he is developing the program "Antioquia, the Best-educated Department in Colombia."

3   I clearly remember that this separation between CC and GPA, and the name "remarkable public management," were proposed (and accepted) by Liliana Caballero and Gustavo Mutis in the workshop carried out at the beginning of 2001 with the whole team in order to construct the Development Plan.

4   See the Corpovisionarios *Cultura Ciudadana* surveys, as well as Murraín's admirably rigorous and Cartesian essay in this volume.

5   Augusto Boal, with his legislative theater, succeeded in getting fourteen ordinances constructed in this way and approved in his State Assembly.

6   The suspicion that this is a sophisticated variation of social control based on recognizing the freedoms of those who are controlled is not fair because the Colombian State is far from being able to ensure such control. Such is its precariousness, on the contrary, that several decades will have to pass before people will be able to legitimately question its apparatuses of discipline and control. In the end, the detailed curriculum was not implemented. The law on education recognized the autonomy of the collective educator (the teaching staff of each school is responsible for the preparation of the corresponding PEI–Institutional Educational Project), and very diverse audiences were able to learn about the pedagogical perspective that had twice governed the city. Part of the task is to understand that there are no miracles and that setbacks should be studied and corrected; we did not discover a panacea, but we did discover that culture is transformable.

7   The title of the Spanish version of the essay is "¿Cara o Culo? Antanas Mockus entre norma y transgresión."

References

Archier, G. and H. Sérieyx. 1984. *L'entreprise du troisième type* [The Third Type of Enterprise]. Paris: Editions du Seuil.

Arendt, Hannah. 1993. *La condición humana* [The Human Condition]. Barcelona: Paidós.

———. 2003. Conferencias sobre la filosofía política de Kant [Lectures of Kant's Political Philosophy]. Barcelona: Paidós.

Baruk, Stella. 1977. *Échec et maths* [Failure and Maths]. Paris: Editions du Seuil.

Bernstein, Basil. 1971-1990. *Class, Codes & Control.* Vol. 1-7. London: Routledge and Kegan Paul.

———. 1984. "Códigos, Modalidades y el Proceso de Reproducción Cultural: Un Modelo" [Codes, Modalities, and the Process of Cultural Reproduction: A Model]. In *Lenguaje y Sociedad* [Language and Society]. Santiago de Cali: Universidad del Valle, Center for Translations.

———. 1996. *Pedagogy, Symbolic Control and Identity: Theory, Research, Critique.* London: Taylor & Francis.

Bourdieu, Pierre and Jean-Claude Passeron. 1970. *La reproduction* [Reproduction]. Paris: Minuit.

Carrillo F., Clara. 1991. "La interacción en la reconstrucción de legalidad y moralidad" [The Interaction in the Reconstruction of Legality and Morality]. Honors Thesis, Department of Philosophy, Universidad Nacional de Colombia, Bogotá.

De Certeau, Michel. [1980] 1990. "L'invention du quotidian" Vol. 1. *Arts de faire* [The Practice of Everyday Life]. Paris: Gallimard.

Elster, Jon. 2009. *Reason and Rationality.* Translated by Steven Rendall. Princeton: Princeton University Press.

Federici, Carlo, et al. 1985. "Limites du Scientisme en éducation" [The Limits of Scientism in Education]. *Fundamenta Scientiae* 6 (3):221-245.

Fisher, Roger and William Ury. 1983. *Getting to Yes: Negotiating Agreement Without Giving In.* New York: Penguin Books.

Habermas, Jürgen. 1970. "La técnica y la ciencia como ideología" [Technique and Science as Ideology]. *ECO Revista de Occidente* [Echo: Journal of the West] 127:9-50.

———. 1987. *Teoría de la acción comunicativa* [The Theory of Communicative Action]. Vol. 1-2. Madrid: Taurus.

———. 1989. *Teoría de la acción comunicativa: complementos y estudios previos* [The Theory of Communicative Action: Complements and prior studies]. Madrid: Cátedra.

————. 1993. *El discurso filosófico de la Modernidad. Doce lecciones.* [The Philosophical Discourse of Modernity. Twelve Lectures]. Madrid: Taurus.

Mackie, Gerry. 1996. "Ending Footbinding and Infibulation: A Convention Account." *American Sociological Review* 61(6): 999-1017.

Milgram, Stanley. 1974. *Obedience to Authority: An Experimental View.* London: Tavistock Publications.

Mockus, Antanas. 1994a. "Anfibios culturales y divorcio entre ley, moral y cultura" [Cultural Amphibians and Divorce Between Law, Morals, and Culture]. *Análisis Político* [Political Analysis] (21):37-48.

————. 1994b. "Anfibios culturales, moral y productividad" [Cultural Amphibians, Morals, and Productivity]. *Revista Colombiana de Psicología* [Colombian Journal of Psychology] (3):125-135.

Rorty, Richard. 1980. *Philosophy and the Mirror of Nature.* Oxford: Basil Blackwell.

Sáenz Obregón, Javier. 2011. "La pedagogía ciudadana en Bogotá: ¿un proyecto autoritario o el mínimo común necesario para la construcción de una democracia radical?" [Civic Pedagogy in Bogotá: An Authoritarian Project or the Common Minimum Necessary for the Construction of a Radical Democracy?] *Revista Educación y Pedagogía* [Education and Pedagogy] 23 (60):137-145.

Sommer, Doris, ed. 2006. *Cultural Agency in the Americas.* Durham and London: Duke University Press.

————. 2014. *The Work of Art in the World.* Durham and London: Duke University Press.

Shklovsky, Viktor. 2004. "Arts as Technique." Pp. 15-21 in *Literary Theory: An Anthology*, edited by Julie Rivkin and Michael Ryan. Malden: Blackwell Pub.

Tognato, Carlo, ed. 2017. *Cultural Agents RELOADED: The Legacy of Antanas Mockus.* Cambridge, Mass.: The Cultural Agents Initiative at Harvard University.

Tomkins, Calvin. 1999. *Duchamp.* Translated by Mónica Martín Berdagué. Barcelona: Anagrama.

Contributors

Paul Bromberg is Assistant Professor at the Institute for Urban Studies of the National University of Colombia, Bogotá. He holds an MSc. in Interdisciplinary Studies–Physics, Biology and History of Science at the University of British Columbia, Vancouver. His research focuses on urban governance, political systems, and *Cultura Ciudadana* (Civic Culture). His publications include: "Ingenieros y profetas, transformaciones dirigidas de comportamientos colectivos" (Engineers and Prophets, Transformations Directed by Collective Behaviors) in *Reflexiones sobre cultura ciudadana en Bogotá* (2003 Reflections on Civic Culture in Bogotá), "¿Qué fue y qué será la *Cultura Ciudadana?*" (2010 What Was and What Will Become of Civic Culture?), and "¿*Cultura Ciudadana* y los retos del gobierno urbano, o el gobierno urbano y los retos de la *Cultura Ciudadana?*" (2010 Civic Culture and the Challenges of Urban Government, or Urban Government and the Challenges of Civic Culture?).

Andrea Bustamante is currently a doctoral candidate in Education at the University of Missouri, Saint Louis. She has an MA in Psychology and a BA in Political Science from the University of the Andes in Bogotá, Colombia. She participated in the design, evaluation, and implementation of the *Aulas en Paz* (Classrooms in Peace) program. In 2008, she received an official recognition by the Colombian Congress for her contributions as a young researcher to the study of corruption prevention. Her publications include: "Aulas en Paz: estrategias pedagógicas" (2008), "Using Research to Set Priorities for Character Education in Schools: A Global Perspective" (2013), and "Reducing Moral Disengagement Mechanisms: A Comparison of Two Interventions" (2014).

Enrique Chaux is Full Professor at the Department of Psychology of the University of the Andes, Bogotá. He holds a doctorate in Education from Harvard University. His main interests include the prevention of aggression, school violence, citizenship competencies, conflicts, bullying, peace education, and humane education. He led the teams that created the Colombian National Standards of Citizenship Competencies, the National Test of Citizenship Competencies, and the school-based program *Aulas en Paz* (Classrooms in Peace). His publications include *Educación, Convivencia y Agresión Escolar* (2010 Education, Peaceful Relationships, and Aggression in Schools), *Competencias Ciudadanas: De los Estándares al Aula* (2004 Citizenship Competencies: From Standards to the Classroom), *Citizenship Competencies in the Midst of a Violent Political Conflict: The Colombian Educational Response* (2009), *Classrooms in Peace within violent contexts: Field evaluation of Aulas en Paz in Colombia* (2015), *Homophobic attitudes and associated factors among adolescents: A comparison of six Latin-American countries* (2016), *Money and age in schools: Bullying and power imbalances* (2015).

Jon Elster is Chair of Rationality and Social Sciences at the Collège de France, Paris. He has a PhD in Philosophy from the University of Paris. He has also taught at Columbia University and the Universities of Oslo and Chicago. His research focuses on the theory of rational choice, the theory of distributional justice, and the history of social thought. His publications include: *Ulysses and the Sirens* (1979), *Sour Grapes* (1983), *Making Sense of Marx* (1985), *The Cement of Society* (1989), *Solomonic Judgements* (1989), *Nuts and Bolts for the Social Sciences* (1989), *Local Justice* (1992), and *Political Psychology* (1993).

José Luis Falconi is the artistic director of *Art Life Laboratory (artlifelaboratory.com)* and Visiting Professor of Latin American Art History at Brandeis University. Until July 2017, he was a fellow at the Department of History of Art and Architecture at Harvard University where he also received his PhD in Romance Languages and Literatures in 2010. In Latin America, he has taught at the Universidad Nacional de Colombia (Bogotá, Colombia), at the Universidad de Chile (Santiago, Chile), at the Universidad San Carlos (Guatemala City, Guatemala) and at the Universidad de Costa Rica (San José, Costa Rica). His publications include: *The Other Latinos* (2008), *Portraits of an Invisible Country: The Photographs of Jorge Mario Múnera* (2012), *A Singular Plurality: The Works of Dario Escobar* (2013), *The Great Swindle* (2014) and *Ad Usum, To Be Used: The Work of Pedro Reyes* (2017).

Fonna Forman is Associate Professor of Political Science at the University of California, San Diego (UCSD), Director of the UCSD Center on Global Justice and Co-Director of the UCSD Cross-Border Initiative. She is a political theorist best known for her revisionist work on Adam Smith, recuperating the ethical, spatial and public dimensions of his political economy. Current work focuses on climate justice in cities, on human rights at the urban scale, and civic participation as a strategy of equitable urbanization. Her publications include: *Adam Smith and the Circles of Sympathy* (2010), Amartya Sen and the Idea of Justice (2013), and with Teddy Cruz, *Informal Market Worlds* (2015); "Latin America and a New Political Leadership: Experimental Acts of Co-Existence" (2017) and "Global Justice at the Municipal Scale: the Case of Medellín, Colombia" (2017).

Marsha Henry is Associate Professor at the London School of Economics Gender Institute and Co-Director of the MPhil/PhD Programme in Gender. She has a PhD in Women and Gender Studies from Warwick University. Her research interests focus on three main areas: gender and development, gender and militarization, and qualitative methodologies. Her publications include: "Gender, Security and Development" (2007), *Insecure Spaces: Peacekeeping, Power and Performance in Haiti, Liberia and Kosovo* (2009), "Peacexploitation? Interrogating Labor Hierarchies and Global Sisterhood Among Indian and Uruguayan Female Peacekeepers" (2012), "Rethinking Masculinity in Conflict and Postconflict Settings" (2012), and *The Sage Handbook of Feminist Theory* (2014).

Carlos Augusto Hernández is Associate Professor at the Department of Physics of the National University of Colombia, Bogotá. He was Academic Vice-Chancellor of the same university between 1992 and 1995. He earned a PhD in Education from the inter-institutional program run by the National Pedagogic University, the Universitdad del Valle, and the District University. His research interests focus on higher education as well as on the history and teaching of sciences. He was a member of the Federici Group. His publications include: *Cultura, artes y humanidades* (2003 Culture, Arts, and the Humanities), *The National Accreditation System in Colombia* (2003), *Galileo: el arte de la ciencia* (2004 Galileo, the Art of Science), *Navegaciones* (2005 Navigations), and *Seis temas centrales asociados a las condiciones básicas de calidad de instituciones y programas de educación superior* (2013 Six Central Themes Associated with the Basic Quality of Institutions and Programs of Superior Education).

Alexandra Jaramillo is Associate Professor and Director of the Literature Department at the National University of Colombia, Bogotá. She has a PhD in Latin American Literature and Cinema from Tulane University. Her research focuses on new decolonial readings of Latin American literature as well as on the cultural studies of urban cultures. Her publications include: *Bogotá Imaginada: narraciones urbanas, cultura y política* (2003 Bogotá Imagined: Urban Narratives, Culture, and Politics), the biographical novel *Manuelita Sáenz. La dama de la libertad* (2005 Manuelita Sáenz. The lady of Liberty), and novels *La ciudad sitiada* (2006 The Besieged City), *Nación y melancolía: narrativas de la violencia en Colombia, 1995-2005* (2006 Nation and Melancholy: Narratives of Violence in Colombia, 1995-2005), and *Mandala* (2014).

Rocío Londoño Botero recently retired from her position as Professor at the Department of Sociology of the National University of Colombia, Bogotá, where she inspired generations of undergraduate and graduate students in her courses on urban sociology. Trained in sociology and with a PhD in history from the National University of Colombia, she is currently coordinating a research project for the *Centro Nacional de Memoria Histórica* (National Center for Historical Memory) about "Lands, Social Organization, and Territory" in conflict zones within Colombia. Her publications include: *Sindicalismo y política* (1986 Syndicalism and Politics), *La ciudad de Dios en Bogotá* (1994 The City of God in Bogotá), *República Liberal: Sociedad y cultura* (2009 Liberal Republic: Society and Culture), *Juan de la Cruz Varela. Sociedad y política en la región de Sumapaz, 1902-1984* (2010 Juan de la Cruz Varela. Society and Politics in the Sumapaz Region, 1902-1984), *Perfiles de los docentes del sector público de Bogotá (2011 Profiles of Public Sector Teachers in Bogotá)*, and *La restauración Conservadora, 1946-1957* (2012 The Conservative Restauration 1946-1957).

Fabio López de la Roche is Associate Professor and Director of the Institute of Political Studies and International Relations (IEPRI) at the National University of Colombia, Bogotá. He has a PhD in Hispanic Languages and Literatures from the University of Pittsburgh. His research interests focus on the critical analysis of media and social communication. His publications include: *Museo, memoria y nación* (2000 Museum, Memory, and Nation), "Historia colombiana reciente, memoria personal y claves identitarias en La Virgen de los Sicarios de Fernando Vallejo" (2007 Recent Colombian History, Personal Memory, and Identity Codes in The Virgin of the Sicarios by Fernando Vallejo), "Discurso presidencial y noticieros de T.V.

La reorientación afectiva de nación" (2010 Presidential Speech and TV News. The Affective Reorientation of the Nation), "Historia de los noticieros de televisión en Colombia y la construcción de una memoria crítica de la sociedad y del oficio del periodismo" (2010 History of Television News in Colombia and the Construction of a Critical Memory of Society and the Journalism Profession), and *Las ficciones del poder: patriotismo, medios de comunicación y reorientación afectiva de los colombianos bajo Uribe Vélez, 2002-2010* (2014 Fictions of Power: Patriotism, Media, and Affective Reorientation of Colombians Under Uribe Vélez, 2002- 2010).

Gerry Mackie is Associate Professor of Political Science and Co-Director of the Center on Global Justice at the University of California, San Diego. In mid-life, he obtained a Ph.D. (U. Chicago) in social and political theory; and has researched or taught at Oxford, ANU, Notre Dame, Princeton, and UCSD. He works on democratic theory; his book, *Democracy Defended,* won the Kamerer Prize from APSA in 2003. Since 1996 he has worked on ending harmful social practices; his ideas on social norms combined with the NGO Tostan's practice of human rights education became the common approach adopted by UN and national development agencies in 2007. Since 2004 he has worked on harmful practices more generally with UNICEF, the NGO Corpovisionarios in Colombia, and more recently with UK DFID. His most recent books (with coauthors) are *Advancing Transformative Human Rights Education* (Open Book Publishers, 2016) and *Values Deliberations and Collective Action: Community Empowerment in Rural Senegal* (Palgrave Macmillan 2017).

Jesús Martín-Barbero is currently Associate Research Fellow at the Center for Social Studies of the National University of Colombia, Bogotá. Before retiring he was Director of the Department of Communication Studies at the Universidad del Valle Cali between 1975 and 1995, and then he taught at the Western Institute of Technology and Higher Education, Guadalajara between 1999 and 2003. He has a PhD in Philosophy from Louvain University. He has been President of Latin American Association of Communication Researchers (ALAIC). Throughout many decades his research has focused on the cultural reception of media communication. His publications include: *De los medios a las mediaciones* (1987 From Media to Mediation), *Comunicación y culturas populares en Latinoamérica* (1987 Communication and Popular Culture in Latin America), *Televisión y melodrama* (1987 Television and Melodrama), *Communication, Culture and Hegemony* (1993), *Pre-textos: conversaciones sobre la comunicación y sus contextos* (1995 Pre-texts: Conversations on Communication and its Contexts), *Proyectar la comunicación* (1997 Projecting Communication), *Mapas nocturnos* (1998 Nocturnal Maps), *Medios, Cultura y Sociedad* (1998 Media, Culture, and Society), y *Los ejercicios del ver. Hegemonía audiovisual y ficción televisiva* (2000 Exercises in Seeing. Audiovisual Hegemony and Televised Fiction).

Antanas Mockus is President of Corpovisionarios. He was Associate Professor in the Department of Mathematics and Chancellor of the National University of Colombia, Bogotá before serving as mayor of Bogotá for two terms. He has an MA in Philosophy from the same university, an MSc. in Mathematics from the University of Dijon, and a PhD Honoris Causa from the University of Paris VIII. He was a member and then director of the Federici Group at the National University of Colombia. He has run as a presidential candidate in Colombia three times. Over the years his work has focused on peaceful coexistence and systematic norm transgression. His publications include: *Representar y disponer: un estudio de la noción de representación orientando hacia el examen de su papel en la comprensión previa del ser como disponibilidad* (1988 Representation and availability: A study examining the notion of representation and its role in the previous understanding of the being as available), "Anfibios culturales y divorcio entre ley, moral y cultura" (1994 Cultural Amphibians and the Divorce Between Law, Morals, and Culture), *Las fronteras de la escuela: articulaciones entre conocimiento escolar y conocimiento extraescolar* (1995 The Borders of School: Articulations Between Scholarly Knowledge and Extra-Scholarly Knowledge), and "Convivencia como armonización de ley, moral y cultura" (Coexistence as Harmonization of Law, Morals, and Culture).

Henry Murraín is currently Executive Director of Corpovisionarios and a student in the Doctoral Program in Human and Social Sciences at the National University of Colombia, Bogotá. His research focuses on the emergence of social norms and on the effects of culture on transgression. His publications include: "A importância de uma agenda pedagógica na Administração Pública" (2007 The Importance of a Pedagogical Agenda in Public Administration), "*Cultura Ciudadana* como política pública: Entre indicadores y arte" (2009 Civic Culture as Public Policy: Between Indicators and Art), and *Antípodas de la violencia: Desafíos de cultura ciudadana para la crisis de (in)seguridad en América Latina* (2012 Antitheses to Violence: Challenges of Citizen Culture for the Crisis of (in)Security in Latin America).

Lucas Ospina is Associate Professor in the Arts Department of the University of the Andes, Bogotá. He has an MFA in Sculpture from Temple University. His exhibits include: *In The Poem About Love You Don't Write the Word Love* (Copenhagen, 2007), *September Show* (Berlin, 2008), *Luleå Art Biennale* (Luleå, 2009), *You Are Insatiable* (Berlin 2009), *The Enlightened / Die Aufgeklärten / Los Ilustrados* (Berlin, 2010), *Esta es la cosa nostra* (Bogotá, 2012 The Ages), and *La imaginada y el seudorretórico* (Cali, 2013 The Imagined and the Pseudo Rhetoric). He also curated *Poesía Museo Filosofía + Arte Degenerado* (Bogotá, 2008 Poetry Museum Philosophy + Degenerate Art), *Malicia Indígena* (Bogotá, 2011 Indian Malice), *Las Edades* (Bogotá, 2012), *Roda: dibujo de un maestro* (Bogotá, 2012 Roda: Sketch of a master). He publishes a monthly column in *Arcadia Magazine*, participates in esferapublica.org and has a blog at lasillavacia.com.

Jaime Ramos is Associate Professor in the Philosophy Department of the National University of Colombia, Bogotá. As a Fulbright Fellow, he earned his PhD in Philosophy at the State University of New York in Buffalo. In 1994, the Colombian "Mission on Science, Education and Development" (formed by ten leading intellectuals, among them, Garcia Marquez and Rodolfo Llinás) commissioned him to write a report on the possible impact of cognitive science on science and education in Colombia. His research interests focus mainly on the philosophy of the mind. After his coedited book *Mentes reales. La ciencia cognitiva y la naturalización de la mente* (2000 Real Minds. Cognitive Science and the Naturalization of the Mind), he has moved away from the dominant Anglo-American paradigm in philosophy, adopting instead a historical and social approach to the understanding of meaning and thought, mainly under the influence of Wittgenstein and Vygotsky. He is now working on a book on the ontology of the social realm.

Javier Sáenz Obregón is Professor at the Department of Sociology and at the Center for Social Studies of the National University of Colombia, Bogotá. He holds a PhD in History and Philosophy of Education from the University of London. As a founding member of the research group on the History of Pedagogical Practices in Colombia, he has published both in Colombia and internationally on the history of pedagogical practices; the relations between pedagogy, philosophy and the human sciences; the pedagogy of John Dewey and Antanas Mockus; the history of childhood and adolescence; historical and contemporary practices of the self; the birth of the "social," and educational and cultural public policy. He also directs a research group on government, subjectivity, and practices of the self. His publications include: *Desconfianza, civilidad y estética: las prácticas formativas estatales por fuera de la escuela en Bogotá, 1994-2003* (2007 Distrust, Civility, and Aesthetics: The State's Out-Of-School Formative Practices in Bogotá, 1994-2003), *Cultura ciudadana y pedagogización de la práctica estatal* (2004 Civic Culture and the Pedagogization of State Practice), and *Mirar la infancia. Pedagogía, moral y modernidad en Colombia: 1903-1946* (1997 Looking at Childhood. Pedagogy, Morals, and Modernity in Colombia: 1903-1946).

Andrés Salcedo is Associate Professor and Director of the Department of Anthropology as well as Research Fellow at the Center for Social Studies at the National University of Colombia, Bogotá. He has a PhD in Anthropology from the University of California, Irvine. His research focuses on forced displacement, internal migration, conflict, and memory. His publications include: Víctimas y trasegares: forjadores de ciudad en Colombia 2002-2005 (2015 Victims and life paths: city builders in Colombia 2002-2005). "Faces da ilegalidade em Bogotá" (2010 Faces of Illegality in Bogota), "Estado y desplazamiento: cartografías históricas de guerra, multiculturalismo y humanitarismo" (2011 State and Displacement: Historical Maps of War, Multiculturalism, and Humanitarianism), *Fricciones sociales en ciudades contemporáneas* (2012 Social Frictions in Contemporary Cities), and "La lucha de los cedros. Reclamo por territorios desde la ciudad" (2012 The struggle of the cedars. Claim for territories from the city).

Fabián Sanabria is Associate Professor in the Department of Sociology and a Research Fellow at the Center for Social Studies-CES at the National University of Colombia, Bogotá. He has a PhD in Sociology from the School for Advanced Studies in the Social Sciences (EHESS), Paris. He has served as General Director of the Colombian Institute of Anthropology and History (ICANH) and Dean of the Faculty of Human Sciences at the National University of Colombia. He currently directs the Research Group on Contemporary Subjectivities and Beliefs (GESCCO). His research focuses on the anthropology and sociology of beliefs, though more recently he has turned to literary fiction. His publications include: *La Virgen se sigue apareciendo. Un estudio antropológico* (2004 The Virgin Keeps Appearing. An Anthropological Study), *Antropologías del creer y creencias antropológicas* (2006 Anthropologies of Belief and Anthropological Beliefs), *Ficciones Contemporáneas*

(2009 Contemporary Fictions), *Tiempos para Planchar* (2011 Times for Ironing), and *Vínculos Virtuales* (2011 Virtual Links).

Efraín Sánchez was Associate Professor of History and Sociology of Arts at the National University of Colombia, Bogotá, served in the Colombian diplomatic service, and was the Director of the Bogotá Observatory of Urban Culture. He holds a PhD in Modern Latin American History from the University of Oxford. His research focuses on cultural history, citizenship, and cultural change. His publications include: *Ramón Torres Méndez, Pintor de la Nueva Granada* (1987 Ramón Torres Méndez, Painter from New Granada), *Tipos y Costumbres de la Nueva Granada* (1989 Emblems and Customs of New Granada), *Santander y los ingleses* (1991 Santander and the English), *Gobierno y Geografía, Agustín Codazzi y la Comisión Corográfica de la Nueva Granada* (1999 Government and Geography, Agustín Codazzi and the Chorographic Commission of New Granada), and *El Mundo del Arte en San Agustín* (2011 The World of Art in San Agustín).

Doris Sommer is Ira Jewell Williams, Jr. Professor of Romance Languages and Literatures, Director of Graduate Studies in Spanish, and founder of Cultural Agents, Inc. Her interests include: nineteenth-century narrative in Latin American women's literature, ethnic literature, and bilingual aesthetics. Her publications include: *Foundational Fictions: The National Romances of Latin America* (1993), *Proceed with Caution, When Engaged by Minority Writing in the Americas* (1999), *Bilingual Aesthetics: A New Sentimental Education* (2004), *Bilingual Games: Some Literary Investigations* (2004), *Cultural Agency in the Americas* (2005), and *The Work of Art in the World: Civic Agency and Public Humanities* (2014).

Francisco Thoumi is currently a member of the International Narcotics Control Board and of the Friedrich Ebert Foundation Observatory of Organized Crime in Latin America and the Caribbean. Until 2014, he was a member of the World Economic Forum's Global Agenda Council on Organized Crime. He was Professor at the University of Texas at Austin, Rosario University at Bogotá, and California State University at Chico. Before that he worked for fifteen years in the research departments of the World Bank and the Inter-American Development Bank. He has a PhD in Economics from the University of Minnesota. His research interests focus on illegal drugs. His publications include: *Political Economy and Illegal Drugs* *in Colombia* (1995), *Illegal Drugs, Economy and Society in the Andes* (2003), "The Colombian Competitive Advantage in Illegal Drugs: The Role of Policies and Institutional Changes" (2005), "The Number Game: Let's All Guess the Size of the Illegal Drug Industry!" (2005), *Vulnerable Societies: Why Antidrug Policies Fail*, and *Why There is a Need for Reforms and Why They are Unlikely to be Implemented* (2012).

Carlo Tognato is Associate Professor at the Department of Sociology and Director of the Center for Social Studies at the National University of Colombia, Bogotá, as well as Director of the Nicanor Restrepo Santamaría Center for Civil Reconstruction. He is also Faculty Fellow at the Center for Cultural Sociology at Yale University. He holds a PhD in Political Science from the University of California, Los Angeles. His research mainly focuses on the study of culture in economic and democratic life. He is author of *Central Bank Independence: Cultural Codes and Symbolic Performance* (Palgrave-Macmillan, 2012), and he has edited a forthcoming book with Jeffrey Alexander (*The Civil Sphere in Latin America*, Cambridge University Press).

Paolo Vignolo is Associate Professor in the Department of History and Research Fellow at the Center for Social Studies of the National University of Colombia, Bogotá. He has a PhD in History of Civilizations at the School for Advanced Studies in the Social Sciences (EHESS), Paris. His research interests focus on the exploration of inverted worlds such as the antipodes, carnivals, and revolutions from the Middle Ages to our time. His publications include: "Nuevo Mundo: ¿un mundo al revés? Las antípodas en el imaginario del Renacimiento" (2003 The New World: A World Upside Down? Antipodes in the Imaginary of the Renaissance), "Santa María de la Antigua del Darién, ¿de lugar del olvido a lugar de la memoria?" (2008 Santa María de la Antigua del Darién, from Place of Oblivion to Place of Memory?), *Cannibali, giganti e selvaggi: creature mostruose del Nuovo Mondo* (2009 Cannibals, Giants and, the Wild: Monstrous Creatures of the New World), *Ciudadanias en Escena* (2009 Citizenship on Stage), "Carnaval, Ciudadanía y Mestizaje en Colombia" (2010 Carnaval, Citizenship, and Miscegenation in Colombia), and *Tierra firme. El Darien en el imaginario de los conquistadores* (2011 Mainland. The Darien in the Imaginary of the Conquerors).

Marta Zambrano is Associate professor in the Department of Anthropology and the Cultural Studies Program at Universidad Nacional de Colombia, Bogota. She has a PhD in Anthropology from the University of Illinois at Urbana Champaign.

Her research interests focus on historical anthropology; memory, history and writing; gender, identities, and multiculturalism. Her publications include: "From *blanqueamiento* to *reindigenización*: paradoxes of *mestizaje* and multiculturalism in contemporary Colombia" (2006), *Trabajadores, villanos y amantes: encuentros entre indígenas y españoles en la ciudad letrada. Santa Fe de Bogotá* (1550-1650) (2008, Workers, Rogues, and Lovers: Encounters between Indians and Spaniards in the Lettered City. Santa Fe de Bogotá (1550-1650), "Entre a reivindicaçao e a exotizaçao: mobilidad etnica, agentes estatais e políticas multiculturais na Colômbia" (2010, Between Vindication and Exotization: Ethnic Mobility, State Agents and Multicultural Policies in Colombia), "Ilegitimidad, cruce de sangres y desigualdad: dilemas del porvenir en Santa Fe colonial" (2011, Illegitimacy, Mixed Blood, and Inequality: The Future as a Dilemma in Colonial Santa Fe), *El valor del patrimonio: mercado, políticas culturales y agenciamientos sociales* (2014, The Value of Heritage: Commodification, Cultural Policies, and Social Agencies).

Image Credits

Cover: Photo: Marcelo Salinas

Back Cover: Photo: Jorge Mario Múnera.

Figure 1: Mockus characterizing Lincoln, 2013. Photo: Alberto Newton. Model: Catalina Londoño. Courtesy of *Publicaciones Semana* / SoHo Magazine.

Figure 2: Antanas Mockus's ID.

Figure 3: Top detail, (*"Everyone Contributes, Everyone Benefits"*), 2014. Courtesy of Futuro Moncada.

Figure 4: Top, 1996. Courtesy of *El Espectador.*

Figure 5: Top and Package, 2014. Courtesy of Futuro Moncada.

Figure 6: Top, 1994. Courtesy of *El Espectador.*

Figure 7: Mimes, 1995. Photo: Eduardo Sotomayor. Courtesy of the Mayor's Office of Bogotá, Secretary General, Central Archive, Photo Archive.

Figure 8: Mimes, 1995. Photo: Leonardo Castro. Courtesy of *El Espectador.*

Figure 9: Mimes Teaching People to Use the Crosswalks, 1995. Courtesy of *El Espectador.*

Figure 10: Mimes Teaching People to Use the Crosswalks, 1995. Courtesy of *El Espectador.*

Figure 11: Mimes Correcting the Behavior of Pedestrians and Drivers, 1995. Photo: Rafael Guerrero. Courtesy of *El Tiempo.*

Figure 12: Mimes Correcting the Behavior of Pedestrians and Drivers, 1995. Photo: Rafael Guerrero. Courtesy of *El Tiempo.*

Figure 13: Mimes Teaching People to Use the Crosswalks, 1995. Courtesy of *El Espectador.*

Figure 14: "Knights of the Crosswalk," 1995-1998. Courtesy of the Personal Archive of Antanas Mockus.

Figure 15: "Knights of the Crosswalk," 1996. Courtesy of *El Espectador.*

Figure 16: Newspaper Classified by Mayor's Office, Bogotá, 1996. Courtesy of *El Tiempo.*

Figure 17: "Super Citizen," 1996. Photo: Juan Castañeda. Courtesy of the Personal Archive of Antanas Mockus.

Figure 18: "Super Citizen," 1996. Photo: Fernando Vergara. Courtesy of *El Tiempo.*

Figure 19: "Super Citizen," 1996. Photo: Fernando Vergara. Courtesy of *El Tiempo.*

Figure 20: Exhibition Case, *"Cultura Ciudadana:* Artists and Architects Give Shape to Public

Politics," 2015. Santa Monica Museum of Art, California. Courtesy of Futuro Moncada.

Figure 21: Still with Bugs Bunny, 1997. Courtesy of the Personal Archive of Antanas Mockus.

Figure 22: Suggestion Slip "I Contribute My Idea," 2014. Courtesy of Futuro Moncada.

Figure 23: "Carrot Kit," 2014. Courtesy of Futuro Moncada.

Figure 24: "Carrot Kit," 2014. Courtesy of Futuro Moncada.

Figure 25: Press Conference, 1997. Photo: Luis Acosta. Courtesy of the Personal Archive of Antanas Mockus.

Figure 26: Press Conference, 1997. Photo: William Martínez. Courtesy of the Personal Archive of Antanas Mockus.

Figure 27: Chingaza Dam, 1995. Photo: Francisco Carranza. Courtesy of *El Espectador*.

Figure 28: Chingaza Dam, 1995. Photo: Juan Castañeda. Courtesy of Personal Archive of Antanas Mockus.

Figure 29: Recording a Telephone Message, 1995. Courtesy of *El Espectador*.

Figure 30: Graphic Work, 2014. Courtesy of Futuro Moncada.

Figure 31: Informative Flyer About Wasting Water, 1995-1998. Courtesy of the Mayor's Office of Bogotá, Secretary General, Central Archive, Photo Archive.

Figure 32: Informative Flyer About Wasting Water, 1995-1998. Courtesy of the Mayor's Office of Bogotá, Secretary General, Central Archive, Photo Archive.

Figure 33: "Family Commissary," 1995-1998. Courtesy of Personal Archive of Antanas Mockus.

Figure 34: Solution to Park Conflicts, 2003. Photo: Ignacio Prieto. Courtesy of the Mayor's Office of Bogotá, Secretary General, Central Archive, Photo Archive.

Figure 35: Solution to Park Conflicts, 2003. Photo by: Ignacio Prieto. Courtesy of the Mayor's Office of Bogotá, Secretary General, Central Archive, Photo Archive.

Figure 36: Solution to Park Conflicts, 2003. Photo by: Ignacio Prieto. Courtesy of the Mayor's Office of Bogotá, Secretary General, Central Archive, Photo Archive.

Figure 37: Solution to Park Conflicts, 2003. Photo: Ignacio Prieto. Courtesy of the Mayor's Office of Bogotá, Secretary General, Central Archive, Photo Archive.

Figure 38: "Tax Serenade," 2001. Photo: Eliseo Rúa. Courtesy of the Mayor's Office of Bogotá, Secretary General, Central Archive, Photo Archive.

Figure 39: "Tax Serenade," 2001. Photo: Eliseo Rúa. Courtesy of the Mayor's Office of Bogotá, Secretary General, Central Archive, Photo Archive.

Figure 40: Construction of the Archive of Bogotá, 1995-2003. Photo: Ignacio Prieto. Courtesy of the Mayor's Office of Bogotá, Secretary General, Central Archive, Photo Archive.

Figure 41: "Tax Serenade," 2001. Photo: Eliseo Rúa. Courtesy of the Mayor's Office of Bogotá, Secretary General, Central Archive, Photo Archive.

Figure 42: Chiva Tax–Contributors Trip, 2001. Courtesy of the Mayor's Office of Bogotá, Secretary General, Central Archive, Photo Archive.

Figure 43: Construction of the Archive of Bogotá, 2001. Photo: Ignacio Prieto. Courtesy of the Mayor's Office of Bogotá, Secretary General, Central Archive, Photo Archive.

Figure 44: Chiva Tax–Contributors Trip, 2001. Courtesy of the Mayor's Office of Bogotá, Secretary General, Central Archive, Photo Archive.

Figure 45: Chiva Tax–Contributors Trip, 2001. Courtesy of the Mayor's Office of Bogotá, Secretary General, Central Archive, Photo Archive.

Figure 46: Chiva Tax–Contributors Trip, 2001. Courtesy of the Mayor's Office of Bogotá, Secretary General, Central Archive, Photo Archive.

Figure 47: Launching "Bogotá Flirts" Citizenship Cards, 1995. Photo: Eduardo Sotomayor. Courtesy of the Mayor's Office of Bogotá, Secretary General, Central Archive, Photo Archive.

Figure 48: Press Conference, "No Car Day", 2003. Photo: Eduardo Sotomayor. Courtesy of the Mayor's Office of Bogotá, Secretary General, Central Archive, Photo Archive.

Figure 49: "Bogotá Flirts," 2005. Courtesy of *El Espectador*.

Figure 50: Newspaper Classified by the Mayor's Office, Bogotá. 1996. Courtesy of *El Espectador*.

Figure 51: "Bogotá Flirts," Logo, 1995-1998. Design by Martha Granados.

Figure 52: "Bogotá Flirts," 2006. Photo: Gabriel Aponte. Courtesy of *El Espectador*.

Figure 53: "Bogotá Flirts," 2006. Photo: Gabriel Aponte. Courtesy of *El Espectador*.

Figure 54: "Carrot Cocktail," 2003. Photo: Eduardo Sotomayor. Courtesy of the Mayor's Office of Bogotá, Secretary General, Central Archive, Photo Archive.

Figure 55: "Carrot Law," 1995. Photo: Gabriel Aponte. Courtesy of *El Espectador*.

Figure 56: "Carrot Law," 1995. Photo: Luis García. Courtesy of *El Espectador*.

Figure 57: "Carrot Law," 1995. Photo: Gabriel Aponte. Courtesy of *El Espectador*.

Figure 58: "Carrot Law," 1995. Photo: Gabriel Aponte. Courtesy of *El Espectador*.

Figure 59: Closing Hour of Public Establishments, "Carrot Law," 1995. Courtesy of *El Espectador*.

Figure 60: Carrots, 2014. Courtesy of Futuro Moncada.

Figure 61: Carrots, 2014. Courtesy of Futuro Moncada.

Figure 62: Launching the New "Police Code," 2003. Photo: Fernando Rodríguez. Courtesy of the Mayor's Office of Bogotá, Secretary General, Central Archive, Photo Archive.

Figure 63: Launching the New "Police Code," 2003. Photo: Carlos Julio Martínez. Courtesy of *El Tiempo*.

Figure 64: Launching the New "Police Code," 2003. Photo: Carlos Julio Martínez. Courtesy of *El Tiempo*.

Figure 90: Decommission of Fireworks, 1995. Photo: Alejandro Rivera. Courtesy of *El Espectador*.

Figure 91: Sanction for Those Whom Use Fireworks, 1996. Photo: Luis Acosta. Courtesy of the Mayor's Office of Bogotá, Secretary General, Central 90Archive, Photo Archive.

Figure 92: Press Conference for Burned Children, 2002. Courtesy of the Mayor's Office of Bogotá, Secretary General, Central Archive, Photo Archive.

Figure 93: Civic Work as Educational Sanction, 1996. Photo: Humberto Pinto. Courtesy of *El Espectador*.

Figure 94: Civic Work as Educational Sanction, 1996. Photo: Humberto Pinto. Courtesy of *El Espectador*.

Figure 95: "Vaccine Against Violence," 2002. Courtesy of the Mayor's Office, Bogotá. Secretary General, Central Archive.

Figure 96: Second Day of "Vaccine Against Violence," 1996. Photo: Juan Castañeda. Courtesy of the Mayor's Office, Bogotá, Secretary General, Central Archive.

Figure 97: "Vaccine Against Violence," 1996. Courtesy of the Mayor's Office, Bogotá. Secretary General, Central Archive.

Figure 98: Mockus at the "Vaccine Against Violence" during his First Administration, 1995-1998. Photo: Jaime García. Courtesy of *El Tiempo*.

Figure 99: Mockus at the "Vaccine Against Violence" during his First Administration, 1995-1998. Courtesy of *El Tiempo*.

Figure 100: "Vaccine Against Forgetfulness." UNICEF, 2002. Photo: Ignacio Prieto. Courtesy of the Mayor's Office of Bogotá, Secretary General, Central Archive, Photo Archive.

Figure 101: Certificate of Vaccination, "Vaccine Against Forgetfulness," 2014. Courtesy of Futuro Moncada.

Figure 102: Exterior of Brochure, "Vaccine Against Forgetfulness," 2014. Courtesy of Futuro Moncada.

Figure 103: Interior of Brochure, "Vaccine Against Forgetfulness," 2014. Courtesy of Futuro Moncada.

Figure 104: Bicycle Day, 1996. Photo: Eduardo Sotomayor. Courtesy of the Mayor's Office, Bogotá. Secretary General, Central Archive.

Figure 105: "Bike Path," 1997. Photo: Felipe Caicedo. Courtesy of *El Tiempo*.

Figure 106: Guardians of the "Bike Path," 2003. Photo: Eduardo Sotomayor. Courtesy of the Mayor's Office of Bogotá, Secretary General, Central Archive, Photo Archive.

Figure 107: Guardian Possession of the "Bike Path," 2003. Courtesy of the Mayor's Office, Bogotá. Secretary General, Central Archive.

Figure 108: "No Car Day," 2003. Courtesy of the Mayor's Office, Bogotá. Secretary General, Central Archive.

Figure 109: "No Car Day," 2003. Courtesy of the Mayor's Office, Bogotá. Secretary General, Central Archive.

Figure 130: Presenting the Education Center for Homeless Children, 2001. Photo: Ignacio Prieto. Courtesy of the Mayor's Office, Bogotá, Secretary General, Central Archive, Photo Archive.

Figure 131: "We Are Going in the Right Direction," 2002. Photo: Arcesio Vega. Courtesy of the Mayor's Office, Bogotá, Secretary General, Central Archive, Photo Archive.

Figure 132: "We Are Going in the Right Direction," 2002. Photo: Arcesio Vega. Courtesy of the Mayor's Office, Bogotá, Secretary General, Central Archive, Photo Archive.

Figure 133: "Bogotá, For All to Live On the Same Side" Logo, 2001-2003. Courtesy of the Mayor's Office, Bogotá, Secretary General, Central Archive, Photo Archive.

Figure 134: "Moebius Strip," 2001-2003. Courtesy of Futuro Moncada.

Figure 135: Presenting the Education Center for Homeless Children, 2001. Photo: Ignacio Prieto. Courtesy of the Mayor's Office, Bogotá, Secretary General, Central Archive, Photo Archive.

Figure 136: "We Are Going in the Right Direction," 2002. Photo: Arcesio Vega. Courtesy of the Mayor's Office of Bogotá, Secretary General, Central Archive, Photo Archive.

Figure 137: "Civil Resistance," 2002. Courtesy of the Mayor's Office, Bogotá, Secretary General, Central Archive, Photo Archive.

Figure 138: "Bulletproof Vest," 2001-2003. Courtesy of the Mayor's Office of Bogotá, Secretary General, Central Archive, Photo Archive.

Figure 139: Mayor Removes "Bulletproof Vest" for Auction, 2002. Photo: Arcesio Vega. Courtesy of the Mayor's Office, Bogotá, Secretary General, Central Archive, Photo Archive.

Figure 140: Mayor Removes "Bulletproof Vest" for Auction, 2002. Photo: Arcesio Vega. Courtesy of the Mayor's Office, Bogotá, Secretary General, Central Archive, Photo Archive.

Figure 141: Mayor Removes "Bulletproof Vest" for Auction, 2002. Photo: Arcesio Vega. Courtesy of the Mayor's Office, Bogotá, Secretary General, Central Archive, Photo Archive.

Figure 142: "Civil Resistance," 2001-2003. Courtesy of the Mayor's Office of Bogotá, Secretary General, Central Archive, Photo Archive.

Figure 143: March for El Nogal, 2003. Photo: Ignacio Prieto. Courtesy of the Mayor's Office of Bogotá, Secretary General, Central Archive, Photo Archive.

Figure 144: March for El Nogal, 2003. Photo: Ignacio Prieto. Courtesy of the Mayor's Office of Bogotá, Secretary General, Central Archive, Photo Archive.

Figure 145: March for El Nogal, 2003. Photo: Ignacio Prieto. Courtesy of the Mayor's Office of Bogotá, Secretary General, Central Archive, Photo Archive.

Figure 146: Walk Against Terrorism, 2003. Photo: Ignacio Prieto. Courtesy of the Mayor's Office of Bogotá, Secretary General, Central Archive, Photo Archive.

Figure 147: March for El Nogal, 2003. Photo: Ignacio Prieto. Courtesy of the Mayor's Office of Bogotá, Secretary General, Central Archive, Photo Archive.

Figure 148: Aerobics, 2002. Photo: Ignacio Prieto. Courtesy of the Mayor's Office of Bogotá, Secretary General, Central Archive, Photo Archive.

Figure 149: "Civil Resistance," 2001-2003. Courtesy of the Mayor's Office, Bogotá, Secretary General, Central Archive, Photo Archive.

Figure 150: Walk Against Terrorism, 2003. Photo: Ignacio Prieto. Courtesy of the Mayor's Office of Bogotá, Secretary General, Central Archive, Photo Archive.

Figure 151: Walk Against Terrorism, 2003. Photo: Ignacio Prieto. Courtesy of the Mayor's Office of Bogotá, Secratary General, Central Archive, Photo Archive.

Figure 152: Signatures for Credit Lines for Women, 2001. Photo: Carlos Martínez Courtesy of *El Tiempo.*

Figure 153: "Ladies' Night," 2001. Photo: Carlos Martínez Courtesy of *El Tiempo.*

Figure 154: "Ladies' Night," 2001. Courtesy of the Mayor's Office, Bogotá, Secretary General, Central Archive, Photo Archive.

Figure 155: Celebration of "Ladies' Night," 2001. Photo: José Barrera. Courtesy of the Mayor's Office, Bogotá, Secretary General, Central Archive, Photo Archive.

Figure 156: Celebration of "Ladies' Night," 2001. Photo: José Barrera. Courtesy of the Mayor's Office, Bogotá, Secretary General, Central Archive, Photo Archive.

Figure 157: "Ladies' Night," 2001. Courtesy of the Mayor's Office of Bogotá, Secretary General, Central Archive, Photo Archive.

Figure 158: "Ladies' Night," 2001. Photo: Carlos Martínez Courtesy of *El Tiempo.*

Figure 159: "Ladies' Night," 2001. Photo: Carlos Martínez Courtesy of *El Tiempo.*

Figure 160: Cemetery of the South, 2002. Photo: Ignacio Prieto. Courtesy of the Mayor's Office of Bogotá, Secretary General, Central Archive, Photo Archive.

Figures 161: Columbariums, 2003. Photo: Ignacio Prieto. Courtesy of the Mayor's Office of Bogotá, Secretary General, Central Archive, Photo Archive.

Figure 162: Press Conference, 2002. Courtesy of the Mayor's Office of Bogotá, Secretary General, Central Archive, Photo Archive.

Figure 163: "Life is Sacred," 2002. Photo: Ignacio Prieto. Courtesy of the Mayor's Office, Bogotá, Secretary General, Central Archive, Photo Archive.

Figure 164. "Life is Sacred," 2002. Photo: Ignacio Prieto. Courtesy of the Mayor's Office, Bogotá, Secretary General, Central Archive, Photo Archive.

Figure 165: Press Conference, Report on the Violence, 2002. Courtesy of the Mayor's Office, Bogotá, Secretary General, Central Archive, Photo Archive.

Figure 166: Press Conference, Report on the Violence, 2002. Courtesy of the Mayor's Office, Bogotá, Secretary General, Central Archive, Photo Archive.

Figure 167: Press Conference, Report on the Violence, 2002. Courtesy of the Mayor's Office, Bogotá, Secretary General, Central Archive, Photo Archive.

Figure 168: Hands and Freedom, 2002. Photo: Ignacio Prieto. Courtesy of the Mayor's Office, Bogotá, Secretary General, Central Archive, Photo Archive.

Figure 169: Homicides Drop. Graph by Sumona Chakravarty.

Figure 170: Income from Tax Increases. Graph by Sumona Chakravarty.

Figure 171: Behavior Regulation Mechanisms Proposed by Mockus. Graph by Corpovisionarios.

Figure 172: Answers to the question "Which feeling do the words 'rule' or 'norm' produce in you?" The figure presents "positive" and "very positive" answers. Graph by Corpovisionarios.

Figure 173: Results of the survey about corruption opinion about both fellow citizens and public officers. Graph by Corpovisionarios.

Figure 174: Regulatory Systems and Reasons to Obey. Graph by Gerry Mackie.

Figure 175: "Moebius Strip." 2001-2003. Courtesy of the Mayor's Office, Bogotá, Secretary General, Central Archive, Photo Archive.

Figure 176: "Citizenship Card." Courtesy of the Mayor's Office, Bogotá, Secretary General, Central Archive, Photo Archive.